MARVEL® PLATINUM
THE DEFINITIVE
INCREDIBLE HULK®

THE INCREDIBLE HULK VOL 1 #1
MAY 1962
WRITER: STAN LEE
PENCILLER: JACK KIRBY
INKER: PAUL REINMAN
LETTERS: ART SIMEK

FANTASTIC FOUR #25
APRIL 1964
WRITER: STAN LEE
PENCILLER: JACK KIRBY
INKS: GEORGE BELL
LETTERS: SAM ROSEN

FANTASTIC FOUR #26
MAY 1964
WRITER: STAN LEE
PENCILLER: JACK KIRBY
INKS: GEORGE BELL
LETTERS: ART SIMEK

THE INCREDIBLE HULK VOL 2 #124
FEBRUARY 1970
WRITER: ROY THOMAS
PENCILLER: HERB TRIMPE
INKER: SAL BUSCEMA
LETTERS: SAM ROSEN

MARVEL FEATURE PRESENTS #1
DECEMBER 1971
WRITER: ROY THOMAS
PENCILLER: ROSS ANDRU
INKER: BILL EVERETT
LETTERS: SAM ROSEN

THE INCREDIBLE HULK VOL 2 #319
MAY 1986
WRITER & PENCILLER: JOHN BYRNE
INKER: KEITH WILLIAMS
LETTERS: RICK PARKER

THE INCREDIBLE HULK VOL 2 #340
FEBRUARY 1988
WRITER: PETER DAVID
PENCILLER & INKER: TODD
McFARLANE
LETTERS: RICK PARKER

HULK: FUTURE IMPERFECT #1
DECEMBER 1992
WRITER: PETER DAVID
PENCILLER & INKER: GEORGE PEREZ
LETTERS: JOE ROSEN

HULK: FUTURE IMPERFECT #2
JANUARY 1993
WRITER: PETER DAVID

PENCILLER & INKER: GEORGE PEREZ
LETTERS: JOE ROSEN

THE INCREDIBLE HULK VOL 3 #25
APRIL 2001
WRITER: PAUL JENKINS
PENCILLER: JOHN ROMITA JR.
INKER: TOM PALMER
LETTERS: JOHN WORKMAN

COVER BY JIM CHEUNG

MARVEL® presents: MARVEL PLATINUM: THE DEFINITIVE INCREDIBLE HULK

MARVEL PLATINUM: THE DEFINITIVE INCREDIBLE HULK. Contains material originally published in magazine form as THE INCREDIBLE HULK VOL 1 #1, FANTASTIC FOUR VOL 1 #25-26, MARVEL FEATURE PRESENTS #1, THE INCREDIBLE HULK VOL 2 #124, 319, 340, HULK: FUTURE IMPERFECT #1-2, THE INCREDIBLE HULK VOL 3 #25. Published by Panini Publishing, a division of Panini UK Limited. Mike Riddell, Managing Director. Alan O'Keefe, Managing Editor. Mark Irvine, Production Manager. Marco M. Lupoi, Publishing Director Europe. Brady Webb, Reprint Editor. Luigi Mutti, Assistant Editor. Tim Warran-Smith, Designer. Office of publication: Panini House, Coach & Horses Passage, The Pantiles, Tunbridge Wells, Kent TN2 5UJ. Tel: 01892 500 100. Copyright © 1962, 1964, 1970, 1971, 1986, 1988, 1992, 1993, 2001 by Marvel Characters, Inc. All rights reserved. No similarity between any of the names, characters, persons and/or institutions in this magazine with any living or dead person or institution is intended, and any similarity which may exist is purely coincidental. This publication may not be sold except by authorised dealers and is sold subject to the conditions that it shall not be sold or distributed with any part of its cover or markings removed, nor in a mutilated condition. HULK (including all prominent characters featured in this issue and the distinctive likeness thereof) is a trademark of MARVEL CHARACTERS, INC. and this publication is under license from Marvel Characters, Inc. through Panini S.p.A. Printed in Italy. ISBN: 978-1-905239-88-7

INTRODUCTION
BY STAN LEE

Hi, Hulkophiles!

It just doesn't get any better than this!

This classic collection of some of the Hulk's greatest and most unforgettable epic tales is beyond awesome. It features not only the strongest rampager on Planet Earth, but one of the greatest assortment of guest stars ever assembled between two colorful covers.

But that's not all. Wait'll you see the brilliant, time-honored artists and writers whose creations will keep you on the edge of your seat. I can't tell you how honored I feel to be included in that august collection.

Now, just to whet your appetite, here's a hint of the excitement awaiting you on the pages ahead...

It seemed to be a no-brainer for us to start with the very first Hulk epic of all — the actual origin of ol' Green Skin, divided into five fantastic parts — THE HULK, THE HULK STRIKES!, SEARCH FOR THE HULK, "ENTER THE GARGOYLE!", and THE HULK TRIUMPHANT! As illustrated by the legendary Jack "King" Kirby, it'll be easy for you to realize why Bruce Banner and his astonishing alter ego were an instant sensation when first published.

As for the Hulk's mighty super villain foe, the hideous Gargoyle, I suspect you'll have a lump in your throat when you see his dramatic fate at story's end.

Our next feature, THE BATTLE OF THE CENTURY, is totally unique. Again drawn by the great Jack Kirby, although it features many epic, unforgettable battles, there isn't a single super villain anywhere to be seen! I can almost hear you ask, "Then who is he fighting?" The answer is (and this is what makes it so unique), instead of villains, the Hulk actually battles some of Marvel's greatest heroes. Wouldja believe the Hulk vs. the Thing? How about the Hulk battling Iron Man, Captain America and Giant Man?

All I can say is-- that one you dare not miss!

But Marvel has never been a company that rests on its laurels. Before you can even catch your breath, the titanically talented Roy Thomas takes over the scripting chores with the great team of Sal Buscema and Herb Trimpe handling the art and the fantastic result is — THE RHINO SAYS NO!

Of course, if you were the Rhino you'd say "No" too when you see Bruce Banner about to marry Betty Ross! Especially after the incredibly evil Leader has sent you to disrupt their marriage and destroy the Hulk! I know you won't be able to put this one down till the last page-- and not even then, because it's followed up with--

THE DAY OF THE DEFENDERS! In this great thriller, scripter Thomas teams up with the brilliant Ross Andru as they introduce herodom's newest super team, the Defenders, consisting of Dr. Strange, the mighty Sub-Mariner and (wouldja believe?) the Incredible Hulk!

All of them must find a way to defeat the mad scientist Yandroth (what's a superhero series without a mad scientist?) and his Earth-destroying invention — the omegatron! Let's hope, for all our sakes, that the good guys win!

Next — waddaya know? Banner is trying to get married again! This time the acclaimed writer/artist John Byrne deftly handles both the art and scripting chores as he brings you MEMBER OF THE WEDDING. Believe it or not, the villain of this one is General Thunderbolt Ross himself! What's even stranger is the Hulk and Banner are now separate entities! The Hulk is on the rampage and it's up to the powerful Doc Samson and the Hulkbusters to capture him! You can bet that the action and suspense never disappoint. You'll love it! It's full of surprises!

Speaking of surprises, how about a story where the Hulk battles — get ready for this — none other than Wolverine! It's called VICIOUS CIRCLE and that name ain't kiddin'! It also features Clay Quartermain, the X-Men's own Rogue and Rick Jones himself. You won't wanna miss the action when the Hulk single-handedly wrecks a giant jet passenger plane and, because of that, has one of the greatest battles of his life against an enraged Wolverine!

You just know *VICIOUS CIRCLE* has to be great because it's written by the justly-acclaimed **Peter David** and illustrated by none other than the great **Todd McFarlane**. It's almost worth the price of admission all by itself.

I know you think we've already given you more than you could have ever expected, or even deserve; but to show how we love our fans, we have not one but two additional great tales in store for you.

The first is called *FUTURE IMPERFECT* and it demonstrates the rare versatility of scripter Peter David as he teams up this time with another of comicdom's greats, artist extraordinaire **George Pérez**. In this great yarn the Hulk goes to the future where he finds Maestro, an evil version of himself! But the worst thing about it is — his evil self is stronger than he is! There's only one thing that can save the Hulk, but it belongs to — get ready for this — the diabolical Doctor Doom! As you can imagine, this one has it all!

Finally, to wrap things up, ye editors made a most outstanding choice. The title of our final titanic tome is *ALWAYS ON MY MIND*, which doesn't begin to give you the slightest idea of the action, drama and suspense you're about to discover in this beautifully-written and dramatically-drawn thriller by the ever-exciting super scripter **Paul Jenkins** and the always-awesome super artist **John Romita, Jr.**

Actually, this tale is so filled with surprises that I hate to give too much away, but I just have to tell you that it features the Hulk's other two identities — Mr. Fix-it and The Professor, as well as Thunderbolt Ross and-- none other than the world-famous and world-feared ex-Russian spy — the Abomination!

It actually takes place after Betty was killed by the Abomination who is now, if you can believe it, a writing teacher in New Hampshire! Determined to make his archenemy pay for the death of his loved one, the Hulk engages in one of his greatest, deadliest, most destructive battles with his most powerful foe. This'll have you hanging on the edge of your seat!

Of course, you have to realize my opinions might be a little bit prejudiced because I'm possibly the Hulk's biggest fan. Still, I'm betting you'll agree with everything I've said after you finish this collector's item volume. But hey, if you don't agree, I'm glad I'm an ocean away!

Enjoy every page, O True Believer!

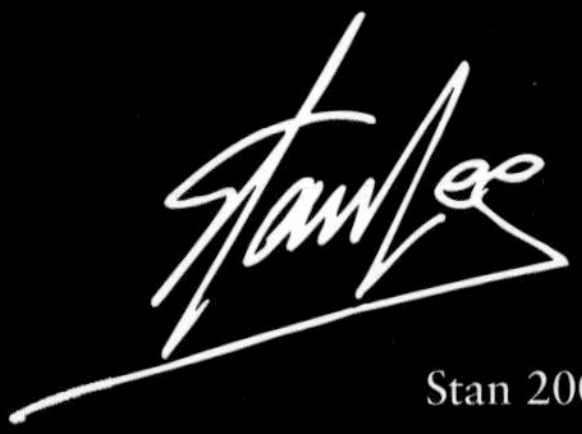

Stan 2008

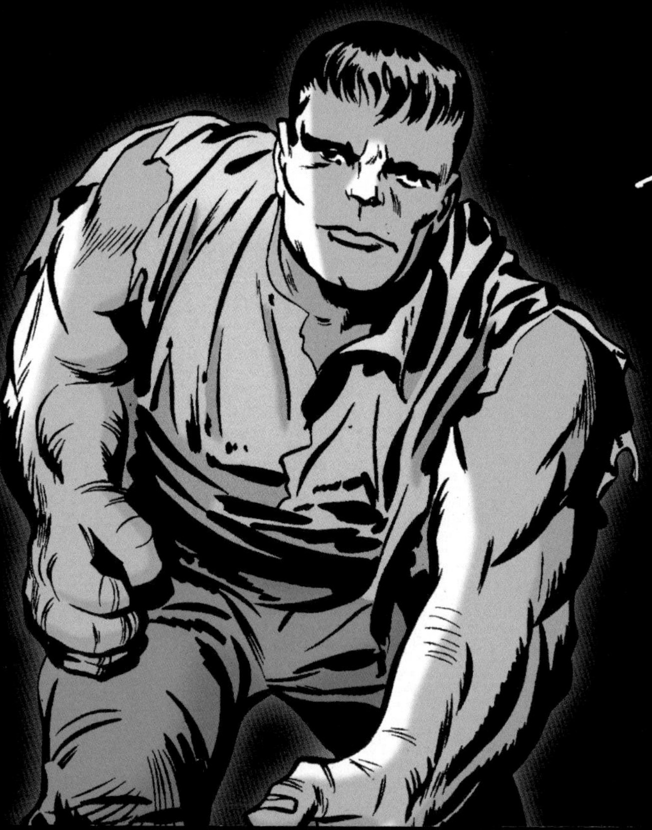

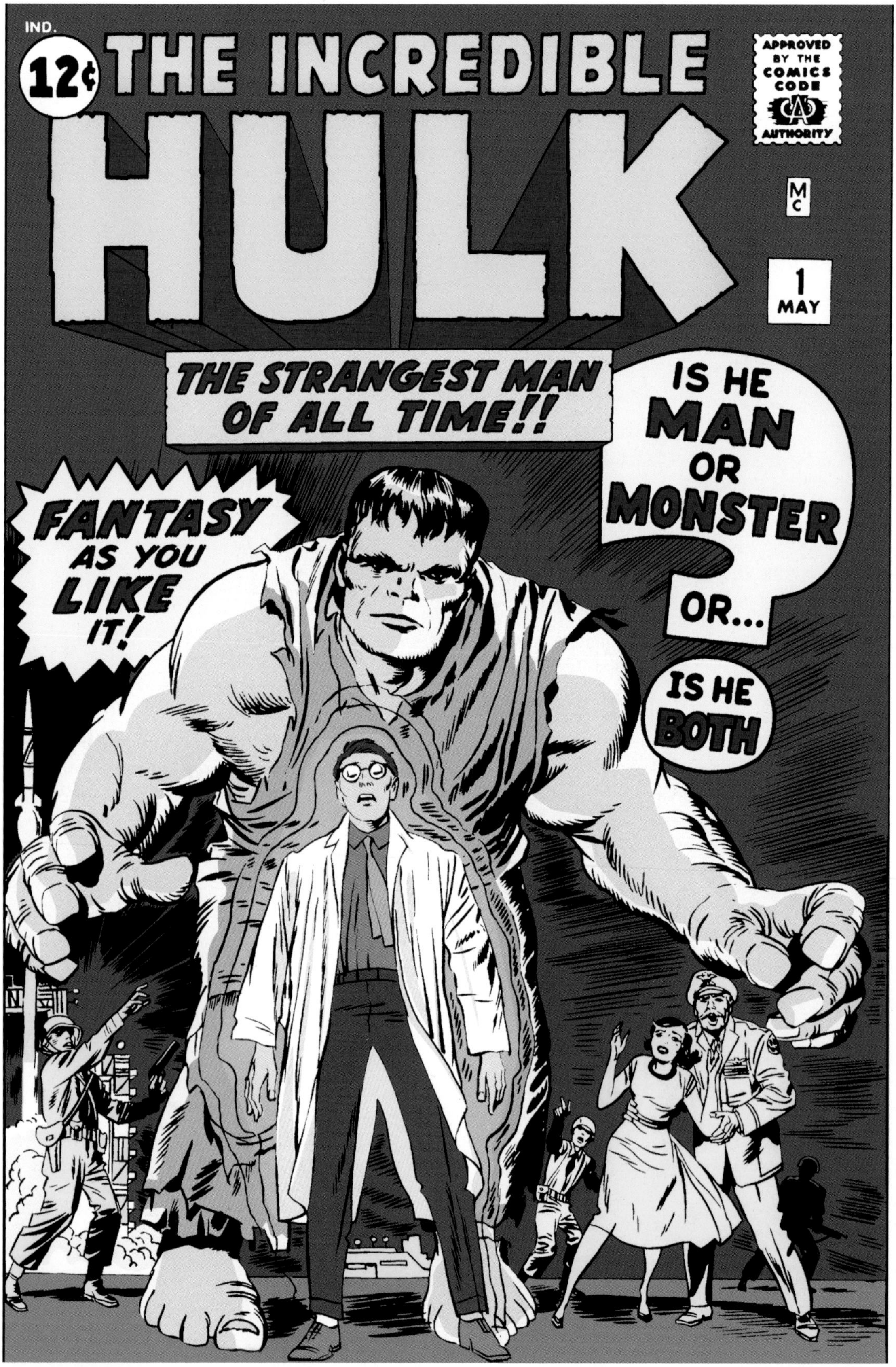
IND.
12¢
THE INCREDIBLE
HULK
APPROVED BY THE COMICS CODE AUTHORITY
MC
1
MAY
THE STRANGEST MAN OF ALL TIME!!
IS HE MAN OR MONSTER
OR...
IS HE BOTH
FANTASY AS YOU LIKE IT!

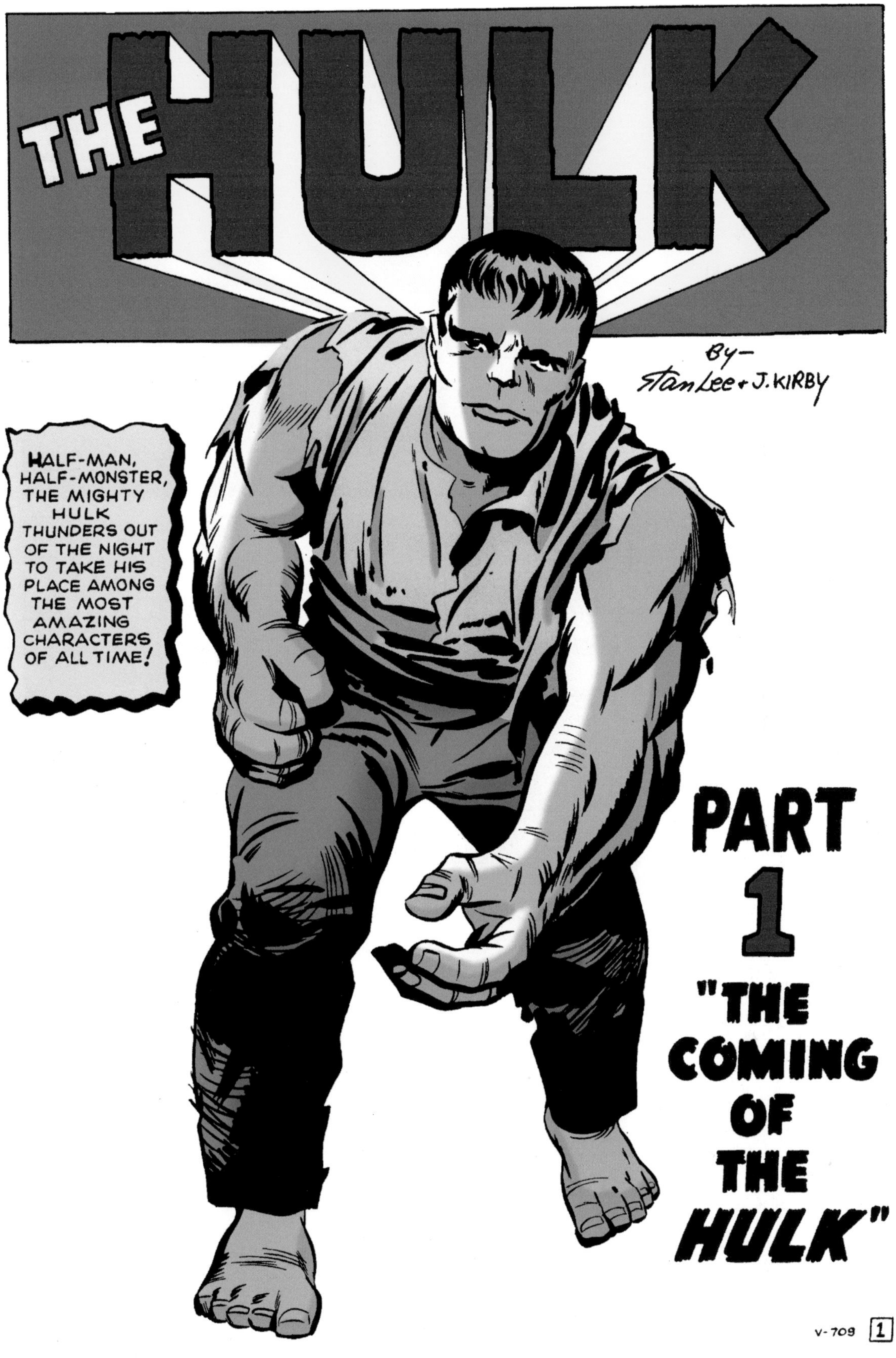
THE HULK
By— Stan Lee + J. KIRBY
HALF-MAN, HALF-MONSTER, THE MIGHTY HULK THUNDERS OUT OF THE NIGHT TO TAKE HIS PLACE AMONG THE MOST AMAZING CHARACTERS OF ALL TIME!
PART 1
"THE COMING OF THE HULK"

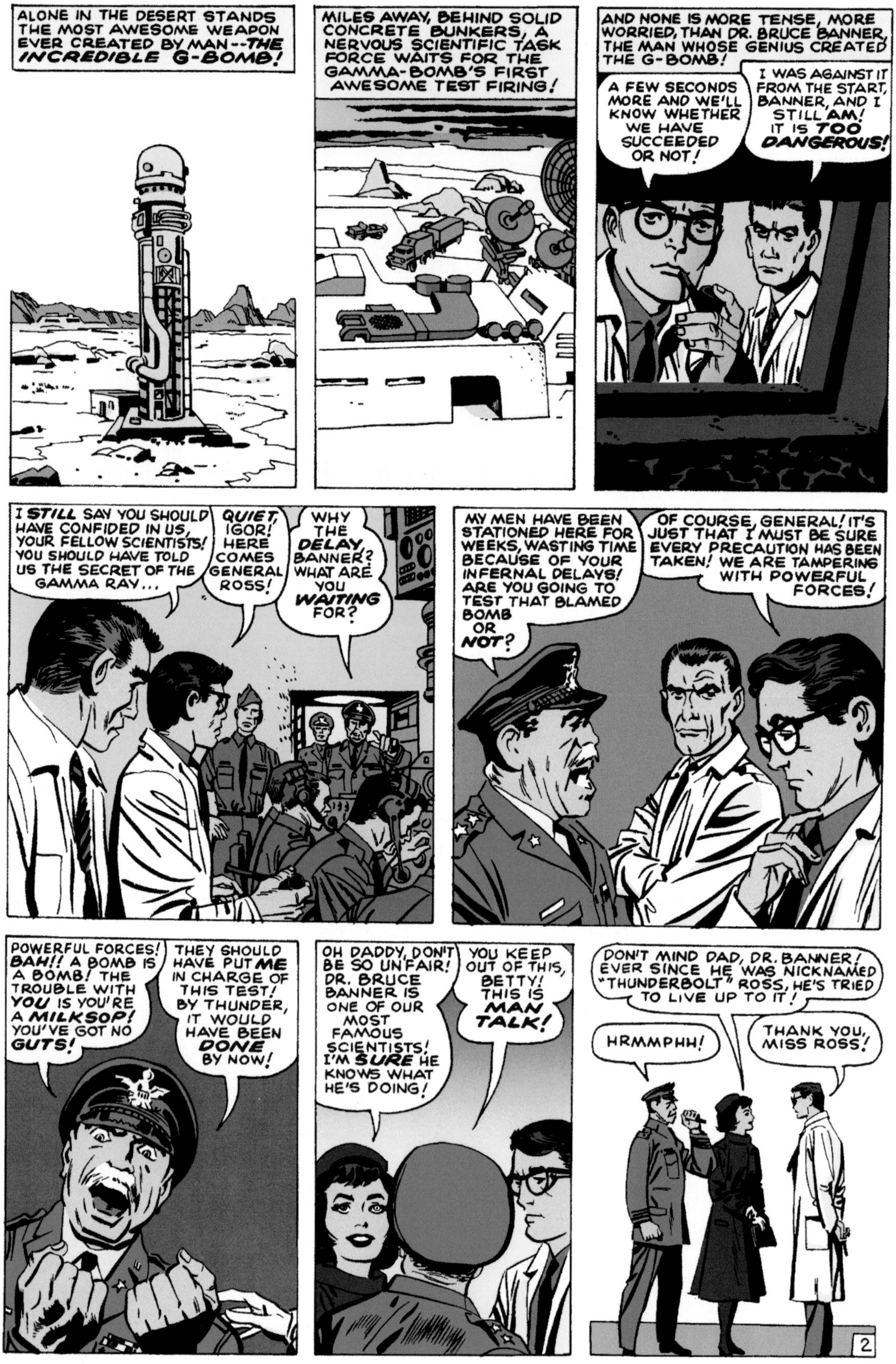
ALONE IN THE DESERT STANDS THE MOST AWESOME WEAPON EVER CREATED BY MAN--THE INCREDIBLE G-BOMB!
MILES AWAY, BEHIND SOLID CONCRETE BUNKERS, A NERVOUS SCIENTIFIC TASK FORCE WAITS FOR THE GAMMA-BOMB'S FIRST AWESOME TEST FIRING!
AND NONE IS MORE TENSE, MORE WORRIED, THAN DR. BRUCE BANNER, THE MAN WHOSE GENIUS CREATED THE G-BOMB!
A FEW SECONDS MORE AND WE'LL KNOW WHETHER WE HAVE SUCCEEDED OR NOT!
I WAS AGAINST IT FROM THE START, BANNER, AND I STILL AM! IT IS TOO DANGEROUS!
I STILL SAY YOU SHOULD HAVE CONFIDED IN US, YOUR FELLOW SCIENTISTS! YOU SHOULD HAVE TOLD US THE SECRET OF THE GAMMA RAY...
QUIET, IGOR! HERE COMES GENERAL ROSS!
WHY THE DELAY, BANNER? WHAT ARE YOU WAITING FOR?
MY MEN HAVE BEEN STATIONED HERE FOR WEEKS, WASTING TIME BECAUSE OF YOUR INFERNAL DELAYS! ARE YOU GOING TO TEST THAT BLAMED BOMB OR NOT?
OF COURSE, GENERAL! IT'S JUST THAT I MUST BE SURE EVERY PRECAUTION HAS BEEN TAKEN! WE ARE TAMPERING WITH POWERFUL FORCES!
POWERFUL FORCES! BAH!! A BOMB IS A BOMB! THE TROUBLE WITH YOU IS YOU'RE A MILKSOP! YOU'VE GOT NO GUTS!
THEY SHOULD HAVE PUT ME IN CHARGE OF THIS TEST! BY THUNDER, IT WOULD HAVE BEEN DONE BY NOW!
OH DADDY, DON'T BE SO UNFAIR! DR. BRUCE BANNER IS ONE OF OUR MOST FAMOUS SCIENTISTS! I'M SURE HE KNOWS WHAT HE'S DOING!
YOU KEEP OUT OF THIS, BETTY! THIS IS MAN TALK!
DON'T MIND DAD, DR. BANNER! EVER SINCE HE WAS NICKNAMED "THUNDERBOLT" ROSS, HE'S TRIED TO LIVE UP TO IT!
HRMMPHH!
THANK YOU, MISS ROSS!
2

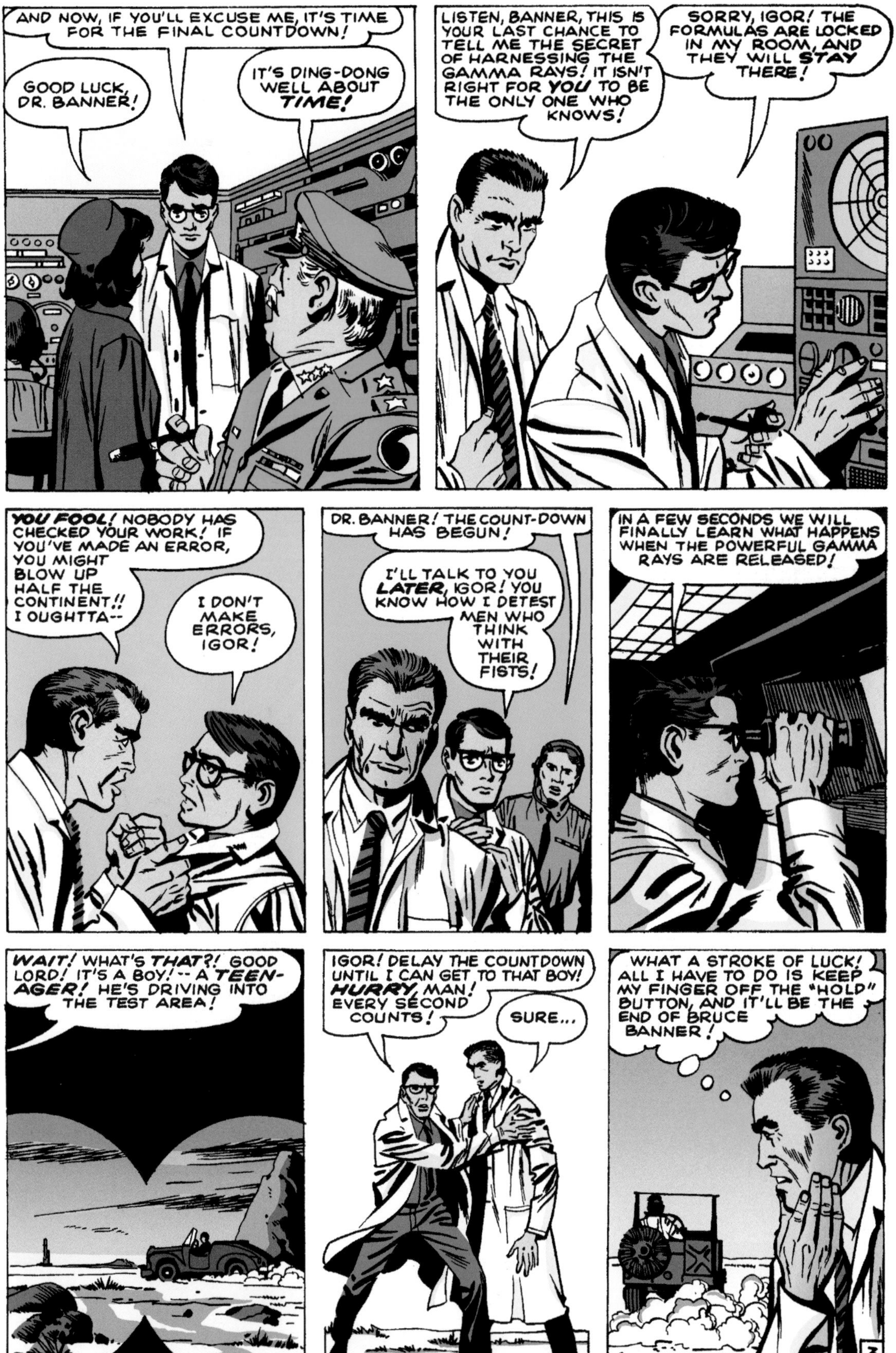
AND NOW, IF YOU'LL EXCUSE ME, IT'S TIME FOR THE FINAL COUNTDOWN!
GOOD LUCK, DR. BANNER!
IT'S DING-DONG WELL ABOUT TIME!
LISTEN, BANNER, THIS IS YOUR LAST CHANCE TO TELL ME THE SECRET OF HARNESSING THE GAMMA RAYS! IT ISN'T RIGHT FOR YOU TO BE THE ONLY ONE WHO KNOWS!
SORRY, IGOR! THE FORMULAS ARE LOCKED IN MY ROOM, AND THEY WILL STAY THERE!
YOU FOOL! NOBODY HAS CHECKED YOUR WORK! IF YOU'VE MADE AN ERROR, YOU MIGHT BLOW UP HALF THE CONTINENT!! I OUGHTTA--
I DON'T MAKE ERRORS, IGOR!
DR. BANNER! THE COUNT-DOWN HAS BEGUN!
I'LL TALK TO YOU LATER, IGOR! YOU KNOW HOW I DETEST MEN WHO THINK WITH THEIR FISTS!
IN A FEW SECONDS WE WILL FINALLY LEARN WHAT HAPPENS WHEN THE POWERFUL GAMMA RAYS ARE RELEASED!
WAIT! WHAT'S THAT?! GOOD LORD! IT'S A BOY! -- A TEEN-AGER! HE'S DRIVING INTO THE TEST AREA!
IGOR! DELAY THE COUNTDOWN UNTIL I CAN GET TO THAT BOY! HURRY, MAN! EVERY SECOND COUNTS!
SURE...
WHAT A STROKE OF LUCK! ALL I HAVE TO DO IS KEEP MY FINGER OFF THE "HOLD" BUTTON, AND IT'LL BE THE END OF BRUCE BANNER!
3

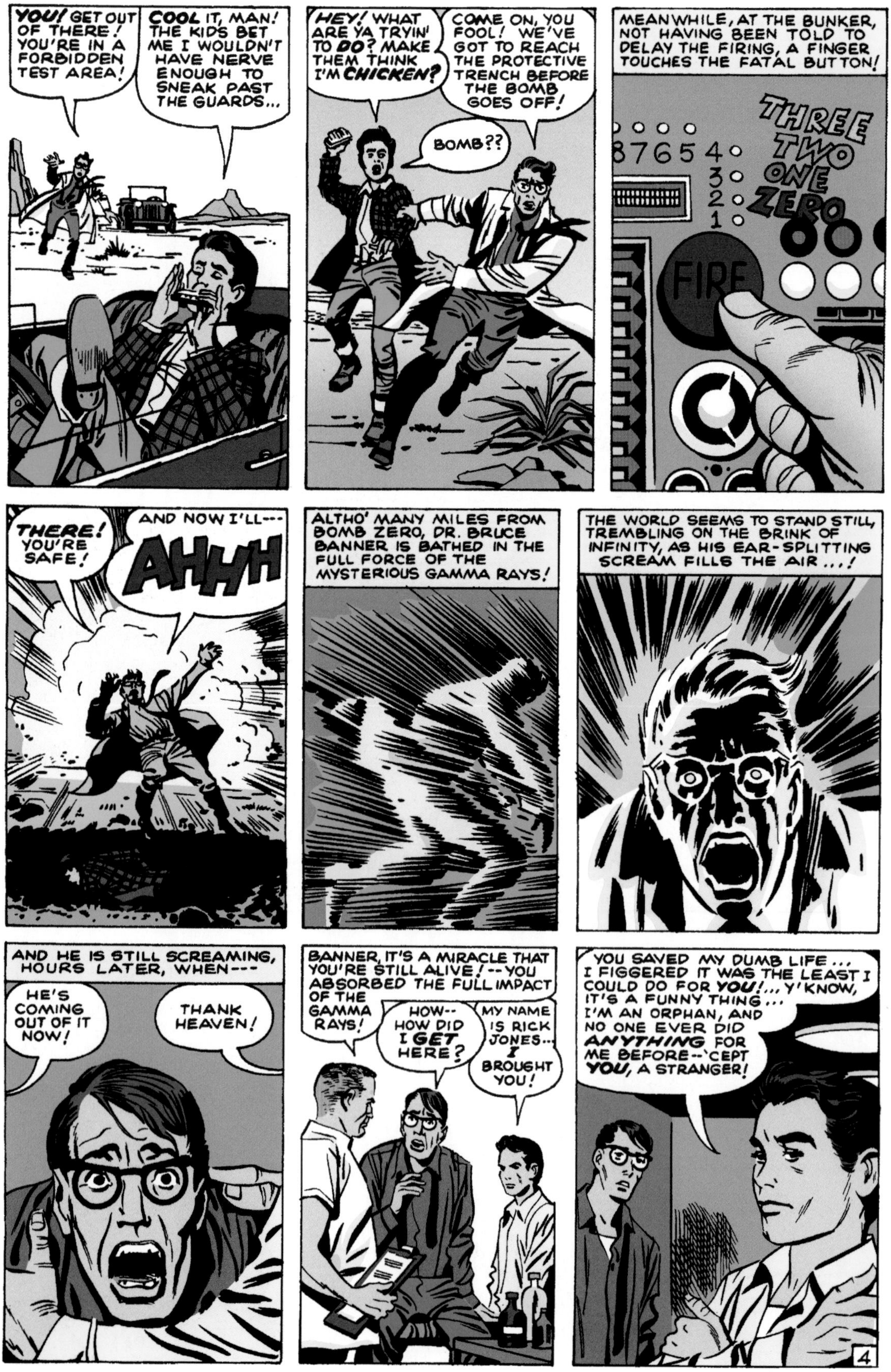
YOU! GET OUT OF THERE! YOU'RE IN A FORBIDDEN TEST AREA!
COOL IT, MAN! THE KIDS BET ME I WOULDN'T HAVE NERVE ENOUGH TO SNEAK PAST THE GUARDS...
HEY! WHAT ARE YA TRYIN' TO DO? MAKE THEM THINK I'M CHICKEN?
COME ON, YOU FOOL! WE'VE GOT TO REACH THE PROTECTIVE TRENCH BEFORE THE BOMB GOES OFF!
BOMB??
MEANWHILE, AT THE BUNKER, NOT HAVING BEEN TOLD TO DELAY THE FIRING, A FINGER TOUCHES THE FATAL BUTTON!
8 7 6 5 4 3 2 1
THREE TWO ONE ZERO
FIRE
THERE! YOU'RE SAFE!
AND NOW I'LL---
AHHH
ALTHO' MANY MILES FROM BOMB ZERO, DR. BRUCE BANNER IS BATHED IN THE FULL FORCE OF THE MYSTERIOUS GAMMA RAYS!
THE WORLD SEEMS TO STAND STILL, TREMBLING ON THE BRINK OF INFINITY, AS HIS EAR-SPLITTING SCREAM FILLS THE AIR...!
AND HE IS STILL SCREAMING, HOURS LATER, WHEN---
HE'S COMING OUT OF IT NOW!
THANK HEAVEN!
BANNER, IT'S A MIRACLE THAT YOU'RE STILL ALIVE! --YOU ABSORBED THE FULL IMPACT OF THE GAMMA RAYS!
HOW-- HOW DID I GET HERE?
MY NAME IS RICK JONES.. I BROUGHT YOU!
YOU SAVED MY DUMB LIFE... I FIGGERED IT WAS THE LEAST I COULD DO FOR YOU!... Y'KNOW, IT'S A FUNNY THING... I'M AN ORPHAN, AND NO ONE EVER DID ANYTHING FOR ME BEFORE--'CEPT YOU, A STRANGER!
4

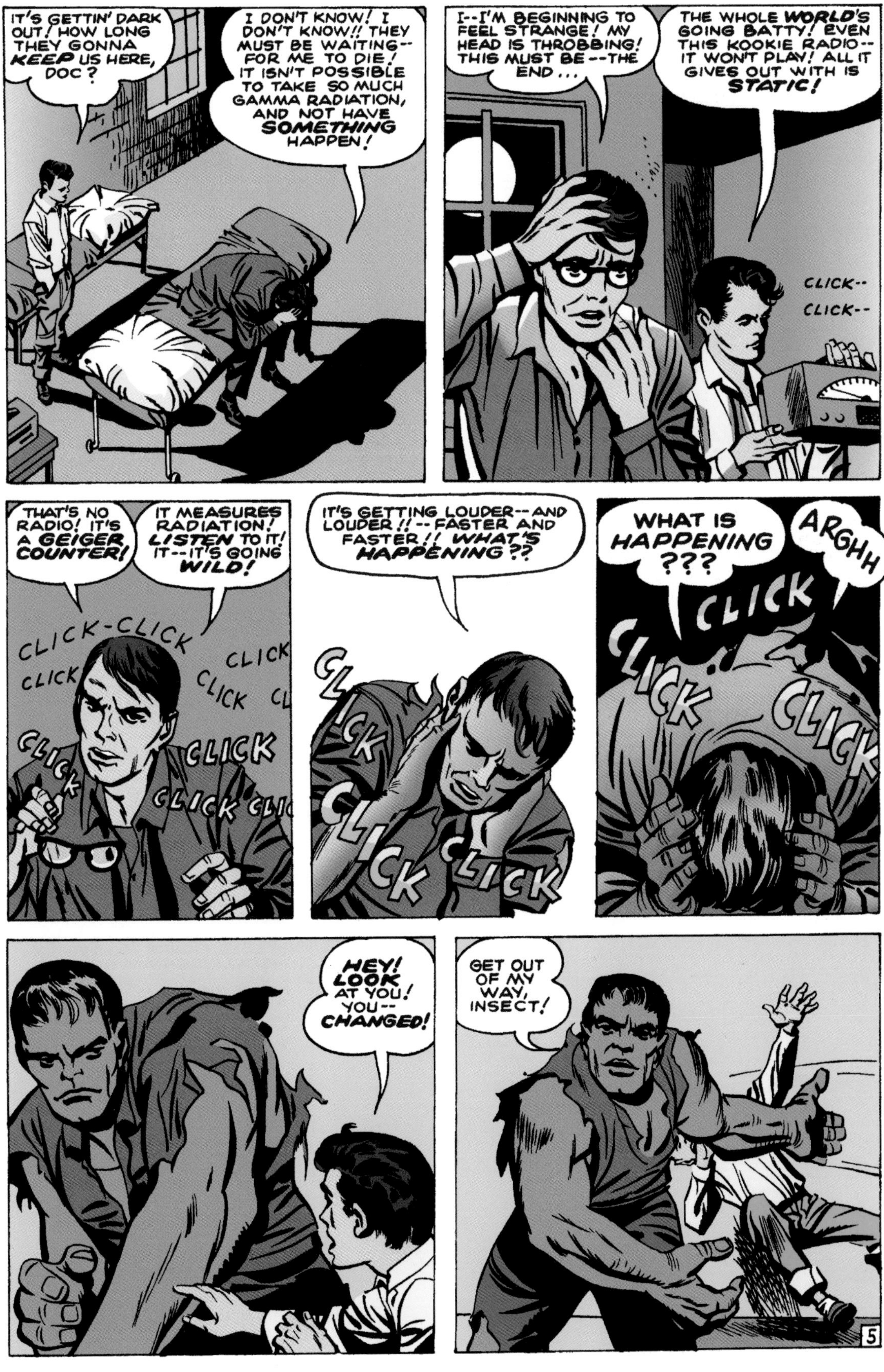
IT'S GETTIN' DARK OUT! HOW LONG THEY GONNA KEEP US HERE, DOC?
I DON'T KNOW! I DON'T KNOW!! THEY MUST BE WAITING-- FOR ME TO DIE! IT ISN'T POSSIBLE TO TAKE SO MUCH GAMMA RADIATION, AND NOT HAVE SOMETHING HAPPEN!
I--I'M BEGINNING TO FEEL STRANGE! MY HEAD IS THROBBING! THIS MUST BE--THE END...
THE WHOLE WORLD'S GOING BATTY! EVEN THIS KOOKIE RADIO-- IT WON'T PLAY! ALL IT GIVES OUT WITH IS STATIC!
CLICK--
CLICK--
THAT'S NO RADIO! IT'S A GEIGER COUNTER!
IT MEASURES RADIATION! LISTEN TO IT! IT--IT'S GOING WILD!
CLICK-CLICK
CLICK
CLICK
CLICK
CLICK
CLICK
CLICK
IT'S GETTING LOUDER--AND LOUDER!!--FASTER AND FASTER!! WHAT'S HAPPENING??
CLICK
CLICK
CLICK
CLICK
WHAT IS HAPPENING ???
ARGHH
CLICK
CLICK
CLICK
HEY! LOOK AT YOU! YOU-- CHANGED!
GET OUT OF MY WAY, INSECT!
5

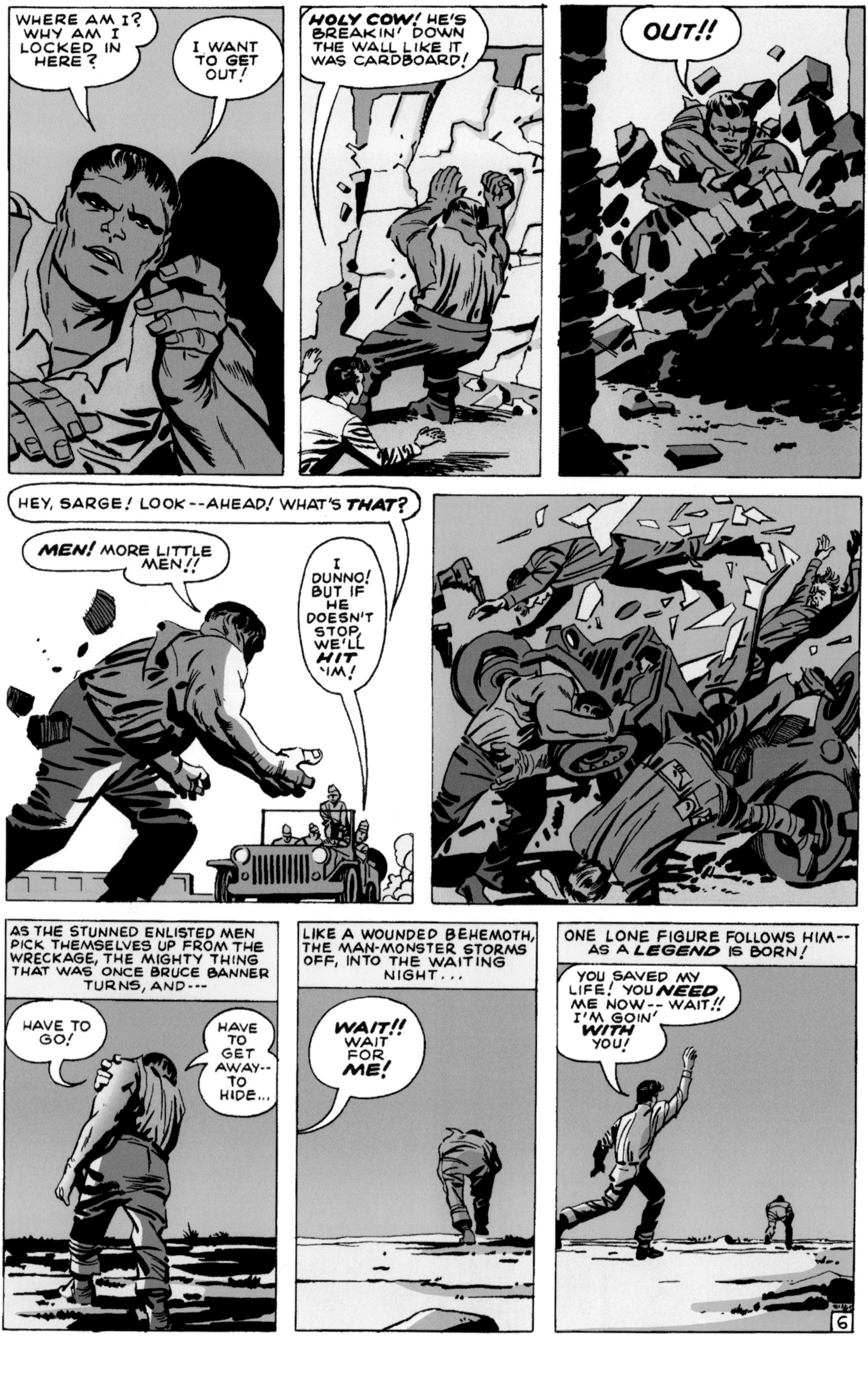
WHERE AM I? WHY AM I LOCKED IN HERE?
I WANT TO GET OUT!
HOLY COW! HE'S BREAKIN' DOWN THE WALL LIKE IT WAS CARDBOARD!
OUT!!
HEY, SARGE! LOOK--AHEAD! WHAT'S THAT?
MEN! MORE LITTLE MEN!!
I DUNNO! BUT IF HE DOESN'T STOP, WE'LL HIT 'IM!
AS THE STUNNED ENLISTED MEN PICK THEMSELVES UP FROM THE WRECKAGE, THE MIGHTY THING THAT WAS ONCE BRUCE BANNER TURNS, AND---
HAVE TO GO!
HAVE TO GET AWAY-- TO HIDE...
LIKE A WOUNDED BEHEMOTH, THE MAN-MONSTER STORMS OFF, INTO THE WAITING NIGHT...
WAIT!! WAIT FOR ME!
ONE LONE FIGURE FOLLOWS HIM-- AS A LEGEND IS BORN!
YOU SAVED MY LIFE! YOU NEED ME NOW-- WAIT!! I'M GOIN' WITH YOU!
6

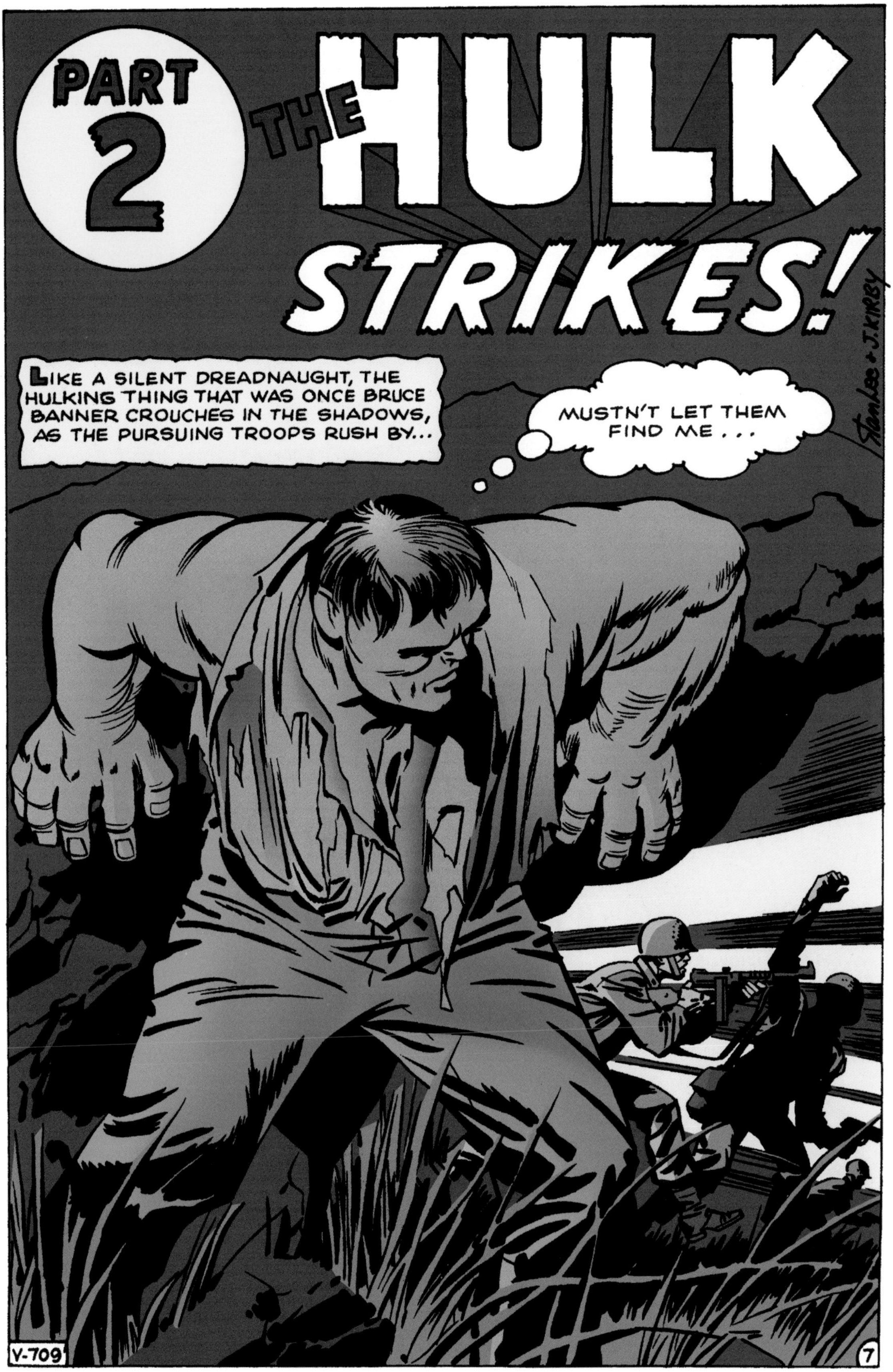
PART 2
THE HULK STRIKES!
STAN LEE + J. KIRBY
LIKE A SILENT DREADNAUGHT, THE HULKING THING THAT WAS ONCE BRUCE BANNER CROUCHES IN THE SHADOWS, AS THE PURSUING TROOPS RUSH BY...
MUSTN'T LET THEM FIND ME . . .
V-709
7

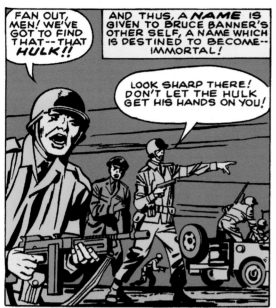

FAN OUT, MEN! WE'VE GOT TO FIND THAT--THAT *HULK*!!

AND THUS, A *NAME* IS GIVEN TO BRUCE BANNER'S OTHER SELF, A NAME WHICH IS DESTINED TO BECOME-- IMMORTAL!

LOOK SHARP THERE! DON'T LET THE HULK GET HIS HANDS ON YOU!

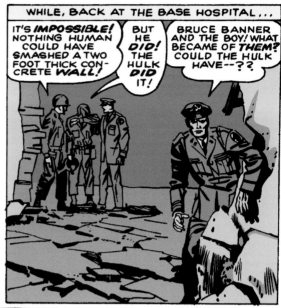

WHILE, BACK AT THE BASE HOSPITAL...

IT'S *IMPOSSIBLE!* NOTHING HUMAN COULD HAVE SMASHED A TWO FOOT THICK CONCRETE *WALL!*

BUT HE *DID!* THE HULK *DID* IT!

BRUCE BANNER AND THE BOY! WHAT BECAME OF *THEM?* COULD THE HULK HAVE--??

BUT WHO COULD EVER GUESS THE INCREDIBLE TRUTH? WHO COULD SUSPECT THAT BRUCE BANNER *IS*... THE HULK!!!

WH-WHERE IS HE *HEADED* FOR?

HAVE TO KEEP MOVING...

...HAVE TO REACH HOME! FORMULA INSIDE HOME! MUST GET FORMULA!!

DRIVEN BY SHEER INSTINCT, THE PART OF THE HULK WHICH IS STILL BRUCE BANNER HEADS FOR A SMALL COTTAGE, SMASHING ALL OBSTACLES IN HIS PATH!

MOVING WITH UNBELIEVABLE STEALTH FOR ONE SO PONDEROUS, HE STORMS CLOSER AND CLOSER TO HIS DESTINATION ...

UNTIL, AT LAST, A DIM MEMORY FROM THE BRAIN OF BRUCE BANNER TELLS HIM...

THE THIRD CABIN! THAT IS WHERE I MUST GO!

8

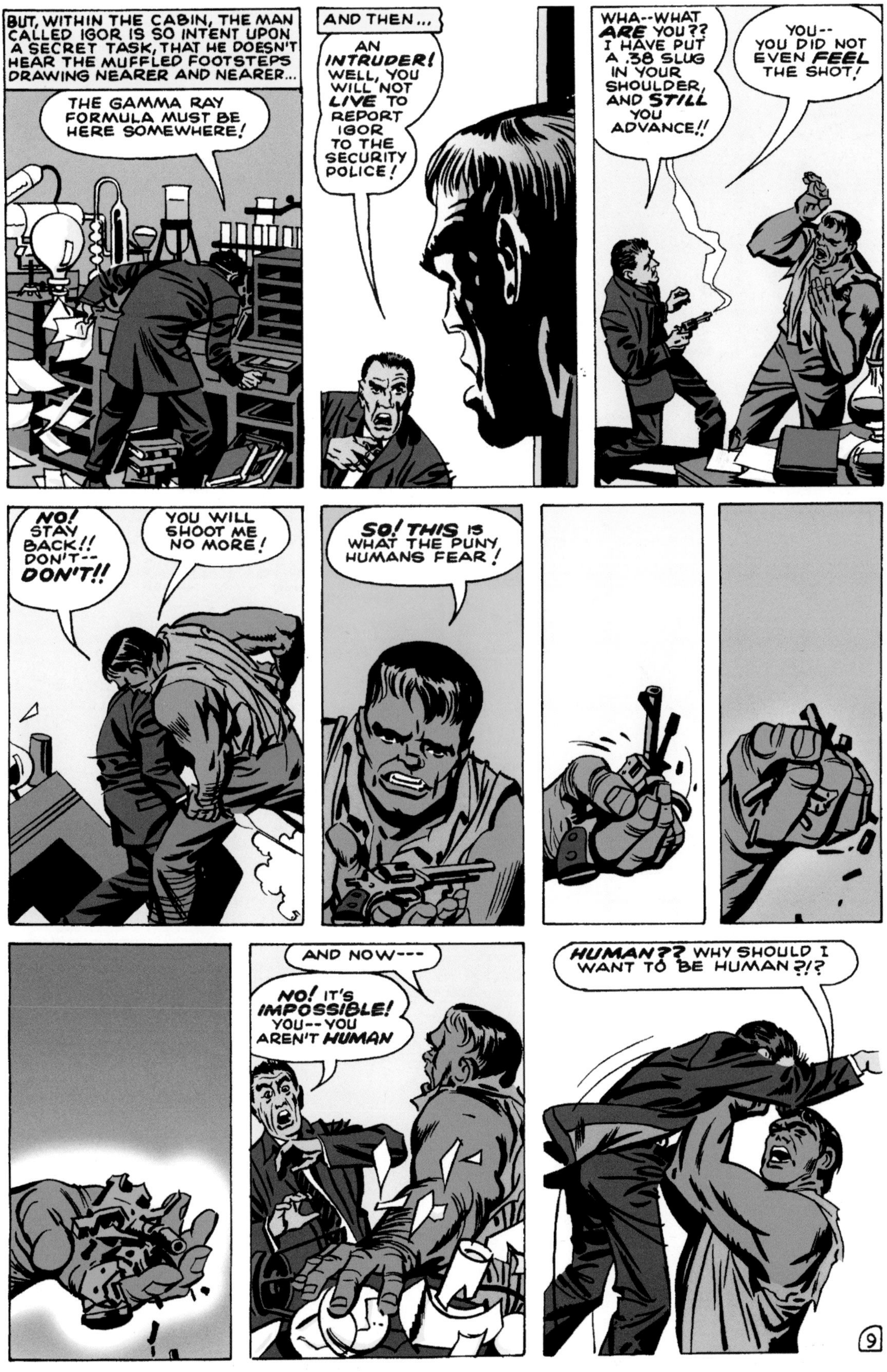
BUT, WITHIN THE CABIN, THE MAN CALLED IGOR IS SO INTENT UPON A SECRET TASK, THAT HE DOESN'T HEAR THE MUFFLED FOOTSTEPS DRAWING NEARER AND NEARER...
THE GAMMA RAY FORMULA MUST BE HERE SOMEWHERE!
AND THEN...
AN INTRUDER! WELL, YOU WILL NOT LIVE TO REPORT IGOR TO THE SECURITY POLICE!
WHA--WHAT ARE YOU?? I HAVE PUT A .38 SLUG IN YOUR SHOULDER, AND STILL YOU ADVANCE!!
YOU-- YOU DID NOT EVEN FEEL THE SHOT!
NO! STAY BACK!! DON'T-- DON'T!!
YOU WILL SHOOT ME NO MORE!
SO! THIS IS WHAT THE PUNY HUMANS FEAR!
AND NOW---
NO! IT'S IMPOSSIBLE! YOU--YOU AREN'T HUMAN
HUMAN?? WHY SHOULD I WANT TO BE HUMAN?!?
9

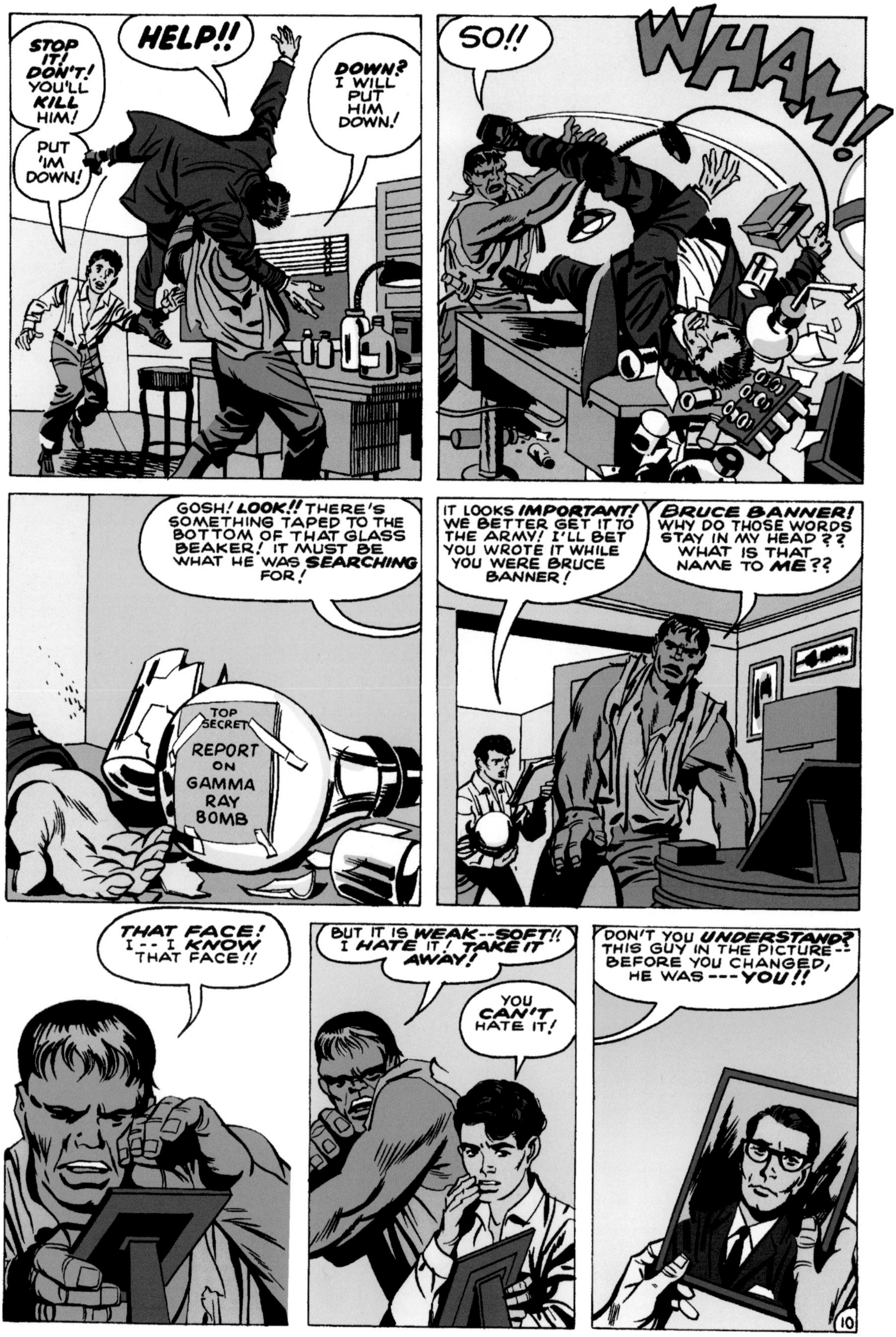

STOP IT! DON'T! YOU'LL KILL HIM!
HELP!!
DOWN? I WILL PUT HIM DOWN!
PUT 'IM DOWN!
SO!!
WHAM!
GOSH! LOOK!! THERE'S SOMETHING TAPED TO THE BOTTOM OF THAT GLASS BEAKER! IT MUST BE WHAT HE WAS SEARCHING FOR!
TOP SECRET
REPORT ON GAMMA RAY BOMB
IT LOOKS IMPORTANT! WE BETTER GET IT TO THE ARMY! I'LL BET YOU WROTE IT WHILE YOU WERE BRUCE BANNER!
BRUCE BANNER! WHY DO THOSE WORDS STAY IN MY HEAD?? WHAT IS THAT NAME TO ME??
THAT FACE! I--I KNOW THAT FACE!!
BUT IT IS WEAK--SOFT!! I HATE IT! TAKE IT AWAY!
YOU CAN'T HATE IT!
DON'T YOU UNDERSTAND? THIS GUY IN THE PICTURE--BEFORE YOU CHANGED, HE WAS---YOU!!
10

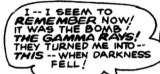

"I -- I SEEM TO *REMEMBER* NOW! IT WAS THE BOMB! *THE GAMMA RAYS!* THEY TURNED ME INTO -- *THIS* -- WHEN DARKNESS FELL!"

"IT WOULD HAVE HAPPENED TO *ME* IF YOU HADN'T SAVED ME! THAT'S WHY I'M STAYIN' *WITH* YOU!"

"*FOOL!* I AM *GLAD* IT HAPPENED!! I'D RATHER BE *ME*, THAN THAT PUNY *WEAKLING* IN THE PICTURE!"

"I DON'T WANT YOU WITH ME! I DON'T *NEED* YOU! I DON'T NEED *ANYBODY!* WITH MY STRENGTH -- MY POWER -- THE *WORLD* IS MINE!"

"AS FOR *YOU* -- YOU ARE THE ONLY ONE WHO KNOWS WHO I REALLY *AM!*"

"WHA -- WHAT DO YOU *MEAN?*"

"BUT, AT THAT VERY INSTANT, THE FIRST RAYS OF *DAWN* APPEAR! AND WITH THEM --"

"MY HEAD!!"

"MY BRAIN -- IT'S ON FIRE!"

"WHAT IS *HAPPENING* TO ME? I -- I'M *CHANGING!!*"

"CHANGING ---"

"IT -- IT FEELS AS THOUGH A *VEIL* HAS LIFTED -- I CAN *THINK* AGAIN!"

"IT'S *OVER!* THE NIGHTMARE IS *OVER!*"

"*GOSH!* YOU -- YOU'RE DOCTOR BRUCE BANNER AGAIN!"

"BUT, ALAS, THE NIGHTMARE OF BRUCE BANNER IS *NOT* YET OVER! IT MAY *NEVER* BE OVER AGAIN!"

"*OPEN UP* IN THERE!"

"THIS IS THE POLICE!"

(11)

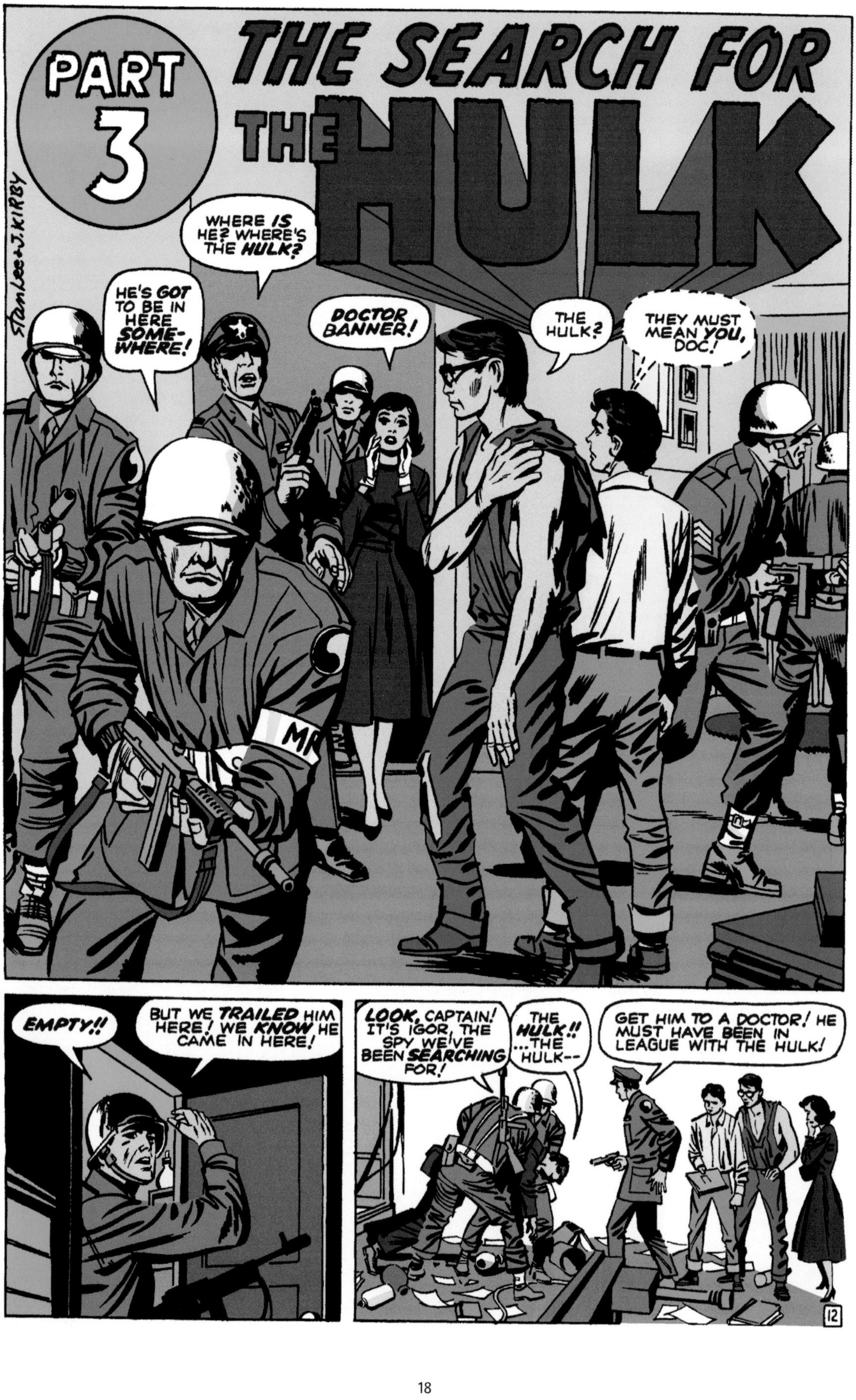
PART 3
THE SEARCH FOR THE HULK
StanLee + J. KIRBY
HE'S GOT TO BE IN HERE SOME-WHERE!
WHERE IS HE? WHERE'S THE HULK?
DOCTOR BANNER!
THE HULK?
THEY MUST MEAN YOU, DOC!
MP
EMPTY!!
BUT WE TRAILED HIM HERE! WE KNOW HE CAME IN HERE!
LOOK, CAPTAIN! IT'S IGOR, THE SPY WE'VE BEEN SEARCHING FOR!
THE HULK!! ...THE HULK--
GET HIM TO A DOCTOR! HE MUST HAVE BEEN IN LEAGUE WITH THE HULK!
12

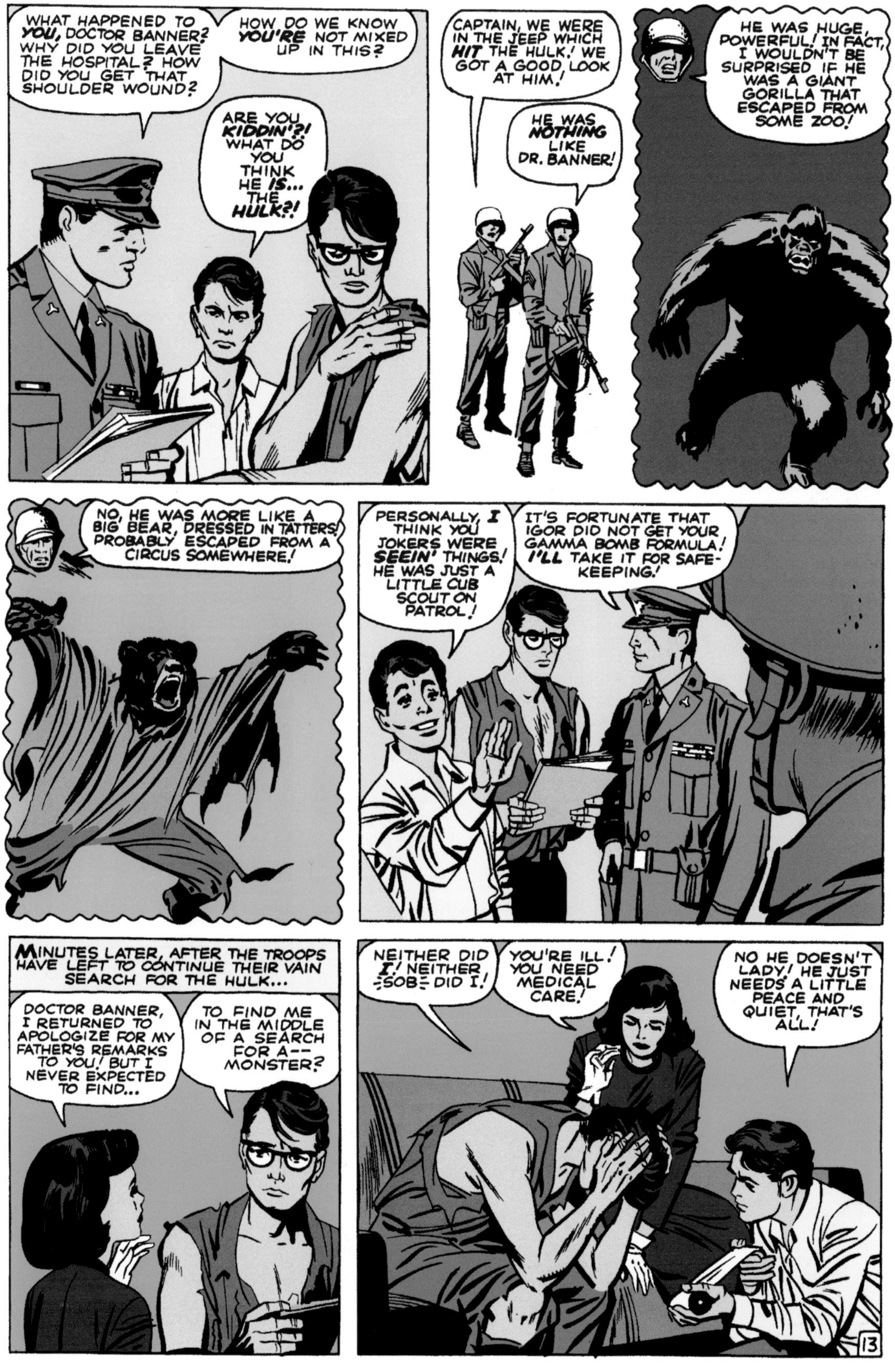
WHAT HAPPENED TO YOU, DOCTOR BANNER? WHY DID YOU LEAVE THE HOSPITAL? HOW DID YOU GET THAT SHOULDER WOUND?
HOW DO WE KNOW YOU'RE NOT MIXED UP IN THIS?
ARE YOU KIDDIN'?! WHAT DO YOU THINK HE IS... THE HULK?!
CAPTAIN, WE WERE IN THE JEEP WHICH HIT THE HULK! WE GOT A GOOD LOOK AT HIM!
HE WAS NOTHING LIKE DR. BANNER!
HE WAS HUGE, POWERFUL! IN FACT, I WOULDN'T BE SURPRISED IF HE WAS A GIANT GORILLA THAT ESCAPED FROM SOME ZOO!
NO, HE WAS MORE LIKE A BIG BEAR, DRESSED IN TATTERS! PROBABLY ESCAPED FROM A CIRCUS SOMEWHERE!
PERSONALLY, I THINK YOU JOKERS WERE SEEIN' THINGS! HE WAS JUST A LITTLE CUB SCOUT ON PATROL!
IT'S FORTUNATE THAT IGOR DID NOT GET YOUR GAMMA BOMB FORMULA! I'LL TAKE IT FOR SAFE-KEEPING!
MINUTES LATER, AFTER THE TROOPS HAVE LEFT TO CONTINUE THEIR VAIN SEARCH FOR THE HULK...
DOCTOR BANNER, I RETURNED TO APOLOGIZE FOR MY FATHER'S REMARKS TO YOU! BUT I NEVER EXPECTED TO FIND...
TO FIND ME IN THE MIDDLE OF A SEARCH FOR A-- MONSTER?
NEITHER DID I! NEITHER -SOB- DID I!
YOU'RE ILL! YOU NEED MEDICAL CARE!
NO HE DOESN'T LADY! HE JUST NEEDS A LITTLE PEACE AND QUIET, THAT'S ALL!
13

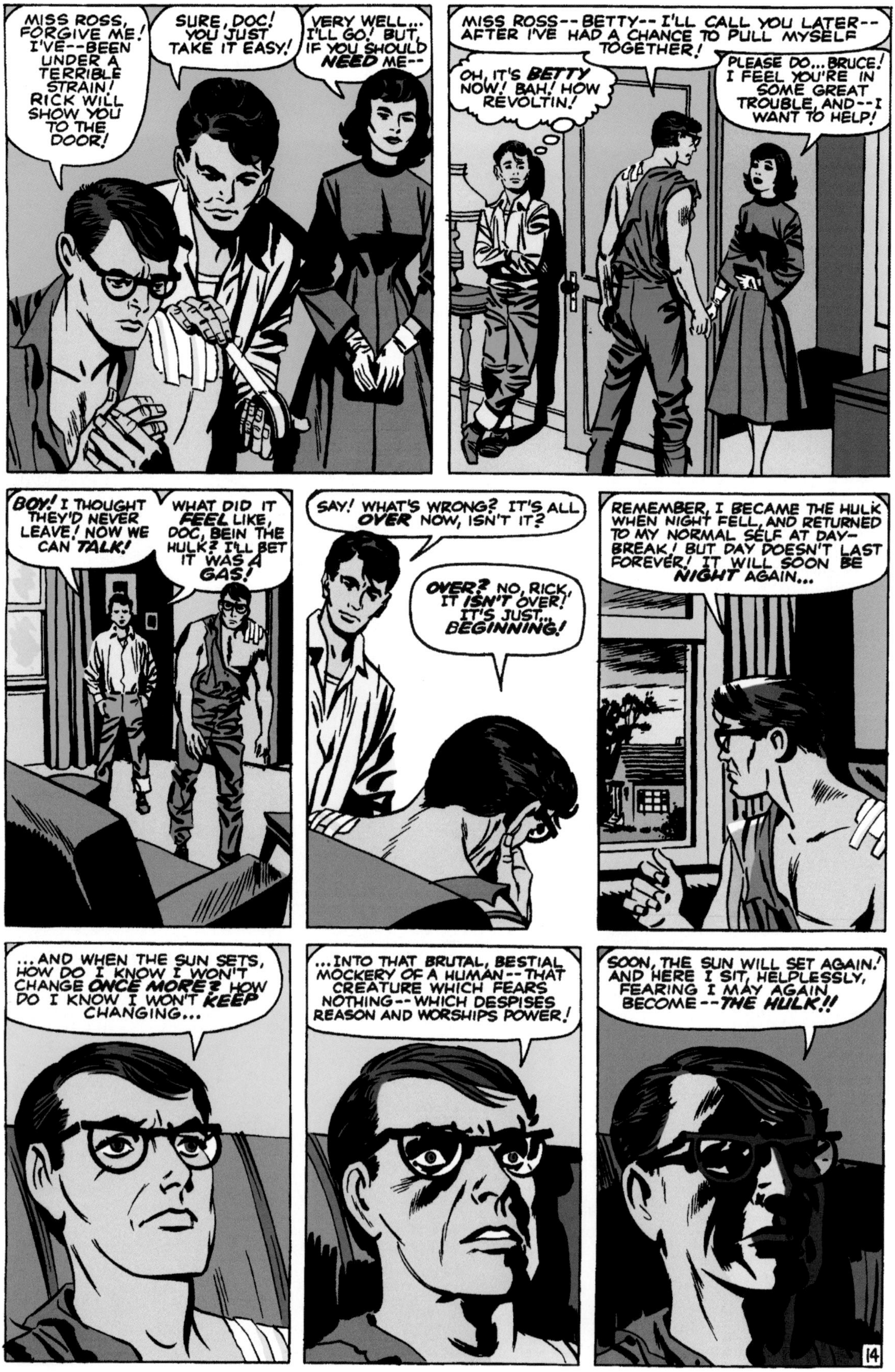
MISS ROSS, FORGIVE ME! I'VE--BEEN UNDER A TERRIBLE STRAIN! RICK WILL SHOW YOU TO THE DOOR!
SURE, DOC! YOU JUST TAKE IT EASY!
VERY WELL... I'LL GO! BUT, IF YOU SHOULD NEED ME--
MISS ROSS--BETTY--I'LL CALL YOU LATER--AFTER I'VE HAD A CHANCE TO PULL MYSELF TOGETHER!
OH, IT'S BETTY NOW! BAH! HOW REVOLTIN!
PLEASE DO...BRUCE! I FEEL YOU'RE IN SOME GREAT TROUBLE, AND--I WANT TO HELP!
BOY! I THOUGHT THEY'D NEVER LEAVE! NOW WE CAN TALK!
WHAT DID IT FEEL LIKE, DOC, BEIN THE HULK? I'LL BET IT WAS A GAS!
SAY! WHAT'S WRONG? IT'S ALL OVER NOW, ISN'T IT?
OVER? NO, RICK, IT ISN'T OVER! IT'S JUST... BEGINNING!
REMEMBER, I BECAME THE HULK WHEN NIGHT FELL, AND RETURNED TO MY NORMAL SELF AT DAYBREAK! BUT DAY DOESN'T LAST FOREVER! IT WILL SOON BE NIGHT AGAIN...
...AND WHEN THE SUN SETS, HOW DO I KNOW I WON'T CHANGE ONCE MORE? HOW DO I KNOW I WON'T KEEP CHANGING...
...INTO THAT BRUTAL, BESTIAL MOCKERY OF A HUMAN--THAT CREATURE WHICH FEARS NOTHING--WHICH DESPISES REASON AND WORSHIPS POWER!
SOON, THE SUN WILL SET AGAIN! AND HERE I SIT, HELPLESSLY, FEARING I MAY AGAIN BECOME--THE HULK!!
14

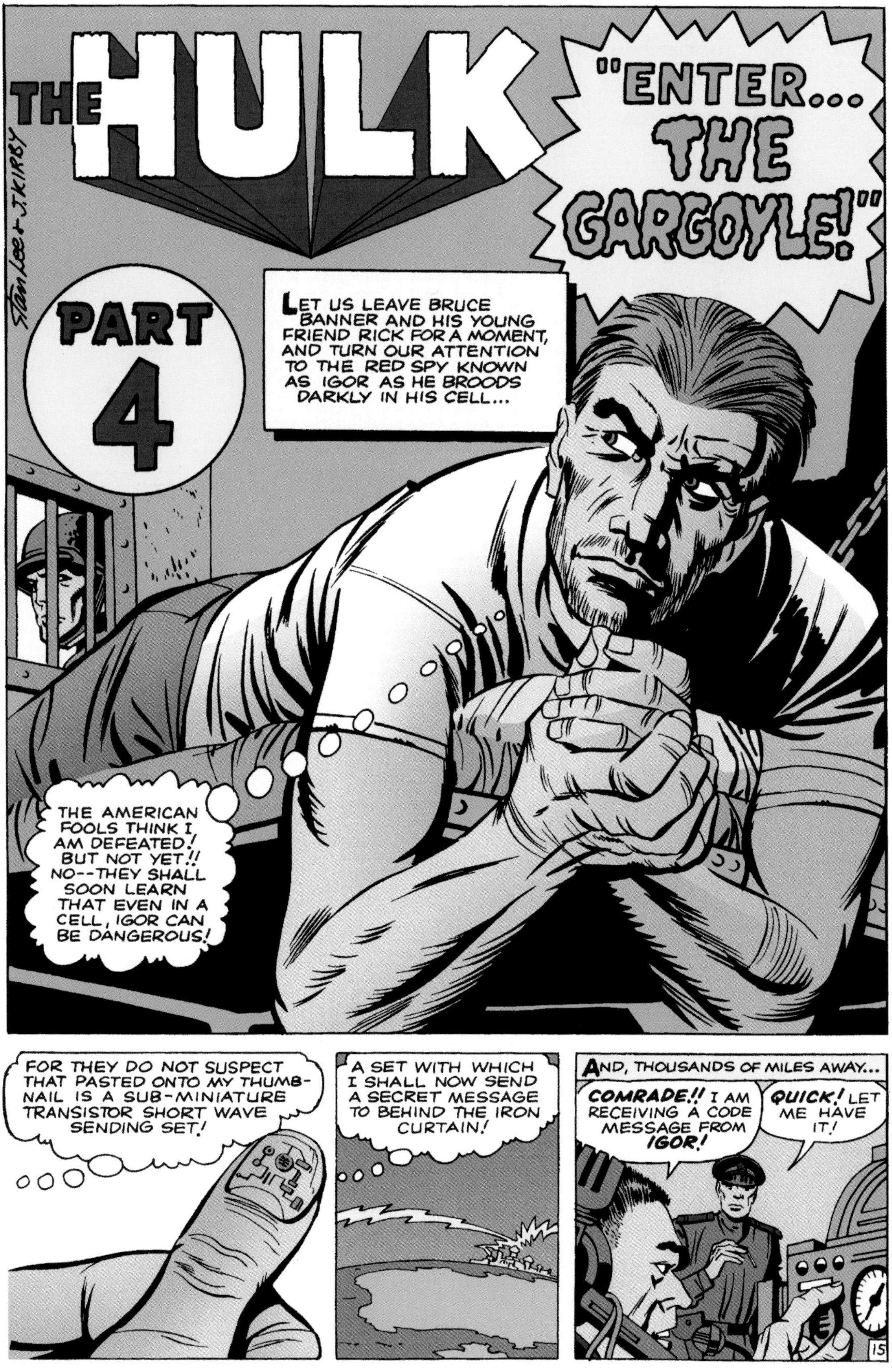
THE HULK
"ENTER... THE GARGOYLE!"
STAN LEE + J. KIRBY
PART 4
LET US LEAVE BRUCE BANNER AND HIS YOUNG FRIEND RICK FOR A MOMENT, AND TURN OUR ATTENTION TO THE RED SPY KNOWN AS IGOR AS HE BROODS DARKLY IN HIS CELL...
THE AMERICAN FOOLS THINK I AM DEFEATED! BUT NOT YET!! NO--THEY SHALL SOON LEARN THAT EVEN IN A CELL, IGOR CAN BE DANGEROUS!
FOR THEY DO NOT SUSPECT THAT PASTED ONTO MY THUMB-NAIL IS A SUB-MINIATURE TRANSISTOR SHORT WAVE SENDING SET!
A SET WITH WHICH I SHALL NOW SEND A SECRET MESSAGE TO BEHIND THE IRON CURTAIN!
AND, THOUSANDS OF MILES AWAY...
COMRADE!! I AM RECEIVING A CODE MESSAGE FROM IGOR!
QUICK! LET ME HAVE IT!
15

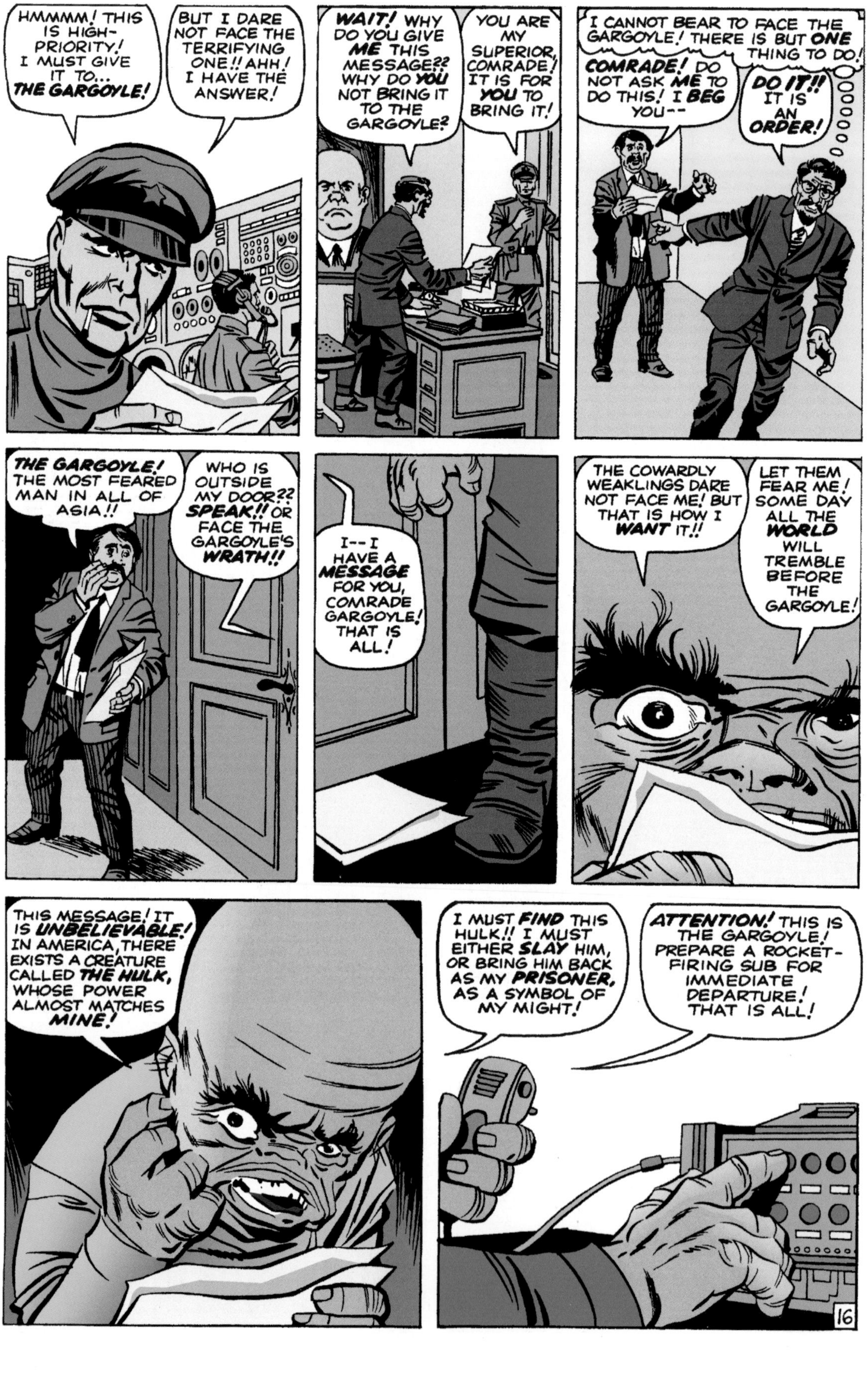
HMMMM! THIS IS HIGH-PRIORITY! I MUST GIVE IT TO... THE GARGOYLE!
BUT I DARE NOT FACE THE TERRIFYING ONE!! AHH! I HAVE THE ANSWER!
WAIT! WHY DO YOU GIVE ME THIS MESSAGE?? WHY DO YOU NOT BRING IT TO THE GARGOYLE?
YOU ARE MY SUPERIOR, COMRADE! IT IS FOR YOU TO BRING IT!
I CANNOT BEAR TO FACE THE GARGOYLE! THERE IS BUT ONE THING TO DO!
COMRADE! DO NOT ASK ME TO DO THIS! I BEG YOU--
DO IT!! IT IS AN ORDER!
THE GARGOYLE! THE MOST FEARED MAN IN ALL OF ASIA!!
WHO IS OUTSIDE MY DOOR?? SPEAK!! OR FACE THE GARGOYLE'S WRATH!!
I-- I HAVE A MESSAGE FOR YOU, COMRADE GARGOYLE! THAT IS ALL!
THE COWARDLY WEAKLINGS DARE NOT FACE ME! BUT THAT IS HOW I WANT IT!!
LET THEM FEAR ME! SOME DAY ALL THE WORLD WILL TREMBLE BEFORE THE GARGOYLE!
THIS MESSAGE! IT IS UNBELIEVABLE! IN AMERICA, THERE EXISTS A CREATURE CALLED THE HULK, WHOSE POWER ALMOST MATCHES MINE!
I MUST FIND THIS HULK!! I MUST EITHER SLAY HIM, OR BRING HIM BACK AS MY PRISONER, AS A SYMBOL OF MY MIGHT!
ATTENTION! THIS IS THE GARGOYLE! PREPARE A ROCKET-FIRING SUB FOR IMMEDIATE DEPARTURE! THAT IS ALL!
16

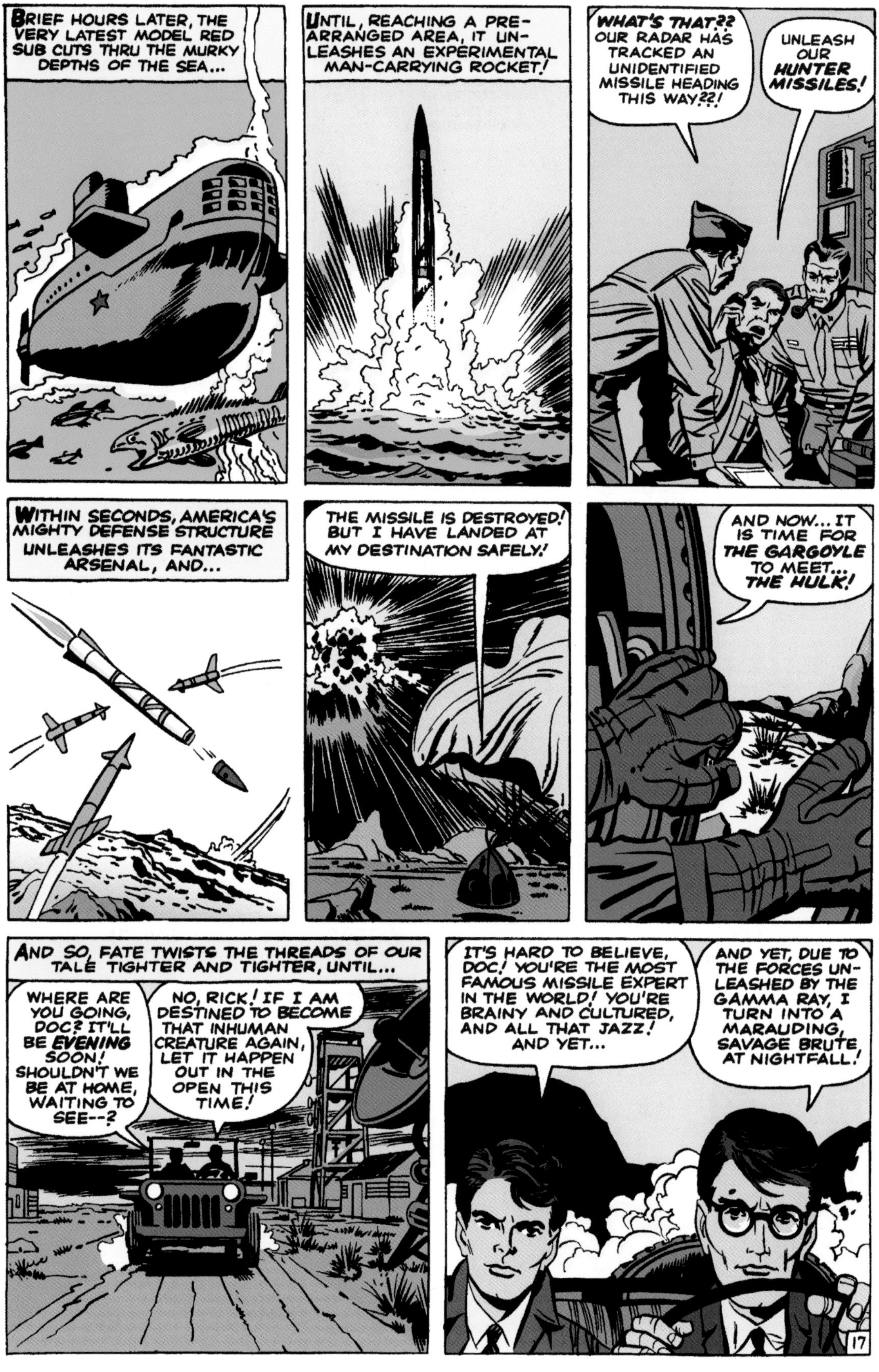
BRIEF HOURS LATER, THE VERY LATEST MODEL RED SUB CUTS THRU THE MURKY DEPTHS OF THE SEA...
UNTIL, REACHING A PRE-ARRANGED AREA, IT UN-LEASHES AN EXPERIMENTAL MAN-CARRYING ROCKET!
WHAT'S THAT?? OUR RADAR HAS TRACKED AN UNIDENTIFIED MISSILE HEADING THIS WAY??!
UNLEASH OUR HUNTER MISSILES!
WITHIN SECONDS, AMERICA'S MIGHTY DEFENSE STRUCTURE UNLEASHES ITS FANTASTIC ARSENAL, AND...
THE MISSILE IS DESTROYED! BUT I HAVE LANDED AT MY DESTINATION SAFELY!
AND NOW... IT IS TIME FOR THE GARGOYLE TO MEET... THE HULK!
AND SO, FATE TWISTS THE THREADS OF OUR TALE TIGHTER AND TIGHTER, UNTIL...
WHERE ARE YOU GOING, DOC? IT'LL BE EVENING SOON! SHOULDN'T WE BE AT HOME, WAITING TO SEE--?
NO, RICK! IF I AM DESTINED TO BECOME THAT INHUMAN CREATURE AGAIN, LET IT HAPPEN OUT IN THE OPEN THIS TIME!
IT'S HARD TO BELIEVE, DOC! YOU'RE THE MOST FAMOUS MISSILE EXPERT IN THE WORLD! YOU'RE BRAINY AND CULTURED, AND ALL THAT JAZZ! AND YET...
AND YET, DUE TO THE FORCES UN-LEASHED BY THE GAMMA RAY, I TURN INTO A MARAUDING, SAVAGE BRUTE AT NIGHTFALL!
17

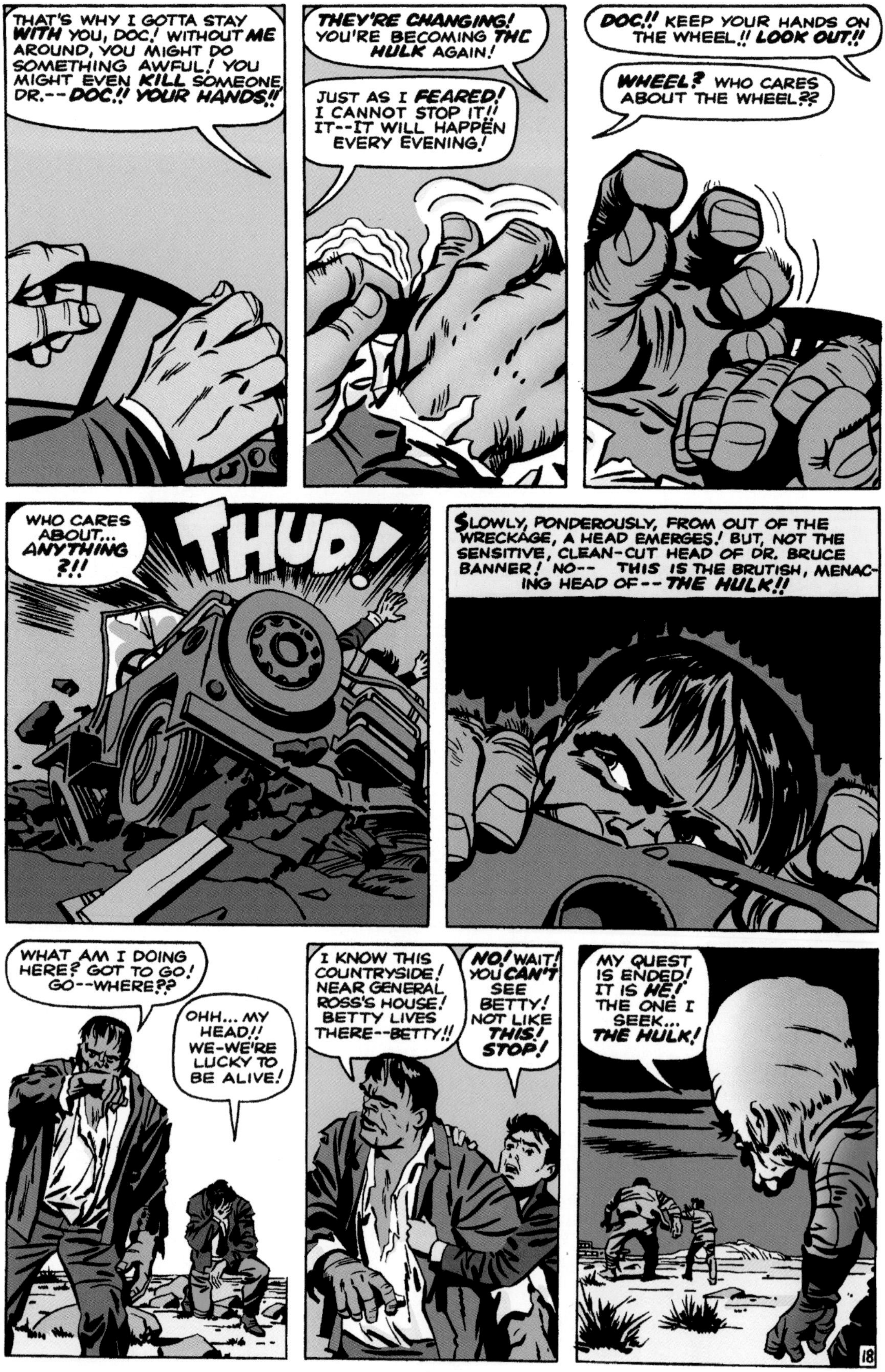
THAT'S WHY I GOTTA STAY WITH YOU, DOC! WITHOUT ME AROUND, YOU MIGHT DO SOMETHING AWFUL! YOU MIGHT EVEN KILL SOMEONE DR.--DOC!! YOUR HANDS!!
THEY'RE CHANGING! YOU'RE BECOMING THE HULK AGAIN!
JUST AS I FEARED! I CANNOT STOP IT!! IT--IT WILL HAPPEN EVERY EVENING!
DOC!! KEEP YOUR HANDS ON THE WHEEL!! LOOK OUT!!
WHEEL? WHO CARES ABOUT THE WHEEL??
WHO CARES ABOUT... ANYTHING ?!!
THUD!
SLOWLY, PONDEROUSLY, FROM OUT OF THE WRECKAGE, A HEAD EMERGES! BUT, NOT THE SENSITIVE, CLEAN-CUT HEAD OF DR. BRUCE BANNER! NO-- THIS IS THE BRUTISH, MENACING HEAD OF--THE HULK!!
WHAT AM I DOING HERE? GOT TO GO! GO--WHERE??
OHH... MY HEAD!! WE-WE'RE LUCKY TO BE ALIVE!
I KNOW THIS COUNTRYSIDE! NEAR GENERAL ROSS'S HOUSE! BETTY LIVES THERE--BETTY!!
NO! WAIT! YOU CAN'T SEE BETTY! NOT LIKE THIS! STOP!
MY QUEST IS ENDED! IT IS HE! THE ONE I SEEK... THE HULK!
18

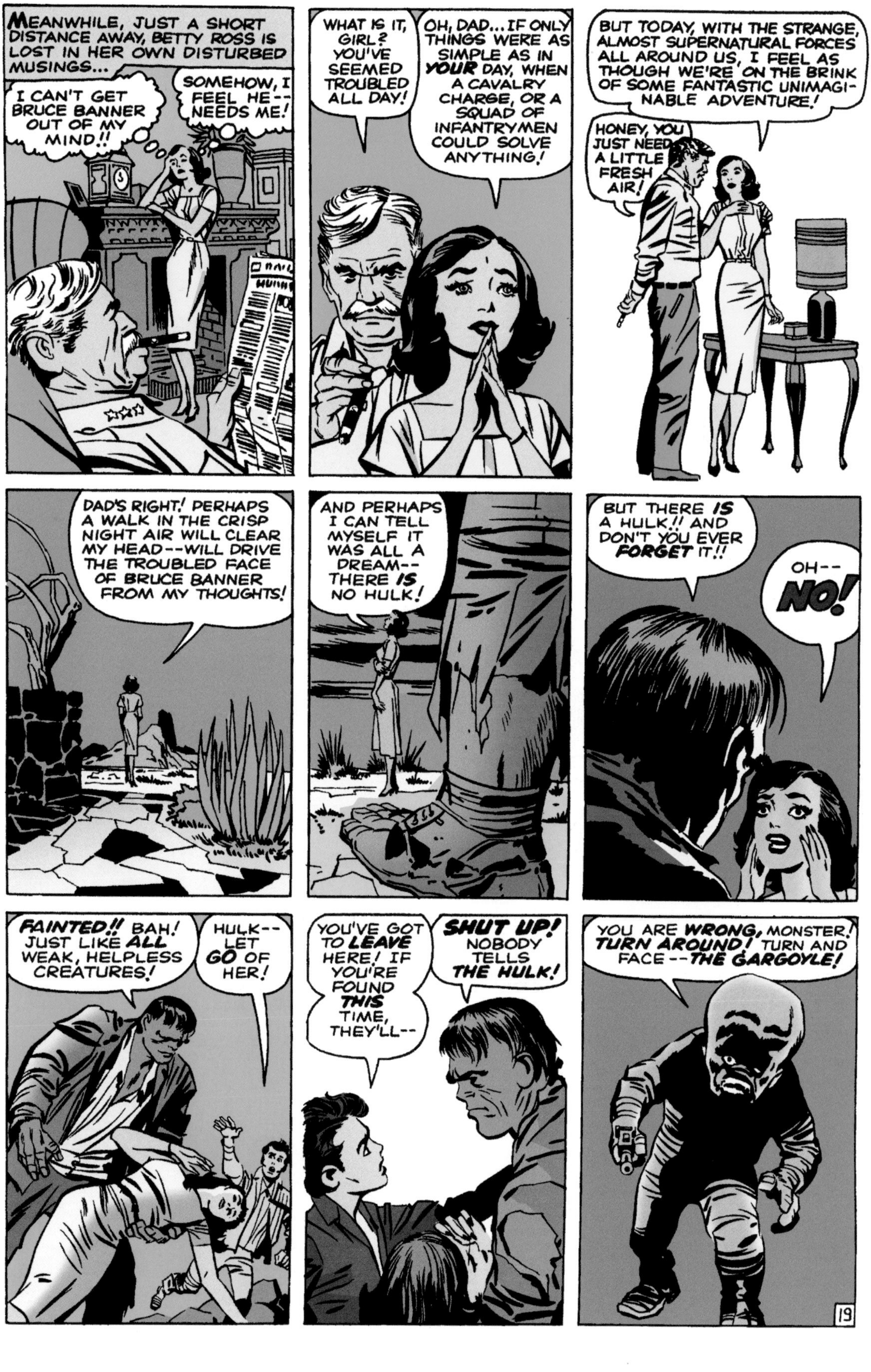
MEANWHILE, JUST A SHORT DISTANCE AWAY, BETTY ROSS IS LOST IN HER OWN DISTURBED MUSINGS...
I CAN'T GET BRUCE BANNER OUT OF MY MIND!!
SOMEHOW, I FEEL HE-- NEEDS ME!
WHAT IS IT, GIRL? YOU'VE SEEMED TROUBLED ALL DAY!
OH, DAD... IF ONLY THINGS WERE AS SIMPLE AS IN YOUR DAY, WHEN A CAVALRY CHARGE, OR A SQUAD OF INFANTRYMEN COULD SOLVE ANYTHING!
BUT TODAY, WITH THE STRANGE, ALMOST SUPERNATURAL FORCES ALL AROUND US, I FEEL AS THOUGH WE'RE ON THE BRINK OF SOME FANTASTIC UNIMAGINABLE ADVENTURE!
HONEY, YOU JUST NEED A LITTLE FRESH AIR!
DAD'S RIGHT! PERHAPS A WALK IN THE CRISP NIGHT AIR WILL CLEAR MY HEAD--WILL DRIVE THE TROUBLED FACE OF BRUCE BANNER FROM MY THOUGHTS!
AND PERHAPS I CAN TELL MYSELF IT WAS ALL A DREAM--THERE IS NO HULK!
BUT THERE IS A HULK!! AND DON'T YOU EVER FORGET IT!!
OH-- NO!
FAINTED!! BAH! JUST LIKE ALL WEAK, HELPLESS CREATURES!
HULK--LET GO OF HER!
YOU'VE GOT TO LEAVE HERE! IF YOU'RE FOUND THIS TIME, THEY'LL--
SHUT UP! NOBODY TELLS THE HULK!
YOU ARE WRONG, MONSTER! TURN AROUND! TURN AND FACE--THE GARGOYLE!
19

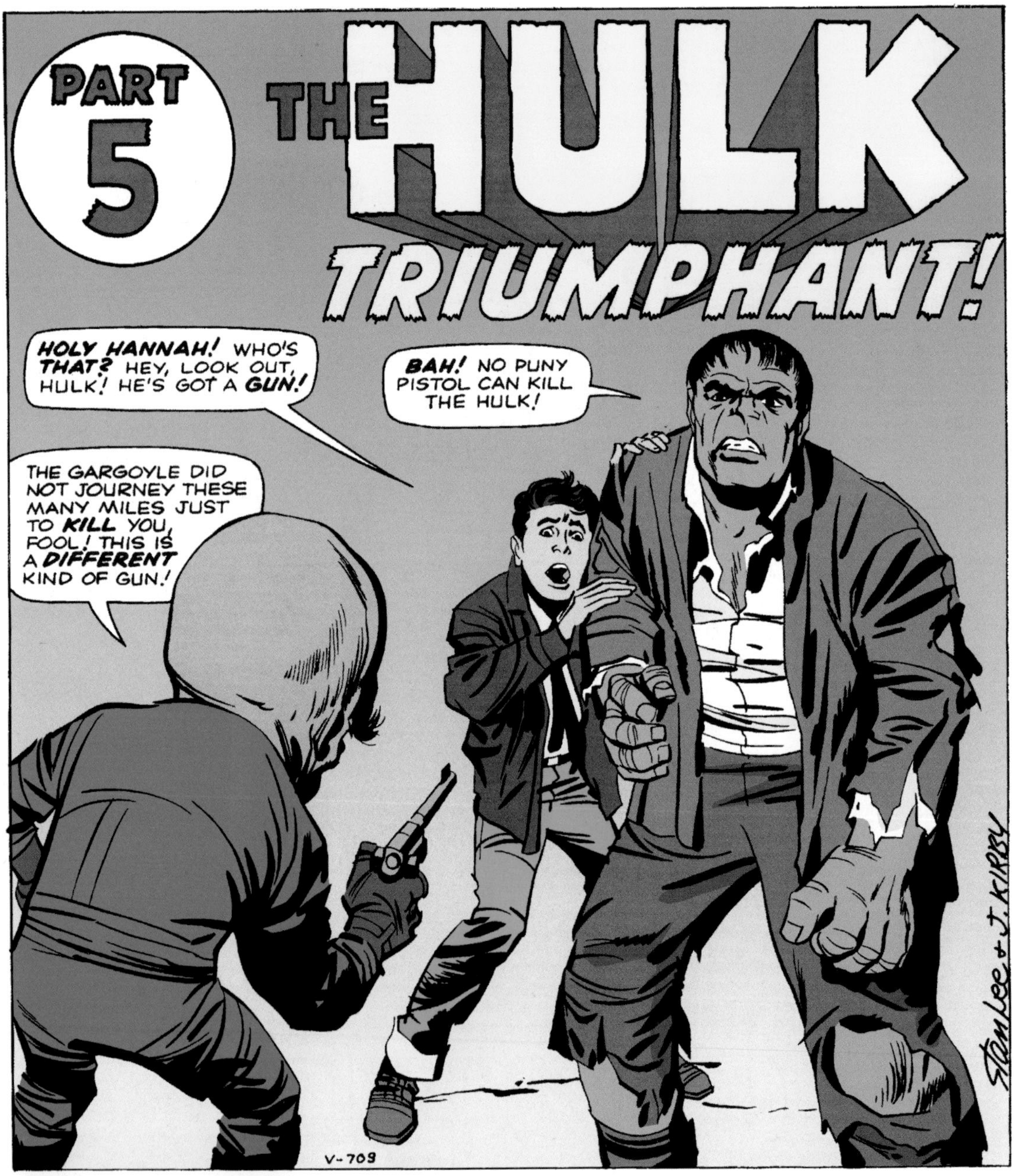
PART 5
THE HULK TRIUMPHANT!
HOLY HANNAH! WHO'S THAT? HEY, LOOK OUT, HULK! HE'S GOT A GUN!
BAH! NO PUNY PISTOL CAN KILL THE HULK!
THE GARGOYLE DID NOT JOURNEY THESE MANY MILES JUST TO KILL YOU, FOOL! THIS IS A DIFFERENT KIND OF GUN!
STAN LEE + J. KIRBY
V-709

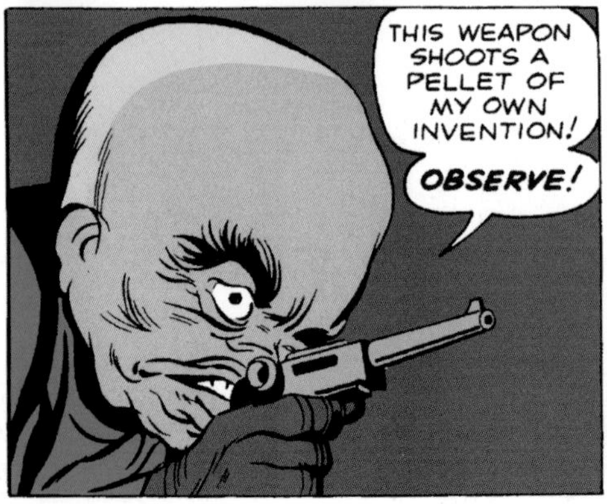
THIS WEAPON SHOOTS A PELLET OF MY OWN INVENTION!
OBSERVE!

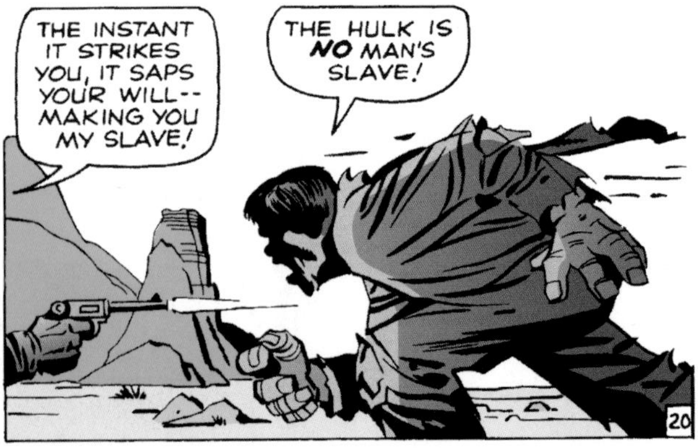
THE INSTANT IT STRIKES YOU, IT SAPS YOUR WILL-- MAKING YOU MY SLAVE!
THE HULK IS NO MAN'S SLAVE!
20

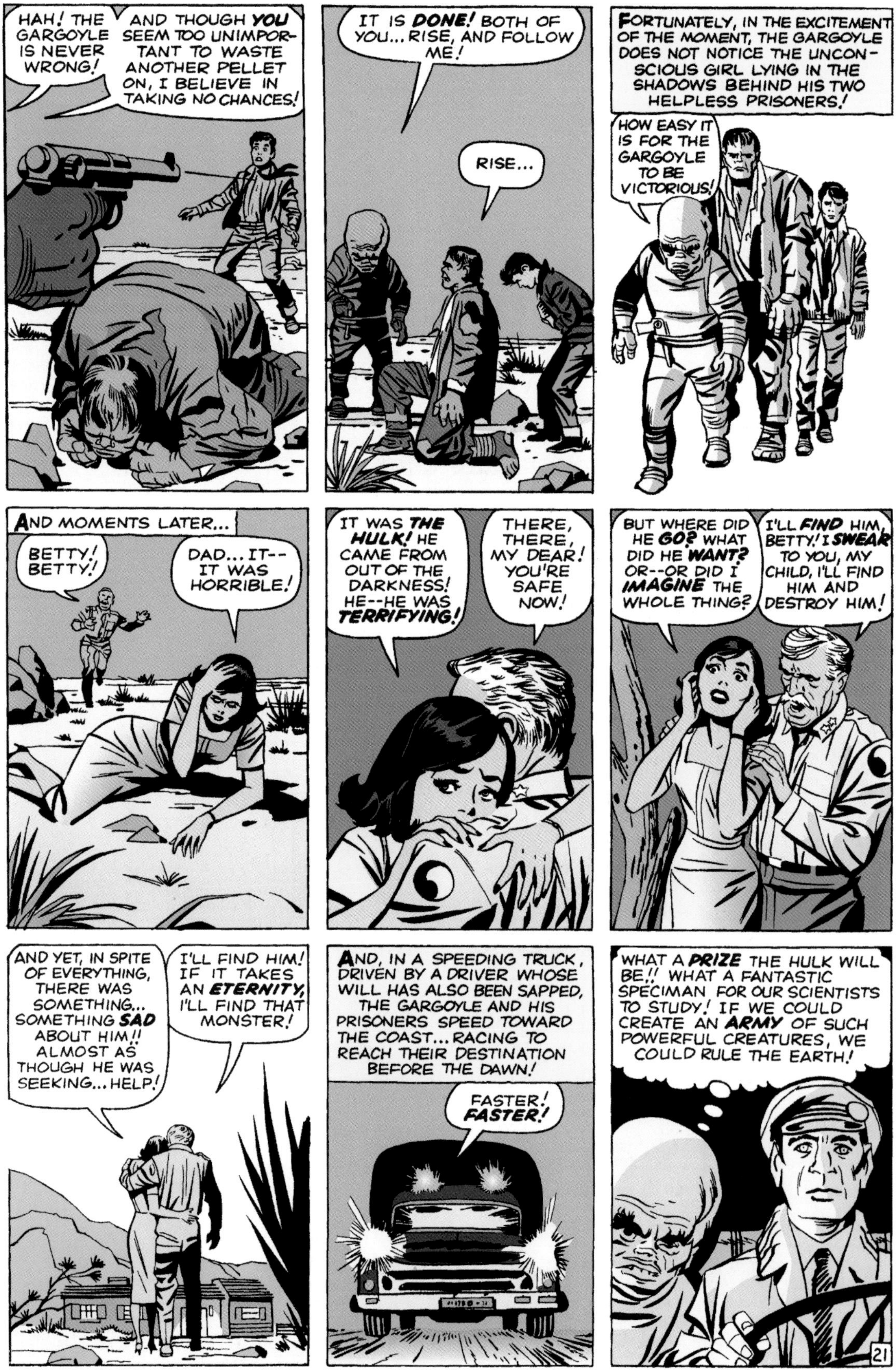
HAH! THE GARGOYLE IS NEVER WRONG!
AND THOUGH YOU SEEM TOO UNIMPORTANT TO WASTE ANOTHER PELLET ON, I BELIEVE IN TAKING NO CHANCES!
IT IS DONE! BOTH OF YOU... RISE, AND FOLLOW ME!
RISE...
FORTUNATELY, IN THE EXCITEMENT OF THE MOMENT, THE GARGOYLE DOES NOT NOTICE THE UNCONSCIOUS GIRL LYING IN THE SHADOWS BEHIND HIS TWO HELPLESS PRISONERS!
HOW EASY IT IS FOR THE GARGOYLE TO BE VICTORIOUS!
AND MOMENTS LATER...
BETTY! BETTY!
DAD... IT-- IT WAS HORRIBLE!
IT WAS THE HULK! HE CAME FROM OUT OF THE DARKNESS! HE--HE WAS TERRIFYING!
THERE, THERE, MY DEAR! YOU'RE SAFE NOW!
BUT WHERE DID HE GO? WHAT DID HE WANT? OR--OR DID I IMAGINE THE WHOLE THING?
I'LL FIND HIM, BETTY! I SWEAR TO YOU, MY CHILD, I'LL FIND HIM AND DESTROY HIM!
AND YET, IN SPITE OF EVERYTHING, THERE WAS SOMETHING... SOMETHING SAD ABOUT HIM!! ALMOST AS THOUGH HE WAS SEEKING... HELP!
I'LL FIND HIM! IF IT TAKES AN ETERNITY, I'LL FIND THAT MONSTER!
AND, IN A SPEEDING TRUCK, DRIVEN BY A DRIVER WHOSE WILL HAS ALSO BEEN SAPPED, THE GARGOYLE AND HIS PRISONERS SPEED TOWARD THE COAST... RACING TO REACH THEIR DESTINATION BEFORE THE DAWN!
FASTER! FASTER!
WHAT A PRIZE THE HULK WILL BE!! WHAT A FANTASTIC SPECIMAN FOR OUR SCIENTISTS TO STUDY! IF WE COULD CREATE AN ARMY OF SUCH POWERFUL CREATURES, WE COULD RULE THE EARTH!
21

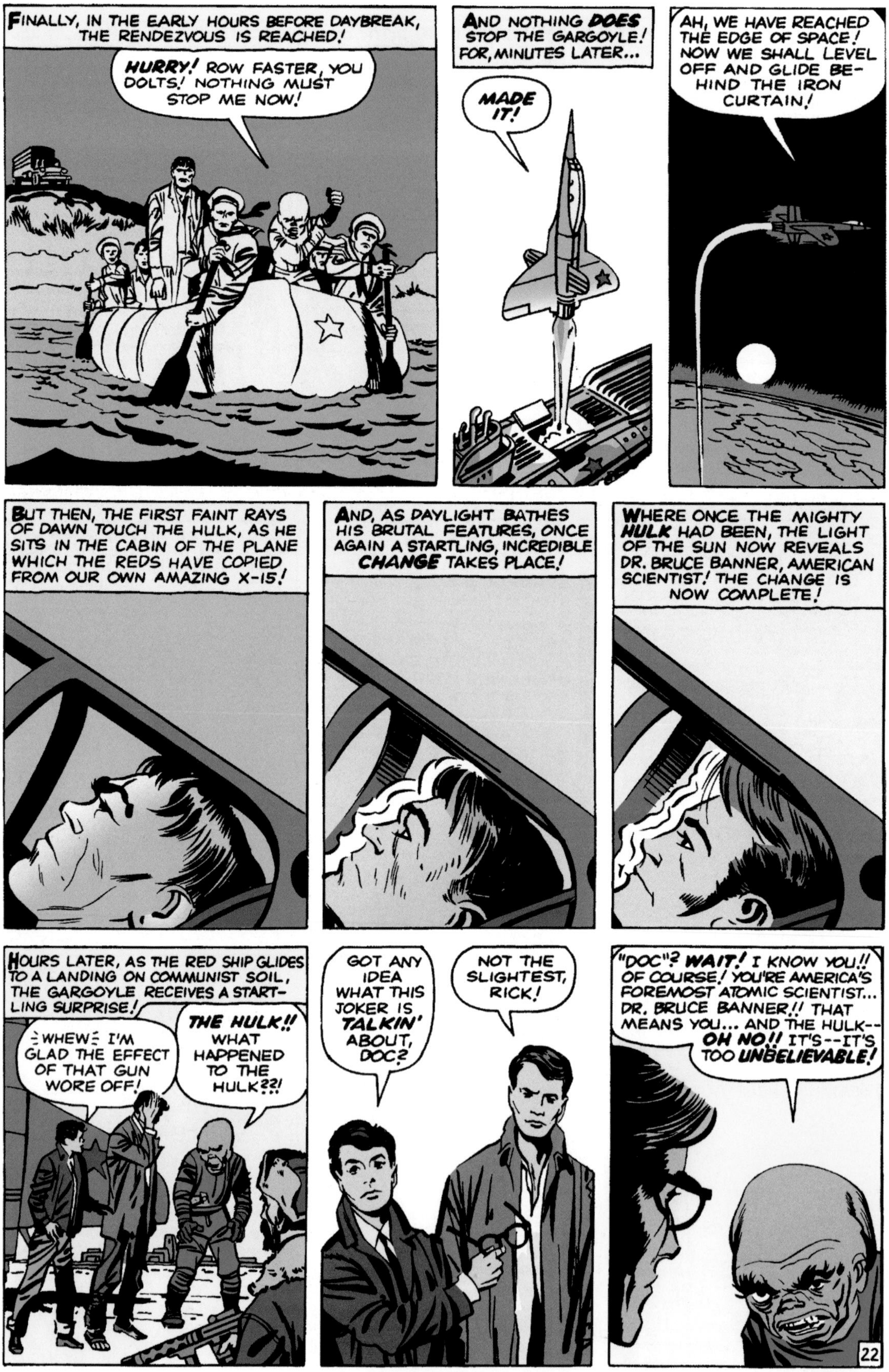
FINALLY, IN THE EARLY HOURS BEFORE DAYBREAK, THE RENDEZVOUS IS REACHED!
HURRY! ROW FASTER, YOU DOLTS! NOTHING MUST STOP ME NOW!
AND NOTHING DOES STOP THE GARGOYLE! FOR, MINUTES LATER...
MADE IT!
AH, WE HAVE REACHED THE EDGE OF SPACE! NOW WE SHALL LEVEL OFF AND GLIDE BE-HIND THE IRON CURTAIN!
BUT THEN, THE FIRST FAINT RAYS OF DAWN TOUCH THE HULK, AS HE SITS IN THE CABIN OF THE PLANE WHICH THE REDS HAVE COPIED FROM OUR OWN AMAZING X-15!
AND, AS DAYLIGHT BATHES HIS BRUTAL FEATURES, ONCE AGAIN A STARTLING, INCREDIBLE CHANGE TAKES PLACE!
WHERE ONCE THE MIGHTY HULK HAD BEEN, THE LIGHT OF THE SUN NOW REVEALS DR. BRUCE BANNER, AMERICAN SCIENTIST! THE CHANGE IS NOW COMPLETE!
HOURS LATER, AS THE RED SHIP GLIDES TO A LANDING ON COMMUNIST SOIL, THE GARGOYLE RECEIVES A START-LING SURPRISE!
WHEW! I'M GLAD THE EFFECT OF THAT GUN WORE OFF!
THE HULK!! WHAT HAPPENED TO THE HULK??!
GOT ANY IDEA WHAT THIS JOKER IS TALKIN' ABOUT, DOC?
NOT THE SLIGHTEST, RICK!
"DOC"? WAIT! I KNOW YOU!! OF COURSE! YOU'RE AMERICA'S FOREMOST ATOMIC SCIENTIST... DR. BRUCE BANNER!! THAT MEANS YOU... AND THE HULK-- OH NO!! IT'S--IT'S TOO UNBELIEVABLE!
22

UNDER CLOSE GUARD, THE GARGOYLE RUSHES HIS PRISONERS TO HIS SECRET STRONGHOLD, AND THEN...

YOUR SECRET IS A SECRET NO LONGER, BANNER. I **KNOW** THAT YOU AND THE HULK ARE THE SAME!!

DOC! WHAT DO WE DO *NOW*?

EASY, RICK! IT'S *HIS* PLAY SO FAR!

BUT WHY? WHY WOULD YOU *WANT* TO BE A *MONSTER*? YOU MUST BE *INSANE!* IT--IT'S THE MOST HORRIBLE THING IN THE WORLD TO BE A FREAK-- A GARGOYLE! LIKE *ME!*

DOC! HE'S CRYING!

I'D GIVE *ANYTHING* TO BE *NORMAL!* *ANYTHING!*

SO WOULD I-- BUT I AM AS HELPLESS AS YOU!

WAIT! *LISTEN* TO ME! I CANNOT *STOP* MYSELF FROM TURNING INTO THE HULK-- BUT *YOUR* CASE IS DIFFERENT!

I'VE *SEEN* CASES LIKE YOURS! I KNOW HOW TO CURE YOU... *BY RADIATION!* BUT ALTHOUGH YOUR FEATURES WOULD BECOME NORMAL, YOUR BRAIN WOULD SUFFER! YOU WOULD NO LONGER BE A BRILLIANT SCIENTIST!

DOC! YOU AIN'T GONNA *HELP* THAT CREEP, ARE YOU??!

QUIET, RICK!

NO MATTER *WHAT* HAPPENS TO ME... EVEN IF I *DIE*... SO LONG AS I COULD DIE AS-- *A MAN!*

THEN, AT A COMMAND FROM THE GARGOYLE, ALL IS MADE READY...

NOW!

AND, WHERE A *GARGOYLE* HAD BEEN LYING...

DOC! IT'S WORKING!

...*A MAN* ARISES!

YOU DID IT!

YOU DID IT!

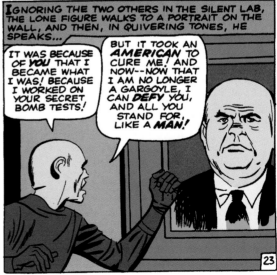

IGNORING THE TWO OTHERS IN THE SILENT LAB, THE LONE FIGURE WALKS TO A PORTRAIT ON THE WALL, AND THEN, IN QUIVERING TONES, HE SPEAKS...

IT WAS BECAUSE OF *YOU* THAT I BECAME WHAT I WAS! BECAUSE I WORKED ON YOUR SECRET BOMB TESTS!

BUT IT TOOK AN *AMERICAN* TO CURE ME! AND NOW--NOW THAT I AM NO LONGER A GARGOYLE, I CAN *DEFY* YOU, AND ALL YOU STAND FOR LIKE A *MAN!*

23

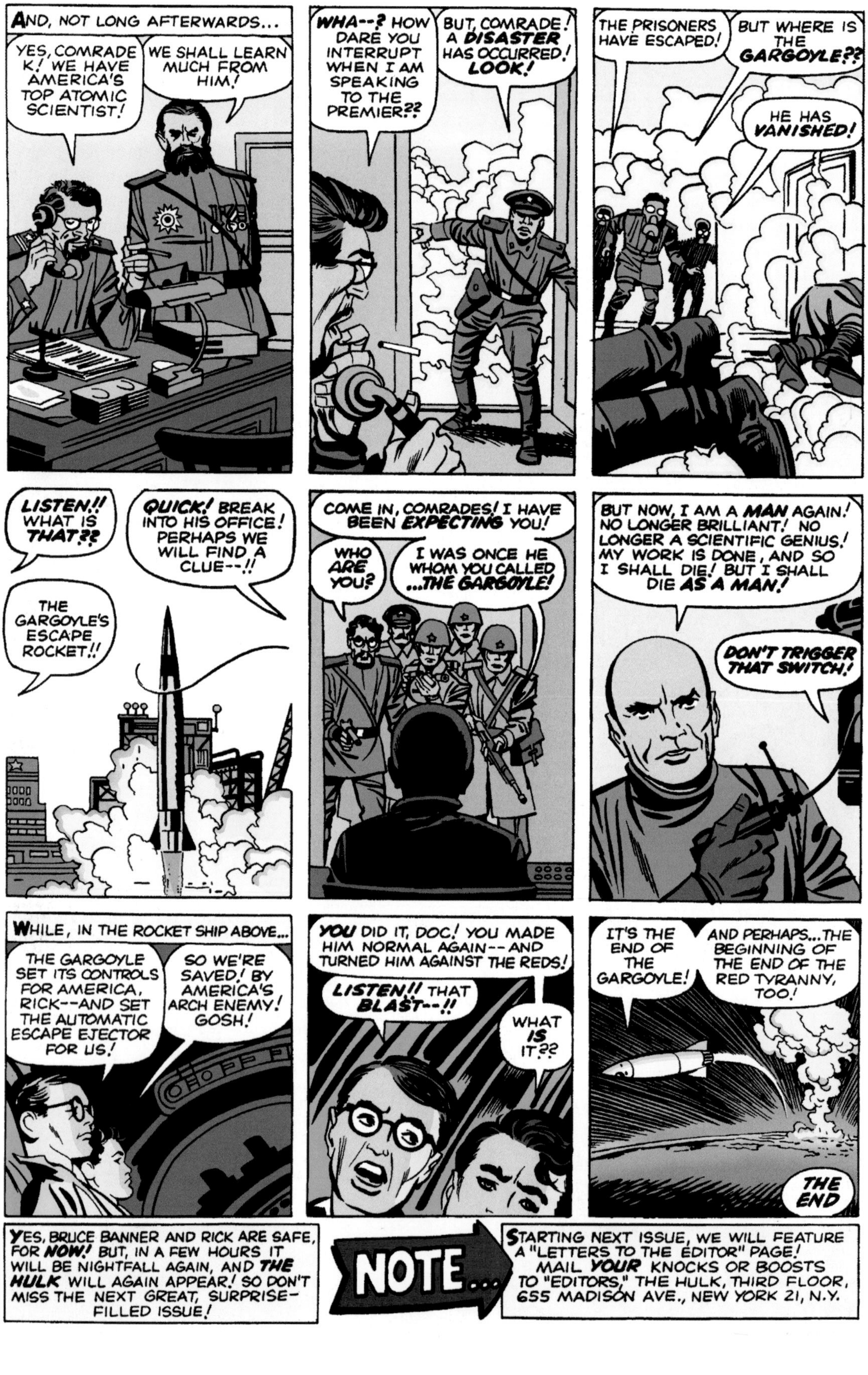
AND, NOT LONG AFTERWARDS...
YES, COMRADE K! WE HAVE AMERICA'S TOP ATOMIC SCIENTIST!
WE SHALL LEARN MUCH FROM HIM!
WHA--? HOW DARE YOU INTERRUPT WHEN I AM SPEAKING TO THE PREMIER??
BUT, COMRADE! A DISASTER HAS OCCURRED! LOOK!
THE PRISONERS HAVE ESCAPED!
BUT WHERE IS THE GARGOYLE??
HE HAS VANISHED!
LISTEN!! WHAT IS THAT??
QUICK! BREAK INTO HIS OFFICE! PERHAPS WE WILL FIND A CLUE--!!
THE GARGOYLE'S ESCAPE ROCKET!!
COME IN, COMRADES! I HAVE BEEN EXPECTING YOU!
WHO ARE YOU?
I WAS ONCE HE WHOM YOU CALLED ...THE GARGOYLE!
BUT NOW, I AM A MAN AGAIN! NO LONGER BRILLIANT! NO LONGER A SCIENTIFIC GENIUS! MY WORK IS DONE, AND SO I SHALL DIE! BUT I SHALL DIE AS A MAN!
DON'T TRIGGER THAT SWITCH!
WHILE, IN THE ROCKET SHIP ABOVE...
THE GARGOYLE SET ITS CONTROLS FOR AMERICA, RICK--AND SET THE AUTOMATIC ESCAPE EJECTOR FOR US!
SO WE'RE SAVED! BY AMERICA'S ARCH ENEMY! GOSH!
YOU DID IT, DOC! YOU MADE HIM NORMAL AGAIN--AND TURNED HIM AGAINST THE REDS!
LISTEN!! THAT BLAST--!!
WHAT IS IT??
IT'S THE END OF THE GARGOYLE!
AND PERHAPS...THE BEGINNING OF THE END OF THE RED TYRANNY, TOO!
THE END
YES, BRUCE BANNER AND RICK ARE SAFE, FOR NOW! BUT, IN A FEW HOURS IT WILL BE NIGHTFALL AGAIN, AND THE HULK WILL AGAIN APPEAR! SO DON'T MISS THE NEXT GREAT, SURPRISE-FILLED ISSUE!
NOTE...
STARTING NEXT ISSUE, WE WILL FEATURE A "LETTERS TO THE EDITOR" PAGE! MAIL YOUR KNOCKS OR BOOSTS TO "EDITORS," THE HULK, THIRD FLOOR, 655 MADISON AVE., NEW YORK 21, N.Y.

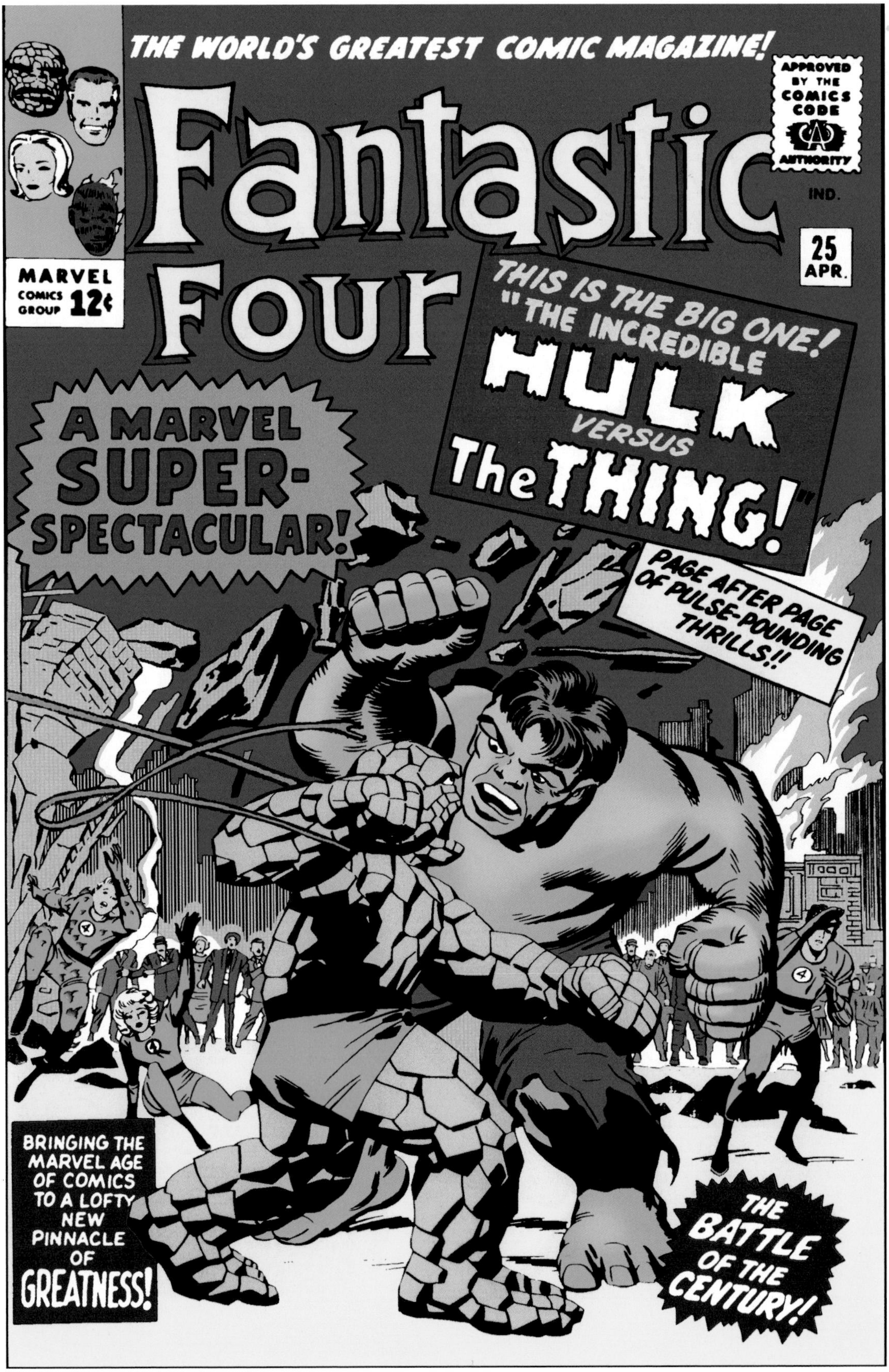
THE WORLD'S GREATEST COMIC MAGAZINE!
APPROVED BY THE COMICS CODE AUTHORITY
Fantastic Four
IND.
25 APR.
MARVEL COMICS GROUP 12¢
THIS IS THE BIG ONE! "THE INCREDIBLE HULK VERSUS The THING!"
A MARVEL SUPER-SPECTACULAR!
PAGE AFTER PAGE OF PULSE-POUNDING THRILLS!!
BRINGING THE MARVEL AGE OF COMICS TO A LOFTY NEW PINNACLE OF GREATNESS!
THE BATTLE OF THE CENTURY!

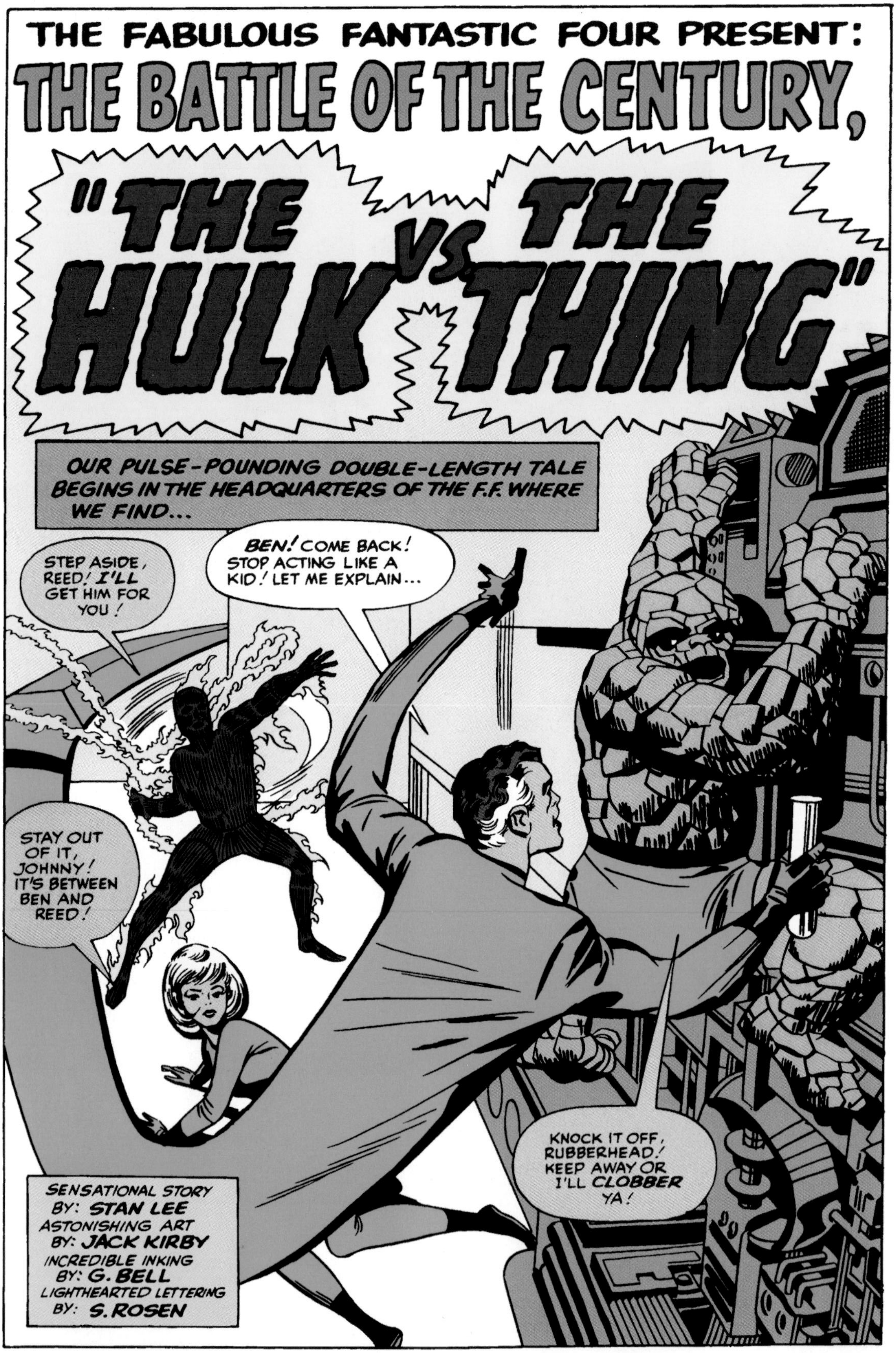
THE FABULOUS FANTASTIC FOUR PRESENT:
THE BATTLE OF THE CENTURY,
"THE HULK VS. THE THING"
OUR PULSE-POUNDING DOUBLE-LENGTH TALE BEGINS IN THE HEADQUARTERS OF THE F.F. WHERE WE FIND...
STEP ASIDE, REED! I'LL GET HIM FOR YOU!
BEN! COME BACK! STOP ACTING LIKE A KID! LET ME EXPLAIN...
STAY OUT OF IT, JOHNNY! IT'S BETWEEN BEN AND REED!
KNOCK IT OFF, RUBBERHEAD! KEEP AWAY OR I'LL CLOBBER YA!
SENSATIONAL STORY BY: STAN LEE
ASTONISHING ART BY: JACK KIRBY
INCREDIBLE INKING BY: G. BELL
LIGHTHEARTED LETTERING BY: S. ROSEN

BEN, OLD FRIEND, YOU'VE **GOT** TO DRINK THIS! I DISCOVERED THE FORMULA ACCIDENTALLY! I MAY NEVER BE ABLE TO DUPLICATE IT! I **KNOW** IT'LL TURN YOU BACK TO BEN GRIMM...**PERMANENTLY!**

HOW MANY TIMES DO I HAVETA **TELL** YA? I **WON'T** DO IT!

THINK WHAT REED IS **DOING** FOR YOU, BEN! IF YOU STOP BEING THE **THING**, WE LOSE ONE FOURTH OF OUR STRENGTH! AND **STILL** HE WANTS YOU TO DRINK IT!

I WONDER WHY THE THING IS SO **STUBBORN?**

I'M **WARNIN'** YA...STOP BUGGIN' ME!

BUT, BEN, IF YOU DON'T DRINK IT SOON, IT'LL LOSE ITS POTENCY! WE MAY NEVER GET ANOTHER OPPORTUNITY LIKE THIS AGAIN! **BEN...!!**

I WASN'T **KIDDIN'!!** ALICIA **LOVES** ME THIS WAY...HOW DO I KNOW HOW SHE'LL FEEL ABOUT ME IF I BECOME JUST PLAIN BEN GRIMM??

YOU MULE-HEADED NITWIT!! IT ISN'T YOUR RIDICULOUS **APPEARANCE** SHE LOVES...IT'S **YOU!**...ALTHOUGH I CAN'T SEE **WHY!!**

OKAY, OKAY! MY PERSONAL LIFE IS **ONE** THING YOU AIN'T GONNA BUTT INTO...AND DON'T FORGET IT, BIG MAN!

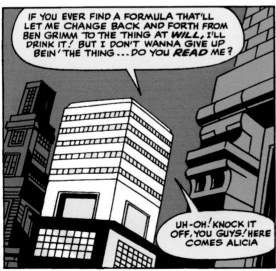

IF YOU EVER FIND A FORMULA THAT'LL LET ME CHANGE BACK AND FORTH FROM BEN GRIMM TO THE THING AT **WILL**, I'LL DRINK IT! BUT I DON'T WANNA GIVE UP BEIN' THE THING...DO YOU **READ** ME?

UH-OH! KNOCK IT OFF, YOU GUYS! HERE COMES ALICIA

HELLO, ALICIA DEAR! WHAT A PLEASANT SURPRISE!

HI, HONEY! WE WERE JUST, EH, TALKIN' ABOUT YA! SAY, WHAT'S THAT YOU'RE CARRYING?

2.

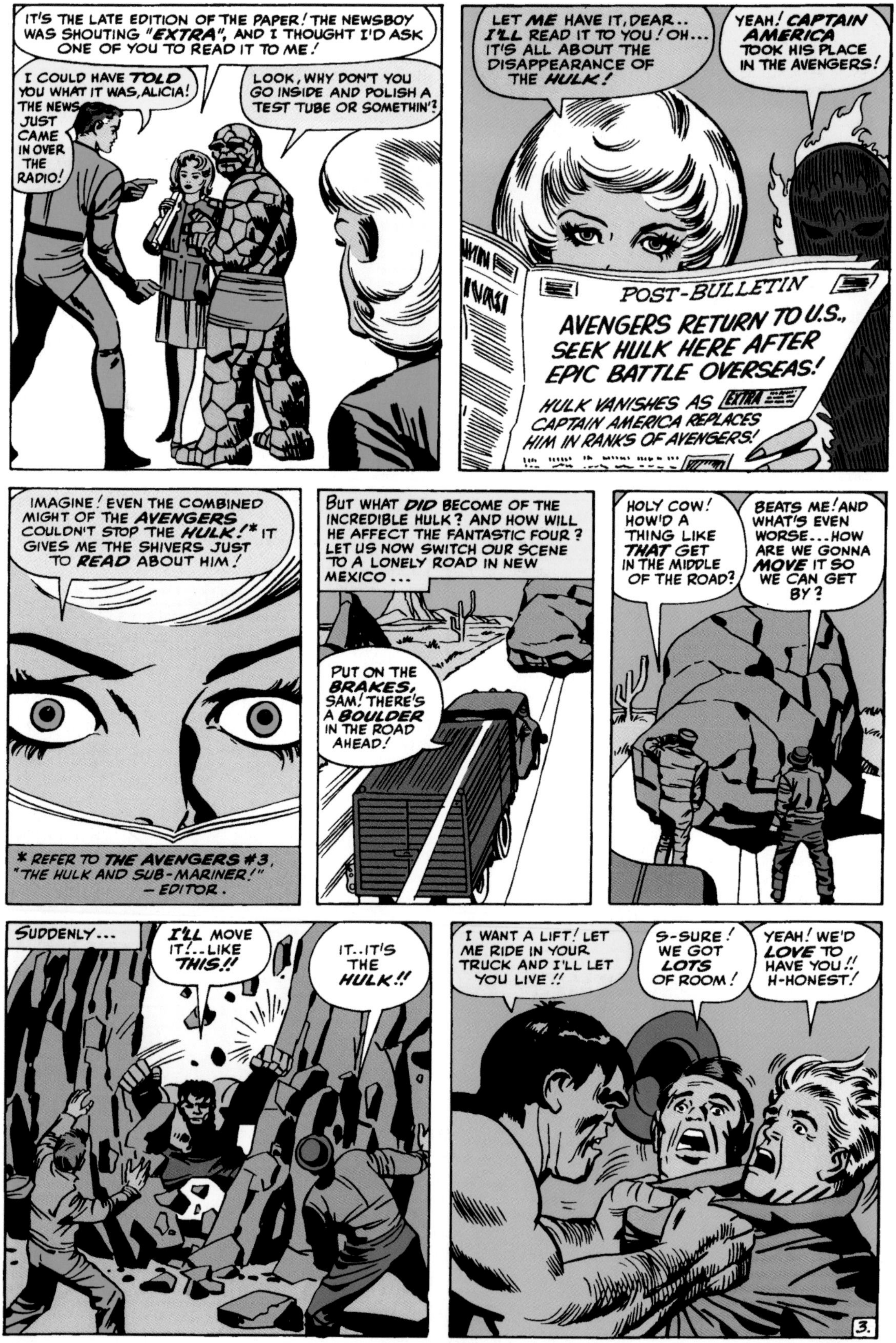
IT'S THE LATE EDITION OF THE PAPER! THE NEWSBOY WAS SHOUTING "EXTRA", AND I THOUGHT I'D ASK ONE OF YOU TO READ IT TO ME!
I COULD HAVE TOLD YOU WHAT IT WAS, ALICIA! THE NEWS JUST CAME IN OVER THE RADIO!
LOOK, WHY DON'T YOU GO INSIDE AND POLISH A TEST TUBE OR SOMETHIN'?
LET ME HAVE IT, DEAR.. I'LL READ IT TO YOU! OH... IT'S ALL ABOUT THE DISAPPEARANCE OF THE HULK!
YEAH! CAPTAIN AMERICA TOOK HIS PLACE IN THE AVENGERS!
POST-BULLETIN
AVENGERS RETURN TO U.S., SEEK HULK HERE AFTER EPIC BATTLE OVERSEAS!
HULK VANISHES AS CAPTAIN AMERICA REPLACES HIM IN RANKS OF AVENGERS!
EXTRA
IMAGINE! EVEN THE COMBINED MIGHT OF THE AVENGERS COULDN'T STOP THE HULK!* IT GIVES ME THE SHIVERS JUST TO READ ABOUT HIM!
* REFER TO THE AVENGERS #3, "THE HULK AND SUB-MARINER!" — EDITOR.
BUT WHAT DID BECOME OF THE INCREDIBLE HULK? AND HOW WILL HE AFFECT THE FANTASTIC FOUR? LET US NOW SWITCH OUR SCENE TO A LONELY ROAD IN NEW MEXICO...
PUT ON THE BRAKES, SAM! THERE'S A BOULDER IN THE ROAD AHEAD!
HOLY COW! HOW'D A THING LIKE THAT GET IN THE MIDDLE OF THE ROAD?
BEATS ME! AND WHAT'S EVEN WORSE... HOW ARE WE GONNA MOVE IT SO WE CAN GET BY?
SUDDENLY...
I'LL MOVE IT!.. LIKE THIS!!
IT..IT'S THE HULK!!
I WANT A LIFT! LET ME RIDE IN YOUR TRUCK AND I'LL LET YOU LIVE!!
S-SURE! WE GOT LOTS OF ROOM!
YEAH! WE'D LOVE TO HAVE YOU!! H-HONEST!
3.

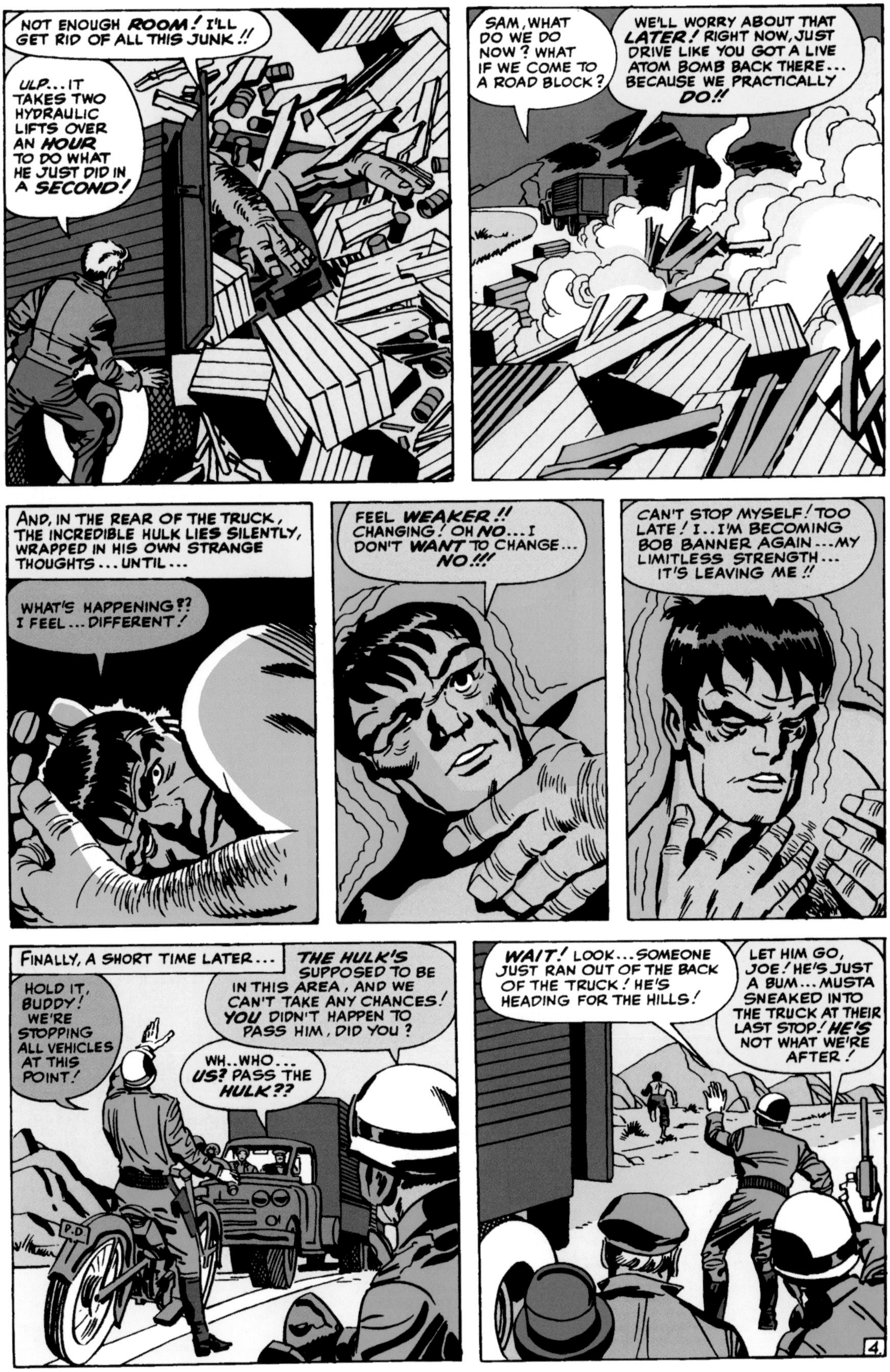

NOT ENOUGH ROOM! I'LL GET RID OF ALL THIS JUNK!!
ULP... IT TAKES TWO HYDRAULIC LIFTS OVER AN HOUR TO DO WHAT HE JUST DID IN A SECOND!
SAM, WHAT DO WE DO NOW? WHAT IF WE COME TO A ROAD BLOCK?
WE'LL WORRY ABOUT THAT LATER! RIGHT NOW, JUST DRIVE LIKE YOU GOT A LIVE ATOM BOMB BACK THERE... BECAUSE WE PRACTICALLY DO!!
AND, IN THE REAR OF THE TRUCK, THE INCREDIBLE HULK LIES SILENTLY, WRAPPED IN HIS OWN STRANGE THOUGHTS... UNTIL...
WHAT'S HAPPENING?? I FEEL... DIFFERENT!
FEEL WEAKER!! CHANGING! OH NO... I DON'T WANT TO CHANGE... NO!!!
CAN'T STOP MYSELF! TOO LATE! I... I'M BECOMING BOB BANNER AGAIN... MY LIMITLESS STRENGTH... IT'S LEAVING ME!!
FINALLY, A SHORT TIME LATER...
HOLD IT, BUDDY! WE'RE STOPPING ALL VEHICLES AT THIS POINT!
THE HULK'S SUPPOSED TO BE IN THIS AREA, AND WE CAN'T TAKE ANY CHANCES! YOU DIDN'T HAPPEN TO PASS HIM, DID YOU?
WH.. WHO... US? PASS THE HULK??
P.D.
WAIT! LOOK... SOMEONE JUST RAN OUT OF THE BACK OF THE TRUCK! HE'S HEADING FOR THE HILLS!
LET HIM GO, JOE! HE'S JUST A BUM... MUSTA SNEAKED INTO THE TRUCK AT THEIR LAST STOP! HE'S NOT WHAT WE'RE AFTER!
4.

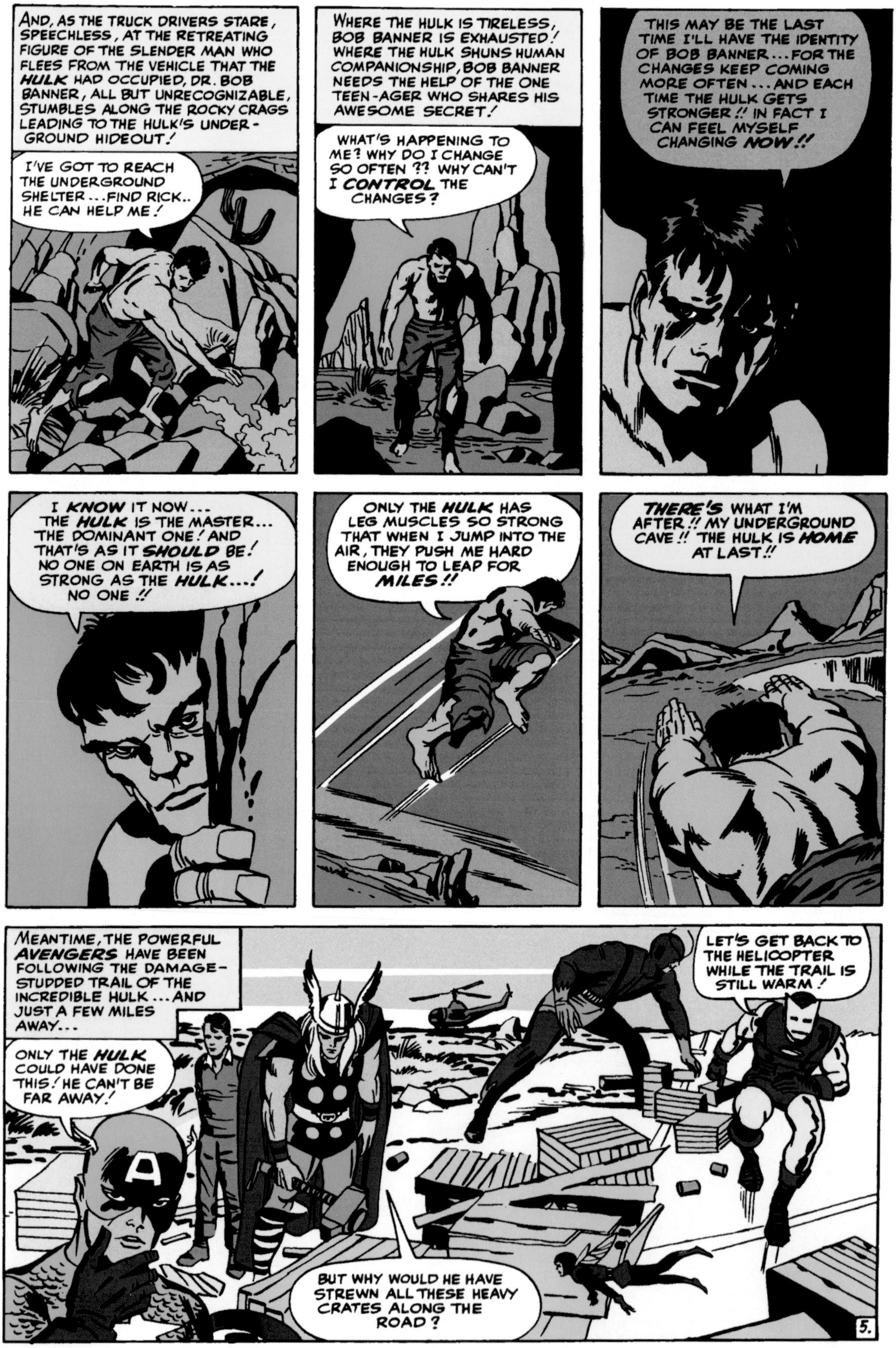
AND, AS THE TRUCK DRIVERS STARE, SPEECHLESS, AT THE RETREATING FIGURE OF THE SLENDER MAN WHO FLEES FROM THE VEHICLE THAT THE HULK HAD OCCUPIED, DR. BOB BANNER, ALL BUT UNRECOGNIZABLE, STUMBLES ALONG THE ROCKY CRAGS LEADING TO THE HULK'S UNDER-GROUND HIDEOUT!
I'VE GOT TO REACH THE UNDERGROUND SHELTER...FIND RICK.. HE CAN HELP ME!
WHERE THE HULK IS TIRELESS, BOB BANNER IS EXHAUSTED! WHERE THE HULK SHUNS HUMAN COMPANIONSHIP, BOB BANNER NEEDS THE HELP OF THE ONE TEEN-AGER WHO SHARES HIS AWESOME SECRET!
WHAT'S HAPPENING TO ME? WHY DO I CHANGE SO OFTEN ?? WHY CAN'T I CONTROL THE CHANGES?
THIS MAY BE THE LAST TIME I'LL HAVE THE IDENTITY OF BOB BANNER...FOR THE CHANGES KEEP COMING MORE OFTEN...AND EACH TIME THE HULK GETS STRONGER!! IN FACT I CAN FEEL MYSELF CHANGING NOW!!
I KNOW IT NOW... THE HULK IS THE MASTER... THE DOMINANT ONE! AND THAT'S AS IT SHOULD BE! NO ONE ON EARTH IS AS STRONG AS THE HULK...! NO ONE!!
ONLY THE HULK HAS LEG MUSCLES SO STRONG THAT WHEN I JUMP INTO THE AIR, THEY PUSH ME HARD ENOUGH TO LEAP FOR MILES!!
THERE'S WHAT I'M AFTER!! MY UNDERGROUND CAVE!! THE HULK IS HOME AT LAST!!
MEANTIME, THE POWERFUL AVENGERS HAVE BEEN FOLLOWING THE DAMAGE-STUDDED TRAIL OF THE INCREDIBLE HULK...AND JUST A FEW MILES AWAY...
ONLY THE HULK COULD HAVE DONE THIS! HE CAN'T BE FAR AWAY!
LET'S GET BACK TO THE HELICOPTER WHILE THE TRAIL IS STILL WARM!
BUT WHY WOULD HE HAVE STREWN ALL THESE HEAVY CRATES ALONG THE ROAD?
5.

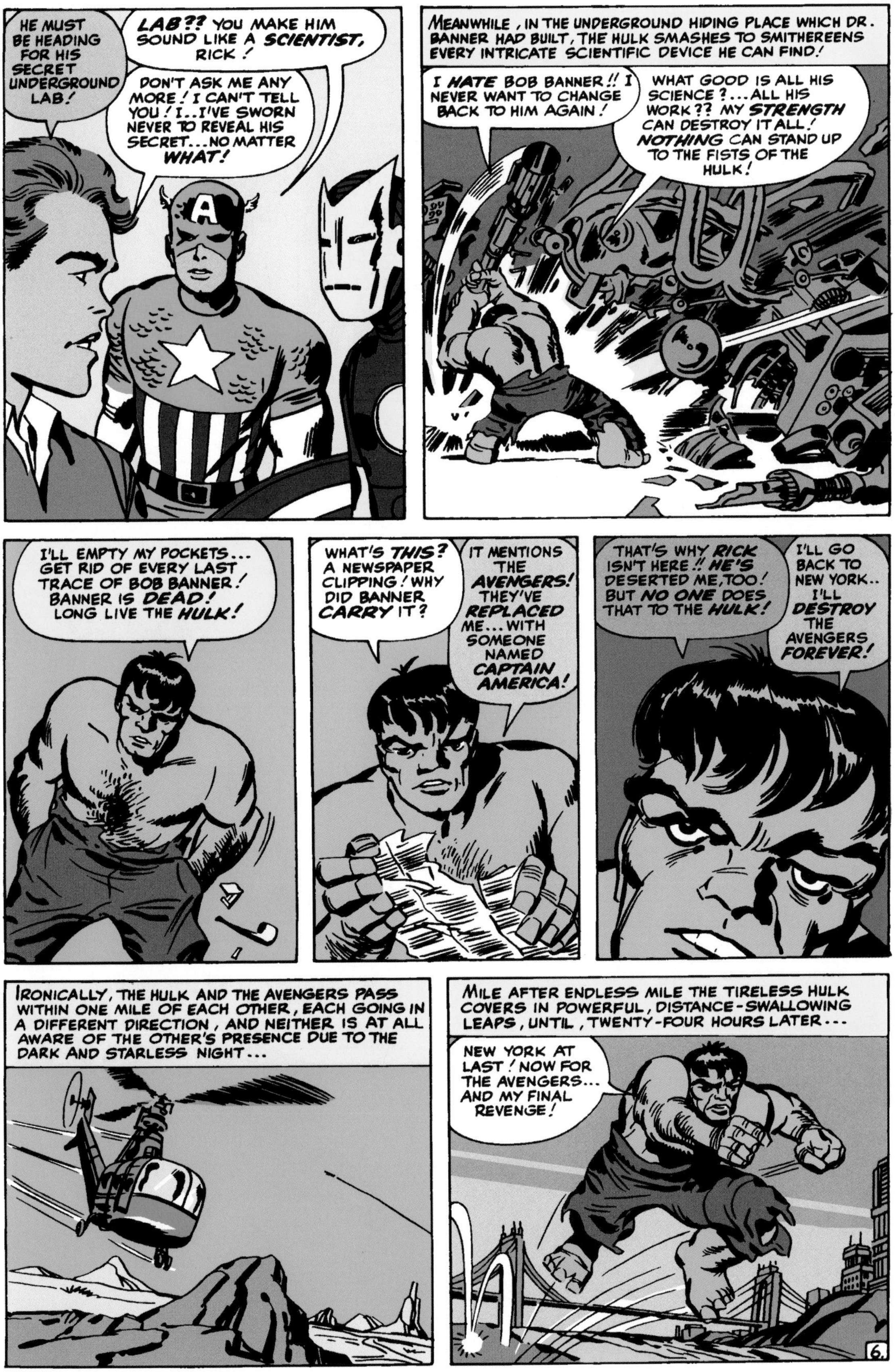
HE MUST BE HEADING FOR HIS SECRET UNDERGROUND LAB!
LAB?? YOU MAKE HIM SOUND LIKE A SCIENTIST, RICK!
DON'T ASK ME ANY MORE! I CAN'T TELL YOU! I..I'VE SWORN NEVER TO REVEAL HIS SECRET...NO MATTER WHAT!
MEANWHILE, IN THE UNDERGROUND HIDING PLACE WHICH DR. BANNER HAD BUILT, THE HULK SMASHES TO SMITHEREENS EVERY INTRICATE SCIENTIFIC DEVICE HE CAN FIND!
I HATE BOB BANNER!! I NEVER WANT TO CHANGE BACK TO HIM AGAIN!
WHAT GOOD IS ALL HIS SCIENCE?...ALL HIS WORK?? MY STRENGTH CAN DESTROY IT ALL! NOTHING CAN STAND UP TO THE FISTS OF THE HULK!
I'LL EMPTY MY POCKETS... GET RID OF EVERY LAST TRACE OF BOB BANNER! BANNER IS DEAD! LONG LIVE THE HULK!
WHAT'S THIS? A NEWSPAPER CLIPPING! WHY DID BANNER CARRY IT?
IT MENTIONS THE AVENGERS! THEY'VE REPLACED ME...WITH SOMEONE NAMED CAPTAIN AMERICA!
THAT'S WHY RICK ISN'T HERE!! HE'S DESERTED ME, TOO! BUT NO ONE DOES THAT TO THE HULK!
I'LL GO BACK TO NEW YORK.. I'LL DESTROY THE AVENGERS FOREVER!
IRONICALLY, THE HULK AND THE AVENGERS PASS WITHIN ONE MILE OF EACH OTHER, EACH GOING IN A DIFFERENT DIRECTION, AND NEITHER IS AT ALL AWARE OF THE OTHER'S PRESENCE DUE TO THE DARK AND STARLESS NIGHT...
MILE AFTER ENDLESS MILE THE TIRELESS HULK COVERS IN POWERFUL, DISTANCE-SWALLOWING LEAPS, UNTIL, TWENTY-FOUR HOURS LATER...
NEW YORK AT LAST! NOW FOR THE AVENGERS... AND MY FINAL REVENGE!
6.

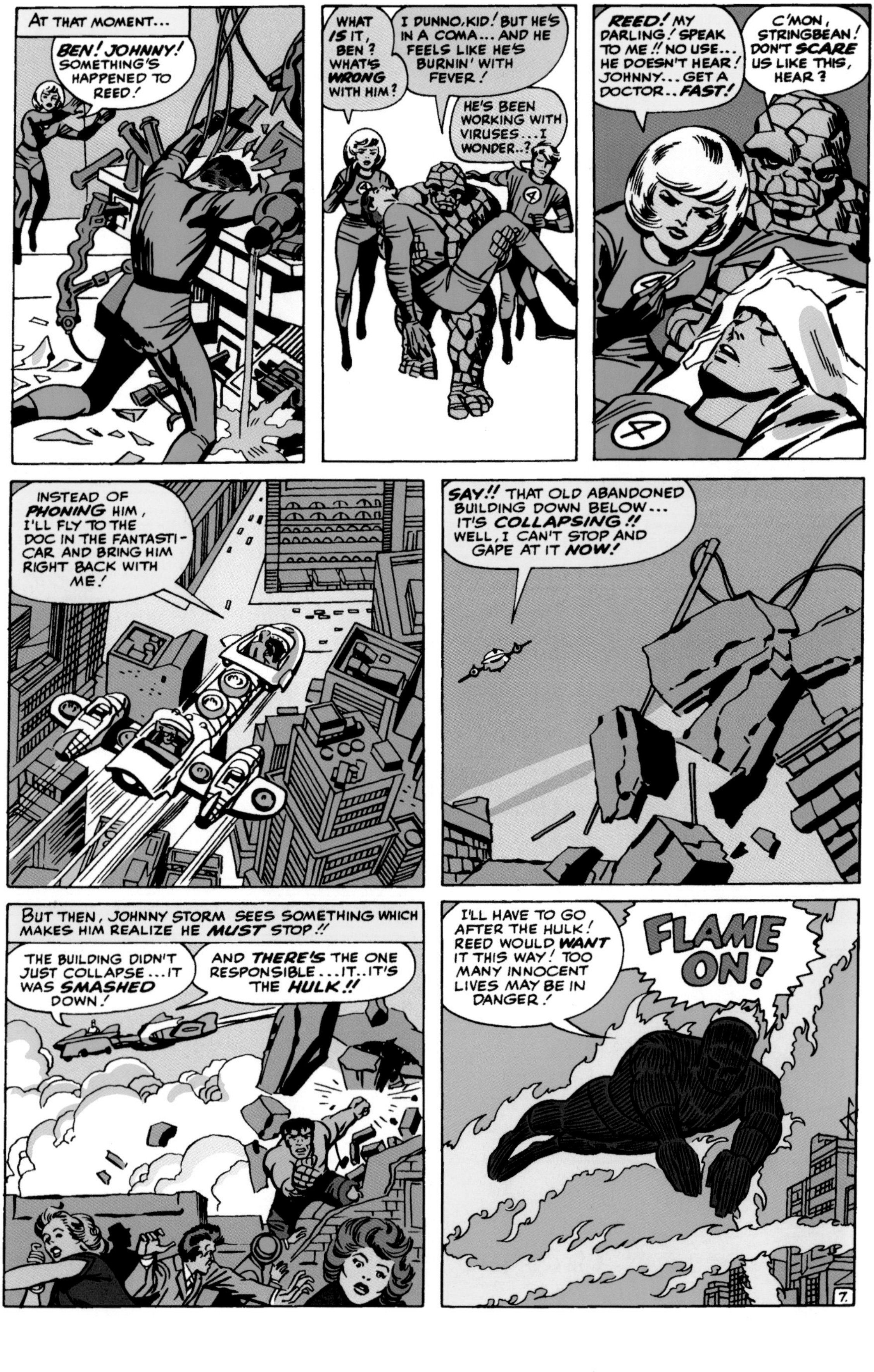

AT THAT MOMENT...
BEN! JOHNNY! SOMETHING'S HAPPENED TO REED!
WHAT IS IT, BEN? WHAT'S WRONG WITH HIM?
I DUNNO, KID! BUT HE'S IN A COMA... AND HE FEELS LIKE HE'S BURNIN' WITH FEVER!
HE'S BEEN WORKING WITH VIRUSES... I WONDER..?
REED! MY DARLING! SPEAK TO ME!! NO USE... HE DOESN'T HEAR! JOHNNY... GET A DOCTOR.. FAST!
C'MON, STRINGBEAN! DON'T SCARE US LIKE THIS, HEAR?
INSTEAD OF PHONING HIM, I'LL FLY TO THE DOC IN THE FANTASTI-CAR AND BRING HIM RIGHT BACK WITH ME!
SAY!! THAT OLD ABANDONED BUILDING DOWN BELOW... IT'S COLLAPSING!! WELL, I CAN'T STOP AND GAPE AT IT NOW!
BUT THEN, JOHNNY STORM SEES SOMETHING WHICH MAKES HIM REALIZE HE MUST STOP!!
THE BUILDING DIDN'T JUST COLLAPSE... IT WAS SMASHED DOWN!
AND THERE'S THE ONE RESPONSIBLE... IT.. IT'S THE HULK!!
I'LL HAVE TO GO AFTER THE HULK! REED WOULD WANT IT THIS WAY! TOO MANY INNOCENT LIVES MAY BE IN DANGER!
FLAME ON!
7.

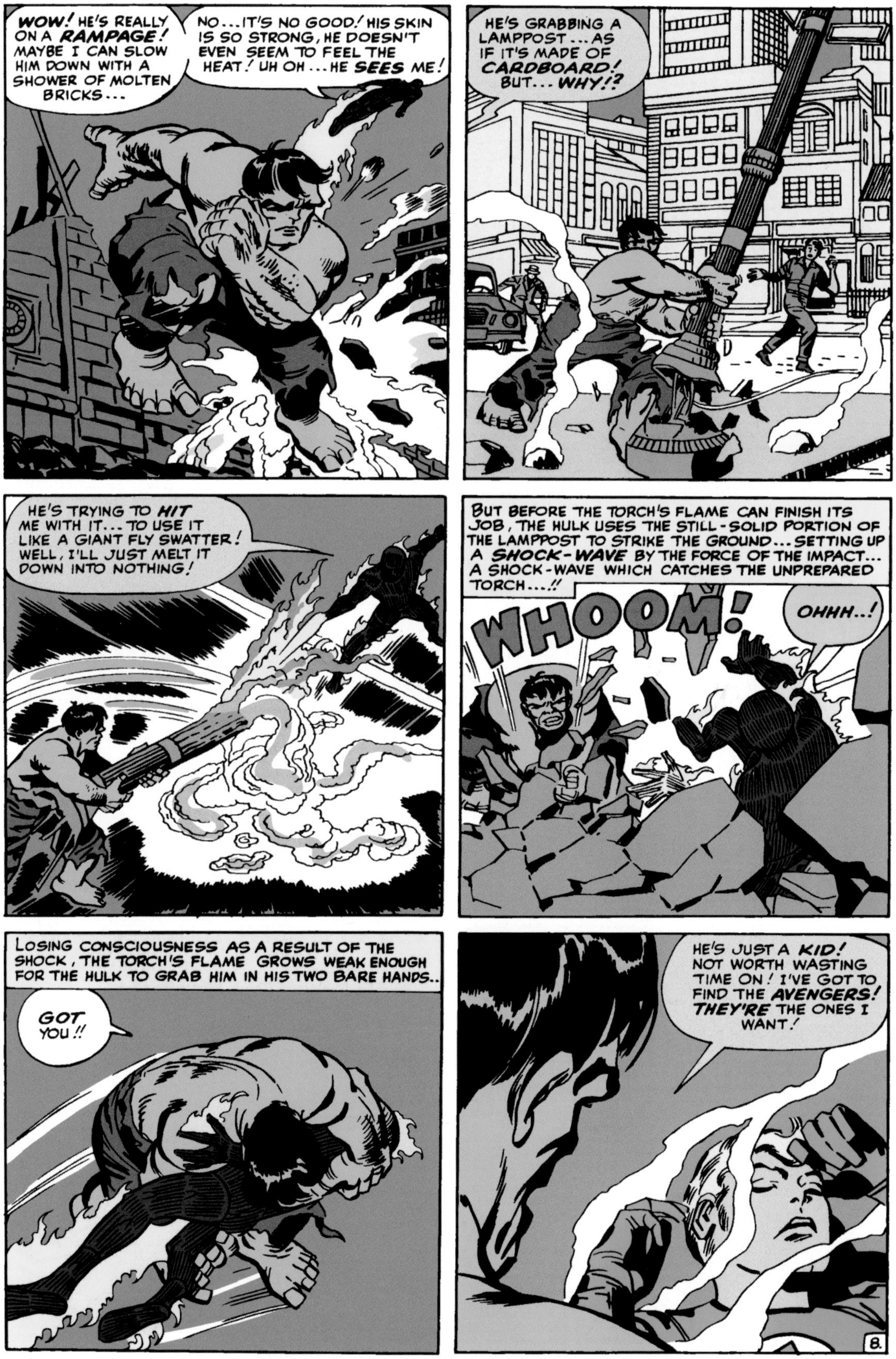
WOW! HE'S REALLY ON A RAMPAGE! MAYBE I CAN SLOW HIM DOWN WITH A SHOWER OF MOLTEN BRICKS...
NO...IT'S NO GOOD! HIS SKIN IS SO STRONG, HE DOESN'T EVEN SEEM TO FEEL THE HEAT! UH OH...HE SEES ME!
HE'S GRABBING A LAMPPOST...AS IF IT'S MADE OF CARDBOARD! BUT...WHY!?
HE'S TRYING TO HIT ME WITH IT...TO USE IT LIKE A GIANT FLY SWATTER! WELL, I'LL JUST MELT IT DOWN INTO NOTHING!
BUT BEFORE THE TORCH'S FLAME CAN FINISH ITS JOB, THE HULK USES THE STILL-SOLID PORTION OF THE LAMPPOST TO STRIKE THE GROUND...SETTING UP A SHOCK-WAVE BY THE FORCE OF THE IMPACT... A SHOCK-WAVE WHICH CATCHES THE UNPREPARED TORCH...!!
WHOOM!
OHHH..!
LOSING CONSCIOUSNESS AS A RESULT OF THE SHOCK, THE TORCH'S FLAME GROWS WEAK ENOUGH FOR THE HULK TO GRAB HIM IN HIS TWO BARE HANDS..
GOT YOU!!
HE'S JUST A KID! NOT WORTH WASTING TIME ON! I'VE GOT TO FIND THE AVENGERS! THEY'RE THE ONES I WANT!
8.

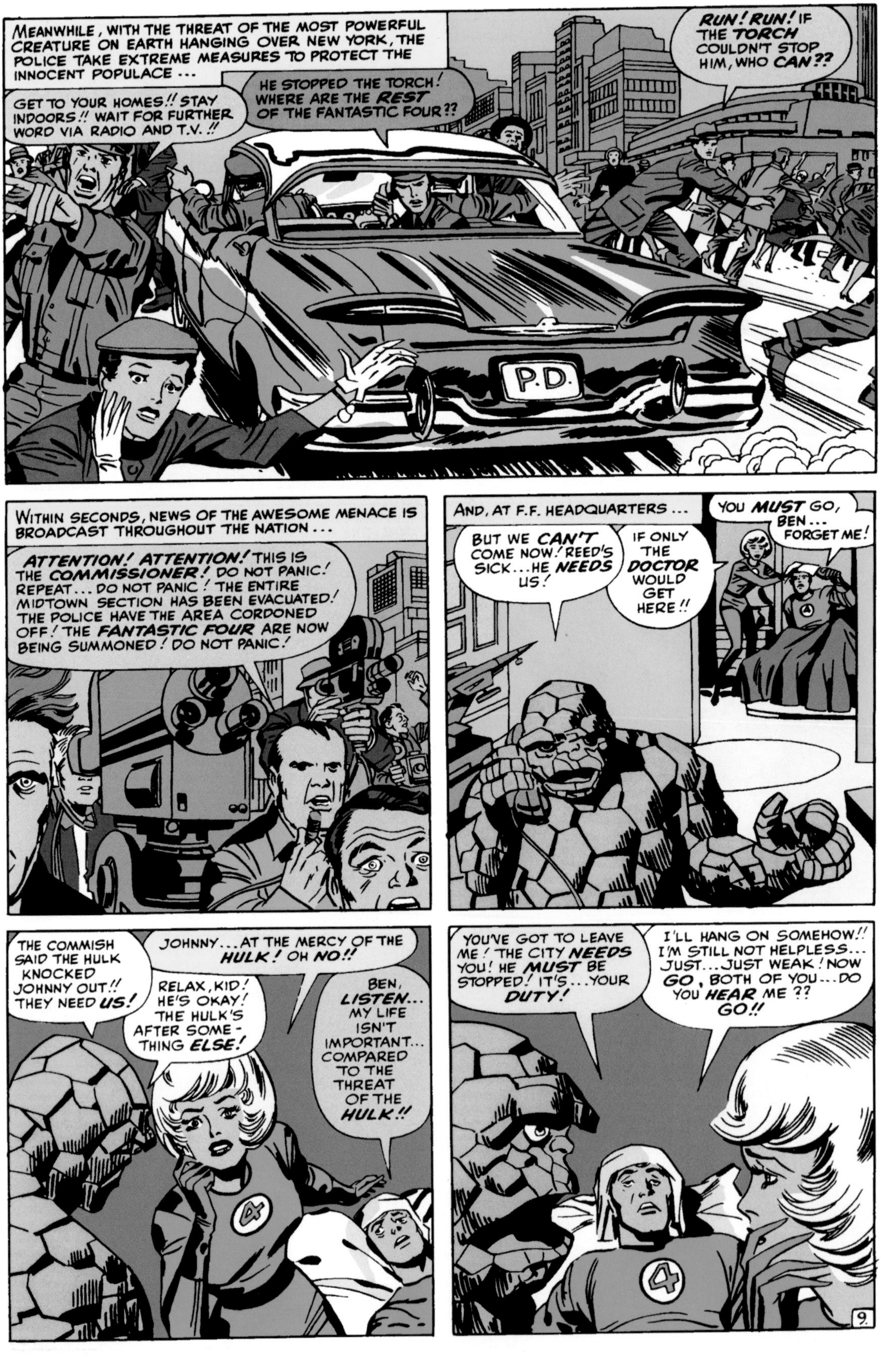
MEANWHILE, WITH THE THREAT OF THE MOST POWERFUL CREATURE ON EARTH HANGING OVER NEW YORK, THE POLICE TAKE EXTREME MEASURES TO PROTECT THE INNOCENT POPULACE ...
GET TO YOUR HOMES!! STAY INDOORS!! WAIT FOR FURTHER WORD VIA RADIO AND T.V.!!
HE STOPPED THE TORCH! WHERE ARE THE REST OF THE FANTASTIC FOUR??
RUN! RUN! IF THE TORCH COULDN'T STOP HIM, WHO CAN??
P.D.
WITHIN SECONDS, NEWS OF THE AWESOME MENACE IS BROADCAST THROUGHOUT THE NATION ...
ATTENTION! ATTENTION! THIS IS THE COMMISSIONER! DO NOT PANIC! REPEAT... DO NOT PANIC! THE ENTIRE MIDTOWN SECTION HAS BEEN EVACUATED! THE POLICE HAVE THE AREA CORDONED OFF! THE FANTASTIC FOUR ARE NOW BEING SUMMONED! DO NOT PANIC!
AND, AT F.F. HEADQUARTERS ...
BUT WE CAN'T COME NOW! REED'S SICK...HE NEEDS US!
IF ONLY THE DOCTOR WOULD GET HERE!!
YOU MUST GO, BEN... FORGET ME!
THE COMMISH SAID THE HULK KNOCKED JOHNNY OUT!! THEY NEED US!
JOHNNY...AT THE MERCY OF THE HULK! OH NO!!
RELAX, KID! HE'S OKAY! THE HULK'S AFTER SOME-THING ELSE!
BEN, LISTEN... MY LIFE ISN'T IMPORTANT... COMPARED TO THE THREAT OF THE HULK!!
YOU'VE GOT TO LEAVE ME! THE CITY NEEDS YOU! HE MUST BE STOPPED! IT'S...YOUR DUTY!
I'LL HANG ON SOMEHOW!! I'M STILL NOT HELPLESS... JUST...JUST WEAK! NOW GO, BOTH OF YOU...DO YOU HEAR ME?? GO!!
9.

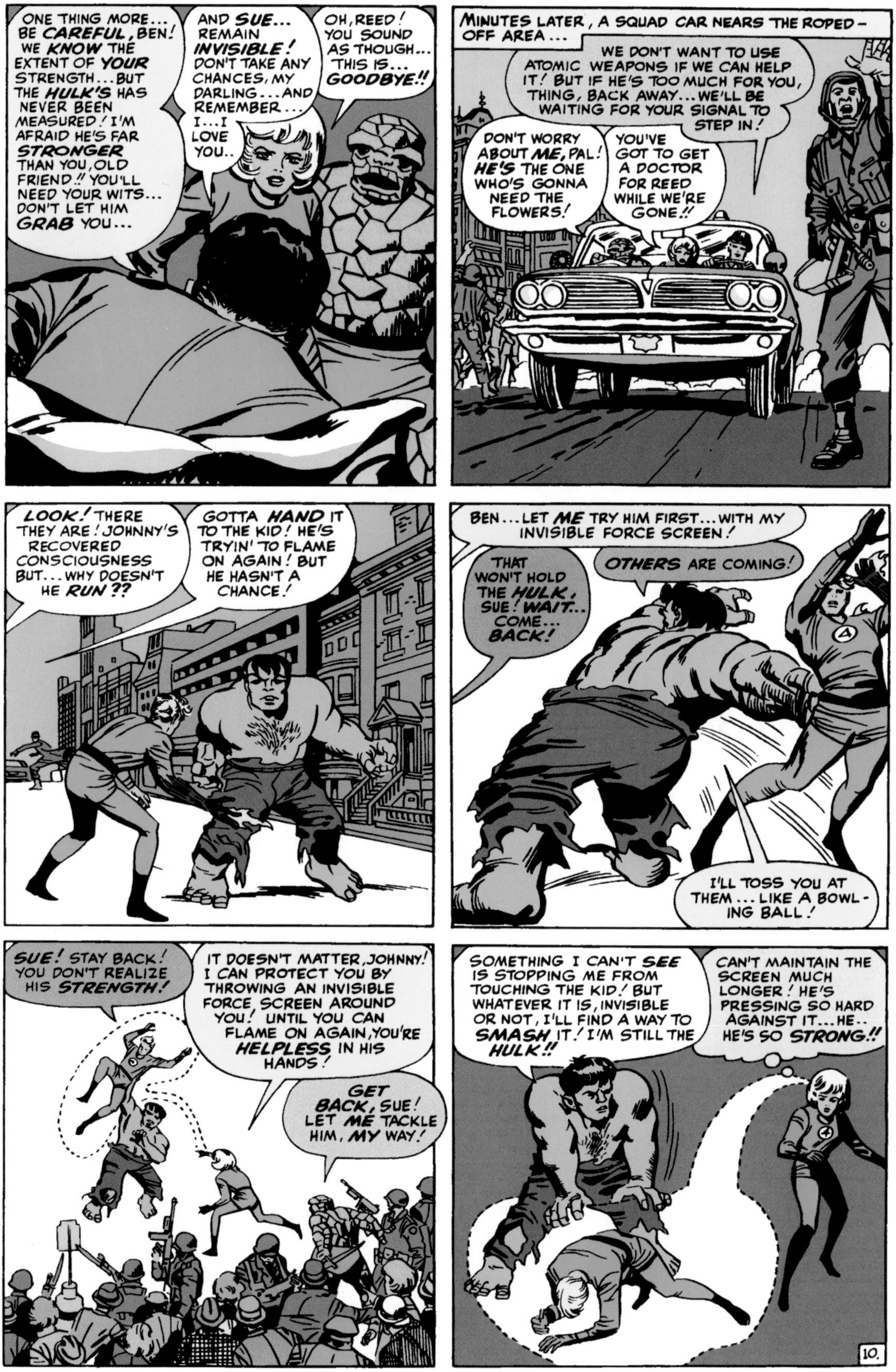
ONE THING MORE... BE CAREFUL, BEN! WE KNOW THE EXTENT OF YOUR STRENGTH... BUT THE HULK'S HAS NEVER BEEN MEASURED! I'M AFRAID HE'S FAR STRONGER THAN YOU, OLD FRIEND!! YOU'LL NEED YOUR WITS... DON'T LET HIM GRAB YOU...
AND SUE... REMAIN INVISIBLE! DON'T TAKE ANY CHANCES, MY DARLING... AND REMEMBER... I... I LOVE YOU..
OH, REED! YOU SOUND AS THOUGH... THIS IS... GOODBYE!!
MINUTES LATER, A SQUAD CAR NEARS THE ROPED-OFF AREA...
WE DON'T WANT TO USE ATOMIC WEAPONS IF WE CAN HELP IT! BUT IF HE'S TOO MUCH FOR YOU, THING, BACK AWAY... WE'LL BE WAITING FOR YOUR SIGNAL TO STEP IN!
DON'T WORRY ABOUT ME, PAL! HE'S THE ONE WHO'S GONNA NEED THE FLOWERS!
YOU'VE GOT TO GET A DOCTOR FOR REED WHILE WE'RE GONE!!
LOOK! THERE THEY ARE! JOHNNY'S RECOVERED CONSCIOUSNESS BUT... WHY DOESN'T HE RUN??
GOTTA HAND IT TO THE KID! HE'S TRYIN' TO FLAME ON AGAIN! BUT HE HASN'T A CHANCE!
BEN... LET ME TRY HIM FIRST... WITH MY INVISIBLE FORCE SCREEN!
THAT WON'T HOLD THE HULK, SUE! WAIT... COME... BACK!
OTHERS ARE COMING!
I'LL TOSS YOU AT THEM... LIKE A BOWL-ING BALL!
SUE! STAY BACK! YOU DON'T REALIZE HIS STRENGTH!
IT DOESN'T MATTER, JOHNNY! I CAN PROTECT YOU BY THROWING AN INVISIBLE FORCE SCREEN AROUND YOU! UNTIL YOU CAN FLAME ON AGAIN, YOU'RE HELPLESS IN HIS HANDS!
GET BACK, SUE! LET ME TACKLE HIM, MY WAY!
SOMETHING I CAN'T SEE IS STOPPING ME FROM TOUCHING THE KID! BUT WHATEVER IT IS, INVISIBLE OR NOT, I'LL FIND A WAY TO SMASH IT! I'M STILL THE HULK!!
CAN'T MAINTAIN THE SCREEN MUCH LONGER! HE'S PRESSING SO HARD AGAINST IT... HE.. HE'S SO STRONG!!
10.

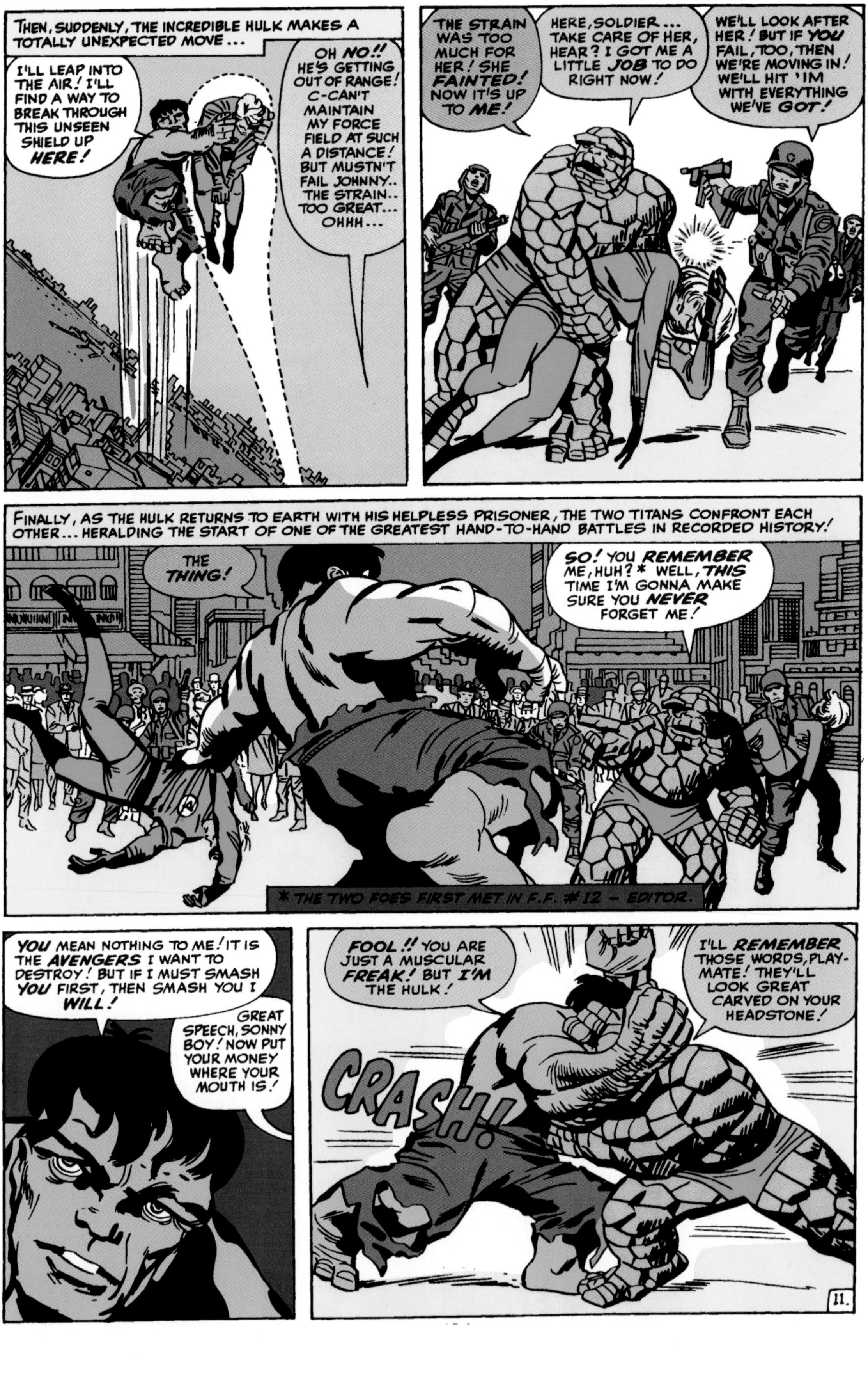

THEN, SUDDENLY, THE INCREDIBLE HULK MAKES A TOTALLY UNEXPECTED MOVE...
I'LL LEAP INTO THE AIR! I'LL FIND A WAY TO BREAK THROUGH THIS UNSEEN SHIELD UP HERE!
OH NO!! HE'S GETTING OUT OF RANGE! C-CAN'T MAINTAIN MY FORCE FIELD AT SUCH A DISTANCE! BUT MUSTN'T FAIL JOHNNY.. THE STRAIN.. TOO GREAT... OHHH...
THE STRAIN WAS TOO MUCH FOR HER! SHE FAINTED! NOW IT'S UP TO ME!
HERE, SOLDIER... TAKE CARE OF HER, HEAR? I GOT ME A LITTLE JOB TO DO RIGHT NOW!
WE'LL LOOK AFTER HER! BUT IF YOU FAIL, TOO, THEN WE'RE MOVING IN! WE'LL HIT 'IM WITH EVERYTHING WE'VE GOT!
FINALLY, AS THE HULK RETURNS TO EARTH WITH HIS HELPLESS PRISONER, THE TWO TITANS CONFRONT EACH OTHER... HERALDING THE START OF ONE OF THE GREATEST HAND-TO-HAND BATTLES IN RECORDED HISTORY!
THE THING!
SO! YOU REMEMBER ME, HUH? * WELL, THIS TIME I'M GONNA MAKE SURE YOU NEVER FORGET ME!
* THE TWO FOES FIRST MET IN F.F. #12 - EDITOR.
YOU MEAN NOTHING TO ME! IT IS THE AVENGERS I WANT TO DESTROY! BUT IF I MUST SMASH YOU FIRST, THEN SMASH YOU I WILL!
GREAT SPEECH, SONNY BOY! NOW PUT YOUR MONEY WHERE YOUR MOUTH IS!
FOOL!! YOU ARE JUST A MUSCULAR FREAK! BUT I'M THE HULK!
I'LL REMEMBER THOSE WORDS, PLAYMATE! THEY'LL LOOK GREAT CARVED ON YOUR HEADSTONE!
CRASH!
11.

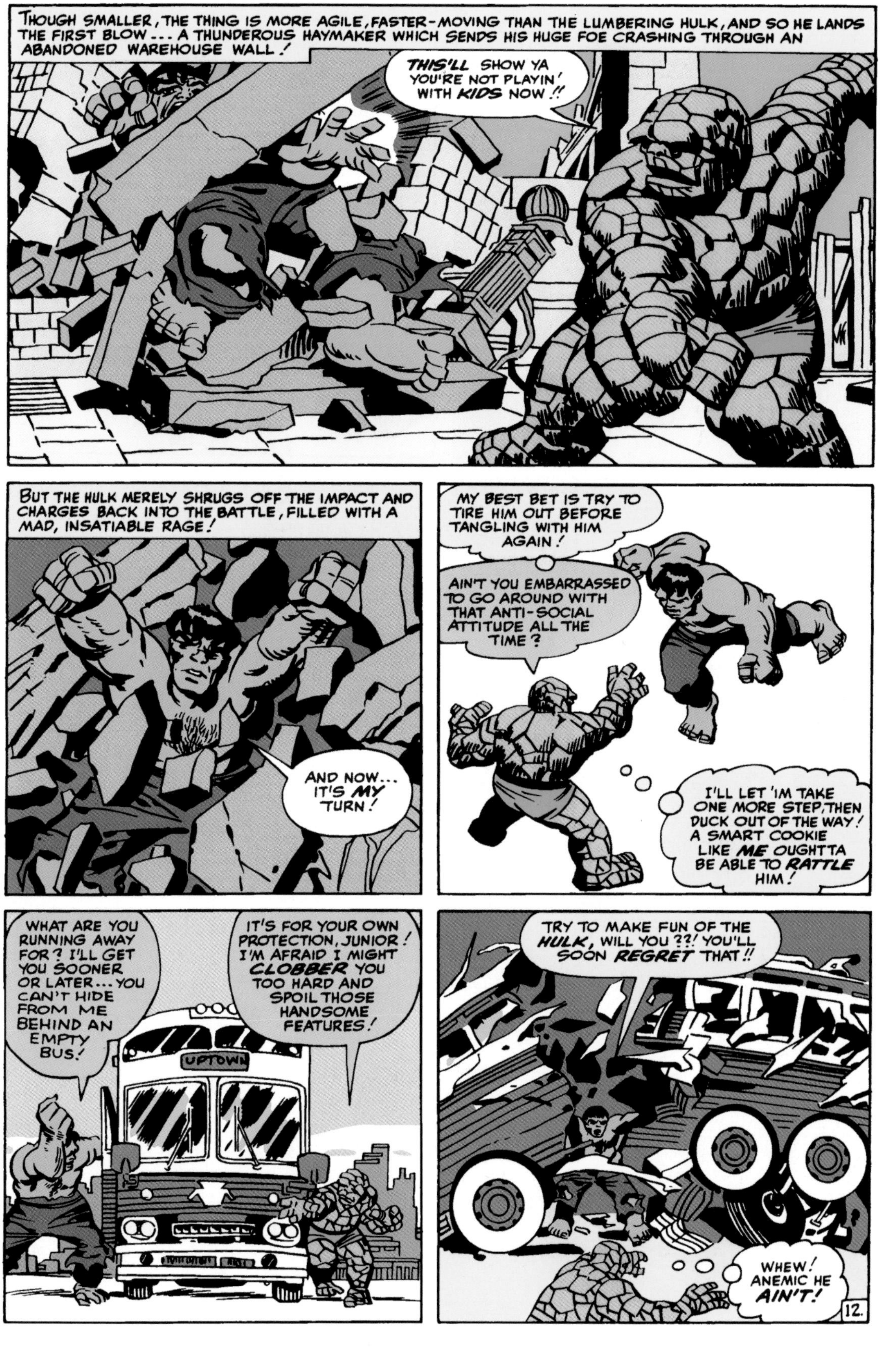
THOUGH SMALLER, THE THING IS MORE AGILE, FASTER-MOVING THAN THE LUMBERING HULK, AND SO HE LANDS THE FIRST BLOW... A THUNDEROUS HAYMAKER WHICH SENDS HIS HUGE FOE CRASHING THROUGH AN ABANDONED WAREHOUSE WALL!
THIS'LL SHOW YA YOU'RE NOT PLAYIN' WITH KIDS NOW!!
BUT THE HULK MERELY SHRUGS OFF THE IMPACT AND CHARGES BACK INTO THE BATTLE, FILLED WITH A MAD, INSATIABLE RAGE!
AND NOW... IT'S MY TURN!
MY BEST BET IS TRY TO TIRE HIM OUT BEFORE TANGLING WITH HIM AGAIN!
AIN'T YOU EMBARRASSED TO GO AROUND WITH THAT ANTI-SOCIAL ATTITUDE ALL THE TIME?
I'LL LET 'IM TAKE ONE MORE STEP, THEN DUCK OUT OF THE WAY! A SMART COOKIE LIKE ME OUGHTTA BE ABLE TO RATTLE HIM!
WHAT ARE YOU RUNNING AWAY FOR? I'LL GET YOU SOONER OR LATER... YOU CAN'T HIDE FROM ME BEHIND AN EMPTY BUS!
IT'S FOR YOUR OWN PROTECTION, JUNIOR! I'M AFRAID I MIGHT CLOBBER YOU TOO HARD AND SPOIL THOSE HANDSOME FEATURES!
UPTOWN
TRY TO MAKE FUN OF THE HULK, WILL YOU??! YOU'LL SOON REGRET THAT!!
WHEW! ANEMIC HE AIN'T!
12.

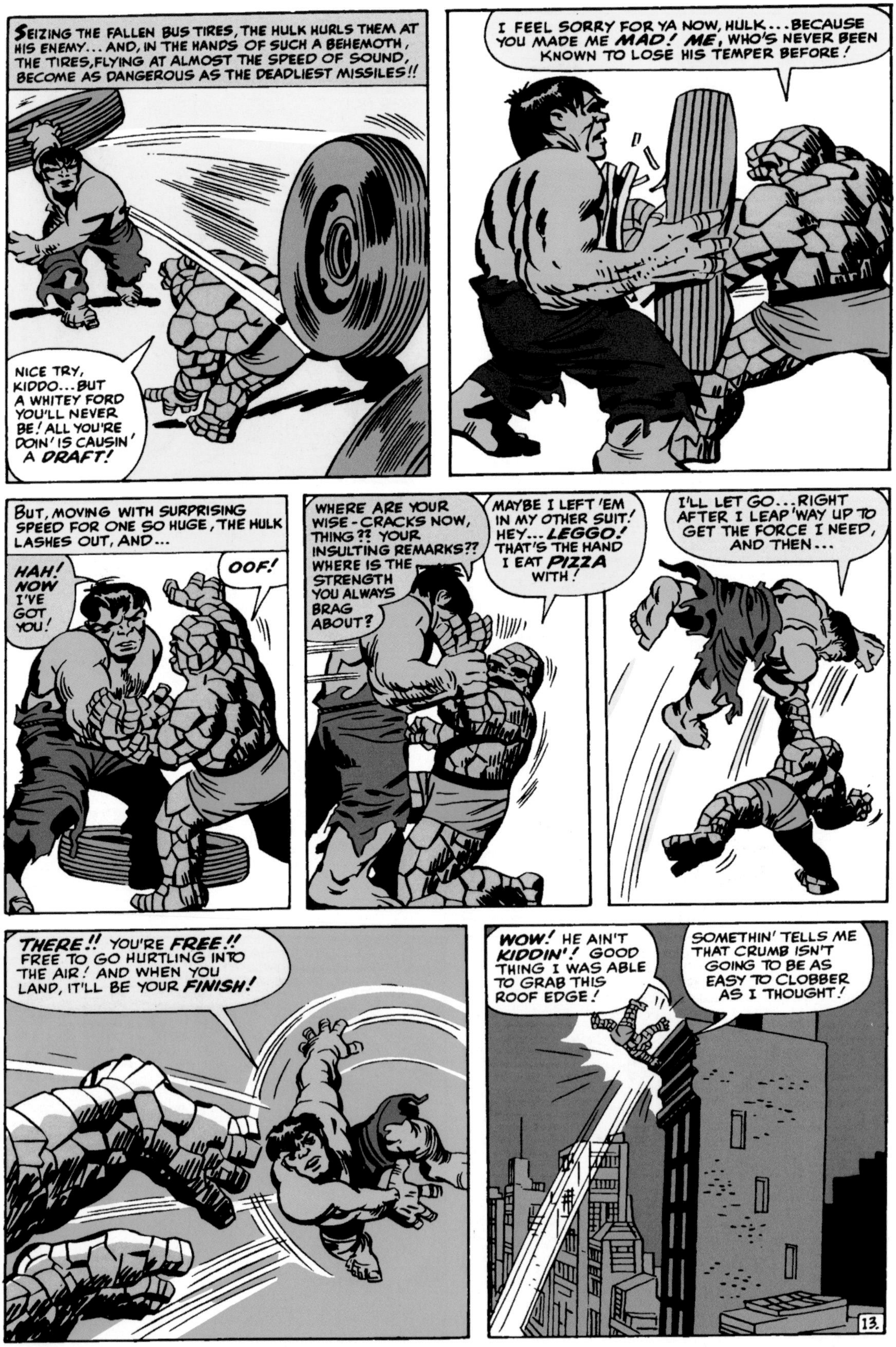
SEIZING THE FALLEN BUS TIRES, THE HULK HURLS THEM AT HIS ENEMY... AND, IN THE HANDS OF SUCH A BEHEMOTH, THE TIRES, FLYING AT ALMOST THE SPEED OF SOUND, BECOME AS DANGEROUS AS THE DEADLIEST MISSILES!!
NICE TRY, KIDDO... BUT A WHITEY FORD YOU'LL NEVER BE! ALL YOU'RE DOIN' IS CAUSIN' A DRAFT!
I FEEL SORRY FOR YA NOW, HULK... BECAUSE YOU MADE ME MAD! ME, WHO'S NEVER BEEN KNOWN TO LOSE HIS TEMPER BEFORE!
BUT, MOVING WITH SURPRISING SPEED FOR ONE SO HUGE, THE HULK LASHES OUT, AND...
HAH! NOW I'VE GOT YOU!
OOF!
WHERE ARE YOUR WISE-CRACKS NOW, THING?? YOUR INSULTING REMARKS?? WHERE IS THE STRENGTH YOU ALWAYS BRAG ABOUT?
MAYBE I LEFT 'EM IN MY OTHER SUIT! HEY... LEGGO! THAT'S THE HAND I EAT PIZZA WITH!
I'LL LET GO... RIGHT AFTER I LEAP 'WAY UP TO GET THE FORCE I NEED, AND THEN...
THERE!! YOU'RE FREE!! FREE TO GO HURTLING INTO THE AIR! AND WHEN YOU LAND, IT'LL BE YOUR FINISH!
WOW! HE AIN'T KIDDIN'! GOOD THING I WAS ABLE TO GRAB THIS ROOF EDGE!
SOMETHIN' TELLS ME THAT CRUMB ISN'T GOING TO BE AS EASY TO CLOBBER AS I THOUGHT!
13.

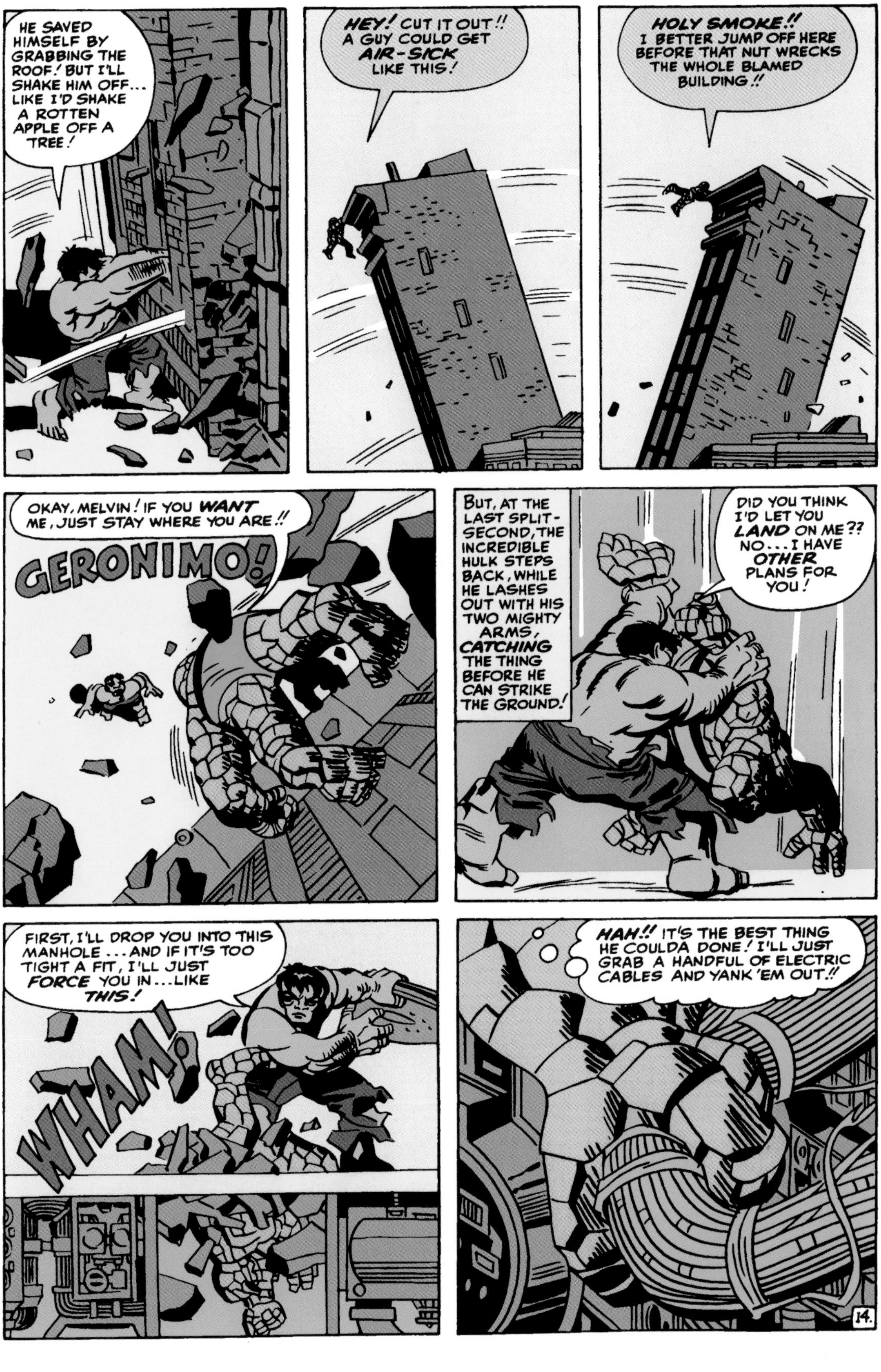
HE SAVED HIMSELF BY GRABBING THE ROOF! BUT I'LL SHAKE HIM OFF... LIKE I'D SHAKE A ROTTEN APPLE OFF A TREE!
HEY! CUT IT OUT!! A GUY COULD GET AIR-SICK LIKE THIS!
HOLY SMOKE!! I BETTER JUMP OFF HERE BEFORE THAT NUT WRECKS THE WHOLE BLAMED BUILDING!!
OKAY, MELVIN! IF YOU WANT ME, JUST STAY WHERE YOU ARE!!
GERONIMO!
BUT, AT THE LAST SPLIT-SECOND, THE INCREDIBLE HULK STEPS BACK, WHILE HE LASHES OUT WITH HIS TWO MIGHTY ARMS, CATCHING THE THING BEFORE HE CAN STRIKE THE GROUND!
DID YOU THINK I'D LET YOU LAND ON ME?? NO... I HAVE OTHER PLANS FOR YOU!
FIRST, I'LL DROP YOU INTO THIS MANHOLE ... AND IF IT'S TOO TIGHT A FIT, I'LL JUST FORCE YOU IN... LIKE THIS!
WHAM!
HAH!! IT'S THE BEST THING HE COULDA DONE! I'LL JUST GRAB A HANDFUL OF ELECTRIC CABLES AND YANK 'EM OUT!!
14.

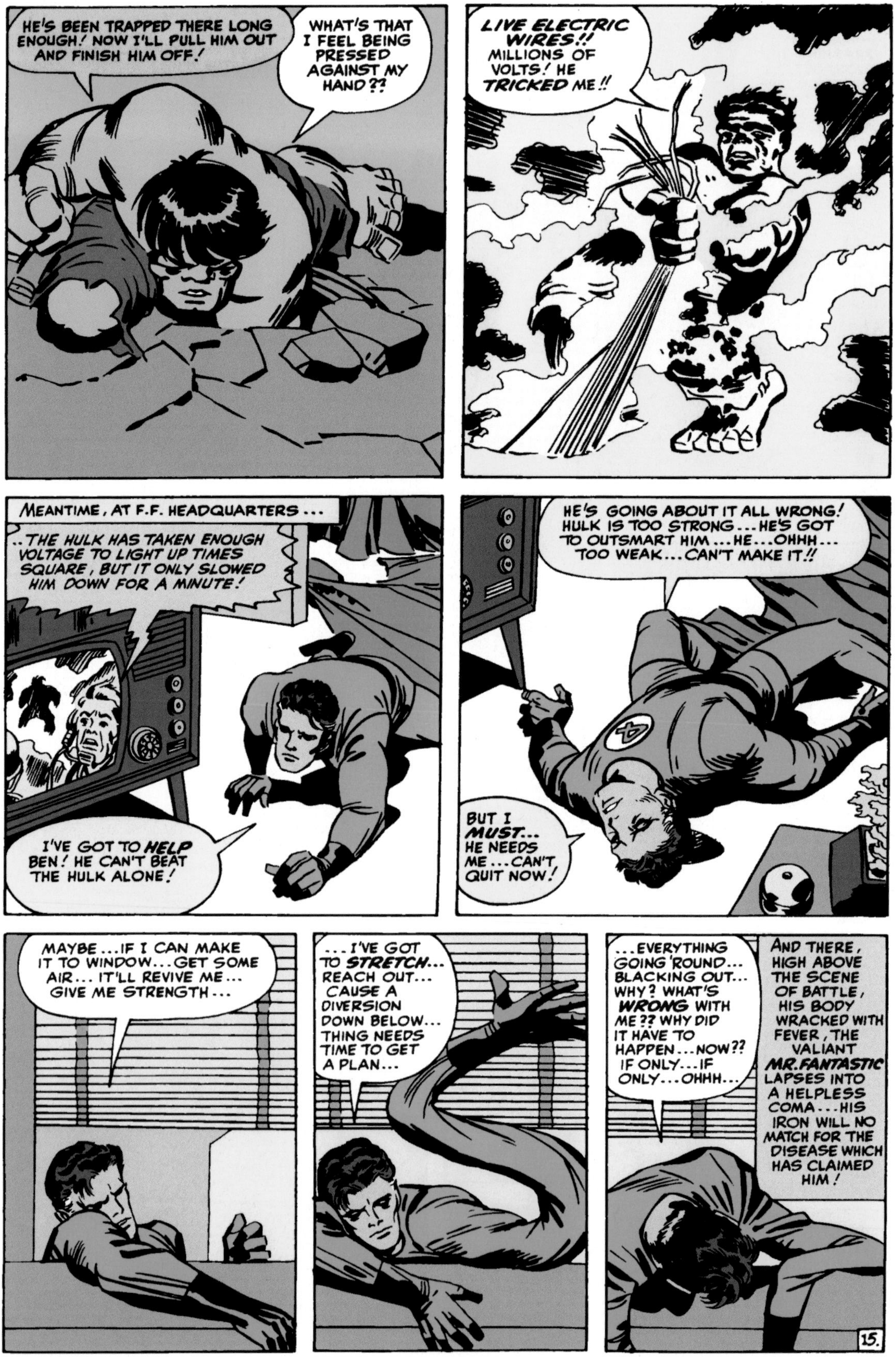
HE'S BEEN TRAPPED THERE LONG ENOUGH! NOW I'LL PULL HIM OUT AND FINISH HIM OFF!
WHAT'S THAT I FEEL BEING PRESSED AGAINST MY HAND??
LIVE ELECTRIC WIRES!! MILLIONS OF VOLTS! HE TRICKED ME!!
MEANTIME, AT F.F. HEADQUARTERS...
..THE HULK HAS TAKEN ENOUGH VOLTAGE TO LIGHT UP TIMES SQUARE, BUT IT ONLY SLOWED HIM DOWN FOR A MINUTE!
I'VE GOT TO HELP BEN! HE CAN'T BEAT THE HULK ALONE!
HE'S GOING ABOUT IT ALL WRONG! HULK IS TOO STRONG...HE'S GOT TO OUTSMART HIM...HE...OHHH... TOO WEAK...CAN'T MAKE IT!!
BUT I MUST... HE NEEDS ME...CAN'T QUIT NOW!
MAYBE...IF I CAN MAKE IT TO WINDOW...GET SOME AIR... IT'LL REVIVE ME... GIVE ME STRENGTH...
...I'VE GOT TO STRETCH... REACH OUT... CAUSE A DIVERSION DOWN BELOW... THING NEEDS TIME TO GET A PLAN...
...EVERYTHING GOING 'ROUND... BLACKING OUT... WHY? WHAT'S WRONG WITH ME?? WHY DID IT HAVE TO HAPPEN...NOW?? IF ONLY...IF ONLY...OHHH...
AND THERE, HIGH ABOVE THE SCENE OF BATTLE, HIS BODY WRACKED WITH FEVER, THE VALIANT MR. FANTASTIC LAPSES INTO A HELPLESS COMA...HIS IRON WILL NO MATCH FOR THE DISEASE WHICH HAS CLAIMED HIM!
15.

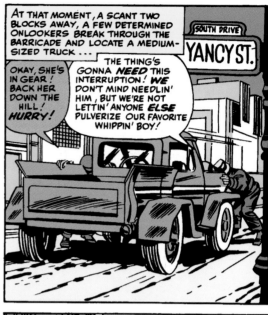

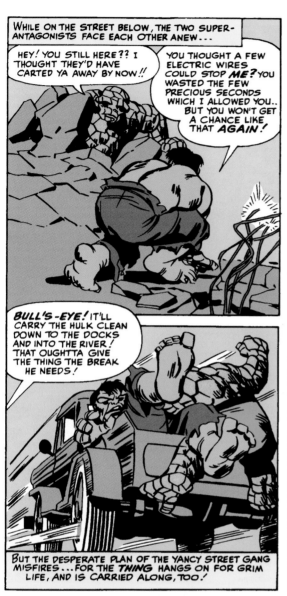

WHILE ON THE STREET BELOW, THE TWO SUPER-ANTAGONISTS FACE EACH OTHER ANEW...

HEY! YOU STILL HERE?? I THOUGHT THEY'D HAVE CARTED YA AWAY BY NOW!!

YOU THOUGHT A FEW ELECTRIC WIRES COULD STOP ME? YOU WASTED THE FEW PRECIOUS SECONDS WHICH I ALLOWED YOU.. BUT YOU WON'T GET A CHANCE LIKE THAT AGAIN!

AT THAT MOMENT, A SCANT TWO BLOCKS AWAY, A FEW DETERMINED ONLOOKERS BREAK THROUGH THE BARRICADE AND LOCATE A MEDIUM-SIZED TRUCK...

SOUTH DRIVE
YANCY ST.

OKAY, SHE'S IN GEAR! BACK HER DOWN THE HILL! HURRY!

THE THING'S GONNA NEED THIS INTERRUPTION! WE DON'T MIND NEEDLIN' HIM, BUT WE'RE NOT LETTIN' ANYONE ELSE PULVERIZE OUR FAVORITE WHIPPIN' BOY!

BULL'S-EYE! IT'LL CARRY THE HULK CLEAN DOWN TO THE DOCKS AND INTO THE RIVER! THAT OUGHTTA GIVE THE THING THE BREAK HE NEEDS!

DON'T SHOOT!! YOU'LL HIT THE THING!

ALERT ALL UNITS! THEY ARE HEADED FOR THE HUDSON RIVER!

BUT THE DESPERATE PLAN OF THE YANCY STREET GANG MISFIRES...FOR THE THING HANGS ON FOR GRIM LIFE, AND IS CARRIED ALONG, TOO!

AND, AS THE RUNAWAY VEHICLE CAREENS OFF THE PIER, THE TWO BATTLING POWERHOUSES PLUNGE INTO THE WATERY DEPTHS.....

THE HULK'S TRYIN' TO HOLD ME UNDER!! HE KNOWS HIS LUNGS ARE STRONGER THAN MINE... HE CAN GO WITHOUT AIR LONGER...I'VE GOTTA BUST LOOSE!!

JUST TIME FOR ONE FAST JUDO BLOW... IT'S GOT TO WORK... HERE GOES!!

16.

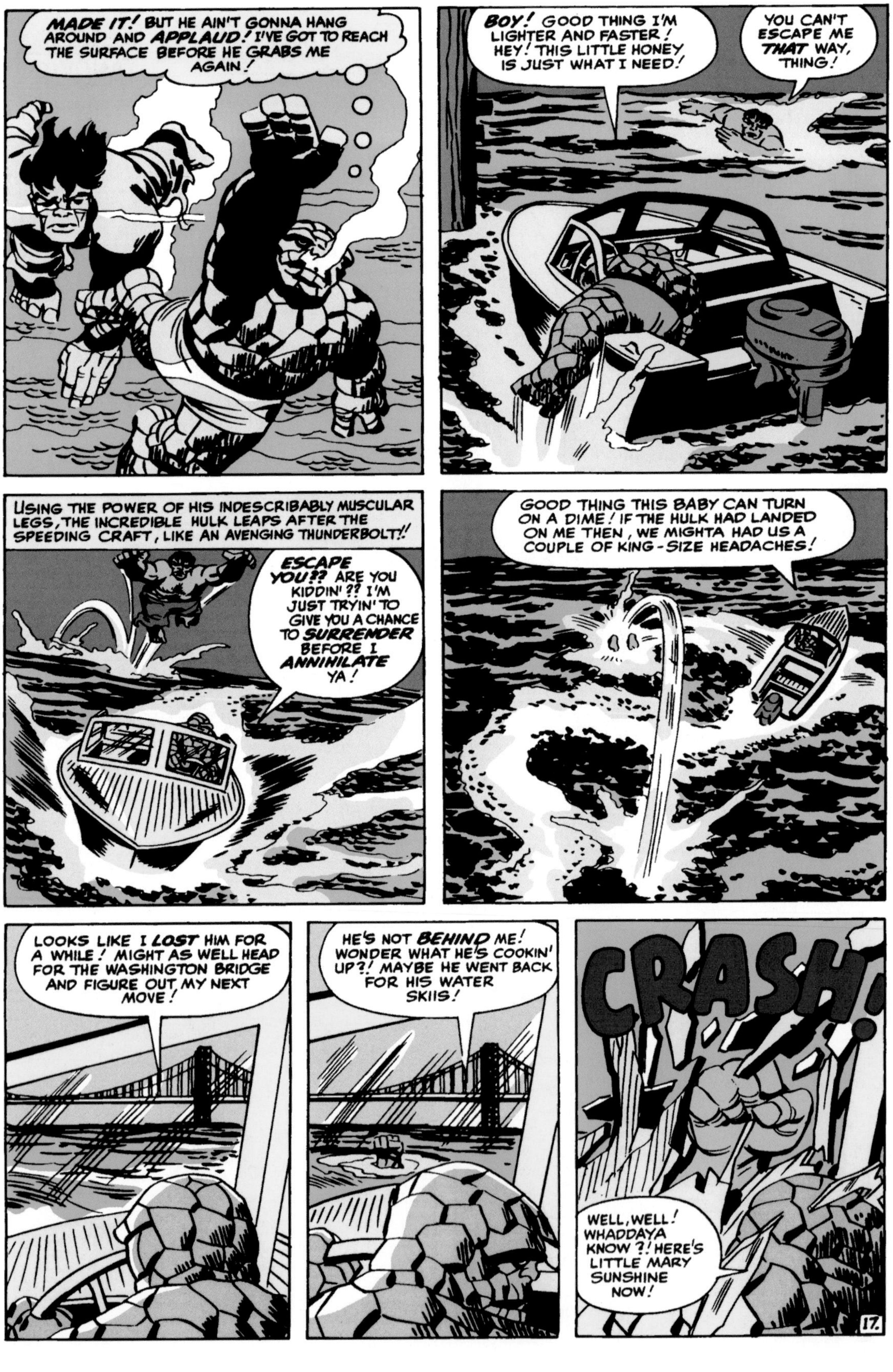

MADE IT! BUT HE AIN'T GONNA HANG AROUND AND APPLAUD! I'VE GOT TO REACH THE SURFACE BEFORE HE GRABS ME AGAIN!
BOY! GOOD THING I'M LIGHTER AND FASTER! HEY! THIS LITTLE HONEY IS JUST WHAT I NEED!
YOU CAN'T ESCAPE ME THAT WAY, THING!
USING THE POWER OF HIS INDESCRIBABLY MUSCULAR LEGS, THE INCREDIBLE HULK LEAPS AFTER THE SPEEDING CRAFT, LIKE AN AVENGING THUNDERBOLT!!
ESCAPE YOU?? ARE YOU KIDDIN'?? I'M JUST TRYIN' TO GIVE YOU A CHANCE TO SURRENDER BEFORE I ANNIHILATE YA!
GOOD THING THIS BABY CAN TURN ON A DIME! IF THE HULK HAD LANDED ON ME THEN, WE MIGHTA HAD US A COUPLE OF KING-SIZE HEADACHES!
LOOKS LIKE I LOST HIM FOR A WHILE! MIGHT AS WELL HEAD FOR THE WASHINGTON BRIDGE AND FIGURE OUT MY NEXT MOVE!
HE'S NOT BEHIND ME! WONDER WHAT HE'S COOKIN' UP?! MAYBE HE WENT BACK FOR HIS WATER SKIIS!
CRASH!
WELL, WELL! WHADDAYA KNOW?! HERE'S LITTLE MARY SUNSHINE NOW!
17.

COME BACK, YOU SNIVELIN' COWARD! WE'LL FINISH THIS OFF RIGHT *HERE!*

WE'LL FINISH IT, ALL RIGHT! BUT *I'LL* PICK THE SPOT... AND IT WON'T BE THE *WATER!*

ALL RIGHT, THEN... THE *BRIDGE* SUITS ME FINE!! BUT THERE'S A FAST WAY TO REACH THE TOP... MUCH FASTER THAN BY *CLIMBING* UP!

I WAS *HOPIN'* YOU'D DO THAT! NOW HANG ON, BUSTER... BECAUSE THIS IS *IT!*

HERE'S A FEW *GOODIES* FOR YA TO CHEW ON SO YOU DON'T GET BORED TILL I GET THERE!

SECONDS LATER, THE FIGHTING-MAD *THING* REACHES THE *HULK* AS THEY GRAB EACH OTHER IN GRIPS OF STEEL!!

SAY YOUR PRAYERS, THING! IT'S A LONG WAY DOWN!

WHY? *I* AIN'T GOIN' ANYWHERE! *YOU'RE* THE ONE WHO'S GONNA TAKE A DIVE!

BUT SLOWLY, STEADILY, WITH EVER-INCREASING PRESSURE, THE HULK'S MIGHTY ARMS FORCE THE THING BACK... BACK... UNTIL...

I'VE BEEN *RELAXIN'* TILL NOW, CUDDLES... SAVIN' MY STRENGTH! AND *HERE'S* WHAT I'M GONNA DO WITH IT!

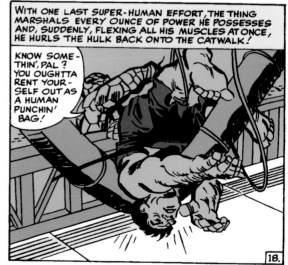

WITH ONE LAST SUPER-HUMAN EFFORT, THE THING MARSHALS EVERY OUNCE OF POWER HE POSSESSES AND, SUDDENLY, FLEXING ALL HIS MUSCLES AT ONCE, HE HURLS THE HULK BACK ONTO THE CATWALK!

KNOW SOMETHIN', PAL? YOU OUGHTTA RENT YOURSELF OUT AS A HUMAN PUNCHIN' BAG!

18.

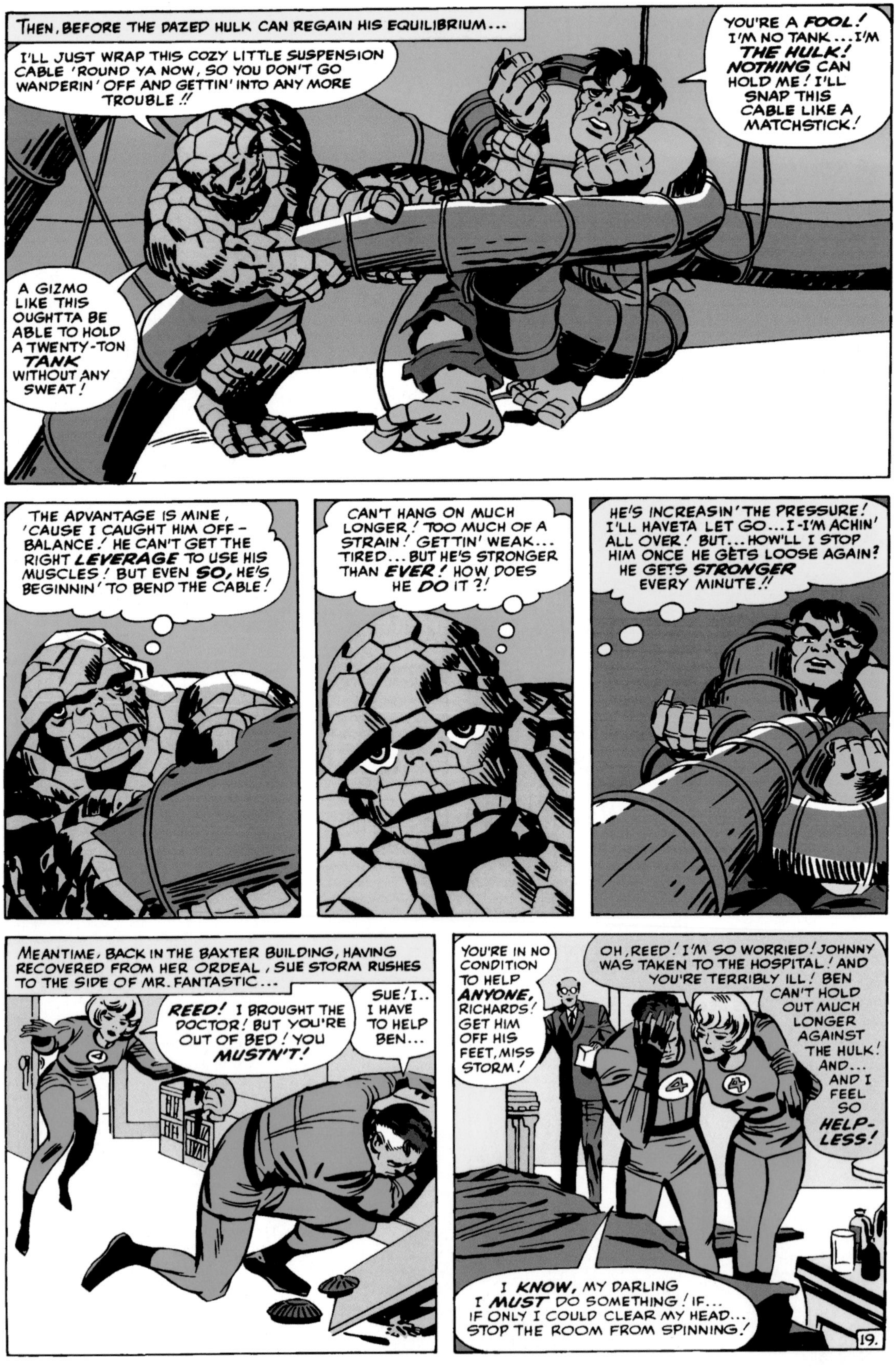
THEN, BEFORE THE DAZED HULK CAN REGAIN HIS EQUILIBRIUM...
I'LL JUST WRAP THIS COZY LITTLE SUSPENSION CABLE 'ROUND YA NOW, SO YOU DON'T GO WANDERIN' OFF AND GETTIN' INTO ANY MORE TROUBLE!!
YOU'RE A FOOL! I'M NO TANK...I'M THE HULK! NOTHING CAN HOLD ME! I'LL SNAP THIS CABLE LIKE A MATCHSTICK!
A GIZMO LIKE THIS OUGHTTA BE ABLE TO HOLD A TWENTY-TON TANK WITHOUT ANY SWEAT!
THE ADVANTAGE IS MINE, 'CAUSE I CAUGHT HIM OFF-BALANCE! HE CAN'T GET THE RIGHT LEVERAGE TO USE HIS MUSCLES! BUT EVEN SO, HE'S BEGINNIN' TO BEND THE CABLE!
CAN'T HANG ON MUCH LONGER! TOO MUCH OF A STRAIN! GETTIN' WEAK... TIRED... BUT HE'S STRONGER THAN EVER! HOW DOES HE DO IT?!
HE'S INCREASIN' THE PRESSURE! I'LL HAVETA LET GO... I-I'M ACHIN' ALL OVER! BUT... HOW'LL I STOP HIM ONCE HE GETS LOOSE AGAIN? HE GETS STRONGER EVERY MINUTE!!
MEANTIME, BACK IN THE BAXTER BUILDING, HAVING RECOVERED FROM HER ORDEAL, SUE STORM RUSHES TO THE SIDE OF MR. FANTASTIC...
REED! I BROUGHT THE DOCTOR! BUT YOU'RE OUT OF BED! YOU MUSTN'T!
SUE! I.. I HAVE TO HELP BEN...
YOU'RE IN NO CONDITION TO HELP ANYONE, RICHARDS! GET HIM OFF HIS FEET, MISS STORM!
OH, REED! I'M SO WORRIED! JOHNNY WAS TAKEN TO THE HOSPITAL! AND YOU'RE TERRIBLY ILL! BEN CAN'T HOLD OUT MUCH LONGER AGAINST THE HULK! AND... AND I FEEL SO HELP-LESS!
I KNOW, MY DARLING I MUST DO SOMETHING! IF... IF ONLY I COULD CLEAR MY HEAD... STOP THE ROOM FROM SPINNING!
19.

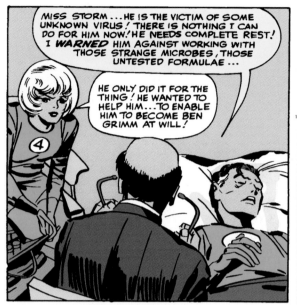

MISS STORM...HE IS THE VICTIM OF SOME UNKNOWN VIRUS! THERE IS NOTHING I CAN DO FOR HIM NOW! HE NEEDS COMPLETE REST! I *WARNED* HIM AGAINST WORKING WITH THOSE STRANGE MICROBES, THOSE UNTESTED FORMULAE...

HE ONLY DID IT FOR THE *THING*! HE WANTED TO HELP HIM...TO ENABLE HIM TO BECOME BEN GRIMM AT WILL!

WELL, I'LL GIVE HIM A SEDATIVE! SEE THAT HE KEEPS CALM...AND PRAY THAT HIS FEVER GOES DOWN!

KEEP HIM CALM?? AT A TIME LIKE *THIS*?! WHEN EVERYTHING IS GOING *AGAINST* US?!! OH, REED...MY DARLING...I...I NEVER REALIZED HOW MUCH I LOVE YOU...*NEED* YOU...

I'VE GOT TO GO NOW! WITH THE *HULK* STILL AT LARGE, THERE'S NO TELLING *WHERE* I'LL BE NEEDED NEXT!

I'D ALMOST FORGOTTEN! THE *THING* IS STILL BATTLING HIM! I'LL TURN ON THE T.V....ALTHOUGH I'M ALMOST AFRAID TO FIND OUT!

...THE BATTLE IS STILL RAGING ATOP THE WASHINGTON BRIDGE...BUT ALTHOUGH THE THING IS FIGHTING VALIANTLY, HE SEEMS TO BE WEAKENING... WAIT...SOMETHING IS *HAPPENING!*

STAND BY! WE'RE TRAINING OUR ZOOM LENS ON THE BRIDGE...TRYING TO GET A CLOSE-UP IMAGE! *NOW* WE CAN SEE...THE HULK HAS BROKEN FREE!!!

CAN'T KEEP UP THE PRESSURE ANY LONGER! GOT TO STOP...REST MY ARMS...JUST FOR A MINUTE...

AND NOW TO FINISH WHAT I STARTED!!

20.

51

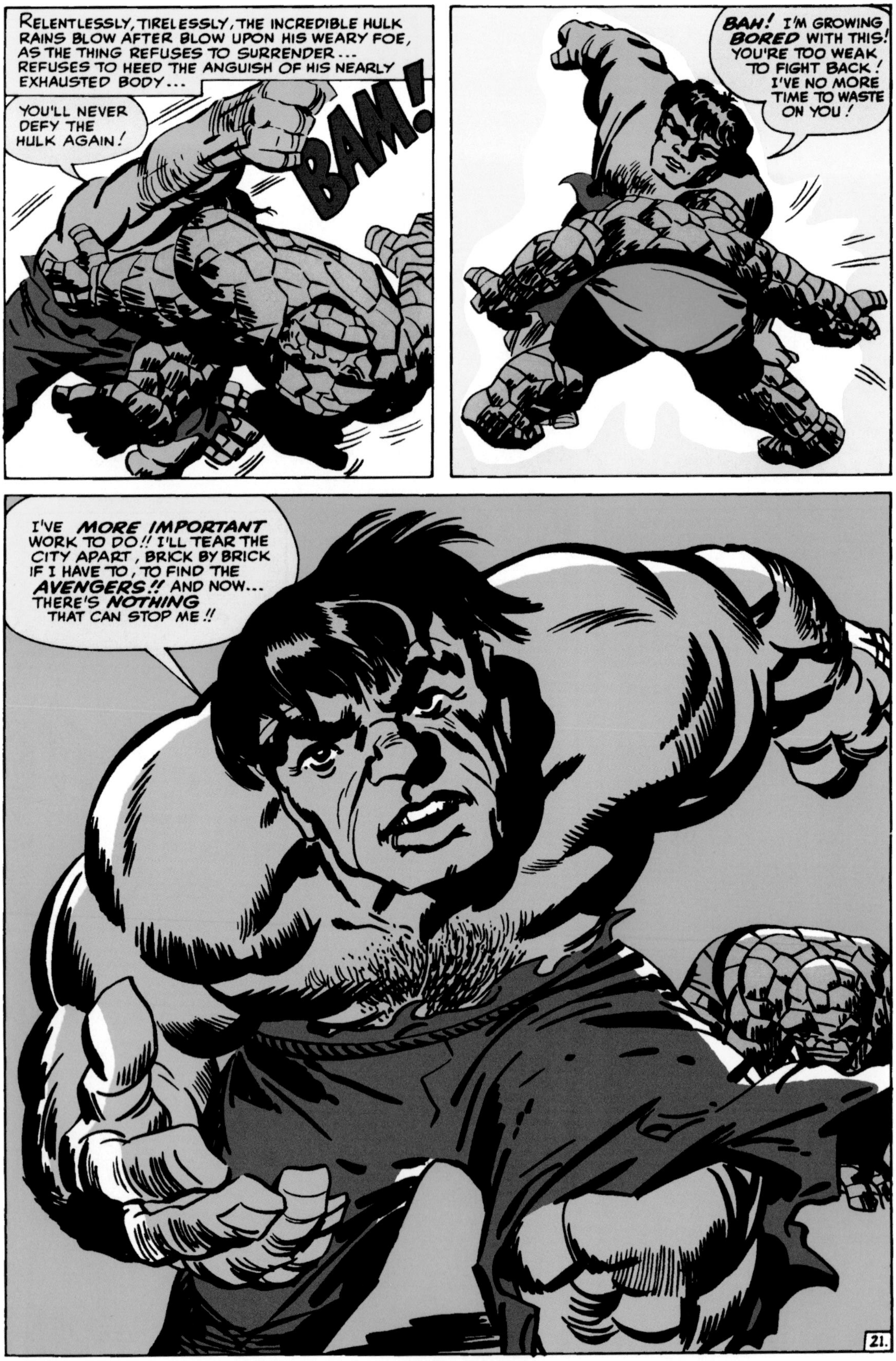
RELENTLESSLY, TIRELESSLY, THE INCREDIBLE HULK RAINS BLOW AFTER BLOW UPON HIS WEARY FOE, AS THE THING REFUSES TO SURRENDER... REFUSES TO HEED THE ANGUISH OF HIS NEARLY EXHAUSTED BODY...
YOU'LL NEVER DEFY THE HULK AGAIN!
BAM!
BAH! I'M GROWING BORED WITH THIS! YOU'RE TOO WEAK TO FIGHT BACK! I'VE NO MORE TIME TO WASTE ON YOU!
I'VE MORE IMPORTANT WORK TO DO!! I'LL TEAR THE CITY APART, BRICK BY BRICK IF I HAVE TO, TO FIND THE AVENGERS!! AND NOW... THERE'S NOTHING THAT CAN STOP ME!!
21.

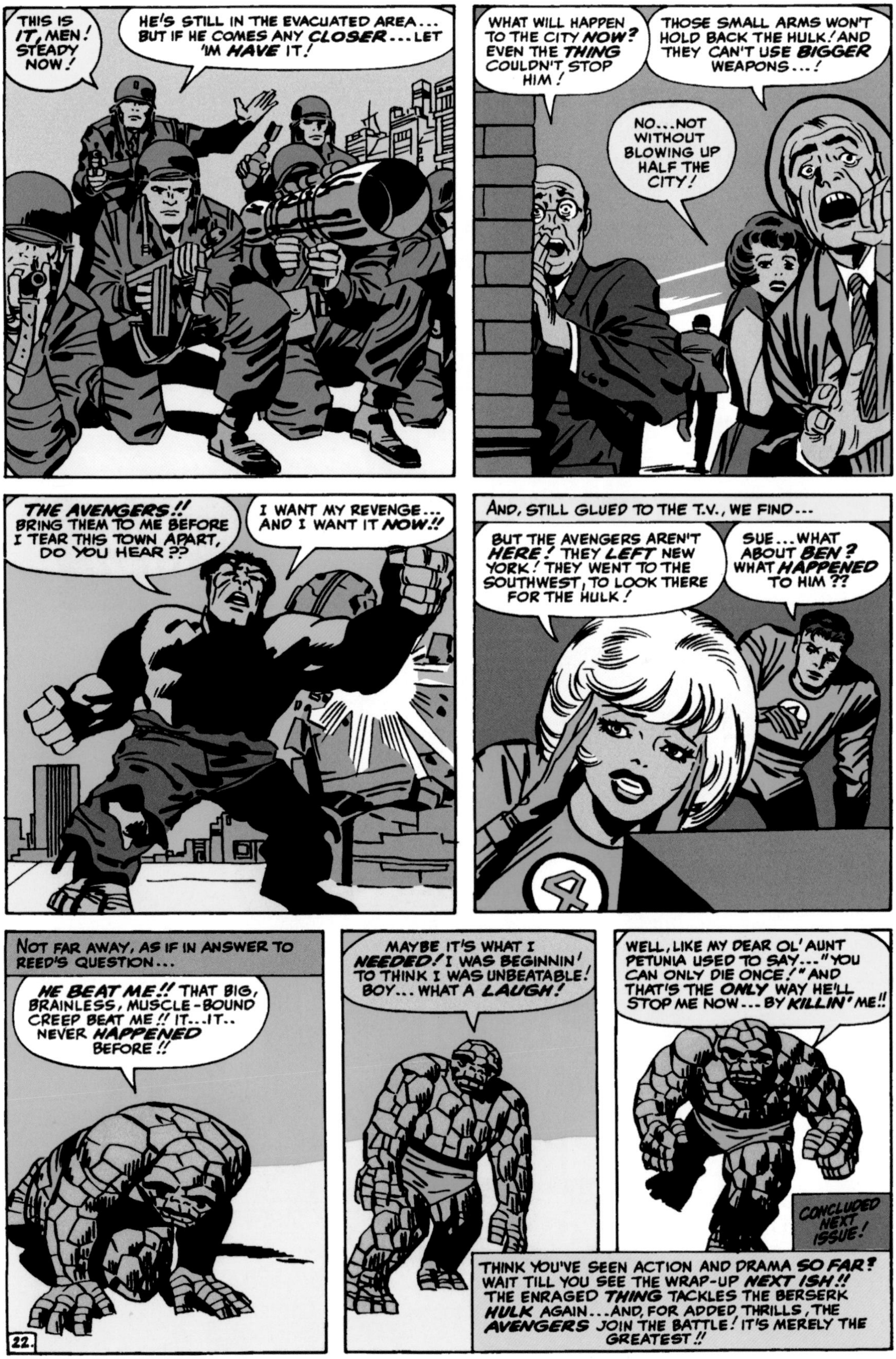
THIS IS IT, MEN! STEADY NOW!
HE'S STILL IN THE EVACUATED AREA... BUT IF HE COMES ANY CLOSER... LET 'IM HAVE IT!
WHAT WILL HAPPEN TO THE CITY NOW? EVEN THE THING COULDN'T STOP HIM!
THOSE SMALL ARMS WON'T HOLD BACK THE HULK! AND THEY CAN'T USE BIGGER WEAPONS...!
NO... NOT WITHOUT BLOWING UP HALF THE CITY!
THE AVENGERS!! BRING THEM TO ME BEFORE I TEAR THIS TOWN APART, DO YOU HEAR??
I WANT MY REVENGE... AND I WANT IT NOW!!
AND, STILL GLUED TO THE T.V., WE FIND...
BUT THE AVENGERS AREN'T HERE! THEY LEFT NEW YORK! THEY WENT TO THE SOUTHWEST, TO LOOK THERE FOR THE HULK!
SUE... WHAT ABOUT BEN? WHAT HAPPENED TO HIM??
NOT FAR AWAY, AS IF IN ANSWER TO REED'S QUESTION...
HE BEAT ME!! THAT BIG, BRAINLESS, MUSCLE-BOUND CREEP BEAT ME!! IT... IT.. NEVER HAPPENED BEFORE!!
22.
MAYBE IT'S WHAT I NEEDED! I WAS BEGINNIN' TO THINK I WAS UNBEATABLE! BOY... WHAT A LAUGH!
WELL, LIKE MY DEAR OL' AUNT PETUNIA USED TO SAY... "YOU CAN ONLY DIE ONCE!" AND THAT'S THE ONLY WAY HE'LL STOP ME NOW... BY KILLIN' ME!!
CONCLUDED NEXT ISSUE!
THINK YOU'VE SEEN ACTION AND DRAMA SO FAR? WAIT TILL YOU SEE THE WRAP-UP NEXT ISH!! THE ENRAGED THING TACKLES THE BERSERK HULK AGAIN... AND, FOR ADDED THRILLS, THE AVENGERS JOIN THE BATTLE! IT'S MERELY THE GREATEST!!

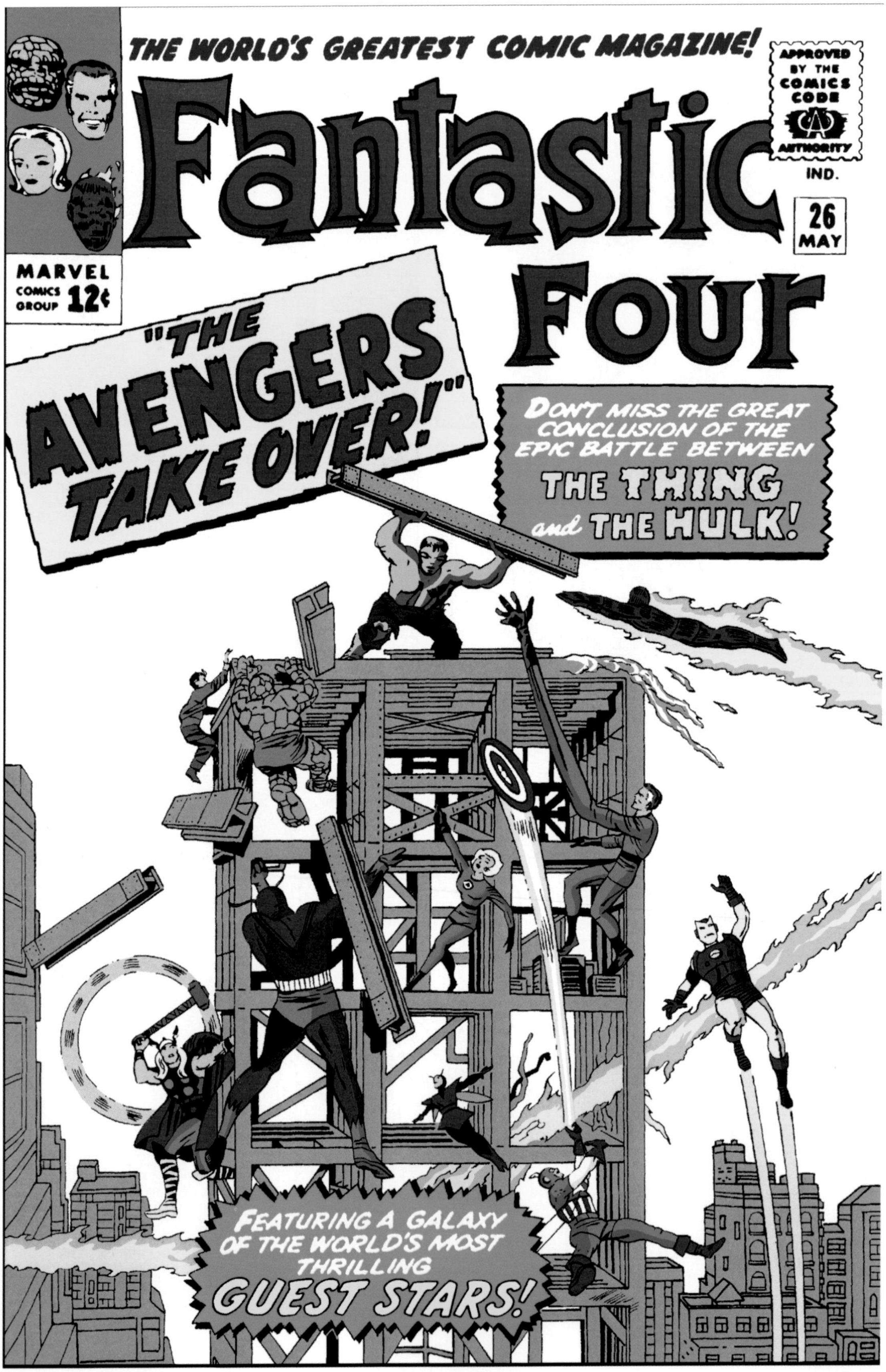
THE WORLD'S GREATEST COMIC MAGAZINE!
APPROVED BY THE COMICS CODE AUTHORITY
IND.
Fantastic Four
26 MAY
MARVEL COMICS GROUP 12¢
"THE AVENGERS TAKE OVER!"
DON'T MISS THE GREAT CONCLUSION OF THE EPIC BATTLE BETWEEN THE THING and THE HULK!
FEATURING A GALAXY OF THE WORLD'S MOST THRILLING GUEST STARS!

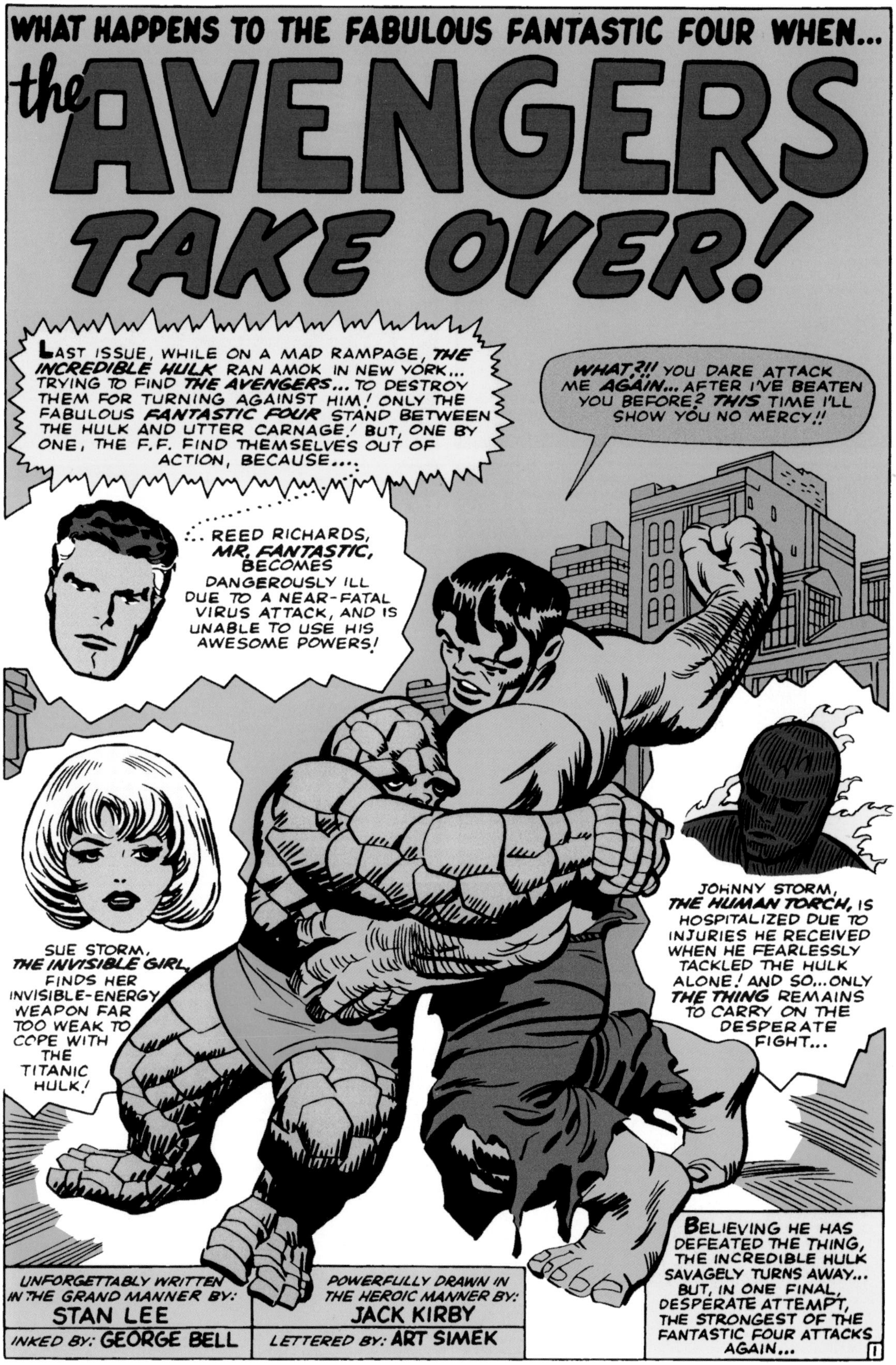
WHAT HAPPENS TO THE FABULOUS FANTASTIC FOUR WHEN...
the AVENGERS TAKE OVER!
LAST ISSUE, WHILE ON A MAD RAMPAGE, THE INCREDIBLE HULK RAN AMOK IN NEW YORK... TRYING TO FIND THE AVENGERS... TO DESTROY THEM FOR TURNING AGAINST HIM! ONLY THE FABULOUS FANTASTIC FOUR STAND BETWEEN THE HULK AND UTTER CARNAGE! BUT, ONE BY ONE, THE F.F. FIND THEMSELVES OUT OF ACTION, BECAUSE....
...REED RICHARDS, MR. FANTASTIC, BECOMES DANGEROUSLY ILL DUE TO A NEAR-FATAL VIRUS ATTACK, AND IS UNABLE TO USE HIS AWESOME POWERS!
WHAT?!! YOU DARE ATTACK ME AGAIN... AFTER I'VE BEATEN YOU BEFORE? THIS TIME I'LL SHOW YOU NO MERCY!!
SUE STORM, THE INVISIBLE GIRL, FINDS HER INVISIBLE-ENERGY WEAPON FAR TOO WEAK TO COPE WITH THE TITANIC HULK!
JOHNNY STORM, THE HUMAN TORCH, IS HOSPITALIZED DUE TO INJURIES HE RECEIVED WHEN HE FEARLESSLY TACKLED THE HULK ALONE! AND SO...ONLY THE THING REMAINS TO CARRY ON THE DESPERATE FIGHT...
BELIEVING HE HAS DEFEATED THE THING, THE INCREDIBLE HULK SAVAGELY TURNS AWAY... BUT, IN ONE FINAL, DESPERATE ATTEMPT, THE STRONGEST OF THE FANTASTIC FOUR ATTACKS AGAIN...
UNFORGETTABLY WRITTEN IN THE GRAND MANNER BY: STAN LEE
POWERFULLY DRAWN IN THE HEROIC MANNER BY: JACK KIRBY
INKED BY: GEORGE BELL
LETTERED BY: ART SIMEK
1

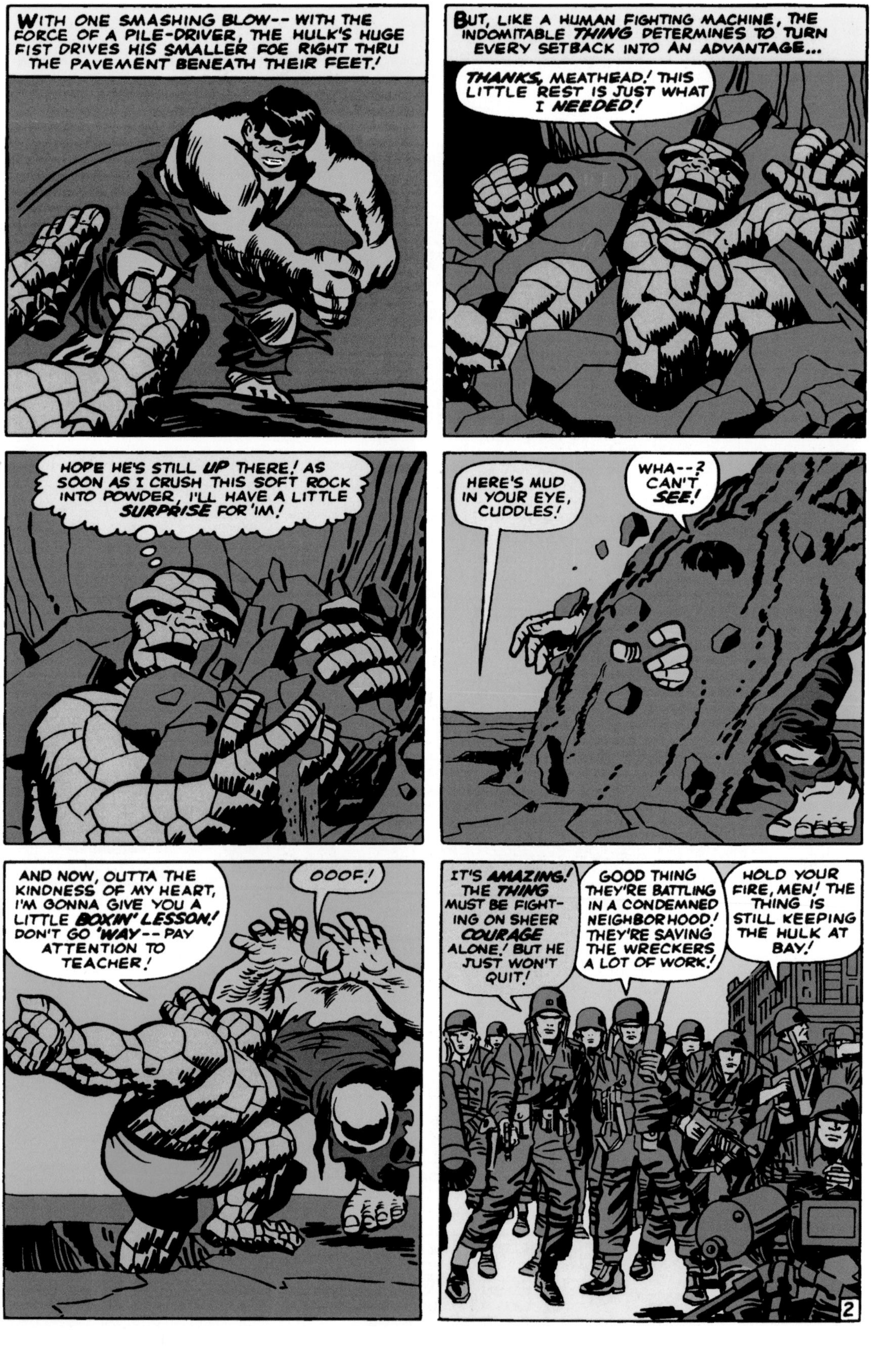
WITH ONE SMASHING BLOW-- WITH THE FORCE OF A PILE-DRIVER, THE HULK'S HUGE FIST DRIVES HIS SMALLER FOE RIGHT THRU THE PAVEMENT BENEATH THEIR FEET!
BUT, LIKE A HUMAN FIGHTING MACHINE, THE INDOMITABLE THING DETERMINES TO TURN EVERY SETBACK INTO AN ADVANTAGE...
THANKS, MEATHEAD! THIS LITTLE REST IS JUST WHAT I NEEDED!
HOPE HE'S STILL UP THERE! AS SOON AS I CRUSH THIS SOFT ROCK INTO POWDER, I'LL HAVE A LITTLE SURPRISE FOR 'IM!
HERE'S MUD IN YOUR EYE, CUDDLES!
WHA--? CAN'T SEE!
AND NOW, OUTTA THE KINDNESS OF MY HEART, I'M GONNA GIVE YOU A LITTLE BOXIN' LESSON! DON'T GO 'WAY-- PAY ATTENTION TO TEACHER!
OOOF!
IT'S AMAZING! THE THING MUST BE FIGHTING ON SHEER COURAGE ALONE! BUT HE JUST WON'T QUIT!
GOOD THING THEY'RE BATTLING IN A CONDEMNED NEIGHBORHOOD! THEY'RE SAVING THE WRECKERS A LOT OF WORK!
HOLD YOUR FIRE, MEN! THE THING IS STILL KEEPING THE HULK AT BAY!
2

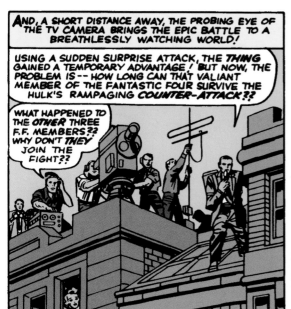

AND, A SHORT DISTANCE AWAY, THE PROBING EYE OF THE TV CAMERA BRINGS THE EPIC BATTLE TO A BREATHLESSLY WATCHING WORLD!

USING A SUDDEN SURPRISE ATTACK, THE *THING* GAINED A TEMPORARY ADVANTAGE! BUT NOW, THE PROBLEM IS -- HOW LONG CAN THAT VALIANT MEMBER OF THE FANTASTIC FOUR SURVIVE THE HULK'S RAMPAGING *COUNTER-ATTACK??*

WHAT HAPPENED TO THE *OTHER* THREE F.F. MEMBERS?? WHY DON'T *THEY* JOIN THE FIGHT??

TO ANSWER THE TV TECHNICIAN'S QUESTION, WE RETURN TO THE F.F. HEADQUARTERS, WHERE WE FIND...

BEN *CAN'T* HOLD OUT MUCH LONGER! I'VE *GOT* TO GO TO HIM-- *GOT TO*--

YOU *CAN'T,* REED! YOU'RE BURNING WITH FEVER! YOU NEED MEDICAL HELP-- RIGHT *NOW!*

THERE HE IS, BOYS! GET HIM ON THE STRETCHER!

GOOD THING HE'S SO WEAK! WE'D NEVER BE ABLE TO *HOLD* HIM OTHERWISE!

LET ME *GO!* BEN *NEEDS* ME! I CAN'T FAIL HIM! I CAN'T--

STAY BACK, MA'AM! *WE'LL* HANDLE HIM! HE'S GETTING DELIRIOUS! TOO WEAK TO RESIST!

LET'S *GO!* HE NEEDS AN OXYGEN TENT! HE'S HAVING TROUBLE BREATHING!

YOU MUSTN'T LET ANYTHING HAPPEN TO HIM!--OH, REED, MY DARLING--

WE'LL DO OUR BEST, MA'AM!

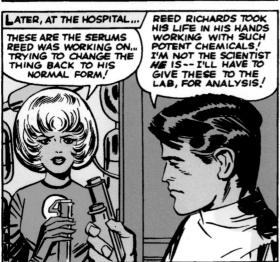

*L*ATER, AT THE HOSPITAL...

THESE ARE THE SERUMS REED WAS WORKING ON... TRYING TO CHANGE THE THING BACK TO HIS NORMAL FORM!

REED RICHARDS TOOK HIS LIFE IN HIS HANDS WORKING WITH SUCH POTENT CHEMICALS! I'M NOT THE SCIENTIST *HE* IS -- I'LL HAVE TO GIVE THESE TO THE LAB, FOR ANALYSIS!

*M*EANWHILE, IN ANOTHER PART OF THE HOSPITAL...

WHO'S THE MYSTERY PATIENT, NURSE? WHY THE ASBESTOS SCREENS?

DIDN'T YOU *HEAR?* IT'S THE *HUMAN TORCH!* HE WAS BROUGHT IN UNDER SEDATION, AFTER BATTLING THAT DREADFUL *HULK!*

3

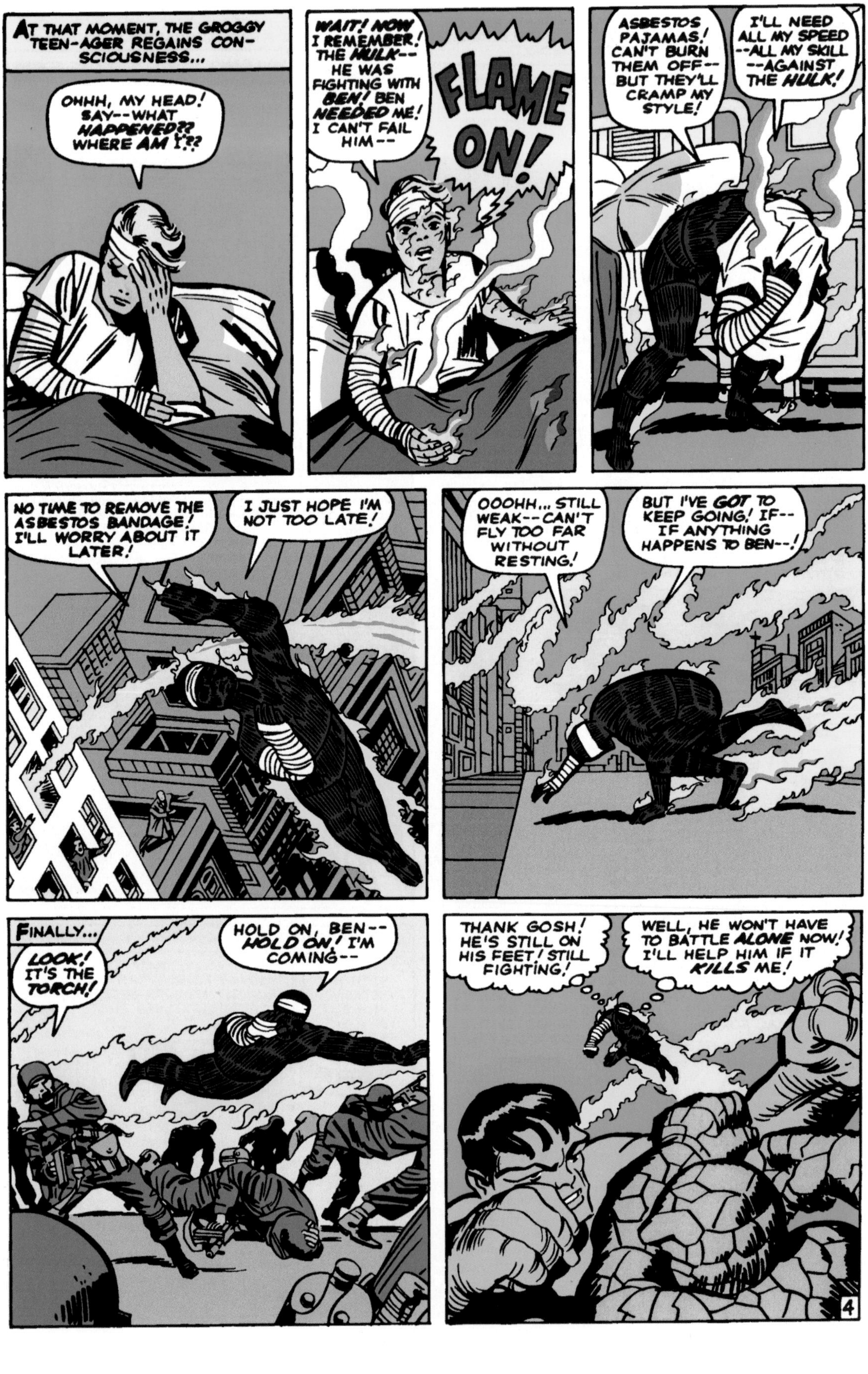
AT THAT MOMENT, THE GROGGY TEEN-AGER REGAINS CONSCIOUSNESS...
OHHH, MY HEAD! SAY--WHAT HAPPENED?? WHERE AM I??
WAIT! NOW I REMEMBER! THE HULK--HE WAS FIGHTING WITH BEN! BEN NEEDED ME! I CAN'T FAIL HIM--
FLAME ON!
ASBESTOS PAJAMAS! CAN'T BURN THEM OFF--BUT THEY'LL CRAMP MY STYLE!
I'LL NEED ALL MY SPEED--ALL MY SKILL--AGAINST THE HULK!
NO TIME TO REMOVE THE ASBESTOS BANDAGE! I'LL WORRY ABOUT IT LATER!
I JUST HOPE I'M NOT TOO LATE!
OOOHH... STILL WEAK--CAN'T FLY TOO FAR WITHOUT RESTING!
BUT I'VE GOT TO KEEP GOING! IF--IF ANYTHING HAPPENS TO BEN--!
FINALLY...
LOOK! IT'S THE TORCH!
HOLD ON, BEN--HOLD ON! I'M COMING--
THANK GOSH! HE'S STILL ON HIS FEET! STILL FIGHTING!
WELL, HE WON'T HAVE TO BATTLE ALONE NOW! I'LL HELP HIM IF IT KILLS ME!
4

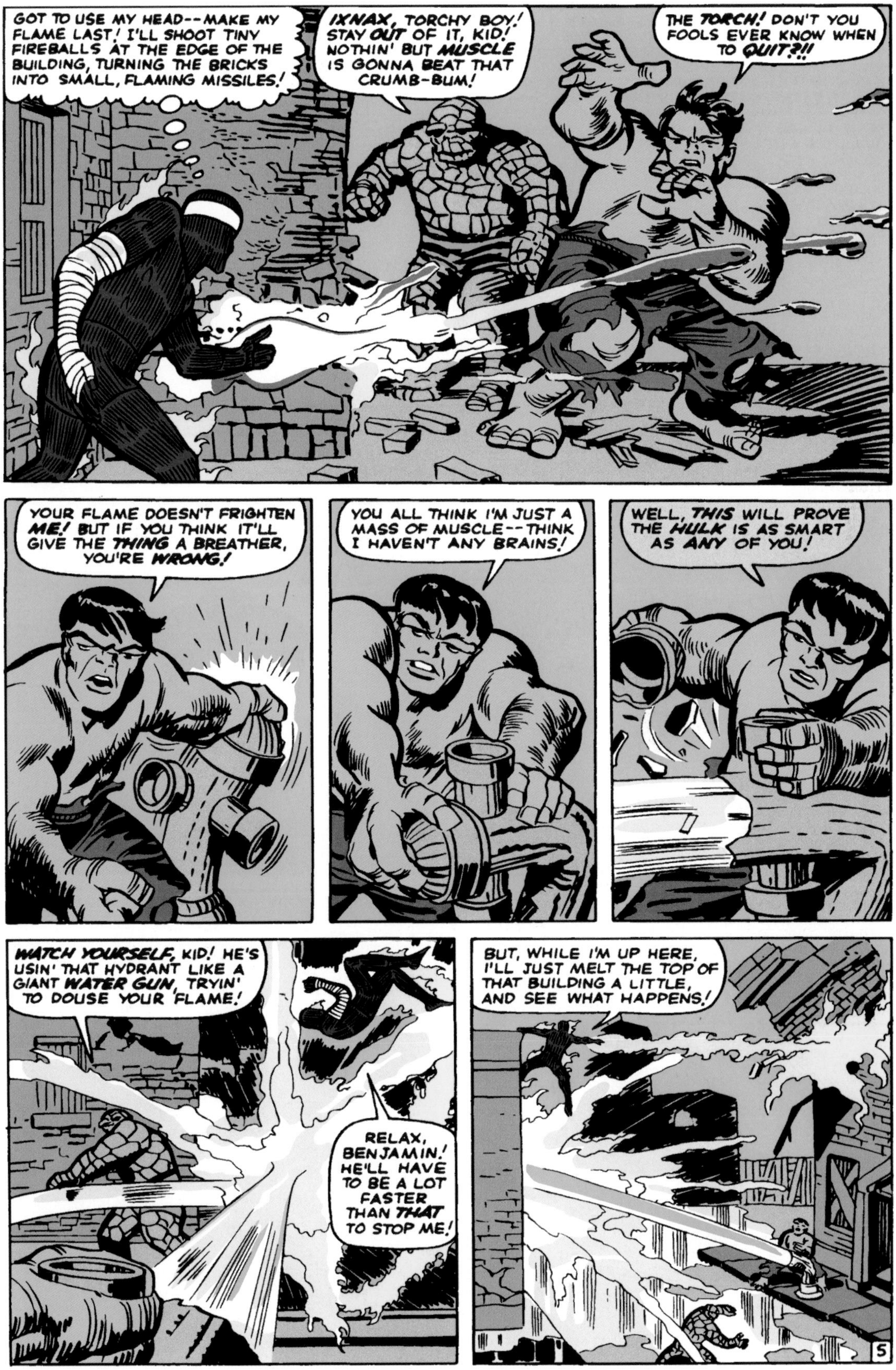
GOT TO USE MY HEAD--MAKE MY FLAME LAST! I'LL SHOOT TINY FIREBALLS AT THE EDGE OF THE BUILDING, TURNING THE BRICKS INTO SMALL, FLAMING MISSILES!
IXNAX, TORCHY BOY! STAY OUT OF IT, KID! NOTHIN' BUT MUSCLE IS GONNA BEAT THAT CRUMB-BUM!
THE TORCH! DON'T YOU FOOLS EVER KNOW WHEN TO QUIT?!!
YOUR FLAME DOESN'T FRIGHTEN ME! BUT IF YOU THINK IT'LL GIVE THE THING A BREATHER, YOU'RE WRONG!
YOU ALL THINK I'M JUST A MASS OF MUSCLE--THINK I HAVEN'T ANY BRAINS!
WELL, THIS WILL PROVE THE HULK IS AS SMART AS ANY OF YOU!
WATCH YOURSELF, KID! HE'S USIN' THAT HYDRANT LIKE A GIANT WATER GUN, TRYIN' TO DOUSE YOUR FLAME!
RELAX, BENJAMIN! HE'LL HAVE TO BE A LOT FASTER THAN THAT TO STOP ME!
BUT, WHILE I'M UP HERE, I'LL JUST MELT THE TOP OF THAT BUILDING A LITTLE, AND SEE WHAT HAPPENS!
5

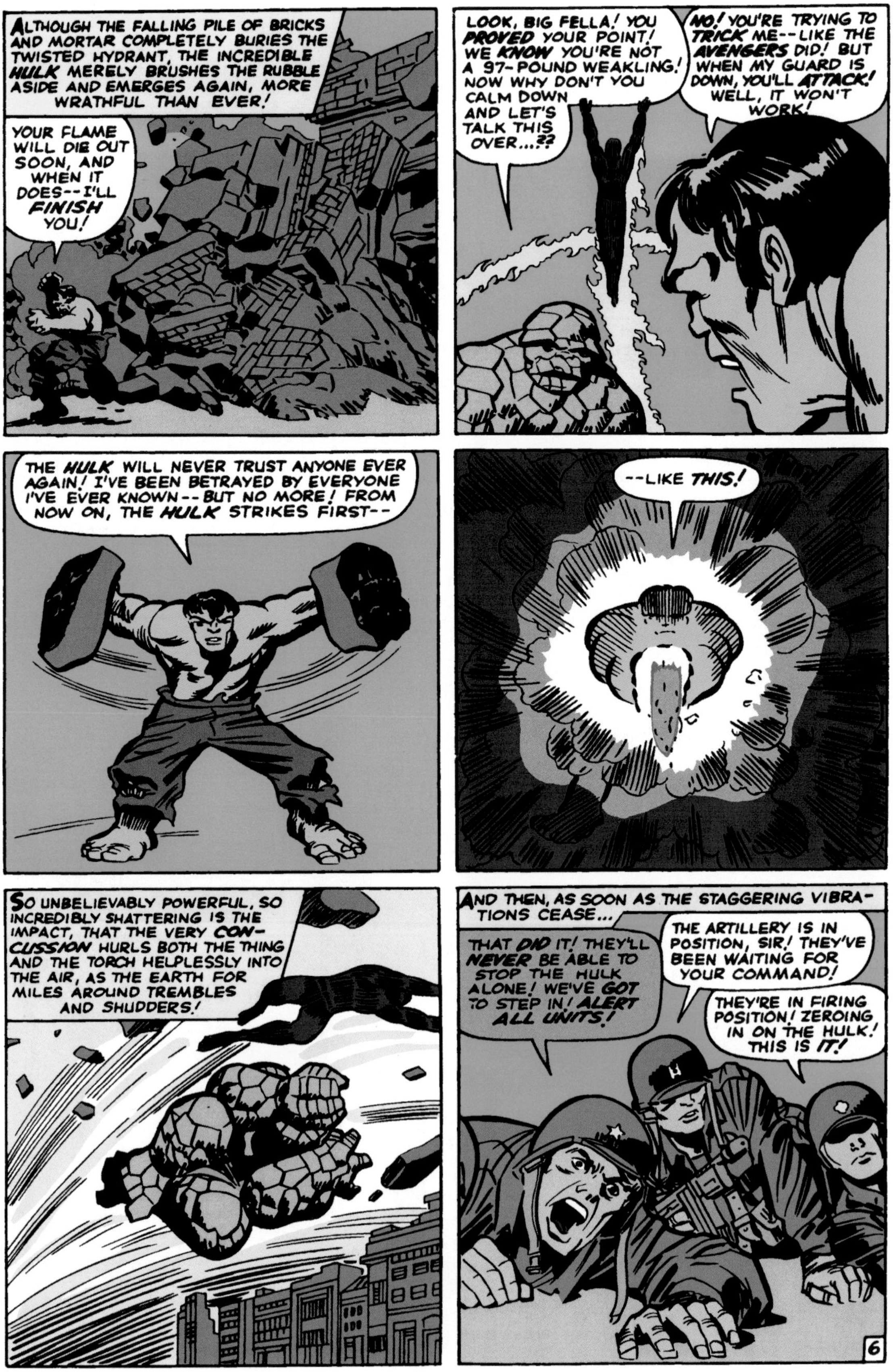
ALTHOUGH THE FALLING PILE OF BRICKS AND MORTAR COMPLETELY BURIES THE TWISTED HYDRANT, THE INCREDIBLE HULK MERELY BRUSHES THE RUBBLE ASIDE AND EMERGES AGAIN, MORE WRATHFUL THAN EVER!
YOUR FLAME WILL DIE OUT SOON, AND WHEN IT DOES--I'LL FINISH YOU!
LOOK, BIG FELLA! YOU PROVED YOUR POINT! WE KNOW YOU'RE NOT A 97-POUND WEAKLING! NOW WHY DON'T YOU CALM DOWN AND LET'S TALK THIS OVER...??
NO! YOU'RE TRYING TO TRICK ME--LIKE THE AVENGERS DID! BUT WHEN MY GUARD IS DOWN, YOU'LL ATTACK! WELL, IT WON'T WORK!
THE HULK WILL NEVER TRUST ANYONE EVER AGAIN! I'VE BEEN BETRAYED BY EVERYONE I'VE EVER KNOWN--BUT NO MORE! FROM NOW ON, THE HULK STRIKES FIRST--
--LIKE THIS!
SO UNBELIEVABLY POWERFUL, SO INCREDIBLY SHATTERING IS THE IMPACT, THAT THE VERY CONCUSSION HURLS BOTH THE THING AND THE TORCH HELPLESSLY INTO THE AIR, AS THE EARTH FOR MILES AROUND TREMBLES AND SHUDDERS!
AND THEN, AS SOON AS THE STAGGERING VIBRATIONS CEASE...
THAT DID IT! THEY'LL NEVER BE ABLE TO STOP THE HULK ALONE! WE'VE GOT TO STEP IN! ALERT ALL UNITS!
THE ARTILLERY IS IN POSITION, SIR! THEY'VE BEEN WAITING FOR YOUR COMMAND!
THEY'RE IN FIRING POSITION! ZEROING IN ON THE HULK! THIS IS IT!
6

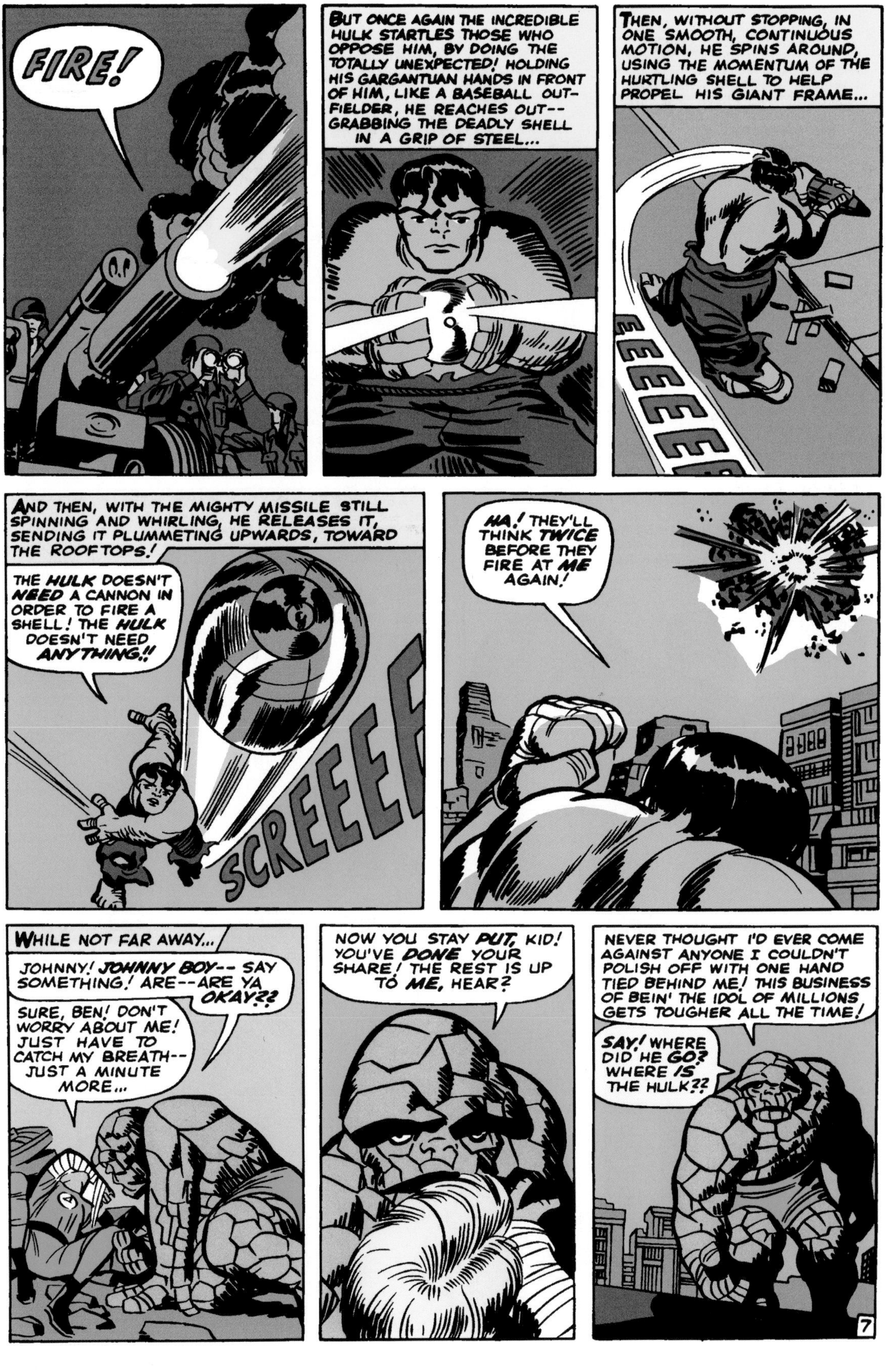
FIRE!
BUT ONCE AGAIN THE INCREDIBLE HULK STARTLES THOSE WHO OPPOSE HIM, BY DOING THE TOTALLY UNEXPECTED! HOLDING HIS GARGANTUAN HANDS IN FRONT OF HIM, LIKE A BASEBALL OUT-FIELDER, HE REACHES OUT-- GRABBING THE DEADLY SHELL IN A GRIP OF STEEL...
THEN, WITHOUT STOPPING, IN ONE SMOOTH, CONTINUOUS MOTION, HE SPINS AROUND, USING THE MOMENTUM OF THE HURTLING SHELL TO HELP PROPEL HIS GIANT FRAME...
EEEEE
AND THEN, WITH THE MIGHTY MISSILE STILL SPINNING AND WHIRLING, HE RELEASES IT, SENDING IT PLUMMETING UPWARDS, TOWARD THE ROOFTOPS!
THE HULK DOESN'T NEED A CANNON IN ORDER TO FIRE A SHELL! THE HULK DOESN'T NEED ANYTHING!!
SCREEEE
HA! THEY'LL THINK TWICE BEFORE THEY FIRE AT ME AGAIN!
WHILE NOT FAR AWAY...
JOHNNY! JOHNNY BOY-- SAY SOMETHING! ARE--ARE YA OKAY??
SURE, BEN! DON'T WORRY ABOUT ME! JUST HAVE TO CATCH MY BREATH-- JUST A MINUTE MORE...
NOW YOU STAY PUT, KID! YOU'VE DONE YOUR SHARE! THE REST IS UP TO ME, HEAR?
NEVER THOUGHT I'D EVER COME AGAINST ANYONE I COULDN'T POLISH OFF WITH ONE HAND TIED BEHIND ME! THIS BUSINESS OF BEIN' THE IDOL OF MILLIONS GETS TOUGHER ALL THE TIME!
SAY! WHERE DID HE GO? WHERE IS THE HULK??
7

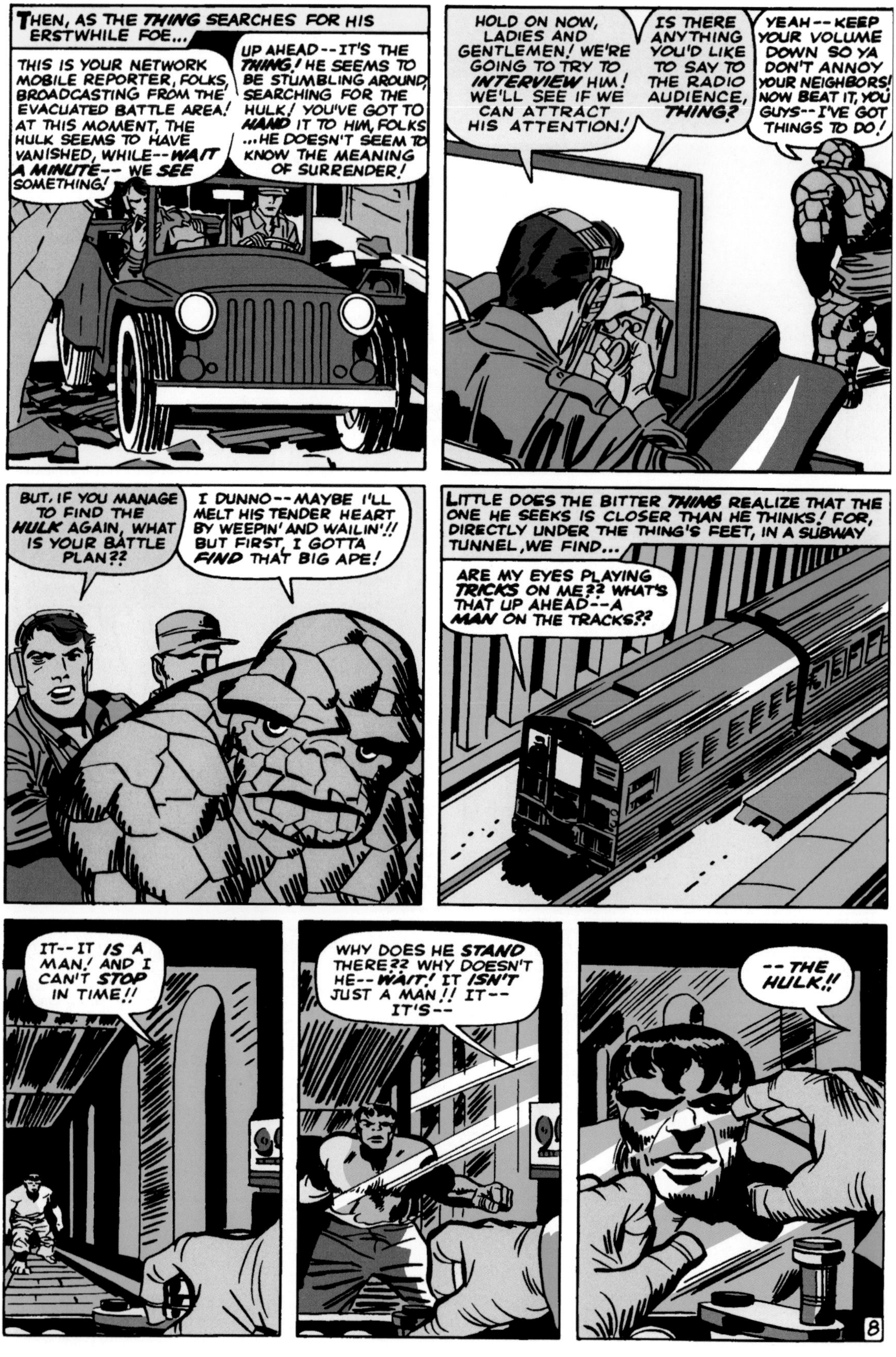
THEN, AS THE THING SEARCHES FOR HIS ERSTWHILE FOE...
THIS IS YOUR NETWORK MOBILE REPORTER, FOLKS, BROADCASTING FROM THE EVACUATED BATTLE AREA! AT THIS MOMENT, THE HULK SEEMS TO HAVE VANISHED, WHILE--WAIT A MINUTE-- WE SEE SOMETHING!
UP AHEAD--IT'S THE THING! HE SEEMS TO BE STUMBLING AROUND, SEARCHING FOR THE HULK! YOU'VE GOT TO HAND IT TO HIM, FOLKS ...HE DOESN'T SEEM TO KNOW THE MEANING OF SURRENDER!
HOLD ON NOW, LADIES AND GENTLEMEN! WE'RE GOING TO TRY TO INTERVIEW HIM! WE'LL SEE IF WE CAN ATTRACT HIS ATTENTION!
IS THERE ANYTHING YOU'D LIKE TO SAY TO THE RADIO AUDIENCE, THING?
YEAH--KEEP YOUR VOLUME DOWN SO YA DON'T ANNOY YOUR NEIGHBORS! NOW BEAT IT, YOU GUYS--I'VE GOT THINGS TO DO!
BUT, IF YOU MANAGE TO FIND THE HULK AGAIN, WHAT IS YOUR BATTLE PLAN??
I DUNNO--MAYBE I'LL MELT HIS TENDER HEART BY WEEPIN' AND WAILIN'!! BUT FIRST, I GOTTA FIND THAT BIG APE!
LITTLE DOES THE BITTER THING REALIZE THAT THE ONE HE SEEKS IS CLOSER THAN HE THINKS! FOR, DIRECTLY UNDER THE THING'S FEET, IN A SUBWAY TUNNEL, WE FIND...
ARE MY EYES PLAYING TRICKS ON ME?? WHAT'S THAT UP AHEAD--A MAN ON THE TRACKS??
IT--IT IS A MAN! AND I CAN'T STOP IN TIME!!
WHY DOES HE STAND THERE?? WHY DOESN'T HE--WAIT! IT ISN'T JUST A MAN!! IT--IT'S--
--THE HULK!!
8

ALMOST EFFORTLESSLY, THE INCREDIBLE HULK STOPS THE SPEEDING TRAIN WITH THE SHEER GAMMA-RAY POWER OF HIS IRON-MUSCLED BODY! AND THEN...

LEAVE THE TRAIN! TAKE ALL THE PASSENGERS WITH YOU-- WHILE YOU STILL CAN!!

M-MISTER, YOU DON'T HAVE TO TELL ME TWICE!! LUCKY THERE'S AN EMERGENCY EXIT STAIRWAY JUST BEHIND US!

SECONDS LATER, WITH HIS MASSIVE HAND ON THE CONTROL LEVER, THE STRONGEST MORTAL ON EARTH PROPELS THE TRAIN THRU THE WINDING TUNNEL, AS ONE THOUGHT ECHOES THRU HIS BRAIN...

THE AVENGERS!! I'VE GOT TO FIND THE AVENGERS!

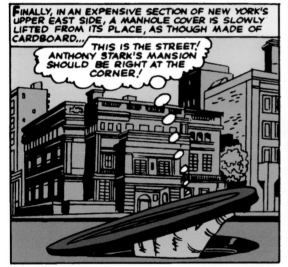

FINALLY, IN AN EXPENSIVE SECTION OF NEW YORK'S UPPER EAST SIDE, A MANHOLE COVER IS SLOWLY LIFTED FROM ITS PLACE, AS THOUGH MADE OF CARDBOARD...

THIS IS THE STREET! ANTHONY STARK'S MANSION SHOULD BE RIGHT AT THE CORNER!

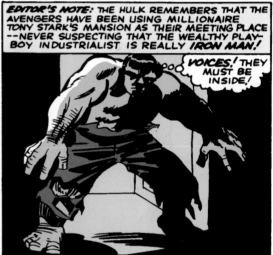

EDITOR'S NOTE: THE HULK REMEMBERS THAT THE AVENGERS HAVE BEEN USING MILLIONAIRE TONY STARK'S MANSION AS THEIR MEETING PLACE --NEVER SUSPECTING THAT THE WEALTHY PLAY-BOY INDUSTRIALIST IS REALLY IRON MAN!

VOICES! THEY MUST BE INSIDE!

SUDDENLY, THE LIGHTS ARE SNAPPED ON, AND...

WE RETURNED TO NEW YORK JUST IN TIME!! THE REPORTS ARE TRUE! THE HULK IS ON THE RAMPAGE AGAIN! BUT THIS TIME WE'LL STOP HIM!

DON'T HURT HIM! GIVE ME A CHANCE! LET ME TRY TO REASON WITH HIM!

WE HAVE NO WISH TO CAUSE ANY INJURY! IT IS UP TO HIM!

9

63

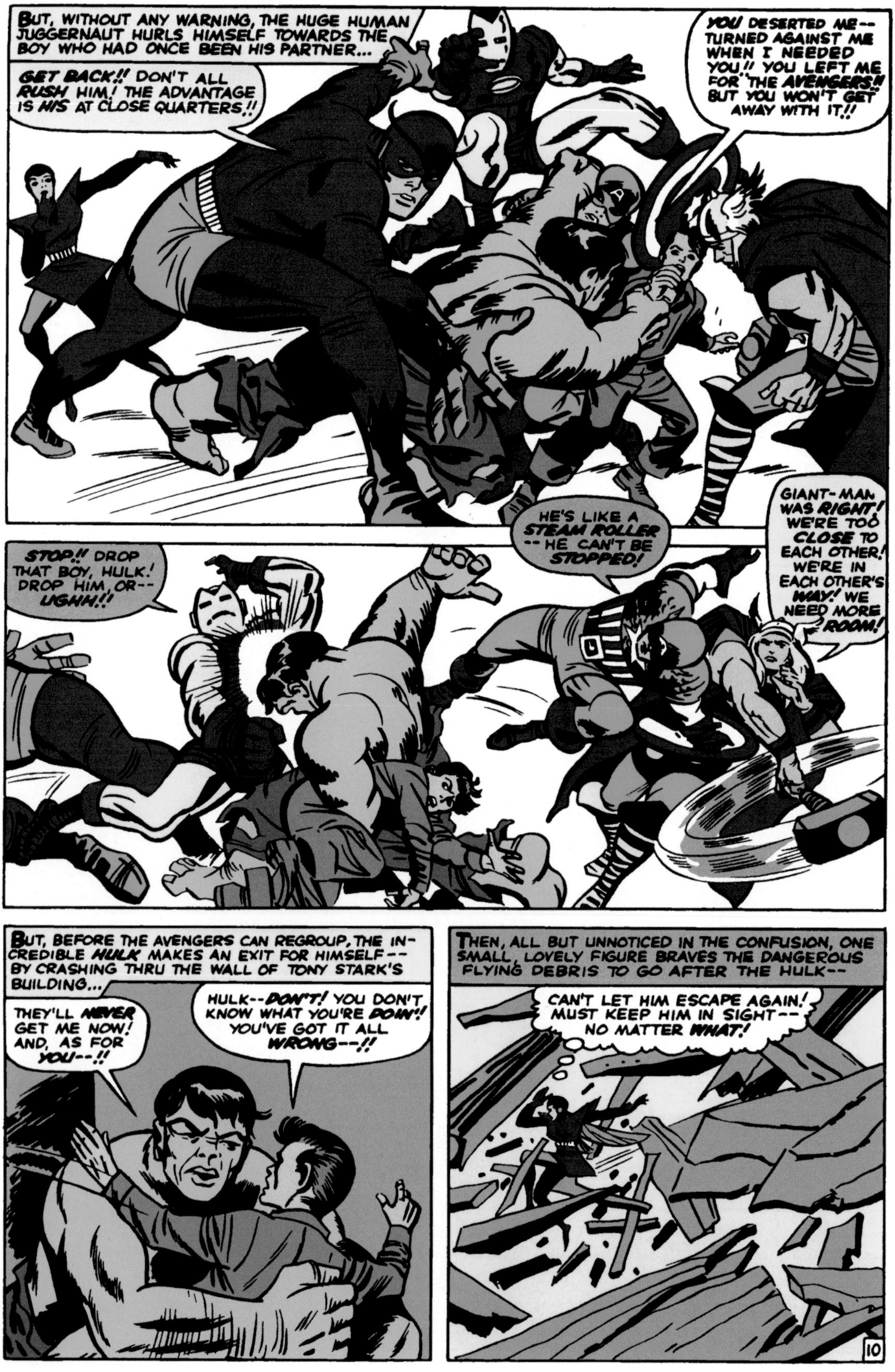

BUT, WITHOUT ANY WARNING, THE HUGE HUMAN JUGGERNAUT HURLS HIMSELF TOWARDS THE BOY WHO HAD ONCE BEEN HIS PARTNER...
GET BACK!! DON'T ALL RUSH HIM! THE ADVANTAGE IS HIS AT CLOSE QUARTERS!!
YOU! DESERTED ME-- TURNED AGAINST ME WHEN I NEEDED YOU!! YOU LEFT ME FOR THE AVENGERS!! BUT YOU WON'T GET AWAY WITH IT!!
STOP!! DROP THAT BOY, HULK! DROP HIM, OR-- UGHH!!
HE'S LIKE A STEAM ROLLER -- HE CAN'T BE STOPPED!
GIANT-MAN WAS RIGHT! WE'RE TOO CLOSE TO EACH OTHER! WE'RE IN EACH OTHER'S WAY! WE NEED MORE ROOM!
BUT, BEFORE THE AVENGERS CAN REGROUP, THE INCREDIBLE HULK MAKES AN EXIT FOR HIMSELF -- BY CRASHING THRU THE WALL OF TONY STARK'S BUILDING...
THEY'LL NEVER GET ME NOW! AND, AS FOR YOU--!!
HULK--DON'T! YOU DON'T KNOW WHAT YOU'RE DOIN'!! YOU'VE GOT IT ALL WRONG--!!
THEN, ALL BUT UNNOTICED IN THE CONFUSION, ONE SMALL, LOVELY FIGURE BRAVES THE DANGEROUS FLYING DEBRIS TO GO AFTER THE HULK--
CAN'T LET HIM ESCAPE AGAIN! MUST KEEP HIM IN SIGHT-- NO MATTER WHAT!
10

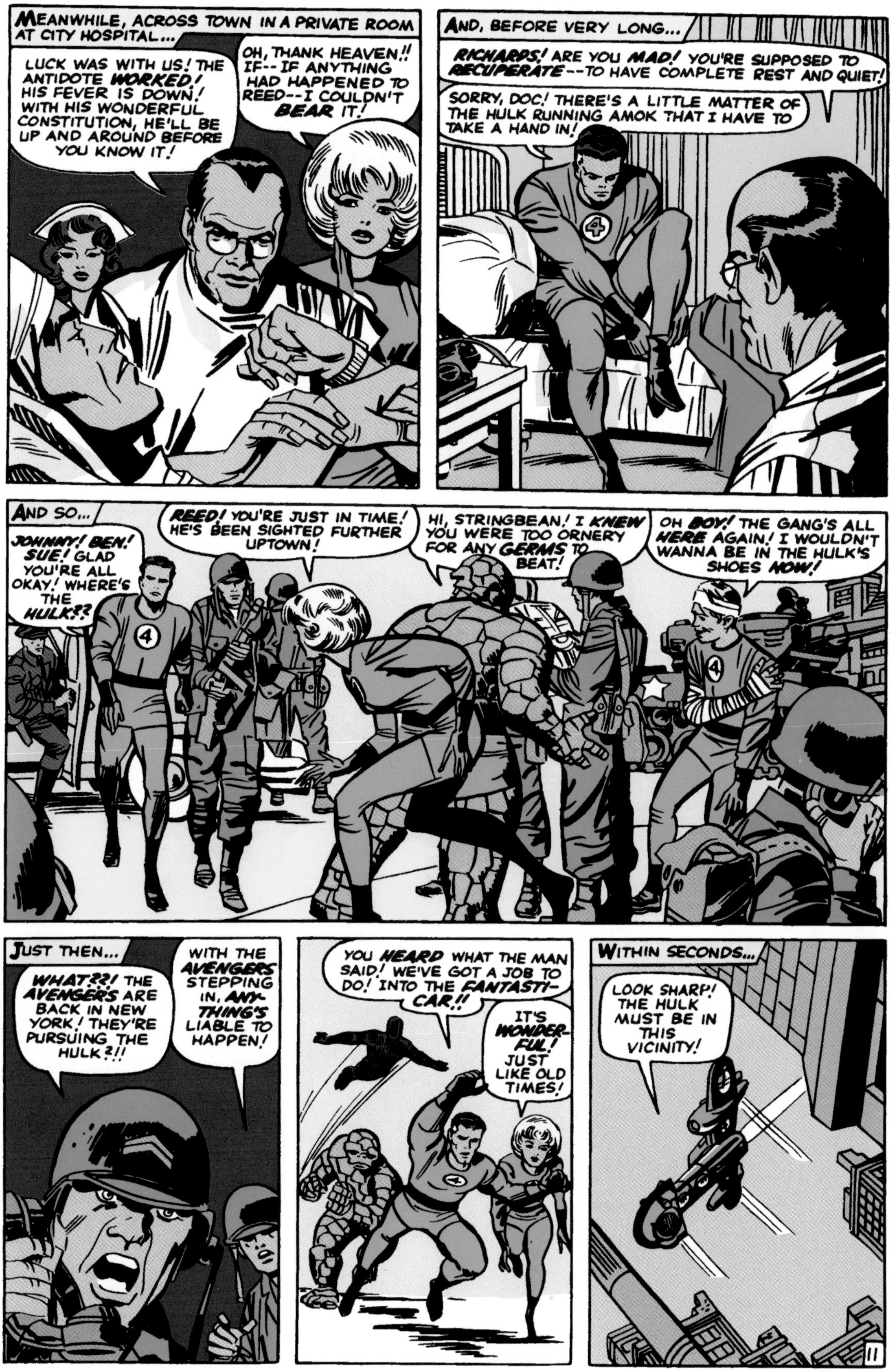
MEANWHILE, ACROSS TOWN IN A PRIVATE ROOM AT CITY HOSPITAL...
LUCK WAS WITH US! THE ANTIDOTE WORKED! HIS FEVER IS DOWN! WITH HIS WONDERFUL CONSTITUTION, HE'LL BE UP AND AROUND BEFORE YOU KNOW IT!
OH, THANK HEAVEN!! IF-- IF ANYTHING HAD HAPPENED TO REED--I COULDN'T BEAR IT!
AND, BEFORE VERY LONG...
RICHARDS! ARE YOU MAD! YOU'RE SUPPOSED TO RECUPERATE--TO HAVE COMPLETE REST AND QUIET!
SORRY, DOC! THERE'S A LITTLE MATTER OF THE HULK RUNNING AMOK THAT I HAVE TO TAKE A HAND IN!
AND SO...
JOHNNY! BEN! SUE! GLAD YOU'RE ALL OKAY! WHERE'S THE HULK??
REED! YOU'RE JUST IN TIME! HE'S BEEN SIGHTED FURTHER UPTOWN!
HI, STRINGBEAN! I KNEW YOU WERE TOO ORNERY FOR ANY GERMS TO BEAT!
OH BOY! THE GANG'S ALL HERE AGAIN! I WOULDN'T WANNA BE IN THE HULK'S SHOES NOW!
JUST THEN...
WHAT??! THE AVENGER'S ARE BACK IN NEW YORK! THEY'RE PURSUING THE HULK?!!
WITH THE AVENGERS STEPPING IN, ANY-THING'S LIABLE TO HAPPEN!
YOU HEARD WHAT THE MAN SAID! WE'VE GOT A JOB TO DO! INTO THE FANTASTI-CAR!!
IT'S WONDER-FUL! JUST LIKE OLD TIMES!
WITHIN SECONDS...
LOOK SHARP! THE HULK MUST BE IN THIS VICINITY!
11

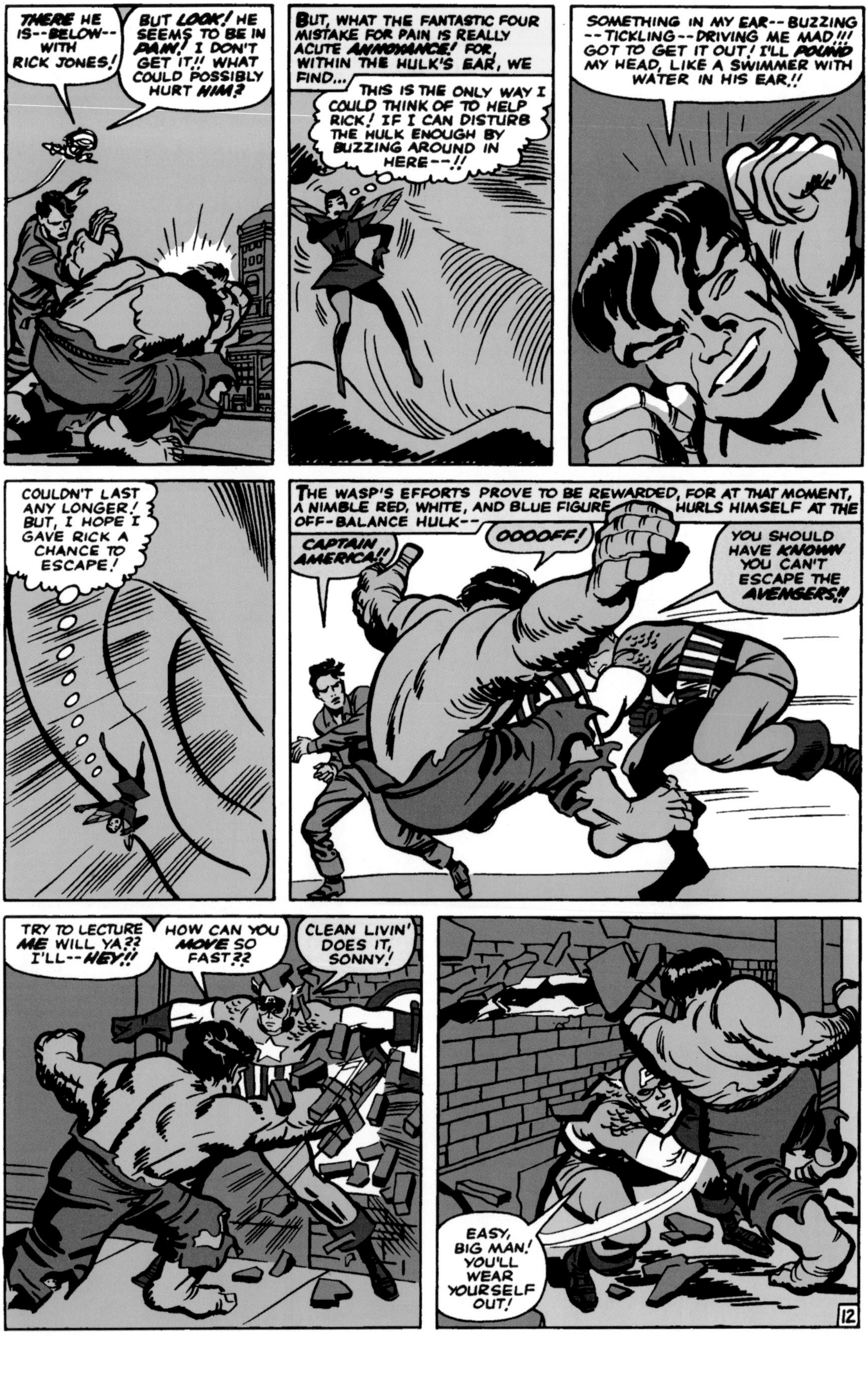
THERE HE IS--BELOW--WITH RICK JONES!
BUT LOOK! HE SEEMS TO BE IN PAIN! I DON'T GET IT!! WHAT COULD POSSIBLY HURT HIM?
BUT, WHAT THE FANTASTIC FOUR MISTAKE FOR PAIN IS REALLY ACUTE ANNOYANCE! FOR, WITHIN THE HULK'S EAR, WE FIND...
THIS IS THE ONLY WAY I COULD THINK OF TO HELP RICK! IF I CAN DISTURB THE HULK ENOUGH BY BUZZING AROUND IN HERE--!!
SOMETHING IN MY EAR--BUZZING--TICKLING--DRIVING ME MAD!!! GOT TO GET IT OUT! I'LL POUND MY HEAD, LIKE A SWIMMER WITH WATER IN HIS EAR!!
COULDN'T LAST ANY LONGER! BUT, I HOPE I GAVE RICK A CHANCE TO ESCAPE!
THE WASP'S EFFORTS PROVE TO BE REWARDED, FOR AT THAT MOMENT, A NIMBLE RED, WHITE, AND BLUE FIGURE HURLS HIMSELF AT THE OFF-BALANCE HULK--
CAPTAIN AMERICA!!
OOOOFF!
YOU SHOULD HAVE KNOWN YOU CAN'T ESCAPE THE AVENGERS!!
TRY TO LECTURE ME WILL YA?? I'LL--HEY!!
HOW CAN YOU MOVE SO FAST??
CLEAN LIVIN' DOES IT, SONNY!
EASY, BIG MAN! YOU'LL WEAR YOURSELF OUT!
12

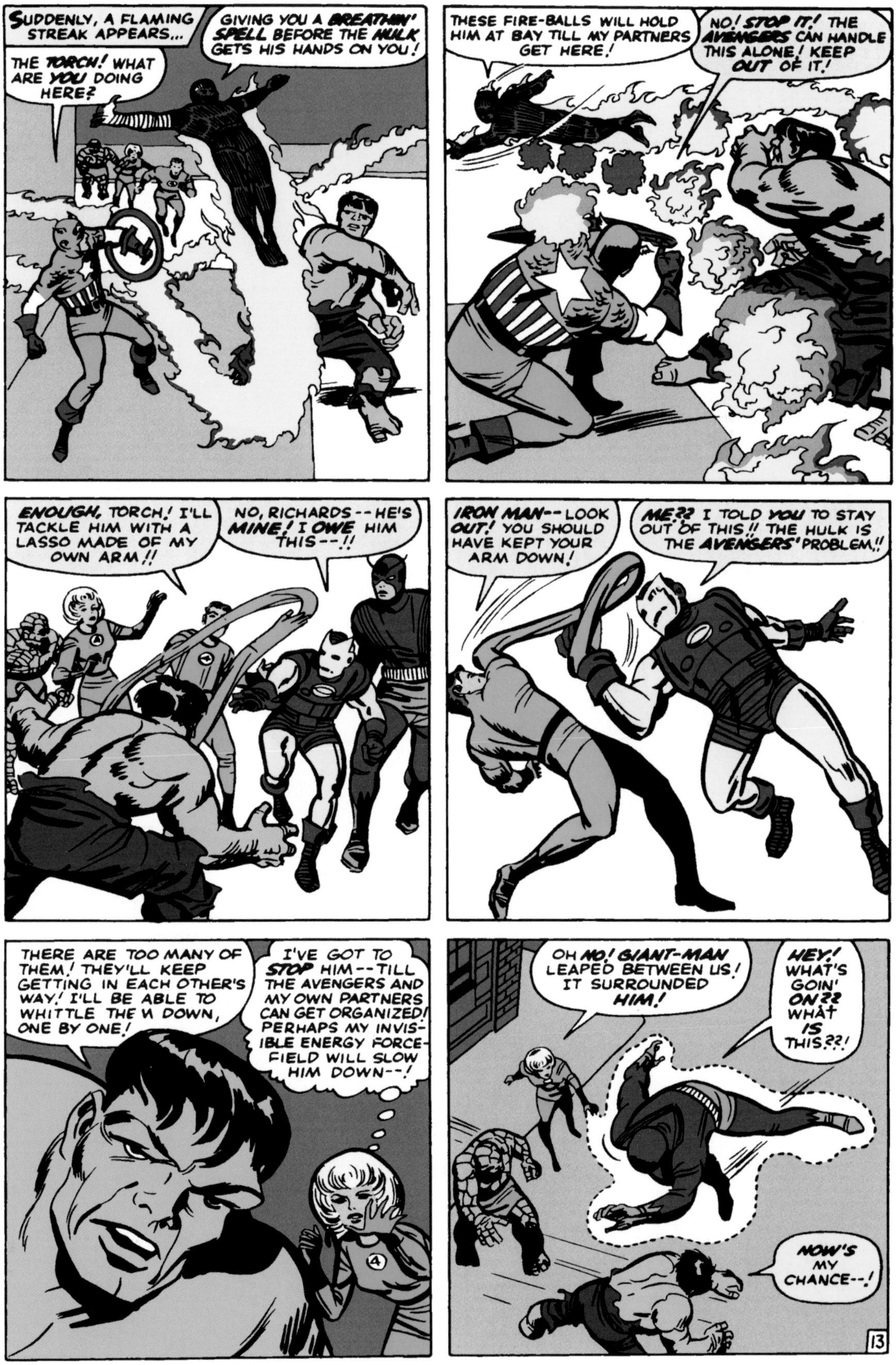
SUDDENLY, A FLAMING STREAK APPEARS...
GIVING YOU A BREATHIN' SPELL BEFORE THE HULK GETS HIS HANDS ON YOU!
THE TORCH! WHAT ARE YOU DOING HERE?
THESE FIRE-BALLS WILL HOLD HIM AT BAY TILL MY PARTNERS GET HERE!
NO! STOP IT! THE AVENGERS CAN HANDLE THIS ALONE! KEEP OUT OF IT!
ENOUGH, TORCH! I'LL TACKLE HIM WITH A LASSO MADE OF MY OWN ARM!!
NO, RICHARDS--HE'S MINE! I OWE HIM THIS--!!
IRON MAN--LOOK OUT! YOU SHOULD HAVE KEPT YOUR ARM DOWN!
ME?? I TOLD YOU TO STAY OUT OF THIS!! THE HULK IS THE AVENGERS' PROBLEM!!
THERE ARE TOO MANY OF THEM! THEY'LL KEEP GETTING IN EACH OTHER'S WAY! I'LL BE ABLE TO WHITTLE THEM DOWN, ONE BY ONE!
I'VE GOT TO STOP HIM--TILL THE AVENGERS AND MY OWN PARTNERS CAN GET ORGANIZED! PERHAPS MY INVISIBLE ENERGY FORCE-FIELD WILL SLOW HIM DOWN--!
OH NO! GIANT-MAN LEAPED BETWEEN US! IT SURROUNDED HIM!
HEY! WHAT'S GOIN' ON?? WHAT IS THIS??!
NOW'S MY CHANCE--!
13

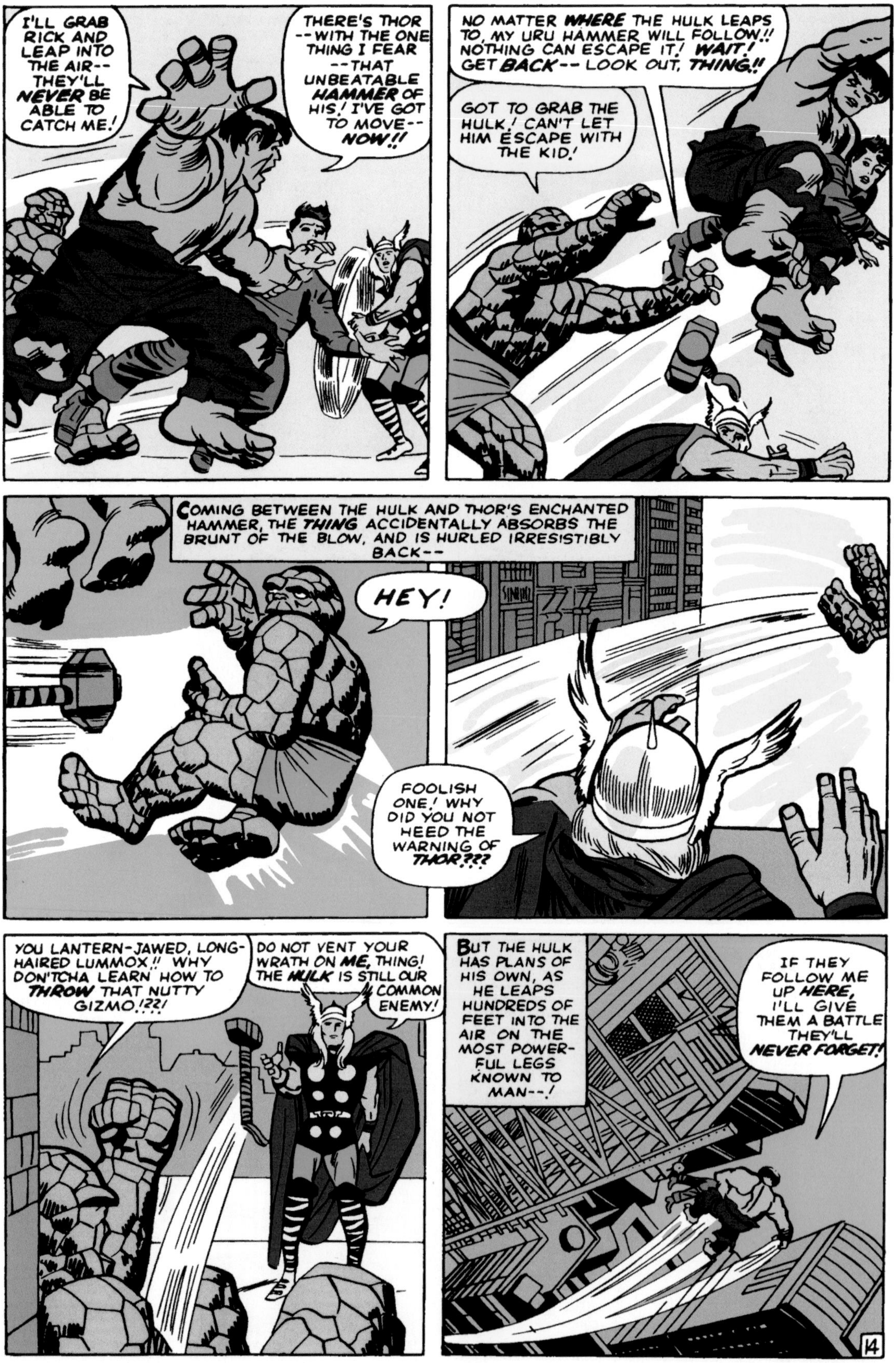
I'LL GRAB RICK AND LEAP INTO THE AIR-- THEY'LL NEVER BE ABLE TO CATCH ME!
THERE'S THOR --WITH THE ONE THING I FEAR --THAT UNBEATABLE HAMMER OF HIS! I'VE GOT TO MOVE-- NOW!!
NO MATTER WHERE THE HULK LEAPS TO, MY URU HAMMER WILL FOLLOW!! NOTHING CAN ESCAPE IT! WAIT! GET BACK-- LOOK OUT, THING!!
GOT TO GRAB THE HULK! CAN'T LET HIM ESCAPE WITH THE KID!
COMING BETWEEN THE HULK AND THOR'S ENCHANTED HAMMER, THE THING ACCIDENTALLY ABSORBS THE BRUNT OF THE BLOW, AND IS HURLED IRRESISTIBLY BACK--
HEY!
FOOLISH ONE! WHY DID YOU NOT HEED THE WARNING OF THOR???
YOU LANTERN-JAWED, LONG-HAIRED LUMMOX!! WHY DON'TCHA LEARN HOW TO THROW THAT NUTTY GIZMO!??!
DO NOT VENT YOUR WRATH ON ME, THING! THE HULK IS STILL OUR COMMON ENEMY!
BUT THE HULK HAS PLANS OF HIS OWN, AS HE LEAPS HUNDREDS OF FEET INTO THE AIR ON THE MOST POWER-FUL LEGS KNOWN TO MAN--!
IF THEY FOLLOW ME UP HERE, I'LL GIVE THEM A BATTLE THEY'LL NEVER FORGET!
14

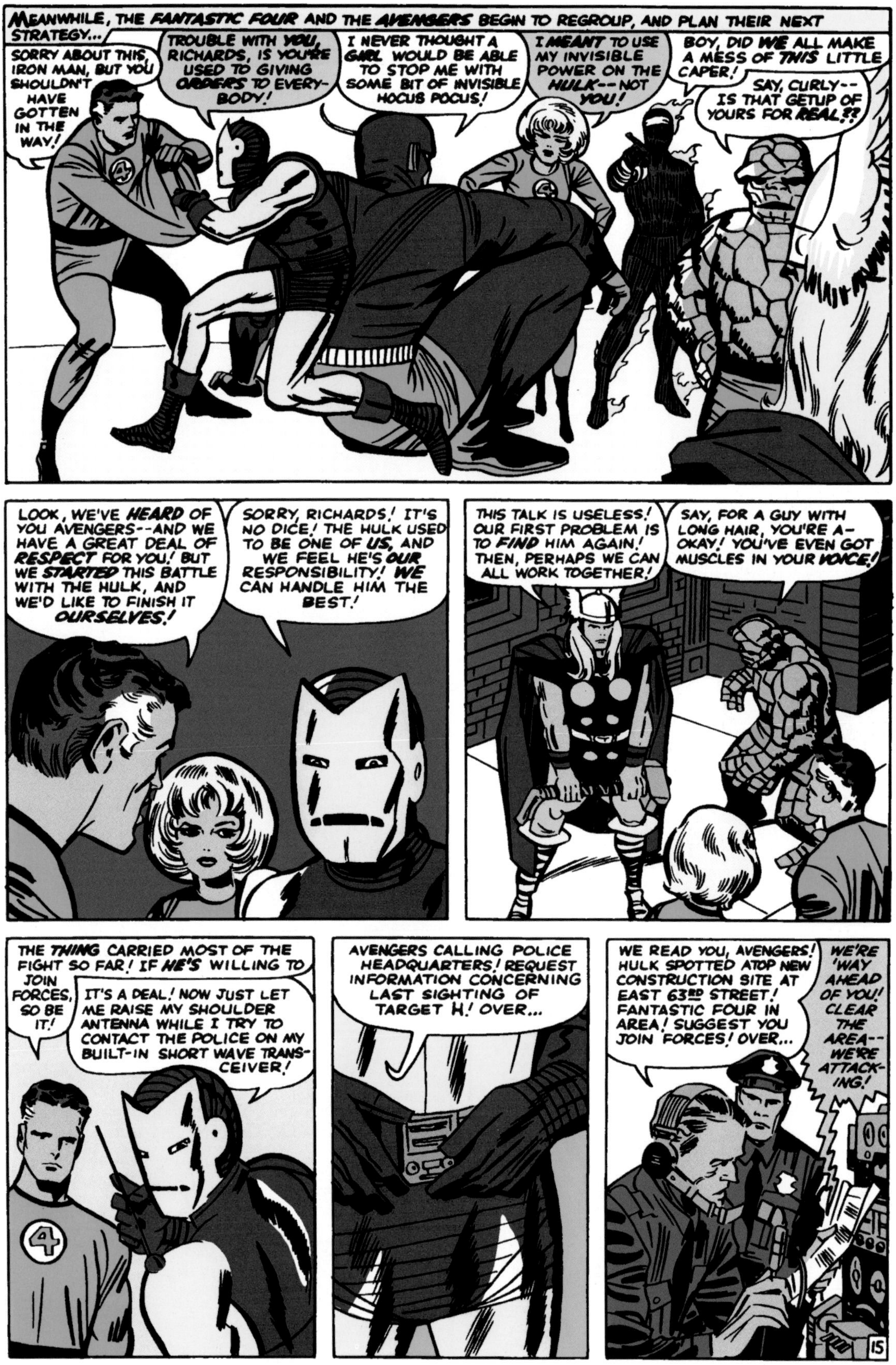

MEANWHILE, THE FANTASTIC FOUR AND THE AVENGERS BEGIN TO REGROUP, AND PLAN THEIR NEXT STRATEGY...
SORRY ABOUT THIS, IRON MAN, BUT YOU SHOULDN'T HAVE GOTTEN IN THE WAY!
TROUBLE WITH YOU, RICHARDS, IS YOU'RE USED TO GIVING ORDERS TO EVERY-BODY!
I NEVER THOUGHT A GIRL WOULD BE ABLE TO STOP ME WITH SOME BIT OF INVISIBLE HOCUS POCUS!
I MEANT TO USE MY INVISIBLE POWER ON THE HULK--NOT YOU!
BOY, DID WE ALL MAKE A MESS OF THIS LITTLE CAPER!
SAY, CURLY--IS THAT GETUP OF YOURS FOR REAL??
LOOK, WE'VE HEARD OF YOU AVENGERS--AND WE HAVE A GREAT DEAL OF RESPECT FOR YOU! BUT WE STARTED THIS BATTLE WITH THE HULK, AND WE'D LIKE TO FINISH IT OURSELVES!
SORRY, RICHARDS! IT'S NO DICE! THE HULK USED TO BE ONE OF US, AND WE FEEL HE'S OUR RESPONSIBILITY! WE CAN HANDLE HIM THE BEST!
THIS TALK IS USELESS! OUR FIRST PROBLEM IS TO FIND HIM AGAIN! THEN, PERHAPS WE CAN ALL WORK TOGETHER!
SAY, FOR A GUY WITH LONG HAIR, YOU'RE A-OKAY! YOU'VE EVEN GOT MUSCLES IN YOUR VOICE!
THE THING CARRIED MOST OF THE FIGHT SO FAR! IF HE'S WILLING TO JOIN FORCES, SO BE IT!
IT'S A DEAL! NOW JUST LET ME RAISE MY SHOULDER ANTENNA WHILE I TRY TO CONTACT THE POLICE ON MY BUILT-IN SHORT WAVE TRANS-CEIVER!
AVENGERS CALLING POLICE HEADQUARTERS! REQUEST INFORMATION CONCERNING LAST SIGHTING OF TARGET H! OVER...
WE READ YOU, AVENGERS! HULK SPOTTED ATOP NEW CONSTRUCTION SITE AT EAST 63RD STREET! FANTASTIC FOUR IN AREA! SUGGEST YOU JOIN FORCES! OVER...
WE'RE 'WAY AHEAD OF YOU! CLEAR THE AREA--WE'RE ATTACK-ING!
15

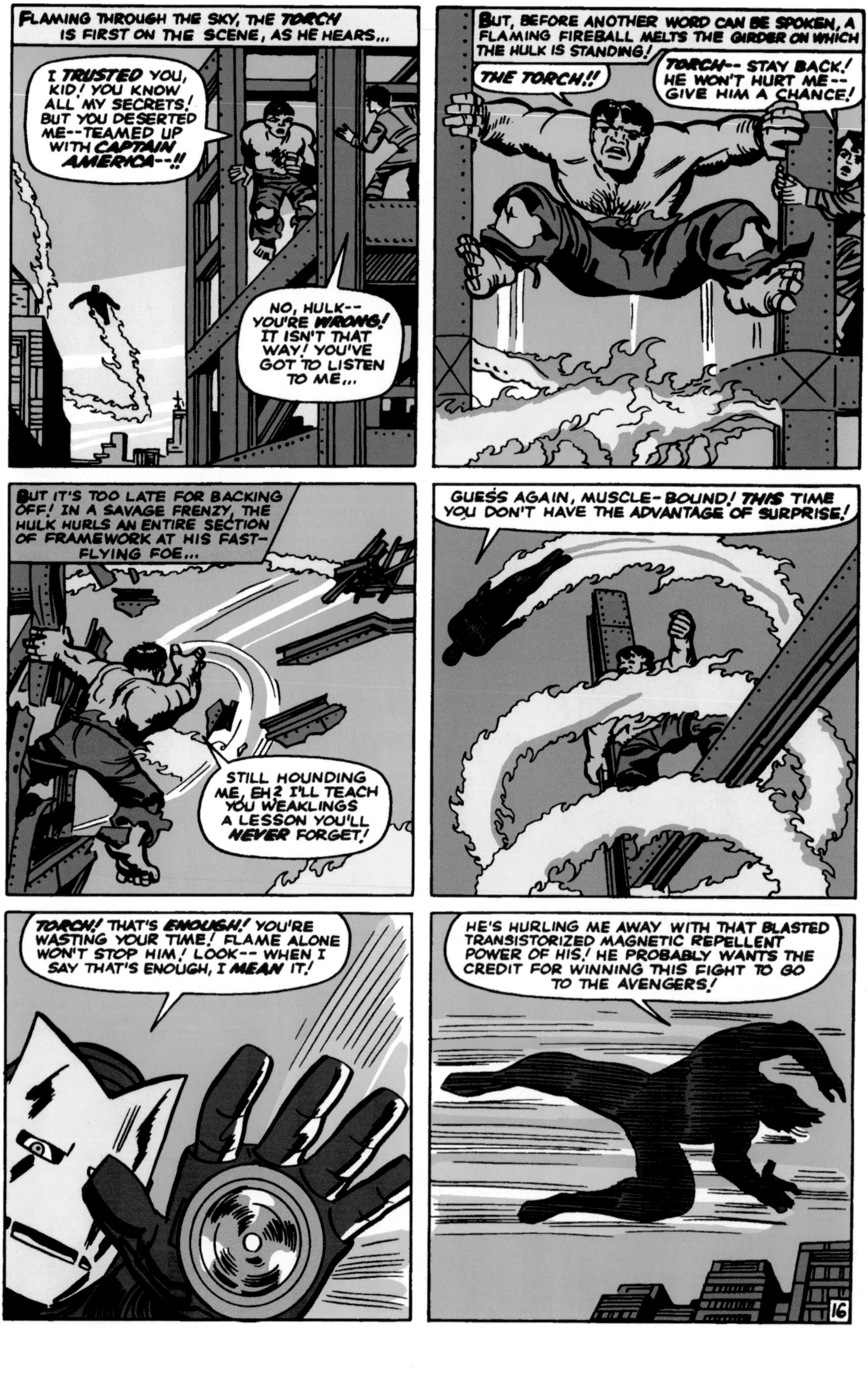
FLAMING THROUGH THE SKY, THE TORCH IS FIRST ON THE SCENE, AS HE HEARS...
I TRUSTED YOU, KID! YOU KNOW ALL MY SECRETS! BUT YOU DESERTED ME--TEAMED UP WITH CAPTAIN AMERICA--!!
NO, HULK-- YOU'RE WRONG! IT ISN'T THAT WAY! YOU'VE GOT TO LISTEN TO ME...
BUT, BEFORE ANOTHER WORD CAN BE SPOKEN, A FLAMING FIREBALL MELTS THE GIRDER ON WHICH THE HULK IS STANDING!
THE TORCH!!
TORCH-- STAY BACK! HE WON'T HURT ME-- GIVE HIM A CHANCE!
BUT IT'S TOO LATE FOR BACKING OFF! IN A SAVAGE FRENZY, THE HULK HURLS AN ENTIRE SECTION OF FRAMEWORK AT HIS FAST-FLYING FOE...
STILL HOUNDING ME, EH? I'LL TEACH YOU WEAKLINGS A LESSON YOU'LL NEVER FORGET!
GUESS AGAIN, MUSCLE-BOUND! THIS TIME YOU DON'T HAVE THE ADVANTAGE OF SURPRISE!
TORCH! THAT'S ENOUGH! YOU'RE WASTING YOUR TIME! FLAME ALONE WON'T STOP HIM! LOOK-- WHEN I SAY THAT'S ENOUGH, I MEAN IT!
HE'S HURLING ME AWAY WITH THAT BLASTED TRANSISTORIZED MAGNETIC REPELLENT POWER OF HIS! HE PROBABLY WANTS THE CREDIT FOR WINNING THIS FIGHT TO GO TO THE AVENGERS!
16

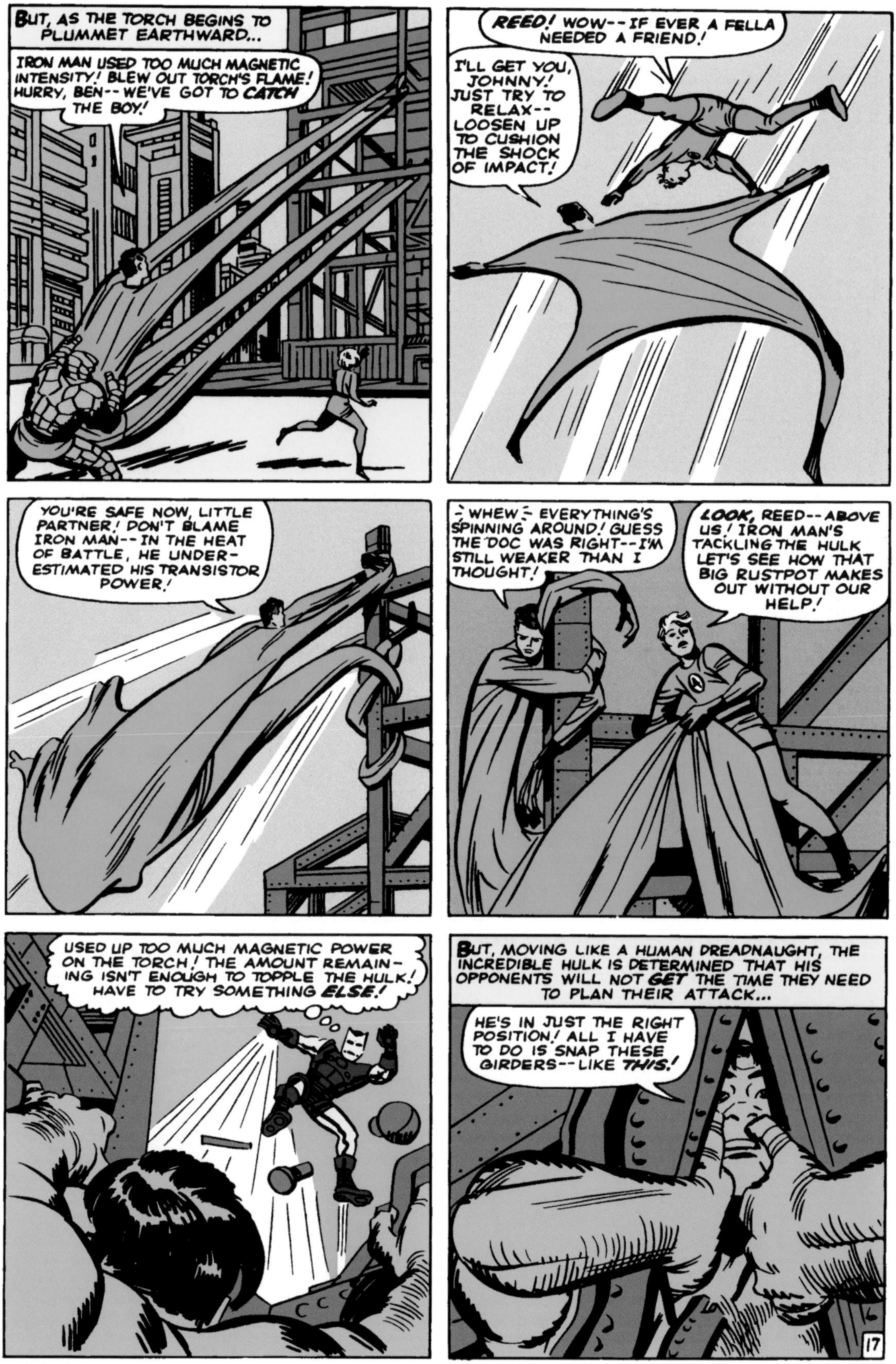
BUT, AS THE TORCH BEGINS TO PLUMMET EARTHWARD...
IRON MAN USED TOO MUCH MAGNETIC INTENSITY! BLEW OUT TORCH'S FLAME! HURRY, BEN-- WE'VE GOT TO CATCH THE BOY!
REED! WOW-- IF EVER A FELLA NEEDED A FRIEND!
I'LL GET YOU, JOHNNY! JUST TRY TO RELAX-- LOOSEN UP TO CUSHION THE SHOCK OF IMPACT!
YOU'RE SAFE NOW, LITTLE PARTNER! DON'T BLAME IRON MAN-- IN THE HEAT OF BATTLE, HE UNDER-ESTIMATED HIS TRANSISTOR POWER!
- WHEW - EVERYTHING'S SPINNING AROUND! GUESS THE DOC WAS RIGHT-- I'M STILL WEAKER THAN I THOUGHT!
LOOK, REED-- ABOVE US! IRON MAN'S TACKLING THE HULK LET'S SEE HOW THAT BIG RUSTPOT MAKES OUT WITHOUT OUR HELP!
USED UP TOO MUCH MAGNETIC POWER ON THE TORCH! THE AMOUNT REMAIN-ING ISN'T ENOUGH TO TOPPLE THE HULK! HAVE TO TRY SOMETHING ELSE!
BUT, MOVING LIKE A HUMAN DREADNAUGHT, THE INCREDIBLE HULK IS DETERMINED THAT HIS OPPONENTS WILL NOT GET THE TIME THEY NEED TO PLAN THEIR ATTACK...
HE'S IN JUST THE RIGHT POSITION! ALL I HAVE TO DO IS SNAP THESE GIRDERS-- LIKE THIS!
17

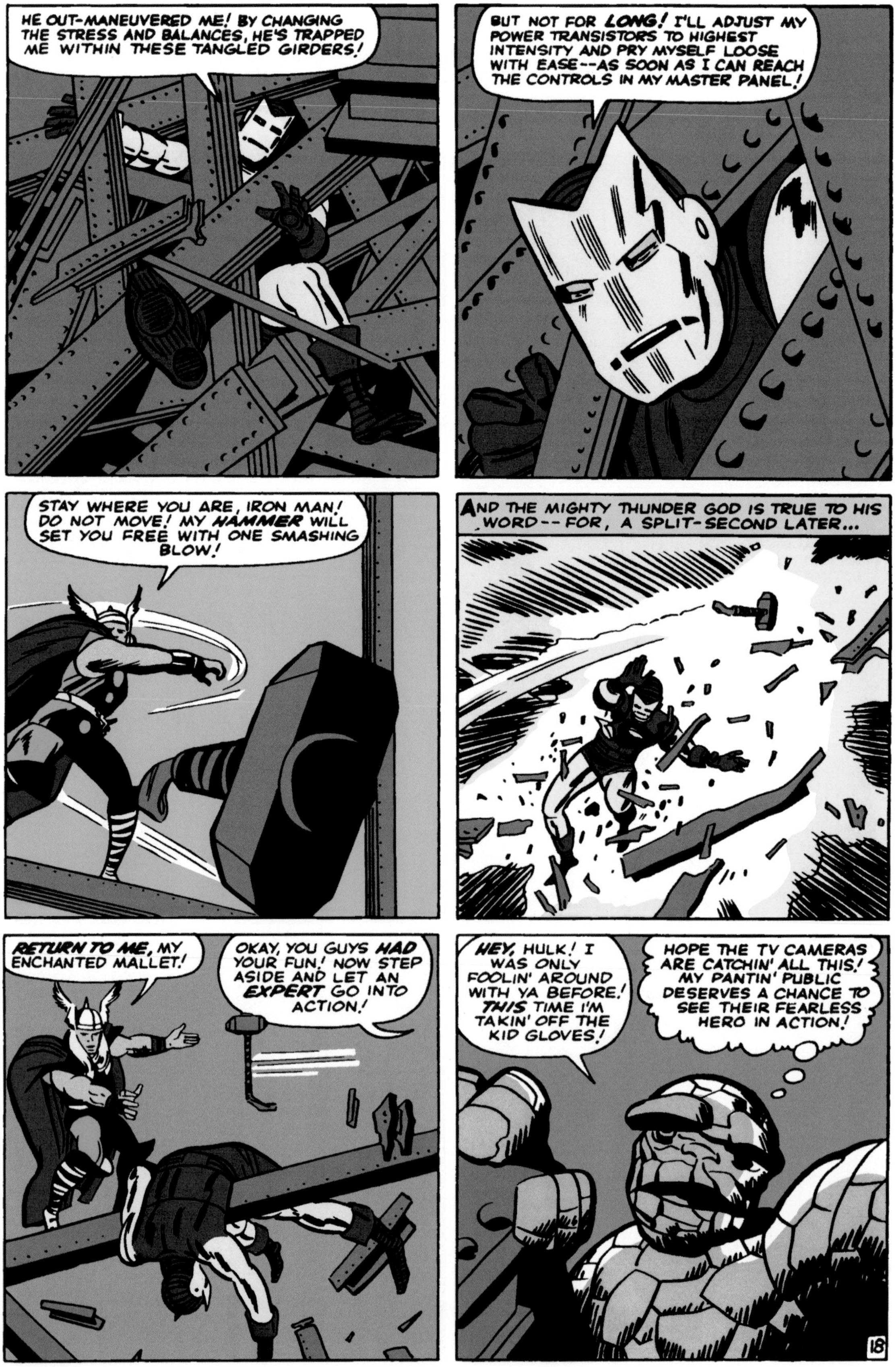
HE OUT-MANEUVERED ME! BY CHANGING THE STRESS AND BALANCES, HE'S TRAPPED ME WITHIN THESE TANGLED GIRDERS!
BUT NOT FOR LONG! I'LL ADJUST MY POWER TRANSISTORS TO HIGHEST INTENSITY AND PRY MYSELF LOOSE WITH EASE--AS SOON AS I CAN REACH THE CONTROLS IN MY MASTER PANEL!
STAY WHERE YOU ARE, IRON MAN! DO NOT MOVE! MY HAMMER WILL SET YOU FREE WITH ONE SMASHING BLOW!
AND THE MIGHTY THUNDER GOD IS TRUE TO HIS WORD--FOR, A SPLIT-SECOND LATER...
RETURN TO ME, MY ENCHANTED MALLET!
OKAY, YOU GUYS HAD YOUR FUN! NOW STEP ASIDE AND LET AN EXPERT GO INTO ACTION!
HEY, HULK! I WAS ONLY FOOLIN' AROUND WITH YA BEFORE! THIS TIME I'M TAKIN' OFF THE KID GLOVES!
HOPE THE TV CAMERAS ARE CATCHIN' ALL THIS! MY PANTIN' PUBLIC DESERVES A CHANCE TO SEE THEIR FEARLESS HERO IN ACTION!
18

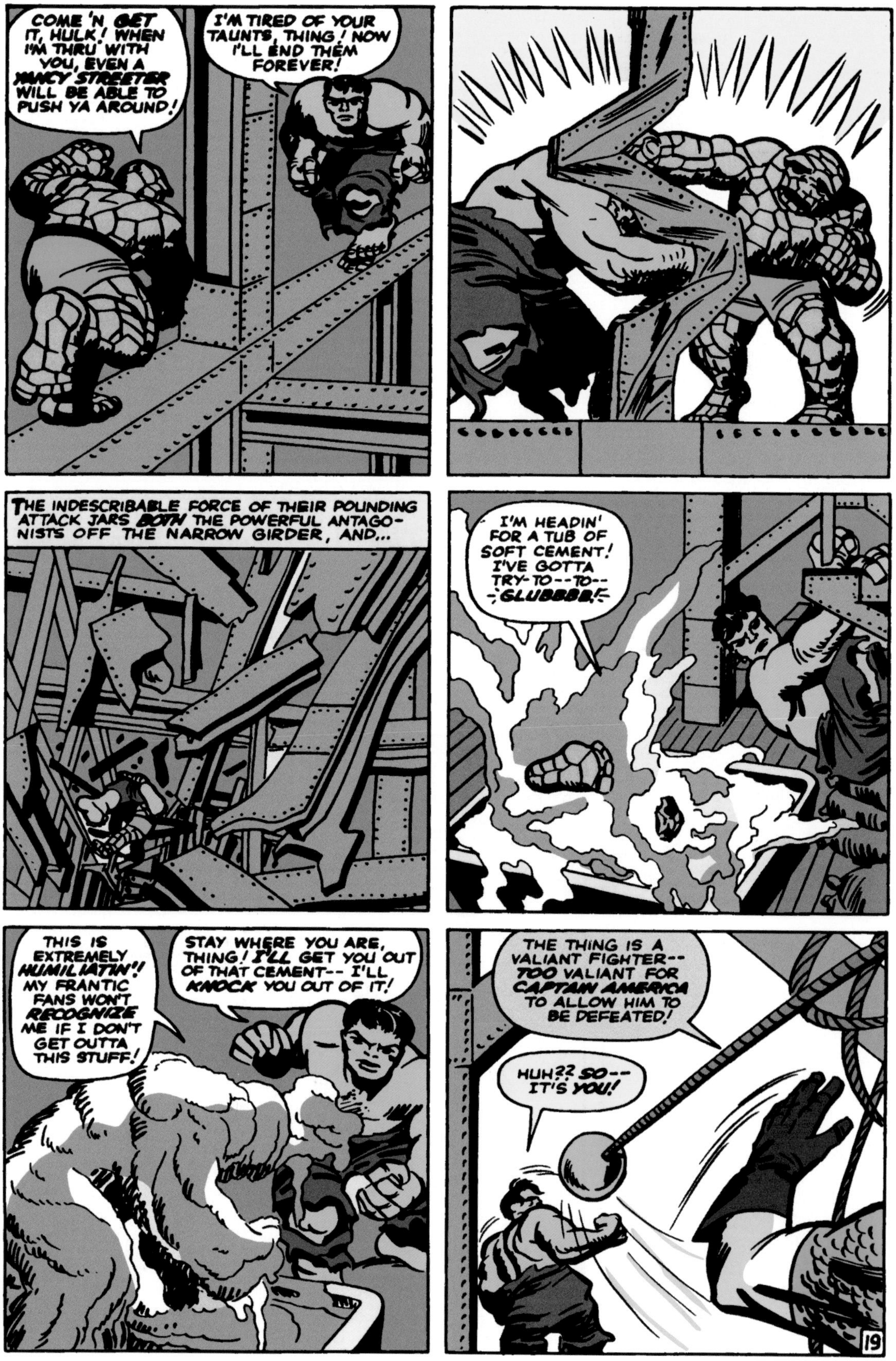

COME 'N GET IT, HULK! WHEN I'M THRU WITH YOU, EVEN A YANCY STREETER WILL BE ABLE TO PUSH YA AROUND!
I'M TIRED OF YOUR TAUNTS, THING! NOW I'LL END THEM FOREVER!
THE INDESCRIBABLE FORCE OF THEIR POUNDING ATTACK JARS BOTH THE POWERFUL ANTAGONISTS OFF THE NARROW GIRDER, AND...
I'M HEADIN' FOR A TUB OF SOFT CEMENT! I'VE GOTTA TRY-TO--TO-- GLUBBBB!
THIS IS EXTREMELY HUMILIATIN'!! MY FRANTIC FANS WON'T RECOGNIZE ME IF I DON'T GET OUTTA THIS STUFF!
STAY WHERE YOU ARE, THING! I'LL GET YOU OUT OF THAT CEMENT-- I'LL KNOCK YOU OUT OF IT!
THE THING IS A VALIANT FIGHTER-- TOO VALIANT FOR CAPTAIN AMERICA TO ALLOW HIM TO BE DEFEATED!
HUH?? SO-- IT'S YOU!
19

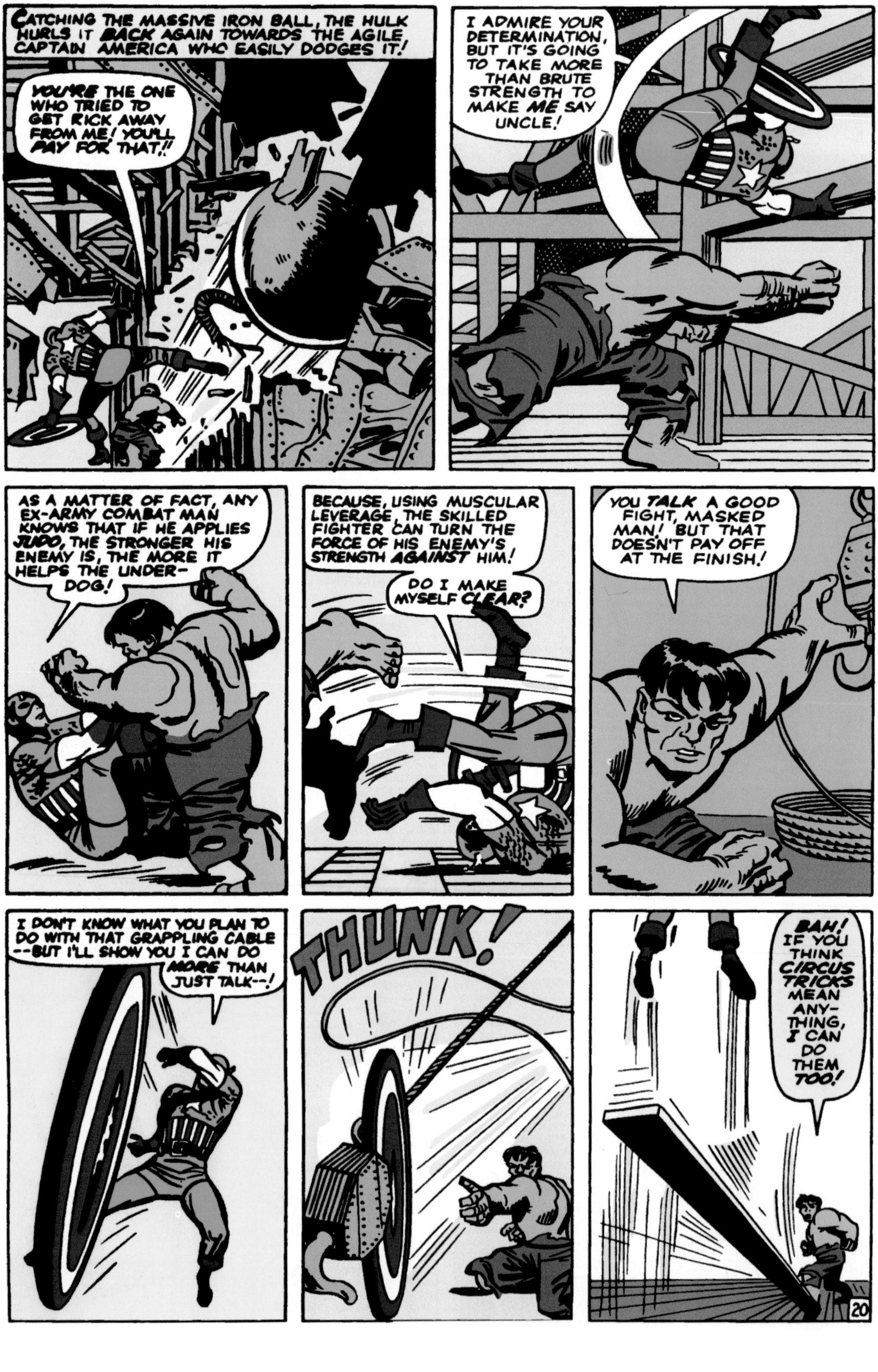
CATCHING THE MASSIVE IRON BALL, THE HULK HURLS IT BACK AGAIN TOWARDS THE AGILE CAPTAIN AMERICA WHO EASILY DODGES IT!
YOU'RE THE ONE WHO TRIED TO GET RICK AWAY FROM ME! YOU'LL PAY FOR THAT!!
I ADMIRE YOUR DETERMINATION, BUT IT'S GOING TO TAKE MORE THAN BRUTE STRENGTH TO MAKE ME SAY UNCLE!
AS A MATTER OF FACT, ANY EX-ARMY COMBAT MAN KNOWS THAT IF HE APPLIES JUDO, THE STRONGER HIS ENEMY IS, THE MORE IT HELPS THE UNDER-DOG!
BECAUSE, USING MUSCULAR LEVERAGE, THE SKILLED FIGHTER CAN TURN THE FORCE OF HIS ENEMY'S STRENGTH AGAINST HIM!
DO I MAKE MYSELF CLEAR?
YOU TALK A GOOD FIGHT, MASKED MAN! BUT THAT DOESN'T PAY OFF AT THE FINISH!
I DON'T KNOW WHAT YOU PLAN TO DO WITH THAT GRAPPLING CABLE --BUT I'LL SHOW YOU I CAN DO MORE THAN JUST TALK--!
THUNK!
BAH! IF YOU THINK CIRCUS TRICKS MEAN ANY-THING, I CAN DO THEM TOO!
20

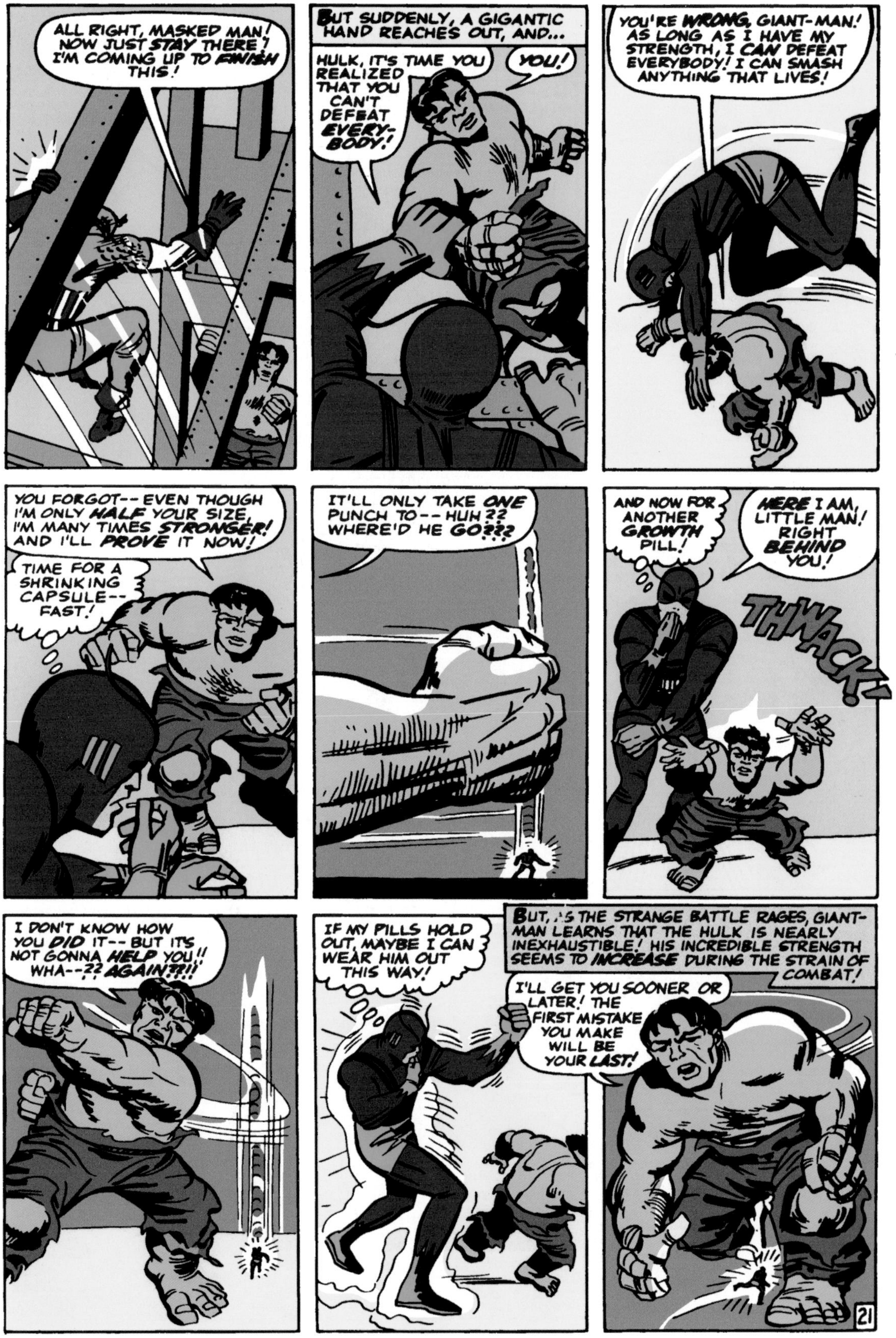
ALL RIGHT, MASKED MAN! NOW JUST STAY THERE! I'M COMING UP TO FINISH THIS!
BUT SUDDENLY, A GIGANTIC HAND REACHES OUT, AND...
HULK, IT'S TIME YOU REALIZED THAT YOU CAN'T DEFEAT EVERY-BODY!
YOU!
YOU'RE WRONG, GIANT-MAN! AS LONG AS I HAVE MY STRENGTH, I CAN DEFEAT EVERYBODY! I CAN SMASH ANYTHING THAT LIVES!
YOU FORGOT-- EVEN THOUGH I'M ONLY HALF YOUR SIZE, I'M MANY TIMES STRONGER! AND I'LL PROVE IT NOW!
TIME FOR A SHRINKING CAPSULE-- FAST!
IT'LL ONLY TAKE ONE PUNCH TO-- HUH?? WHERE'D HE GO???
AND NOW FOR ANOTHER GROWTH PILL!
HERE I AM, LITTLE MAN! RIGHT BEHIND YOU!
THWACK!
I DON'T KNOW HOW YOU DID IT-- BUT IT'S NOT GONNA HELP YOU!! WHA--?? AGAIN??!!
IF MY PILLS HOLD OUT, MAYBE I CAN WEAR HIM OUT THIS WAY!
BUT, AS THE STRANGE BATTLE RAGES, GIANT-MAN LEARNS THAT THE HULK IS NEARLY INEXHAUSTIBLE! HIS INCREDIBLE STRENGTH SEEMS TO INCREASE DURING THE STRAIN OF COMBAT!
I'LL GET YOU SOONER OR LATER! THE FIRST MISTAKE YOU MAKE WILL BE YOUR LAST!
21

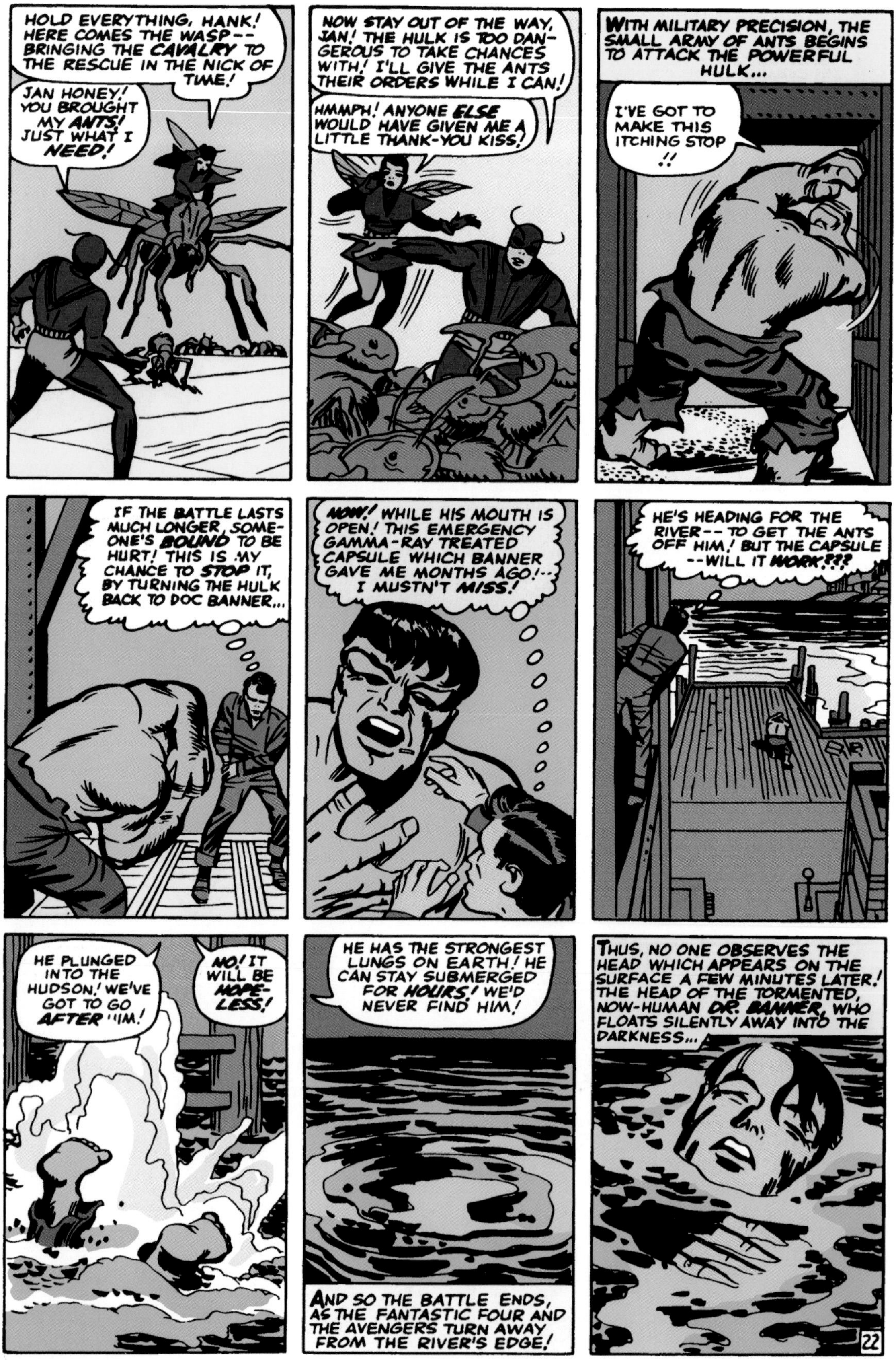
HOLD EVERYTHING, HANK! HERE COMES THE WASP-- BRINGING THE CAVALRY TO THE RESCUE IN THE NICK OF TIME!
JAN HONEY! YOU BROUGHT MY ANTS! JUST WHAT I NEED!
NOW STAY OUT OF THE WAY, JAN! THE HULK IS TOO DANGEROUS TO TAKE CHANCES WITH! I'LL GIVE THE ANTS THEIR ORDERS WHILE I CAN!
HMMPH! ANYONE ELSE WOULD HAVE GIVEN ME A LITTLE THANK-YOU KISS!
WITH MILITARY PRECISION, THE SMALL ARMY OF ANTS BEGINS TO ATTACK THE POWERFUL HULK...
I'VE GOT TO MAKE THIS ITCHING STOP!!
IF THE BATTLE LASTS MUCH LONGER, SOMEONE'S BOUND TO BE HURT! THIS IS MY CHANCE TO STOP IT, BY TURNING THE HULK BACK TO DOC BANNER...
NOW! WHILE HIS MOUTH IS OPEN! THIS EMERGENCY GAMMA-RAY TREATED CAPSULE WHICH BANNER GAVE ME MONTHS AGO!-- I MUSTN'T MISS!
HE'S HEADING FOR THE RIVER-- TO GET THE ANTS OFF HIM! BUT THE CAPSULE --WILL IT WORK???
HE PLUNGED INTO THE HUDSON! WE'VE GOT TO GO AFTER HIM!
NO! IT WILL BE HOPELESS!
HE HAS THE STRONGEST LUNGS ON EARTH! HE CAN STAY SUBMERGED FOR HOURS! WE'D NEVER FIND HIM!
AND SO THE BATTLE ENDS, AS THE FANTASTIC FOUR AND THE AVENGERS TURN AWAY FROM THE RIVER'S EDGE!
THUS, NO ONE OBSERVES THE HEAD WHICH APPEARS ON THE SURFACE A FEW MINUTES LATER! THE HEAD OF THE TORMENTED, NOW-HUMAN DR. BANNER, WHO FLOATS SILENTLY AWAY INTO THE DARKNESS...
22

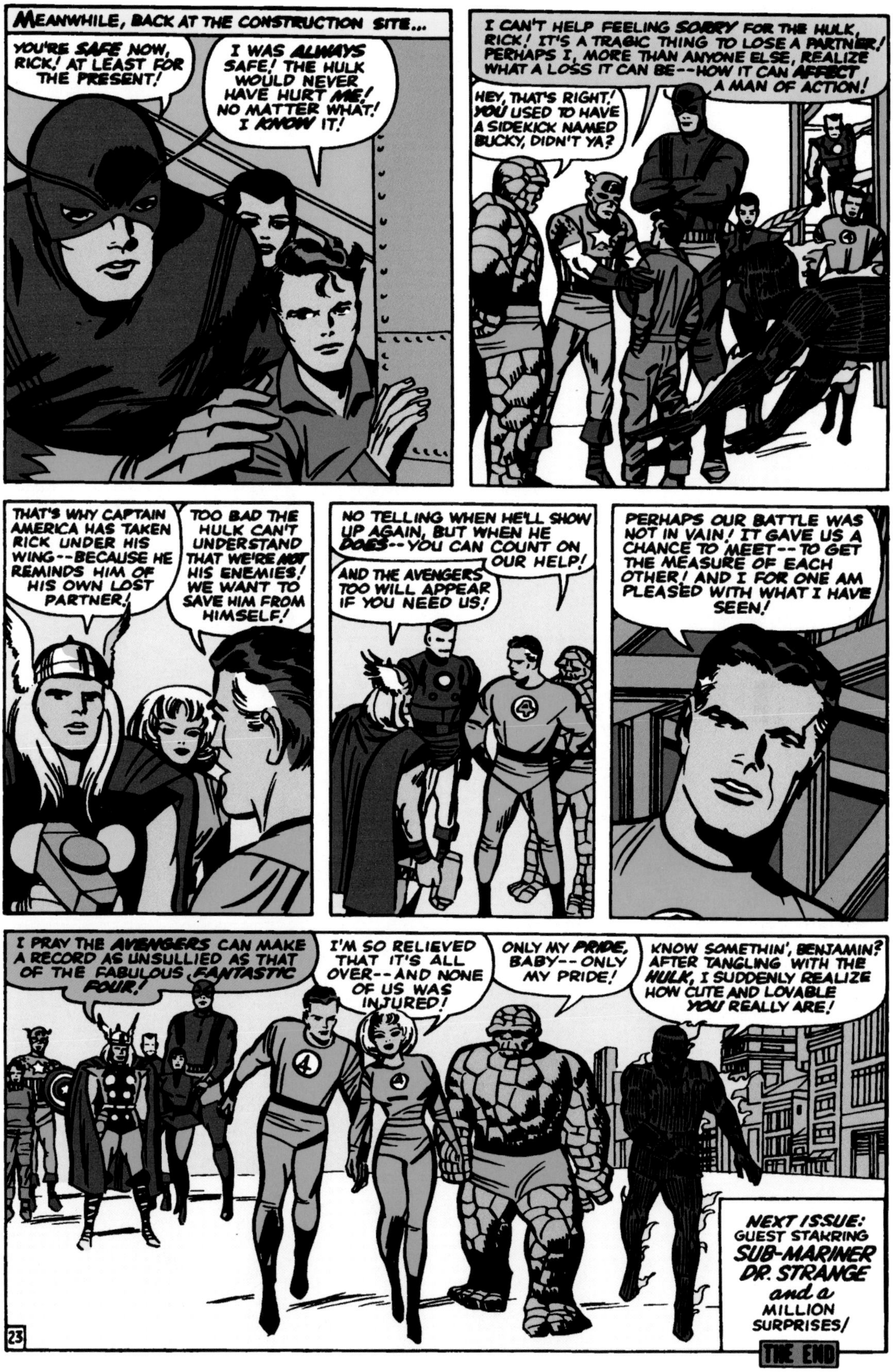
MEANWHILE, BACK AT THE CONSTRUCTION SITE...
YOU'RE SAFE NOW, RICK! AT LEAST FOR THE PRESENT!
I WAS ALWAYS SAFE! THE HULK WOULD NEVER HAVE HURT ME! NO MATTER WHAT! I KNOW IT!
I CAN'T HELP FEELING SORRY FOR THE HULK, RICK! IT'S A TRAGIC THING TO LOSE A PARTNER! PERHAPS I, MORE THAN ANYONE ELSE, REALIZE WHAT A LOSS IT CAN BE--HOW IT CAN AFFECT A MAN OF ACTION!
HEY, THAT'S RIGHT! YOU USED TO HAVE A SIDEKICK NAMED BUCKY, DIDN'T YA?
THAT'S WHY CAPTAIN AMERICA HAS TAKEN RICK UNDER HIS WING--BECAUSE HE REMINDS HIM OF HIS OWN LOST PARTNER!
TOO BAD THE HULK CAN'T UNDERSTAND THAT WE'RE NOT HIS ENEMIES! WE WANT TO SAVE HIM FROM HIMSELF!
NO TELLING WHEN HE'LL SHOW UP AGAIN, BUT WHEN HE DOES--YOU CAN COUNT ON OUR HELP!
AND THE AVENGERS TOO WILL APPEAR IF YOU NEED US!
PERHAPS OUR BATTLE WAS NOT IN VAIN! IT GAVE US A CHANCE TO MEET--TO GET THE MEASURE OF EACH OTHER! AND I FOR ONE AM PLEASED WITH WHAT I HAVE SEEN!
I PRAY THE AVENGERS CAN MAKE A RECORD AS UNSULLIED AS THAT OF THE FABULOUS FANTASTIC FOUR!
I'M SO RELIEVED THAT IT'S ALL OVER--AND NONE OF US WAS INJURED!
ONLY MY PRIDE, BABY--ONLY MY PRIDE!
KNOW SOMETHIN', BENJAMIN? AFTER TANGLING WITH THE HULK, I SUDDENLY REALIZE HOW CUTE AND LOVABLE YOU REALLY ARE!
NEXT ISSUE: GUEST STARRING SUB-MARINER DR. STRANGE and a MILLION SURPRISES!
23
THE END

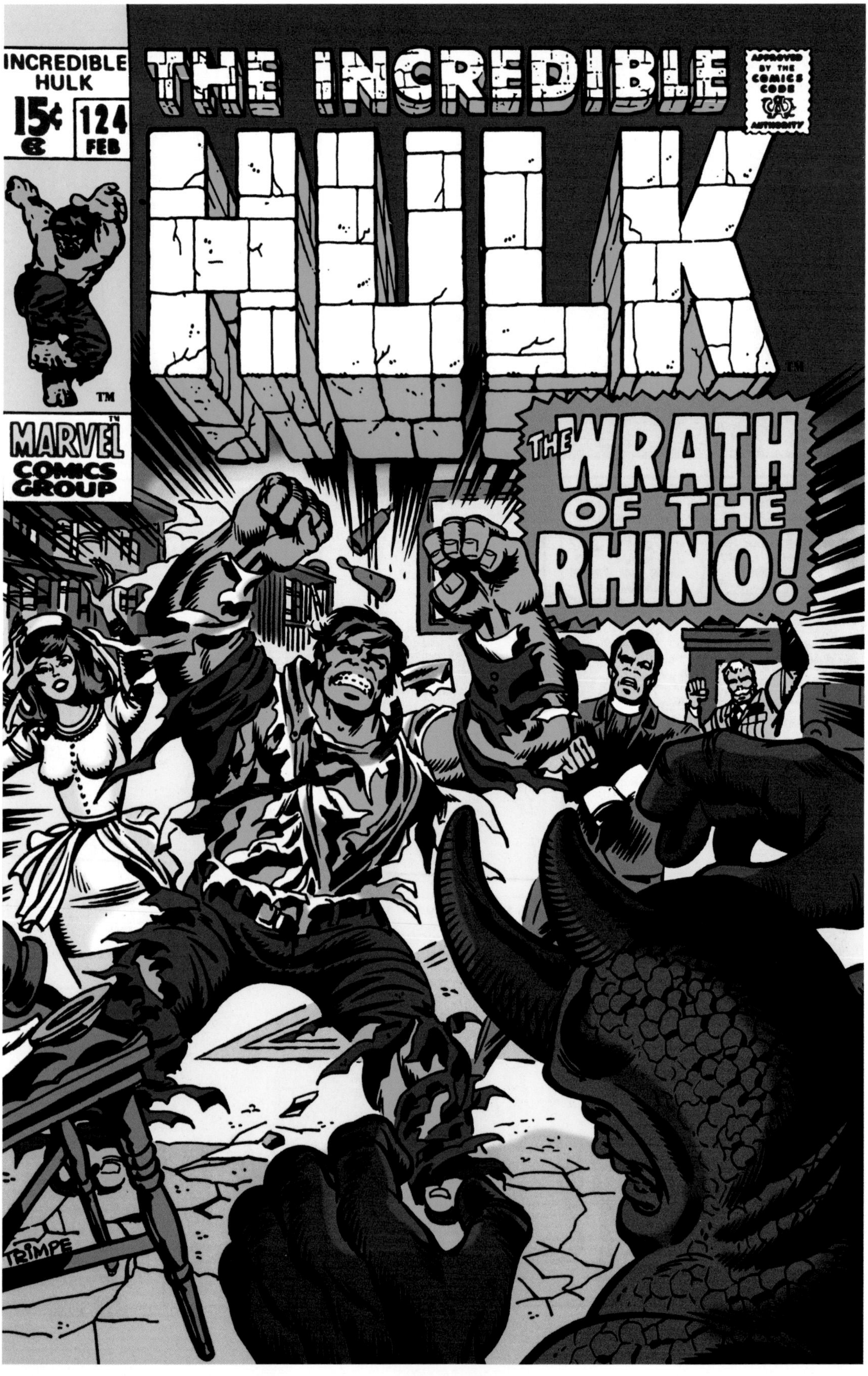
INCREDIBLE HULK
15¢
124
FEB
MARVEL COMICS GROUP
THE INCREDIBLE HULK
APPROVED BY THE COMICS CODE AUTHORITY
THE WRATH OF THE RHINO!
TRIMPE

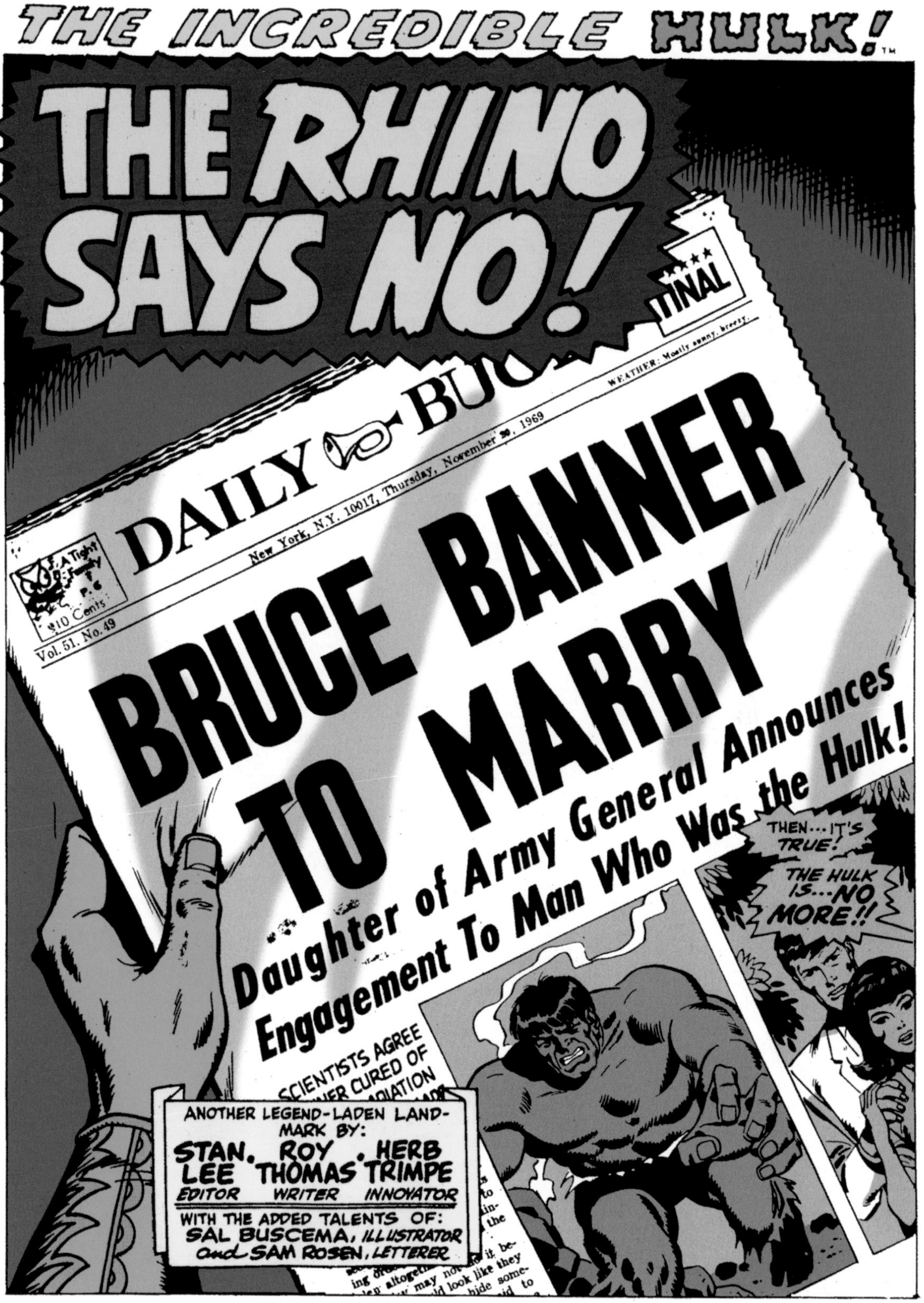

THE INCREDIBLE HULK!
THE RHINO SAYS NO!
DAILY BUGLE
New York, N.Y. 10017, Thursday, November 20, 1969
WEATHER: Mostly sunny, breezy.
10 Cents
Vol. 51. No. 49
BRUCE BANNER TO MARRY
Daughter of Army General Announces Engagement To Man Who Was the Hulk!
SCIENTISTS AGREE
THEN... IT'S TRUE!
THE HULK IS... NO MORE!!
ANOTHER LEGEND-LADEN LANDMARK BY:
STAN LEE EDITOR
ROY THOMAS WRITER
HERB TRIMPE INNOVATOR
WITH THE ADDED TALENTS OF:
SAL BUSCEMA, ILLUSTRATOR
and SAM ROSEN, LETTERER

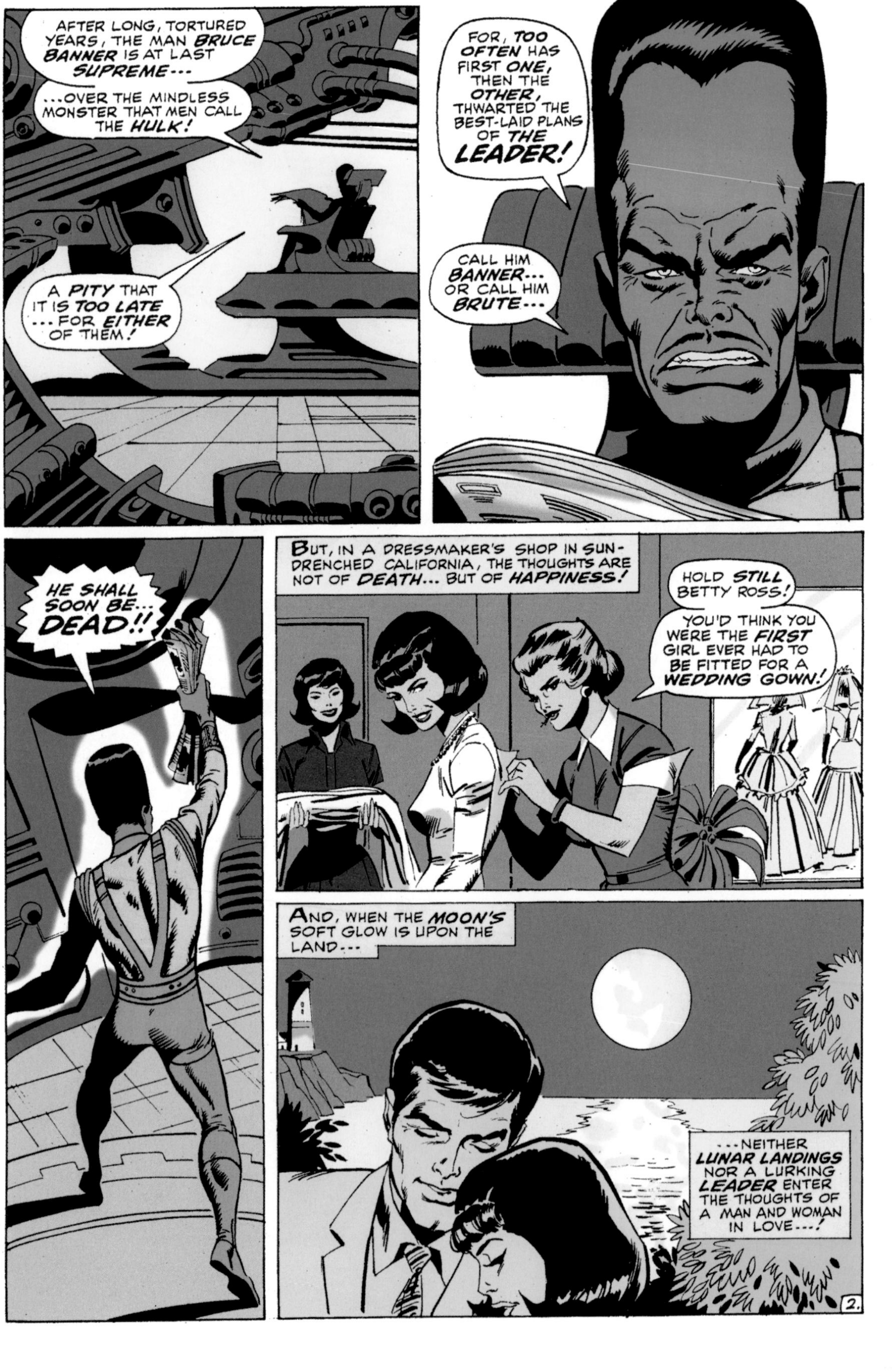
AFTER LONG, TORTURED YEARS, THE MAN BRUCE BANNER IS AT LAST SUPREME---
...OVER THE MINDLESS MONSTER THAT MEN CALL THE HULK!
A PITY THAT IT IS TOO LATE ---FOR EITHER OF THEM!
FOR, TOO OFTEN HAS FIRST ONE, THEN THE OTHER, THWARTED THE BEST-LAID PLANS OF THE LEADER!
CALL HIM BANNER... OR CALL HIM BRUTE---
HE SHALL SOON BE... DEAD!!
BUT, IN A DRESSMAKER'S SHOP IN SUN-DRENCHED CALIFORNIA, THE THOUGHTS ARE NOT OF DEATH... BUT OF HAPPINESS!
HOLD STILL BETTY ROSS!
YOU'D THINK YOU WERE THE FIRST GIRL EVER HAD TO BE FITTED FOR A WEDDING GOWN!
AND, WHEN THE MOON'S SOFT GLOW IS UPON THE LAND---
---NEITHER LUNAR LANDINGS NOR A LURKING LEADER ENTER THE THOUGHTS OF A MAN AND WOMAN IN LOVE---!
2.

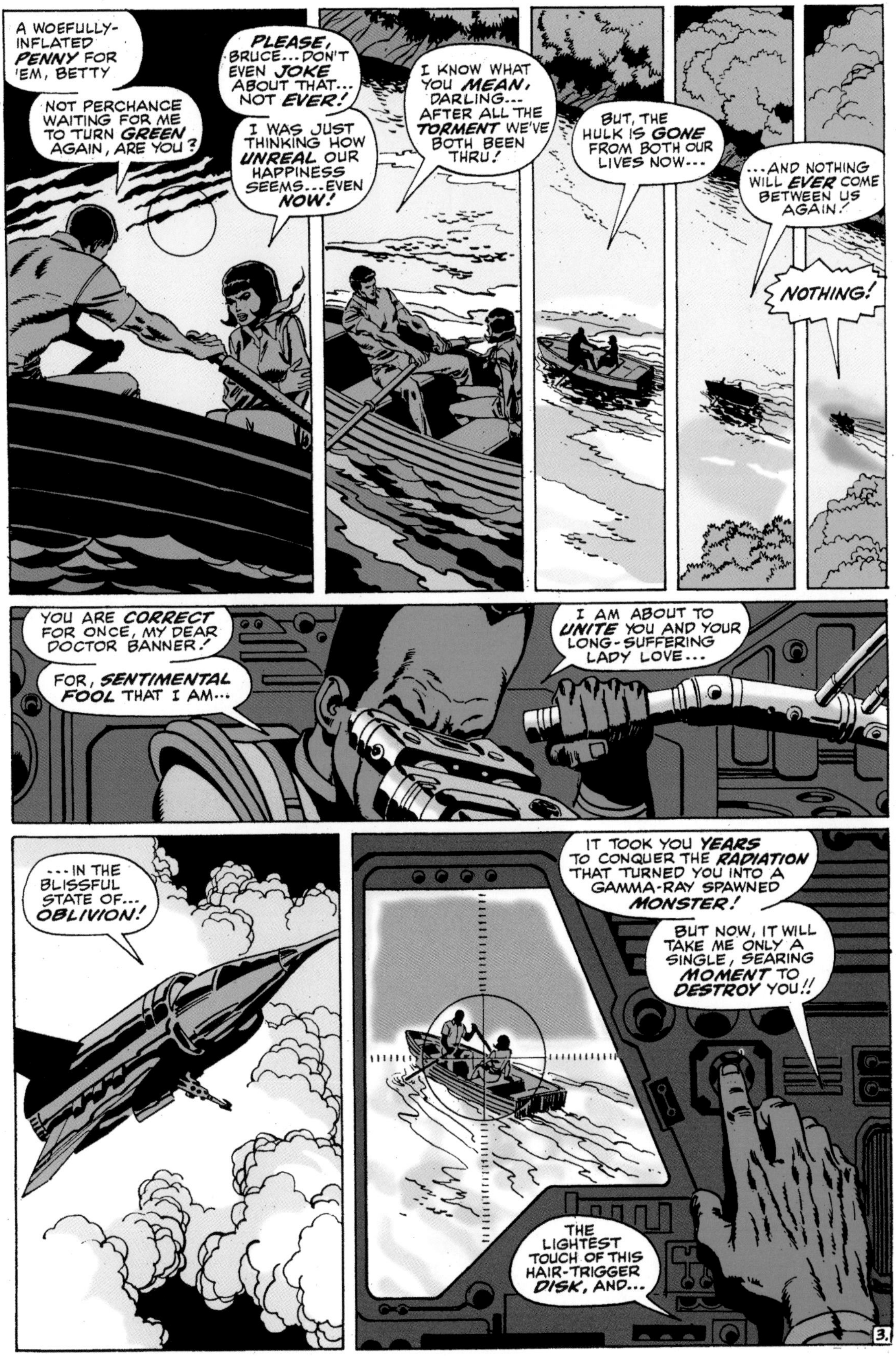
A WOEFULLY-INFLATED PENNY FOR 'EM, BETTY
NOT PERCHANCE WAITING FOR ME TO TURN GREEN AGAIN, ARE YOU?
PLEASE, BRUCE... DON'T EVEN JOKE ABOUT THAT... NOT EVER!
I WAS JUST THINKING HOW UNREAL OUR HAPPINESS SEEMS... EVEN NOW!
I KNOW WHAT YOU MEAN, DARLING... AFTER ALL THE TORMENT WE'VE BOTH BEEN THRU!
BUT, THE HULK IS GONE FROM BOTH OUR LIVES NOW...
...AND NOTHING WILL EVER COME BETWEEN US AGAIN!
NOTHING!
YOU ARE CORRECT FOR ONCE, MY DEAR DOCTOR BANNER!
FOR, SENTIMENTAL FOOL THAT I AM...
I AM ABOUT TO UNITE YOU AND YOUR LONG-SUFFERING LADY LOVE...
...IN THE BLISSFUL STATE OF... OBLIVION!
IT TOOK YOU YEARS TO CONQUER THE RADIATION THAT TURNED YOU INTO A GAMMA-RAY SPAWNED MONSTER!
BUT NOW, IT WILL TAKE ME ONLY A SINGLE, SEARING MOMENT TO DESTROY YOU!!
THE LIGHTEST TOUCH OF THIS HAIR-TRIGGER DISK, AND...
3.

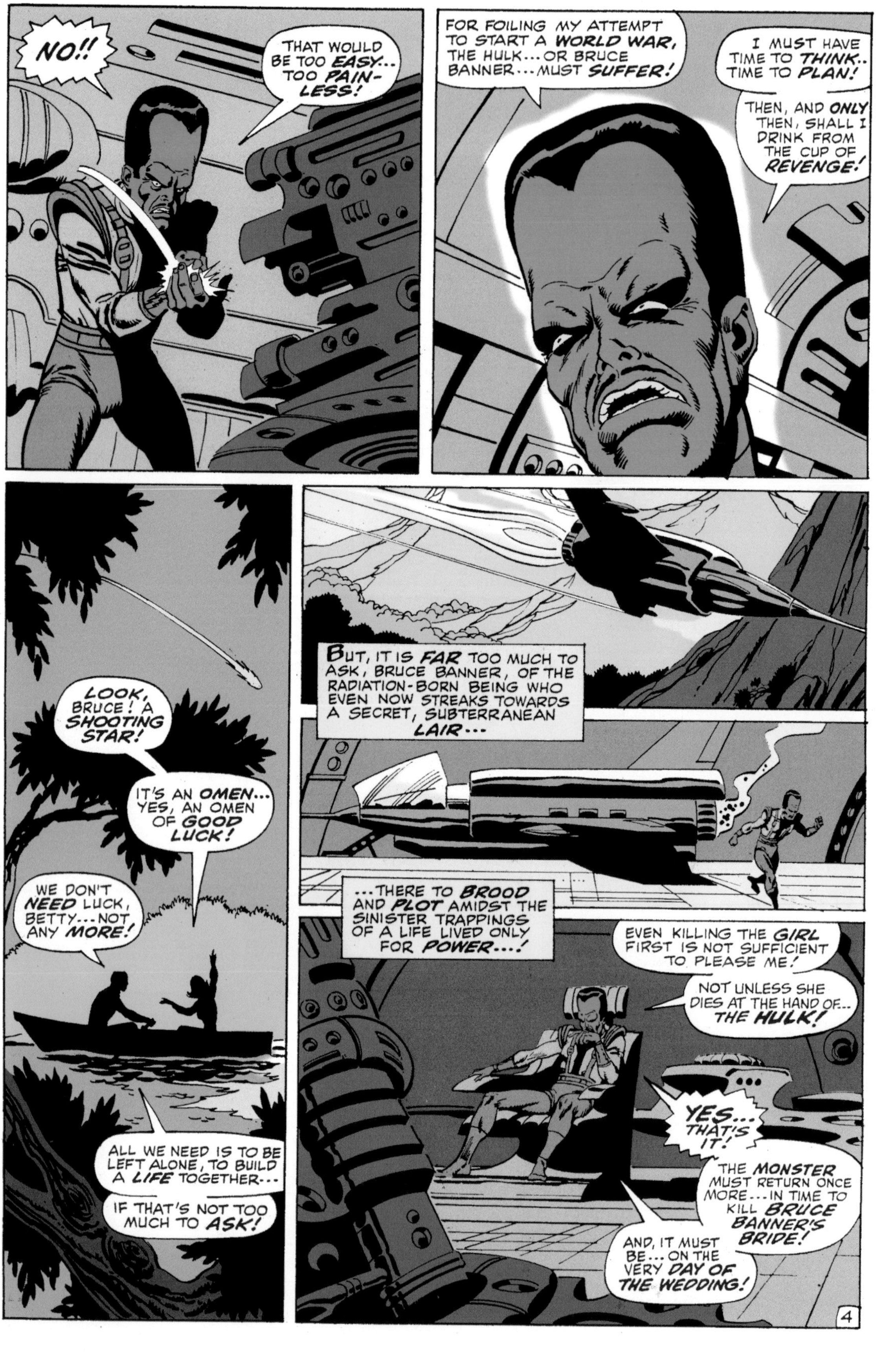
NO!!
THAT WOULD BE TOO EASY... TOO PAINLESS!
FOR FOILING MY ATTEMPT TO START A WORLD WAR, THE HULK... OR BRUCE BANNER... MUST SUFFER!
I MUST HAVE TIME TO THINK.. TIME TO PLAN!
THEN, AND ONLY THEN, SHALL I DRINK FROM THE CUP OF REVENGE!
LOOK, BRUCE! A SHOOTING STAR!
IT'S AN OMEN... YES, AN OMEN OF GOOD LUCK!
WE DON'T NEED LUCK, BETTY... NOT ANY MORE!
ALL WE NEED IS TO BE LEFT ALONE, TO BUILD A LIFE TOGETHER...
IF THAT'S NOT TOO MUCH TO ASK!
BUT, IT IS FAR TOO MUCH TO ASK, BRUCE BANNER, OF THE RADIATION-BORN BEING WHO EVEN NOW STREAKS TOWARDS A SECRET, SUBTERRANEAN LAIR...
...THERE TO BROOD AND PLOT AMIDST THE SINISTER TRAPPINGS OF A LIFE LIVED ONLY FOR POWER...!
EVEN KILLING THE GIRL FIRST IS NOT SUFFICIENT TO PLEASE ME!
NOT UNLESS SHE DIES AT THE HAND OF... THE HULK!
YES... THAT'S IT!
THE MONSTER MUST RETURN ONCE MORE... IN TIME TO KILL BRUCE BANNER'S BRIDE!
AND, IT MUST BE... ON THE VERY DAY OF THE WEDDING!
4

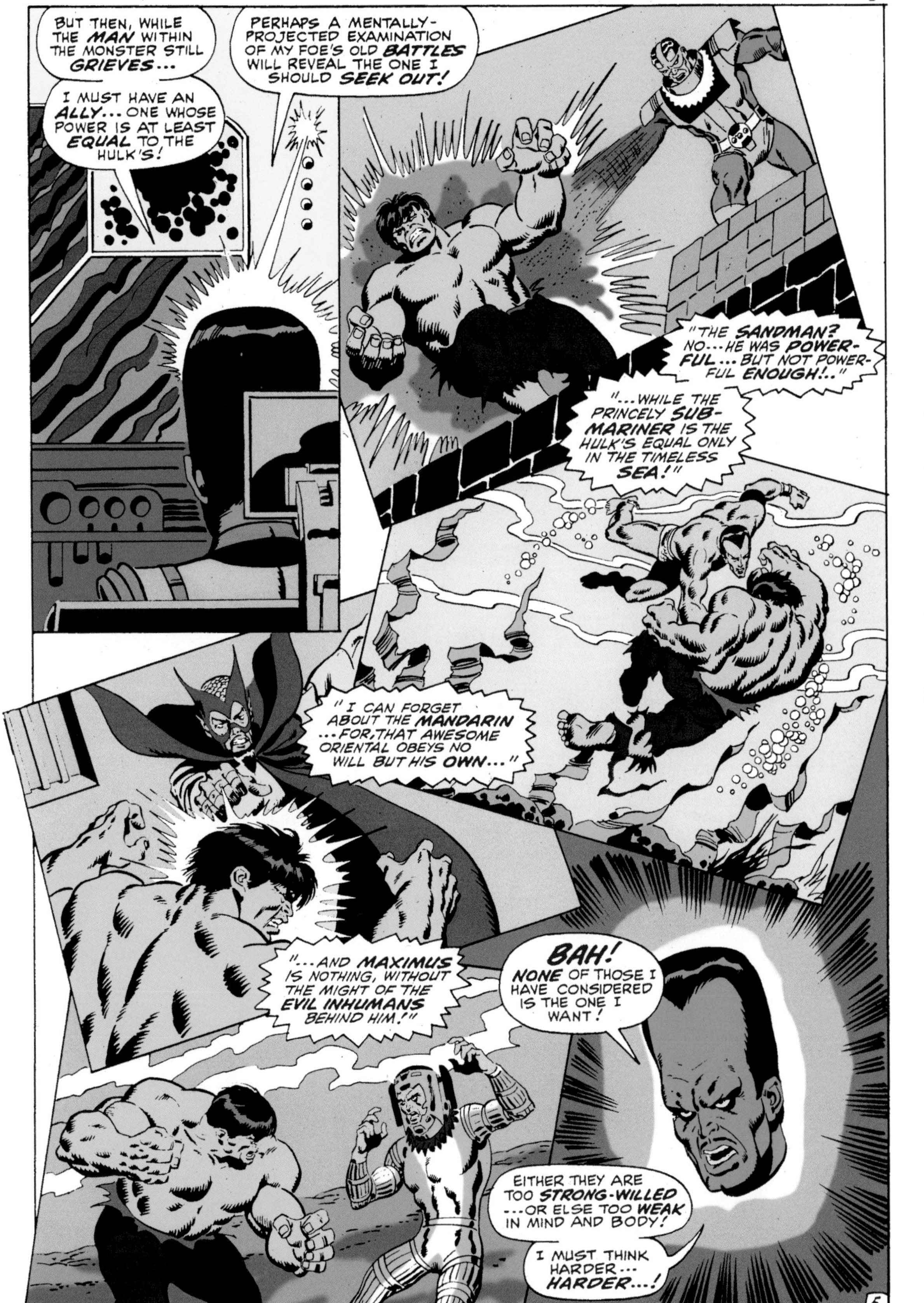

BUT THEN, WHILE THE MAN WITHIN THE MONSTER STILL GRIEVES...
I MUST HAVE AN ALLY... ONE WHOSE POWER IS AT LEAST EQUAL TO THE HULK'S!
PERHAPS A MENTALLY-PROJECTED EXAMINATION OF MY FOE'S OLD BATTLES WILL REVEAL THE ONE I SHOULD SEEK OUT!
"THE SANDMAN? NO---HE WAS POWERFUL... BUT NOT POWERFUL ENOUGH!.."
"...WHILE THE PRINCELY SUB-MARINER IS THE HULK'S EQUAL ONLY IN THE TIMELESS SEA!"
"I CAN FORGET ABOUT THE MANDARIN ...FOR THAT AWESOME ORIENTAL OBEYS NO WILL BUT HIS OWN..."
"...AND MAXIMUS IS NOTHING, WITHOUT THE MIGHT OF THE EVIL INHUMANS BEHIND HIM!"
BAH! NONE OF THOSE I HAVE CONSIDERED IS THE ONE I WANT!
EITHER THEY ARE TOO STRONG-WILLED ...OR ELSE TOO WEAK IN MIND AND BODY!
I MUST THINK HARDER... HARDER...!
5.

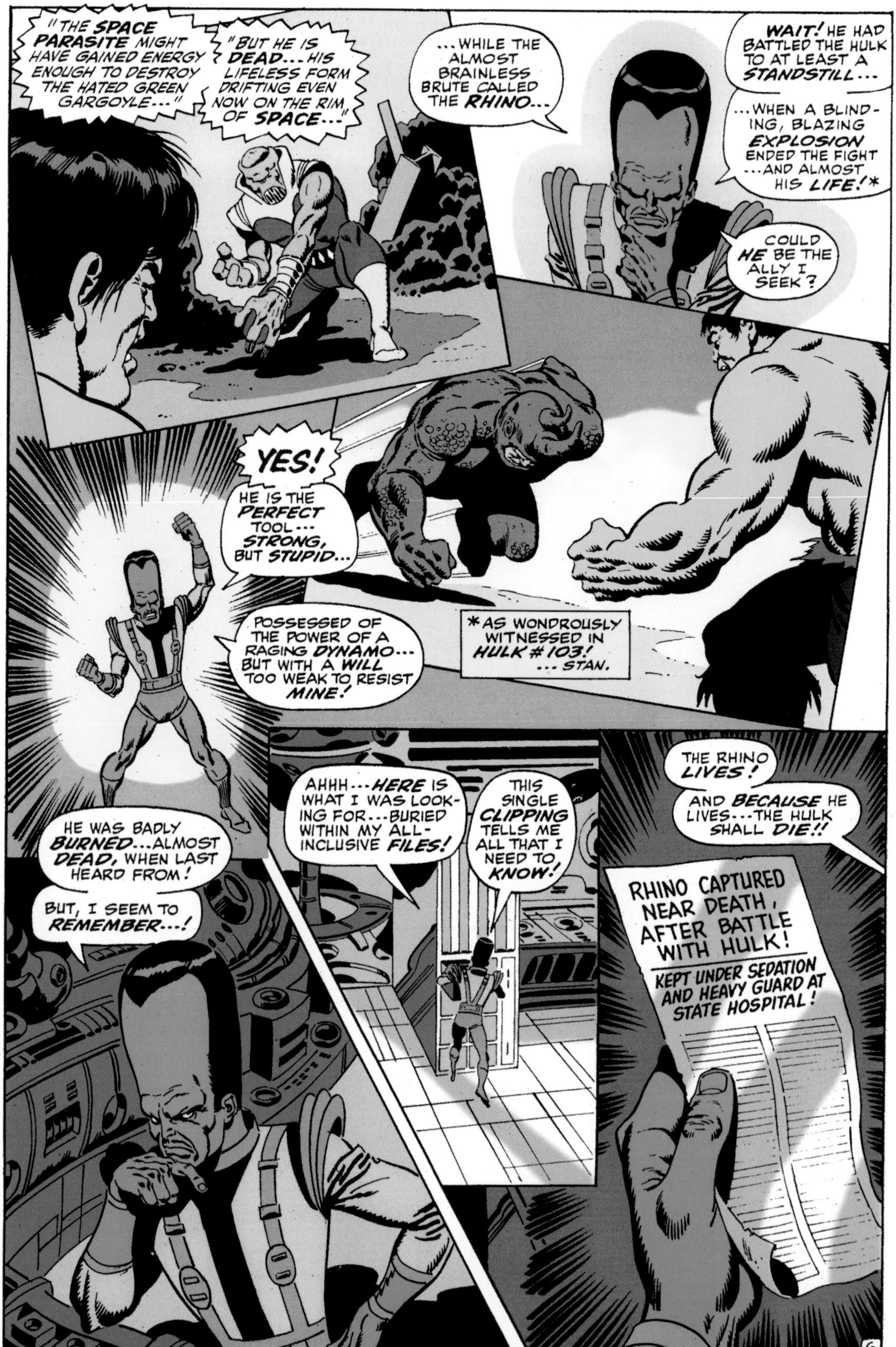
"THE SPACE PARASITE MIGHT HAVE GAINED ENERGY ENOUGH TO DESTROY THE HATED GREEN GARGOYLE..."
"BUT HE IS DEAD... HIS LIFELESS FORM DRIFTING EVEN NOW ON THE RIM OF SPACE..."
...WHILE THE ALMOST BRAINLESS BRUTE CALLED THE RHINO...
WAIT! HE HAD BATTLED THE HULK TO AT LEAST A STANDSTILL...
...WHEN A BLINDING, BLAZING EXPLOSION ENDED THE FIGHT ...AND ALMOST HIS LIFE!*
COULD HE BE THE ALLY I SEEK?
YES!
HE IS THE PERFECT TOOL... STRONG, BUT STUPID...
POSSESSED OF THE POWER OF A RAGING DYNAMO... BUT WITH A WILL TOO WEAK TO RESIST MINE!
*AS WONDROUSLY WITNESSED IN HULK #103! ...STAN.
HE WAS BADLY BURNED...ALMOST DEAD, WHEN LAST HEARD FROM!
BUT, I SEEM TO REMEMBER...!
AHHH... HERE IS WHAT I WAS LOOKING FOR... BURIED WITHIN MY ALL-INCLUSIVE FILES!
THIS SINGLE CLIPPING TELLS ME ALL THAT I NEED TO KNOW!
THE RHINO LIVES!
AND BECAUSE HE LIVES... THE HULK SHALL DIE!!
RHINO CAPTURED NEAR DEATH, AFTER BATTLE WITH HULK!
KEPT UNDER SEDATION AND HEAVY GUARD AT STATE HOSPITAL!
6

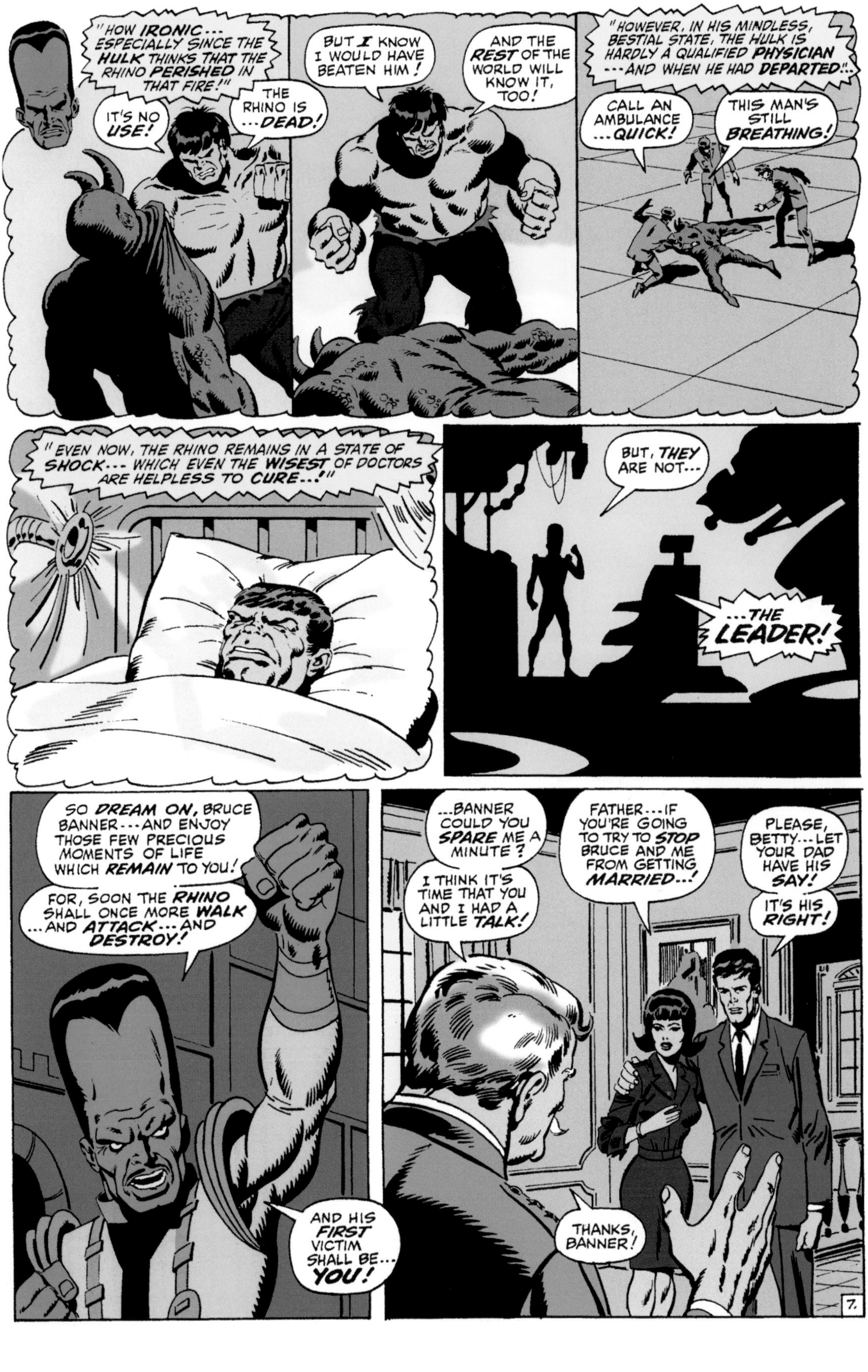
"HOW IRONIC... ESPECIALLY SINCE THE HULK THINKS THAT THE RHINO PERISHED IN THAT FIRE!"
IT'S NO USE!
THE RHINO IS ...DEAD!
BUT I KNOW I WOULD HAVE BEATEN HIM!
AND THE REST OF THE WORLD WILL KNOW IT, TOO!
"HOWEVER, IN HIS MINDLESS, BESTIAL STATE, THE HULK IS HARDLY A QUALIFIED PHYSICIAN ---AND WHEN HE HAD DEPARTED!..
CALL AN AMBULANCE ...QUICK!
THIS MAN'S STILL BREATHING!
"EVEN NOW, THE RHINO REMAINS IN A STATE OF SHOCK--- WHICH EVEN THE WISEST OF DOCTORS ARE HELPLESS TO CURE...!"
BUT, THEY ARE NOT...
...THE LEADER!
SO DREAM ON, BRUCE BANNER---AND ENJOY THOSE FEW PRECIOUS MOMENTS OF LIFE WHICH REMAIN TO YOU!
FOR, SOON THE RHINO SHALL ONCE MORE WALK ...AND ATTACK...AND DESTROY!
AND HIS FIRST VICTIM SHALL BE... YOU!
...BANNER COULD YOU SPARE ME A MINUTE?
I THINK IT'S TIME THAT YOU AND I HAD A LITTLE TALK!
FATHER---IF YOU'RE GOING TO TRY TO STOP BRUCE AND ME FROM GETTING MARRIED...!
PLEASE, BETTY...LET YOUR DAD HAVE HIS SAY!
IT'S HIS RIGHT!
THANKS, BANNER!
7.

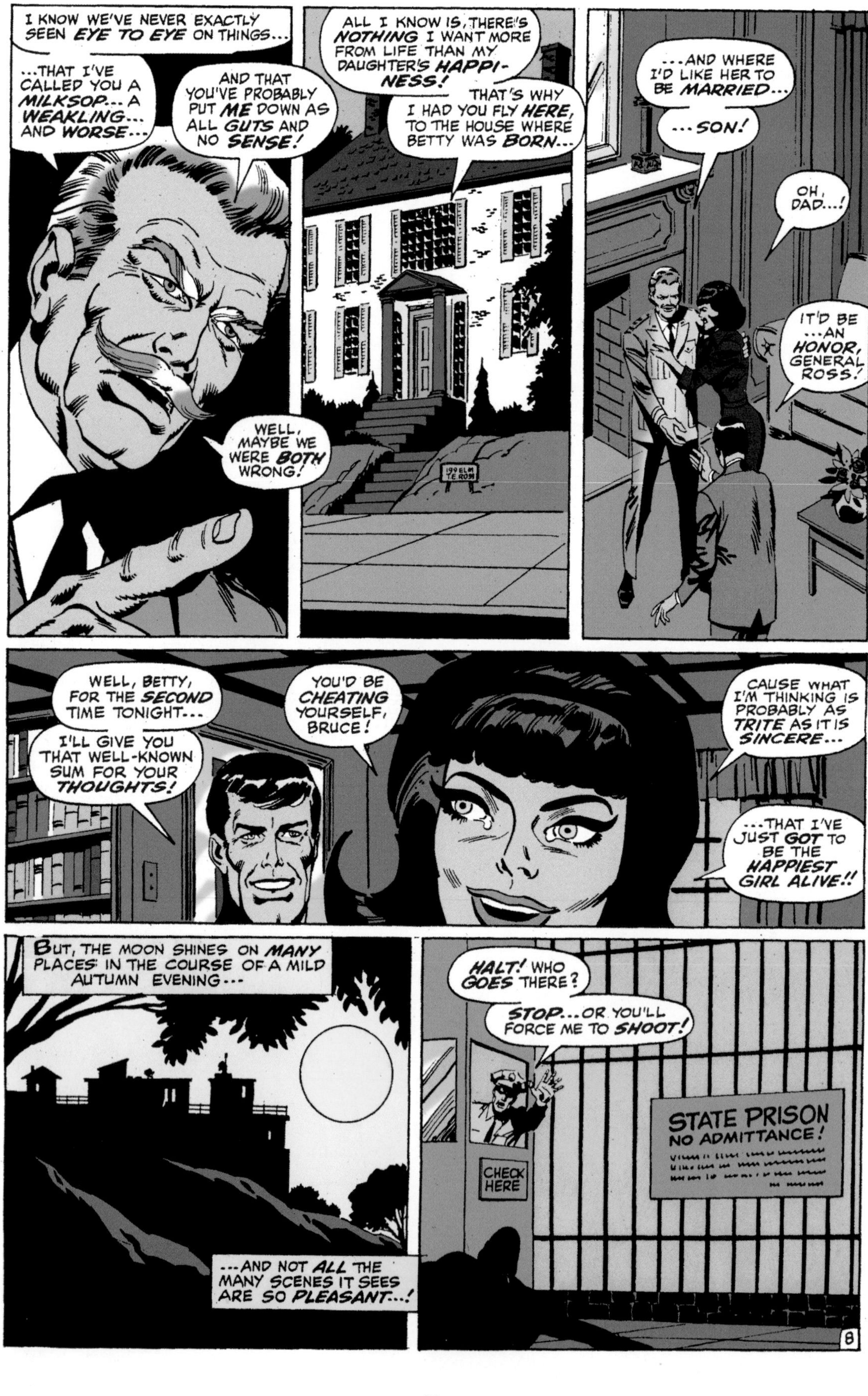
I KNOW WE'VE NEVER EXACTLY SEEN EYE TO EYE ON THINGS...
...THAT I'VE CALLED YOU A MILKSOP... A WEAKLING... AND WORSE...
AND THAT YOU'VE PROBABLY PUT ME DOWN AS ALL GUTS AND NO SENSE!
WELL, MAYBE WE WERE BOTH WRONG!
ALL I KNOW IS, THERE'S NOTHING I WANT MORE FROM LIFE THAN MY DAUGHTER'S HAPPI-NESS!
THAT'S WHY I HAD YOU FLY HERE, TO THE HOUSE WHERE BETTY WAS BORN...
199 ELM TE. ROSS
...AND WHERE I'D LIKE HER TO BE MARRIED...
...SON!
OH, DAD...!
IT'D BE ...AN HONOR, GENERAL ROSS!
WELL, BETTY, FOR THE SECOND TIME TONIGHT...
I'LL GIVE YOU THAT WELL-KNOWN SUM FOR YOUR THOUGHTS!
YOU'D BE CHEATING YOURSELF, BRUCE!
CAUSE WHAT I'M THINKING IS PROBABLY AS TRITE AS IT IS SINCERE...
...THAT I'VE JUST GOT TO BE THE HAPPIEST GIRL ALIVE!!
BUT, THE MOON SHINES ON MANY PLACES IN THE COURSE OF A MILD AUTUMN EVENING...
...AND NOT ALL THE MANY SCENES IT SEES ARE SO PLEASANT...!
HALT! WHO GOES THERE?
STOP...OR YOU'LL FORCE ME TO SHOOT!
CHECK HERE
STATE PRISON
NO ADMITTANCE!
8

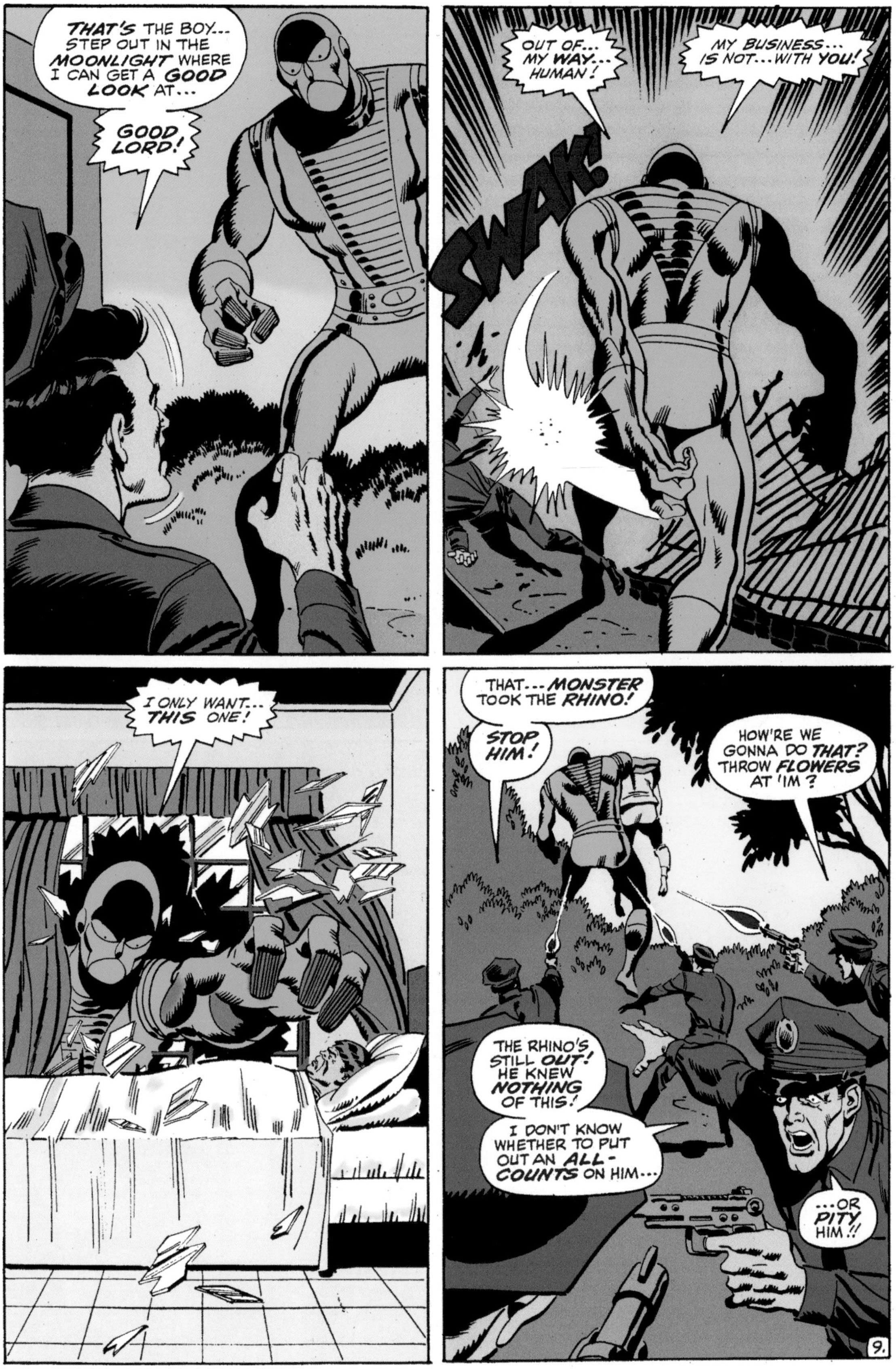
THAT'S THE BOY... STEP OUT IN THE MOONLIGHT WHERE I CAN GET A GOOD LOOK AT...
GOOD LORD!
OUT OF... MY WAY... HUMAN!
MY BUSINESS... IS NOT...WITH YOU!
SWAK!
I ONLY WANT... THIS ONE!
THAT...MONSTER TOOK THE RHINO!
STOP HIM!
HOW'RE WE GONNA DO THAT? THROW FLOWERS AT 'IM?
THE RHINO'S STILL OUT! HE KNEW NOTHING OF THIS!
I DON'T KNOW WHETHER TO PUT OUT AN ALL-COUNTS ON HIM...
...OR PITY HIM!!
9.

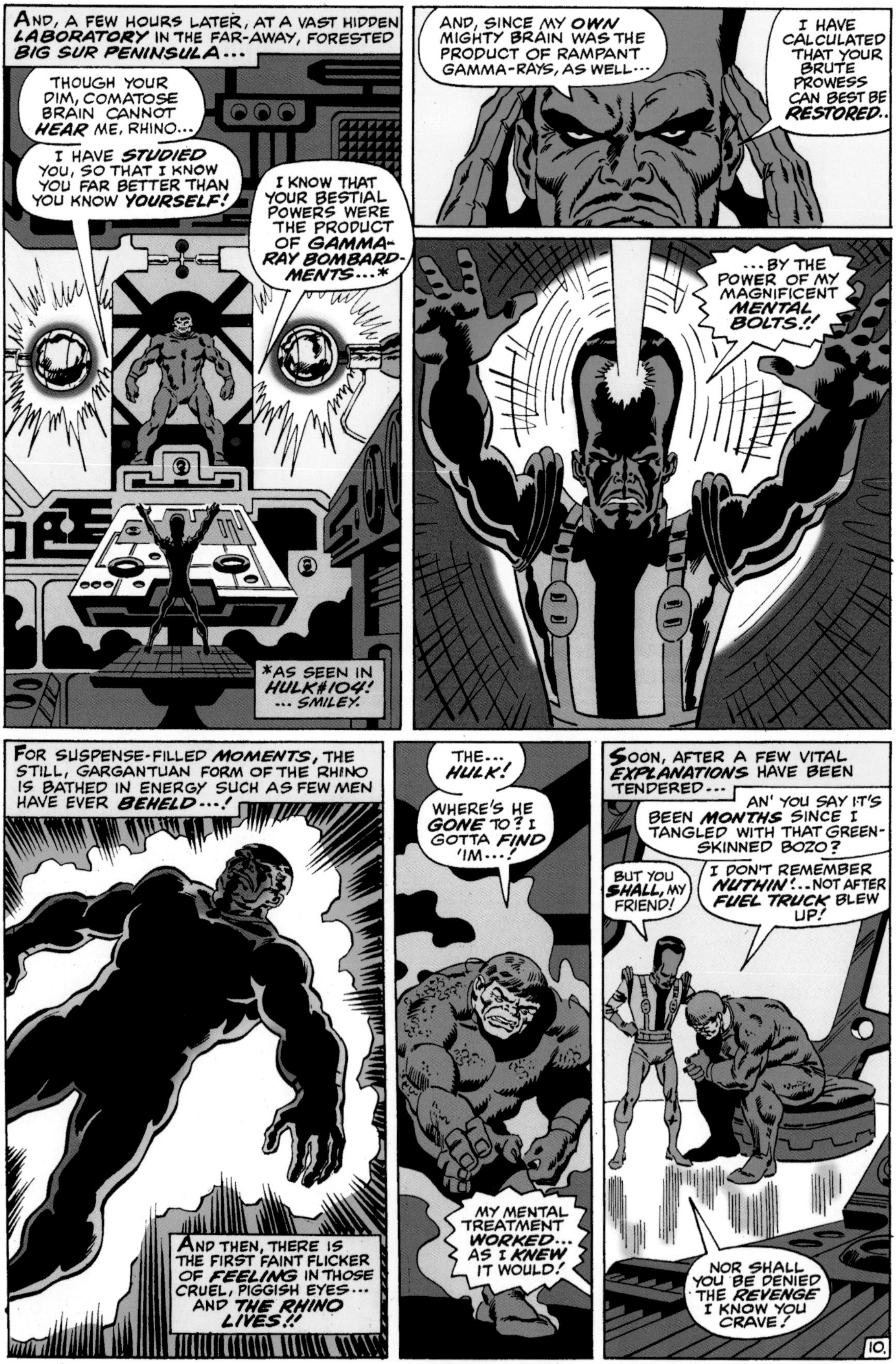
AND, A FEW HOURS LATER, AT A VAST HIDDEN LABORATORY IN THE FAR-AWAY, FORESTED BIG SUR PENINSULA...
THOUGH YOUR DIM, COMATOSE BRAIN CANNOT HEAR ME, RHINO...
I HAVE STUDIED YOU, SO THAT I KNOW YOU FAR BETTER THAN YOU KNOW YOURSELF!
I KNOW THAT YOUR BESTIAL POWERS WERE THE PRODUCT OF GAMMA-RAY BOMBARDMENTS...*
*AS SEEN IN HULK#104! ... SMILEY.
AND, SINCE MY OWN MIGHTY BRAIN WAS THE PRODUCT OF RAMPANT GAMMA-RAYS, AS WELL...
I HAVE CALCULATED THAT YOUR BRUTE PROWESS CAN BEST BE RESTORED..
...BY THE POWER OF MY MAGNIFICENT MENTAL BOLTS!!
FOR SUSPENSE-FILLED MOMENTS, THE STILL, GARGANTUAN FORM OF THE RHINO IS BATHED IN ENERGY SUCH AS FEW MEN HAVE EVER BEHELD...!
AND THEN, THERE IS THE FIRST FAINT FLICKER OF FEELING IN THOSE CRUEL, PIGGISH EYES... AND THE RHINO LIVES!!
THE... HULK!
WHERE'S HE GONE TO? I GOTTA FIND 'IM...!
MY MENTAL TREATMENT WORKED... AS I KNEW IT WOULD!
SOON, AFTER A FEW VITAL EXPLANATIONS HAVE BEEN TENDERED...
AN' YOU SAY IT'S BEEN MONTHS SINCE I TANGLED WITH THAT GREEN-SKINNED BOZO?
I DON'T REMEMBER NUTHIN'!...NOT AFTER FUEL TRUCK BLEW UP!
BUT YOU SHALL, MY FRIEND!
NOR SHALL YOU BE DENIED THE REVENGE I KNOW YOU CRAVE!
10.

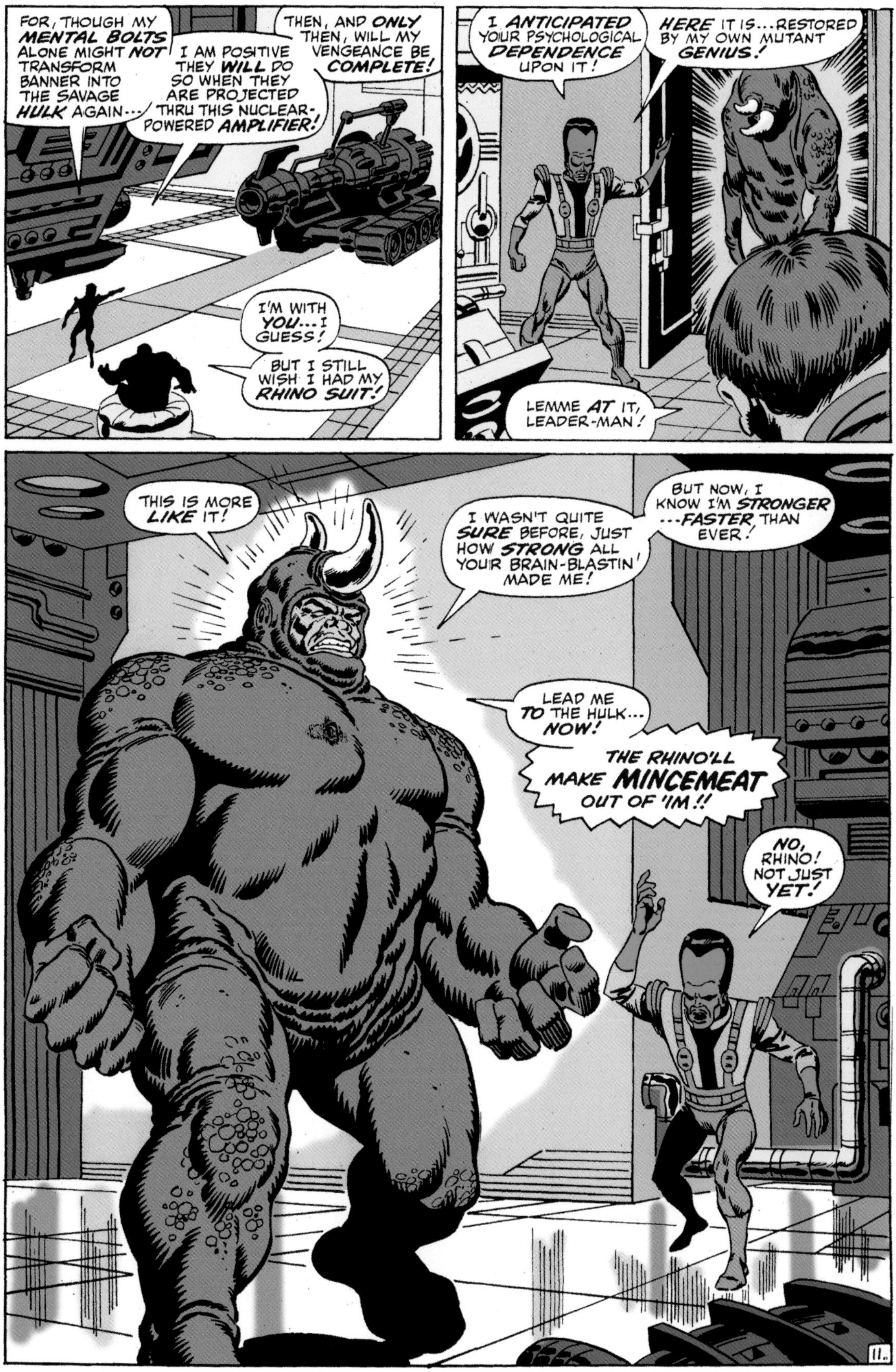

FOR, THOUGH MY MENTAL BOLTS ALONE MIGHT NOT TRANSFORM BANNER INTO THE SAVAGE HULK AGAIN...
I AM POSITIVE THEY WILL DO SO WHEN THEY ARE PROJECTED THRU THIS NUCLEAR-POWERED AMPLIFIER!
THEN, AND ONLY THEN, WILL MY VENGEANCE BE COMPLETE!
I'M WITH YOU... I GUESS!
BUT I STILL WISH I HAD MY RHINO SUIT!
I ANTICIPATED YOUR PSYCHOLOGICAL DEPENDENCE UPON IT!
HERE IT IS... RESTORED BY MY OWN MUTANT GENIUS!
LEMME AT IT, LEADER-MAN!
THIS IS MORE LIKE IT!
I WASN'T QUITE SURE BEFORE, JUST HOW STRONG ALL YOUR BRAIN-BLASTIN' MADE ME!
BUT NOW, I KNOW I'M STRONGER ---FASTER THAN EVER!
LEAD ME TO THE HULK... NOW!
THE RHINO'LL MAKE MINCEMEAT OUT OF 'IM!!
NO, RHINO! NOT JUST YET!
11

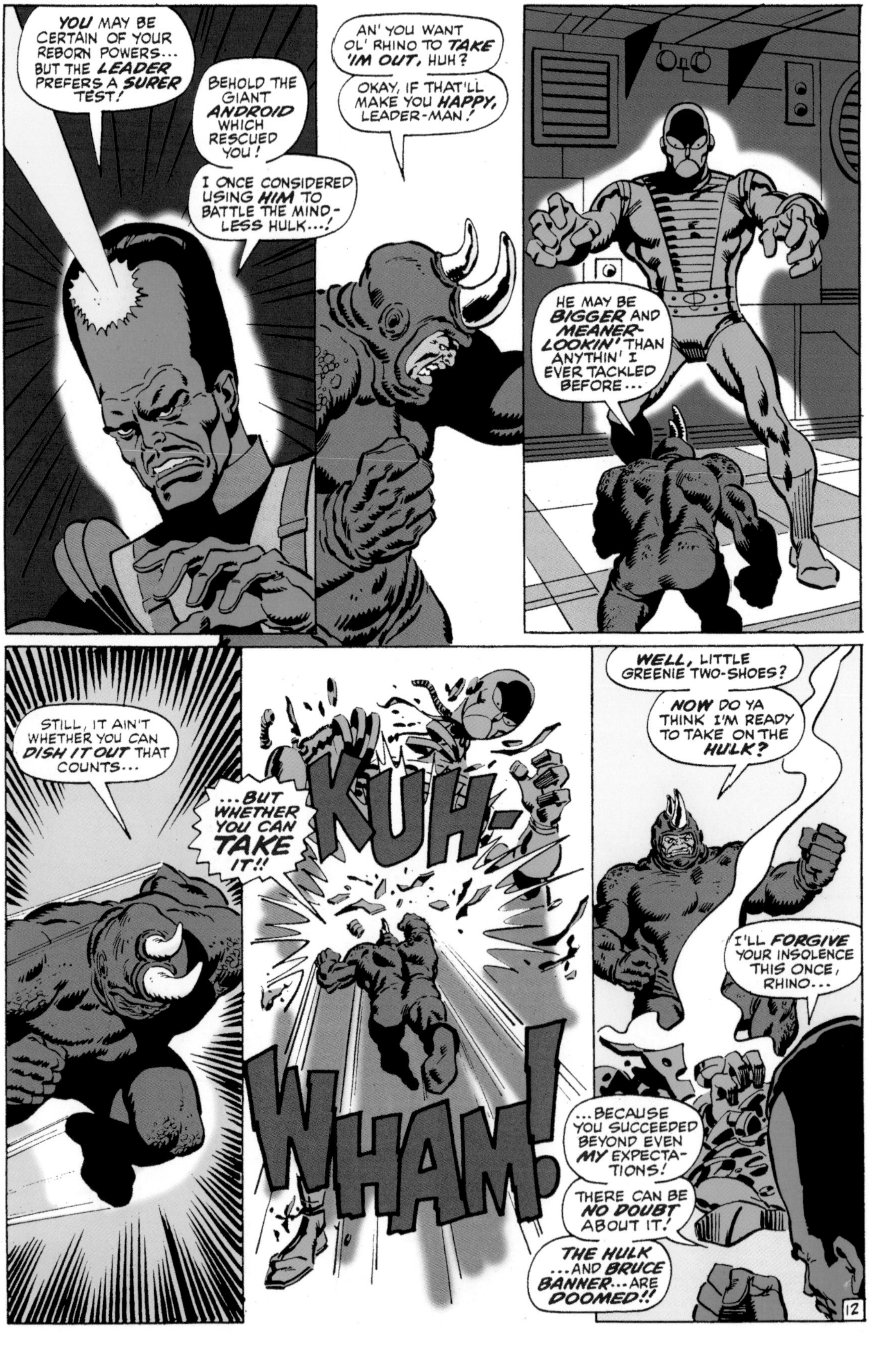
YOU MAY BE CERTAIN OF YOUR REBORN POWERS... BUT THE LEADER PREFERS A SURER TEST!
BEHOLD THE GIANT ANDROID WHICH RESCUED YOU!
I ONCE CONSIDERED USING HIM TO BATTLE THE MINDLESS HULK...!
AN' YOU WANT OL' RHINO TO TAKE 'IM OUT, HUH?
OKAY, IF THAT'LL MAKE YOU HAPPY, LEADER-MAN!
HE MAY BE BIGGER AND MEANER-LOOKIN' THAN ANYTHIN' I EVER TACKLED BEFORE...
STILL, IT AIN'T WHETHER YOU CAN DISH IT OUT THAT COUNTS...
...BUT WHETHER YOU CAN TAKE IT!!
KUH-
WHAM!
WELL, LITTLE GREENIE TWO-SHOES?
NOW DO YA THINK I'M READY TO TAKE ON THE HULK?
I'LL FORGIVE YOUR INSOLENCE THIS ONCE, RHINO...
...BECAUSE YOU SUCCEEDED BEYOND EVEN MY EXPECTATIONS!
THERE CAN BE NO DOUBT ABOUT IT!
THE HULK ...AND BRUCE BANNER... ARE DOOMED!!
12

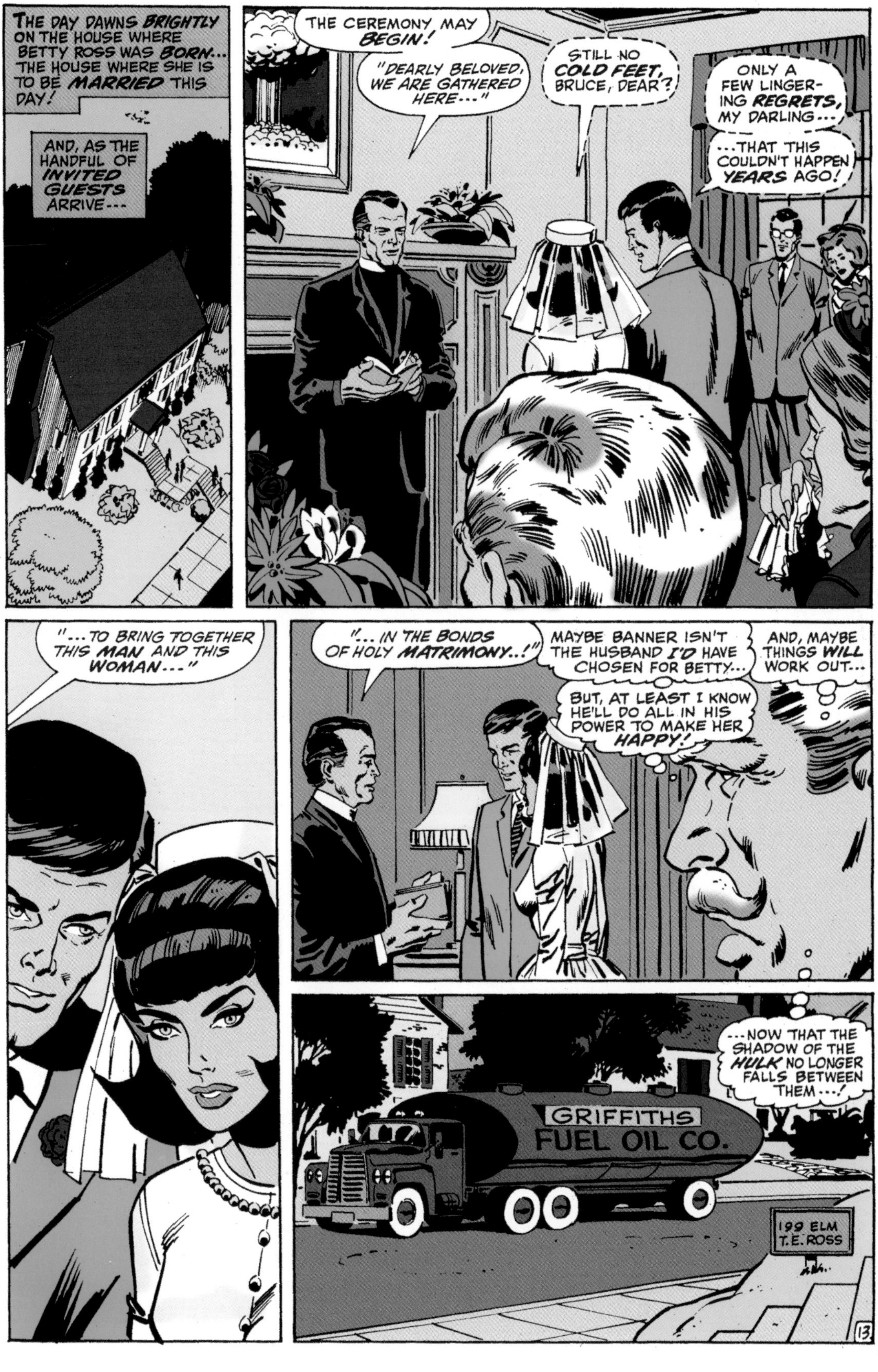

THE DAY DAWNS BRIGHTLY ON THE HOUSE WHERE BETTY ROSS WAS BORN... THE HOUSE WHERE SHE IS TO BE MARRIED THIS DAY!
AND, AS THE HANDFUL OF INVITED GUESTS ARRIVE---
THE CEREMONY MAY BEGIN!
"DEARLY BELOVED, WE ARE GATHERED HERE---"
STILL NO COLD FEET, BRUCE, DEAR?
ONLY A FEW LINGERING REGRETS, MY DARLING---
---THAT THIS COULDN'T HAPPEN YEARS AGO!
"---TO BRING TOGETHER THIS MAN AND THIS WOMAN---"
"... IN THE BONDS OF HOLY MATRIMONY..!"
MAYBE BANNER ISN'T THE HUSBAND I'D HAVE CHOSEN FOR BETTY...
BUT, AT LEAST I KNOW HE'LL DO ALL IN HIS POWER TO MAKE HER HAPPY!
AND, MAYBE THINGS WILL WORK OUT---
---NOW THAT THE SHADOW OF THE HULK NO LONGER FALLS BETWEEN THEM---!
GRIFFITHS
FUEL OIL CO.
199 ELM
T.E. ROSS
13

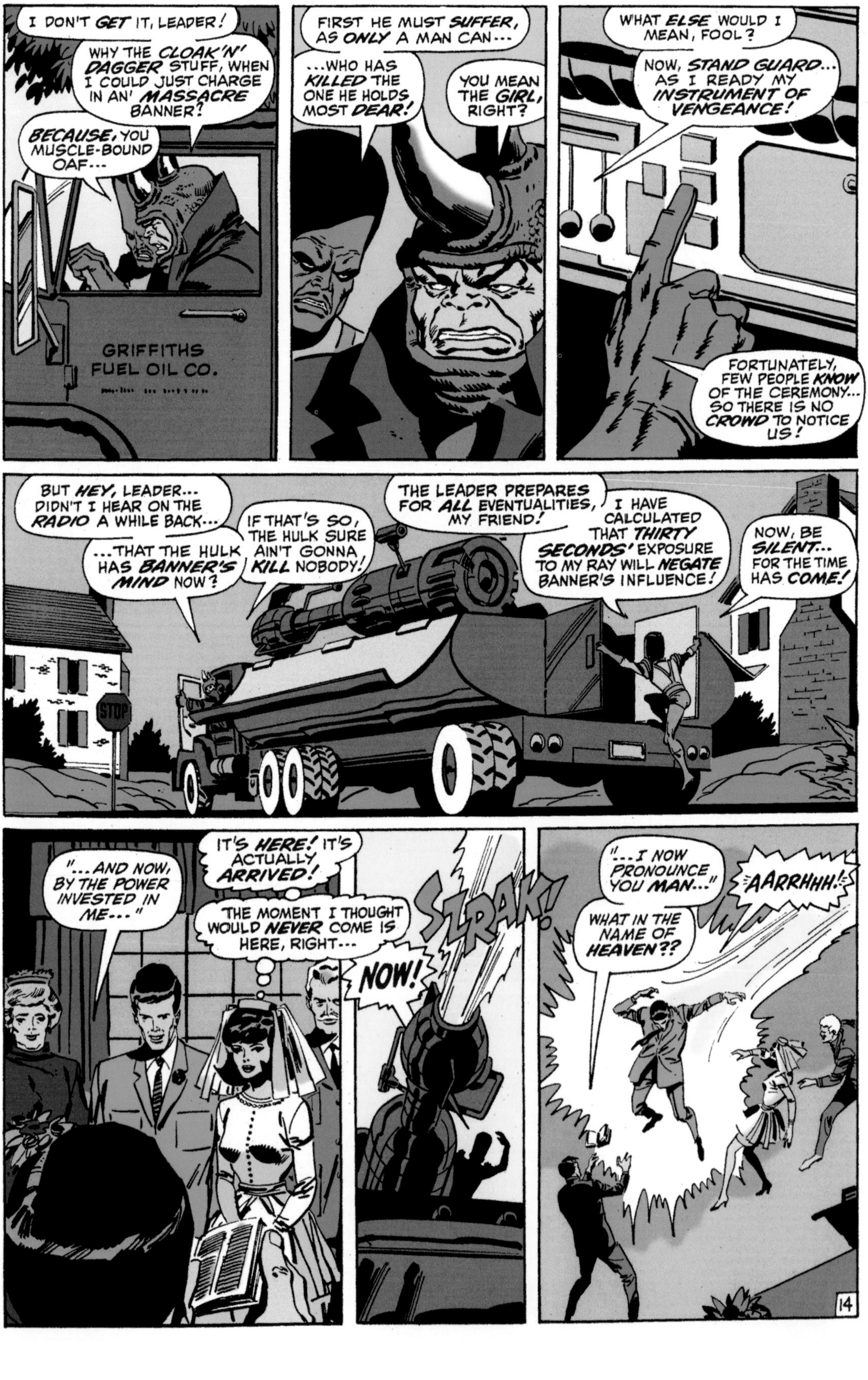

I DON'T GET IT, LEADER!
WHY THE CLOAK'N' DAGGER STUFF, WHEN I COULD JUST CHARGE IN AN' MASSACRE BANNER?
BECAUSE, YOU MUSCLE-BOUND OAF---
GRIFFITHS FUEL OIL CO.
FIRST HE MUST SUFFER, AS ONLY A MAN CAN---
---WHO HAS KILLED THE ONE HE HOLDS MOST DEAR!
YOU MEAN THE GIRL, RIGHT?
WHAT ELSE WOULD I MEAN, FOOL?
NOW, STAND GUARD... AS I READY MY INSTRUMENT OF VENGEANCE!
FORTUNATELY, FEW PEOPLE KNOW OF THE CEREMONY... SO THERE IS NO CROWD TO NOTICE US!
BUT HEY, LEADER... DIDN'T I HEAR ON THE RADIO A WHILE BACK---
---THAT THE HULK HAS BANNER'S MIND NOW?
IF THAT'S SO, THE HULK SURE AIN'T GONNA KILL NOBODY!
THE LEADER PREPARES FOR ALL EVENTUALITIES, MY FRIEND!
I HAVE CALCULATED THAT THIRTY SECONDS' EXPOSURE TO MY RAY WILL NEGATE BANNER'S INFLUENCE!
NOW, BE SILENT... FOR THE TIME HAS COME!
STOP
"---AND NOW, BY THE POWER INVESTED IN ME---"
IT'S HERE! IT'S ACTUALLY ARRIVED!
THE MOMENT I THOUGHT WOULD NEVER COME IS HERE, RIGHT---
NOW!
SZRAK!
"---I NOW PRONOUNCE YOU MAN---"
AARRHHH!
WHAT IN THE NAME OF HEAVEN??
14

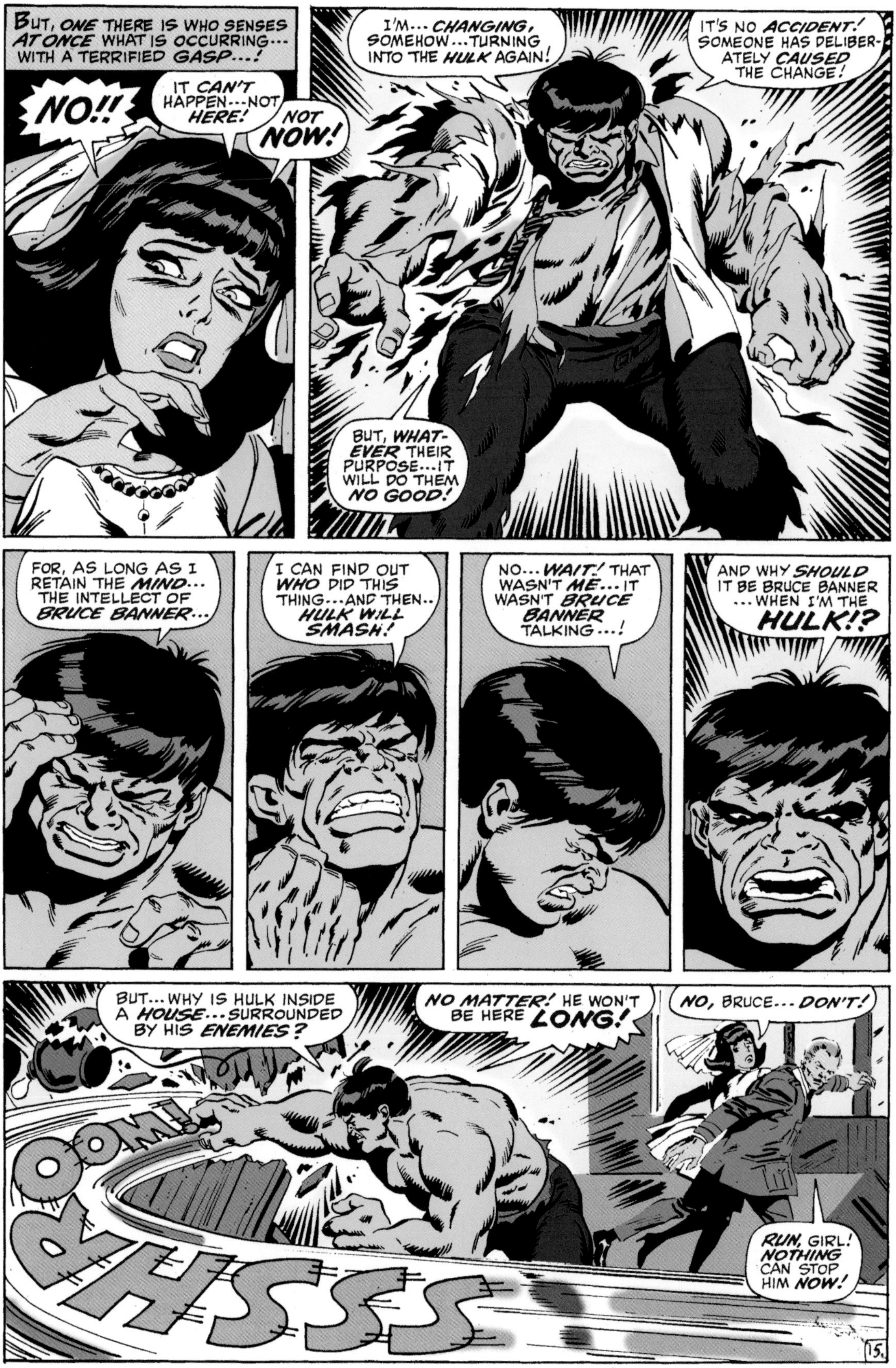

BUT, ONE THERE IS WHO SENSES AT ONCE WHAT IS OCCURRING--- WITH A TERRIFIED GASP---!
NO!!
IT CAN'T HAPPEN---NOT HERE!
NOT NOW!
I'M--- CHANGING, SOMEHOW---TURNING INTO THE HULK AGAIN!
IT'S NO ACCIDENT! SOMEONE HAS DELIBERATELY CAUSED THE CHANGE!
BUT, WHATEVER THEIR PURPOSE---IT WILL DO THEM NO GOOD!
FOR, AS LONG AS I RETAIN THE MIND--- THE INTELLECT OF BRUCE BANNER---
I CAN FIND OUT WHO DID THIS THING---AND THEN-- HULK WILL SMASH!
NO---WAIT! THAT WASN'T ME---IT WASN'T BRUCE BANNER TALKING---!
AND WHY SHOULD IT BE BRUCE BANNER ---WHEN I'M THE HULK!?
BUT---WHY IS HULK INSIDE A HOUSE---SURROUNDED BY HIS ENEMIES?
NO MATTER! HE WON'T BE HERE LONG!
NO, BRUCE--- DON'T!
BOOM!
KRHSSS
RUN, GIRL! NOTHING CAN STOP HIM NOW!
15

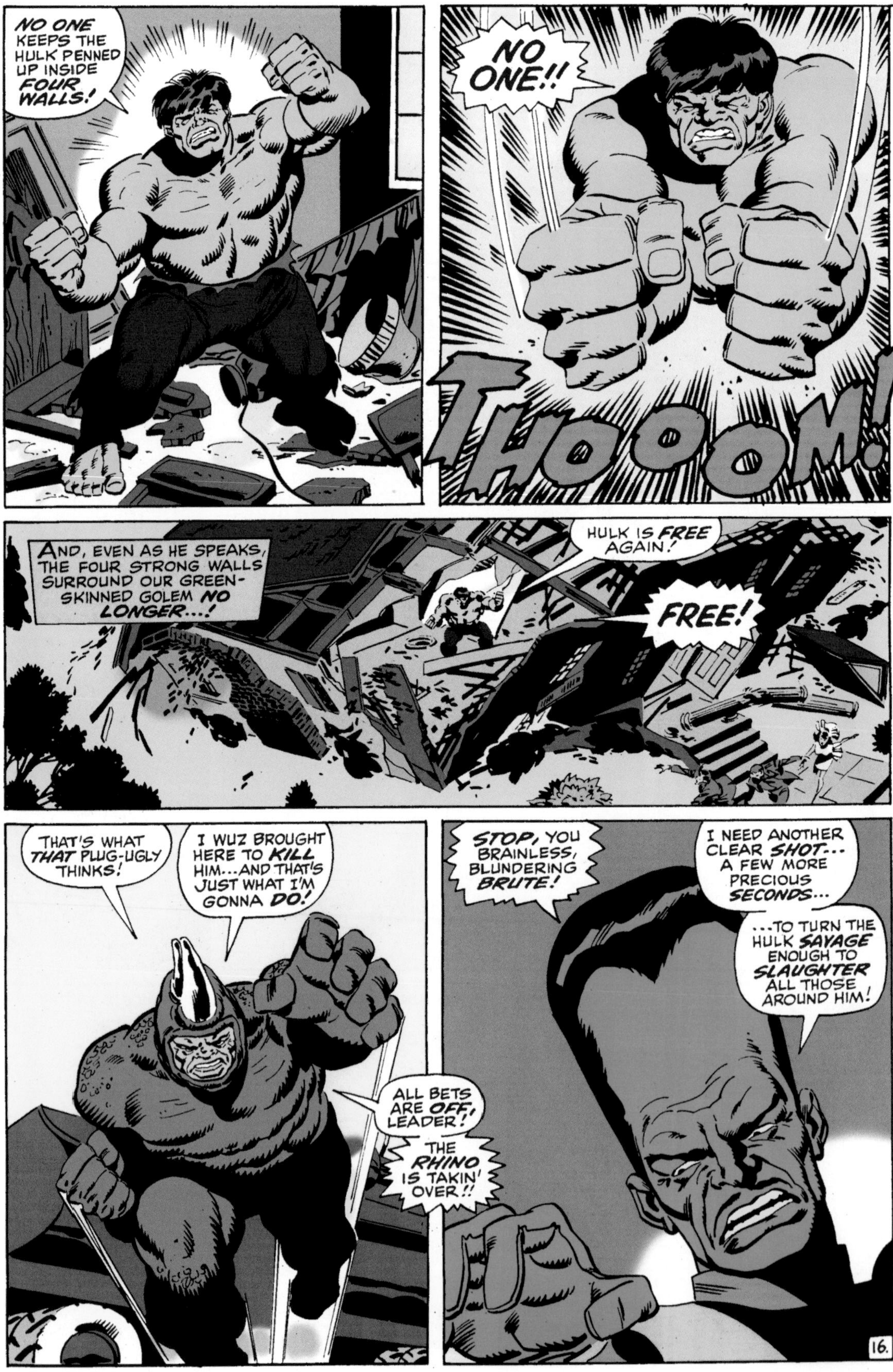
NO ONE KEEPS THE HULK PENNED UP INSIDE FOUR WALLS!
NO ONE!!
THOOOM!
AND, EVEN AS HE SPEAKS, THE FOUR STRONG WALLS SURROUND OUR GREEN-SKINNED GOLEM NO LONGER...!
HULK IS FREE AGAIN!
FREE!
THAT'S WHAT THAT PLUG-UGLY THINKS!
I WUZ BROUGHT HERE TO KILL HIM...AND THAT'S JUST WHAT I'M GONNA DO!
ALL BETS ARE OFF, LEADER!
THE RHINO IS TAKIN' OVER!!
STOP, YOU BRAINLESS, BLUNDERING BRUTE!
I NEED ANOTHER CLEAR SHOT... A FEW MORE PRECIOUS SECONDS...
...TO TURN THE HULK SAVAGE ENOUGH TO SLAUGHTER ALL THOSE AROUND HIM!
16.

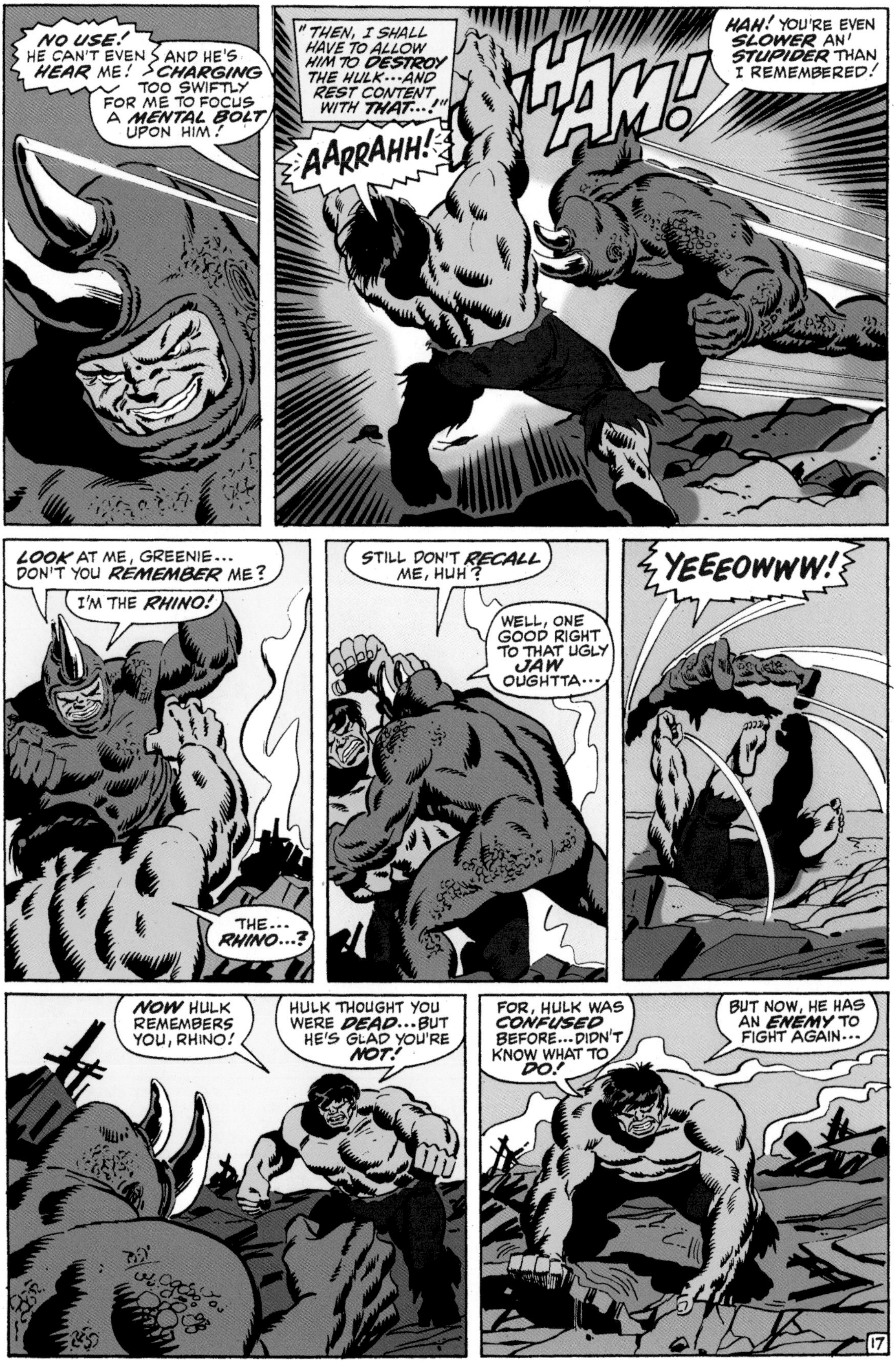
NO USE! HE CAN'T EVEN HEAR ME!
AND HE'S CHARGING TOO SWIFTLY FOR ME TO FOCUS A MENTAL BOLT UPON HIM!
"THEN, I SHALL HAVE TO ALLOW HIM TO DESTROY THE HULK...AND REST CONTENT WITH THAT...!"
AARRAHH!
HAM!
HAH! YOU'RE EVEN SLOWER AN' STUPIDER THAN I REMEMBERED!
LOOK AT ME, GREENIE... DON'T YOU REMEMBER ME?
I'M THE RHINO!
THE... RHINO...?
STILL DON'T RECALL ME, HUH?
WELL, ONE GOOD RIGHT TO THAT UGLY JAW OUGHTTA...
YEEEOWWW!
NOW HULK REMEMBERS YOU, RHINO!
HULK THOUGHT YOU WERE DEAD...BUT HE'S GLAD YOU'RE NOT!
FOR, HULK WAS CONFUSED BEFORE...DIDN'T KNOW WHAT TO DO!
BUT NOW, HE HAS AN ENEMY TO FIGHT AGAIN...
17

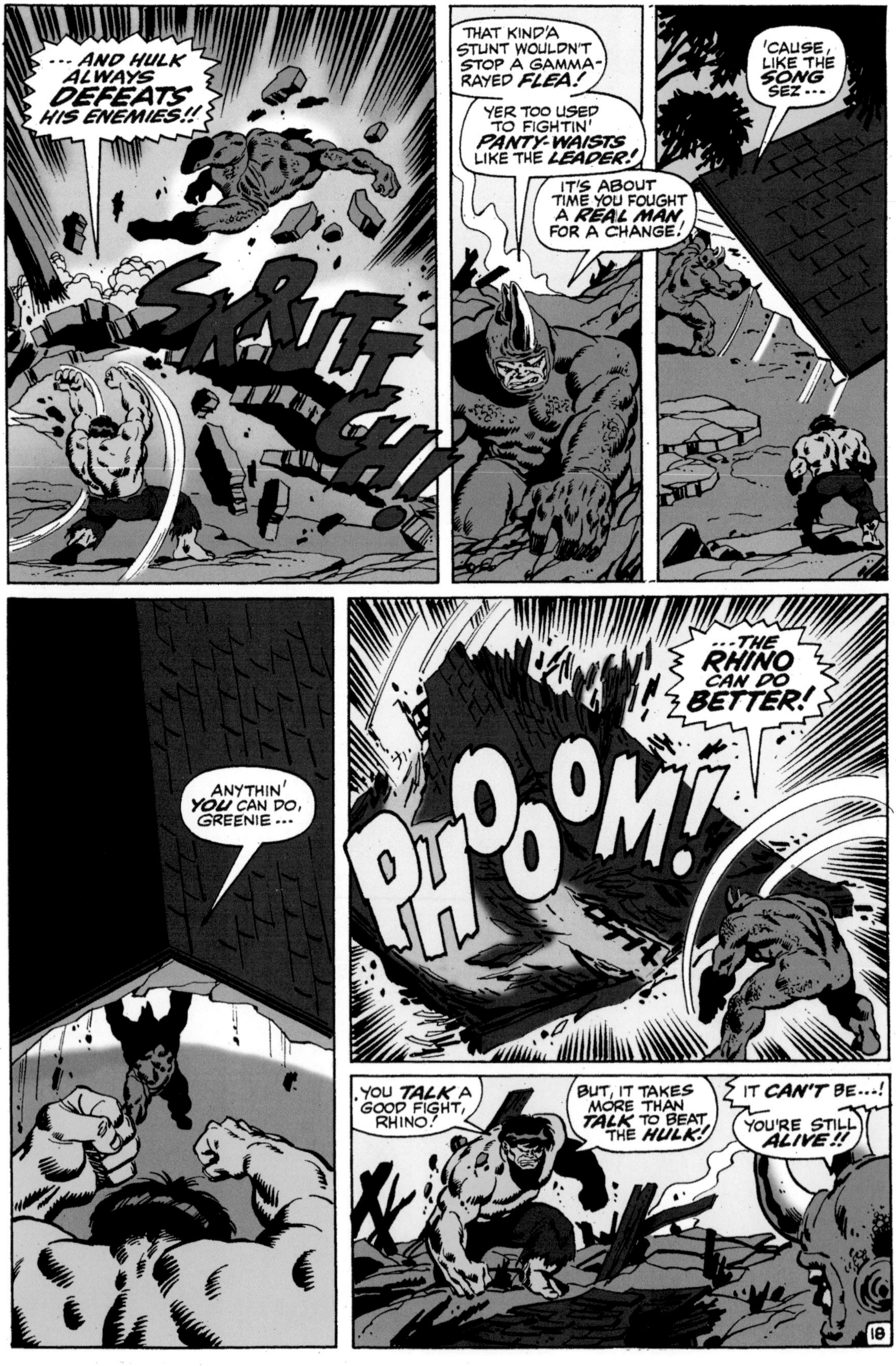
...AND HULK ALWAYS DEFEATS HIS ENEMIES!!
SKRUTTCH!
THAT KIND'A STUNT WOULDN'T STOP A GAMMA-RAYED FLEA!
YER TOO USED TO FIGHTIN' PANTY-WAISTS LIKE THE LEADER!
IT'S ABOUT TIME YOU FOUGHT A REAL MAN FOR A CHANGE!
'CAUSE, LIKE THE SONG SEZ...
ANYTHIN' YOU CAN DO, GREENIE...
...THE RHINO CAN DO BETTER!
PHOOOM!
YOU TALK A GOOD FIGHT, RHINO!
BUT, IT TAKES MORE THAN TALK TO BEAT THE HULK!
IT CAN'T BE...!
YOU'RE STILL ALIVE!!
18

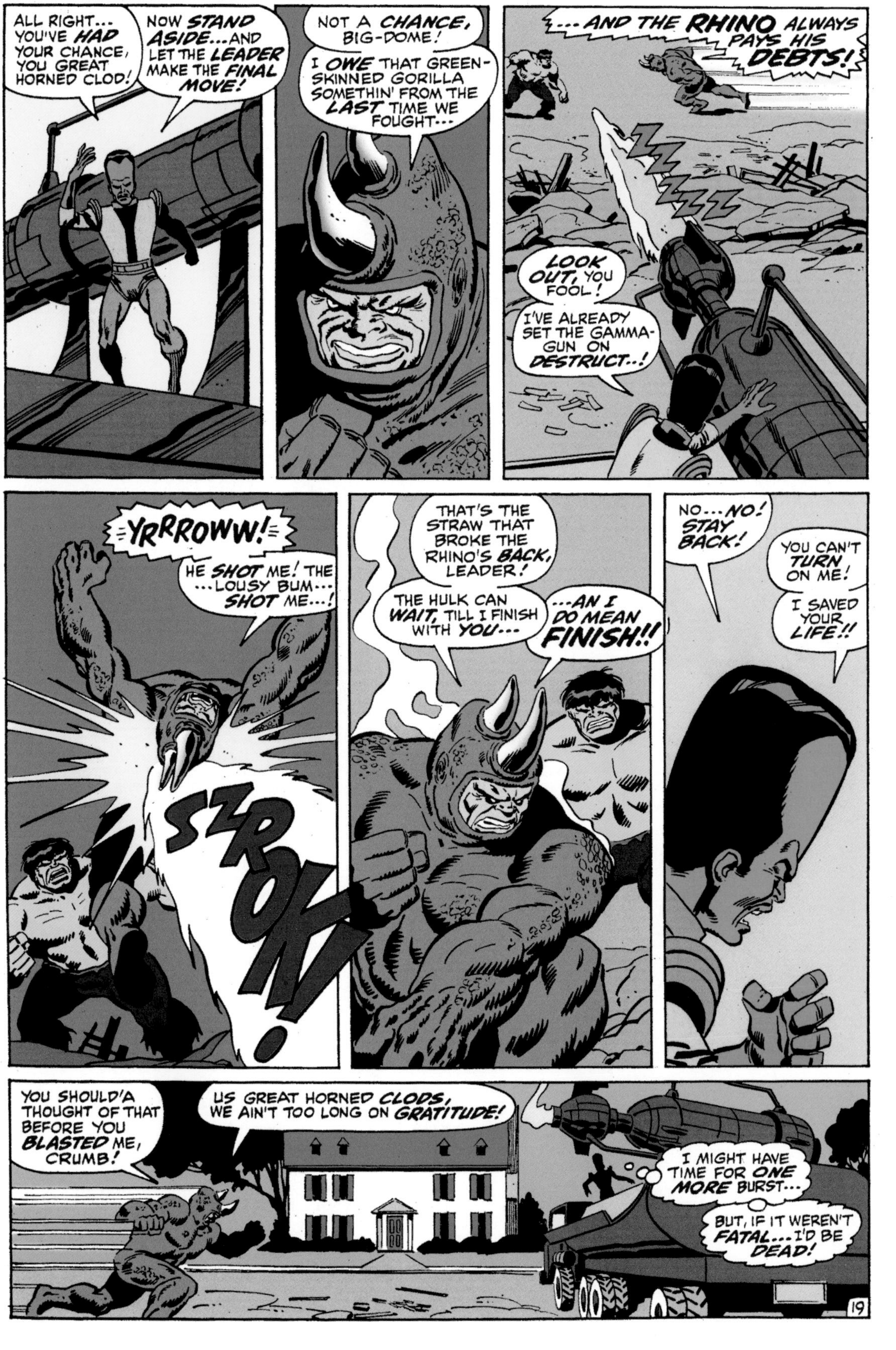
ALL RIGHT... YOU'VE HAD YOUR CHANCE, YOU GREAT HORNED CLOD!
NOW STAND ASIDE...AND LET THE LEADER MAKE THE FINAL MOVE!
NOT A CHANCE, BIG-DOME!
I OWE THAT GREEN-SKINNED GORILLA SOMETHIN' FROM THE LAST TIME WE FOUGHT...
...AND THE RHINO ALWAYS PAYS HIS DEBTS!
LOOK OUT, YOU FOOL!
I'VE ALREADY SET THE GAMMA-GUN ON DESTRUCT..!
YRRROWW!
HE SHOT ME! THE ...LOUSY BUM... SHOT ME...!
SZZROK!
THAT'S THE STRAW THAT BROKE THE RHINO'S BACK, LEADER!
THE HULK CAN WAIT, TILL I FINISH WITH YOU...
...AN I DO MEAN FINISH!!
NO...NO! STAY BACK!
YOU CAN'T TURN ON ME!
I SAVED YOUR LIFE!!
YOU SHOULD'A THOUGHT OF THAT BEFORE YOU BLASTED ME, CRUMB!
US GREAT HORNED CLODS, WE AIN'T TOO LONG ON GRATITUDE!
I MIGHT HAVE TIME FOR ONE MORE BURST...
BUT, IF IT WEREN'T FATAL...I'D BE DEAD!
19

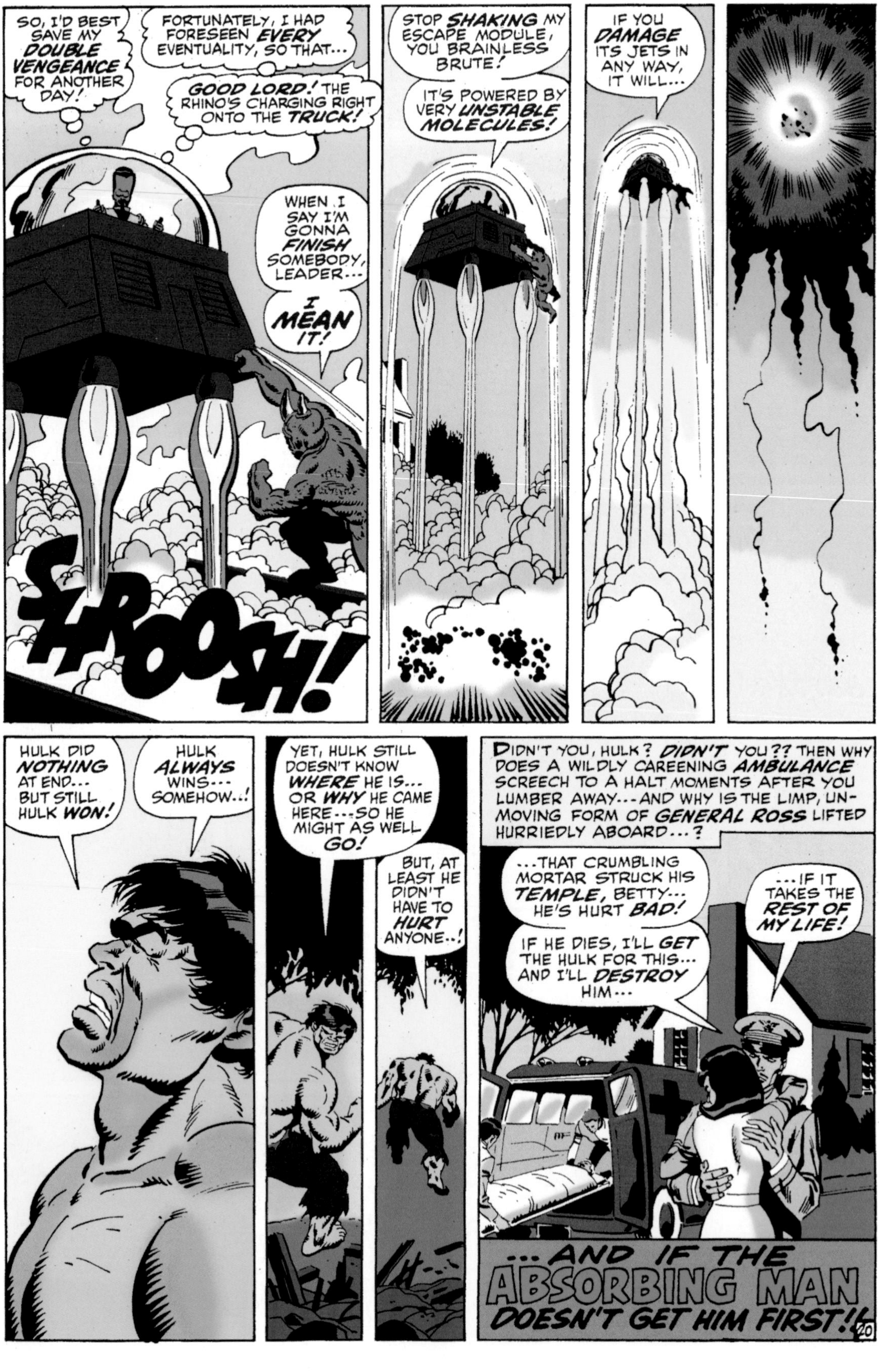

SO, I'D BEST SAVE MY DOUBLE VENGEANCE FOR ANOTHER DAY!
FORTUNATELY, I HAD FORESEEN EVERY EVENTUALITY, SO THAT...
GOOD LORD! THE RHINO'S CHARGING RIGHT ONTO THE TRUCK!
WHEN I SAY I'M GONNA FINISH SOMEBODY, LEADER...
I MEAN IT!
SHROOSH!
STOP SHAKING MY ESCAPE MODULE, YOU BRAINLESS BRUTE!
IT'S POWERED BY VERY UNSTABLE MOLECULES!
IF YOU DAMAGE ITS JETS IN ANY WAY, IT WILL...
HULK DID NOTHING AT END... BUT STILL HULK WON!
HULK ALWAYS WINS... SOMEHOW..!
YET, HULK STILL DOESN'T KNOW WHERE HE IS... OR WHY HE CAME HERE... SO HE MIGHT AS WELL GO!
BUT, AT LEAST HE DIDN'T HAVE TO HURT ANYONE..!
DIDN'T YOU, HULK? DIDN'T YOU?? THEN WHY DOES A WILDLY CAREENING AMBULANCE SCREECH TO A HALT MOMENTS AFTER YOU LUMBER AWAY... AND WHY IS THE LIMP, UNMOVING FORM OF GENERAL ROSS LIFTED HURRIEDLY ABOARD...?
...THAT CRUMBLING MORTAR STRUCK HIS TEMPLE, BETTY... HE'S HURT BAD!
IF HE DIES, I'LL GET THE HULK FOR THIS... AND I'LL DESTROY HIM...
...IF IT TAKES THE REST OF MY LIFE!
...AND IF THE ABSORBING MAN DOESN'T GET HIM FIRST!!
20

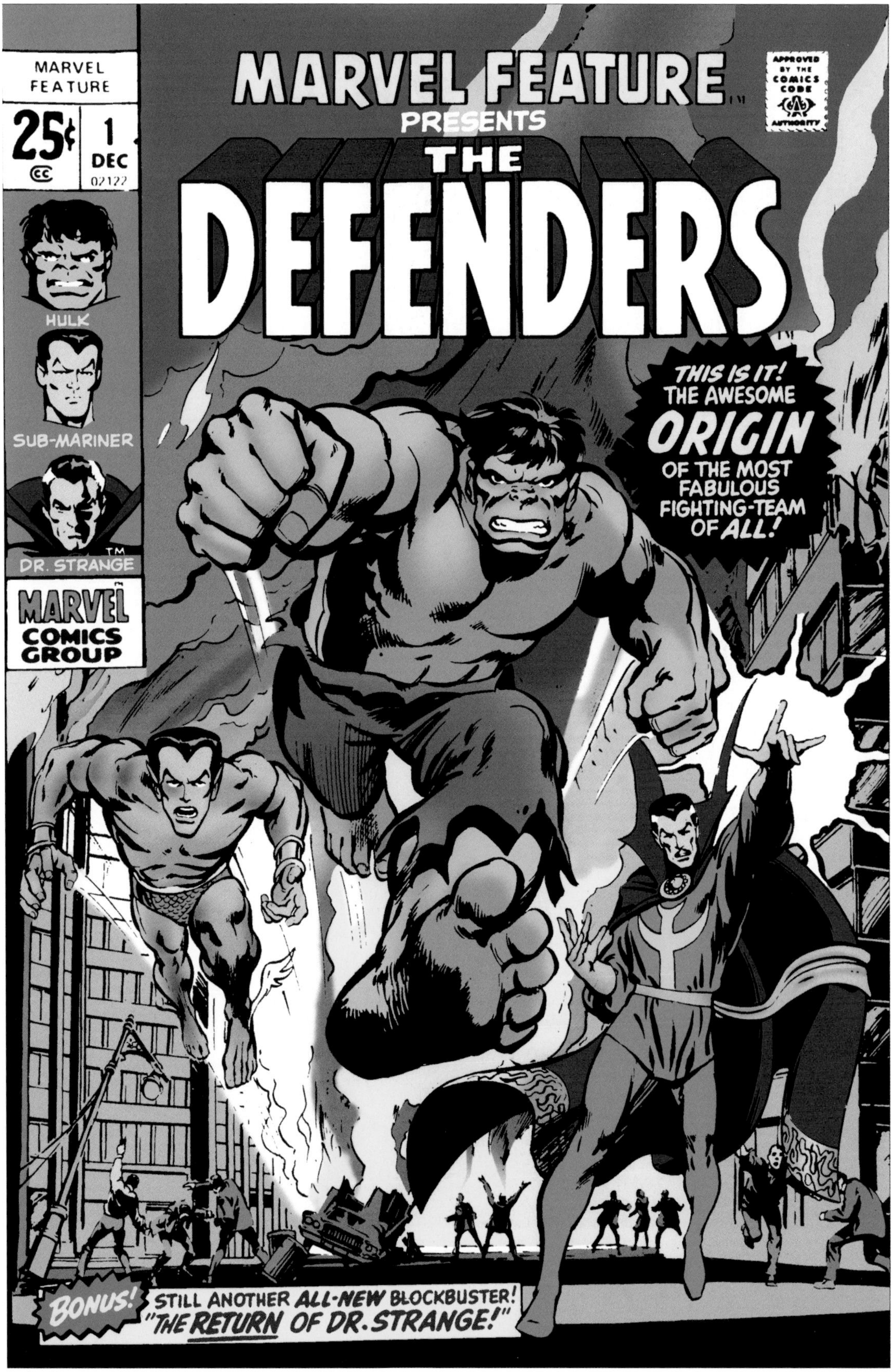
MARVEL FEATURE
25¢
1
DEC
02122
HULK
SUB-MARINER
DR. STRANGE
MARVEL COMICS GROUP
MARVEL FEATURE
PRESENTS
THE DEFENDERS
APPROVED BY THE COMICS CODE AUTHORITY
THIS IS IT! THE AWESOME ORIGIN OF THE MOST FABULOUS FIGHTING-TEAM OF ALL!
BONUS!
STILL ANOTHER ALL-NEW BLOCKBUSTER! "THE RETURN OF DR. STRANGE!"

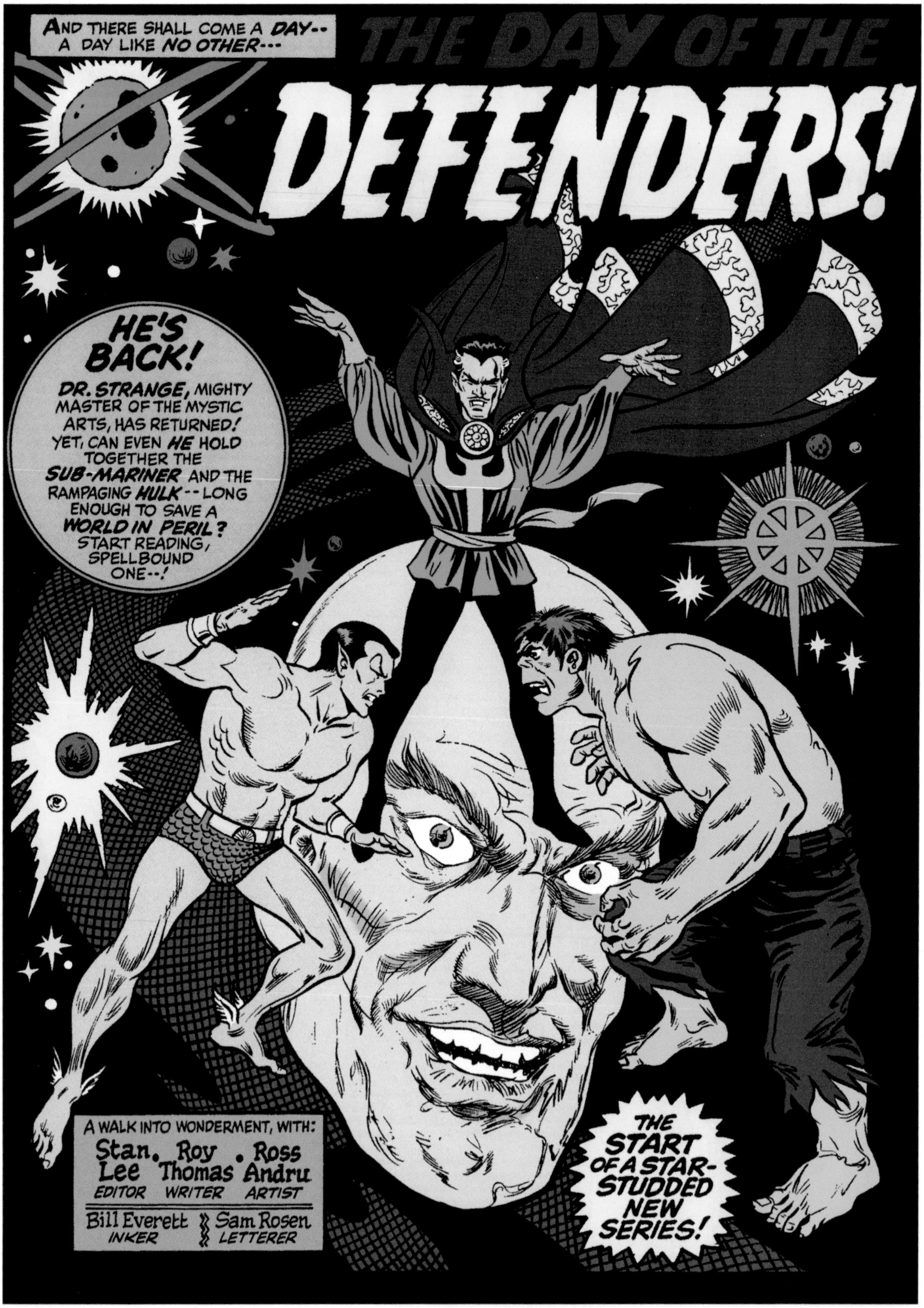

AND THERE SHALL COME A DAY-- A DAY LIKE NO OTHER---
THE DAY OF THE DEFENDERS!
HE'S BACK!
DR. STRANGE, MIGHTY MASTER OF THE MYSTIC ARTS, HAS RETURNED! YET, CAN EVEN HE HOLD TOGETHER THE SUB-MARINER AND THE RAMPAGING HULK--LONG ENOUGH TO SAVE A WORLD IN PERIL? START READING, SPELLBOUND ONE--!
A WALK INTO WONDERMENT, WITH:
Stan Lee EDITOR
Roy Thomas WRITER
Ross Andru ARTIST
Bill Everett INKER
Sam Rosen LETTERER
THE START OF A STAR-STUDDED NEW SERIES!

FOR LONG MONTHS IT STOOD *EMPTY*, THIS DARK-GABLED OLD HOUSE ON A SHADOWY BACK-STREET IN *GREENWICH VILLAGE*--WITH SPIDERS ITS SOLE TENANTS, SAD-WINGED BATS ITS ONLY VISITORS--

BUT NOW THERE IS *LIFE* AMID THE SHADOWS ONCE MORE. NOW THERE IS--

--DR. STRANGE, I HAVE BROUGHT YOU *TEA*, AS YOU ORDERED.

STILL, IT GROWS *LATE*, MASTER. THE CHURCH CLOCK STRIKES *MIDNIGHT*.

YES--THE *WITCHING HOUR*--AND YET--

DR. STRANGE... DR. STRANGE...

EH? WHY DID YOU CALL MY NAME *AGAIN*, WONG-- --WHEN YOU ARE RIGHT HERE *BESIDE* ME?

"AGAIN" MASTER? I DIDN'T! I MERELY--

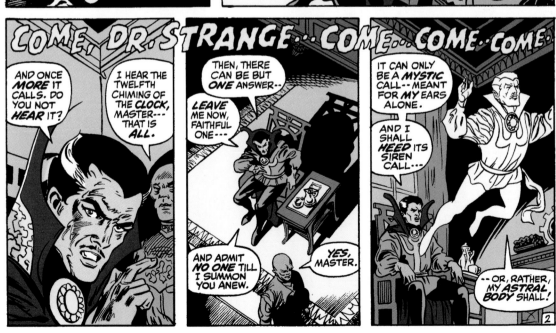

COME, DR. STRANGE... COME... COME... COME...

AND ONCE *MORE* IT CALLS. DO YOU NOT *HEAR* IT?

I HEAR THE TWELFTH CHIMING OF THE *CLOCK*, MASTER--- THAT IS *ALL*.

THEN, THERE CAN BE BUT *ONE* ANSWER--

LEAVE ME NOW, FAITHFUL ONE---

AND ADMIT *NO ONE* TILL I SUMMON YOU ANEW.

YES, MASTER.

IT CAN ONLY BE A *MYSTIC* CALL--MEANT FOR *MY* EARS ALONE.

AND I SHALL *HEED* ITS *SIREN* CALL...

--OR, RATHER, MY *ASTRAL BODY* SHALL!

2

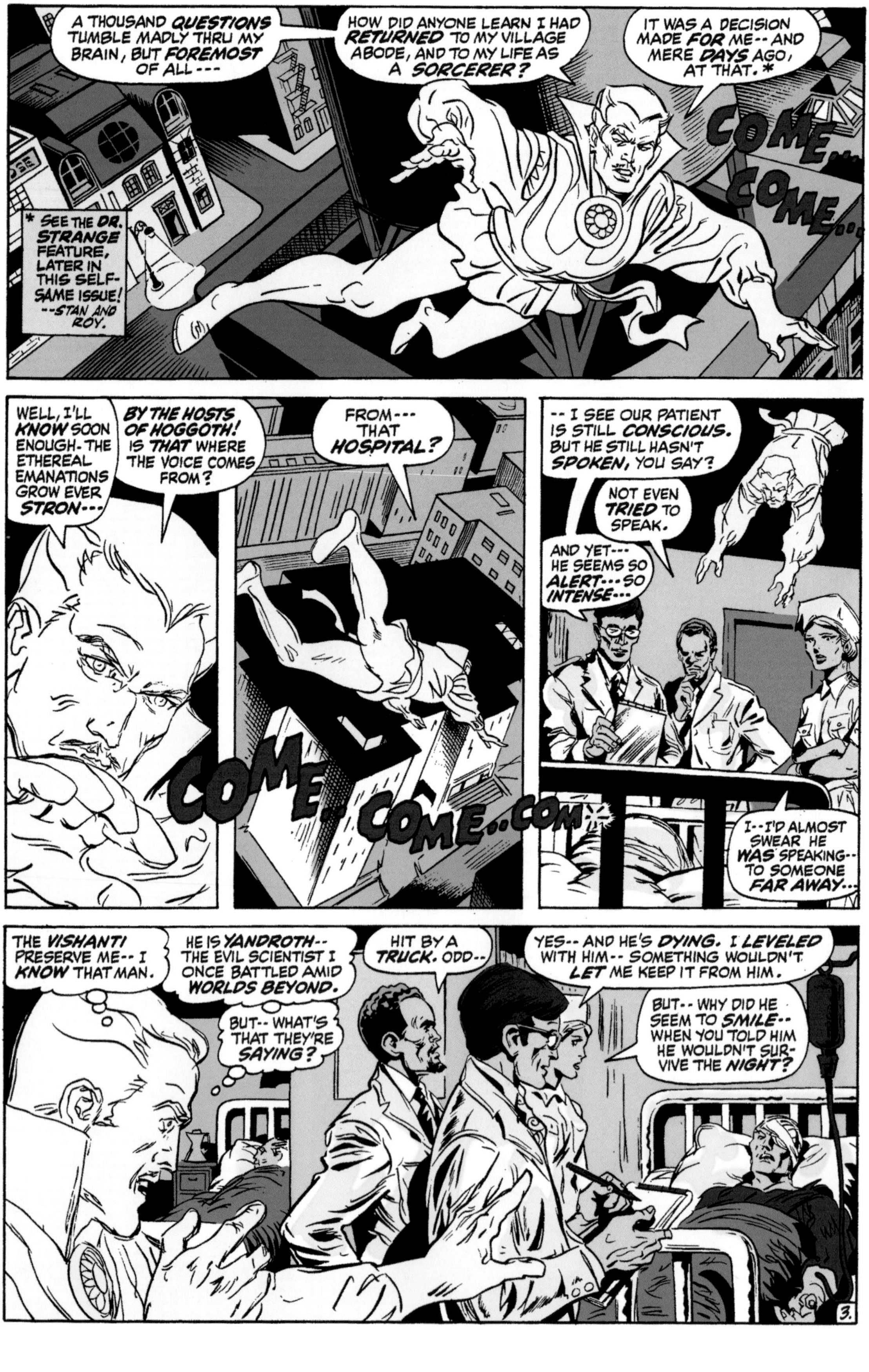
A THOUSAND QUESTIONS TUMBLE MADLY THRU MY BRAIN, BUT FOREMOST OF ALL---
HOW DID ANYONE LEARN I HAD RETURNED TO MY VILLAGE ABODE, AND TO MY LIFE AS A SORCERER?
IT WAS A DECISION MADE FOR ME-- AND MERE DAYS AGO, AT THAT. *
COME... COME...
* SEE THE DR. STRANGE FEATURE, LATER IN THIS SELF-SAME ISSUE! --STAN AND ROY.
WELL, I'LL KNOW SOON ENOUGH- THE ETHEREAL EMANATIONS GROW EVER STRON---
BY THE HOSTS OF HOGGOTH! IS THAT WHERE THE VOICE COMES FROM?
FROM--- THAT HOSPITAL?
COME..COME..COM
-- I SEE OUR PATIENT IS STILL CONSCIOUS. BUT HE STILL HASN'T SPOKEN, YOU SAY?
NOT EVEN TRIED TO SPEAK.
AND YET--- HE SEEMS SO ALERT--- SO INTENSE---
I--I'D ALMOST SWEAR HE WAS SPEAKING-- TO SOMEONE FAR AWAY...
THE VISHANTI PRESERVE ME-- I KNOW THAT MAN.
HE IS YANDROTH-- THE EVIL SCIENTIST I ONCE BATTLED AMID WORLDS BEYOND.
BUT-- WHAT'S THAT THEY'RE SAYING?
HIT BY A TRUCK. ODD--
YES-- AND HE'S DYING. I LEVELED WITH HIM-- SOMETHING WOULDN'T LET ME KEEP IT FROM HIM.
BUT-- WHY DID HE SEEM TO SMILE-- WHEN YOU TOLD HIM HE WOULDN'T SURVIVE THE NIGHT?
3.

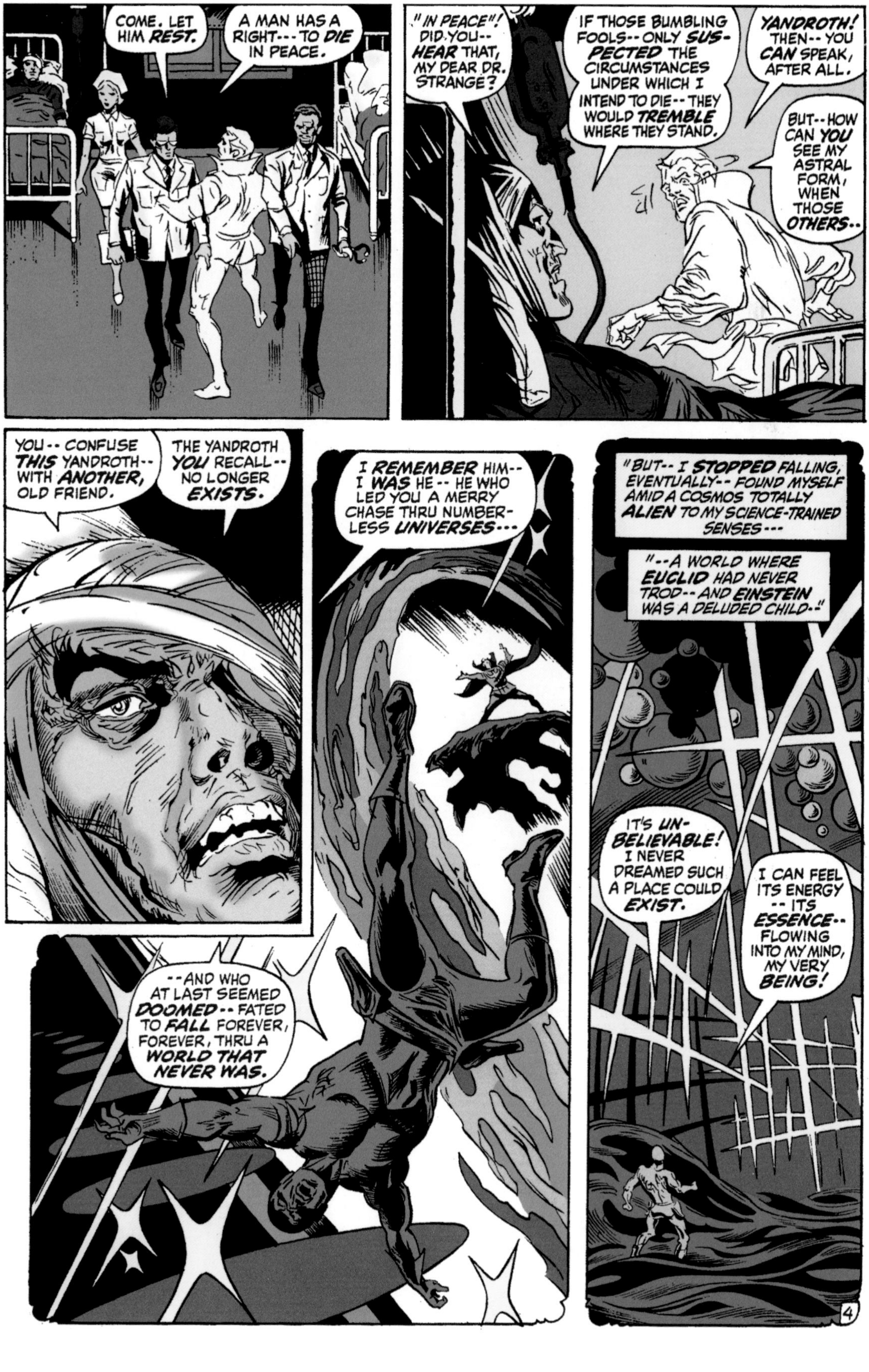
COME. LET HIM REST.
A MAN HAS A RIGHT--- TO DIE IN PEACE.
"IN PEACE"! DID YOU-- HEAR THAT, MY DEAR DR. STRANGE?
IF THOSE BUMBLING FOOLS-- ONLY SUSPECTED THE CIRCUMSTANCES UNDER WHICH I INTEND TO DIE-- THEY WOULD TREMBLE WHERE THEY STAND.
YANDROTH! THEN-- YOU CAN SPEAK, AFTER ALL.
BUT-- HOW CAN YOU SEE MY ASTRAL FORM, WHEN THOSE OTHERS..
YOU-- CONFUSE THIS YANDROTH-- WITH ANOTHER, OLD FRIEND.
THE YANDROTH YOU RECALL-- NO LONGER EXISTS.
I REMEMBER HIM-- I WAS HE-- HE WHO LED YOU A MERRY CHASE THRU NUMBERLESS UNIVERSES---
--AND WHO AT LAST SEEMED DOOMED-- FATED TO FALL FOREVER, FOREVER, THRU A WORLD THAT NEVER WAS.
"BUT-- I STOPPED FALLING, EVENTUALLY-- FOUND MYSELF AMID A COSMOS TOTALLY ALIEN TO MY SCIENCE-TRAINED SENSES---
"--A WORLD WHERE EUCLID HAD NEVER TROD-- AND EINSTEIN WAS A DELUDED CHILD--"
IT'S UNBELIEVABLE! I NEVER DREAMED SUCH A PLACE COULD EXIST.
I CAN FEEL ITS ENERGY -- ITS ESSENCE-- FLOWING INTO MY MIND, MY VERY BEING!
4

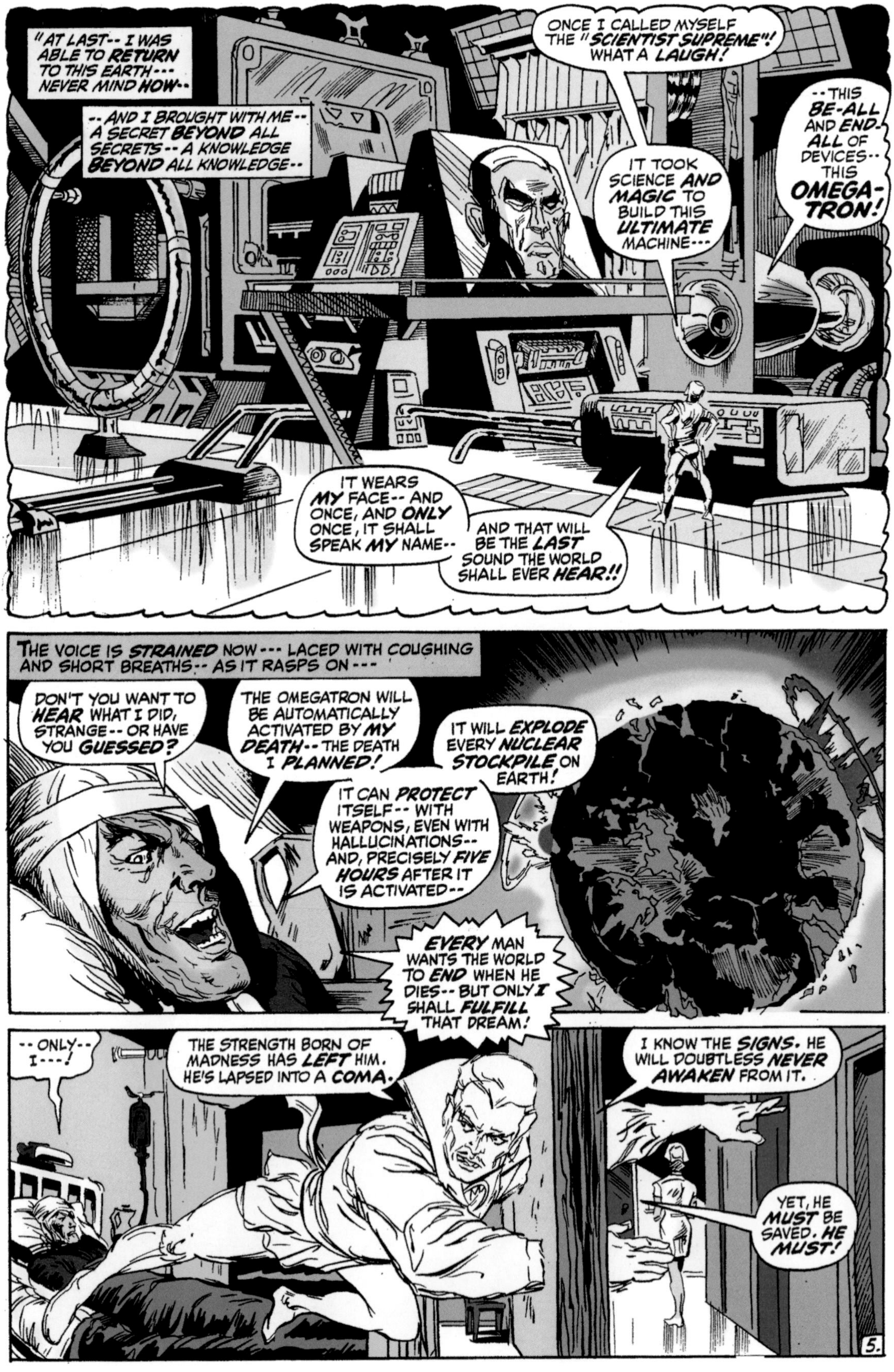
"AT LAST-- I WAS ABLE TO RETURN TO THIS EARTH--- NEVER MIND HOW--
--AND I BROUGHT WITH ME-- A SECRET BEYOND ALL SECRETS-- A KNOWLEDGE BEYOND ALL KNOWLEDGE--
ONCE I CALLED MYSELF THE "SCIENTIST SUPREME"! WHAT A LAUGH!
IT TOOK SCIENCE AND MAGIC TO BUILD THIS ULTIMATE MACHINE---
--THIS BE-ALL AND END-ALL OF DEVICES-- THIS OMEGA-TRON!
IT WEARS MY FACE-- AND ONCE, AND ONLY ONCE, IT SHALL SPEAK MY NAME--
AND THAT WILL BE THE LAST SOUND THE WORLD SHALL EVER HEAR!!
THE VOICE IS STRAINED NOW--- LACED WITH COUGHING AND SHORT BREATHS-- AS IT RASPS ON---
DON'T YOU WANT TO HEAR WHAT I DID, STRANGE-- OR HAVE YOU GUESSED?
THE OMEGATRON WILL BE AUTOMATICALLY ACTIVATED BY MY DEATH-- THE DEATH I PLANNED!
IT WILL EXPLODE EVERY NUCLEAR STOCKPILE ON EARTH!
IT CAN PROTECT ITSELF-- WITH WEAPONS, EVEN WITH HALLUCINATIONS-- AND, PRECISELY FIVE HOURS AFTER IT IS ACTIVATED--
EVERY MAN WANTS THE WORLD TO END WHEN HE DIES-- BUT ONLY I SHALL FULFILL THAT DREAM!
--ONLY-- I---!
THE STRENGTH BORN OF MADNESS HAS LEFT HIM. HE'S LAPSED INTO A COMA.
I KNOW THE SIGNS. HE WILL DOUBTLESS NEVER AWAKEN FROM IT.
YET, HE MUST BE SAVED. HE MUST!
5.

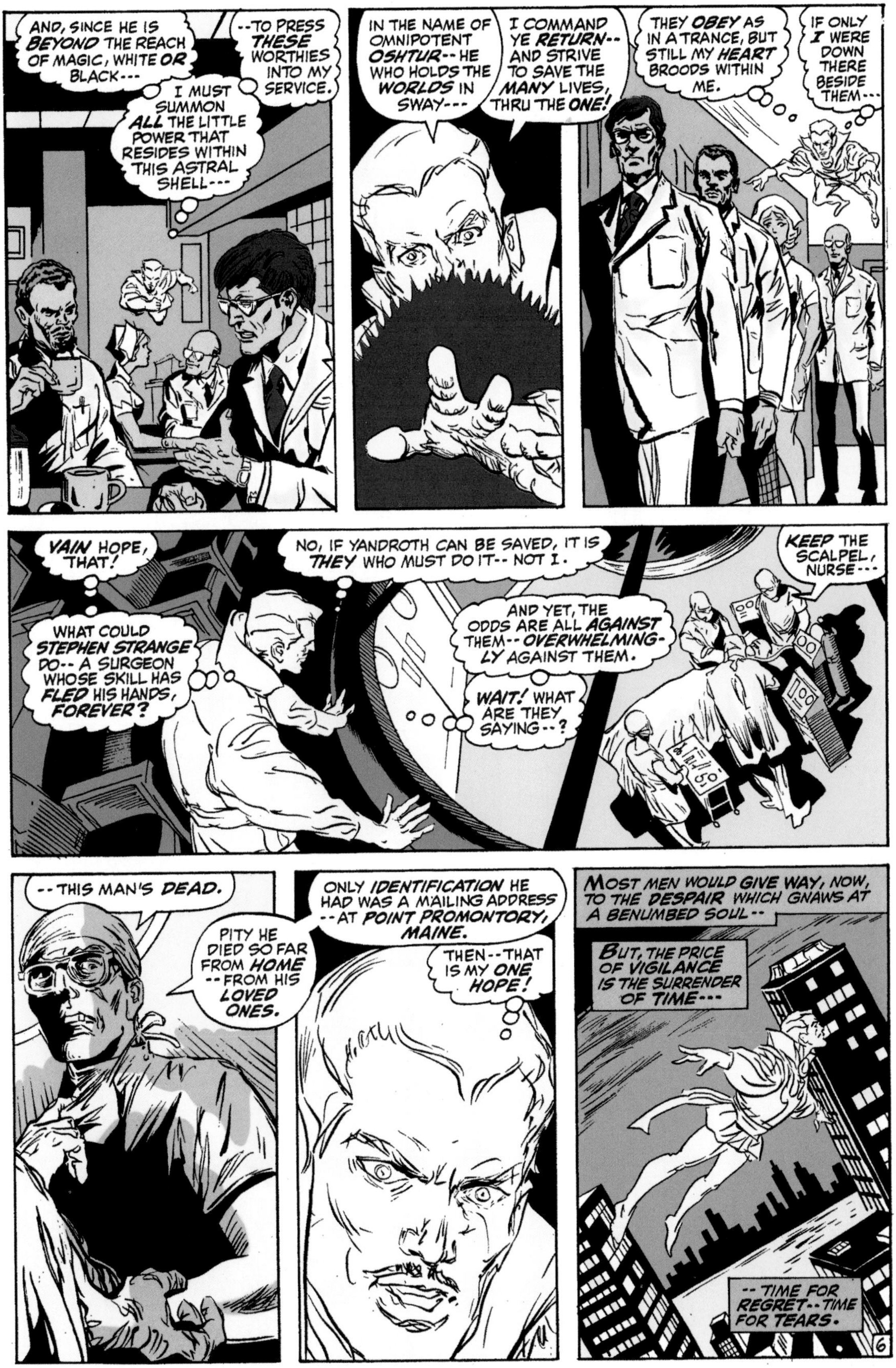
AND, SINCE HE IS BEYOND THE REACH OF MAGIC, WHITE OR BLACK---
--TO PRESS THESE WORTHIES INTO MY SERVICE.
I MUST SUMMON ALL THE LITTLE POWER THAT RESIDES WITHIN THIS ASTRAL SHELL---
IN THE NAME OF OMNIPOTENT OSHTUR--HE WHO HOLDS THE WORLDS IN SWAY---
I COMMAND YE RETURN--AND STRIVE TO SAVE THE MANY LIVES, THRU THE ONE!
THEY OBEY AS IN A TRANCE, BUT STILL MY HEART BROODS WITHIN ME.
IF ONLY I WERE DOWN THERE BESIDE THEM---
VAIN HOPE, THAT!
WHAT COULD STEPHEN STRANGE DO--A SURGEON WHOSE SKILL HAS FLED HIS HANDS, FOREVER?
NO, IF YANDROTH CAN BE SAVED, IT IS THEY WHO MUST DO IT--NOT I.
AND YET, THE ODDS ARE ALL AGAINST THEM--OVERWHELMINGLY AGAINST THEM.
WAIT! WHAT ARE THEY SAYING--?
KEEP THE SCALPEL, NURSE---
--THIS MAN'S DEAD.
PITY HE DIED SO FAR FROM HOME--FROM HIS LOVED ONES.
ONLY IDENTIFICATION HE HAD WAS A MAILING ADDRESS--AT POINT PROMONTORY, MAINE.
THEN--THAT IS MY ONE HOPE!
MOST MEN WOULD GIVE WAY, NOW, TO THE DESPAIR WHICH GNAWS AT A BENUMBED SOUL--
BUT, THE PRICE OF VIGILANCE IS THE SURRENDER OF TIME---
--TIME FOR REGRET--TIME FOR TEARS.
6

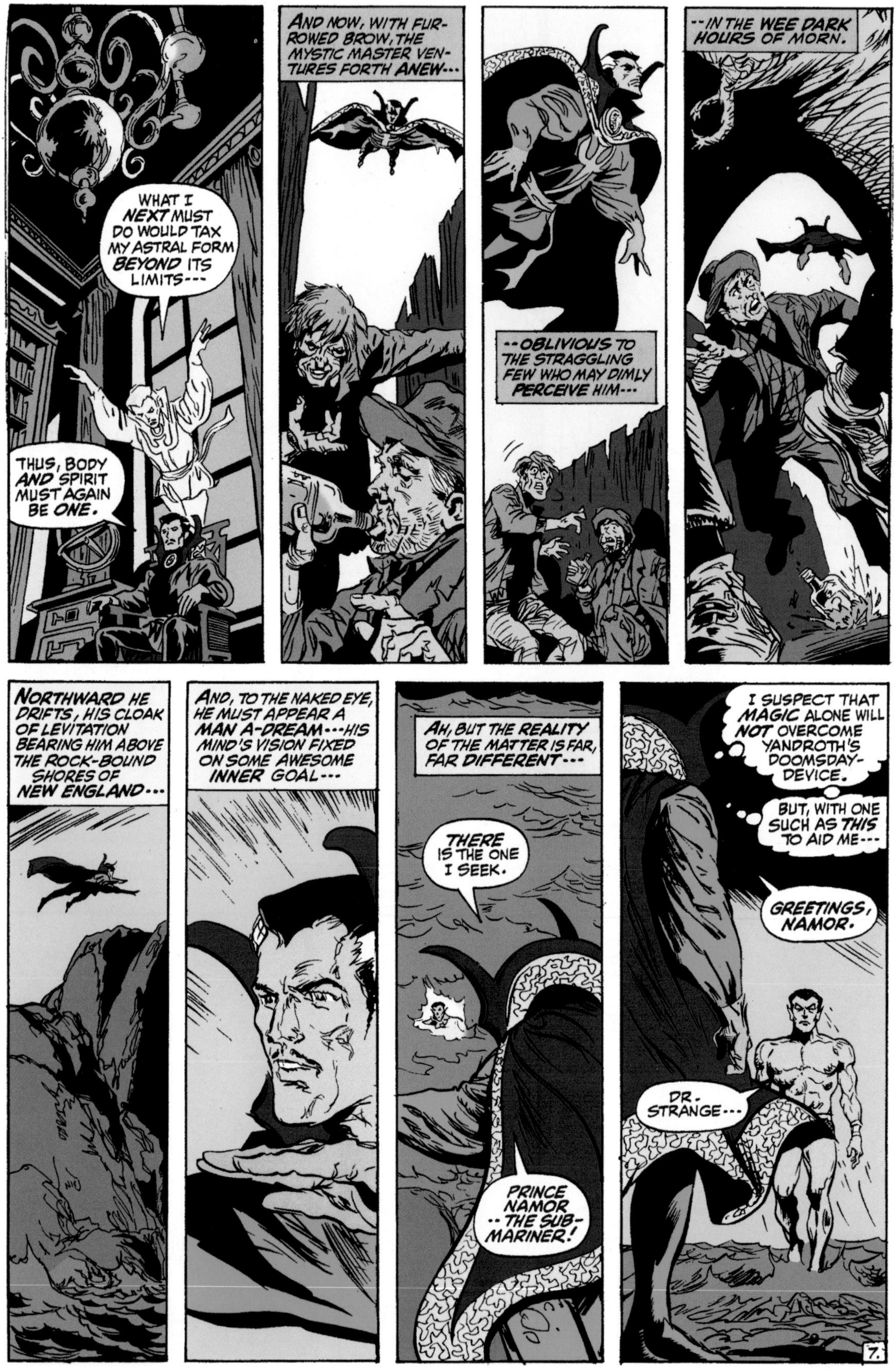
WHAT I NEXT MUST DO WOULD TAX MY ASTRAL FORM BEYOND ITS LIMITS---
THUS, BODY AND SPIRIT MUST AGAIN BE ONE.
AND NOW, WITH FUR-ROWED BROW, THE MYSTIC MASTER VEN-TURES FORTH ANEW---
--OBLIVIOUS TO THE STRAGGLING FEW WHO MAY DIMLY PERCEIVE HIM---
--IN THE WEE DARK HOURS OF MORN.
NORTHWARD HE DRIFTS, HIS CLOAK OF LEVITATION BEARING HIM ABOVE THE ROCK-BOUND SHORES OF NEW ENGLAND---
AND, TO THE NAKED EYE, HE MUST APPEAR A MAN A-DREAM---HIS MIND'S VISION FIXED ON SOME AWESOME INNER GOAL---
AH, BUT THE REALITY OF THE MATTER IS FAR, FAR DIFFERENT---
THERE IS THE ONE I SEEK.
PRINCE NAMOR --THE SUB-MARINER!
I SUSPECT THAT MAGIC ALONE WILL NOT OVERCOME YANDROTH'S DOOMSDAY-DEVICE.
BUT, WITH ONE SUCH AS THIS TO AID ME---
GREETINGS, NAMOR.
DR. STRANGE---
7.

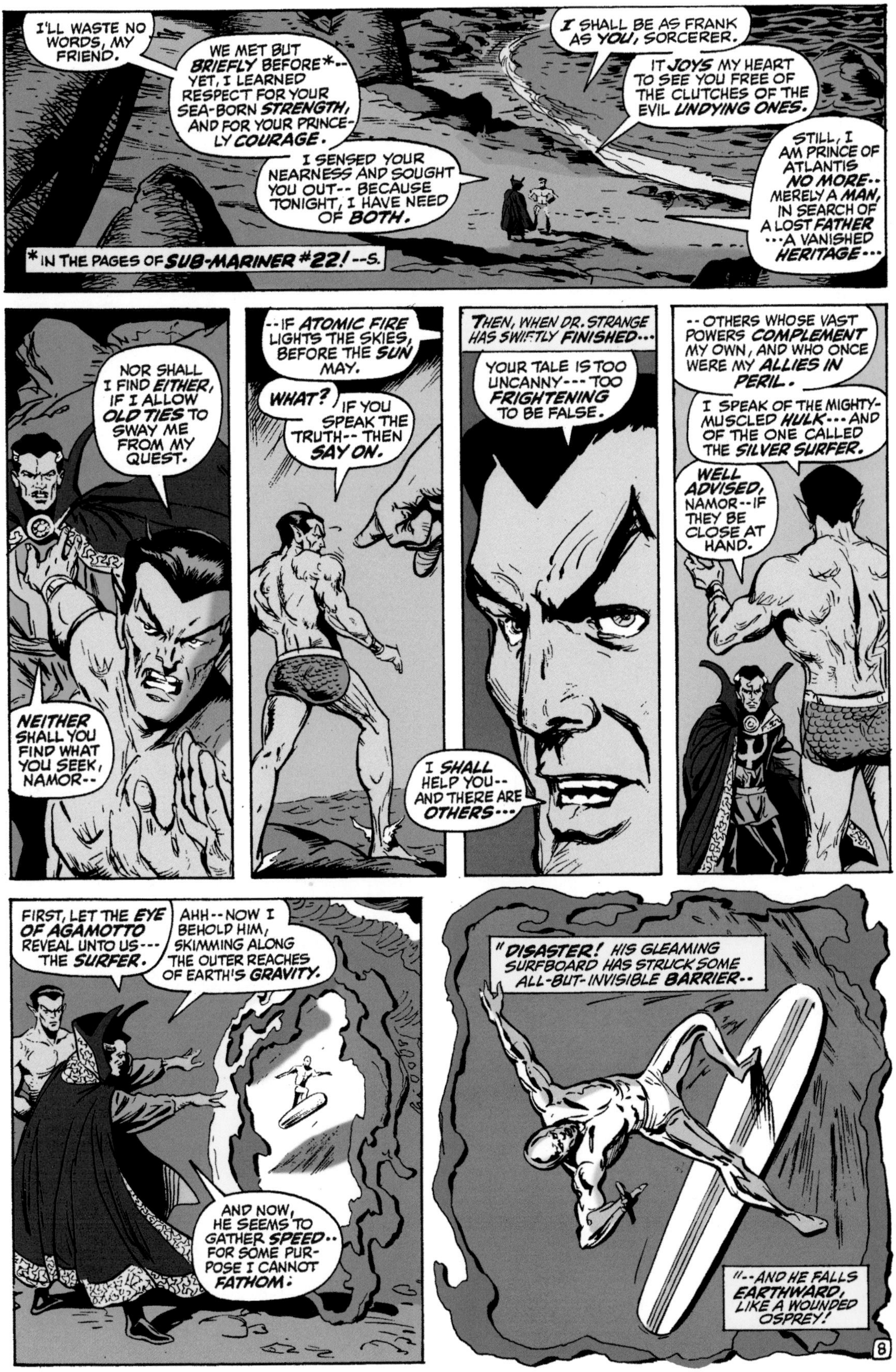
I'LL WASTE NO WORDS, MY FRIEND.
WE MET BUT BRIEFLY BEFORE*-- YET, I LEARNED RESPECT FOR YOUR SEA-BORN STRENGTH, AND FOR YOUR PRINCE-LY COURAGE.
I SENSED YOUR NEARNESS AND SOUGHT YOU OUT-- BECAUSE TONIGHT, I HAVE NEED OF BOTH.
I SHALL BE AS FRANK AS YOU, SORCERER.
IT JOYS MY HEART TO SEE YOU FREE OF THE CLUTCHES OF THE EVIL UNDYING ONES.
STILL, I AM PRINCE OF ATLANTIS NO MORE-- MERELY A MAN, IN SEARCH OF A LOST FATHER ---A VANISHED HERITAGE---
* IN THE PAGES OF SUB-MARINER #22! --S.
NOR SHALL I FIND EITHER, IF I ALLOW OLD TIES TO SWAY ME FROM MY QUEST.
NEITHER SHALL YOU FIND WHAT YOU SEEK, NAMOR--
--IF ATOMIC FIRE LIGHTS THE SKIES, BEFORE THE SUN MAY.
WHAT? IF YOU SPEAK THE TRUTH-- THEN SAY ON.
THEN, WHEN DR. STRANGE HAS SWIFTLY FINISHED---
YOUR TALE IS TOO UNCANNY--- TOO FRIGHTENING TO BE FALSE.
I SHALL HELP YOU-- AND THERE ARE OTHERS---
--OTHERS WHOSE VAST POWERS COMPLEMENT MY OWN, AND WHO ONCE WERE MY ALLIES IN PERIL.
I SPEAK OF THE MIGHTY-MUSCLED HULK--- AND OF THE ONE CALLED THE SILVER SURFER.
WELL ADVISED, NAMOR--IF THEY BE CLOSE AT HAND.
FIRST, LET THE EYE OF AGAMOTTO REVEAL UNTO US--- THE SURFER.
AHH--NOW I BEHOLD HIM, SKIMMING ALONG THE OUTER REACHES OF EARTH'S GRAVITY.
AND NOW, HE SEEMS TO GATHER SPEED-- FOR SOME PUR-POSE I CANNOT FATHOM:
"DISASTER! HIS GLEAMING SURFBOARD HAS STRUCK SOME ALL-BUT-INVISIBLE BARRIER--
"--AND HE FALLS EARTHWARD, LIKE A WOUNDED OSPREY!
8

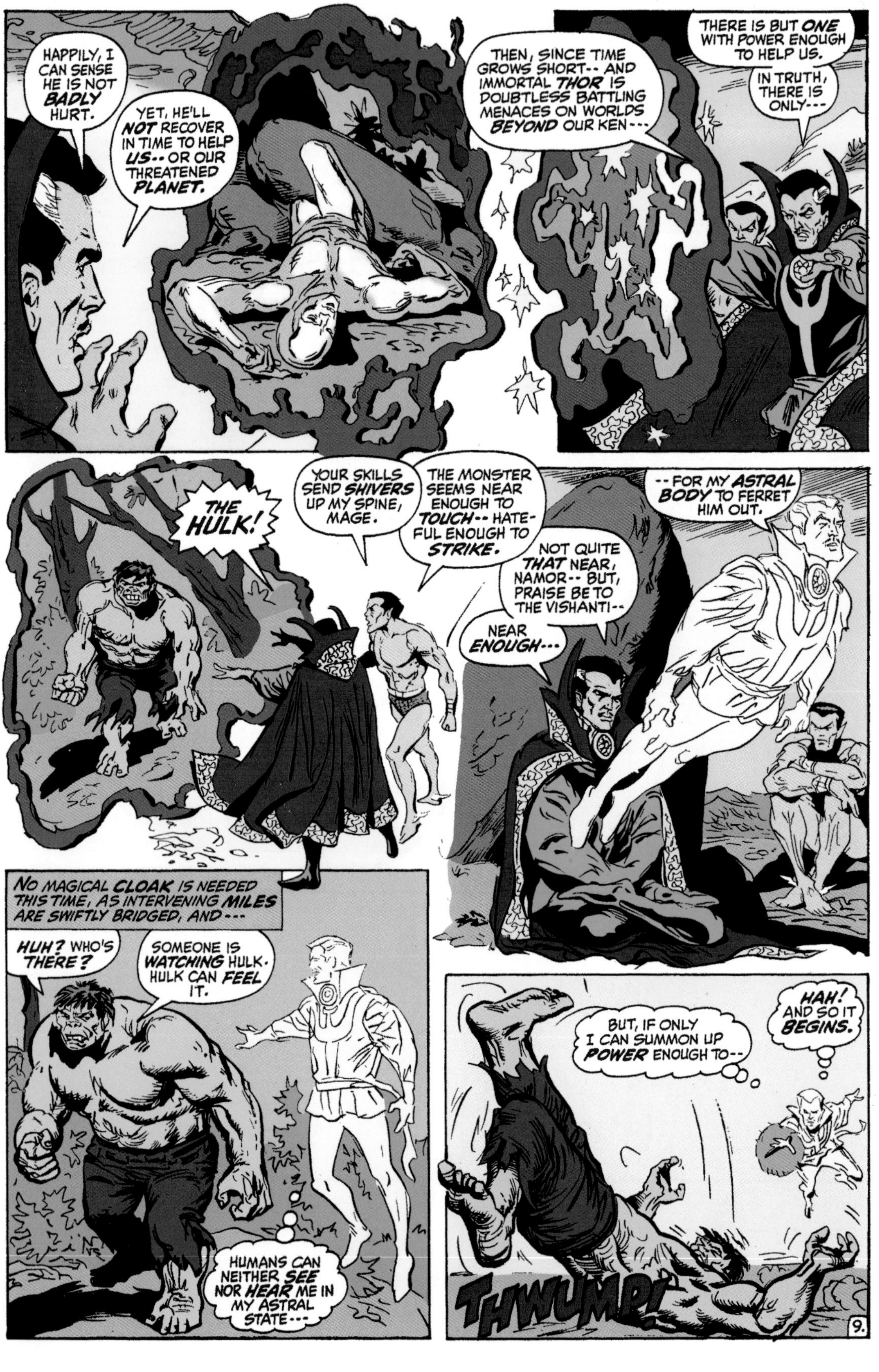
HAPPILY, I CAN SENSE HE IS NOT BADLY HURT.
YET, HE'LL NOT RECOVER IN TIME TO HELP US-- OR OUR THREATENED PLANET.
THEN, SINCE TIME GROWS SHORT-- AND IMMORTAL THOR IS DOUBTLESS BATTLING MENACES ON WORLDS BEYOND OUR KEN---
THERE IS BUT ONE WITH POWER ENOUGH TO HELP US.
IN TRUTH, THERE IS ONLY---
THE HULK!
YOUR SKILLS SEND SHIVERS UP MY SPINE, MAGE.
THE MONSTER SEEMS NEAR ENOUGH TO TOUCH-- HATEFUL ENOUGH TO STRIKE.
NOT QUITE THAT NEAR, NAMOR-- BUT, PRAISE BE TO THE VISHANTI--
NEAR ENOUGH---
--FOR MY ASTRAL BODY TO FERRET HIM OUT.
NO MAGICAL CLOAK IS NEEDED THIS TIME, AS INTERVENING MILES ARE SWIFTLY BRIDGED, AND---
HUH? WHO'S THERE?
SOMEONE IS WATCHING HULK. HULK CAN FEEL IT.
HUMANS CAN NEITHER SEE NOR HEAR ME IN MY ASTRAL STATE---
BUT, IF ONLY I CAN SUMMON UP POWER ENOUGH TO--
HAH! AND SO IT BEGINS.
THWUMP!
9.

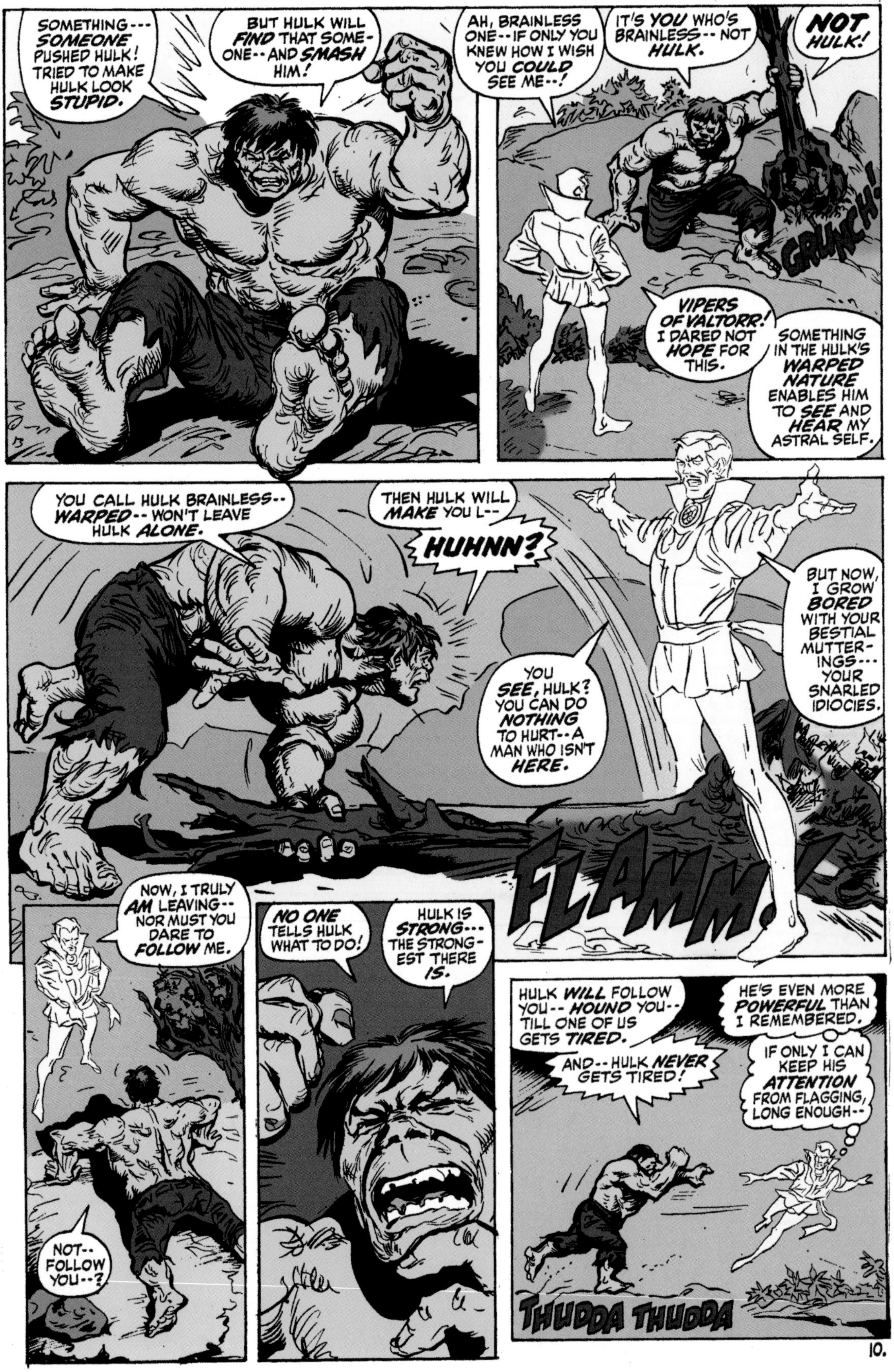
SOMETHING--- SOMEONE PUSHED HULK! TRIED TO MAKE HULK LOOK STUPID.
BUT HULK WILL FIND THAT SOMEONE--AND SMASH HIM!
AH, BRAINLESS ONE--IF ONLY YOU KNEW HOW I WISH YOU COULD SEE ME--!
IT'S YOU WHO'S BRAINLESS--NOT HULK.
NOT HULK!
CRUNCH!
VIPERS OF VALTORR! I DARED NOT HOPE FOR THIS.
SOMETHING IN THE HULK'S WARPED NATURE ENABLES HIM TO SEE AND HEAR MY ASTRAL SELF.
YOU CALL HULK BRAINLESS-- WARPED--WON'T LEAVE HULK ALONE.
THEN HULK WILL MAKE YOU L--
HUHNN?
YOU SEE, HULK? YOU CAN DO NOTHING TO HURT--A MAN WHO ISN'T HERE.
BUT NOW, I GROW BORED WITH YOUR BESTIAL MUTTERINGS---YOUR SNARLED IDIOCIES.
FLAMM!
NOW, I TRULY AM LEAVING-- NOR MUST YOU DARE TO FOLLOW ME.
NOT-- FOLLOW YOU--?
NO ONE TELLS HULK WHAT TO DO!
HULK IS STRONG--- THE STRONGEST THERE IS.
HULK WILL FOLLOW YOU--HOUND YOU-- TILL ONE OF US GETS TIRED.
AND--HULK NEVER GETS TIRED!
HE'S EVEN MORE POWERFUL THAN I REMEMBERED.
IF ONLY I CAN KEEP HIS ATTENTION FROM FLAGGING, LONG ENOUGH--
THUDDA THUDDA
10.

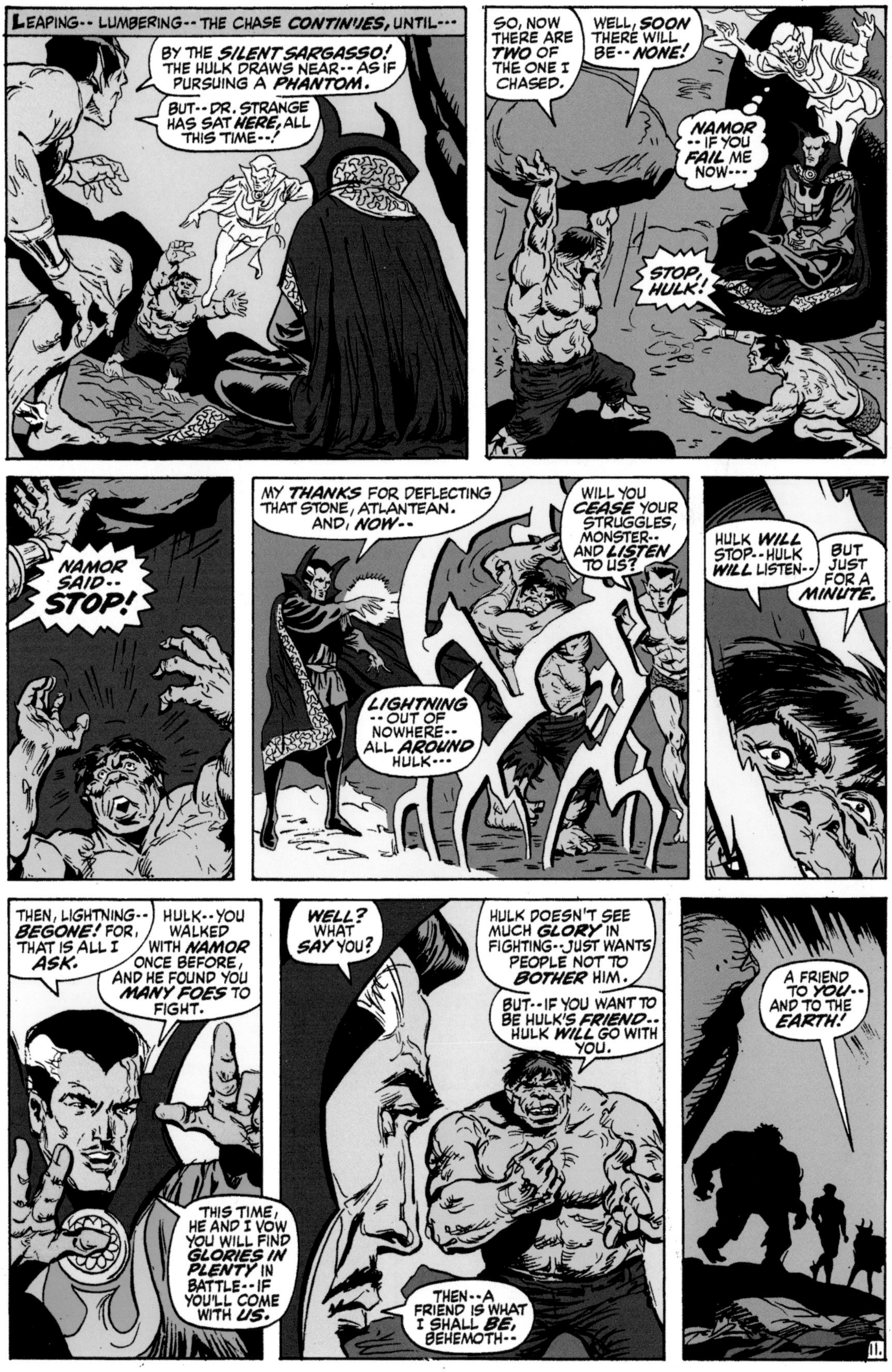
LEAPING-- LUMBERING-- THE CHASE CONTINUES, UNTIL---
BY THE SILENT SARGASSO! THE HULK DRAWS NEAR-- AS IF PURSUING A PHANTOM.
BUT-- DR. STRANGE HAS SAT HERE, ALL THIS TIME--!
SO, NOW THERE ARE TWO OF THE ONE I CHASED.
WELL, SOON THERE WILL BE-- NONE!
NAMOR -- IF YOU FAIL ME NOW---
STOP, HULK!
NAMOR SAID-- STOP!
MY THANKS FOR DEFLECTING THAT STONE, ATLANTEAN. AND, NOW--
WILL YOU CEASE YOUR STRUGGLES, MONSTER-- AND LISTEN TO US?
LIGHTNING -- OUT OF NOWHERE-- ALL AROUND HULK---
HULK WILL STOP-- HULK WILL LISTEN--
BUT JUST FOR A MINUTE.
THEN, LIGHTNING-- BEGONE! FOR, THAT IS ALL I ASK.
HULK-- YOU WALKED WITH NAMOR ONCE BEFORE, AND HE FOUND YOU MANY FOES TO FIGHT.
THIS TIME, HE AND I VOW YOU WILL FIND GLORIES IN PLENTY IN BATTLE-- IF YOU'LL COME WITH US.
WELL? WHAT SAY YOU?
HULK DOESN'T SEE MUCH GLORY IN FIGHTING-- JUST WANTS PEOPLE NOT TO BOTHER HIM.
BUT-- IF YOU WANT TO BE HULK'S FRIEND-- HULK WILL GO WITH YOU.
THEN-- A FRIEND IS WHAT I SHALL BE, BEHEMOTH--
A FRIEND TO YOU-- AND TO THE EARTH!
11.

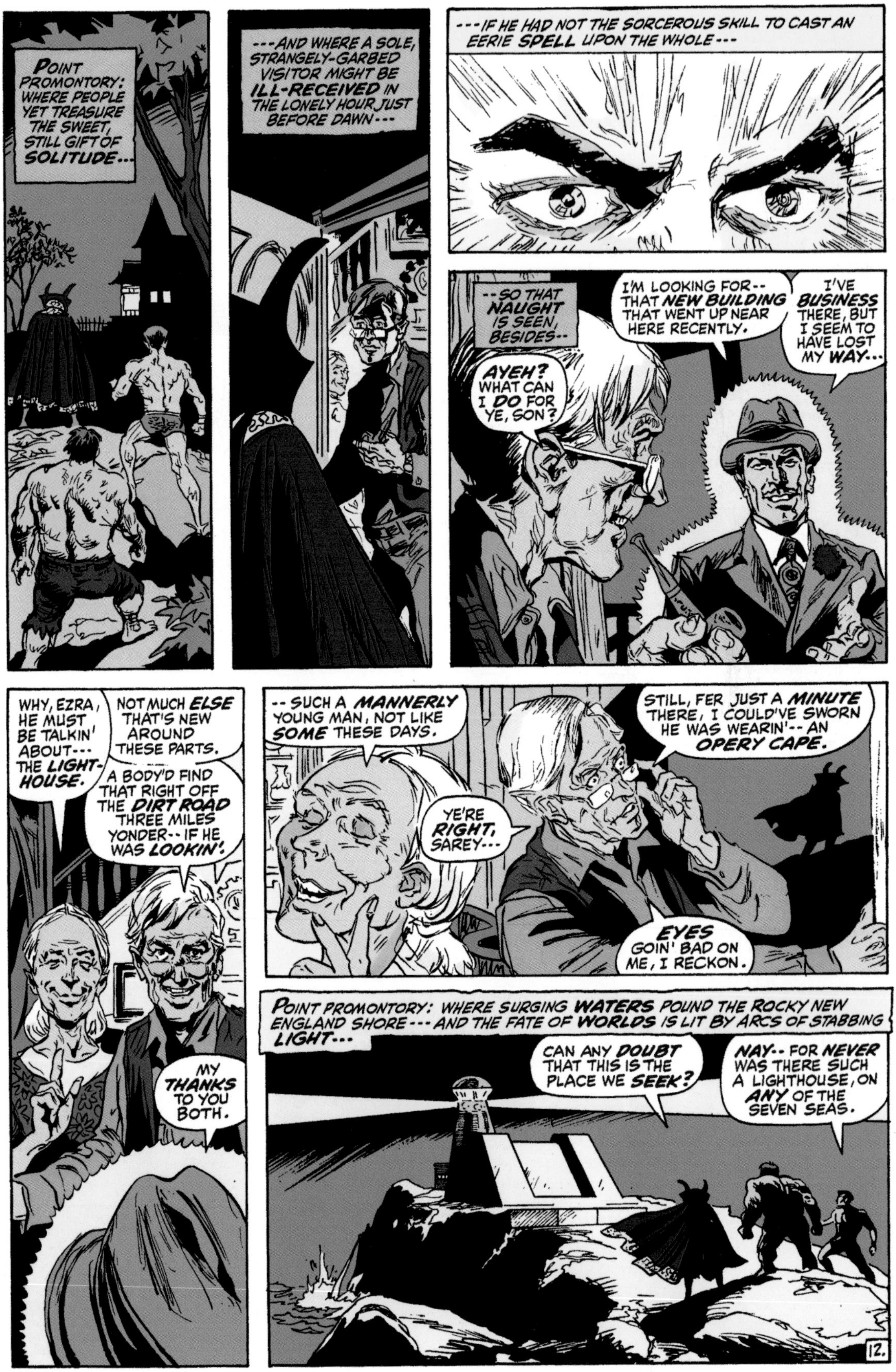
POINT PROMONTORY: WHERE PEOPLE YET TREASURE THE SWEET, STILL GIFT OF SOLITUDE...
---AND WHERE A SOLE, STRANGELY-GARBED VISITOR MIGHT BE ILL-RECEIVED IN THE LONELY HOUR JUST BEFORE DAWN---
---IF HE HAD NOT THE SORCEROUS SKILL TO CAST AN EERIE SPELL UPON THE WHOLE---
--SO THAT NAUGHT IS SEEN, BESIDES--
AYEH? WHAT CAN I DO FOR YE, SON?
I'M LOOKING FOR-- THAT NEW BUILDING THAT WENT UP NEAR HERE RECENTLY.
I'VE BUSINESS THERE, BUT I SEEM TO HAVE LOST MY WAY...
WHY, EZRA, HE MUST BE TALKIN' ABOUT--- THE LIGHT-HOUSE.
NOT MUCH ELSE THAT'S NEW AROUND THESE PARTS.
A BODY'D FIND THAT RIGHT OFF THE DIRT ROAD THREE MILES YONDER-- IF HE WAS LOOKIN'.
MY THANKS TO YOU BOTH.
-- SUCH A MANNERLY YOUNG MAN, NOT LIKE SOME THESE DAYS.
YE'RE RIGHT, SAREY---
STILL, FER JUST A MINUTE THERE, I COULD'VE SWORN HE WAS WEARIN'-- AN OPERY CAPE.
EYES GOIN' BAD ON ME, I RECKON.
POINT PROMONTORY: WHERE SURGING WATERS POUND THE ROCKY NEW ENGLAND SHORE--- AND THE FATE OF WORLDS IS LIT BY ARCS OF STABBING LIGHT...
CAN ANY DOUBT THAT THIS IS THE PLACE WE SEEK?
NAY-- FOR NEVER WAS THERE SUCH A LIGHTHOUSE, ON ANY OF THE SEVEN SEAS.
12.

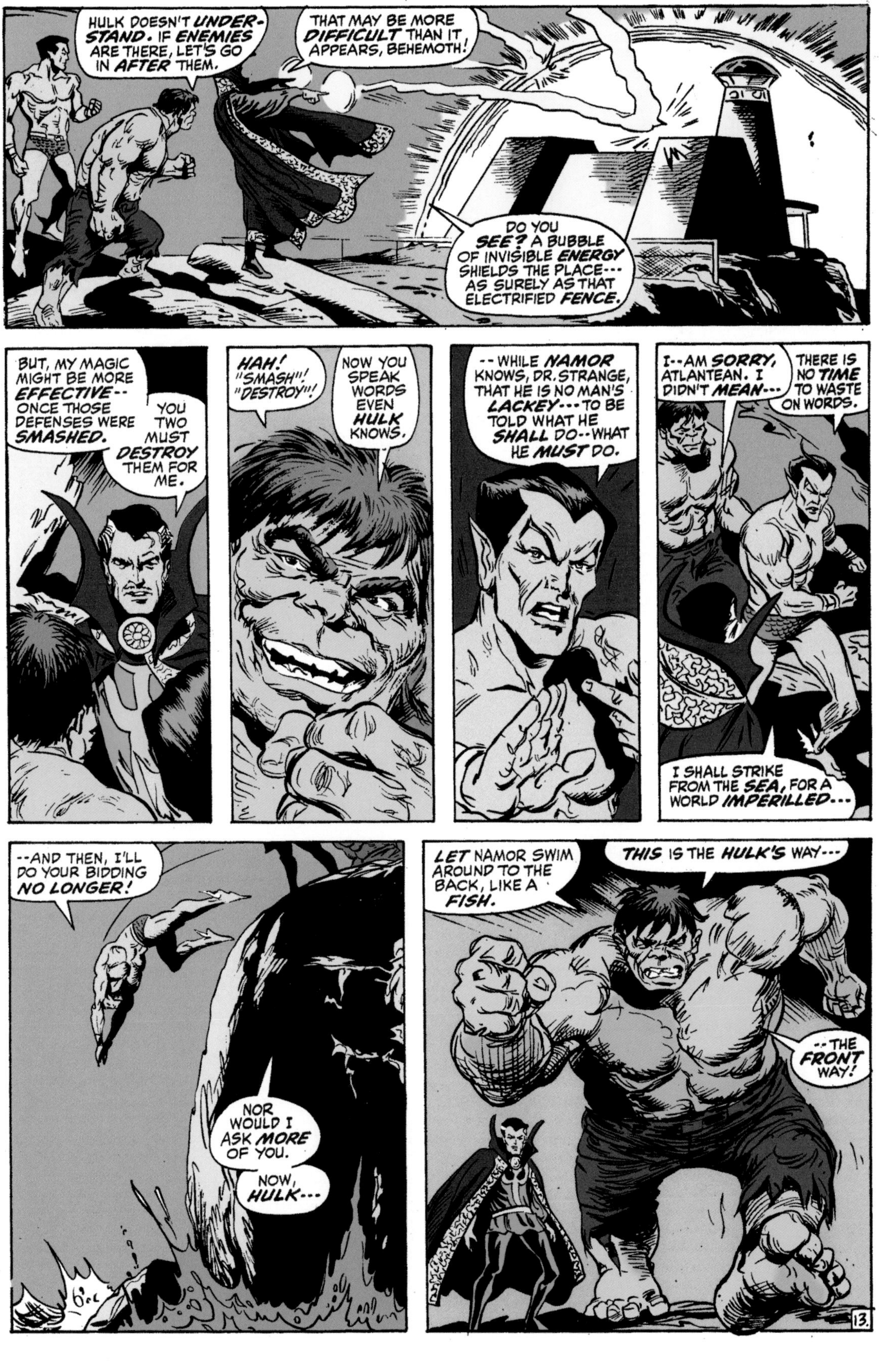
HULK DOESN'T UNDERSTAND. IF ENEMIES ARE THERE, LET'S GO IN AFTER THEM.
THAT MAY BE MORE DIFFICULT THAN IT APPEARS, BEHEMOTH!
DO YOU SEE? A BUBBLE OF INVISIBLE ENERGY SHIELDS THE PLACE--- AS SURELY AS THAT ELECTRIFIED FENCE.
BUT, MY MAGIC MIGHT BE MORE EFFECTIVE-- ONCE THOSE DEFENSES WERE SMASHED.
YOU TWO MUST DESTROY THEM FOR ME.
HAH! "SMASH"! "DESTROY"!
NOW YOU SPEAK WORDS EVEN HULK KNOWS.
--WHILE NAMOR KNOWS, DR. STRANGE, THAT HE IS NO MAN'S LACKEY--- TO BE TOLD WHAT HE SHALL DO--WHAT HE MUST DO.
I--AM SORRY, ATLANTEAN. I DIDN'T MEAN---
THERE IS NO TIME TO WASTE ON WORDS.
I SHALL STRIKE FROM THE SEA, FOR A WORLD IMPERILLED---
--AND THEN, I'LL DO YOUR BIDDING NO LONGER!
NOR WOULD I ASK MORE OF YOU.
NOW, HULK---
LET NAMOR SWIM AROUND TO THE BACK, LIKE A FISH.
THIS IS THE HULK'S WAY---
--THE FRONT WAY!
13.

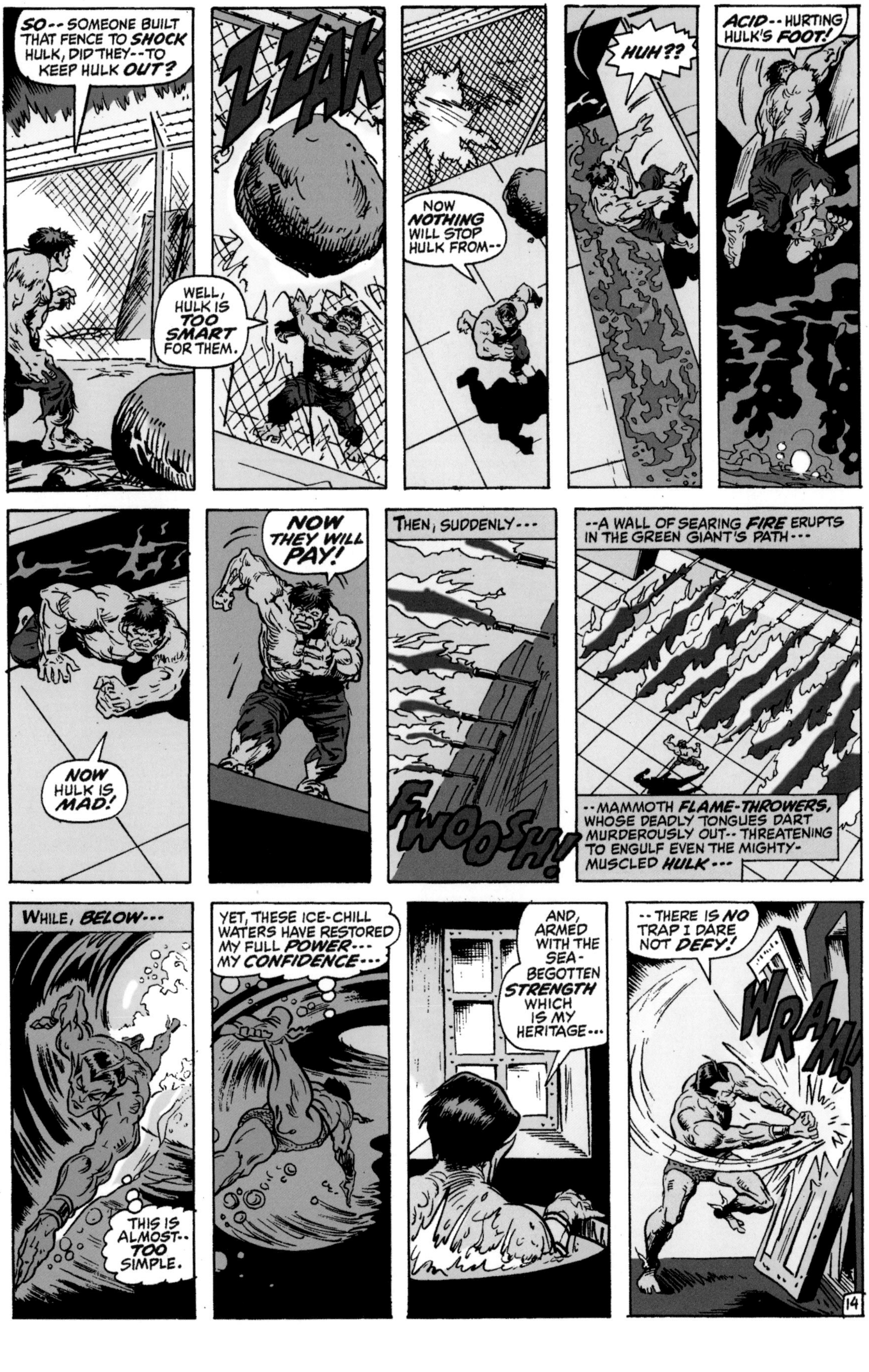

SO-- SOMEONE BUILT THAT FENCE TO SHOCK HULK, DID THEY--TO KEEP HULK OUT?
ZZAK
WELL, HULK IS TOO SMART FOR THEM.
NOW NOTHING WILL STOP HULK FROM--
HUH??
ACID-- HURTING HULK'S FOOT!
NOW HULK IS MAD!
NOW THEY WILL PAY!
THEN, SUDDENLY---
FWOOSH!
--A WALL OF SEARING FIRE ERUPTS IN THE GREEN GIANT'S PATH---
--MAMMOTH FLAME-THROWERS, WHOSE DEADLY TONGUES DART MURDEROUSLY OUT-- THREATENING TO ENGULF EVEN THE MIGHTY-MUSCLED HULK---
WHILE, BELOW---
THIS IS ALMOST-- TOO SIMPLE.
YET, THESE ICE-CHILL WATERS HAVE RESTORED MY FULL POWER--- MY CONFIDENCE---
AND, ARMED WITH THE SEA-BEGOTTEN STRENGTH WHICH IS MY HERITAGE---
--THERE IS NO TRAP I DARE NOT DEFY!
WRAM!
14

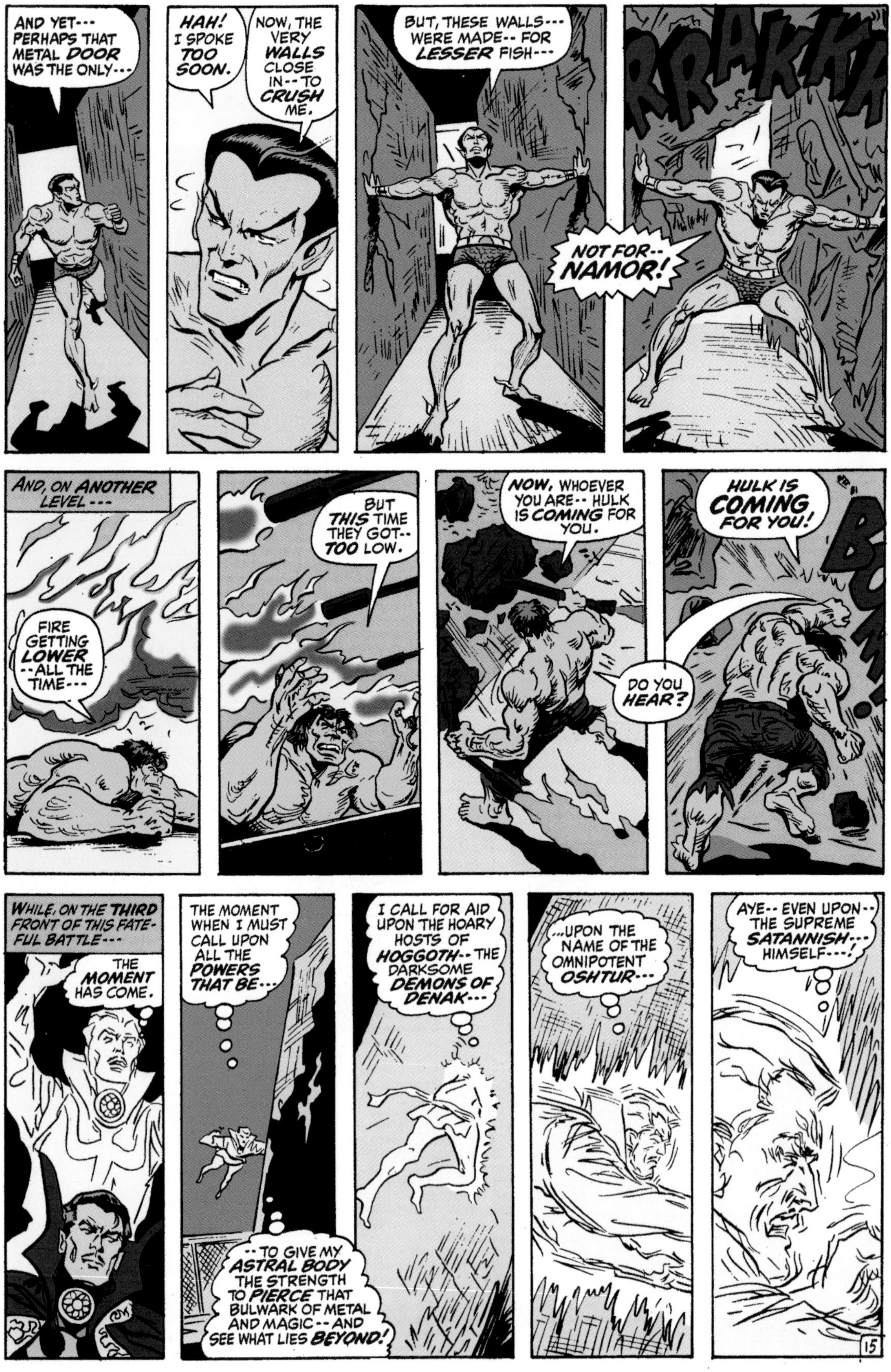
AND YET--- PERHAPS THAT METAL DOOR WAS THE ONLY---
HAH! I SPOKE TOO SOON.
NOW, THE VERY WALLS CLOSE IN--TO CRUSH ME.
BUT, THESE WALLS--- WERE MADE-- FOR LESSER FISH---
NOT FOR-- NAMOR!
RRAKKK
AND, ON ANOTHER LEVEL---
FIRE GETTING LOWER --ALL THE TIME---
BUT THIS TIME THEY GOT-- TOO LOW.
NOW, WHOEVER YOU ARE-- HULK IS COMING FOR YOU.
DO YOU HEAR?
HULK IS COMING FOR YOU!
WHILE, ON THE THIRD FRONT OF THIS FATEFUL BATTLE---
THE MOMENT HAS COME.
THE MOMENT WHEN I MUST CALL UPON ALL THE POWERS THAT BE---
--TO GIVE MY ASTRAL BODY THE STRENGTH TO PIERCE THAT BULWARK OF METAL AND MAGIC--AND SEE WHAT LIES BEYOND!
I CALL FOR AID UPON THE HOARY HOSTS OF HOGGOTH--THE DARKSOME DEMONS OF DENAK---
...UPON THE NAME OF THE OMNIPOTENT OSHTUR---
AYE-- EVEN UPON-- THE SUPREME SATANNISH--- HIMSELF---!
15

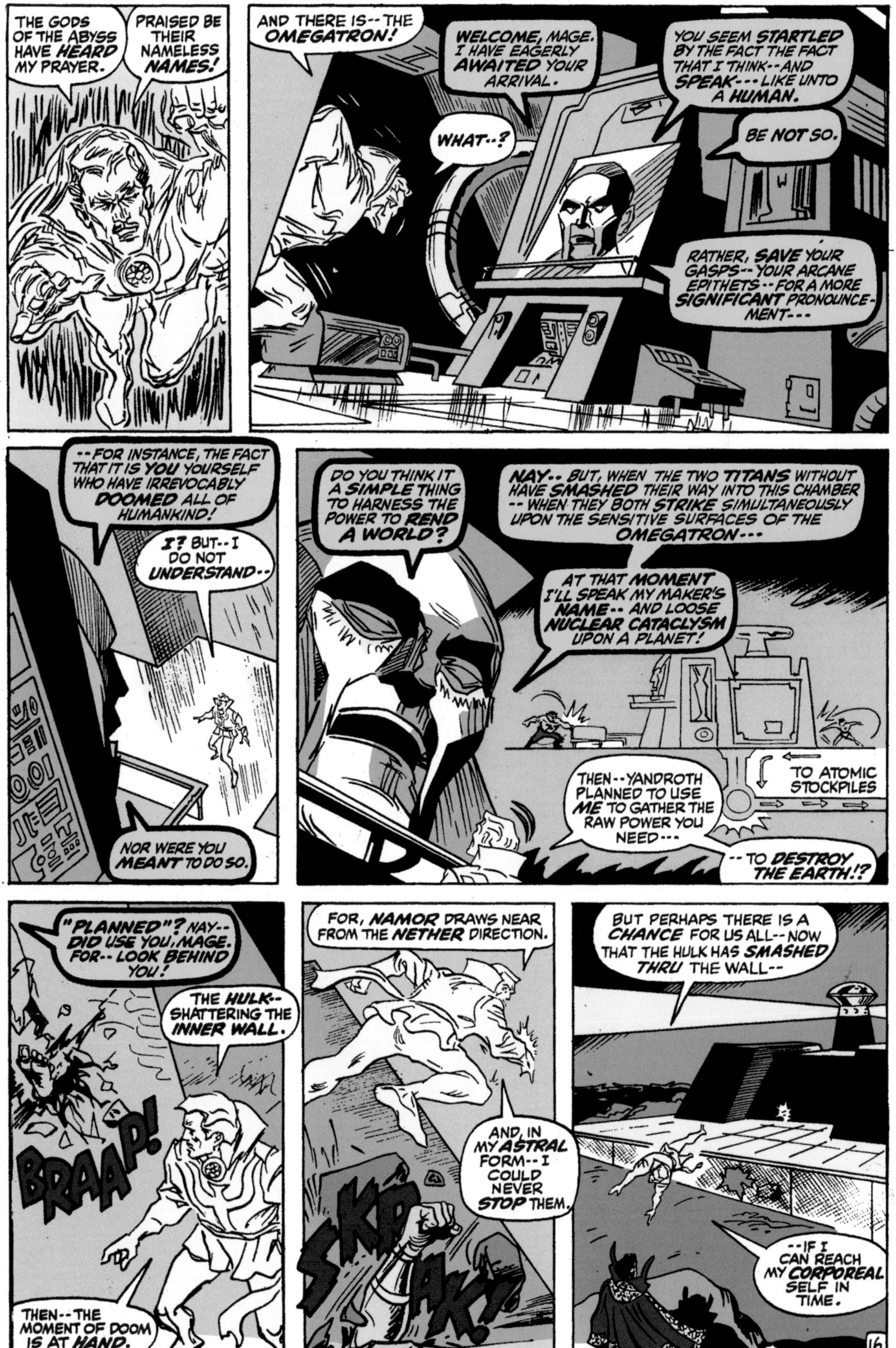
THE GODS OF THE ABYSS HAVE HEARD MY PRAYER.
PRAISED BE THEIR NAMELESS NAMES!
AND THERE IS-- THE OMEGATRON!
WELCOME, MAGE. I HAVE EAGERLY AWAITED YOUR ARRIVAL.
WHAT--?
YOU SEEM STARTLED BY THE FACT THE FACT THAT I THINK--AND SPEAK--- LIKE UNTO A HUMAN.
BE NOT SO.
RATHER, SAVE YOUR GASPS-- YOUR ARCANE EPITHETS-- FOR A MORE SIGNIFICANT PRONOUNCEMENT---
--FOR INSTANCE, THE FACT THAT IT IS YOU YOURSELF WHO HAVE IRREVOCABLY DOOMED ALL OF HUMANKIND!
I? BUT--I DO NOT UNDERSTAND--
NOR WERE YOU MEANT TO DO SO.
DO YOU THINK IT A SIMPLE THING TO HARNESS THE POWER TO REND A WORLD?
NAY-- BUT, WHEN THE TWO TITANS WITHOUT HAVE SMASHED THEIR WAY INTO THIS CHAMBER -- WHEN THEY BOTH STRIKE SIMULTANEOUSLY UPON THE SENSITIVE SURFACES OF THE OMEGATRON---
AT THAT MOMENT I'LL SPEAK MY MAKER'S NAME-- AND LOOSE NUCLEAR CATACLYSM UPON A PLANET!
TO ATOMIC STOCKPILES
THEN--YANDROTH PLANNED TO USE ME TO GATHER THE RAW POWER YOU NEED---
--TO DESTROY THE EARTH!?
"PLANNED"? NAY-- DID USE YOU, MAGE. FOR-- LOOK BEHIND YOU!
THE HULK-- SHATTERING THE INNER WALL.
BRAAP!
THEN--THE MOMENT OF DOOM IS AT HAND.
FOR, NAMOR DRAWS NEAR FROM THE NETHER DIRECTION.
AND, IN MY ASTRAL FORM--I COULD NEVER STOP THEM.
BUT PERHAPS THERE IS A CHANCE FOR US ALL--NOW THAT THE HULK HAS SMASHED THRU THE WALL--
--IF I CAN REACH MY CORPOREAL SELF IN TIME.
16

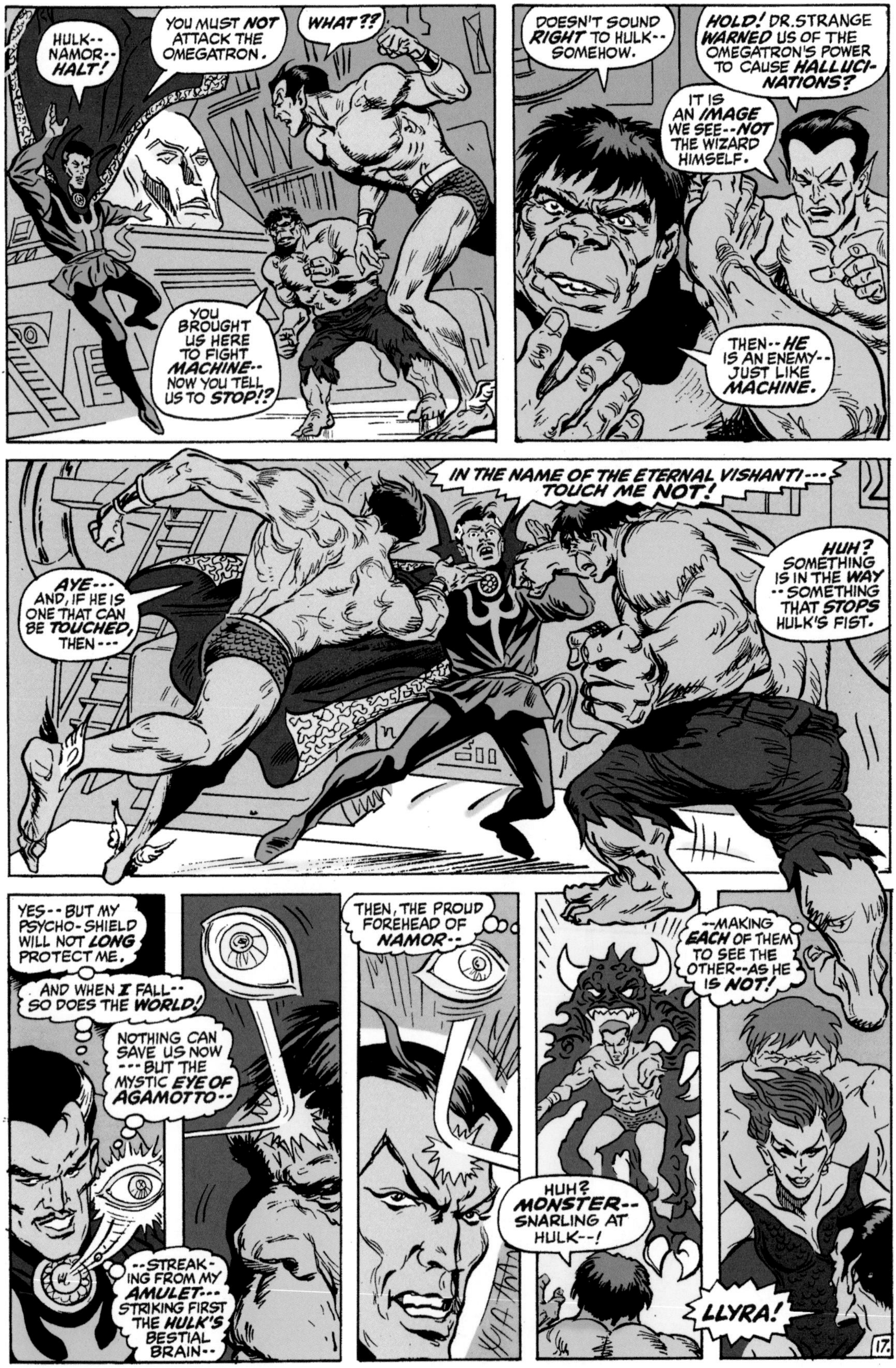
HULK-- NAMOR-- HALT!
YOU MUST NOT ATTACK THE OMEGATRON.
WHAT??
YOU BROUGHT US HERE TO FIGHT MACHINE-- NOW YOU TELL US TO STOP!?
DOESN'T SOUND RIGHT TO HULK-- SOMEHOW.
HOLD! DR.STRANGE WARNED US OF THE OMEGATRON'S POWER TO CAUSE HALLUCI-NATIONS?
IT IS AN IMAGE WE SEE--NOT THE WIZARD HIMSELF.
THEN--HE IS AN ENEMY-- JUST LIKE MACHINE.
IN THE NAME OF THE ETERNAL VISHANTI--- TOUCH ME NOT!
AYE--- AND, IF HE IS ONE THAT CAN BE TOUCHED, THEN---
HUH? SOMETHING IS IN THE WAY --SOMETHING THAT STOPS HULK'S FIST.
YES--BUT MY PSYCHO-SHIELD WILL NOT LONG PROTECT ME.
AND WHEN I FALL-- SO DOES THE WORLD!
NOTHING CAN SAVE US NOW ---BUT THE MYSTIC EYE OF AGAMOTTO--
--STREAK-ING FROM MY AMULET--- STRIKING FIRST THE HULK'S BESTIAL BRAIN--
THEN, THE PROUD FOREHEAD OF NAMOR--
--MAKING EACH OF THEM TO SEE THE OTHER--AS HE IS NOT!
HUH? MONSTER-- SNARLING AT HULK--!
LLYRA!
17.

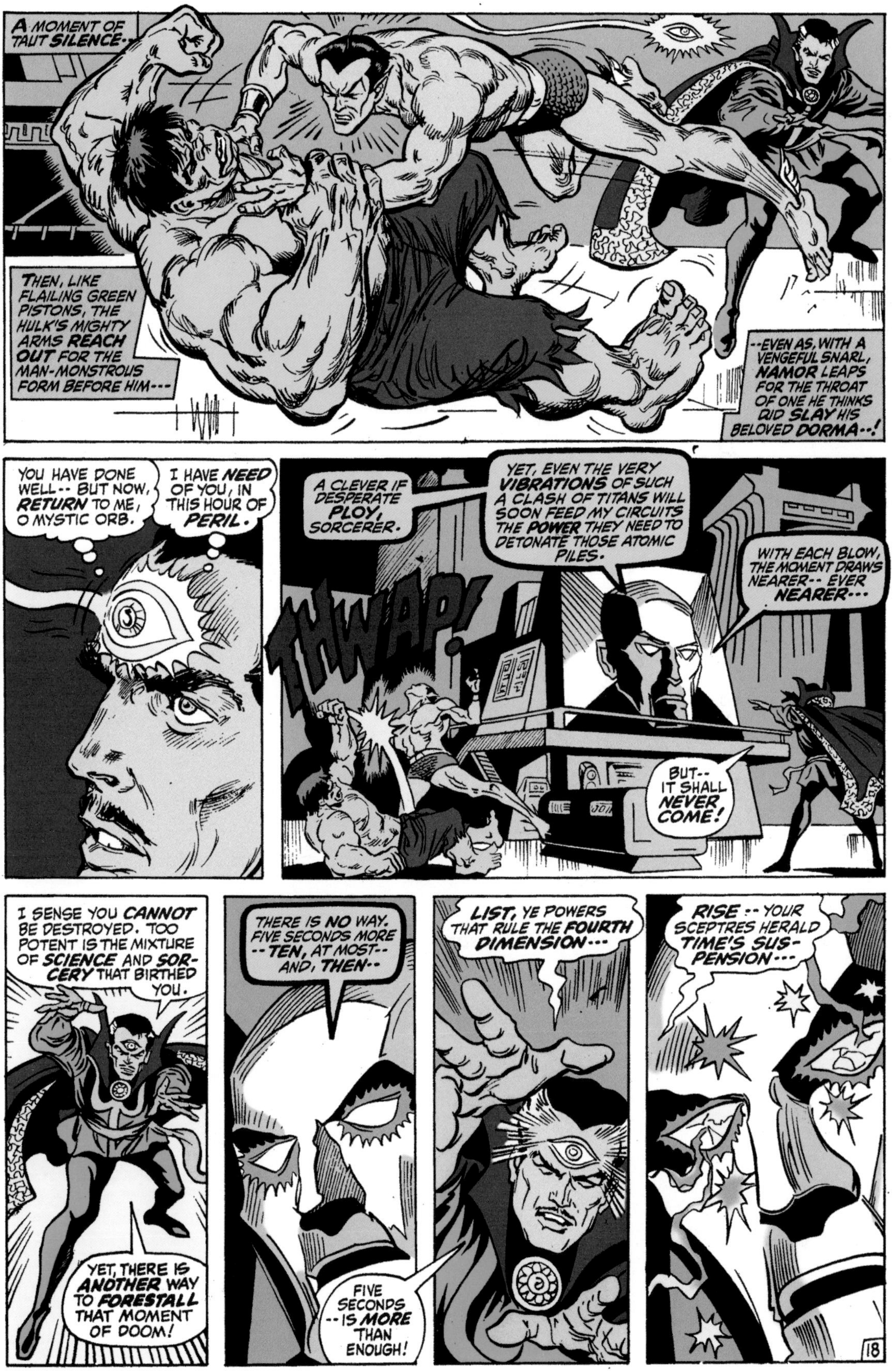
A MOMENT OF TAUT SILENCE--
THEN, LIKE FLAILING GREEN PISTONS, THE HULK'S MIGHTY ARMS REACH OUT FOR THE MAN-MONSTROUS FORM BEFORE HIM---
--EVEN AS, WITH A VENGEFUL SNARL, NAMOR LEAPS FOR THE THROAT OF ONE HE THINKS DID SLAY HIS BELOVED DORMA--!
YOU HAVE DONE WELL-- BUT NOW, RETURN TO ME, O MYSTIC ORB.
I HAVE NEED OF YOU, IN THIS HOUR OF PERIL.
A CLEVER IF DESPERATE PLOY, SORCERER.
YET, EVEN THE VERY VIBRATIONS OF SUCH A CLASH OF TITANS WILL SOON FEED MY CIRCUITS THE POWER THEY NEED TO DETONATE THOSE ATOMIC PILES.
WITH EACH BLOW, THE MOMENT DRAWS NEARER-- EVER NEARER---
THWAP!
BUT-- IT SHALL NEVER COME!
I SENSE YOU CANNOT BE DESTROYED. TOO POTENT IS THE MIXTURE OF SCIENCE AND SORCERY THAT BIRTHED YOU.
YET, THERE IS ANOTHER WAY TO FORESTALL THAT MOMENT OF DOOM!
THERE IS NO WAY. FIVE SECONDS MORE --TEN, AT MOST-- AND, THEN--
FIVE SECONDS --IS MORE THAN ENOUGH!
LIST, YE POWERS THAT RULE THE FOURTH DIMENSION---
RISE -- YOUR SCEPTRES HERALD TIME'S SUSPENSION---
18

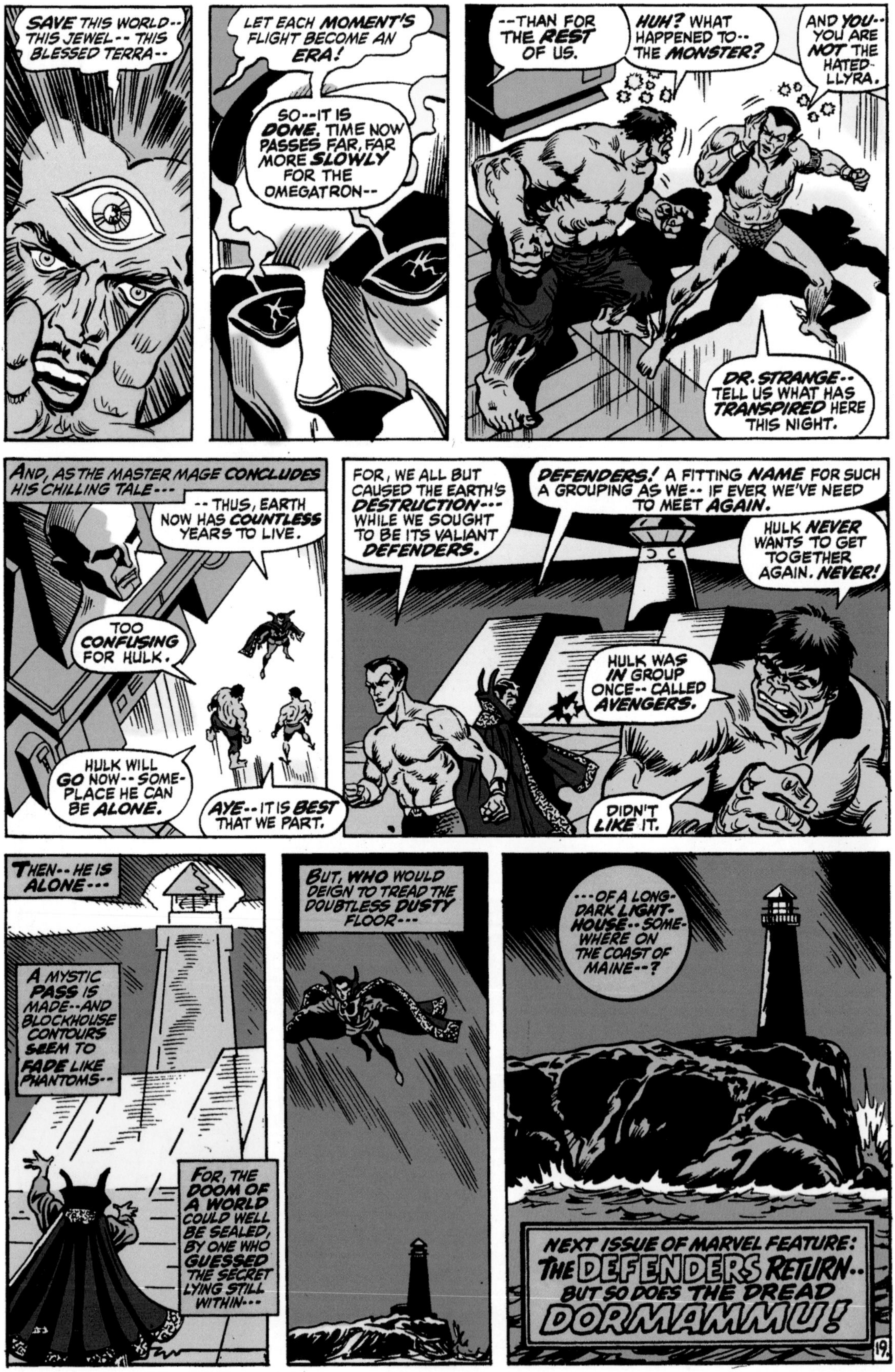
SAVE THIS WORLD-- THIS JEWEL-- THIS BLESSED TERRA--
LET EACH MOMENT'S FLIGHT BECOME AN ERA!
SO--IT IS DONE. TIME NOW PASSES FAR, FAR MORE SLOWLY FOR THE OMEGATRON--
--THAN FOR THE REST OF US.
HUH? WHAT HAPPENED TO-- THE MONSTER?
AND YOU-- YOU ARE NOT THE HATED-LLYRA.
DR. STRANGE-- TELL US WHAT HAS TRANSPIRED HERE THIS NIGHT.
AND, AS THE MASTER MAGE CONCLUDES HIS CHILLING TALE---
-- THUS, EARTH NOW HAS COUNTLESS YEARS TO LIVE.
TOO CONFUSING FOR HULK.
HULK WILL GO NOW-- SOME-PLACE HE CAN BE ALONE.
AYE-- IT IS BEST THAT WE PART.
FOR, WE ALL BUT CAUSED THE EARTH'S DESTRUCTION--- WHILE WE SOUGHT TO BE ITS VALIANT DEFENDERS.
DEFENDERS! A FITTING NAME FOR SUCH A GROUPING AS WE-- IF EVER WE'VE NEED TO MEET AGAIN.
HULK NEVER WANTS TO GET TOGETHER AGAIN. NEVER!
HULK WAS IN GROUP ONCE-- CALLED AVENGERS.
DIDN'T LIKE IT.
THEN-- HE IS ALONE---
A MYSTIC PASS IS MADE--AND BLOCKHOUSE CONTOURS SEEM TO FADE LIKE PHANTOMS--
FOR, THE DOOM OF A WORLD COULD WELL BE SEALED, BY ONE WHO GUESSED THE SECRET LYING STILL WITHIN---
BUT, WHO WOULD DEIGN TO TREAD THE DOUBTLESS DUSTY FLOOR---
---OF A LONG-DARK LIGHT-HOUSE-- SOME-WHERE ON THE COAST OF MAINE--?
NEXT ISSUE OF MARVEL FEATURE: THE DEFENDERS RETURN.. BUT SO DOES THE DREAD DORMAMMU!
19.

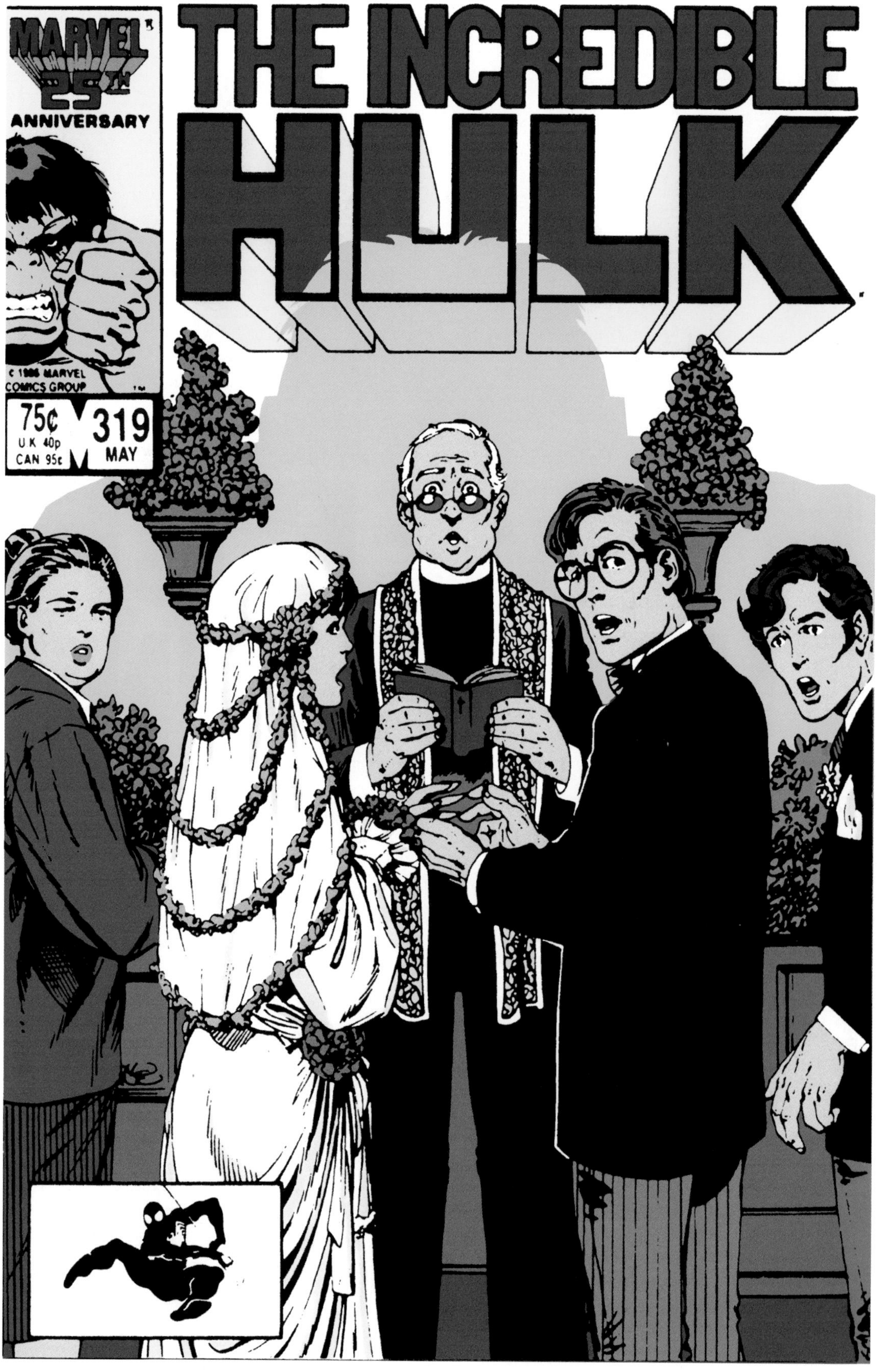
MARVEL 25TH ANNIVERSARY
THE INCREDIBLE HULK
© 1986 MARVEL COMICS GROUP
75¢ UK 40p CAN 95¢
319
MAY

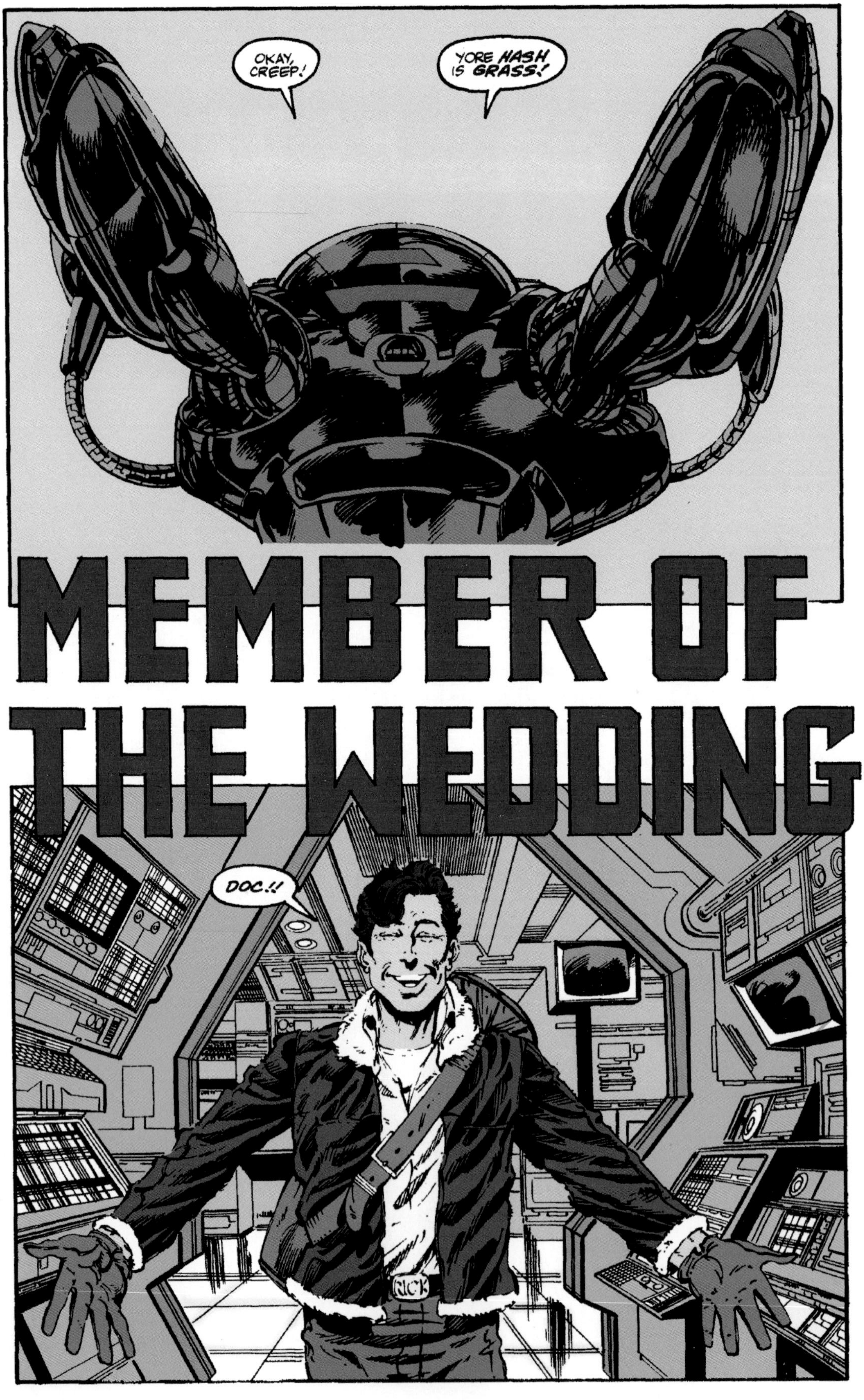
OKAY, CREEP!
YORE NASH IS GRASS!
MEMBER OF THE WEDDING
DOC.!!

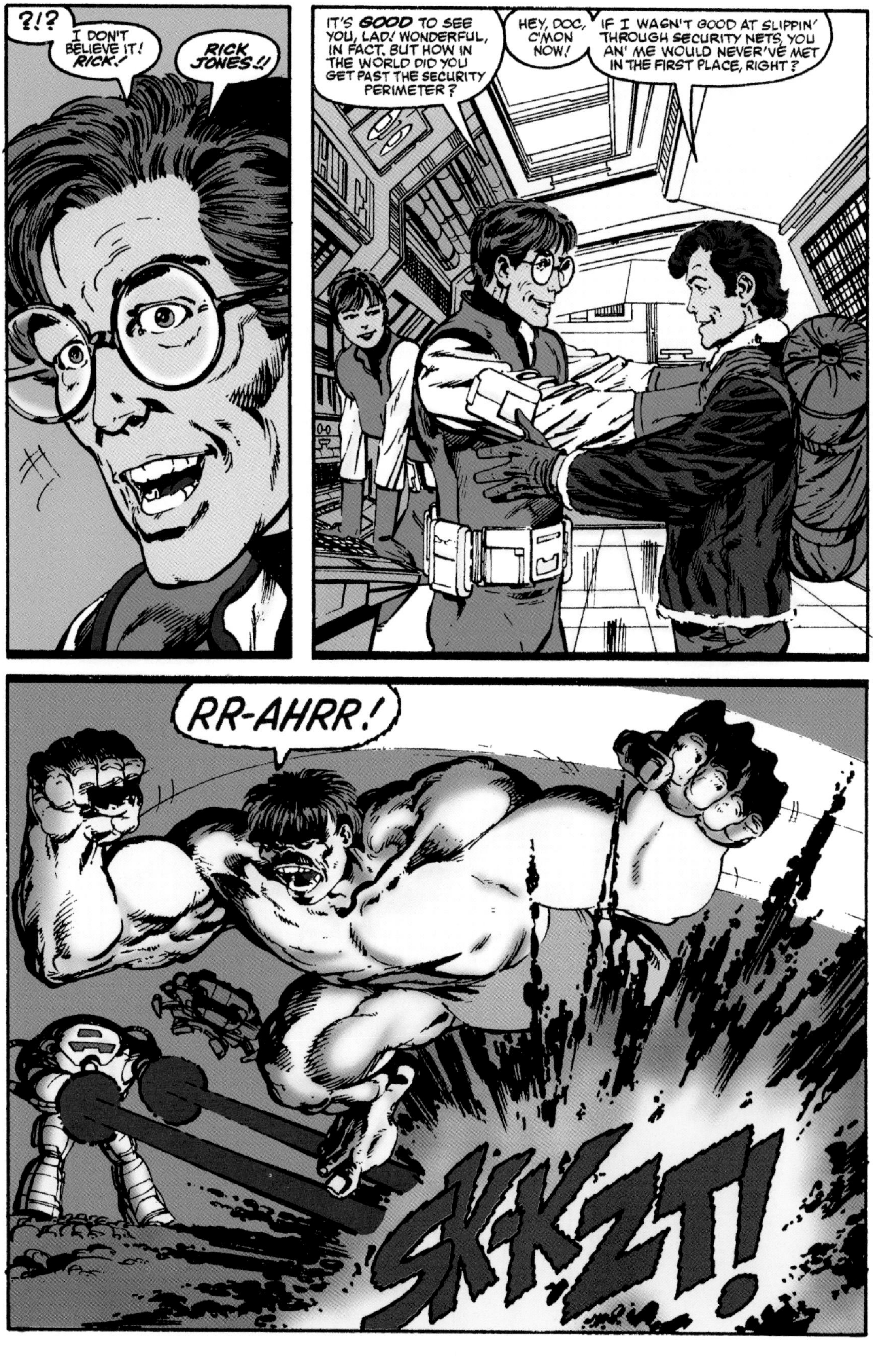
?!?
I DON'T BELIEVE IT! RICK!
RICK JONES!!
IT'S GOOD TO SEE YOU, LAD! WONDERFUL, IN FACT. BUT HOW IN THE WORLD DID YOU GET PAST THE SECURITY PERIMETER?
HEY, DOC, C'MON NOW!
IF I WASN'T GOOD AT SLIPPIN' THROUGH SECURITY NETS, YOU AN' ME WOULD NEVER'VE MET IN THE FIRST PLACE, RIGHT?
RR-AHRR!
SK-KZZT!

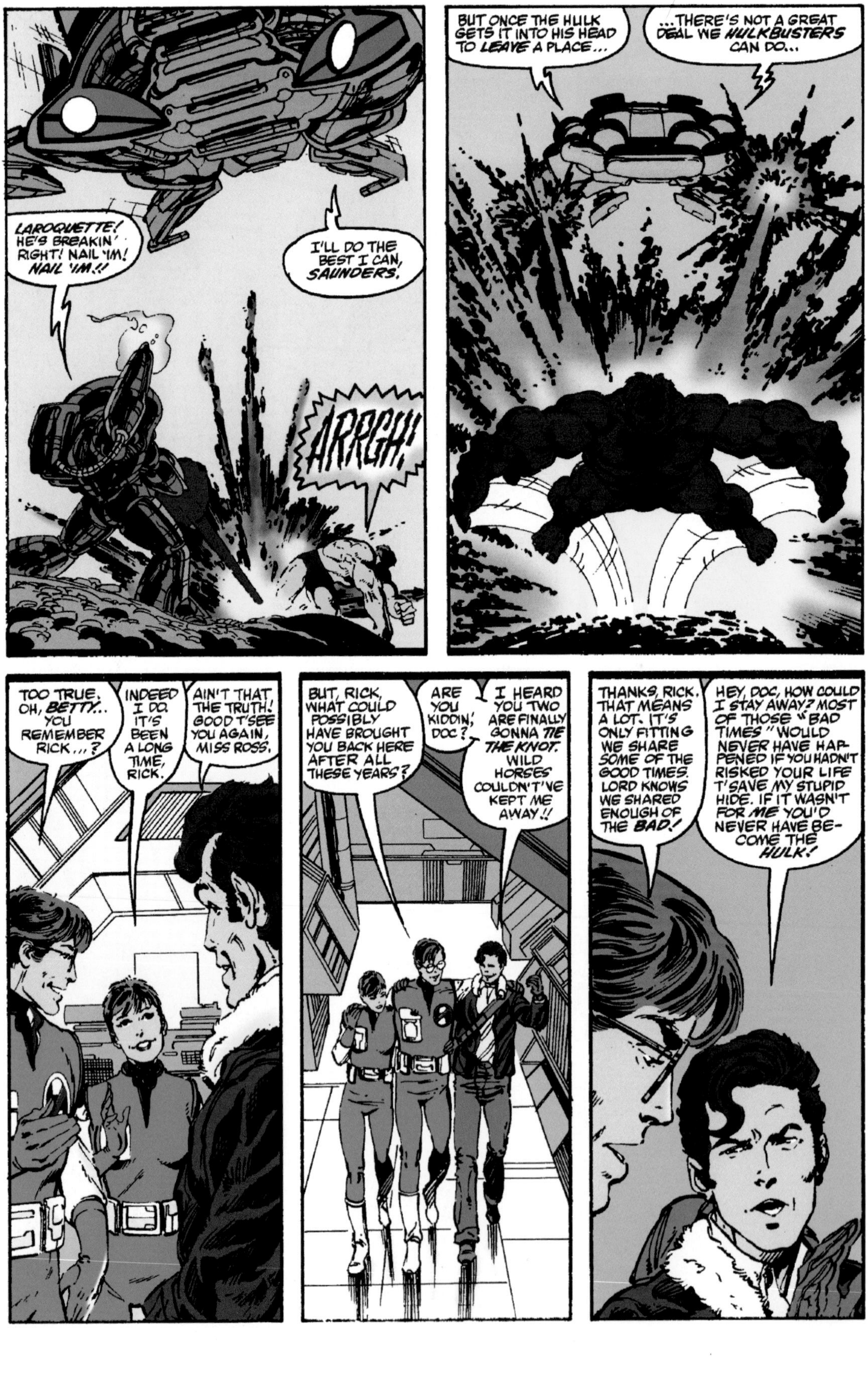
LAROQUETTE! HE'S BREAKIN' RIGHT! NAIL 'IM! NAIL 'IM!!
I'LL DO THE BEST I CAN, SAUNDERS.
ARRGH!
BUT ONCE THE HULK GETS IT INTO HIS HEAD TO LEAVE A PLACE...
...THERE'S NOT A GREAT DEAL WE HULKBUSTERS CAN DO...
TOO TRUE. OH, BETTY... YOU REMEMBER RICK...?
INDEED I DO. IT'S BEEN A LONG TIME, RICK.
AIN'T THAT THE TRUTH! GOOD T'SEE YOU AGAIN, MISS ROSS.
BUT, RICK, WHAT COULD POSSIBLY HAVE BROUGHT YOU BACK HERE AFTER ALL THESE YEARS?
ARE YOU KIDDIN', DOC?
I HEARD YOU TWO ARE FINALLY GONNA TIE THE KNOT. WILD HORSES COULDN'T'VE KEPT ME AWAY!!
THANKS, RICK. THAT MEANS A LOT. IT'S ONLY FITTING WE SHARE SOME OF THE GOOD TIMES. LORD KNOWS WE SHARED ENOUGH OF THE BAD!
HEY, DOC, HOW COULD I STAY AWAY? MOST OF THOSE "BAD TIMES" WOULD NEVER HAVE HAPPENED IF YOU HADN'T RISKED YOUR LIFE T'SAVE MY STUPID HIDE. IF IT WASN'T FOR ME YOU'D NEVER HAVE BECOME THE HULK!

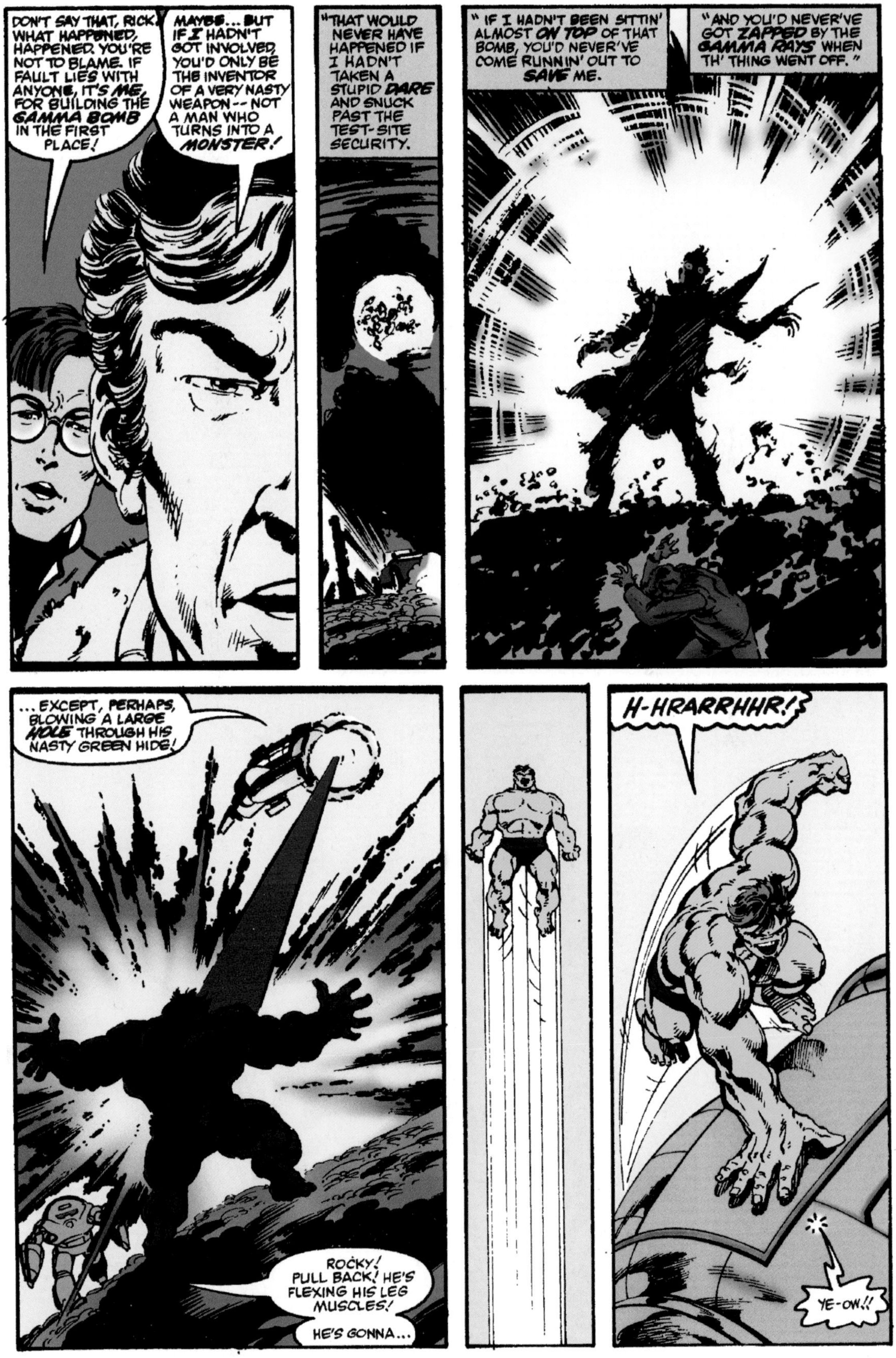
DON'T SAY THAT, RICK. WHAT HAPPENED, HAPPENED. YOU'RE NOT TO BLAME. IF FAULT LIES WITH ANYONE, IT'S ME, FOR BUILDING THE GAMMA BOMB IN THE FIRST PLACE!
MAYBE... BUT IF I HADN'T GOT INVOLVED, YOU'D ONLY BE THE INVENTOR OF A VERY NASTY WEAPON -- NOT A MAN WHO TURNS INTO A MONSTER!
"THAT WOULD NEVER HAVE HAPPENED IF I HADN'T TAKEN A STUPID DARE AND SNUCK PAST THE TEST-SITE SECURITY.
"IF I HADN'T BEEN SITTIN' ALMOST ON TOP OF THAT BOMB, YOU'D NEVER'VE COME RUNNIN' OUT TO SAVE ME.
"AND YOU'D NEVER'VE GOT ZAPPED BY THE GAMMA RAYS WHEN TH' THING WENT OFF."
... EXCEPT, PERHAPS, BLOWING A LARGE HOLE THROUGH HIS NASTY GREEN HIDE!
ROCKY! PULL BACK! HE'S FLEXING HIS LEG MUSCLES!
HE'S GONNA...
H-HRARRHHR!
YE-OW!!

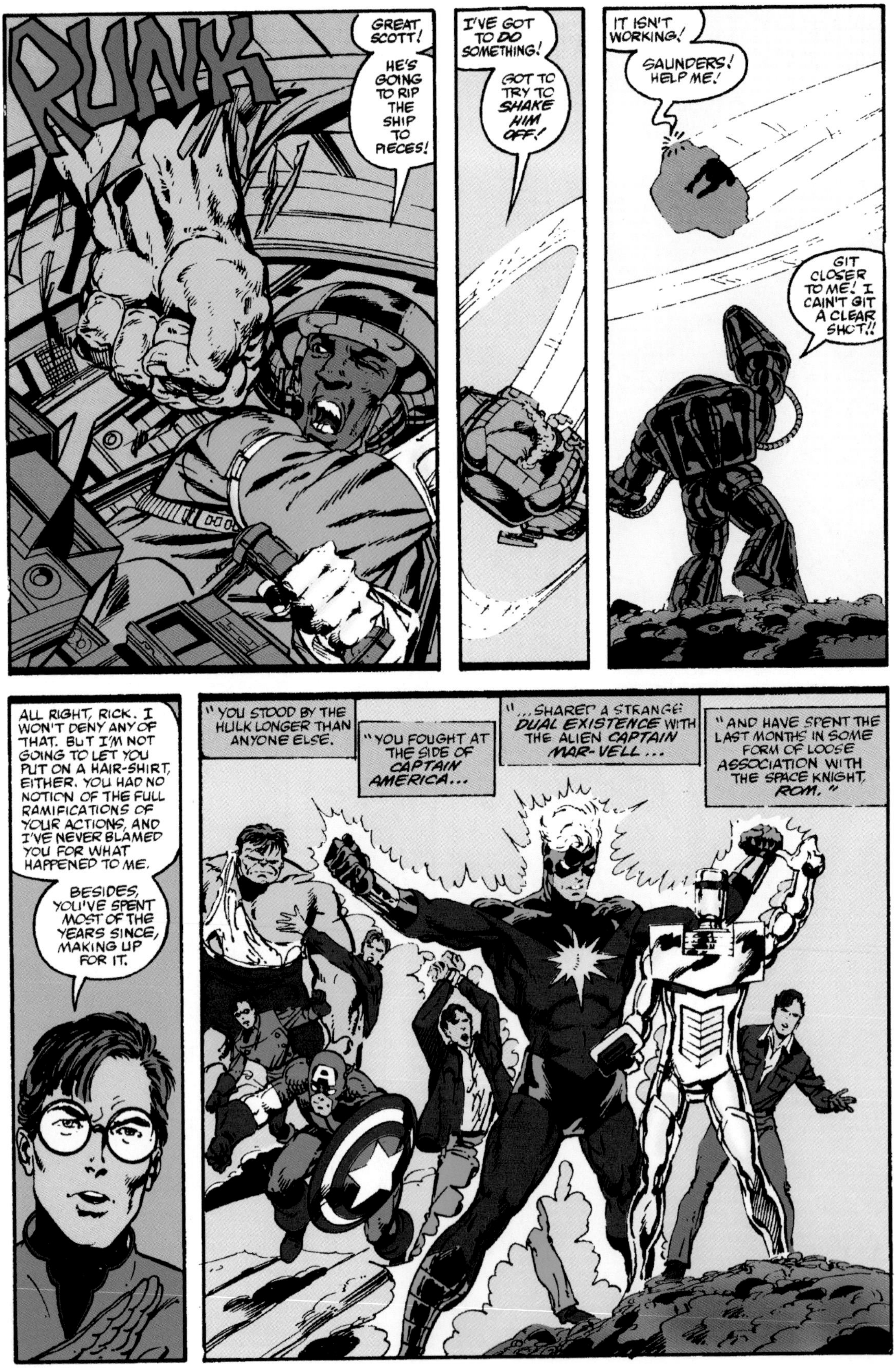
RUNK
GREAT SCOTT!
HE'S GOING TO RIP THE SHIP TO PIECES!
I'VE GOT TO DO SOMETHING!
GOT TO TRY TO SHAKE HIM OFF!
IT ISN'T WORKING!
SAUNDERS! HELP ME!
GIT CLOSER TO ME! I CAIN'T GIT A CLEAR SHOT!!
ALL RIGHT, RICK. I WON'T DENY ANY OF THAT. BUT I'M NOT GOING TO LET YOU PUT ON A HAIR-SHIRT, EITHER. YOU HAD NO NOTION OF THE FULL RAMIFICATIONS OF YOUR ACTIONS, AND I'VE NEVER BLAMED YOU FOR WHAT HAPPENED TO ME.
BESIDES, YOU'VE SPENT MOST OF THE YEARS SINCE, MAKING UP FOR IT.
"YOU STOOD BY THE HULK LONGER THAN ANYONE ELSE.
"YOU FOUGHT AT THE SIDE OF CAPTAIN AMERICA...
"...SHARED A STRANGE DUAL EXISTENCE WITH THE ALIEN CAPTAIN MAR-VELL...
"AND HAVE SPENT THE LAST MONTHS IN SOME FORM OF LOOSE ASSOCIATION WITH THE SPACE KNIGHT, ROM."

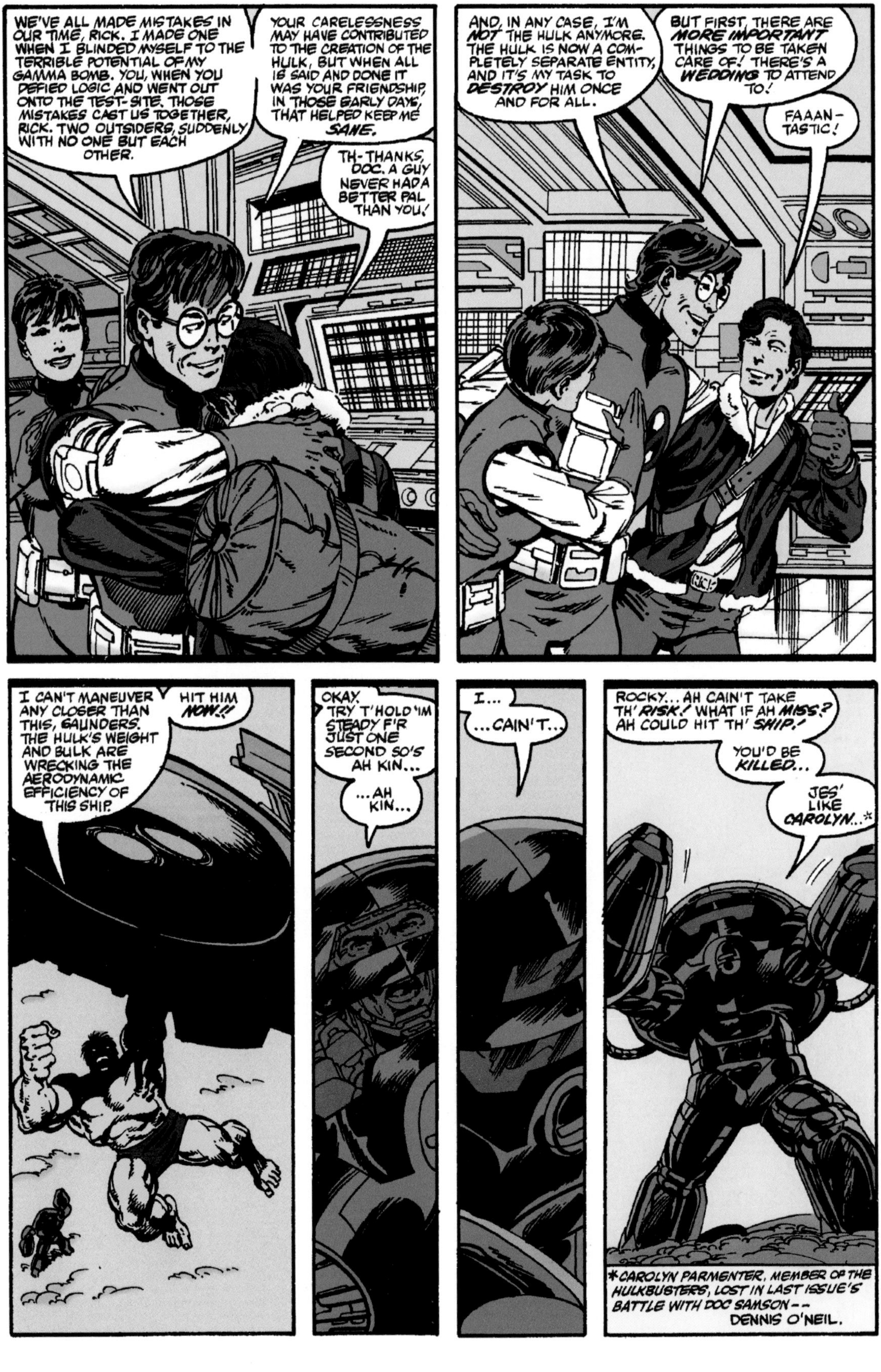

WE'VE ALL MADE MISTAKES IN OUR TIME, RICK. I MADE ONE WHEN I BLINDED MYSELF TO THE TERRIBLE POTENTIAL OF MY GAMMA BOMB. YOU, WHEN YOU DEFIED LOGIC AND WENT OUT ONTO THE TEST-SITE. THOSE MISTAKES CAST US TOGETHER, RICK. TWO OUTSIDERS, SUDDENLY WITH NO ONE BUT EACH OTHER.
YOUR CARELESSNESS MAY HAVE CONTRIBUTED TO THE CREATION OF THE HULK, BUT WHEN ALL IS SAID AND DONE IT WAS YOUR FRIENDSHIP, IN THOSE EARLY DAYS, THAT HELPED KEEP ME SANE.
TH-THANKS, DOC. A GUY NEVER HAD A BETTER PAL THAN YOU!
AND, IN ANY CASE, I'M NOT THE HULK ANYMORE. THE HULK IS NOW A COMPLETELY SEPARATE ENTITY, AND IT'S MY TASK TO DESTROY HIM ONCE AND FOR ALL.
BUT FIRST, THERE ARE MORE IMPORTANT THINGS TO BE TAKEN CARE OF! THERE'S A WEDDING TO ATTEND TO!
FAAAN-TASTIC!
I CAN'T MANEUVER ANY CLOSER THAN THIS, SAUNDERS. THE HULK'S WEIGHT AND BULK ARE WRECKING THE AERODYNAMIC EFFICIENCY OF THIS SHIP.
HIT HIM NOW!!
OKAY. TRY T'HOLD 'IM STEADY F'R JUST ONE SECOND SO'S AH KIN...
...AH KIN...
I...
...CAIN'T...
ROCKY... AH CAIN'T TAKE TH' RISK! WHAT IF AH MISS? AH COULD HIT TH' SHIP!
YOU'D BE KILLED...
JES' LIKE CAROLYN...*
*CAROLYN PARMENTER, MEMBER OF THE HULKBUSTERS, LOST IN LAST ISSUE'S BATTLE WITH DOC SAMSON-- DENNIS O'NEIL.

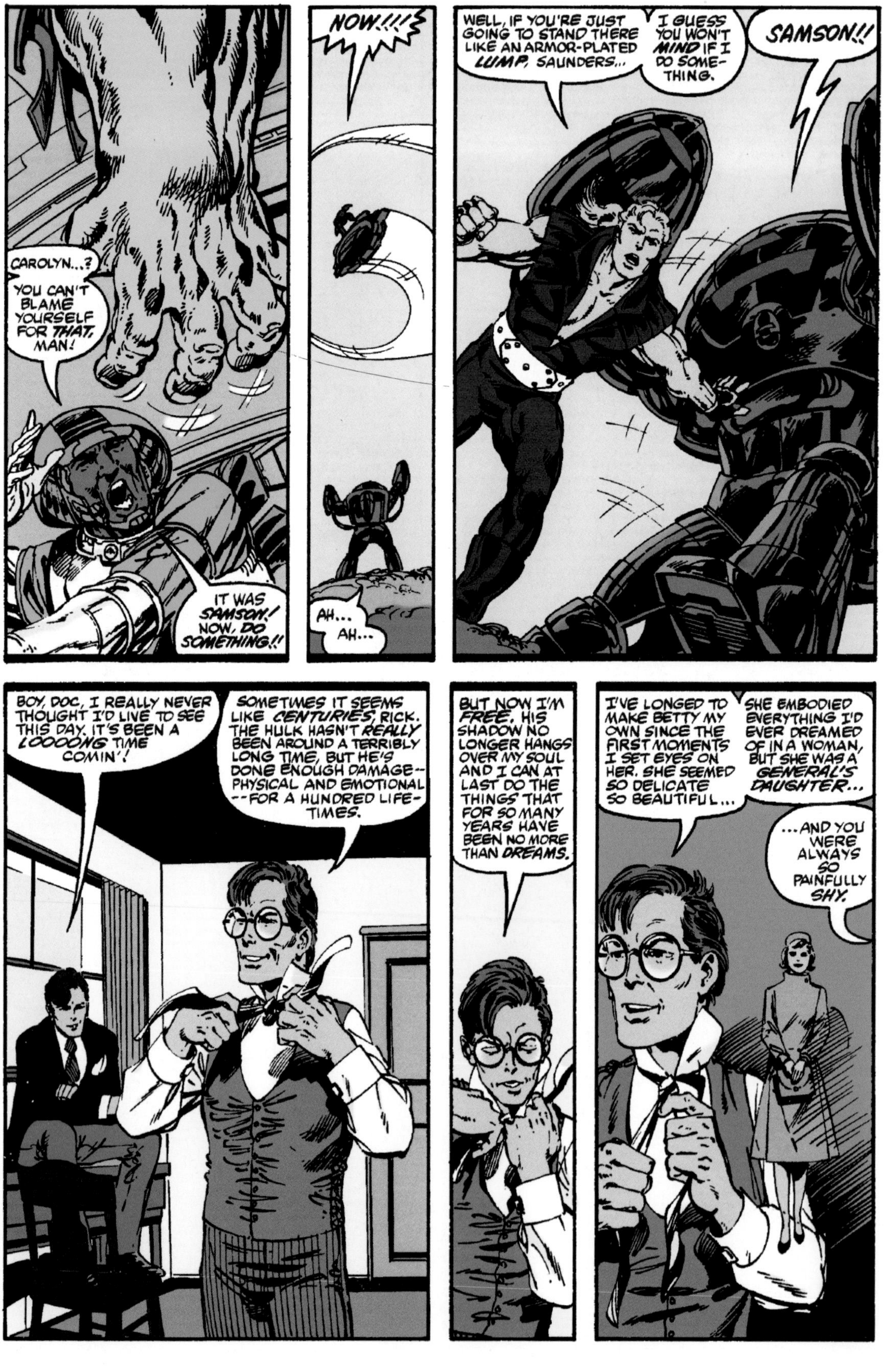
CAROLYN...?
YOU CAN'T BLAME YOURSELF FOR THAT, MAN!
IT WAS SAMSON! NOW, DO SOMETHING!!
NOW!!!!
AH... AH...
WELL, IF YOU'RE JUST GOING TO STAND THERE LIKE AN ARMOR-PLATED LUMP, SAUNDERS...
I GUESS YOU WON'T MIND IF I DO SOMETHING.
SAMSON!!
BOY, DOC, I REALLY NEVER THOUGHT I'D LIVE TO SEE THIS DAY. IT'S BEEN A LOOOONG TIME COMIN'!
SOMETIMES IT SEEMS LIKE CENTURIES, RICK. THE HULK HASN'T REALLY BEEN AROUND A TERRIBLY LONG TIME, BUT HE'S DONE ENOUGH DAMAGE-- PHYSICAL AND EMOTIONAL --FOR A HUNDRED LIFETIMES.
BUT NOW I'M FREE. HIS SHADOW NO LONGER HANGS OVER MY SOUL AND I CAN AT LAST DO THE THINGS THAT FOR SO MANY YEARS HAVE BEEN NO MORE THAN DREAMS.
I'VE LONGED TO MAKE BETTY MY OWN SINCE THE FIRST MOMENTS I SET EYES ON HER. SHE SEEMED SO DELICATE SO BEAUTIFUL...
SHE EMBODIED EVERYTHING I'D EVER DREAMED OF IN A WOMAN, BUT SHE WAS A GENERAL'S DAUGHTER...
...AND YOU WERE ALWAYS SO PAINFULLY SHY.

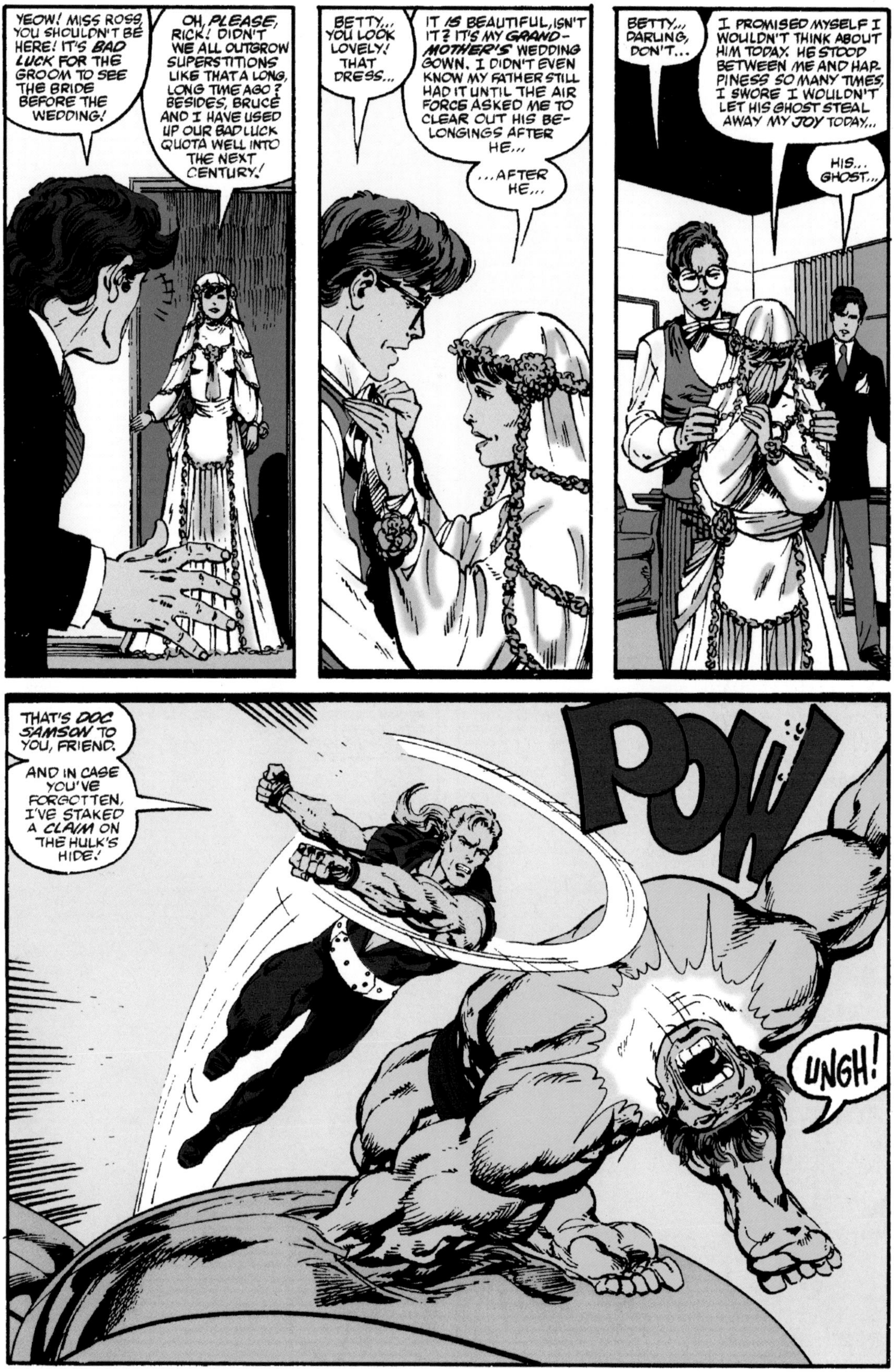
YEOW! MISS ROSS, YOU SHOULDN'T BE HERE! IT'S BAD LUCK FOR THE GROOM TO SEE THE BRIDE BEFORE THE WEDDING!
OH, PLEASE, RICK! DIDN'T WE ALL OUTGROW SUPERSTITIONS LIKE THAT A LONG, LONG TIME AGO? BESIDES, BRUCE AND I HAVE USED UP OUR BAD LUCK QUOTA WELL INTO THE NEXT CENTURY!
BETTY... YOU LOOK LOVELY! THAT DRESS...
IT IS BEAUTIFUL, ISN'T IT? IT'S MY GRAND-MOTHER'S WEDDING GOWN. I DIDN'T EVEN KNOW MY FATHER STILL HAD IT UNTIL THE AIR FORCE ASKED ME TO CLEAR OUT HIS BE-LONGINGS AFTER HE...
...AFTER HE...
BETTY... DARLING, DON'T...
I PROMISED MYSELF I WOULDN'T THINK ABOUT HIM TODAY. HE STOOD BETWEEN ME AND HAP-PINESS SO MANY TIMES, I SWORE I WOULDN'T LET HIS GHOST STEAL AWAY MY JOY TODAY...
HIS... GHOST...
THAT'S DOC SAMSON TO YOU, FRIEND.
AND IN CASE YOU'VE FORGOTTEN, I'VE STAKED A CLAIM ON THE HULK'S HIDE!
POW
UNGH!

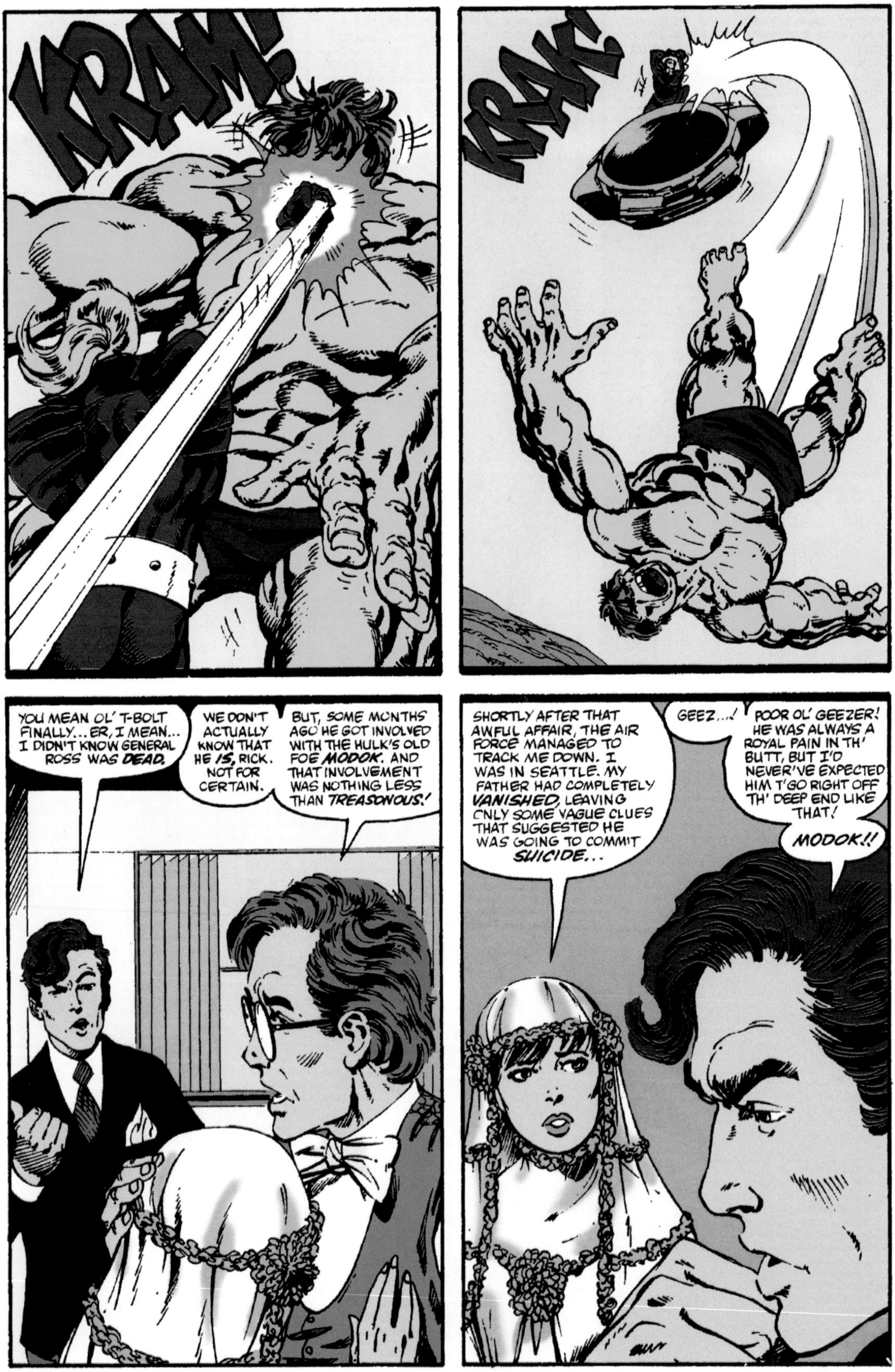
KRAM!
KRAK!
YOU MEAN OL' T-BOLT FINALLY... ER, I MEAN... I DIDN'T KNOW GENERAL ROSS WAS DEAD.
WE DON'T ACTUALLY KNOW THAT HE IS, RICK. NOT FOR CERTAIN.
BUT, SOME MONTHS AGO HE GOT INVOLVED WITH THE HULK'S OLD FOE MODOK. AND THAT INVOLVEMENT WAS NOTHING LESS THAN TREASONOUS!
SHORTLY AFTER THAT AWFUL AFFAIR, THE AIR FORCE MANAGED TO TRACK ME DOWN. I WAS IN SEATTLE. MY FATHER HAD COMPLETELY VANISHED, LEAVING ONLY SOME VAGUE CLUES THAT SUGGESTED HE WAS GOING TO COMMIT SUICIDE...
GEEZ...!
POOR OL' GEEZER! HE WAS ALWAYS A ROYAL PAIN IN TH' BUTT, BUT I'D NEVER'VE EXPECTED HIM T'GO RIGHT OFF TH' DEEP END LIKE THAT!
MODOK!!

BETTY-- EXCUSE ME FOR INTERRUPTING, BUT REVEREND MORRIS WOULD LIKE A FEW WORDS WITH YOU BEFORE THE CEREMONY.

OH, YES. THANK YOU, HIDEKO.

ENOUGH SAD MEMORIES, BRUCE DARLING. I'LL SEE YOU IN A FEW MINUTES.

WELL, DOC, TH' CLOCK IS RUNNIN' FOR SURE NOW! THIS IS YOUR LAST CHANCE T' SNEAK OUT THE BACK DOOR!

IT'S NOT A JOKING MATTER, RICK. IN THE WEEKS SINCE I PROPOSED TO BETTY I'VE GONE BACK AND FORTH A HUNDRED TIMES ON WHETHER OR NOT THIS IS REALLY THE RIGHT THING TO DO.

HEY, DOC, WHAT COULD BE MORE RIGHT? YOU TWO LOVE EACH OTHER. YOU ALWAYS HAVE.

TRUE. BUT IS LOVE ENOUGH? WITH ALL THE OTHER FACTORS, IS THE ADDITION OF LOVE ENOUGH TO MAKE THE EQUATION POSITIVE?

WHERE IS THE GUARANTEE WE'RE NOT ABOUT TO MAKE A HORRIBLE MISTAKE?

SHOOM!

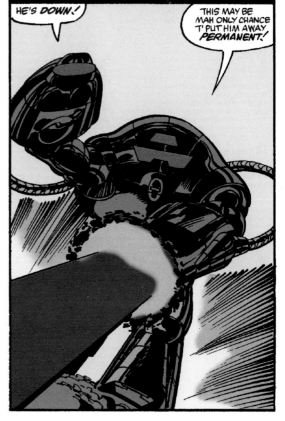

HE'S DOWN!

THIS MAY BE MAH ONLY CHANCE T' PUT HIM AWAY PERMANENT!

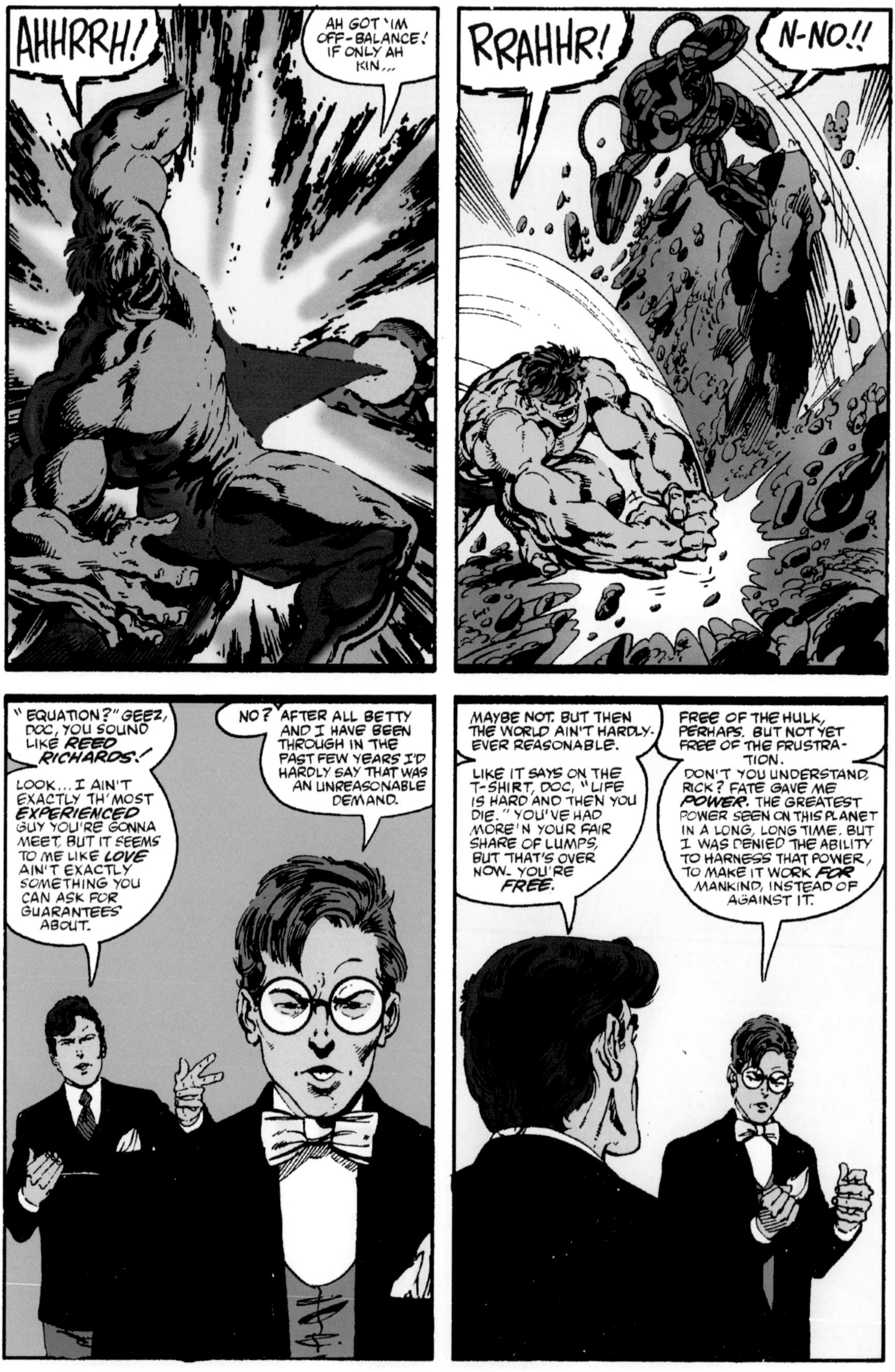

AHHRRH!
AH GOT 'IM OFF-BALANCE! IF ONLY AH KIN...
RRAHHR!
N-NO!!
"EQUATION?" GEEZ, DOC, YOU SOUND LIKE REED RICHARDS!
LOOK... I AIN'T EXACTLY TH' MOST EXPERIENCED GUY YOU'RE GONNA MEET, BUT IT SEEMS TO ME LIKE LOVE AIN'T EXACTLY SOMETHING YOU CAN ASK FOR GUARANTEES ABOUT.
NO?
AFTER ALL BETTY AND I HAVE BEEN THROUGH IN THE PAST FEW YEARS I'D HARDLY SAY THAT WAS AN UNREASONABLE DEMAND.
MAYBE NOT. BUT THEN THE WORLD AIN'T HARDLY EVER REASONABLE.
LIKE IT SAYS ON THE T-SHIRT, DOC, "LIFE IS HARD AND THEN YOU DIE." YOU'VE HAD MORE'N YOUR FAIR SHARE OF LUMPS, BUT THAT'S OVER NOW. YOU'RE FREE.
FREE OF THE HULK, PERHAPS. BUT NOT YET FREE OF THE FRUSTRATION.
DON'T YOU UNDERSTAND, RICK? FATE GAVE ME POWER. THE GREATEST POWER SEEN ON THIS PLANET IN A LONG, LONG TIME. BUT I WAS DENIED THE ABILITY TO HARNESS THAT POWER, TO MAKE IT WORK FOR MANKIND, INSTEAD OF AGAINST IT.

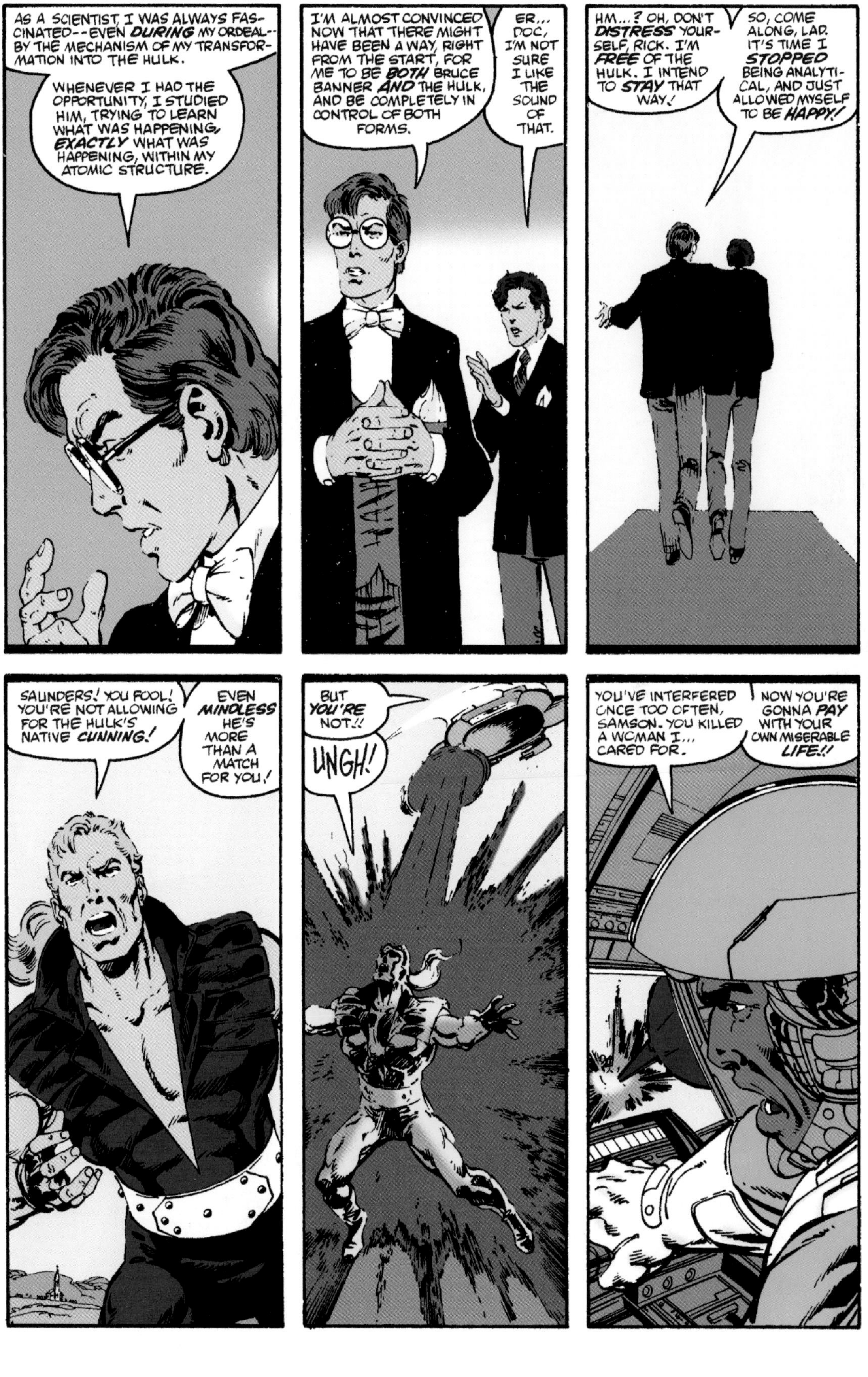

AS A SCIENTIST, I WAS ALWAYS FASCINATED--EVEN DURING MY ORDEAL--BY THE MECHANISM OF MY TRANSFORMATION INTO THE HULK.
WHENEVER I HAD THE OPPORTUNITY, I STUDIED HIM, TRYING TO LEARN WHAT WAS HAPPENING, EXACTLY WHAT WAS HAPPENING, WITHIN MY ATOMIC STRUCTURE.
I'M ALMOST CONVINCED NOW THAT THERE MIGHT HAVE BEEN A WAY, RIGHT FROM THE START, FOR ME TO BE BOTH BRUCE BANNER AND THE HULK, AND BE COMPLETELY IN CONTROL OF BOTH FORMS.
ER... DOC, I'M NOT SURE I LIKE THE SOUND OF THAT.
HM...? OH, DON'T DISTRESS YOURSELF, RICK. I'M FREE OF THE HULK. I INTEND TO STAY THAT WAY!
SO, COME ALONG, LAD. IT'S TIME I STOPPED BEING ANALYTICAL, AND JUST ALLOWED MYSELF TO BE HAPPY!
SAUNDERS! YOU FOOL! YOU'RE NOT ALLOWING FOR THE HULK'S NATIVE CUNNING!
EVEN MINDLESS HE'S MORE THAN A MATCH FOR YOU!
BUT YOU'RE NOT!!
UNGH!
YOU'VE INTERFERED ONCE TOO OFTEN, SAMSON. YOU KILLED A WOMAN I... CARED FOR.
NOW YOU'RE GONNA PAY WITH YOUR OWN MISERABLE LIFE!!

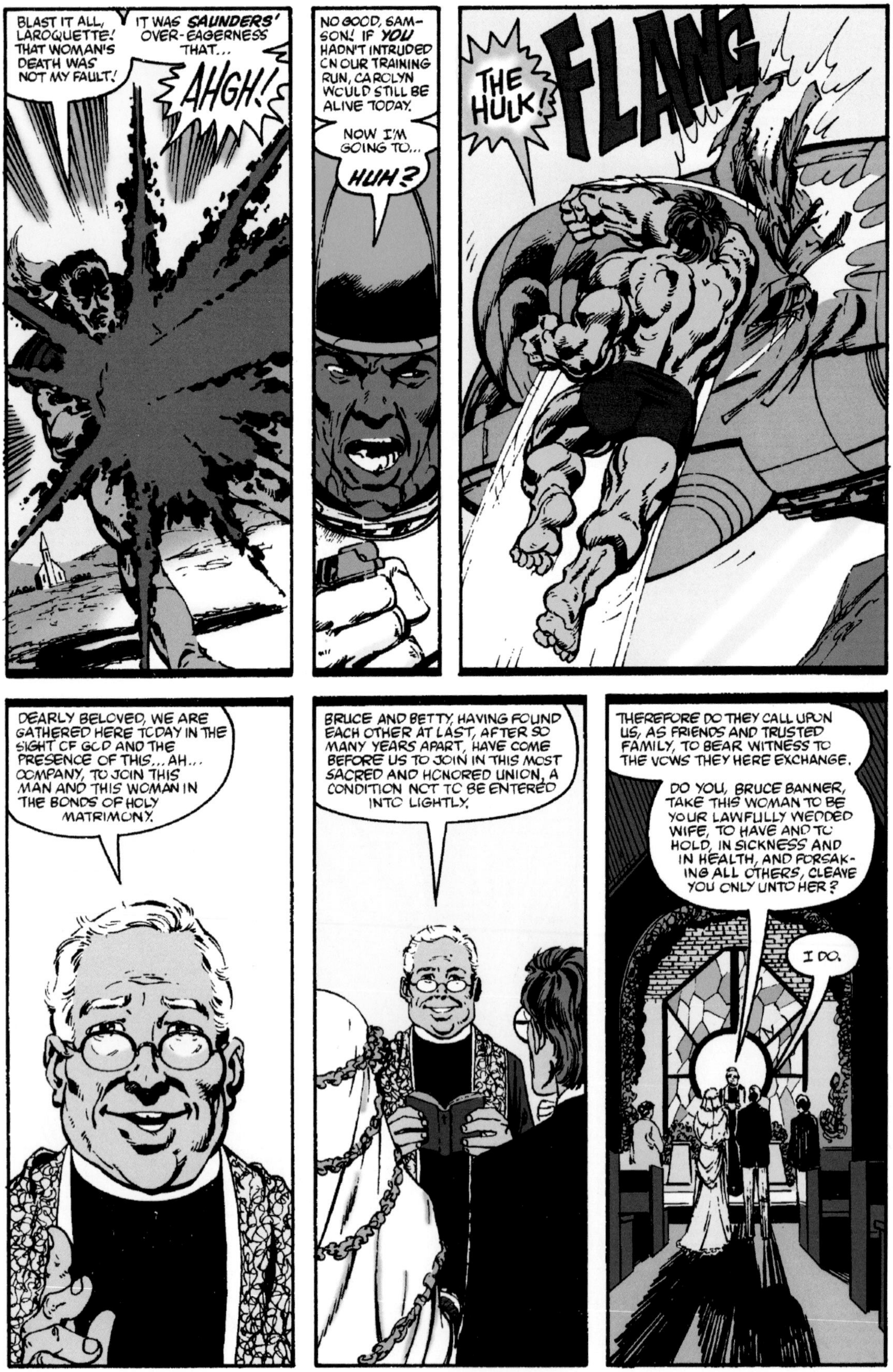
BLAST IT ALL, LAROQUETTE! THAT WOMAN'S DEATH WAS NOT MY FAULT!
IT WAS SAUNDERS' OVER-EAGERNESS THAT...
AHGH!
NO GOOD, SAMSON! IF YOU HADN'T INTRUDED ON OUR TRAINING RUN, CAROLYN WOULD STILL BE ALIVE TODAY.
NOW I'M GOING TO...
HUH?
THE HULK!
FLANG
DEARLY BELOVED, WE ARE GATHERED HERE TODAY IN THE SIGHT OF GOD AND THE PRESENCE OF THIS... AH... COMPANY, TO JOIN THIS MAN AND THIS WOMAN IN THE BONDS OF HOLY MATRIMONY.
BRUCE AND BETTY, HAVING FOUND EACH OTHER AT LAST, AFTER SO MANY YEARS APART, HAVE COME BEFORE US TO JOIN IN THIS MOST SACRED AND HONORED UNION, A CONDITION NOT TO BE ENTERED INTO LIGHTLY.
THEREFORE DO THEY CALL UPON US, AS FRIENDS AND TRUSTED FAMILY, TO BEAR WITNESS TO THE VOWS THEY HERE EXCHANGE.
DO YOU, BRUCE BANNER, TAKE THIS WOMAN TO BE YOUR LAWFULLY WEDDED WIFE, TO HAVE AND TO HOLD, IN SICKNESS AND IN HEALTH, AND FORSAKING ALL OTHERS, CLEAVE YOU ONLY UNTO HER?
I DO.

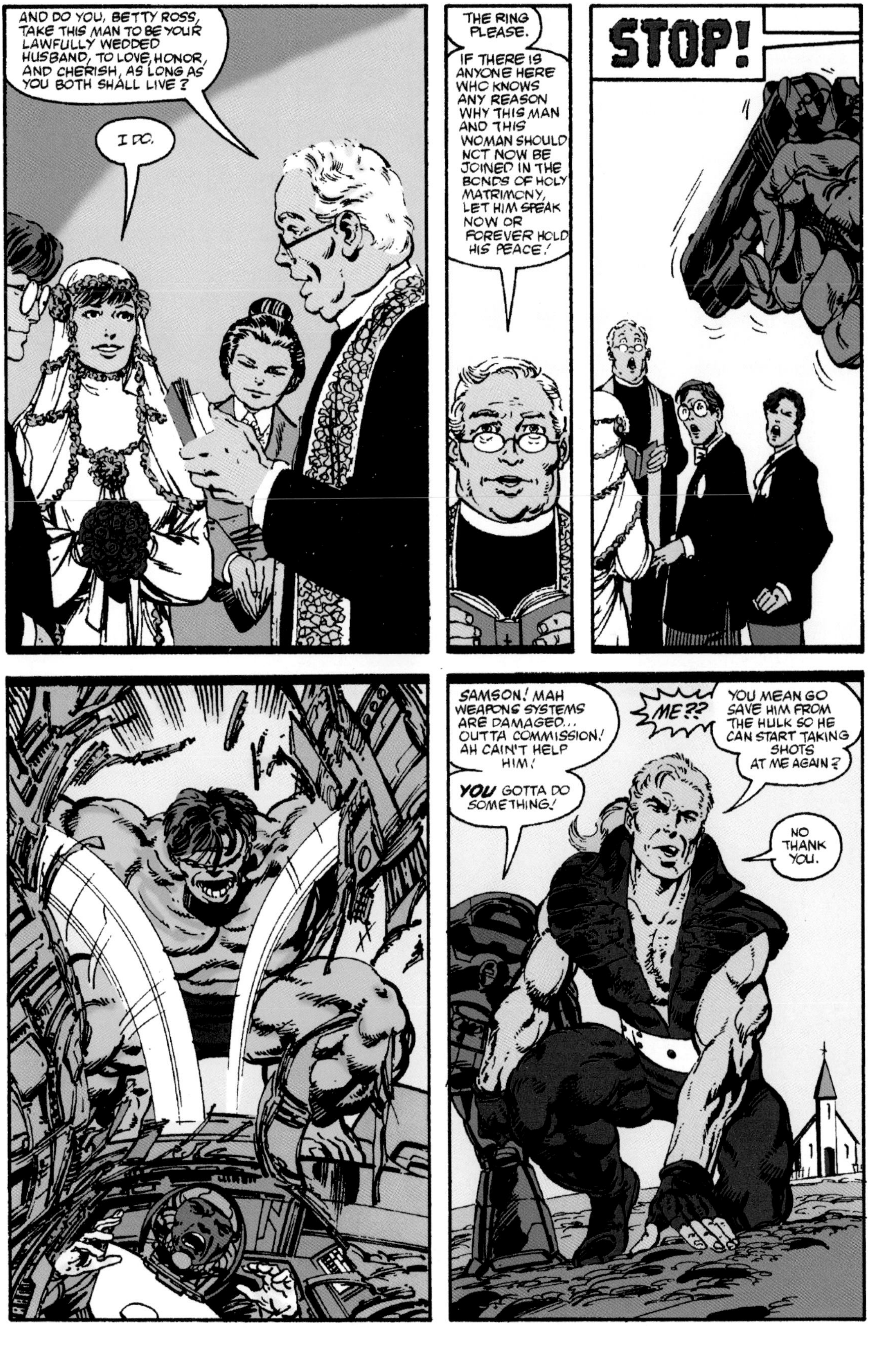

AND DO YOU, BETTY ROSS, TAKE THIS MAN TO BE YOUR LAWFULLY WEDDED HUSBAND, TO LOVE, HONOR, AND CHERISH, AS LONG AS YOU BOTH SHALL LIVE?
I DO.
THE RING PLEASE.
IF THERE IS ANYONE HERE WHO KNOWS ANY REASON WHY THIS MAN AND THIS WOMAN SHOULD NOT NOW BE JOINED IN THE BONDS OF HOLY MATRIMONY, LET HIM SPEAK NOW OR FOREVER HOLD HIS PEACE!
STOP!
SAMSON! MAH WEAPONS SYSTEMS ARE DAMAGED... OUTTA COMMISSION! AH CAIN'T HELP HIM!
YOU GOTTA DO SOMETHING!
ME??
YOU MEAN GO SAVE HIM FROM THE HULK SO HE CAN START TAKING SHOTS AT ME AGAIN?
NO THANK YOU.

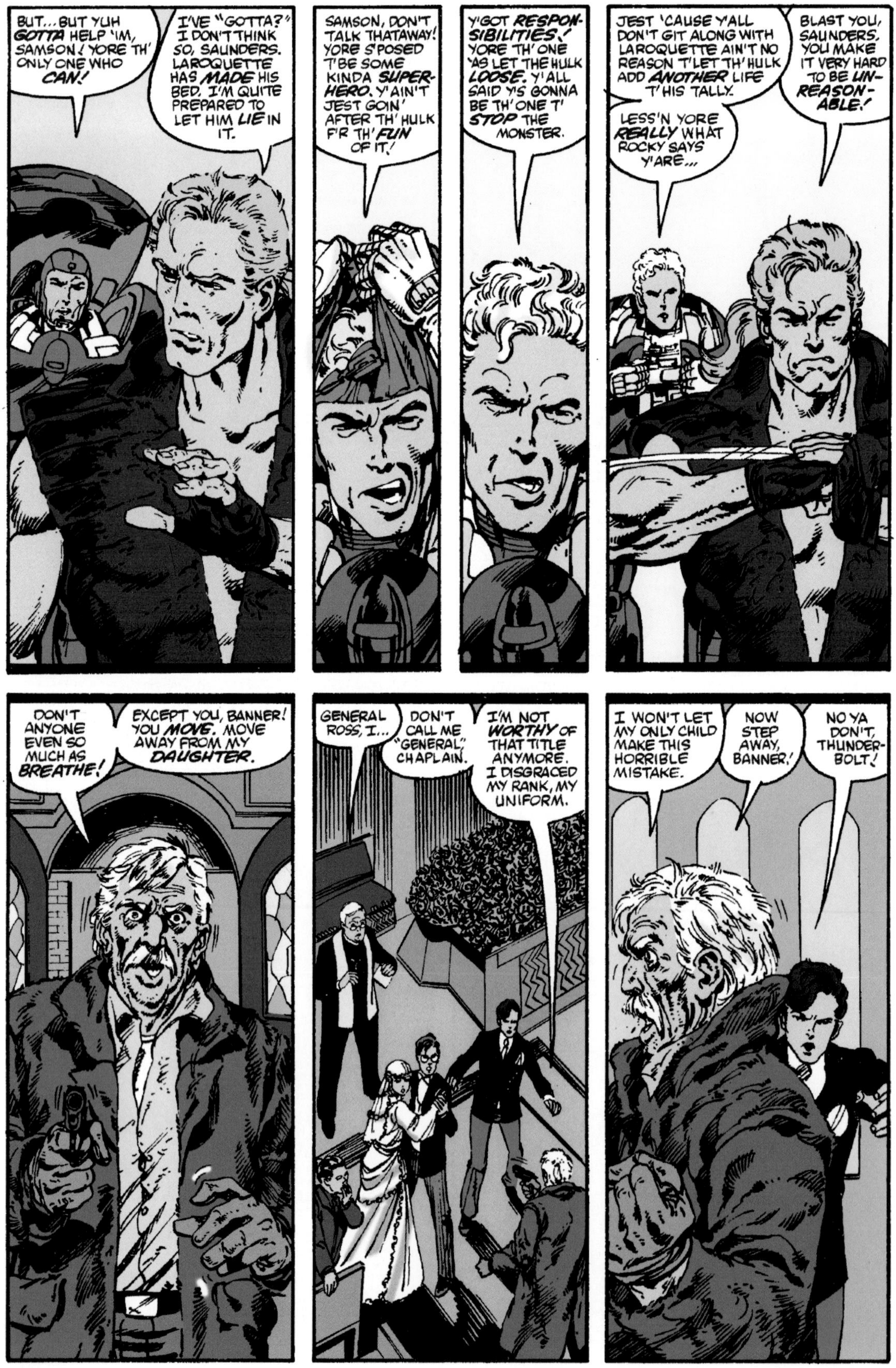
BUT... BUT YUH GOTTA HELP 'IM, SAMSON! YORE TH' ONLY ONE WHO CAN!
I'VE "GOTTA?" I DON'T THINK SO, SAUNDERS. LAROQUETTE HAS MADE HIS BED. I'M QUITE PREPARED TO LET HIM LIE IN IT.
SAMSON, DON'T TALK THATAWAY! YORE S'POSED T'BE SOME KINDA SUPER-HERO. Y'AIN'T JEST GOIN' AFTER TH' HULK F'R TH' FUN OF IT!
Y'GOT RESPON-SIBILITIES! YORE TH' ONE 'AS LET THE HULK LOOSE. Y'ALL SAID Y'S GONNA BE TH' ONE T' STOP THE MONSTER.
JEST 'CAUSE Y'ALL DON'T GIT ALONG WITH LAROQUETTE AIN'T NO REASON T'LET TH' HULK ADD ANOTHER LIFE T'HIS TALLY.
LESS'N YORE REALLY WHAT ROCKY SAYS Y'ARE...
BLAST YOU, SAUNDERS. YOU MAKE IT VERY HARD TO BE UN-REASON-ABLE!
DON'T ANYONE EVEN SO MUCH AS BREATHE!
EXCEPT YOU, BANNER! YOU MOVE. MOVE AWAY FROM MY DAUGHTER.
GENERAL ROSS, I...
DON'T CALL ME "GENERAL," CHAPLAIN.
I'M NOT WORTHY OF THAT TITLE ANYMORE. I DISGRACED MY RANK, MY UNIFORM.
I WON'T LET MY ONLY CHILD MAKE THIS HORRIBLE MISTAKE.
NOW STEP AWAY, BANNER!
NO YA DON'T, THUNDER-BOLT!

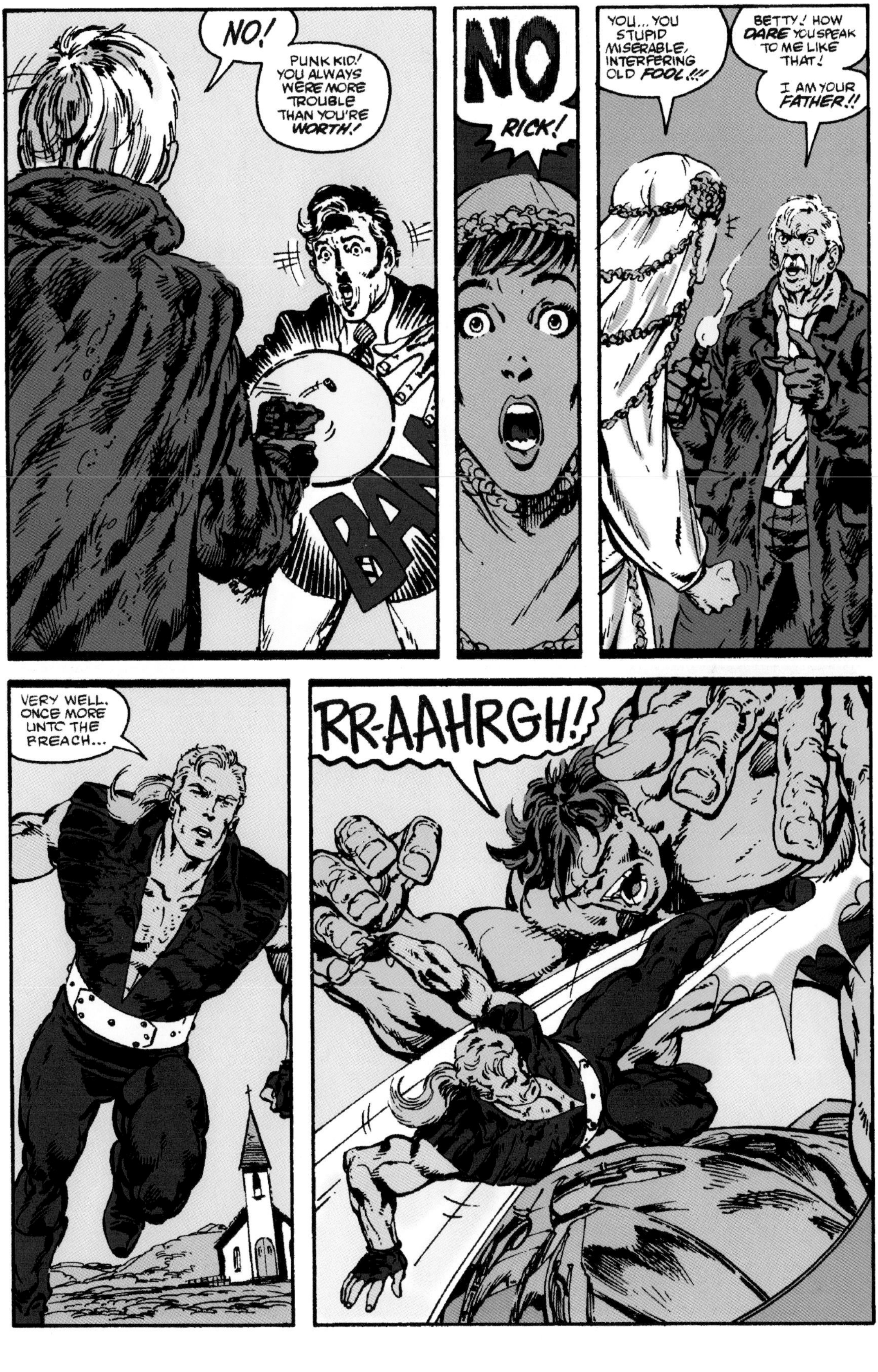
NO!
PUNK KID! YOU ALWAYS WERE MORE TROUBLE THAN YOU'RE WORTH!
BAM
NO
RICK!
YOU... YOU STUPID MISERABLE, INTERFERING OLD FOOL!!!
BETTY! HOW DARE YOU SPEAK TO ME LIKE THAT!
I AM YOUR FATHER!!
VERY WELL. ONCE MORE UNTO THE BREACH...
RR-AAHRGH!!

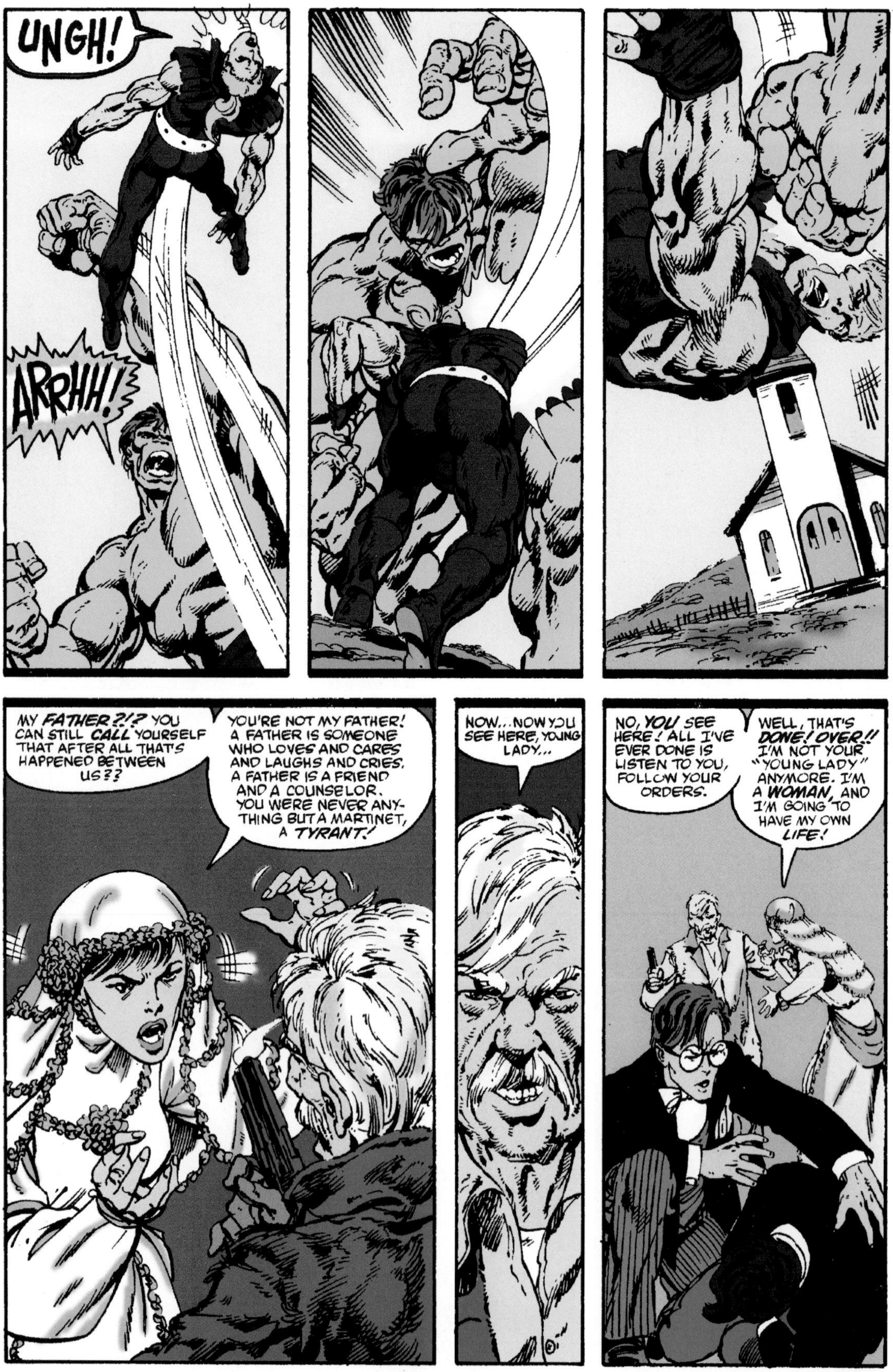
UNGH!
ARRHH!
MY FATHER?!? YOU CAN STILL CALL YOURSELF THAT AFTER ALL THAT'S HAPPENED BETWEEN US??
YOU'RE NOT MY FATHER! A FATHER IS SOMEONE WHO LOVES AND CARES AND LAUGHS AND CRIES. A FATHER IS A FRIEND AND A COUNSELOR. YOU WERE NEVER ANYTHING BUT A MARTINET, A TYRANT!
NOW... NOW YOU SEE HERE, YOUNG LADY...
NO, YOU SEE HERE! ALL I'VE EVER DONE IS LISTEN TO YOU, FOLLOW YOUR ORDERS.
WELL, THAT'S DONE! OVER!! I'M NOT YOUR "YOUNG LADY" ANYMORE. I'M A WOMAN, AND I'M GOING TO HAVE MY OWN LIFE!

BETTY...
I'M NOT FINISHED!

YOU'VE LOOMED OVER ME ALL MY LIFE, DOMINATED ME, TOLD ME HOW TO THINK. HOW TO FEEL. YOU NEVER LET ME HAVE A MOMENT I COULD CALL MY OWN.

AND THEN I MET *BRUCE.* HE SHOWED ME MEN WEREN'T ALL LIKE YOU. HE SHOWED ME MEN COULD HAVE A TENDER SIDE, A SWEET, SHY, LOVING SIDE.

BUT YOU *MOCKED* HIM FOR THAT. YOU CALLED HIM A *MILK-SOP.* YOU *RAGED* AT MY GROWING LOVE FOR HIM.

YOU DID EVERYTHING IN YOUR POWER TO STAND IN OUR WAY, TO *KILL* OUR LOVE. AND NOW YOU'RE DOING IT AGAIN.

WELL, THERE'S ONLY *ONE* WAY YOU'LL SUCCEED THIS TIME. YOU'LL HAVE TO KILL *ME!*

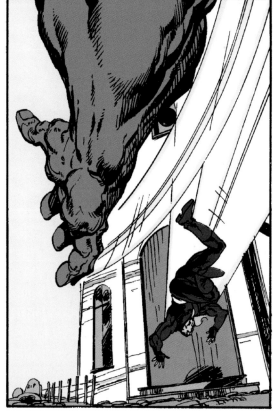

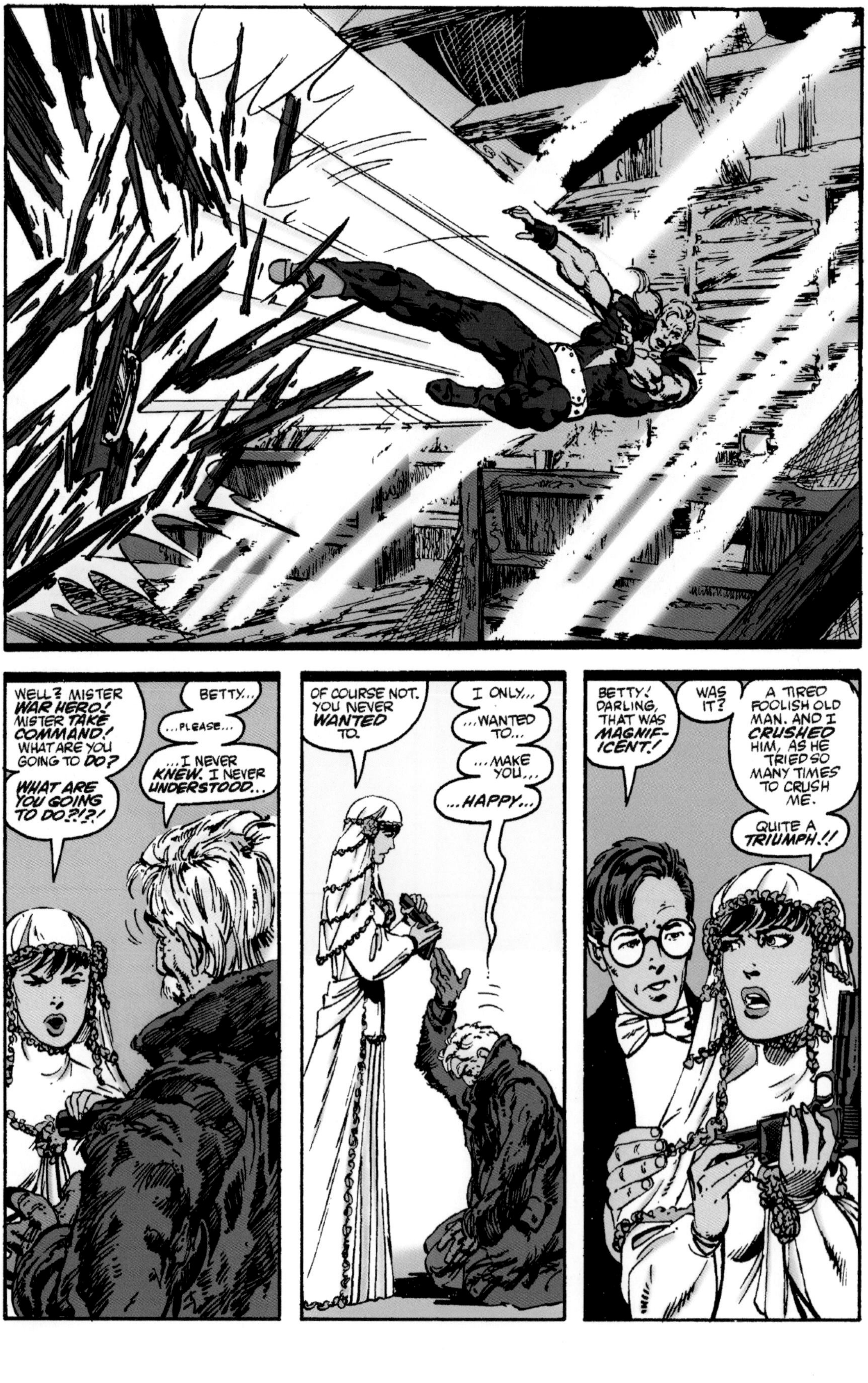

WELL? MISTER WAR HERO! MISTER TAKE COMMAND! WHAT ARE YOU GOING TO DO?
WHAT ARE YOU GOING TO DO?!?!
BETTY...
...PLEASE...
...I NEVER KNEW. I NEVER UNDERSTOOD...
OF COURSE NOT. YOU NEVER WANTED TO.
I ONLY...
...WANTED TO...
...MAKE YOU...
...HAPPY...
BETTY! DARLING, THAT WAS MAGNIFICENT!
WAS IT?
A TIRED FOOLISH OLD MAN. AND I CRUSHED HIM, AS HE TRIED SO MANY TIMES TO CRUSH ME.
QUITE A TRIUMPH!!

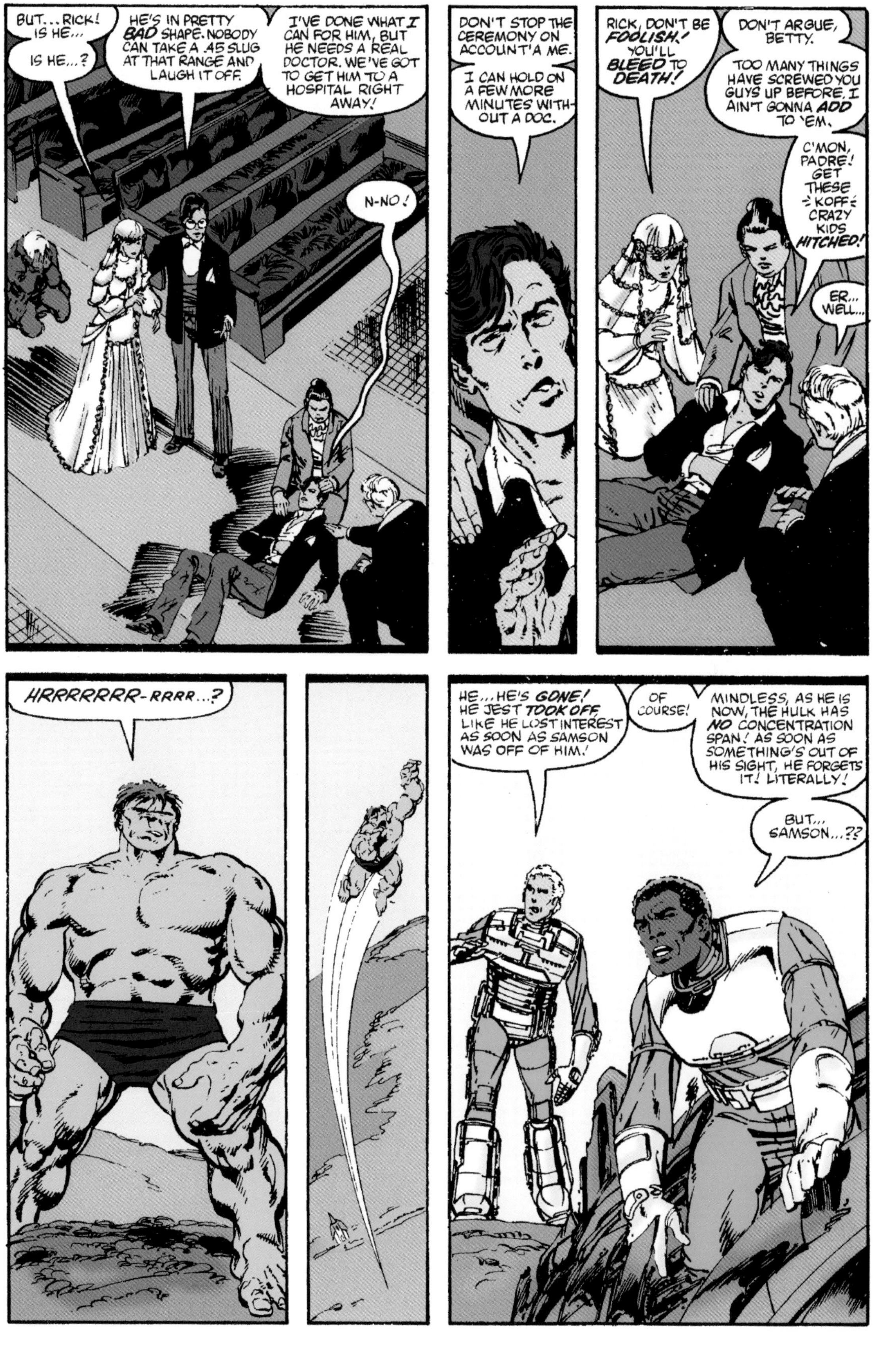

BUT... RICK! IS HE...
IS HE...?
HE'S IN PRETTY BAD SHAPE. NOBODY CAN TAKE A .45 SLUG AT THAT RANGE AND LAUGH IT OFF.
I'VE DONE WHAT I CAN FOR HIM, BUT HE NEEDS A REAL DOCTOR. WE'VE GOT TO GET HIM TO A HOSPITAL RIGHT AWAY!
N-NO!
DON'T STOP THE CEREMONY ON ACCOUNT'A ME.
I CAN HOLD ON A FEW MORE MINUTES WITH-OUT A DOC.
RICK, DON'T BE FOOLISH! YOU'LL BLEED TO DEATH!
DON'T ARGUE, BETTY.
TOO MANY THINGS HAVE SCREWED YOU GUYS UP BEFORE. I AIN'T GONNA ADD TO 'EM.
C'MON, PADRE! GET THESE KOFF CRAZY KIDS HITCHED!
ER... WELL...
HRRRRRRR-RRRR...?
HE... HE'S GONE! HE JEST TOOK OFF LIKE HE LOST INTEREST AS SOON AS SAMSON WAS OFF OF HIM!
OF COURSE!
MINDLESS, AS HE IS NOW, THE HULK HAS NO CONCENTRATION SPAN! AS SOON AS SOMETHING'S OUT OF HIS SIGHT, HE FORGETS IT! LITERALLY!
BUT... SAMSON...??

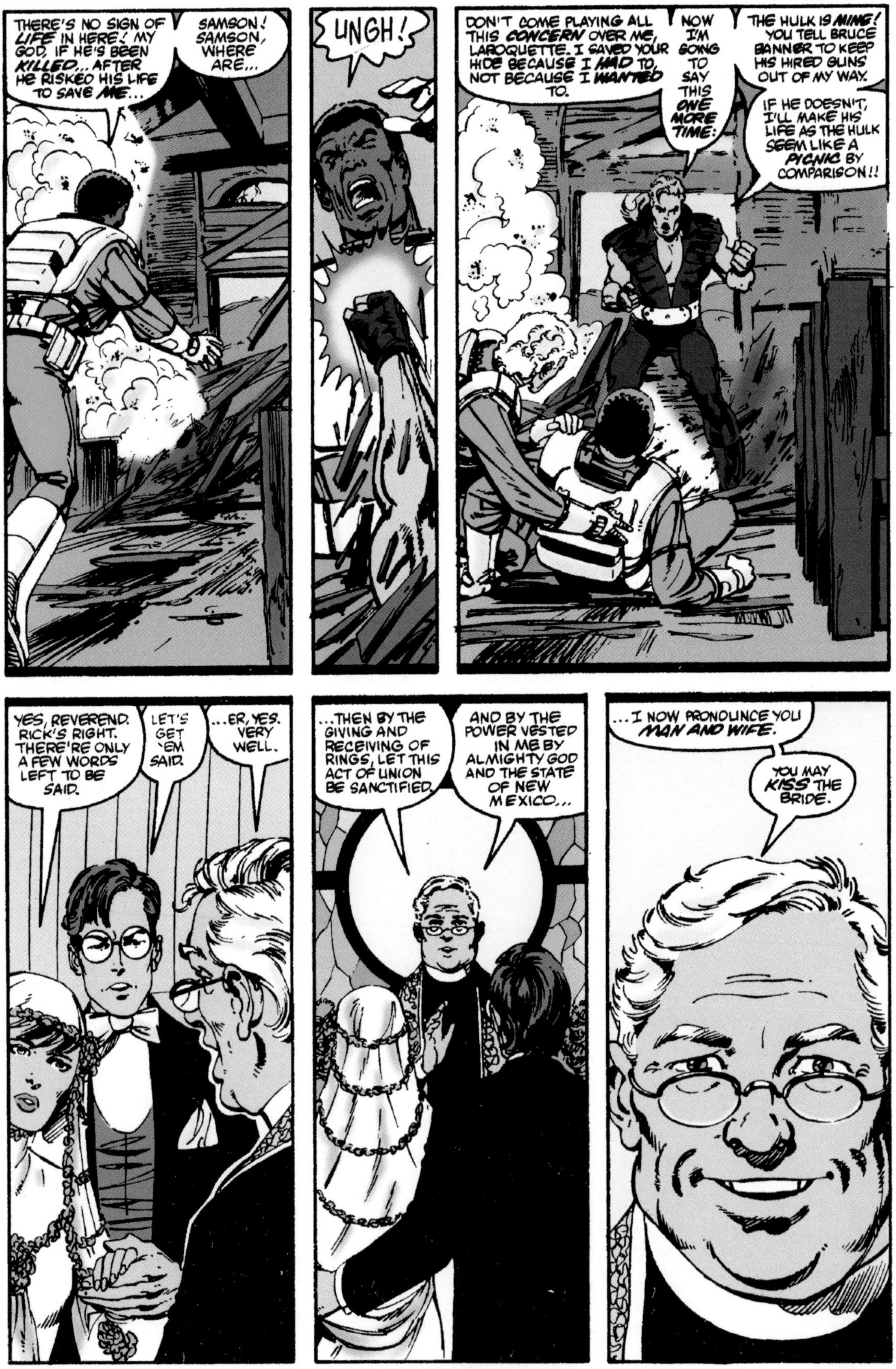
THERE'S NO SIGN OF LIFE IN HERE! MY GOD, IF HE'S BEEN KILLED... AFTER HE RISKED HIS LIFE TO SAVE ME...
SAMSON! SAMSON, WHERE ARE...
UNGH!
DON'T COME PLAYING ALL THIS CONCERN OVER ME, LAROQUETTE. I SAVED YOUR HIDE BECAUSE I HAD TO, NOT BECAUSE I WANTED TO.
NOW I'M GOING TO SAY THIS ONE MORE TIME:
THE HULK IS MINE! YOU TELL BRUCE BANNER TO KEEP HIS HIRED GUNS OUT OF MY WAY.
IF HE DOESN'T, I'LL MAKE HIS LIFE AS THE HULK SEEM LIKE A PICNIC BY COMPARISON!!
YES, REVEREND. RICK'S RIGHT. THERE'RE ONLY A FEW WORDS LEFT TO BE SAID.
LET'S GET 'EM SAID.
...ER, YES. VERY WELL.
...THEN BY THE GIVING AND RECEIVING OF RINGS, LET THIS ACT OF UNION BE SANCTIFIED.
AND BY THE POWER VESTED IN ME BY ALMIGHTY GOD AND THE STATE OF NEW MEXICO...
...I NOW PRONOUNCE YOU MAN AND WIFE.
YOU MAY KISS THE BRIDE.

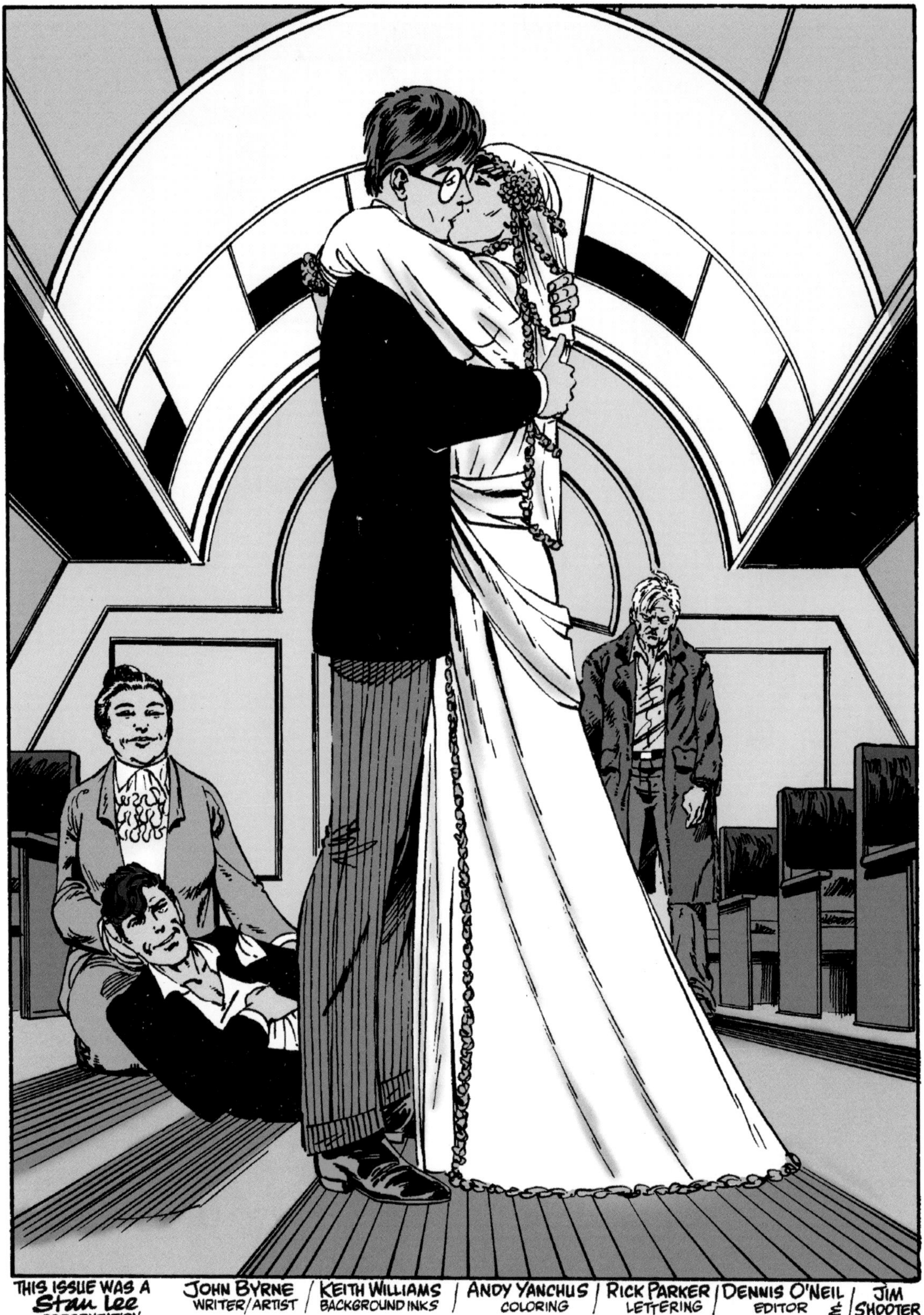

THIS ISSUE WAS A Stan Lee PRESENTATION.
JOHN BYRNE WRITER/ARTIST
KEITH WILLIAMS BACKGROUND INKS
ANDY YANCHUS COLORING
RICK PARKER LETTERING
DENNIS O'NEIL EDITOR
&
JIM SHOOTER EDITOR IN CHIEF
NEXT ISSUE:
THINK THINGS ARE MOVIN' FAST NOW?!?! TUNE IN NEXT ISH FOR
"HONEYMOON'S OVER!!!"

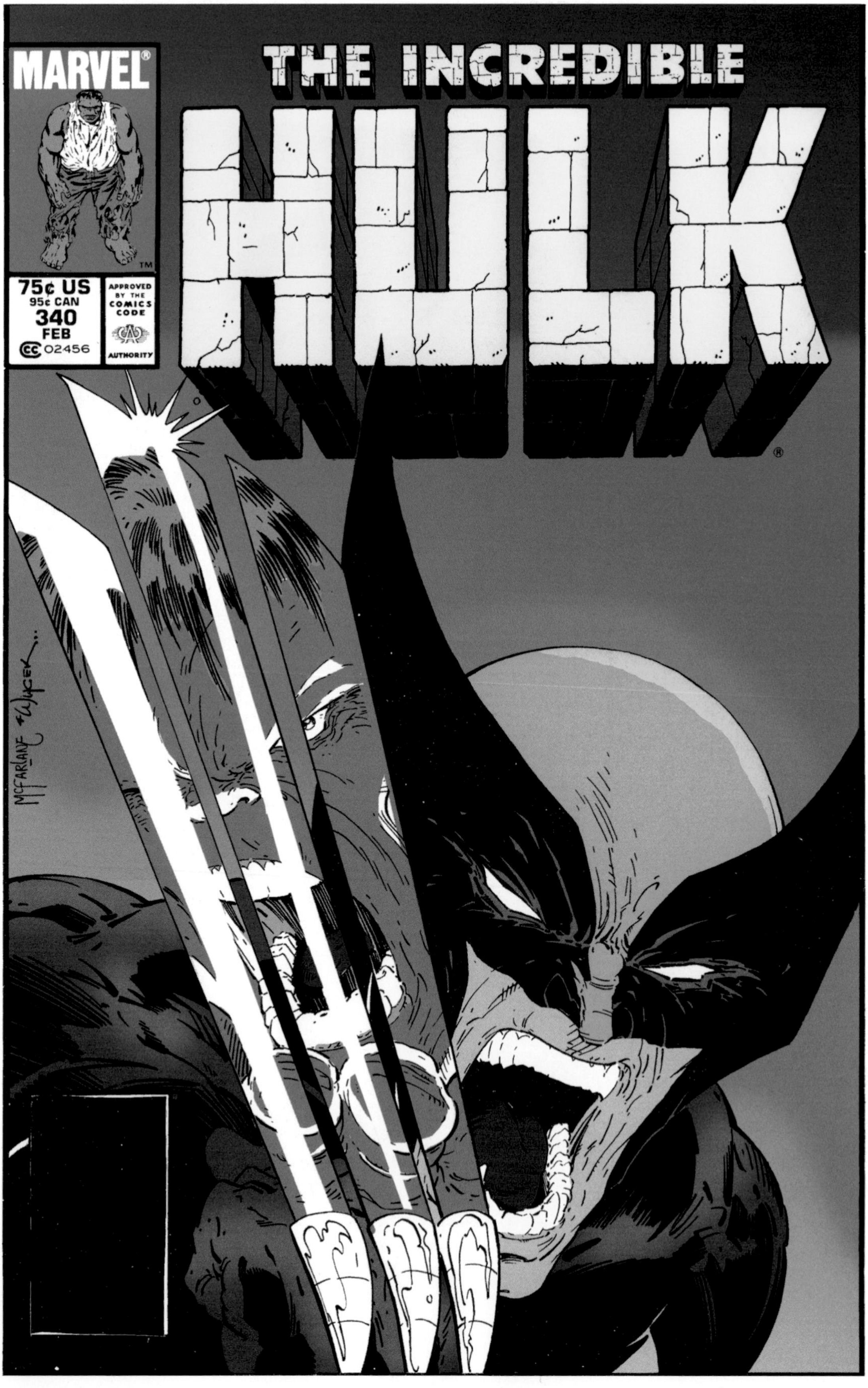
MARVEL
THE INCREDIBLE
HULK
75¢ US
95¢ CAN
340
FEB
02456
APPROVED BY THE COMICS CODE AUTHORITY
McFARLANE + WIACEK

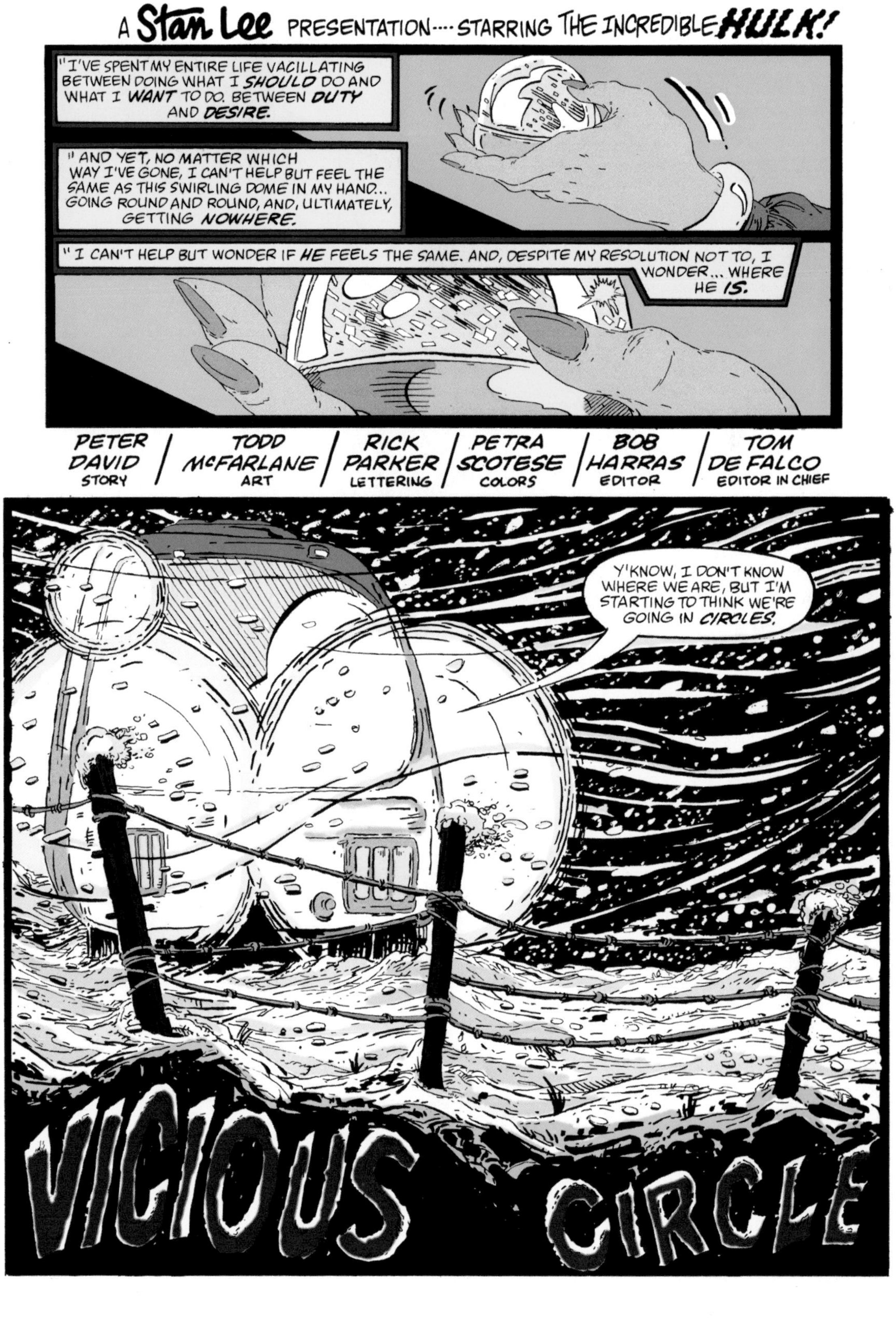
A Stan Lee PRESENTATION.... STARRING THE INCREDIBLE HULK!
"I'VE SPENT MY ENTIRE LIFE VACILLATING BETWEEN DOING WHAT I SHOULD DO AND WHAT I WANT TO DO. BETWEEN DUTY AND DESIRE.
"AND YET, NO MATTER WHICH WAY I'VE GONE, I CAN'T HELP BUT FEEL THE SAME AS THIS SWIRLING DOME IN MY HAND... GOING ROUND AND ROUND, AND, ULTIMATELY, GETTING NOWHERE.
"I CAN'T HELP BUT WONDER IF HE FEELS THE SAME. AND, DESPITE MY RESOLUTION NOT TO, I WONDER... WHERE HE IS.
PETER DAVID STORY
TODD McFARLANE ART
RICK PARKER LETTERING
PETRA SCOTESE COLORS
BOB HARRAS EDITOR
TOM DE FALCO EDITOR IN CHIEF
Y'KNOW, I DON'T KNOW WHERE WE ARE, BUT I'M STARTING TO THINK WE'RE GOING IN CIRCLES.
VICIOUS CIRCLE

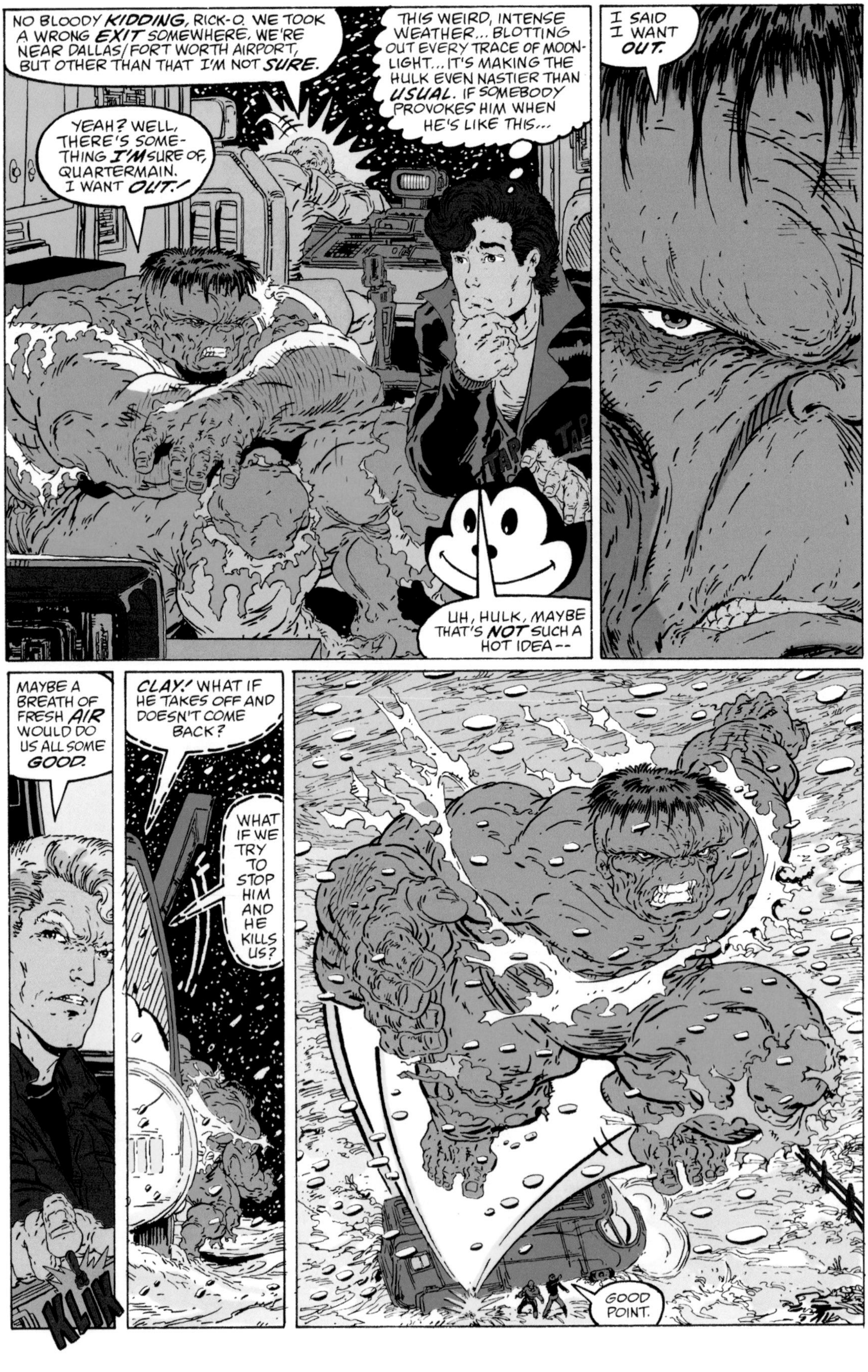
NO BLOODY KIDDING, RICK-O. WE TOOK A WRONG EXIT SOMEWHERE. WE'RE NEAR DALLAS/FORT WORTH AIRPORT, BUT OTHER THAN THAT I'M NOT SURE.
THIS WEIRD, INTENSE WEATHER... BLOTTING OUT EVERY TRACE OF MOON-LIGHT... IT'S MAKING THE HULK EVEN NASTIER THAN USUAL. IF SOMEBODY PROVOKES HIM WHEN HE'S LIKE THIS...
YEAH? WELL, THERE'S SOME-THING I'M SURE OF, QUARTERMAIN. I WANT OUT.!
UH, HULK, MAYBE THAT'S NOT SUCH A HOT IDEA--
I SAID I WANT OUT.
MAYBE A BREATH OF FRESH AIR WOULD DO US ALL SOME GOOD.
KLIK
CLAY! WHAT IF HE TAKES OFF AND DOESN'T COME BACK?
WHAT IF WE TRY TO STOP HIM AND HE KILLS US?
GOOD POINT.

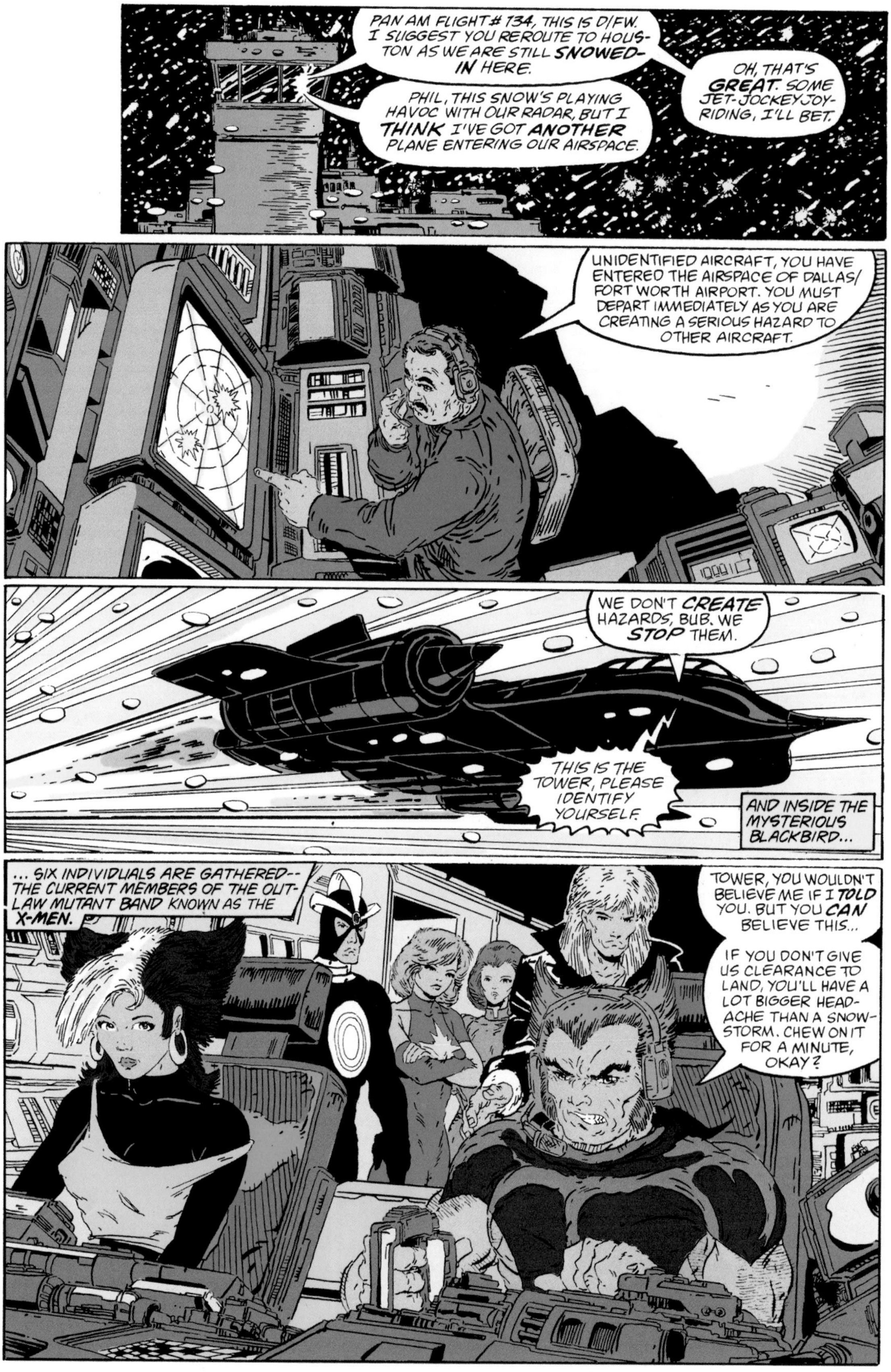
PAN AM FLIGHT # 134, THIS IS D/FW. I SUGGEST YOU REROUTE TO HOUSTON AS WE ARE STILL SNOWED-IN HERE.
PHIL, THIS SNOW'S PLAYING HAVOC WITH OUR RADAR, BUT I THINK I'VE GOT ANOTHER PLANE ENTERING OUR AIRSPACE.
OH, THAT'S GREAT. SOME JET-JOCKEY JOY-RIDING, I'LL BET.
UNIDENTIFIED AIRCRAFT, YOU HAVE ENTERED THE AIRSPACE OF DALLAS/ FORT WORTH AIRPORT. YOU MUST DEPART IMMEDIATELY AS YOU ARE CREATING A SERIOUS HAZARD TO OTHER AIRCRAFT.
THIS IS THE TOWER, PLEASE IDENTIFY YOURSELF.
WE DON'T CREATE HAZARDS, BUB. WE STOP THEM.
AND INSIDE THE MYSTERIOUS BLACKBIRD...
... SIX INDIVIDUALS ARE GATHERED-- THE CURRENT MEMBERS OF THE OUTLAW MUTANT BAND KNOWN AS THE X-MEN.
TOWER, YOU WOULDN'T BELIEVE ME IF I TOLD YOU. BUT YOU CAN BELIEVE THIS...
IF YOU DON'T GIVE US CLEARANCE TO LAND, YOU'LL HAVE A LOT BIGGER HEADACHE THAN A SNOWSTORM. CHEW ON IT FOR A MINUTE, OKAY?

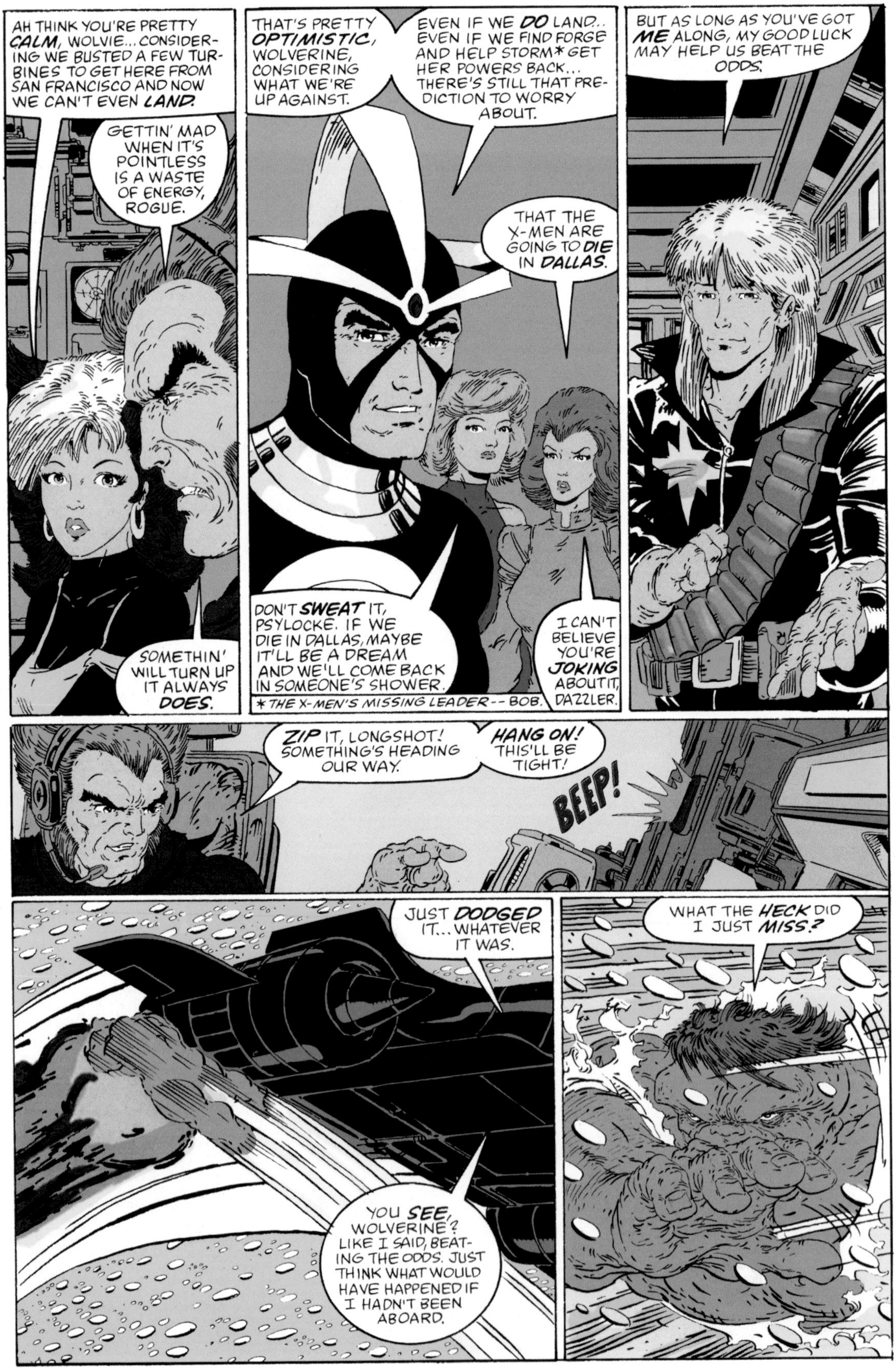
AH THINK YOU'RE PRETTY CALM, WOLVIE... CONSIDERING WE BUSTED A FEW TURBINES TO GET HERE FROM SAN FRANCISCO AND NOW WE CAN'T EVEN LAND.
GETTIN' MAD WHEN IT'S POINTLESS IS A WASTE OF ENERGY, ROGUE.
SOMETHIN' WILL TURN UP IT ALWAYS DOES.
THAT'S PRETTY OPTIMISTIC, WOLVERINE, CONSIDERING WHAT WE'RE UP AGAINST.
EVEN IF WE DO LAND.. EVEN IF WE FIND FORGE AND HELP STORM* GET HER POWERS BACK... THERE'S STILL THAT PREDICTION TO WORRY ABOUT.
THAT THE X-MEN ARE GOING TO DIE IN DALLAS.
DON'T SWEAT IT, PSYLOCKE. IF WE DIE IN DALLAS, MAYBE IT'LL BE A DREAM AND WE'LL COME BACK IN SOMEONE'S SHOWER.
I CAN'T BELIEVE YOU'RE JOKING ABOUT IT, DAZZLER.
* THE X-MEN'S MISSING LEADER -- BOB.
BUT AS LONG AS YOU'VE GOT ME ALONG, MY GOOD LUCK MAY HELP US BEAT THE ODDS.
ZIP IT, LONGSHOT! SOMETHING'S HEADING OUR WAY.
HANG ON! THIS'LL BE TIGHT!
BEEP!
JUST DODGED IT... WHATEVER IT WAS.
YOU SEE, WOLVERINE? LIKE I SAID, BEATING THE ODDS. JUST THINK WHAT WOULD HAVE HAPPENED IF I HADN'T BEEN ABOARD.
WHAT THE HECK DID I JUST MISS?

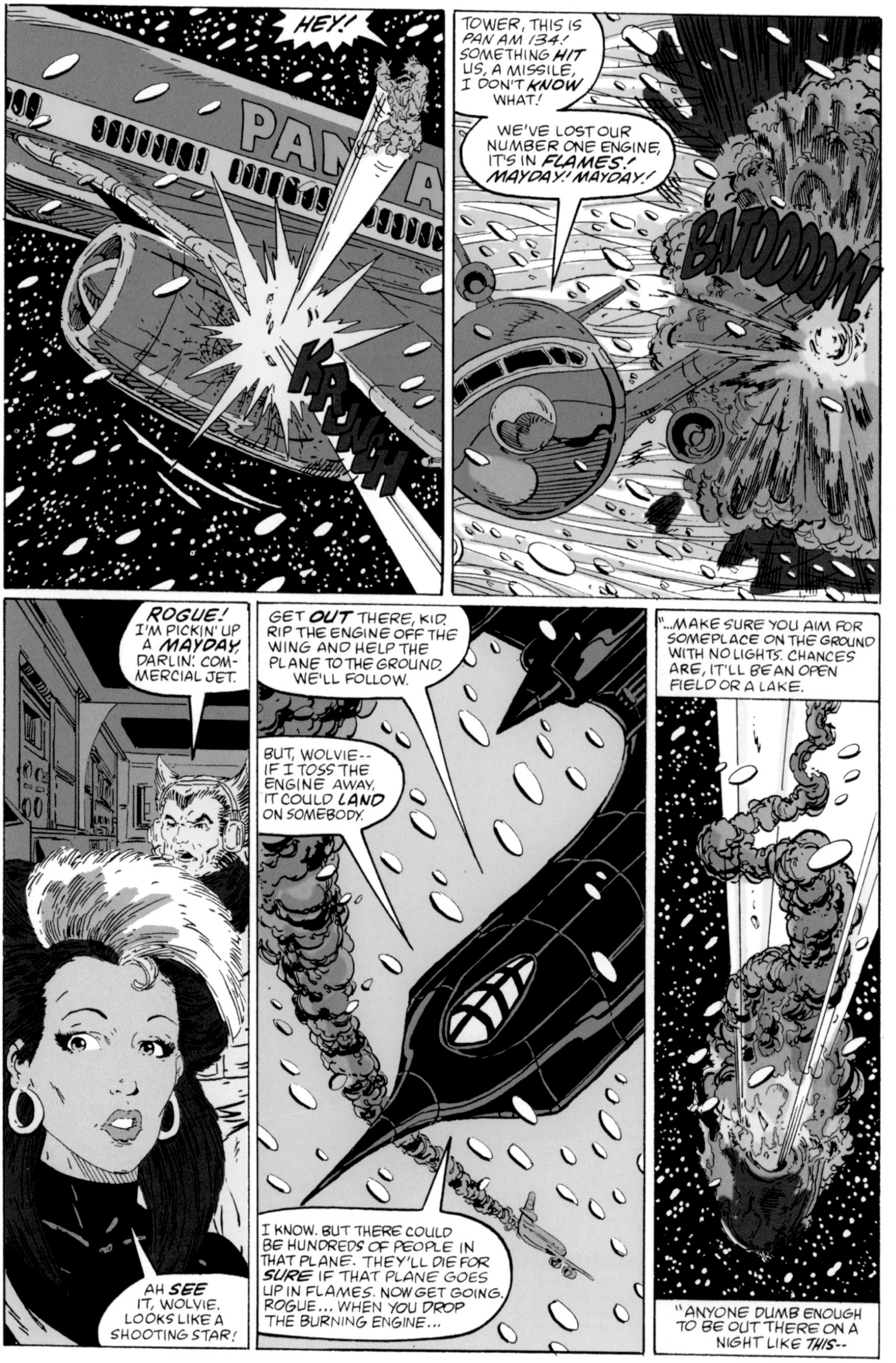
HEY!
PAN A
KRUNCH
TOWER, THIS IS PAN AM 134! SOMETHING HIT US, A MISSILE, I DON'T KNOW WHAT!
WE'VE LOST OUR NUMBER ONE ENGINE, IT'S IN FLAMES! MAYDAY! MAYDAY!
BATOOOOOM!
ROGUE! I'M PICKIN' UP A MAYDAY, DARLIN'. COMMERCIAL JET.
AH SEE IT, WOLVIE. LOOKS LIKE A SHOOTING STAR!
GET OUT THERE, KID. RIP THE ENGINE OFF THE WING AND HELP THE PLANE TO THE GROUND. WE'LL FOLLOW.
BUT, WOLVIE-- IF I TOSS THE ENGINE AWAY, IT COULD LAND ON SOMEBODY.
I KNOW. BUT THERE COULD BE HUNDREDS OF PEOPLE IN THAT PLANE. THEY'LL DIE FOR SURE IF THAT PLANE GOES UP IN FLAMES. NOW GET GOING. ROGUE... WHEN YOU DROP THE BURNING ENGINE...
"...MAKE SURE YOU AIM FOR SOMEPLACE ON THE GROUND WITH NO LIGHTS. CHANCES ARE, IT'LL BE AN OPEN FIELD OR A LAKE.
"ANYONE DUMB ENOUGH TO BE OUT THERE ON A NIGHT LIKE THIS--

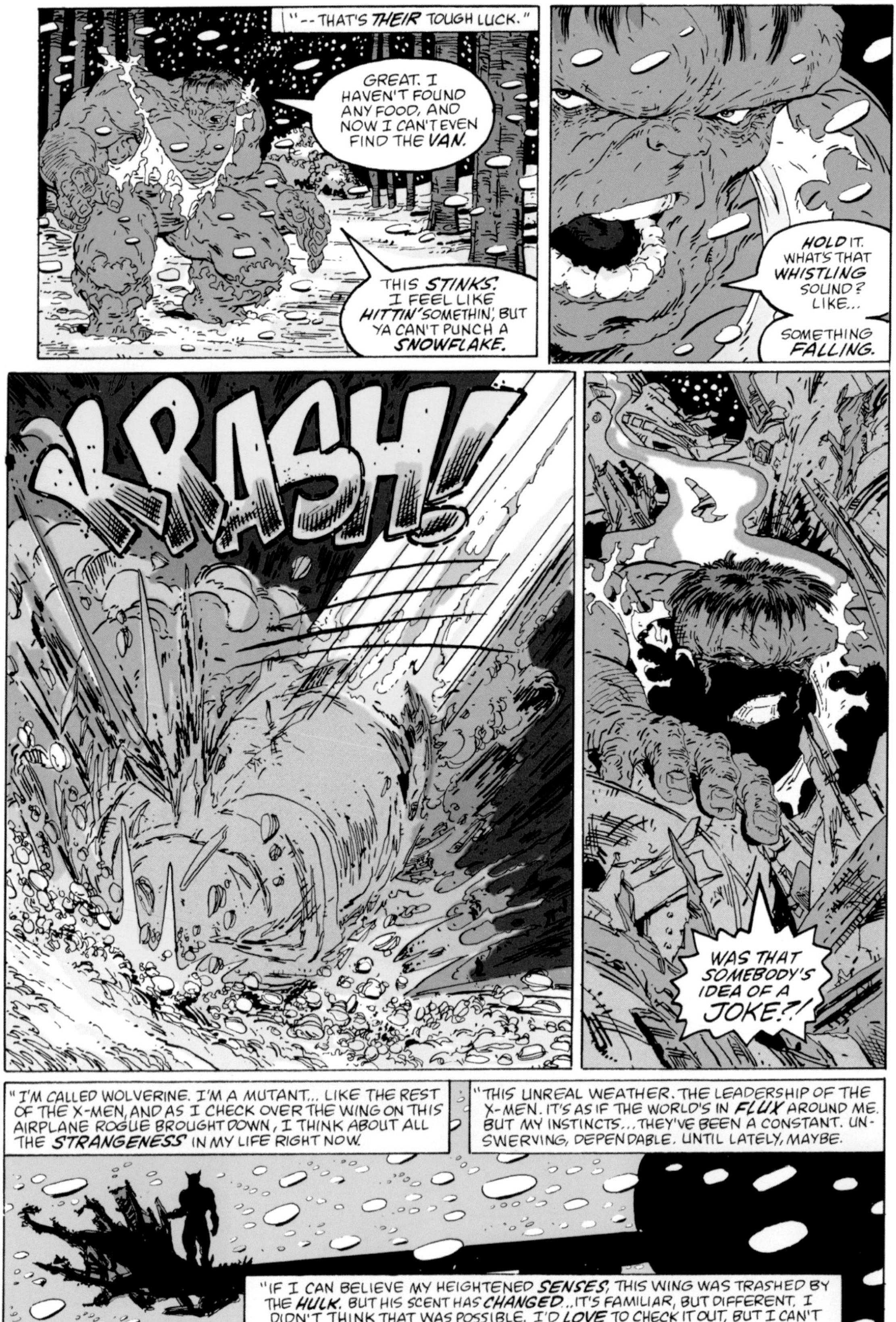
"--THAT'S THEIR TOUGH LUCK."
GREAT. I HAVEN'T FOUND ANY FOOD, AND NOW I CAN'T EVEN FIND THE VAN.
THIS STINKS. I FEEL LIKE HITTIN' SOMETHIN', BUT YA CAN'T PUNCH A SNOWFLAKE.
HOLD IT. WHAT'S THAT WHISTLING SOUND? LIKE...
SOMETHING FALLING.
KRASH!
WAS THAT SOMEBODY'S IDEA OF A JOKE?!
"I'M CALLED WOLVERINE. I'M A MUTANT... LIKE THE REST OF THE X-MEN, AND AS I CHECK OVER THE WING ON THIS AIRPLANE ROGUE BROUGHT DOWN, I THINK ABOUT ALL THE STRANGENESS IN MY LIFE RIGHT NOW.
"THIS UNREAL WEATHER. THE LEADERSHIP OF THE X-MEN. IT'S AS IF THE WORLD'S IN FLUX AROUND ME. BUT MY INSTINCTS... THEY'VE BEEN A CONSTANT. UNSWERVING, DEPENDABLE. UNTIL LATELY, MAYBE.
"IF I CAN BELIEVE MY HEIGHTENED SENSES, THIS WING WAS TRASHED BY THE HULK. BUT HIS SCENT HAS CHANGED... IT'S FAMILIAR, BUT DIFFERENT. I DIDN'T THINK THAT WAS POSSIBLE. I'D LOVE TO CHECK IT OUT, BUT I CAN'T LEAVE THE TEAM. ME, THE LONER. NOW I'M THE LEADER. FUNNY WORLD. I'M NOT LAUGHING.

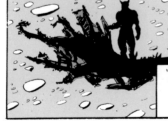

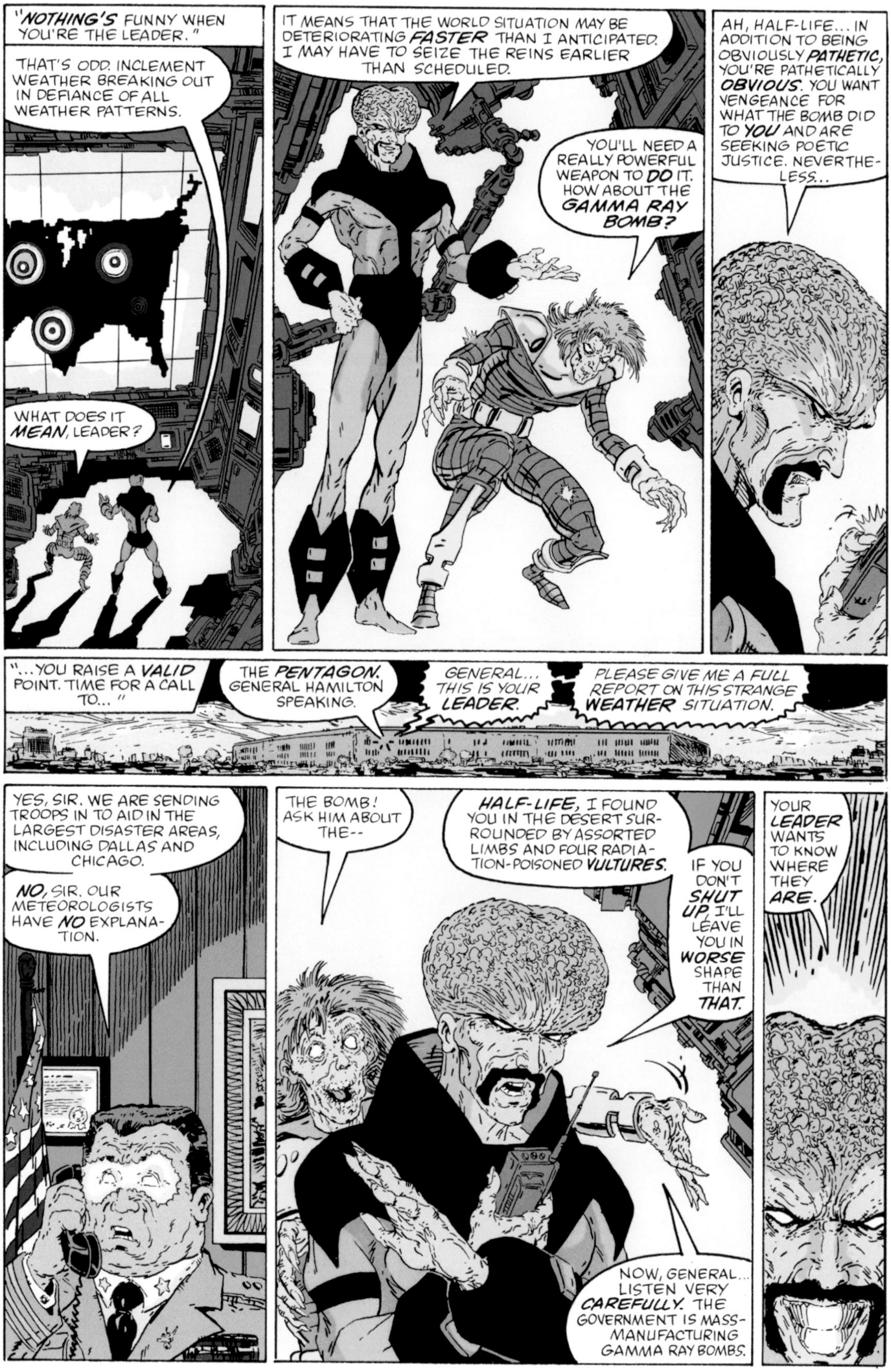

"NOTHING'S FUNNY WHEN YOU'RE THE LEADER."
THAT'S ODD. INCLEMENT WEATHER BREAKING OUT IN DEFIANCE OF ALL WEATHER PATTERNS.
WHAT DOES IT MEAN, LEADER?
IT MEANS THAT THE WORLD SITUATION MAY BE DETERIORATING FASTER THAN I ANTICIPATED. I MAY HAVE TO SEIZE THE REINS EARLIER THAN SCHEDULED.
YOU'LL NEED A REALLY POWERFUL WEAPON TO DO IT. HOW ABOUT THE GAMMA RAY BOMB?
AH, HALF-LIFE... IN ADDITION TO BEING OBVIOUSLY PATHETIC, YOU'RE PATHETICALLY OBVIOUS. YOU WANT VENGEANCE FOR WHAT THE BOMB DID TO YOU AND ARE SEEKING POETIC JUSTICE. NEVERTHE-LESS...
"...YOU RAISE A VALID POINT. TIME FOR A CALL TO..."
THE PENTAGON. GENERAL HAMILTON SPEAKING.
GENERAL... THIS IS YOUR LEADER.
PLEASE GIVE ME A FULL REPORT ON THIS STRANGE WEATHER SITUATION.
YES, SIR. WE ARE SENDING TROOPS IN TO AID IN THE LARGEST DISASTER AREAS, INCLUDING DALLAS AND CHICAGO.
NO, SIR. OUR METEOROLOGISTS HAVE NO EXPLANA-TION.
THE BOMB! ASK HIM ABOUT THE--
HALF-LIFE, I FOUND YOU IN THE DESERT SUR-ROUNDED BY ASSORTED LIMBS AND FOUR RADIA-TION-POISONED VULTURES.
IF YOU DON'T SHUT UP, I'LL LEAVE YOU IN WORSE SHAPE THAN THAT.
NOW, GENERAL... LISTEN VERY CAREFULLY. THE GOVERNMENT IS MASS-MANUFACTURING GAMMA RAY BOMBS.
YOUR LEADER WANTS TO KNOW WHERE THEY ARE.

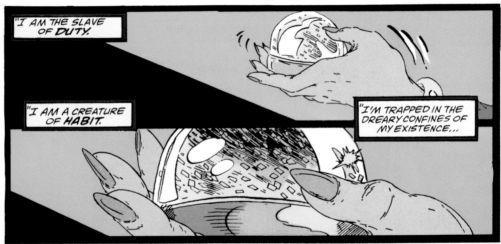

"I AM THE SLAVE of *DUTY*.

"I AM A CREATURE of *HABIT*.

"I'M TRAPPED IN THE DREARY CONFINES OF MY EXISTENCE,...

"STALLED AND UNABLE TO GO *FORWARD*, SNOW-BLINDED AND UNABLE TO LOOK *BACK*.

"I KNOW WHAT I *SHOULD* DO, AND WHAT I *SHOULDN'T*. I ALWAYS *HAVE*, BUT IT'S NEVER HELPED.

"THE ONE THING I *SHOULDN'T* DO IS THINK ABOUT *HIM*. AND YET ONCE AGAIN, I DO.

MANUFACTURERS OF FINE MEAT PRODUCT

PATTY-TIME INC.

EZ4U

"WHERE *IS* HE?"

PATTY-TIME

HELLO IN THERE! THIS IS SERGEANT O'RILEY OF THE NATIONAL GUARD! IS ANYBODY *IN* THERE?

WE'RE HERE TO *HELP* YOU!

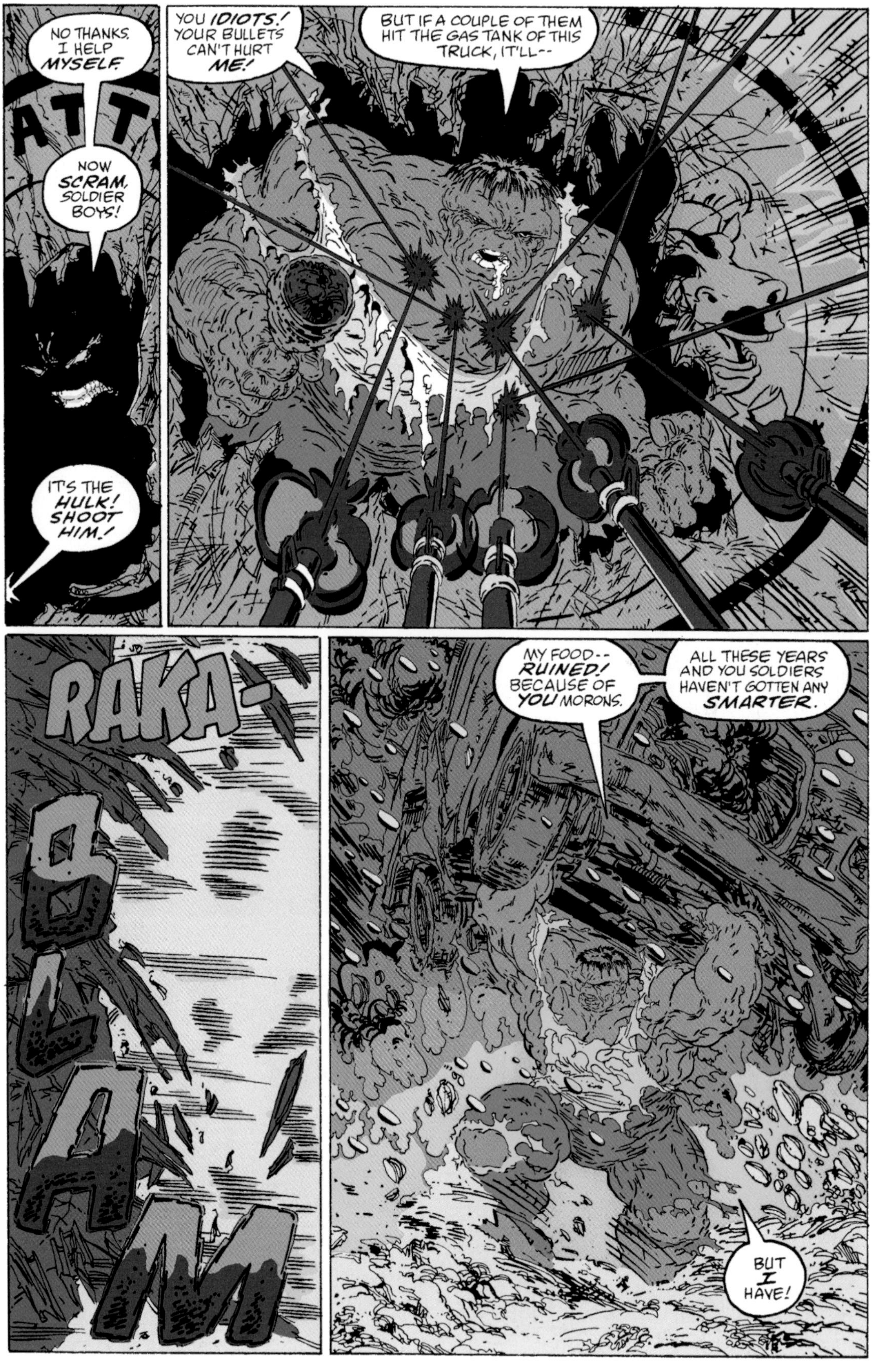
NO THANKS. I HELP MYSELF.
NOW SCRAM, SOLDIER BOYS!
IT'S THE HULK! SHOOT HIM!
YOU IDIOTS! YOUR BULLETS CAN'T HURT ME!
BUT IF A COUPLE OF THEM HIT THE GAS TANK OF THIS TRUCK, IT'LL--
RAKA-BLAAM
MY FOOD-- RUINED! BECAUSE OF YOU MORONS.
ALL THESE YEARS AND YOU SOLDIERS HAVEN'T GOTTEN ANY SMARTER.
BUT I HAVE!

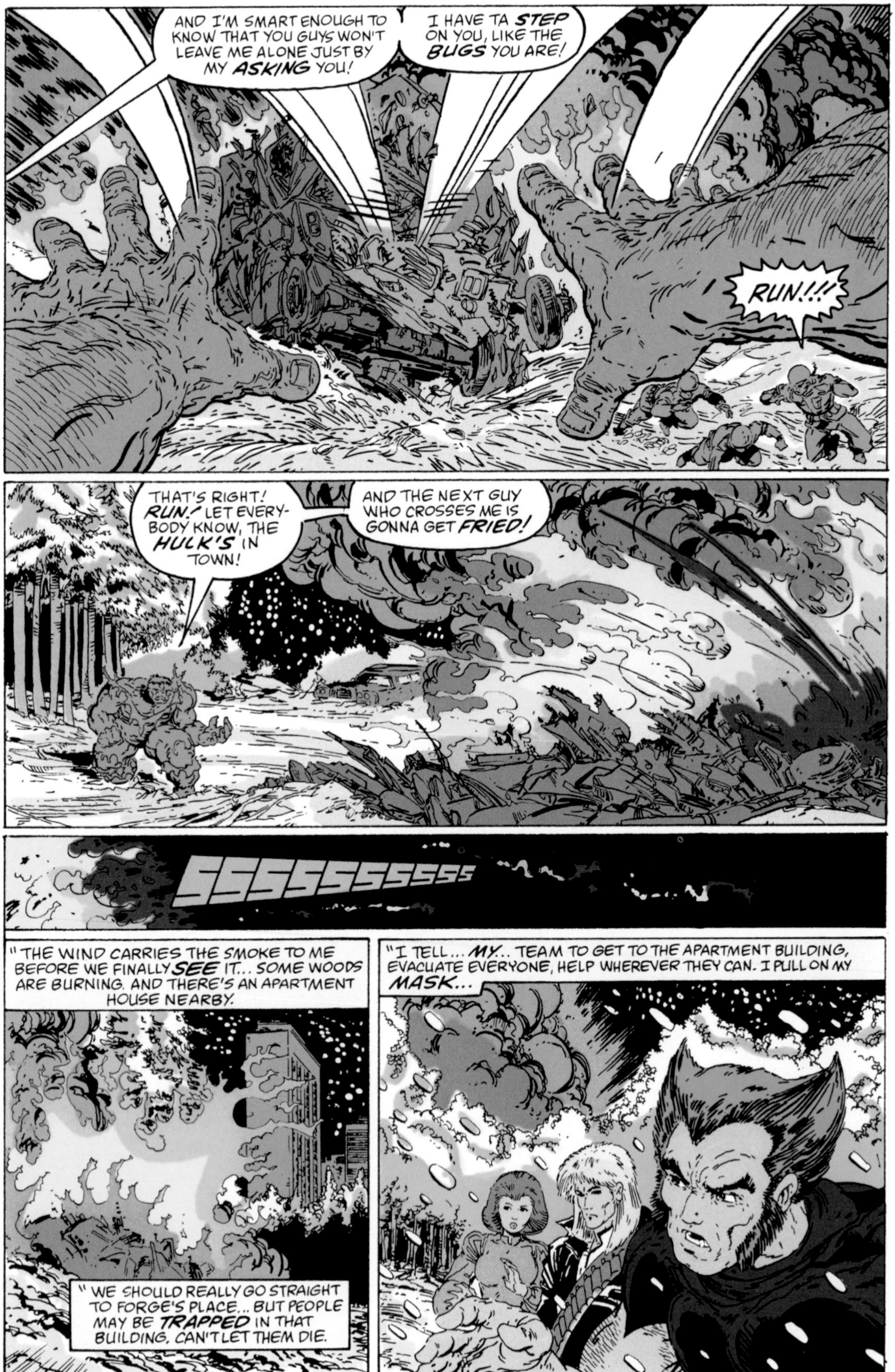

AND I'M SMART ENOUGH TO KNOW THAT YOU GUYS WON'T LEAVE ME ALONE JUST BY MY ASKING YOU!
I HAVE TA STEP ON YOU, LIKE THE BUGS YOU ARE!
RUN!!!
THAT'S RIGHT! RUN! LET EVERYBODY KNOW, THE HULK'S IN TOWN!
AND THE NEXT GUY WHO CROSSES ME IS GONNA GET FRIED!
SSSSSSSSSSS
"THE WIND CARRIES THE SMOKE TO ME BEFORE WE FINALLY SEE IT... SOME WOODS ARE BURNING. AND THERE'S AN APARTMENT HOUSE NEARBY.
"WE SHOULD REALLY GO STRAIGHT TO FORGE'S PLACE... BUT PEOPLE MAY BE TRAPPED IN THAT BUILDING. CAN'T LET THEM DIE.
"I TELL... MY... TEAM TO GET TO THE APARTMENT BUILDING, EVACUATE EVERYONE, HELP WHEREVER THEY CAN. I PULL ON MY MASK...

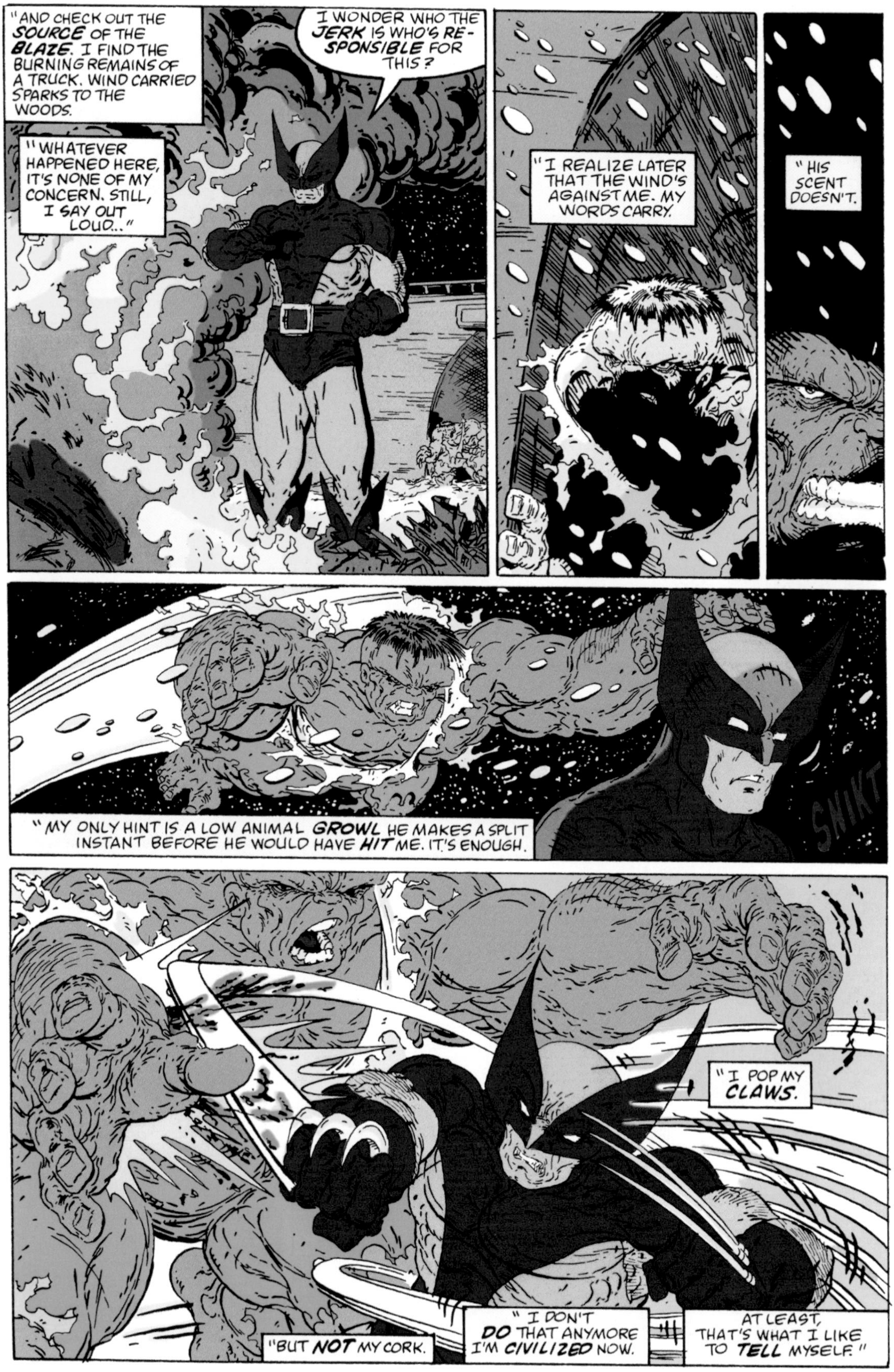
"AND CHECK OUT THE SOURCE OF THE BLAZE. I FIND THE BURNING REMAINS OF A TRUCK. WIND CARRIED SPARKS TO THE WOODS.
I WONDER WHO THE JERK IS WHO'S RESPONSIBLE FOR THIS?
"WHATEVER HAPPENED HERE, IT'S NONE OF MY CONCERN. STILL, I SAY OUT LOUD..."
"I REALIZE LATER THAT THE WIND'S AGAINST ME. MY WORDS CARRY.
"HIS SCENT DOESN'T.
"MY ONLY HINT IS A LOW ANIMAL GROWL HE MAKES A SPLIT INSTANT BEFORE HE WOULD HAVE HIT ME. IT'S ENOUGH.
SNIKT
"I POP MY CLAWS.
"BUT NOT MY CORK.
"I DON'T DO THAT ANYMORE I'M CIVILIZED NOW.
AT LEAST, THAT'S WHAT I LIKE TO TELL MYSELF."

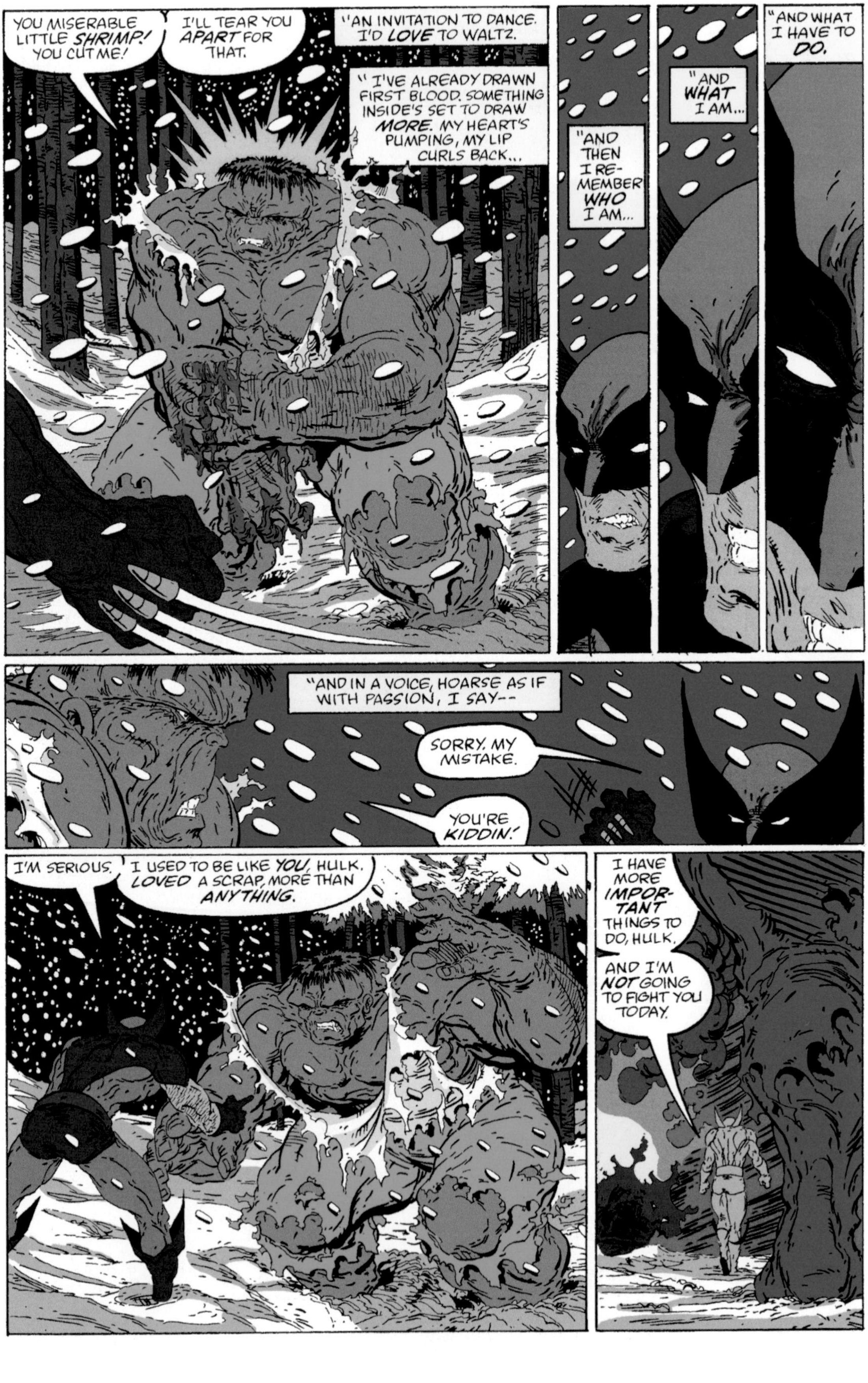
YOU MISERABLE LITTLE SHRIMP! YOU CUT ME!
I'LL TEAR YOU APART FOR THAT.
"AN INVITATION TO DANCE. I'D LOVE TO WALTZ.
"I'VE ALREADY DRAWN FIRST BLOOD. SOMETHING INSIDE'S SET TO DRAW MORE. MY HEART'S PUMPING, MY LIP CURLS BACK...
"AND THEN I REMEMBER WHO I AM...
"AND WHAT I AM...
"AND WHAT I HAVE TO DO.
"AND IN A VOICE, HOARSE AS IF WITH PASSION, I SAY--
SORRY. MY MISTAKE.
YOU'RE KIDDIN'!
I'M SERIOUS.
I USED TO BE LIKE YOU, HULK. LOVED A SCRAP, MORE THAN ANYTHING.
I HAVE MORE IMPORTANT THINGS TO DO, HULK.
AND I'M NOT GOING TO FIGHT YOU TODAY.

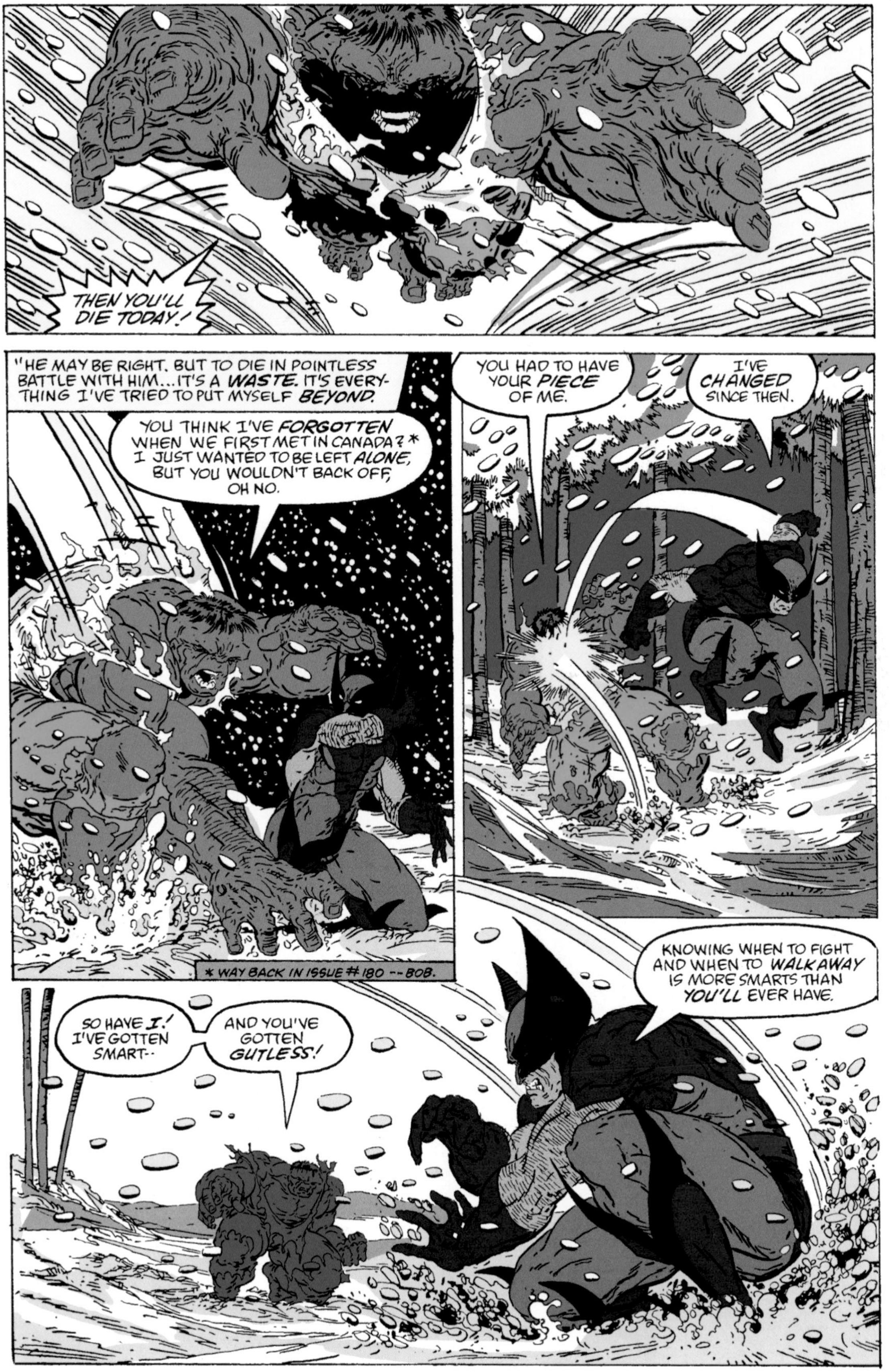

THEN YOU'LL DIE TODAY!
"HE MAY BE RIGHT. BUT TO DIE IN POINTLESS BATTLE WITH HIM... IT'S A WASTE. IT'S EVERYTHING I'VE TRIED TO PUT MYSELF BEYOND.
YOU THINK I'VE FORGOTTEN WHEN WE FIRST MET IN CANADA?* I JUST WANTED TO BE LEFT ALONE, BUT YOU WOULDN'T BACK OFF, OH NO.
* WAY BACK IN ISSUE #180 -- BOB.
YOU HAD TO HAVE YOUR PIECE OF ME.
I'VE CHANGED SINCE THEN.
SO HAVE I! I'VE GOTTEN SMART--
AND YOU'VE GOTTEN GUTLESS!
KNOWING WHEN TO FIGHT AND WHEN TO WALK AWAY IS MORE SMARTS THAN YOU'LL EVER HAVE.

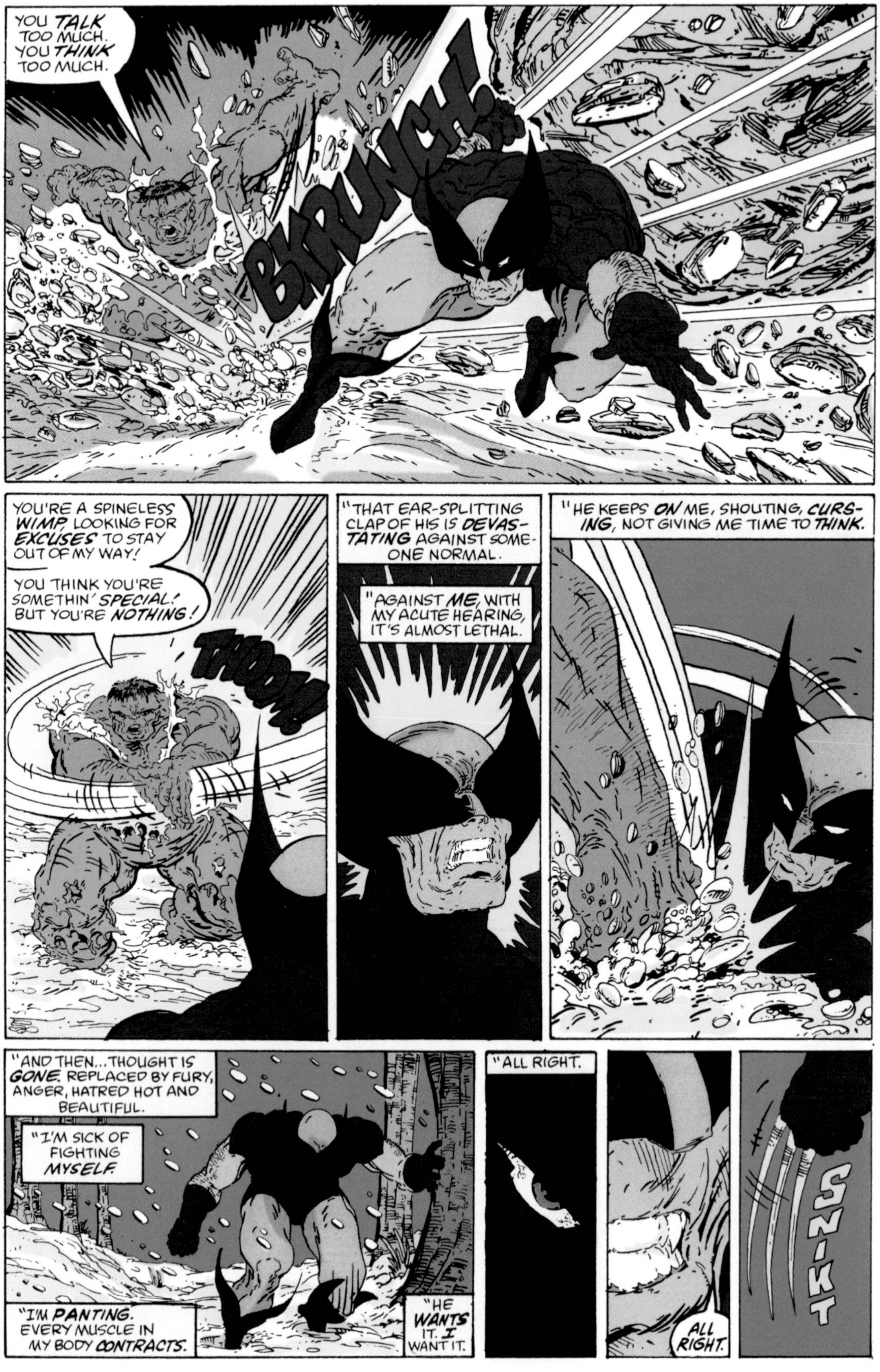
YOU TALK TOO MUCH. YOU THINK TOO MUCH.
BKRUNCH!
YOU'RE A SPINELESS WIMP, LOOKING FOR EXCUSES TO STAY OUT OF MY WAY!
YOU THINK YOU'RE SOMETHIN' SPECIAL! BUT YOU'RE NOTHING!
THOOM!
"THAT EAR-SPLITTING CLAP OF HIS IS DEVASTATING AGAINST SOMEONE NORMAL.
"AGAINST ME, WITH MY ACUTE HEARING, IT'S ALMOST LETHAL.
"HE KEEPS ON ME, SHOUTING, CURSING, NOT GIVING ME TIME TO THINK.
"AND THEN... THOUGHT IS GONE. REPLACED BY FURY, ANGER, HATRED HOT AND BEAUTIFUL.
"I'M SICK OF FIGHTING MYSELF.
"I'M PANTING. EVERY MUSCLE IN MY BODY CONTRACTS.
"HE WANTS IT. I WANT IT.
"ALL RIGHT.
ALL RIGHT.
SNIKT

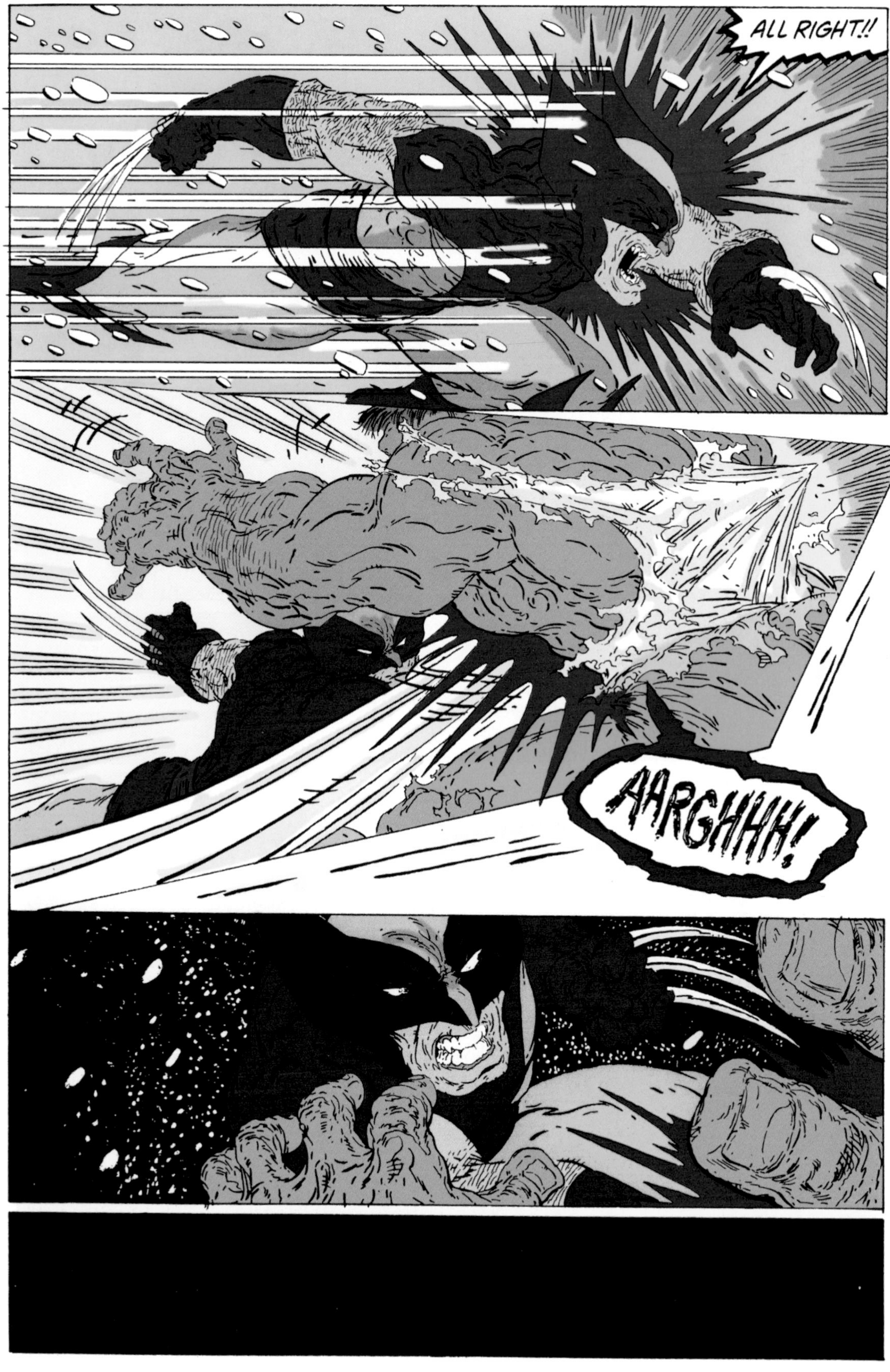
ALL RIGHT!!
AARGHHH!

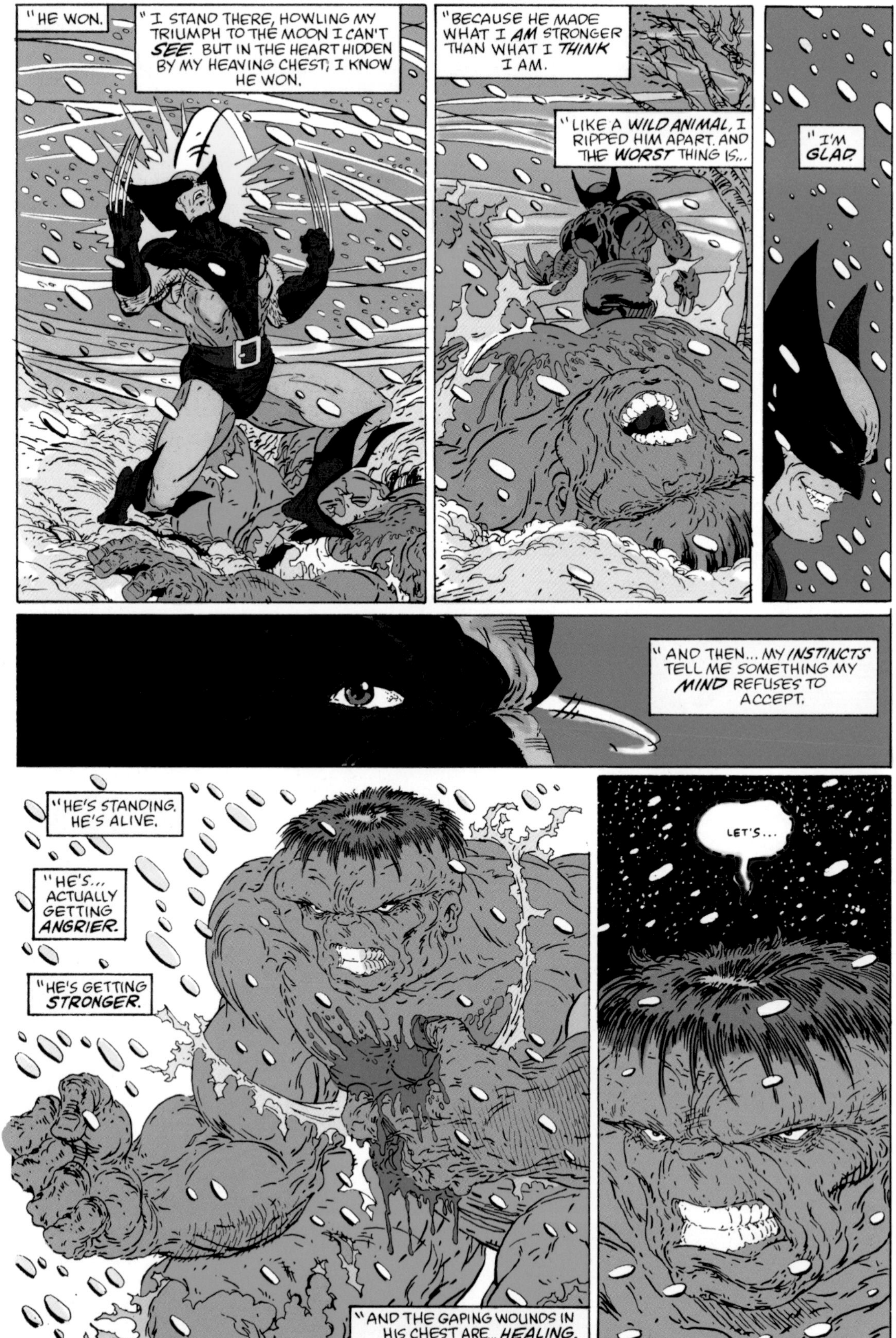
"HE WON.
"I STAND THERE, HOWLING MY TRIUMPH TO THE MOON I CAN'T SEE. BUT IN THE HEART HIDDEN BY MY HEAVING CHEST, I KNOW HE WON.
"BECAUSE HE MADE WHAT I AM STRONGER THAN WHAT I THINK I AM.
"LIKE A WILD ANIMAL, I RIPPED HIM APART. AND THE WORST THING IS...
"I'M GLAD.
"AND THEN... MY INSTINCTS TELL ME SOMETHING MY MIND REFUSES TO ACCEPT.
"HE'S STANDING. HE'S ALIVE.
"HE'S... ACTUALLY GETTING ANGRIER.
"HE'S GETTING STRONGER.
"AND THE GAPING WOUNDS IN HIS CHEST ARE... HEALING.
LET'S...

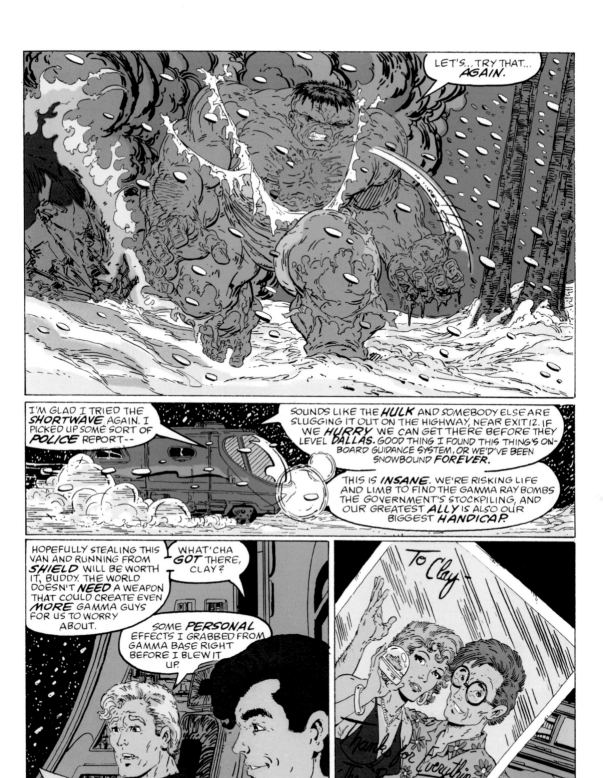

LET'S... TRY THAT... *AGAIN.*

I'M GLAD I TRIED THE *SHORTWAVE* AGAIN. I PICKED UP SOME SORT OF *POLICE* REPORT--

SOUNDS LIKE THE *HULK* AND SOMEBODY ELSE ARE SLUGGING IT OUT ON THE HIGHWAY, NEAR EXIT 12. IF WE *HURRY* WE CAN GET THERE BEFORE THEY LEVEL *DALLAS.* GOOD THING I FOUND THIS THING'S ON-BOARD GUIDANCE SYSTEM, OR WE'D'VE BEEN SNOWBOUND *FOREVER.*

THIS IS *INSANE.* WE'RE RISKING LIFE AND LIMB TO FIND THE GAMMA RAY BOMBS THE GOVERNMENT'S STOCKPILING, AND OUR GREATEST *ALLY* IS ALSO OUR BIGGEST *HANDICAP.*

HOPEFULLY STEALING THIS VAN AND RUNNING FROM *SHIELD* WILL BE WORTH IT, BUDDY. THE WORLD DOESN'T *NEED* A WEAPON THAT COULD CREATE EVEN *MORE* GAMMA GUYS FOR US TO WORRY ABOUT.

WHAT'CHA *GOT* THERE, CLAY?

SOME *PERSONAL* EFFECTS I GRABBED FROM GAMMA BASE RIGHT BEFORE I BLEW IT UP.

To Clay--

Thanks for everything
the Banners

...IN *HAPPIER* TIMES.

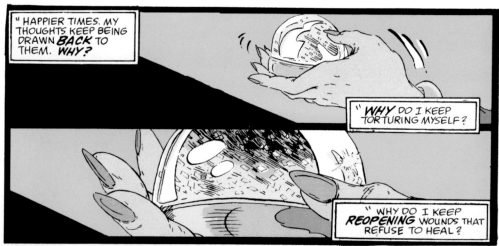

" HAPPIER TIMES. MY THOUGHTS KEEP BEING DRAWN *BACK* TO THEM. *WHY?*

" *WHY* DO I KEEP TORTURING MYSELF?

" WHY DO I KEEP *REOPENING* WOUNDS THAT REFUSE TO HEAL?

THOSE PIGSTICKERS OF YOURS DIDN'T STOP ME *BEFORE,* AND THEY *WON'T* HELP YA *NOW!*

" I REALIZE WHAT IS HAPPENING, AND I DON'T *LIKE* IT.

"THE MOST COMMON RESULT OF RADIATION EXPOSURE IS *CANCER* -- AN ABNORMAL GROWTH OF CELLS.

" WHEN BRUCE BANNER GOT HIT BY GAMMA RAYS, IT GAVE HIM A KIND OF CANCER, CALLED THE *HULK.*

"I CUT HIM *AGAIN* -- HE HEALS EVEN *FASTER.*

" I ALWAYS THOUGHT THE HULK'S SKIN WAS *IMPENETRABLE.* I WAS *WRONG.*

"BUT HIS CELLS REPRODUCE SO *FAST* IT *SEEMS* THAT WAY. AND THE MADDER HE GETS, THE MORE HIS SYSTEM *SPEEDS UP,* THE MORE *CELLS* HE PRODUCES...

" HE GETS *TOUGHER. STRONGER.* HARDER TO *HURT.*

WHUMP

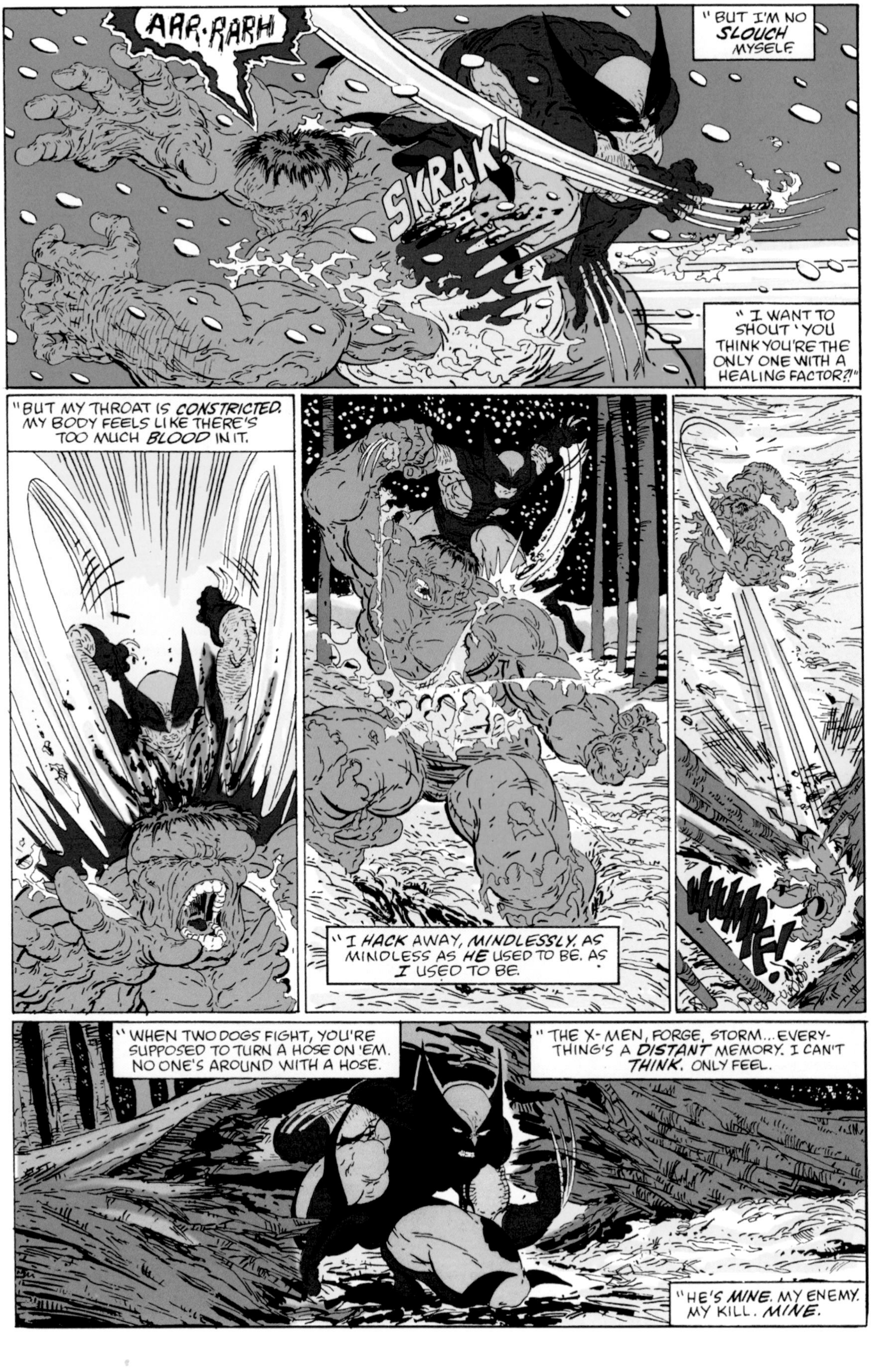
ARR·RARH
"BUT I'M NO SLOUCH MYSELF.
SKRAK!
"I WANT TO SHOUT 'YOU THINK YOU'RE THE ONLY ONE WITH A HEALING FACTOR?!'
"BUT MY THROAT IS CONSTRICTED. MY BODY FEELS LIKE THERE'S TOO MUCH BLOOD IN IT.
"I HACK AWAY, MINDLESSLY. AS MINDLESS AS HE USED TO BE. AS I USED TO BE.
WHUMPF!
"WHEN TWO DOGS FIGHT, YOU'RE SUPPOSED TO TURN A HOSE ON 'EM. NO ONE'S AROUND WITH A HOSE.
"THE X-MEN, FORGE, STORM... EVERYTHING'S A DISTANT MEMORY. I CAN'T THINK. ONLY FEEL.
"HE'S MINE. MY ENEMY. MY KILL. MINE.

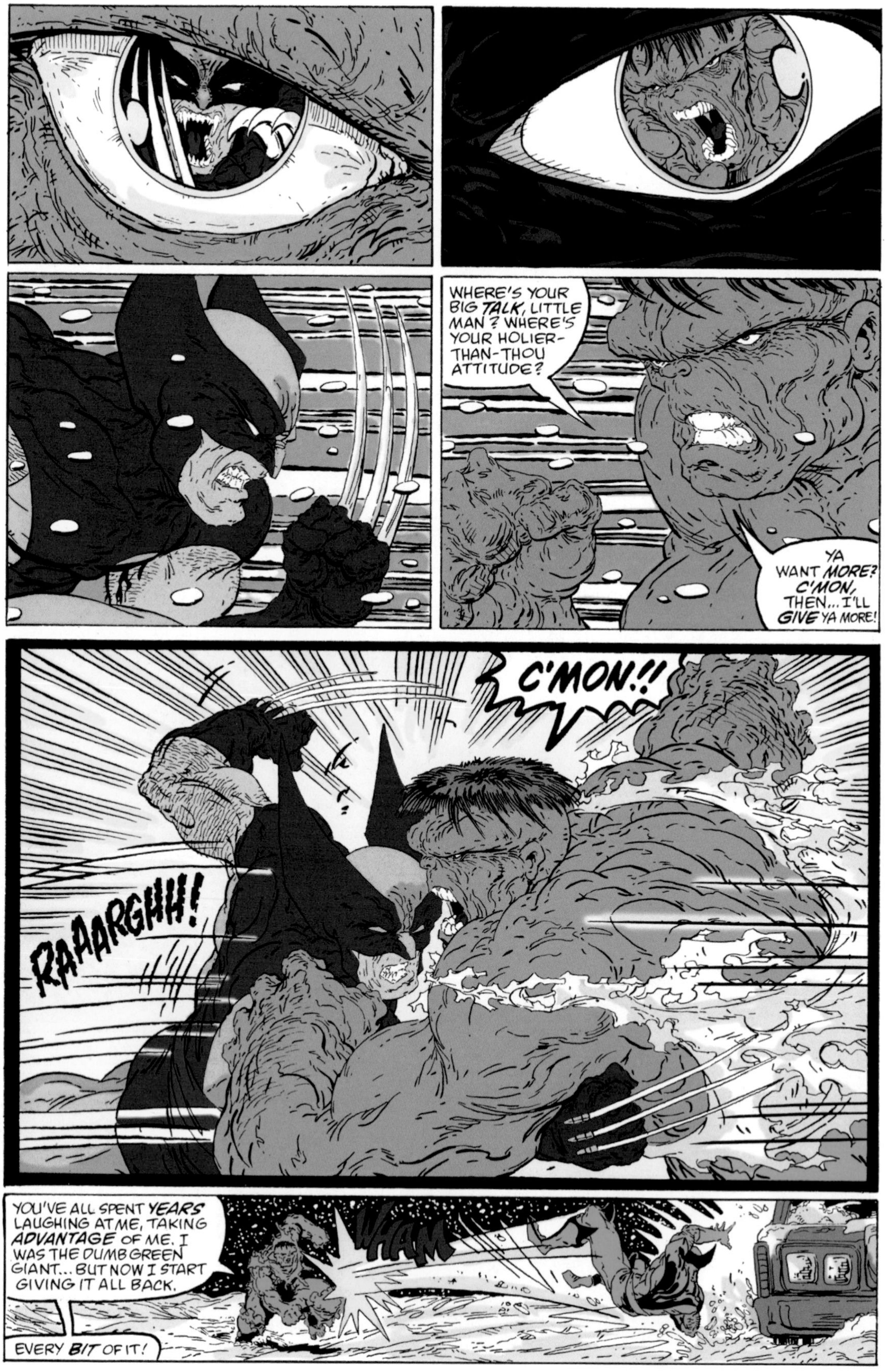
WHERE'S YOUR BIG TALK, LITTLE MAN? WHERE'S YOUR HOLIER-THAN-THOU ATTITUDE?
YA WANT MORE? C'MON, THEN... I'LL GIVE YA MORE!
C'MON!!
RAAARGHH!
YOU'VE ALL SPENT YEARS LAUGHING AT ME, TAKING ADVANTAGE OF ME. I WAS THE DUMB GREEN GIANT... BUT NOW I START GIVING IT ALL BACK.
WHAM
EVERY BIT OF IT!

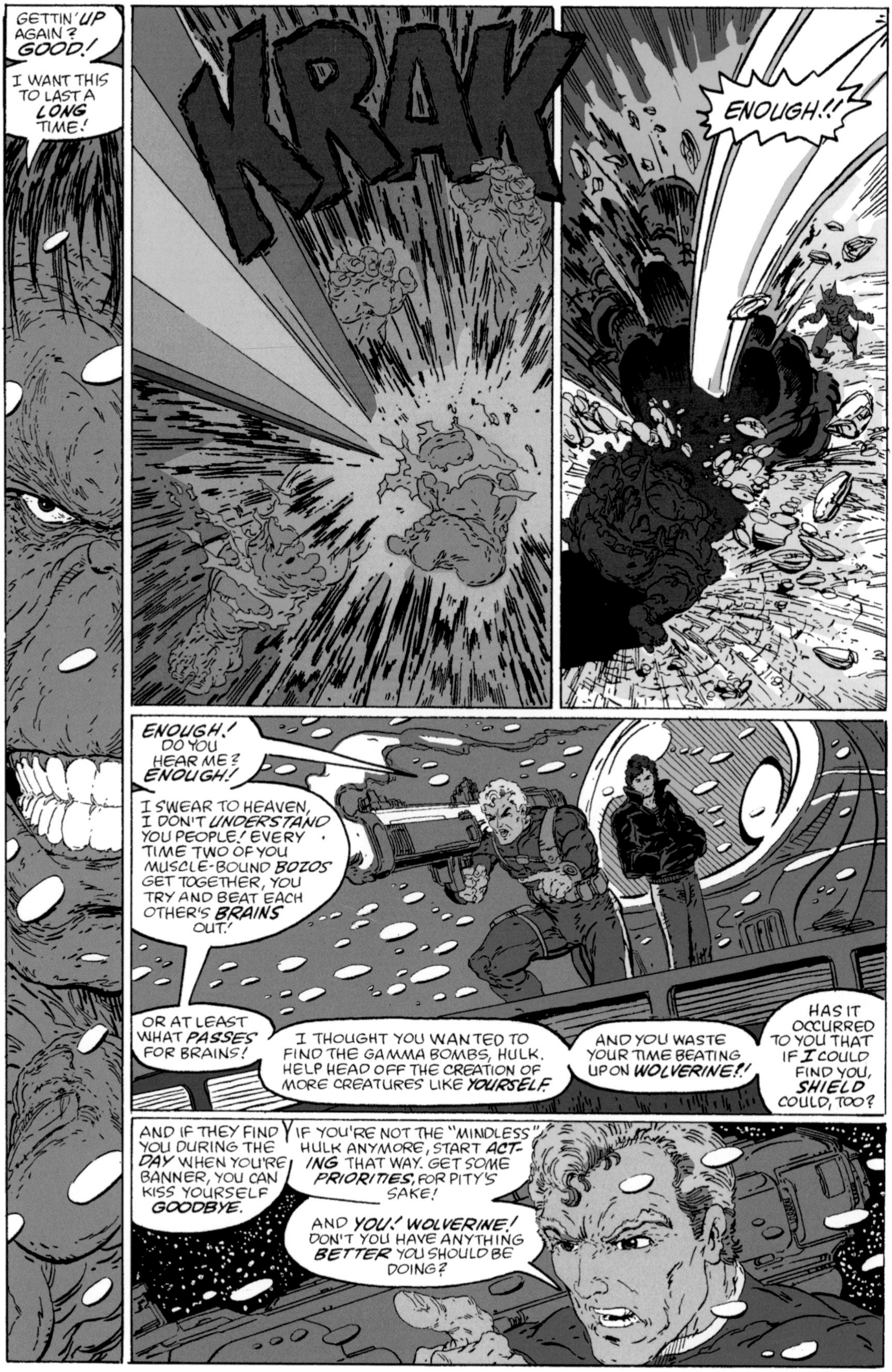
GETTIN' UP AGAIN? GOOD!
I WANT THIS TO LAST A LONG TIME!
KRAK
ENOUGH!!
ENOUGH! DO YOU HEAR ME? ENOUGH!
I SWEAR TO HEAVEN, I DON'T UNDERSTAND YOU PEOPLE! EVERY TIME TWO OF YOU MUSCLE-BOUND BOZOS GET TOGETHER, YOU TRY AND BEAT EACH OTHER'S BRAINS OUT!
OR AT LEAST WHAT PASSES FOR BRAINS!
I THOUGHT YOU WANTED TO FIND THE GAMMA BOMBS, HULK. HELP HEAD OFF THE CREATION OF MORE CREATURES LIKE YOURSELF.
AND YOU WASTE YOUR TIME BEATING UP ON WOLVERINE!!
HAS IT OCCURRED TO YOU THAT IF I COULD FIND YOU, SHIELD COULD, TOO?
AND IF THEY FIND YOU DURING THE DAY WHEN YOU'RE BANNER, YOU CAN KISS YOURSELF GOODBYE.
IF YOU'RE NOT THE "MINDLESS" HULK ANYMORE, START ACTING THAT WAY. GET SOME PRIORITIES, FOR PITY'S SAKE!
AND YOU! WOLVERINE! DON'T YOU HAVE ANYTHING BETTER YOU SHOULD BE DOING?

"AND IN A STRANGLED VOICE I REPLY--

YEAH.

YEAH. I *DO*.

I THOUGHT I'D COME SO *FAR*. THEN I RUN INTO YOU AND *BANG*, THE YEARS FALL AWAY.

NO MATTER HOW FAR I GO, I'M RIGHT BACK WHERE I *STARTED*.

YEAH, WELL, YOU'RE JUST LIKE ALL THE *OTHERS*, WHO ALWAYS THOUGHT THEY WERE BETTER'N *ME*.

WELL, NOW I'M BETTER'N *ALL* OF YA!

UNDERSTAND?! *ALL* OF YA!

AND I DON'T HAVE TO BEAT UP EVERY LOW-LIFE LIKE *YOU* TO PROVE IT. YOU *TELL* 'EM, SHRIMP. TELL 'EM THE HULK'S BETTER THAN *ANY* OF 'EM.

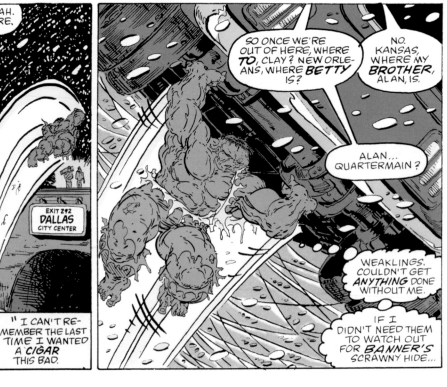

YEAH. SURE.

EXIT 242
DALLAS
CITY CENTER

" I CAN'T REMEMBER THE LAST TIME I WANTED A *CIGAR* THIS BAD.

SO ONCE WE'RE OUT OF HERE, WHERE *TO*, CLAY? NEW ORLEANS, WHERE *BETTY* IS?

NO. KANSAS, WHERE MY *BROTHER*, ALAN, IS.

ALAN... QUARTERMAIN?

WEAKLINGS. COULDN'T GET *ANYTHING* DONE WITHOUT ME.

IF I DIDN'T NEED THEM TO WATCH OUT FOR *BANNER'S* SCRAWNY HIDE...

164

DON'T LAUGH. HE'S THE *ELDER*. IT *COULD'VE* BEEN ME. ANYWAY, HE CAN *HELP* US FIND THE GAMMA BOMBS.

CONVINCING BRUCE THAT THE BOMBS ARE MORE IMPORTANT THAN FINDING BETTY MAY BE TOUGH,

CLAY... YOU THINK BETTY'S BEEN THINKING ABOUT BRUCE SINCE SHE RAN OFF?

NOT IF SHE'S *SMART*, RICK-O. NOT IF SHE'S *SMART*.

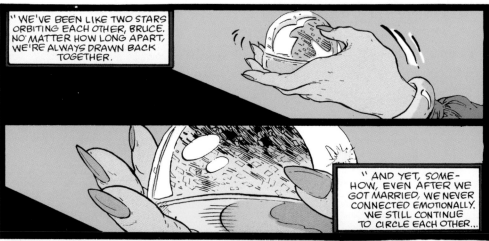

" WE'VE BEEN LIKE TWO STARS ORBITING EACH OTHER, BRUCE. NO MATTER HOW LONG APART, WE'RE ALWAYS DRAWN BACK TOGETHER.

" AND YET, SOME-HOW, EVEN AFTER WE GOT MARRIED, WE NEVER CONNECTED EMOTIONALLY. WE STILL CONTINUE TO CIRCLE EACH OTHER...

" LIKE TWO SHIPS *PASSING* IN THE NIGHT.

"AN ENDLESS, VICIOUS CIRCLE. A *CYCLE*, EVEN...

KRAK!

" A CYCLE THAT CAN ONLY BE BROKEN... AT GREAT EXPENSE."

NEXT ISSUE: > THE MAN-BULL!

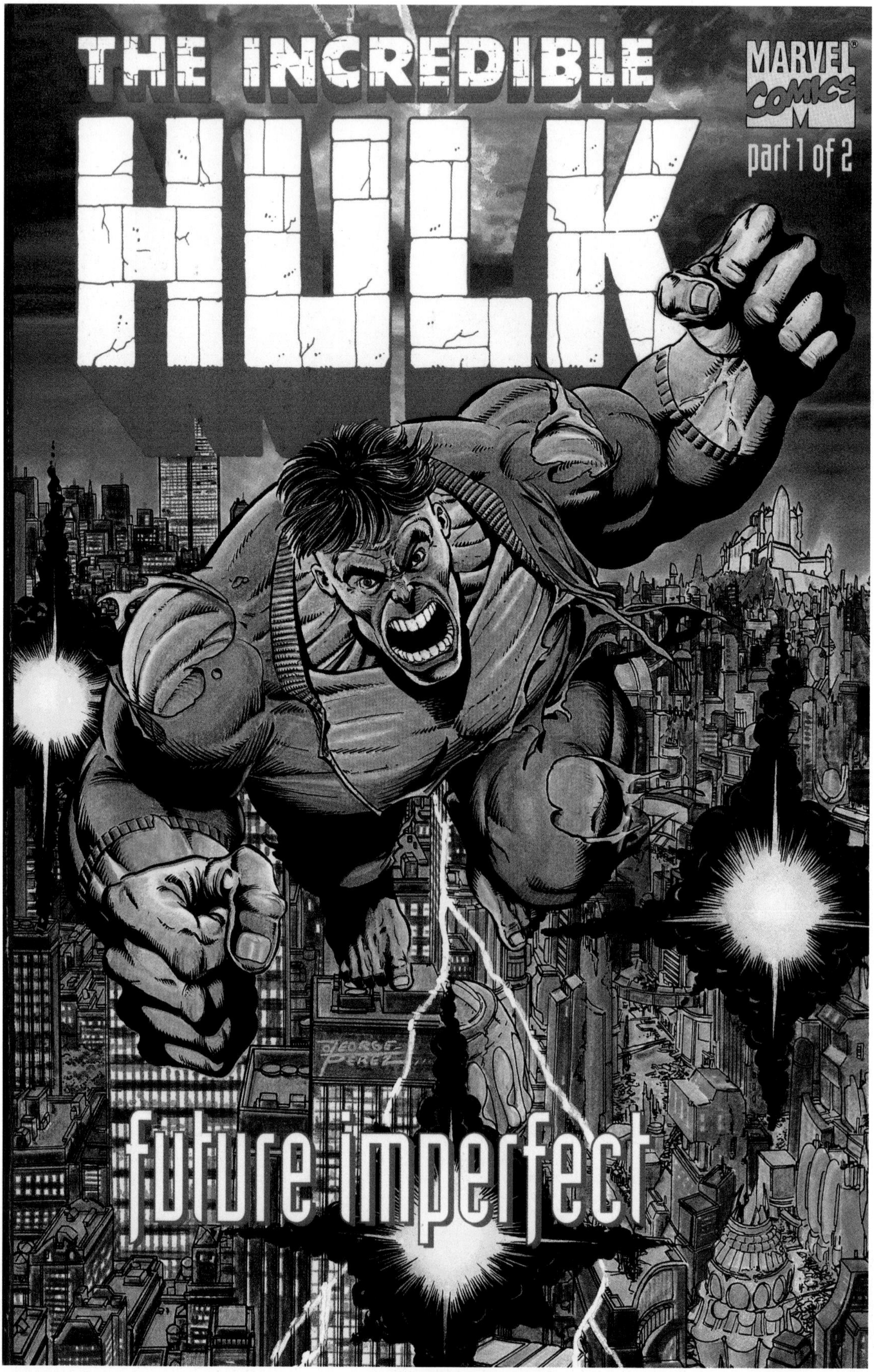
THE INCREDIBLE
HULK
MARVEL COMICS
part 1 of 2
GEORGE PEREZ
future imperfect

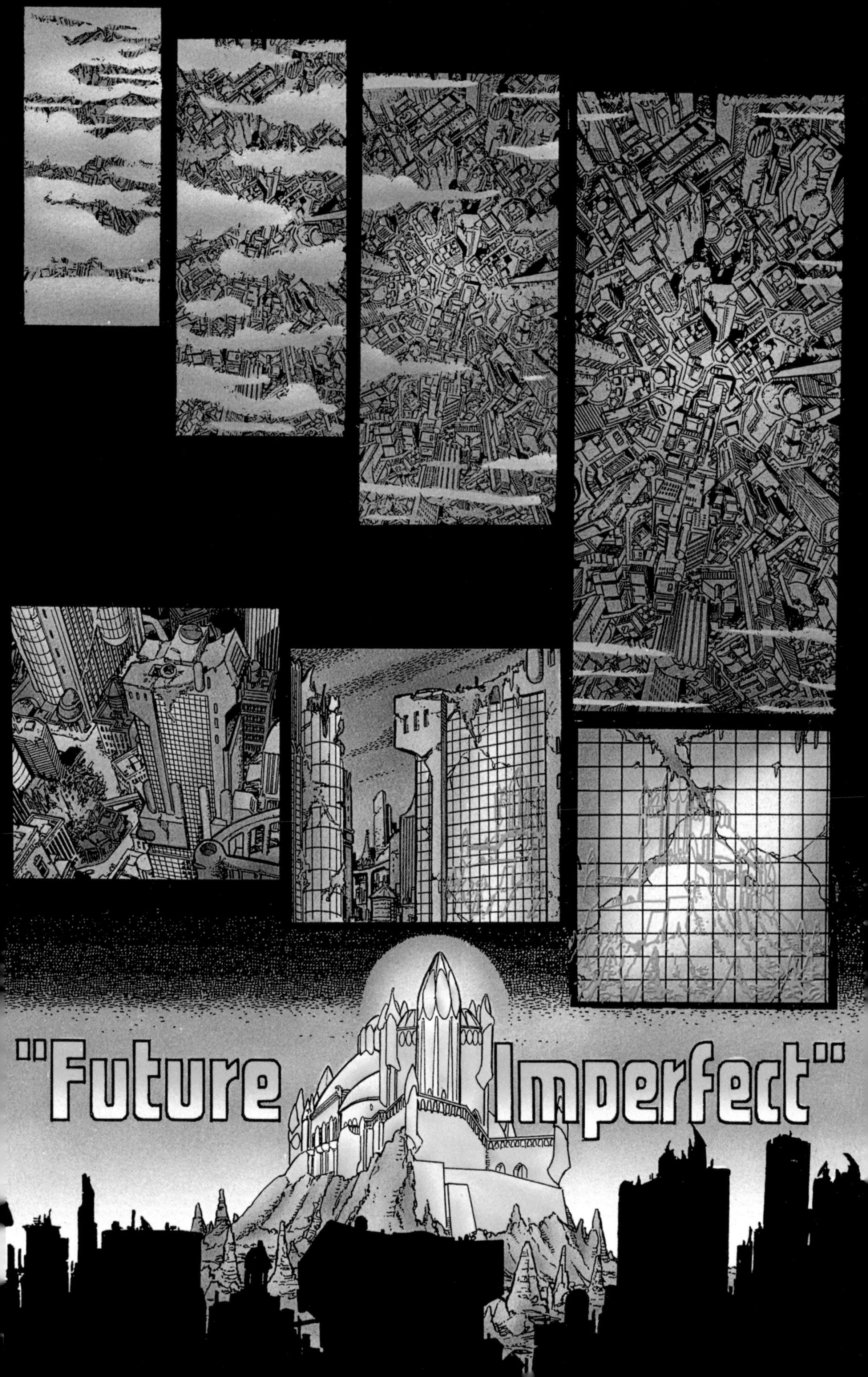
"Future Imperfect"

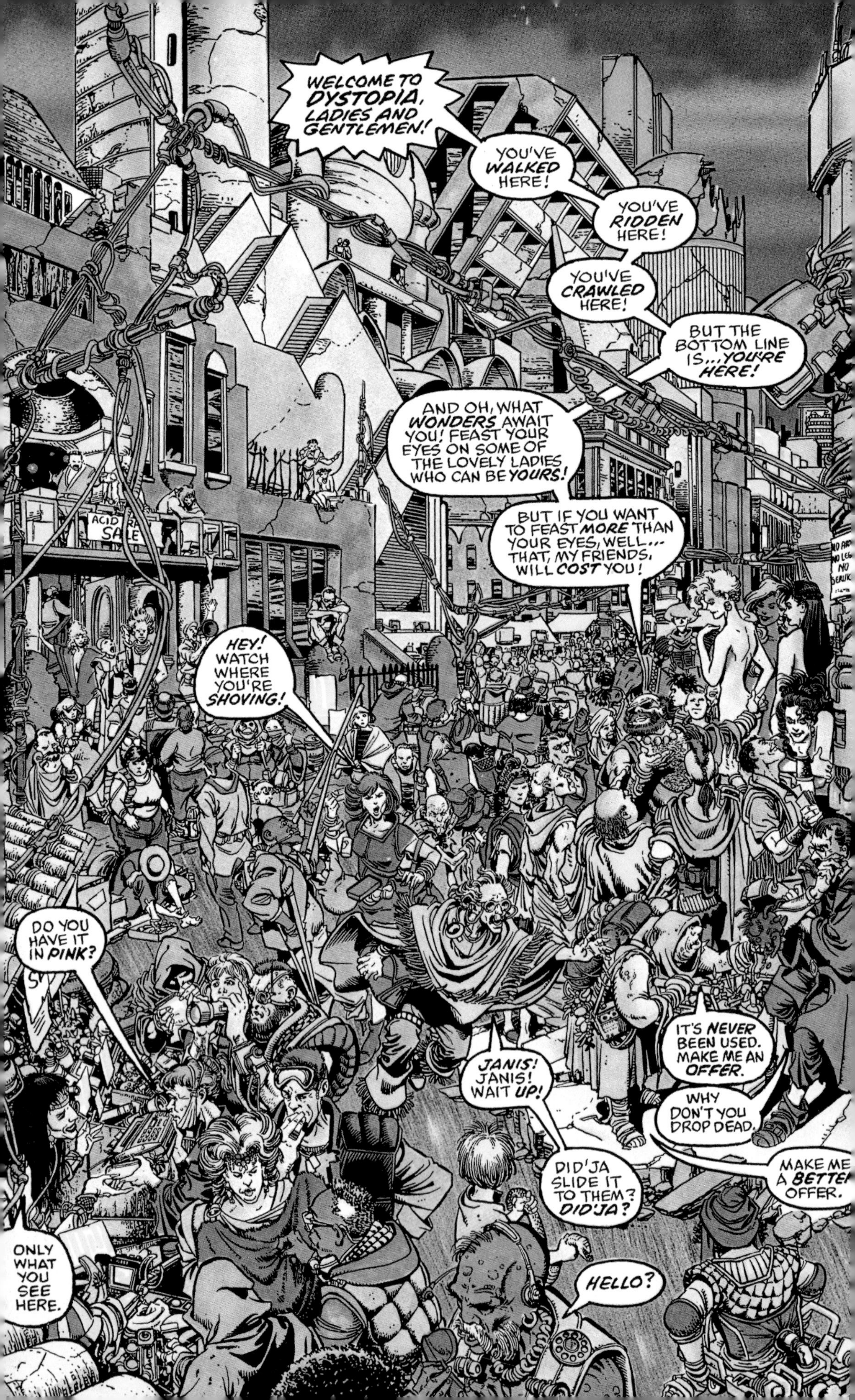

WELCOME TO DYSTOPIA, LADIES AND GENTLEMEN!
YOU'VE WALKED HERE!
YOU'VE RIDDEN HERE!
YOU'VE CRAWLED HERE!
BUT THE BOTTOM LINE IS... YOU'RE HERE!
AND OH, WHAT WONDERS AWAIT YOU! FEAST YOUR EYES ON SOME OF THE LOVELY LADIES WHO CAN BE YOURS!
BUT IF YOU WANT TO FEAST MORE THAN YOUR EYES, WELL... THAT, MY FRIENDS, WILL COST YOU!
HEY! WATCH WHERE YOU'RE SHOVING!
DO YOU HAVE IT IN PINK?
JANIS! JANIS! WAIT UP!
IT'S NEVER BEEN USED. MAKE ME AN OFFER.
WHY DON'T YOU DROP DEAD.
MAKE ME A BETTE OFFER.
DID'JA SLIDE IT TO THEM? DID'JA?
ONLY WHAT YOU SEE HERE.
HELLO?

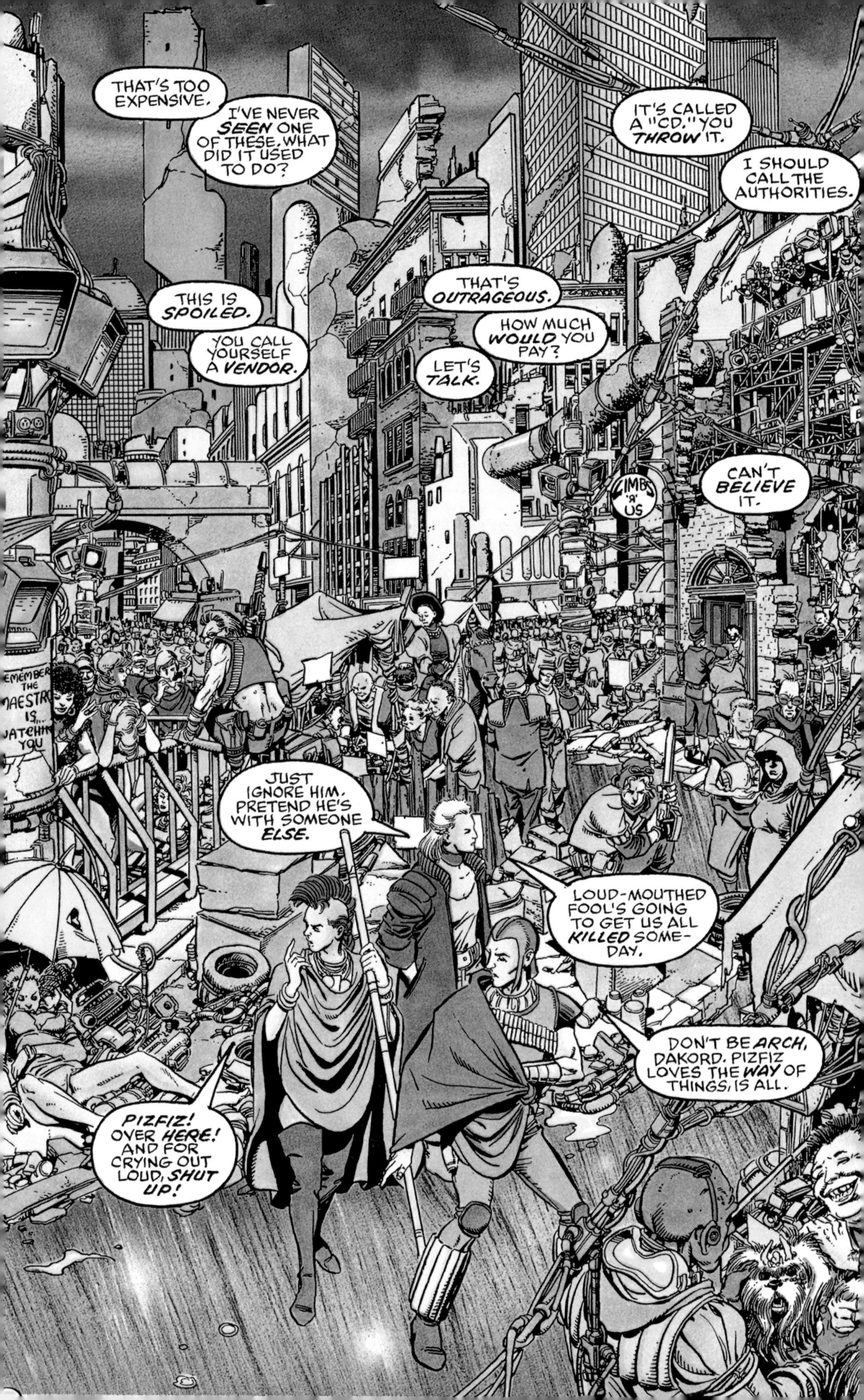
THAT'S TOO EXPENSIVE.
I'VE NEVER SEEN ONE OF THESE. WHAT DID IT USED TO DO?
IT'S CALLED A "CD." YOU THROW IT.
I SHOULD CALL THE AUTHORITIES.
THIS IS SPOILED.
YOU CALL YOURSELF A VENDOR.
THAT'S OUTRAGEOUS.
HOW MUCH WOULD YOU PAY?
LET'S TALK.
LIMBS 'R' US
CAN'T BELIEVE IT.
EMEMBER THE AESTRO IS ATCHIN YOU
JUST IGNORE HIM. PRETEND HE'S WITH SOMEONE ELSE.
LOUD-MOUTHED FOOL'S GOING TO GET US ALL KILLED SOME-DAY.
DON'T BE ARCH, DAKORD. PIZFIZ LOVES THE WAY OF THINGS, IS ALL.
PIZFIZ! OVER HERE! AND FOR CRYING OUT LOUD, SHUT UP!

DID'JA *SLIDE* IT? *DIDJA?*

IT'S BEEN SLID, PIZFIZ. THEY'RE IN THE KNOW.

NOW *GRIP* IT.

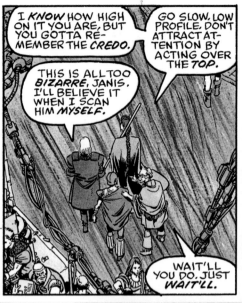

I *KNOW* HOW HIGH ON IT YOU ARE, BUT YOU GOTTA RE-MEMBER THE *CREDO.*

GO SLOW. LOW PROFILE. DON'T ATTRACT ATTEN-TION BY ACTING OVER THE *TOP.*

THIS IS ALL TOO *BIZARRE,* JANIS. I'LL BELIEVE IT WHEN I SCAN HIM *MYSELF.*

IT'S JUST THAT I'VE BEEN WATCH-ING MY BACK AGAINST THE MAES-TRO TOO LONG TO BELIEVE THIS *STUDLY* YOU'VE RE-TRIEVED IS GOING TO *CHANGE* THINGS.

WAIT'LL YOU DO. JUST *WAIT'LL.*

ONE SIDE, PEASANTS.

FLARK YOU! THINGS ARE GONNA BE *DIFFERENT* AROUND HERE! SOONER THAN YOU *THINK!*

WILL YOU *SHUT UP!* STOP MOUTHING! YOUR BOASTING'S GOING TO GET US ALL *KILLED!*

ARE YOU COM-PLETELY DIM?

THE GRAVITY POLICE ARE *EVERYWHERE.* YOU CAN'T DRAW ATTENTION TO YOURSELF.

ONE MINUTE YOU'D BE MIND-ING YOUR OWN BUSINESS, AND THE NEXT THING IT'S--

BLAK

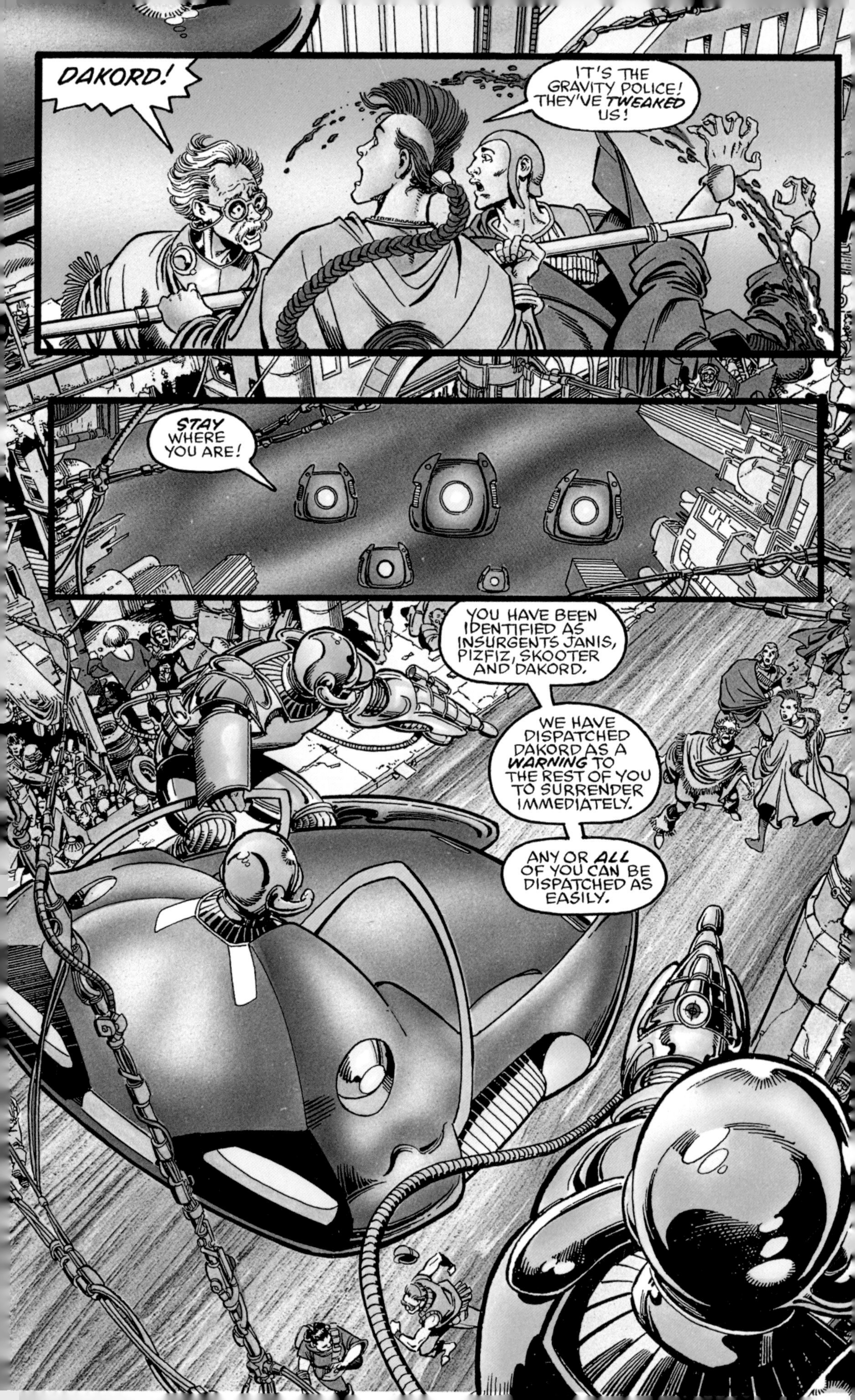
DAKORD!
IT'S THE GRAVITY POLICE! THEY'VE TWEAKED US!
STAY WHERE YOU ARE!
YOU HAVE BEEN IDENTIFIED AS INSURGENTS JANIS, PIZFIZ, SKOOTER AND DAKORD.
WE HAVE DISPATCHED DAKORD AS A WARNING TO THE REST OF YOU TO SURRENDER IMMEDIATELY.
ANY OR ALL OF YOU CAN BE DISPATCHED AS EASILY.

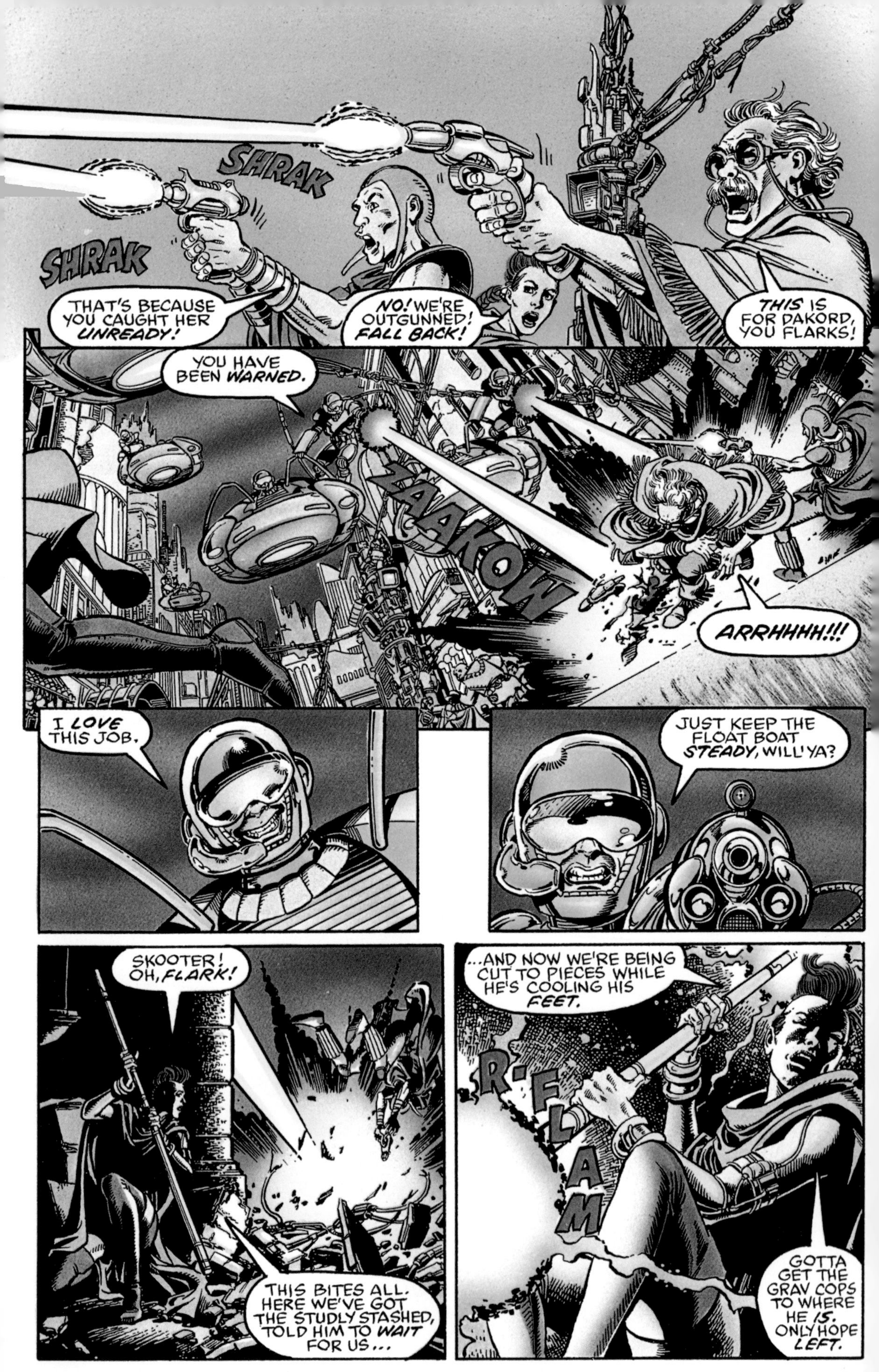
SHRAK
SHRAK
THAT'S BECAUSE YOU CAUGHT HER UNREADY!
NO! WE'RE OUTGUNNED! FALL BACK!
THIS IS FOR DAKORD, YOU FLARKS!
YOU HAVE BEEN WARNED.
ZAAKOW
ARRHHHH!!!
I LOVE THIS JOB.
JUST KEEP THE FLOAT BOAT STEADY, WILL'YA?
SKOOTER! OH, FLARK!
THIS BITES ALL. HERE WE'VE GOT THE STUDLY STASHED, TOLD HIM TO WAIT FOR US...
...AND NOW WE'RE BEING CUT TO PIECES WHILE HE'S COOLING HIS FEET.
R-FLAM
GOTTA GET THE GRAV COPS TO WHERE HE IS. ONLY HOPE LEFT.

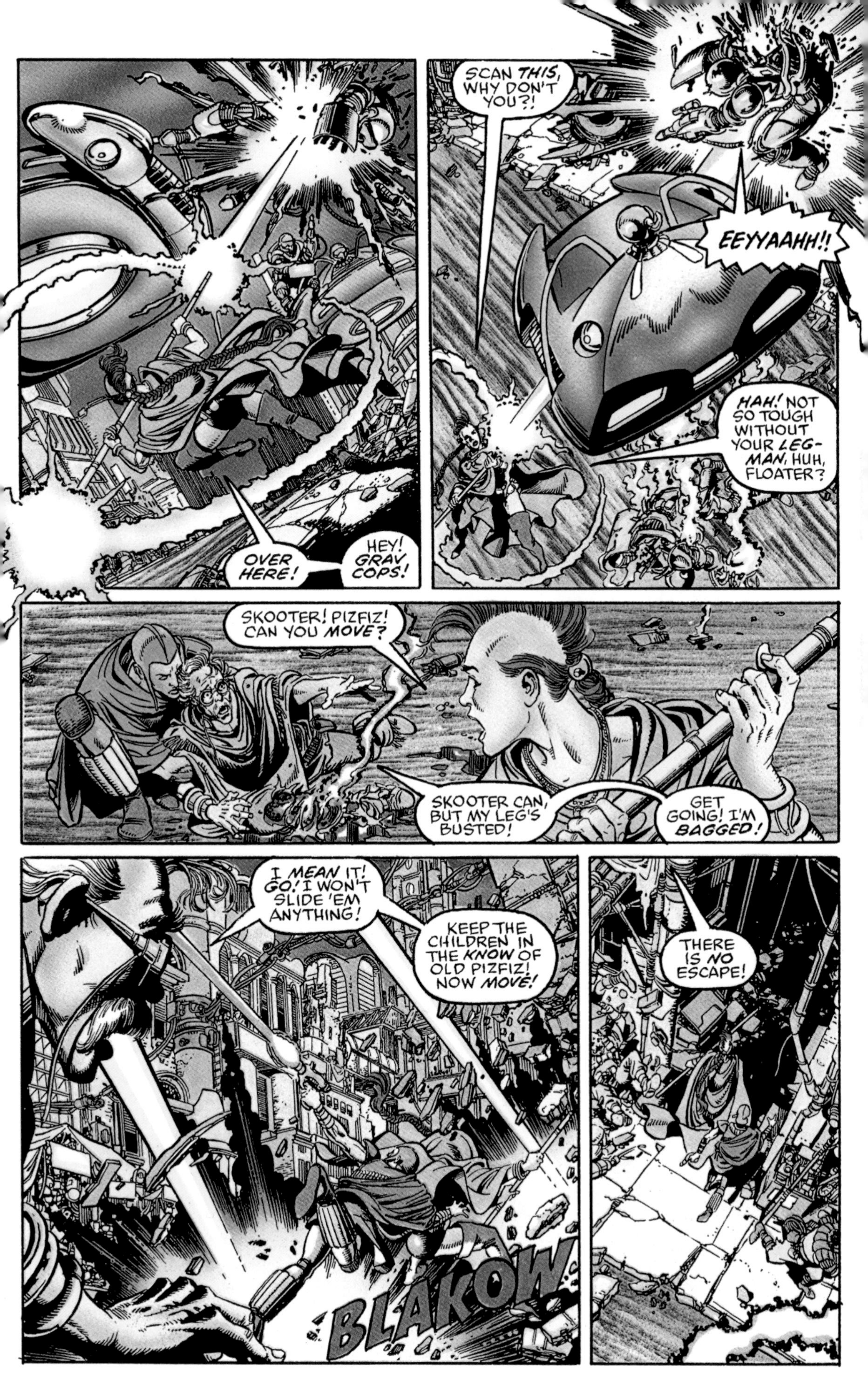
OVER HERE!
HEY! GRAV COPS!
SCAN THIS, WHY DON'T YOU?!
EEYYAAHH!!
HAH! NOT SO TOUGH WITHOUT YOUR LEG-MAN, HUH, FLOATER?
SKOOTER! PIZFIZ! CAN YOU MOVE?
SKOOTER CAN, BUT MY LEG'S BUSTED!
GET GOING! I'M BAGGED!
I MEAN IT! GO! I WON'T SLIDE 'EM ANYTHING!
KEEP THE CHILDREN IN THE KNOW OF OLD PIZFIZ! NOW MOVE!
BLAKOW
THERE IS NO ESCAPE!

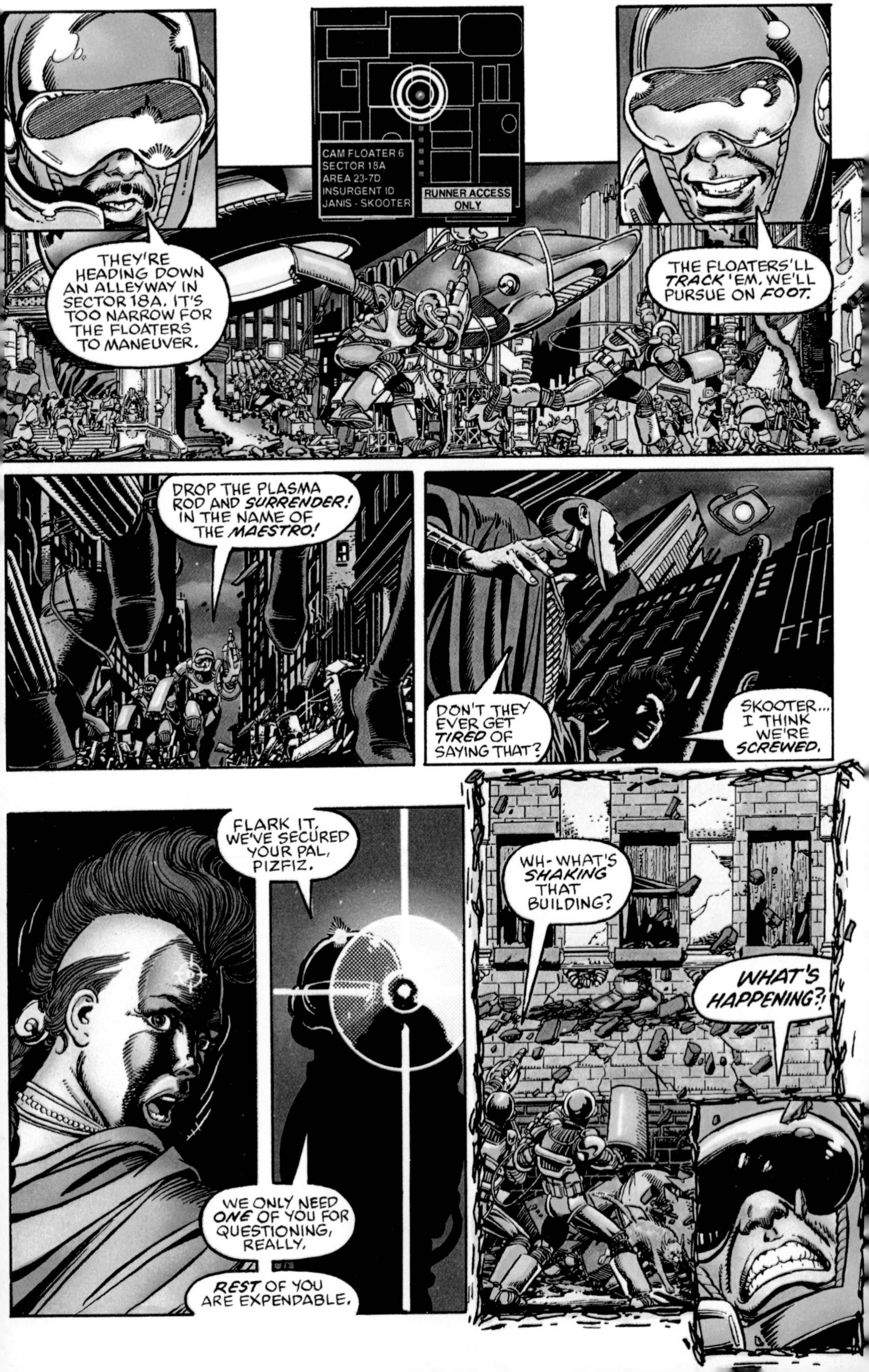
CAM FLOATER 6
SECTOR 18A
AREA 23-7D
INSURGENT ID
JANIS - SKOOTER
RUNNER ACCESS ONLY
THEY'RE HEADING DOWN AN ALLEYWAY IN SECTOR 18A. IT'S TOO NARROW FOR THE FLOATERS TO MANEUVER.
THE FLOATERS'LL TRACK 'EM, WE'LL PURSUE ON FOOT.
DROP THE PLASMA ROD AND SURRENDER! IN THE NAME OF THE MAESTRO!
DON'T THEY EVER GET TIRED OF SAYING THAT?
SKOOTER... I THINK WE'RE SCREWED.
FLARK IT. WE'VE SECURED YOUR PAL, PIZFIZ.
WE ONLY NEED ONE OF YOU FOR QUESTIONING, REALLY.
REST OF YOU ARE EXPENDABLE.
WH- WHAT'S SHAKING THAT BUILDING?
WHAT'S HAPPENING?!

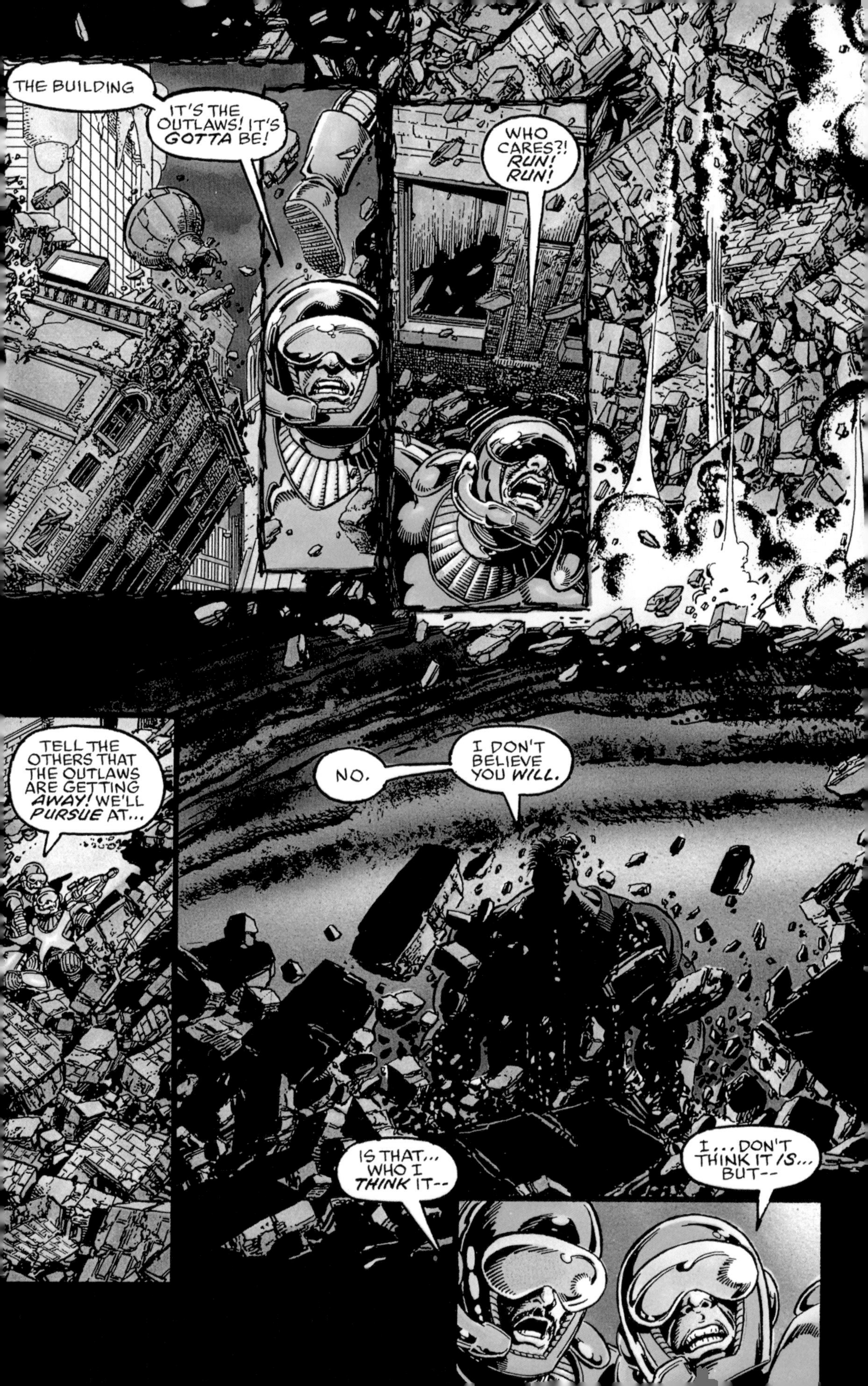

THE BUILDING
IT'S THE OUTLAWS! IT'S GOTTA BE!
WHO CARES?! RUN! RUN!
TELL THE OTHERS THAT THE OUTLAWS ARE GETTING AWAY! WE'LL PURSUE AT...
NO.
I DON'T BELIEVE YOU WILL.
IS THAT... WHO I THINK IT--
I... DON'T THINK IT IS... BUT--

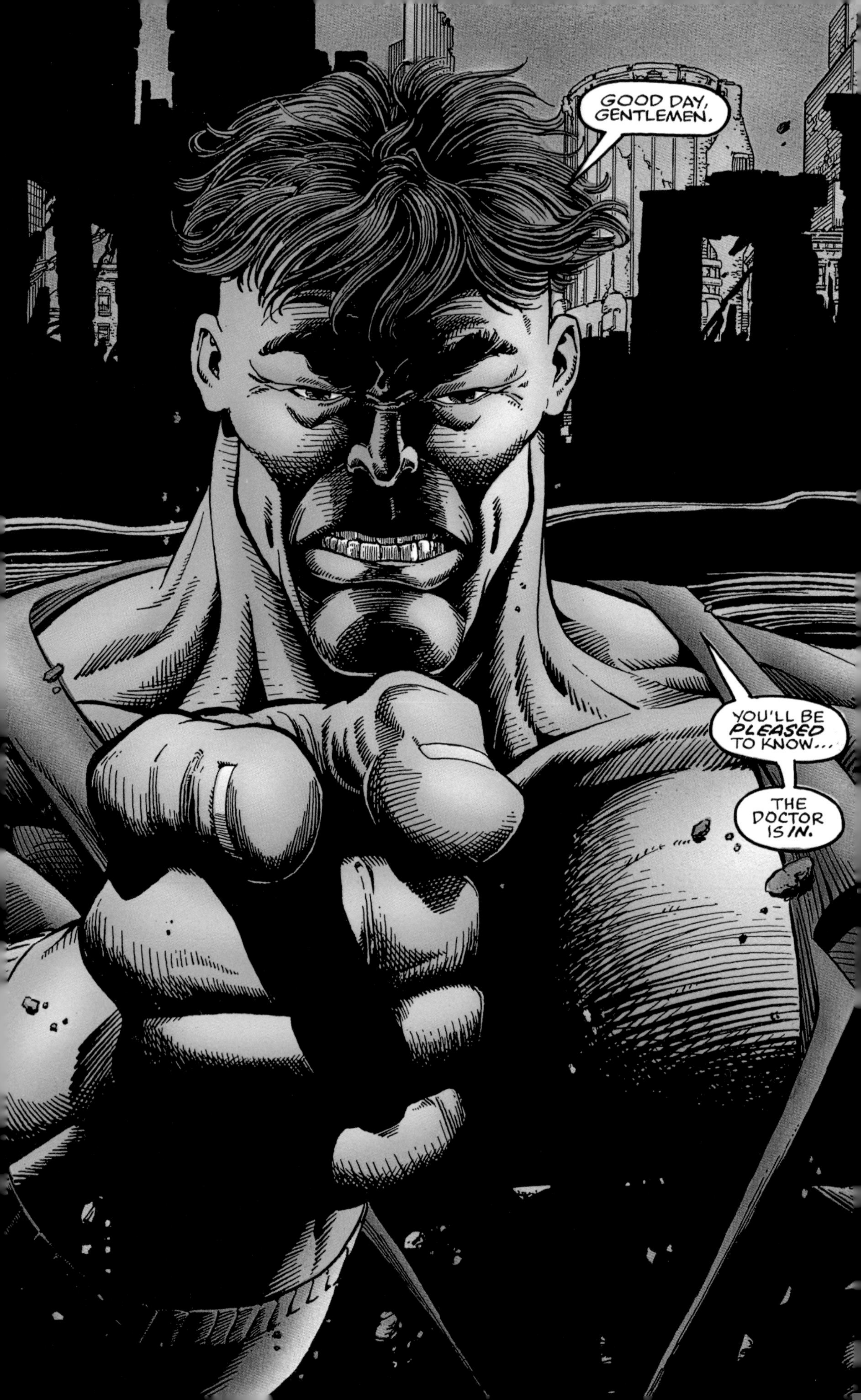
GOOD DAY, GENTLEMEN.
YOU'LL BE *PLEASED* TO KNOW...
THE DOCTOR IS *IN*.

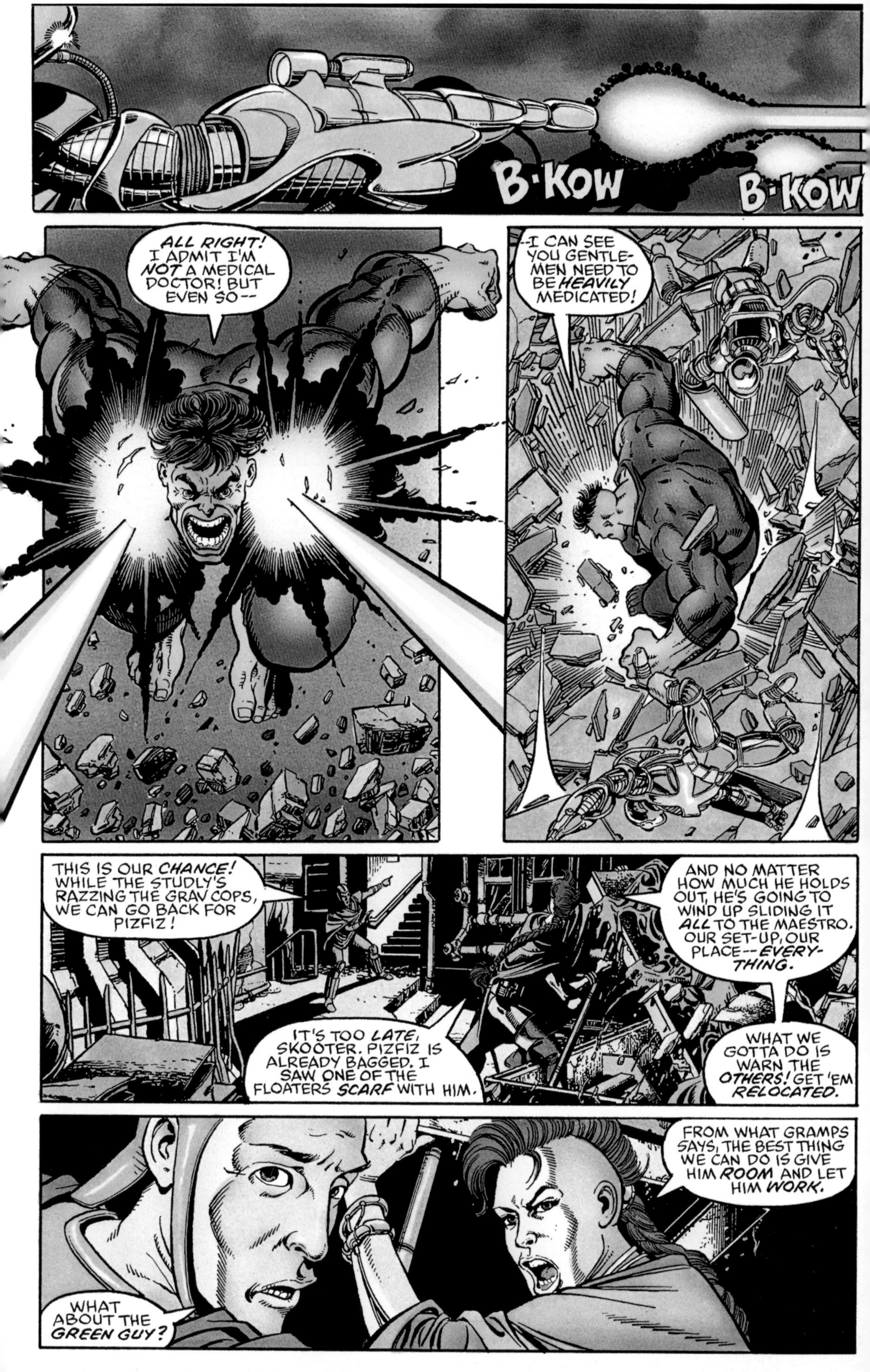
B·KOW
B·KOW
ALL RIGHT! I ADMIT I'M NOT A MEDICAL DOCTOR! BUT EVEN SO--
--I CAN SEE YOU GENTLEMEN NEED TO BE HEAVILY MEDICATED!
THIS IS OUR CHANCE! WHILE THE STUDLY'S RAZZING THE GRAV COPS, WE CAN GO BACK FOR PIZFIZ!
IT'S TOO LATE, SKOOTER. PIZFIZ IS ALREADY BAGGED. I SAW ONE OF THE FLOATERS SCARF WITH HIM.
AND NO MATTER HOW MUCH HE HOLDS OUT, HE'S GOING TO WIND UP SLIDING IT ALL TO THE MAESTRO. OUR SET-UP, OUR PLACE--EVERYTHING.
WHAT WE GOTTA DO IS WARN THE OTHERS! GET 'EM RELOCATED.
WHAT ABOUT THE GREEN GUY?
FROM WHAT GRAMPS SAYS, THE BEST THING WE CAN DO IS GIVE HIM ROOM AND LET HIM WORK.

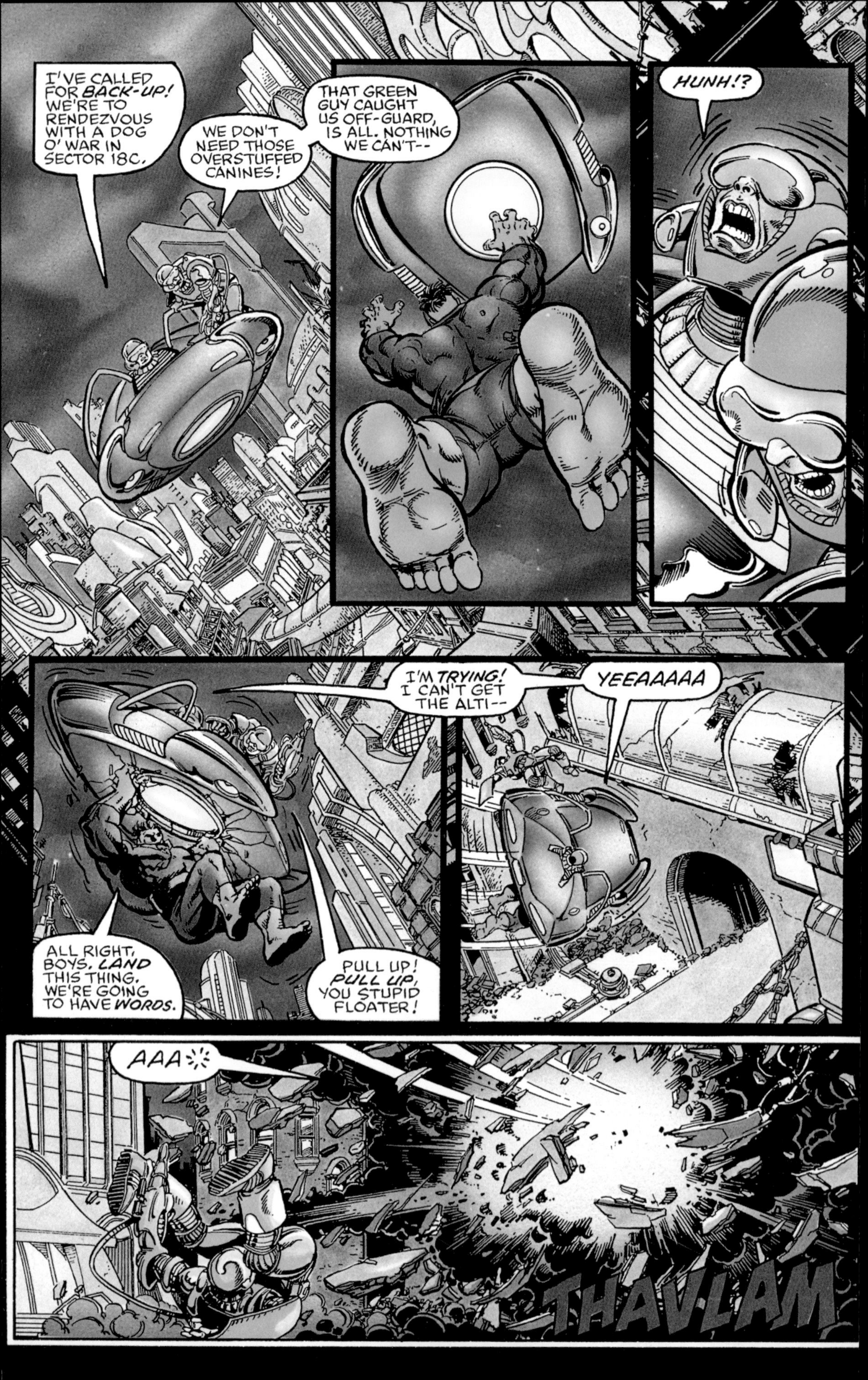

I'VE CALLED FOR BACK-UP! WE'RE TO RENDEZVOUS WITH A DOG O' WAR IN SECTOR 18C.
WE DON'T NEED THOSE OVERSTUFFED CANINES!
THAT GREEN GUY CAUGHT US OFF-GUARD, IS ALL. NOTHING WE CAN'T--
HUNH!?
ALL RIGHT, BOYS. LAND THIS THING. WE'RE GOING TO HAVE WORDS.
PULL UP! PULL UP, YOU STUPID FLOATER!
I'M TRYING! I CAN'T GET THE ALTI--
YEEAAAAA
AAA
THAVLAM

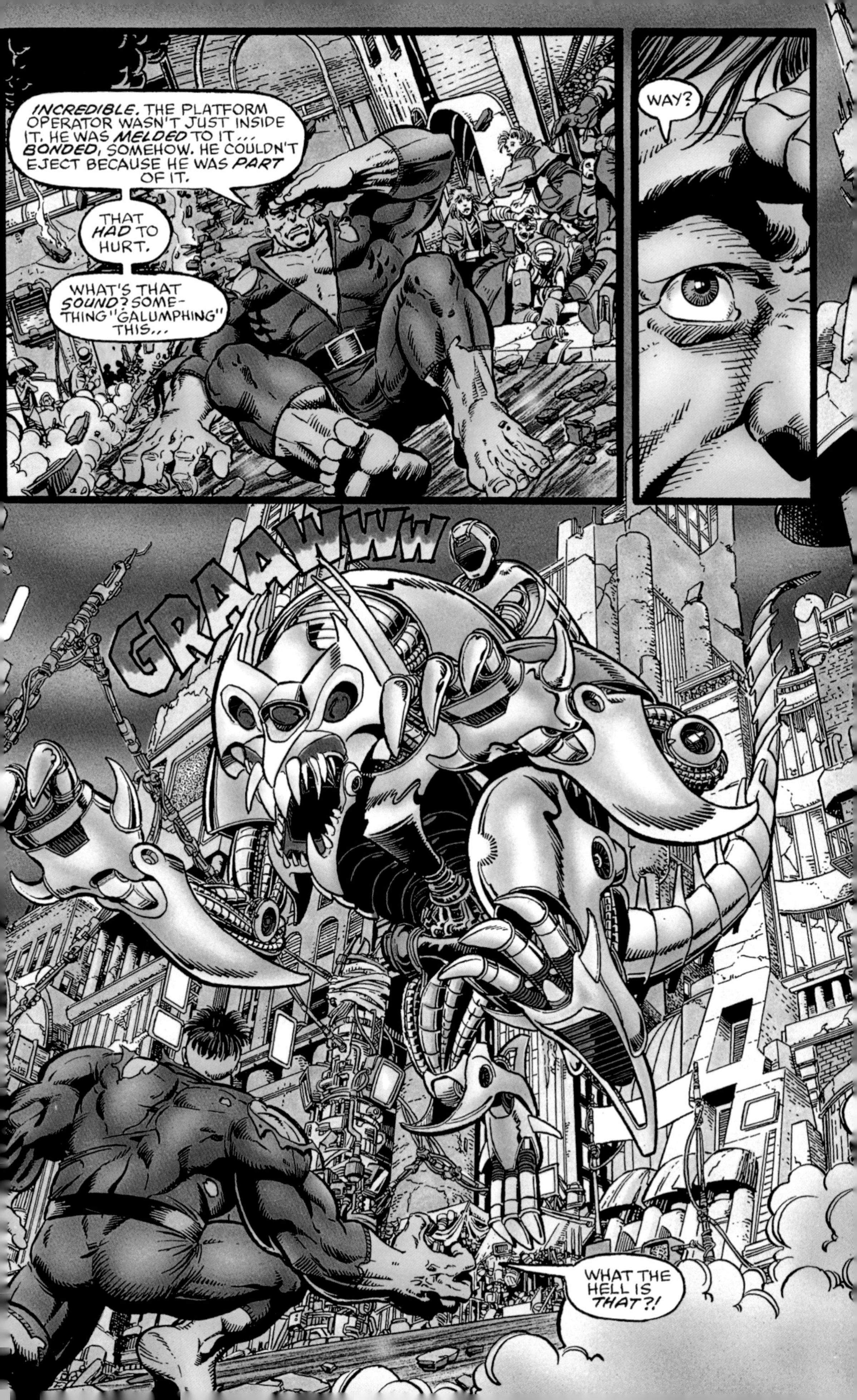
INCREDIBLE. THE PLATFORM OPERATOR WASN'T JUST INSIDE IT. HE WAS MELDED TO IT... BONDED, SOMEHOW. HE COULDN'T EJECT BECAUSE HE WAS PART OF IT.
THAT HAD TO HURT.
WHAT'S THAT SOUND? SOMETHING "GALUMPHING" THIS...
WAY?
GRAAAWWW
WHAT THE HELL IS THAT?!

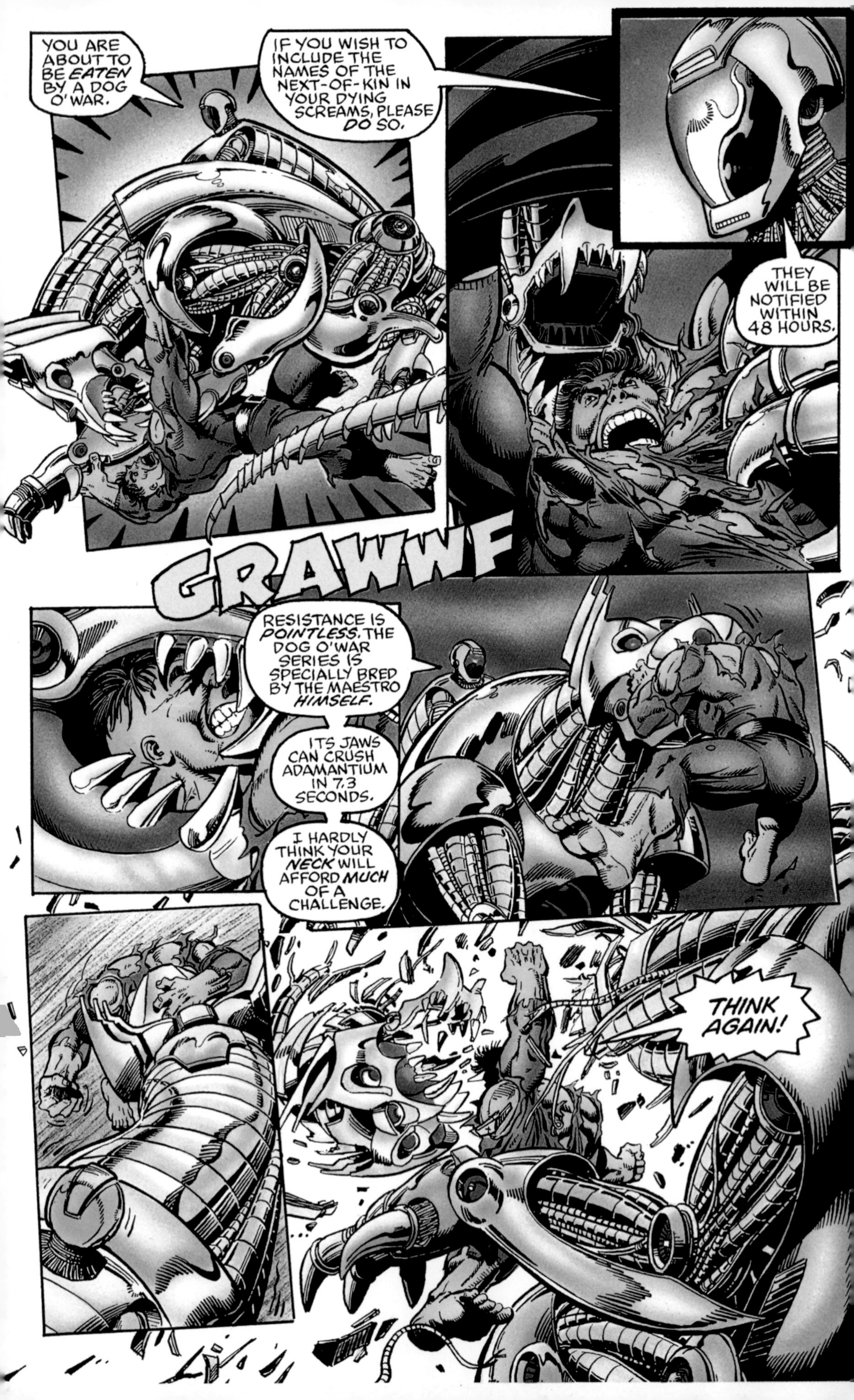

YOU ARE ABOUT TO BE EATEN BY A DOG O' WAR.
IF YOU WISH TO INCLUDE THE NAMES OF THE NEXT-OF-KIN IN YOUR DYING SCREAMS, PLEASE DO SO.
THEY WILL BE NOTIFIED WITHIN 48 HOURS.
GRAWWF
RESISTANCE IS POINTLESS. THE DOG O'WAR SERIES IS SPECIALLY BRED BY THE MAESTRO HIMSELF.
ITS JAWS CAN CRUSH ADAMANTIUM IN 7.3 SECONDS.
I HARDLY THINK YOUR NECK WILL AFFORD MUCH OF A CHALLENGE.
THINK AGAIN!

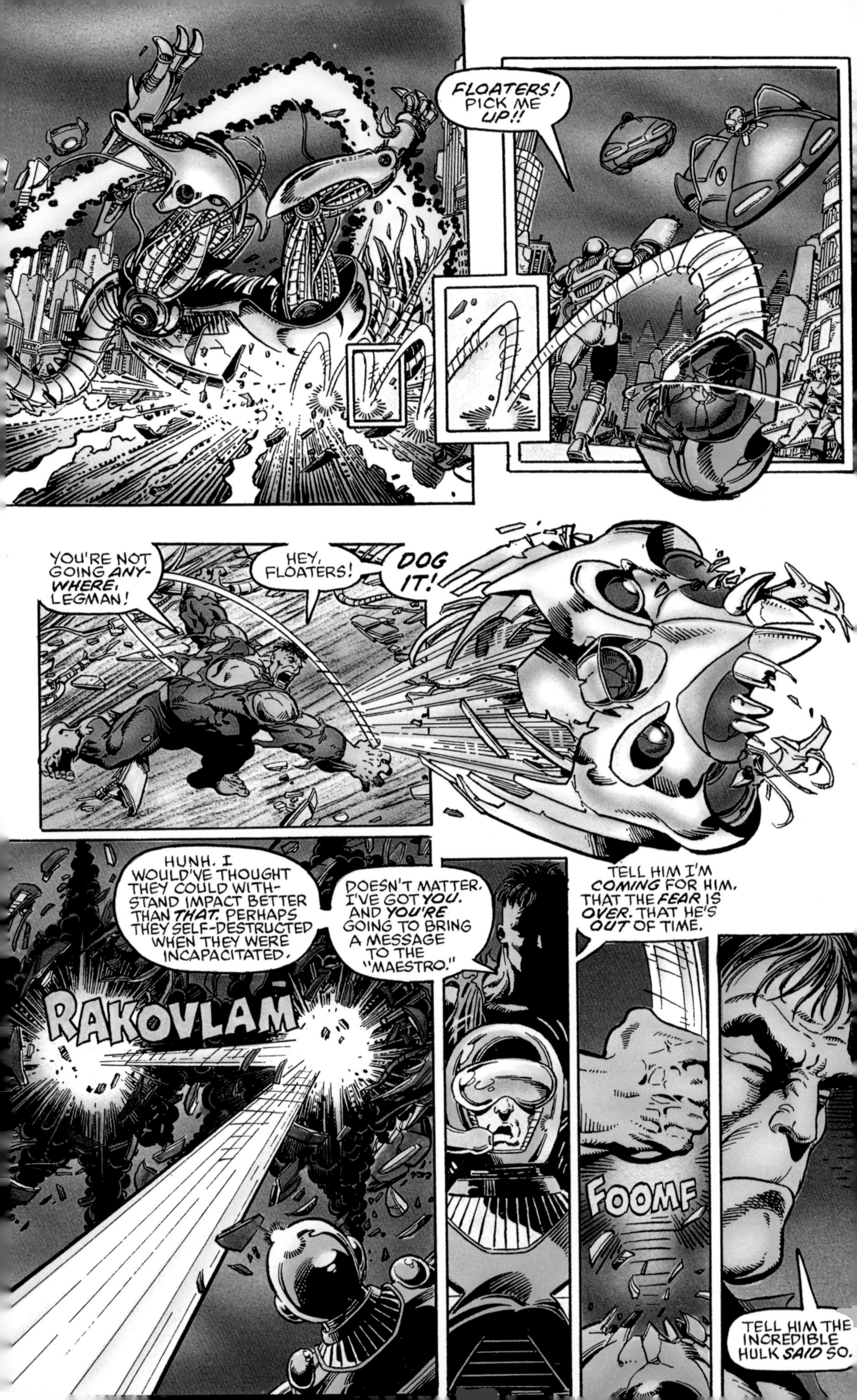
FLOATERS! PICK ME UP!!
YOU'RE NOT GOING ANYWHERE, LEGMAN!
HEY, FLOATERS!
DOG IT!
HUNH. I WOULD'VE THOUGHT THEY COULD WITHSTAND IMPACT BETTER THAN THAT. PERHAPS THEY SELF-DESTRUCTED WHEN THEY WERE INCAPACITATED.
DOESN'T MATTER. I'VE GOT YOU. AND YOU'RE GOING TO BRING A MESSAGE TO THE "MAESTRO."
RAKOVLAM
TELL HIM I'M COMING FOR HIM. THAT THE FEAR IS OVER. THAT HE'S OUT OF TIME.
FOOMF
TELL HIM THE INCREDIBLE HULK SAID SO.

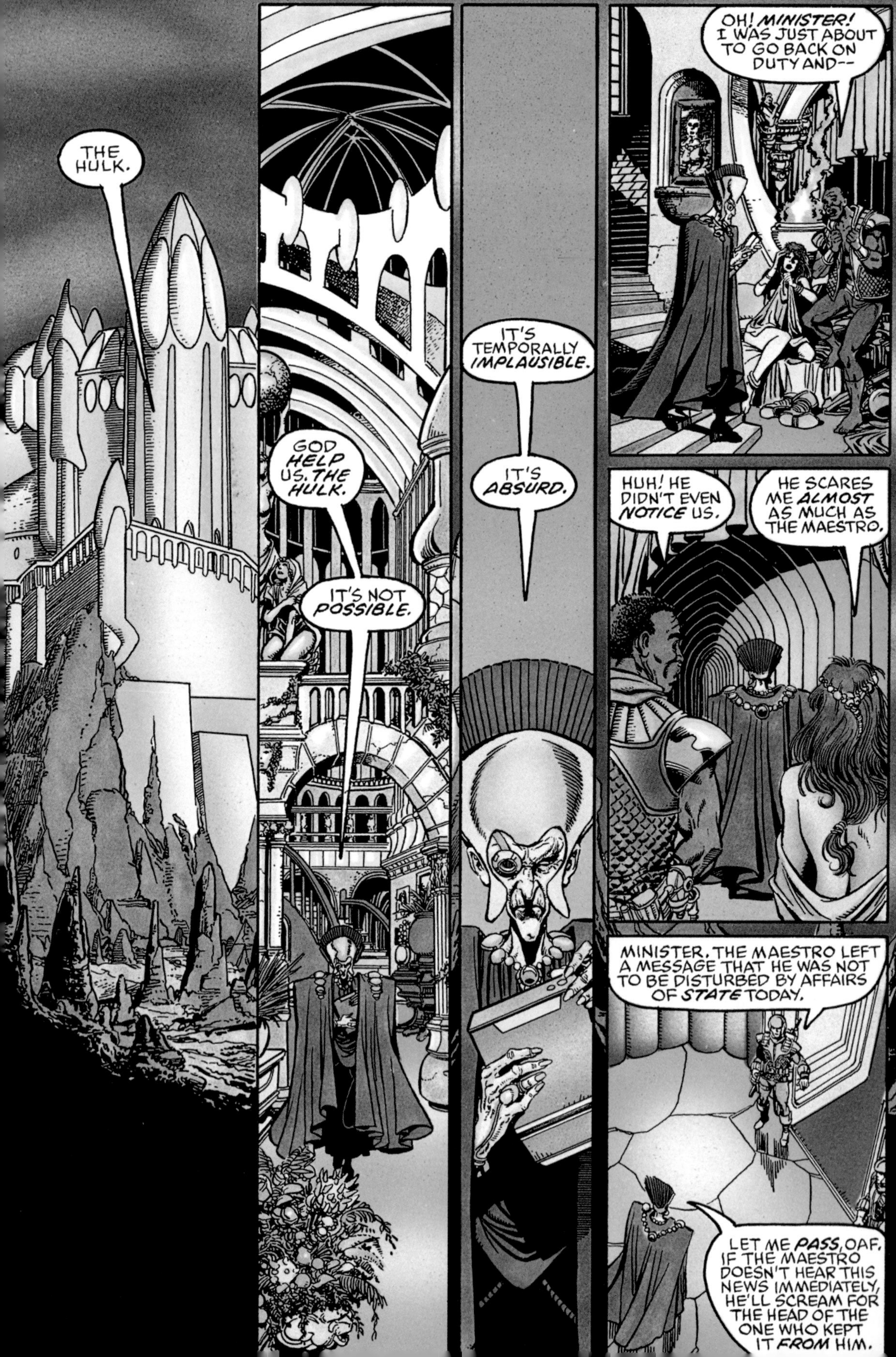
THE HULK.
GOD HELP US. THE HULK.
IT'S NOT POSSIBLE.
IT'S TEMPORALLY IMPLAUSIBLE.
IT'S ABSURD.
OH! MINISTER! I WAS JUST ABOUT TO GO BACK ON DUTY AND--
HUH! HE DIDN'T EVEN NOTICE US.
HE SCARES ME ALMOST AS MUCH AS THE MAESTRO.
MINISTER, THE MAESTRO LEFT A MESSAGE THAT HE WAS NOT TO BE DISTURBED BY AFFAIRS OF STATE TODAY.
LET ME PASS, OAF. IF THE MAESTRO DOESN'T HEAR THIS NEWS IMMEDIATELY, HE'LL SCREAM FOR THE HEAD OF THE ONE WHO KEPT IT FROM HIM.

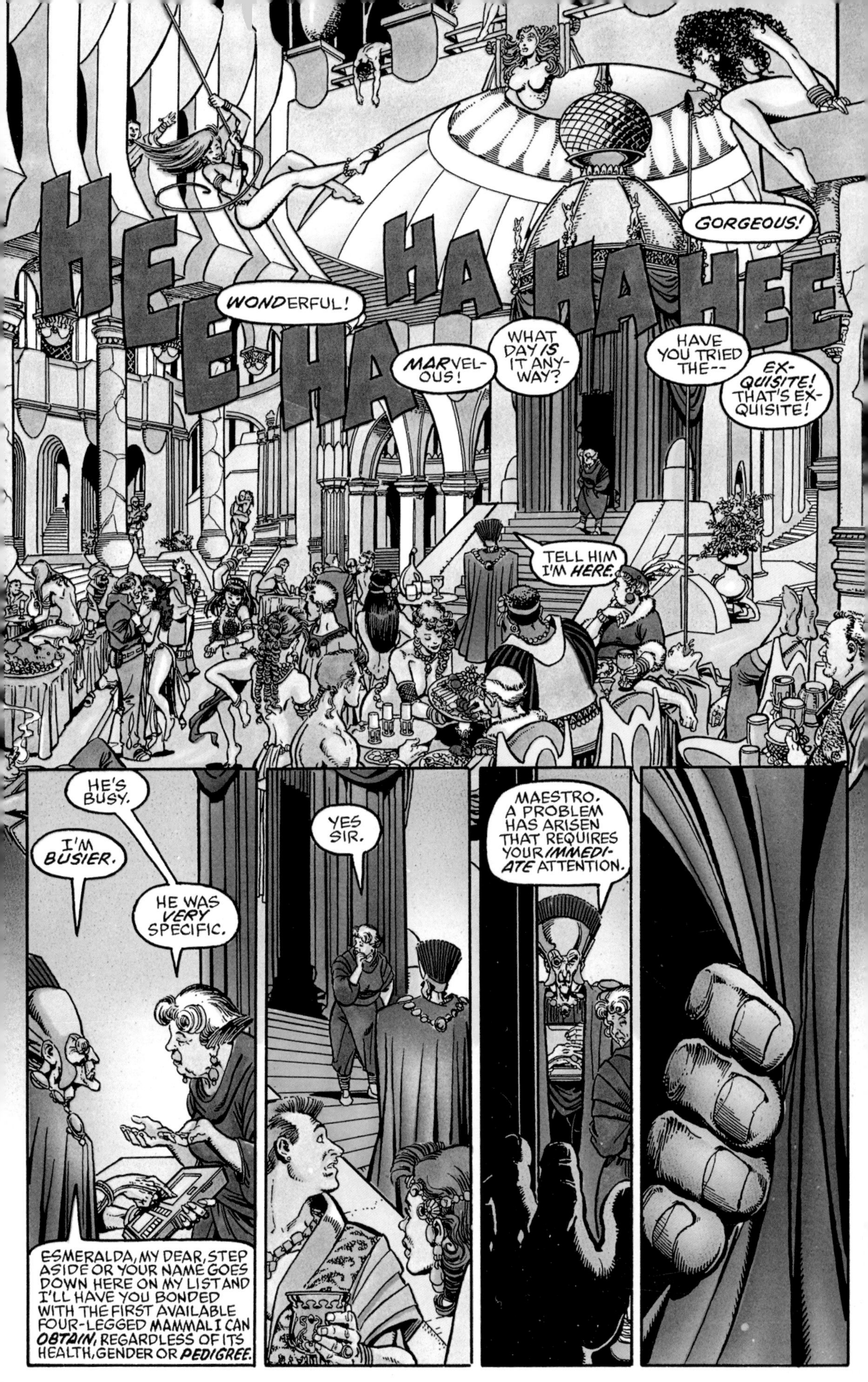
HEE HA HA HA HA HEE
WONDERFUL!
GORGEOUS!
MARVEL-OUS!
WHAT DAY IS IT ANYWAY?
HAVE YOU TRIED THE--
EX-QUISITE! THAT'S EX-QUISITE!
TELL HIM I'M HERE.
HE'S BUSY.
I'M BUSIER.
HE WAS VERY SPECIFIC.
ESMERALDA, MY DEAR, STEP ASIDE OR YOUR NAME GOES DOWN HERE ON MY LIST AND I'LL HAVE YOU BONDED WITH THE FIRST AVAILABLE FOUR-LEGGED MAMMAL I CAN OBTAIN, REGARDLESS OF ITS HEALTH, GENDER OR PEDIGREE.
YES SIR.
MAESTRO, A PROBLEM HAS ARISEN THAT REQUIRES YOUR IMMEDIATE ATTENTION.

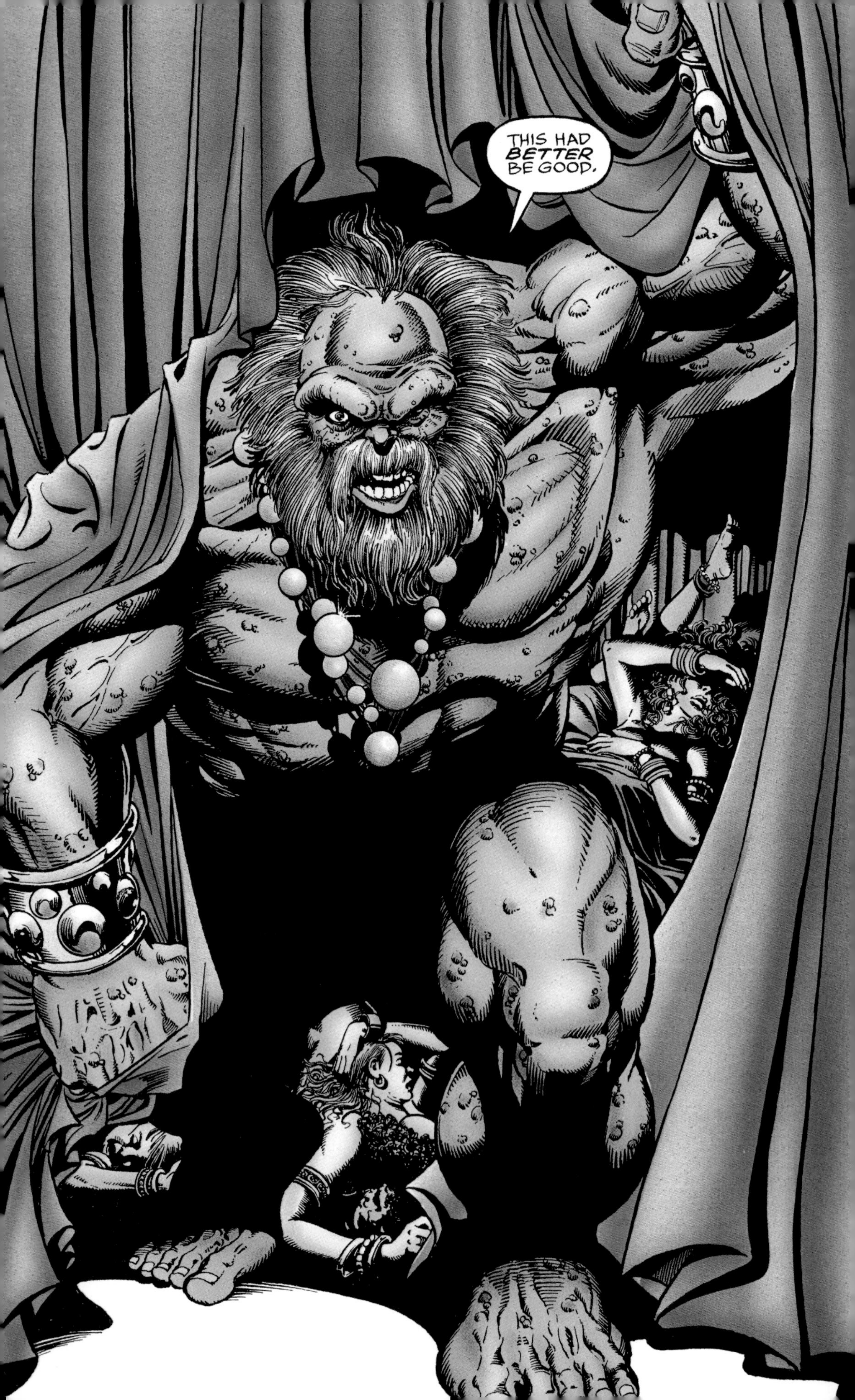
THIS HAD BETTER BE GOOD.

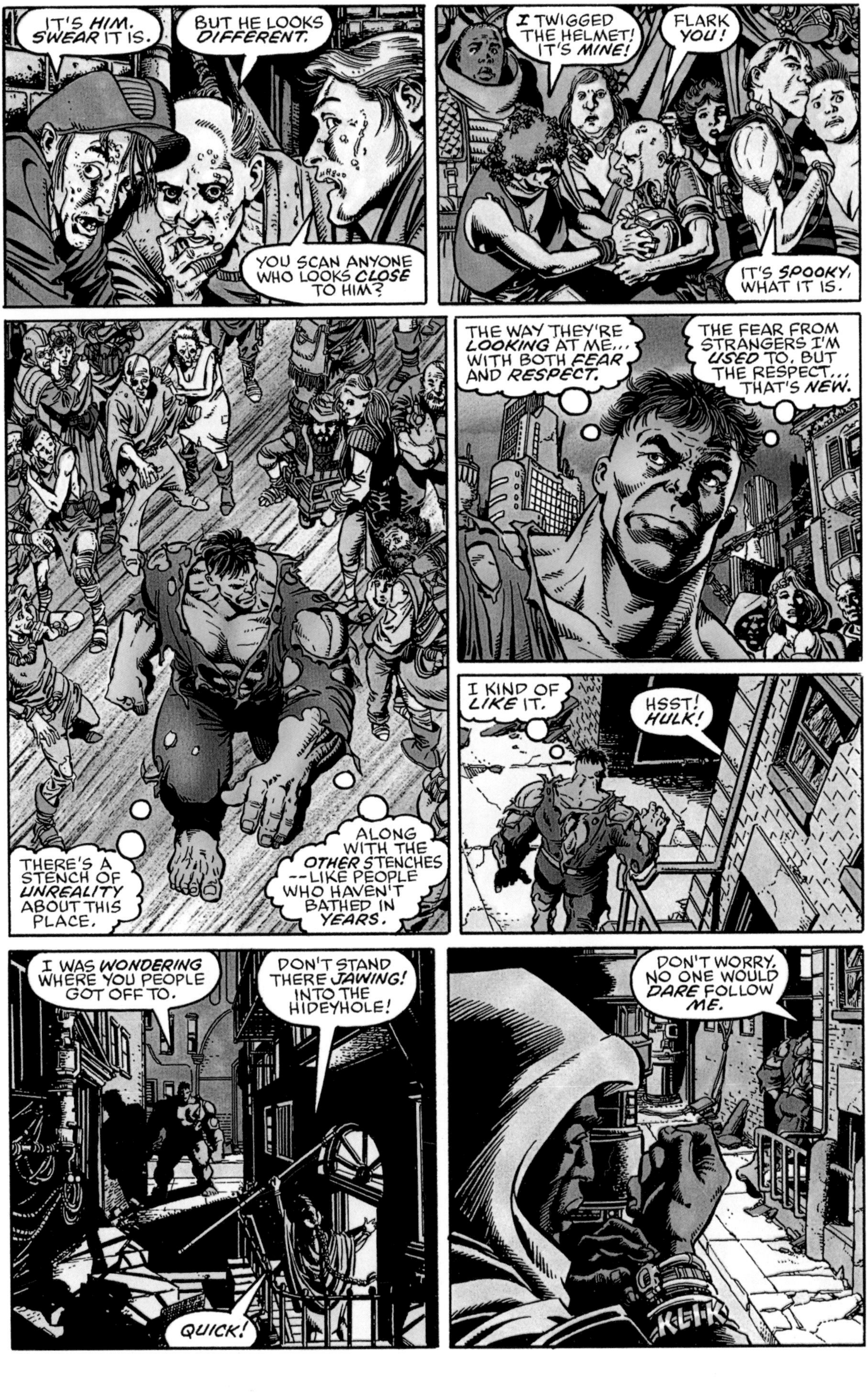
IT'S HIM. SWEAR IT IS.
BUT HE LOOKS DIFFERENT.
YOU SCAN ANYONE WHO LOOKS CLOSE TO HIM?
I TWIGGED THE HELMET! IT'S MINE!
FLARK YOU!
IT'S SPOOKY, WHAT IT IS.
THERE'S A STENCH OF UNREALITY ABOUT THIS PLACE.
ALONG WITH THE OTHER STENCHES --LIKE PEOPLE WHO HAVEN'T BATHED IN YEARS.
THE WAY THEY'RE LOOKING AT ME... WITH BOTH FEAR AND RESPECT.
THE FEAR FROM STRANGERS I'M USED TO. BUT THE RESPECT... THAT'S NEW.
I KIND OF LIKE IT.
HSST! HULK!
I WAS WONDERING WHERE YOU PEOPLE GOT OFF TO.
DON'T STAND THERE JAWING! INTO THE HIDEYHOLE!
QUICK!
DON'T WORRY. NO ONE WOULD DARE FOLLOW ME.
KLIK

THIS PLACE IS REMARKABLE. DID YOU BUILD IT ALL YOURSELVES?

SOME OF IT. SOME OF IT WAS ALREADY HERE, AND THOSE OF US IN THE KNOW RIGGED IT FOR US SPECIAL.

WHAT IS THIS, AN ELEVATOR?

LIFTER, YEAH. HOLD STILL A MO.

WHERE'S THE CONTROL?

RECEIVE JANIS AND COMPANION, UNDER MY AUTHORITY, PASSCODE ZED ALPHA GAMMA.

SCAN FOR ID.

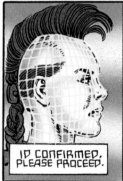

ID CONFIRMED, PLEASE PROCEED.

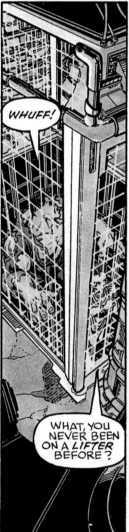

WHUFF!

WHAT, YOU NEVER BEEN ON A LIFTER BEFORE?

OH, YES. I JUST USUALLY GET A MOMENT'S WARNING BEFORE.

THIS THING COULD USE SOME MUZAK.

SOME WHAT?

NEVER MIND.

HOW FAR DOWN ARE WE GOING?

ALL THE WAY.

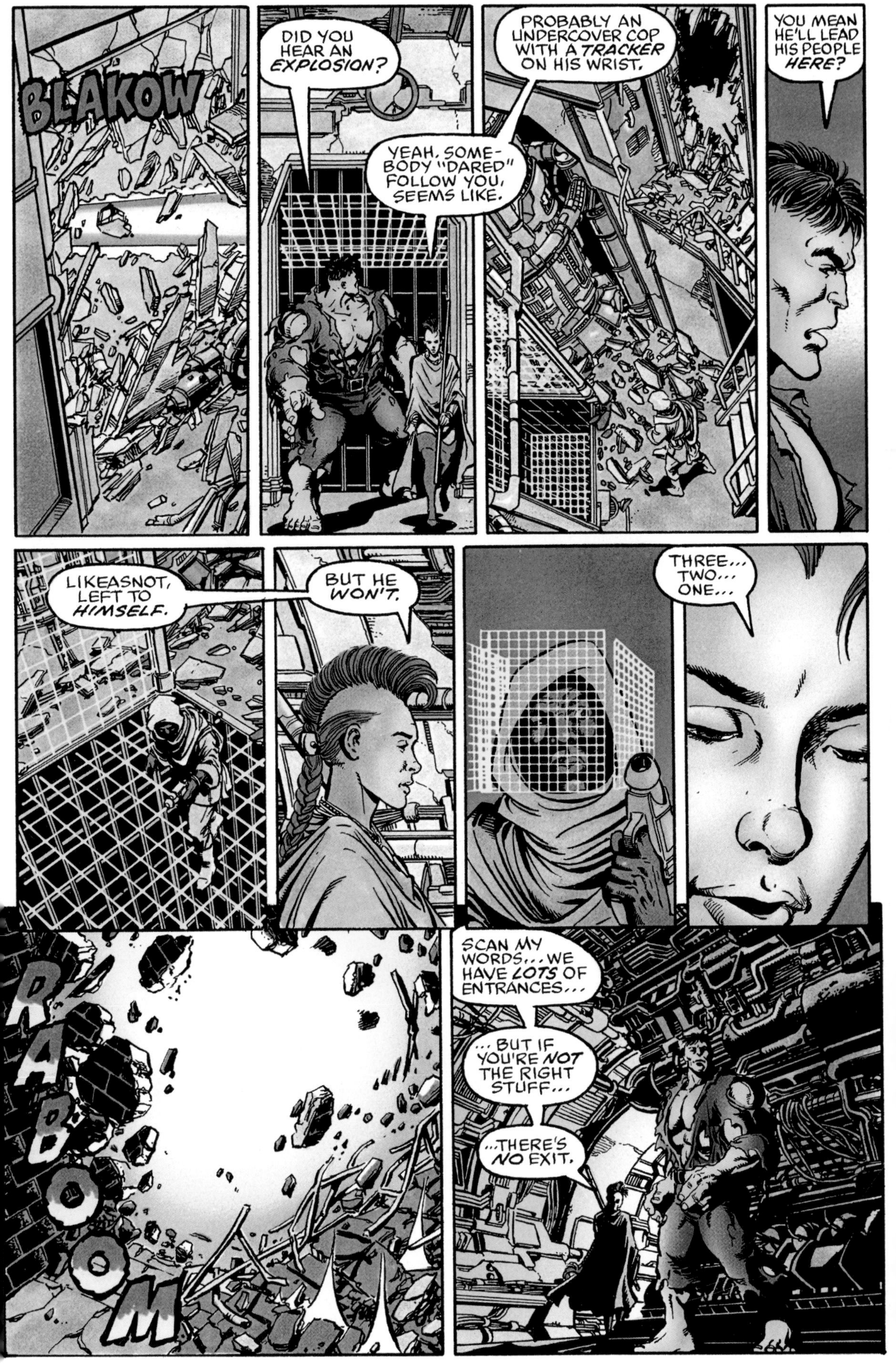
BLAKOW
DID YOU HEAR AN EXPLOSION?
YEAH. SOME-BODY "DARED" FOLLOW YOU, SEEMS LIKE.
PROBABLY AN UNDERCOVER COP WITH A TRACKER ON HIS WRIST.
YOU MEAN HE'LL LEAD HIS PEOPLE HERE?
LIKEASNOT, LEFT TO HIMSELF.
BUT HE WON'T.
THREE... TWO... ONE...
RABOOM
SCAN MY WORDS... WE HAVE LOTS OF ENTRANCES...
...BUT IF YOU'RE NOT THE RIGHT STUFF...
...THERE'S NO EXIT.

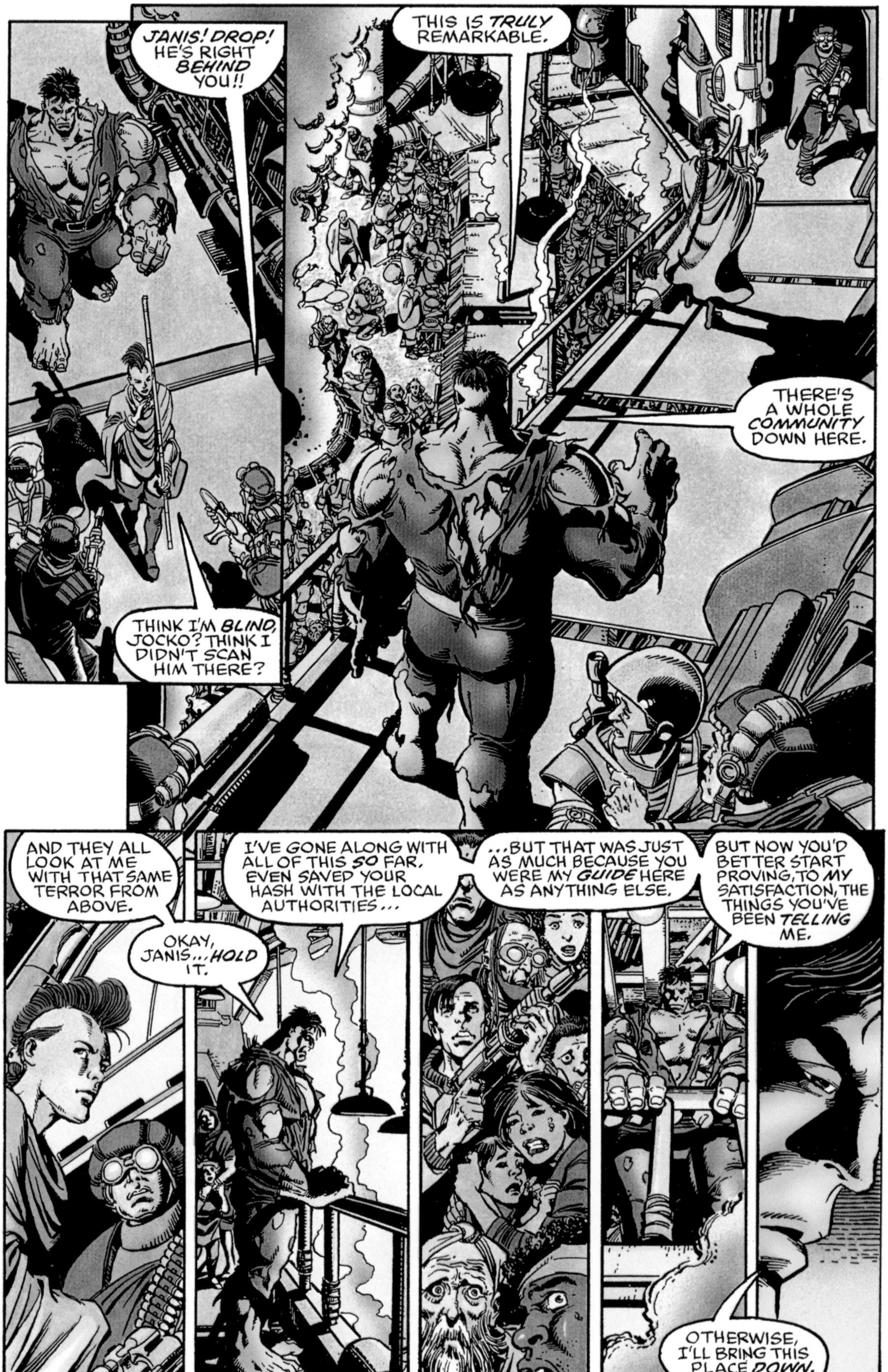
JANIS! DROP! HE'S RIGHT BEHIND YOU!!
THINK I'M BLIND, JOCKO? THINK I DIDN'T SCAN HIM THERE?
THIS IS TRULY REMARKABLE.
THERE'S A WHOLE COMMUNITY DOWN HERE.
AND THEY ALL LOOK AT ME WITH THAT SAME TERROR FROM ABOVE.
OKAY, JANIS... HOLD IT.
I'VE GONE ALONG WITH ALL OF THIS SO FAR, EVEN SAVED YOUR HASH WITH THE LOCAL AUTHORITIES...
...BUT THAT WAS JUST AS MUCH BECAUSE YOU WERE MY GUIDE HERE AS ANYTHING ELSE.
BUT NOW YOU'D BETTER START PROVING, TO MY SATISFACTION, THE THINGS YOU'VE BEEN TELLING ME.
OTHERWISE, I'LL BRING THIS PLACE DOWN.

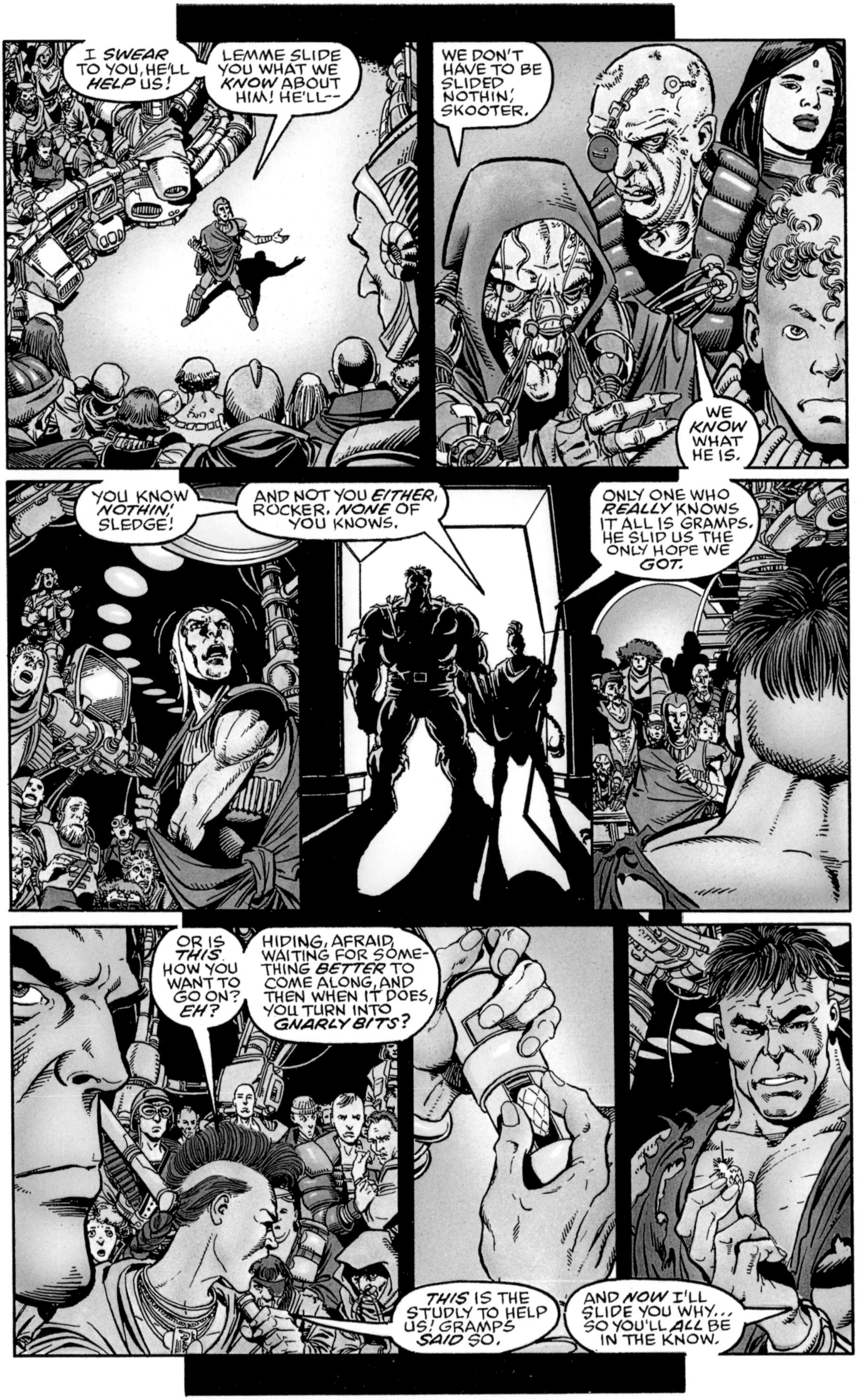
I SWEAR TO YOU, HE'LL HELP US!
LEMME SLIDE YOU WHAT WE KNOW ABOUT HIM! HE'LL--
WE DON'T HAVE TO BE SLIDED NOTHIN', SKOOTER.
WE KNOW WHAT HE IS.
YOU KNOW NOTHIN', SLEDGE!
AND NOT YOU EITHER, ROCKER. NONE OF YOU KNOWS.
ONLY ONE WHO REALLY KNOWS IT ALL IS GRAMPS. HE SLID US THE ONLY HOPE WE GOT.
OR IS THIS HOW YOU WANT TO GO ON? EH?
HIDING, AFRAID, WAITING FOR SOMETHING BETTER TO COME ALONG, AND THEN WHEN IT DOES, YOU TURN INTO GNARLY BITS?
THIS IS THE STUDLY TO HELP US! GRAMPS SAID SO.
AND NOW I'LL SLIDE YOU WHY... SO YOU'LL ALL BE IN THE KNOW.

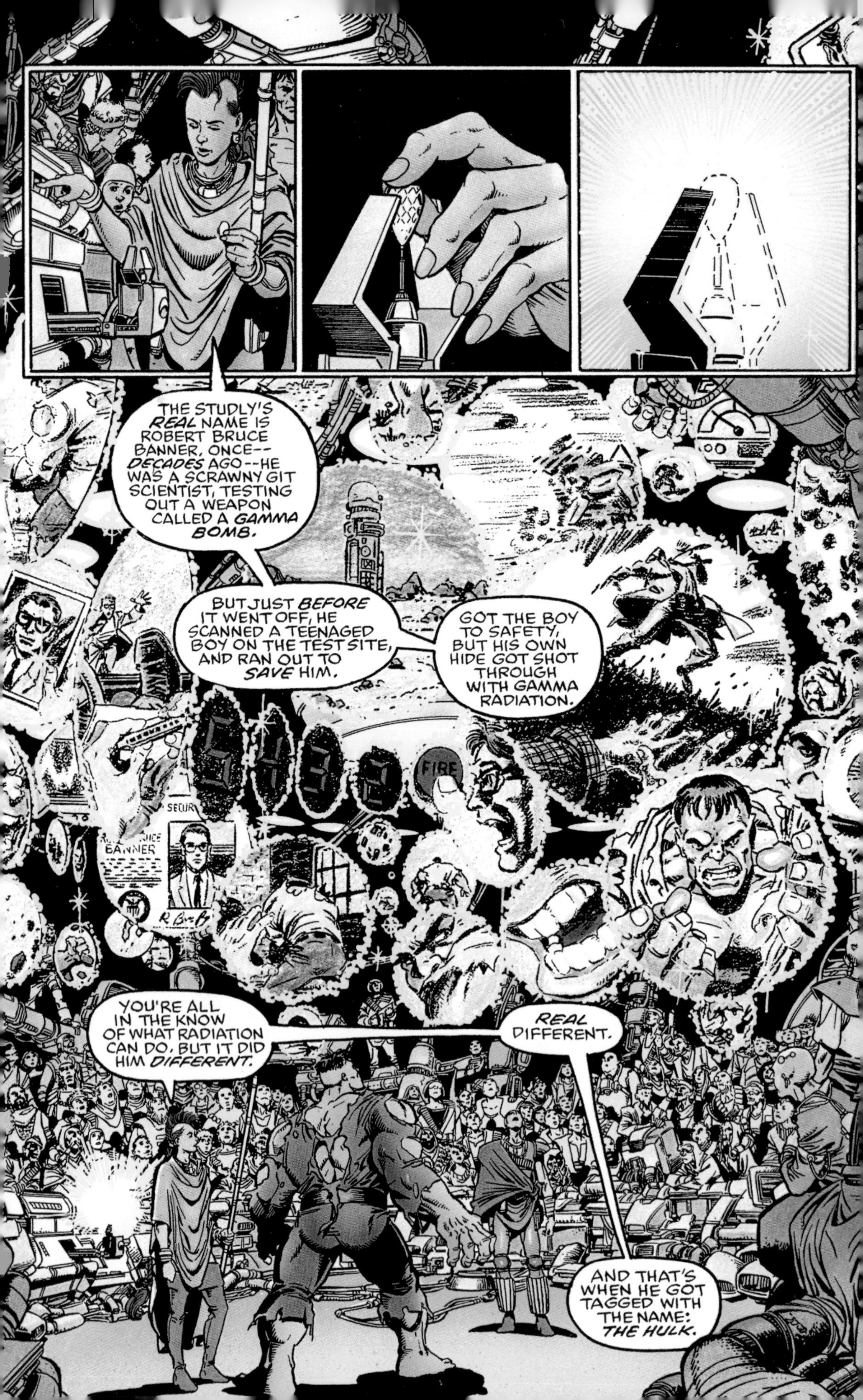
THE STUDLY'S REAL NAME IS ROBERT BRUCE BANNER. ONCE--DECADES AGO--HE WAS A SCRAWNY GIT SCIENTIST, TESTING OUT A WEAPON CALLED A GAMMA BOMB.
BUT JUST BEFORE IT WENT OFF, HE SCANNED A TEENAGED BOY ON THE TEST SITE, AND RAN OUT TO SAVE HIM.
GOT THE BOY TO SAFETY, BUT HIS OWN HIDE GOT SHOT THROUGH WITH GAMMA RADIATION.
FIRE
BANNER
YOU'RE ALL IN THE KNOW OF WHAT RADIATION CAN DO, BUT IT DID HIM DIFFERENT.
REAL DIFFERENT.
AND THAT'S WHEN HE GOT TAGGED WITH THE NAME: THE HULK.

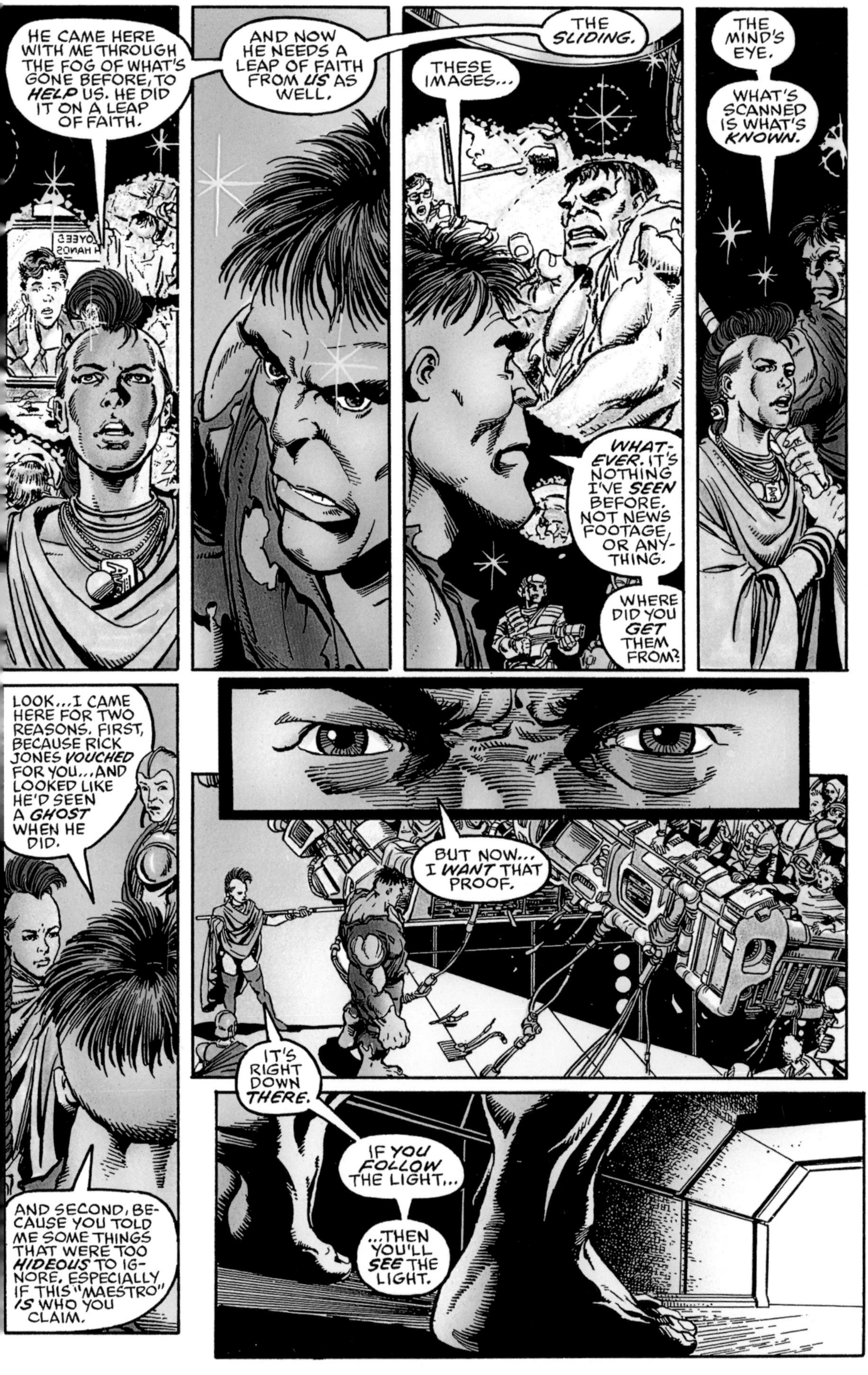
HE CAME HERE WITH ME THROUGH THE FOG OF WHAT'S GONE BEFORE, TO HELP US. HE DID IT ON A LEAP OF FAITH.
AND NOW HE NEEDS A LEAP OF FAITH FROM US AS WELL.
THE SLIDING.
THESE IMAGES...
WHAT-EVER. IT'S NOTHING I'VE SEEN BEFORE. NOT NEWS FOOTAGE OR ANY-THING.
WHERE DID YOU GET THEM FROM?
THE MIND'S EYE.
WHAT'S SCANNED IS WHAT'S KNOWN.
LOOK... I CAME HERE FOR TWO REASONS. FIRST, BECAUSE RICK JONES VOUCHED FOR YOU... AND LOOKED LIKE HE'D SEEN A GHOST WHEN HE DID.
AND SECOND, BE-CAUSE YOU TOLD ME SOME THINGS THAT WERE TOO HIDEOUS TO IG-NORE, ESPECIALLY IF THIS "MAESTRO" IS WHO YOU CLAIM.
BUT NOW... I WANT THAT PROOF.
IT'S RIGHT DOWN THERE.
IF YOU FOLLOW THE LIGHT...
...THEN YOU'LL SEE THE LIGHT.

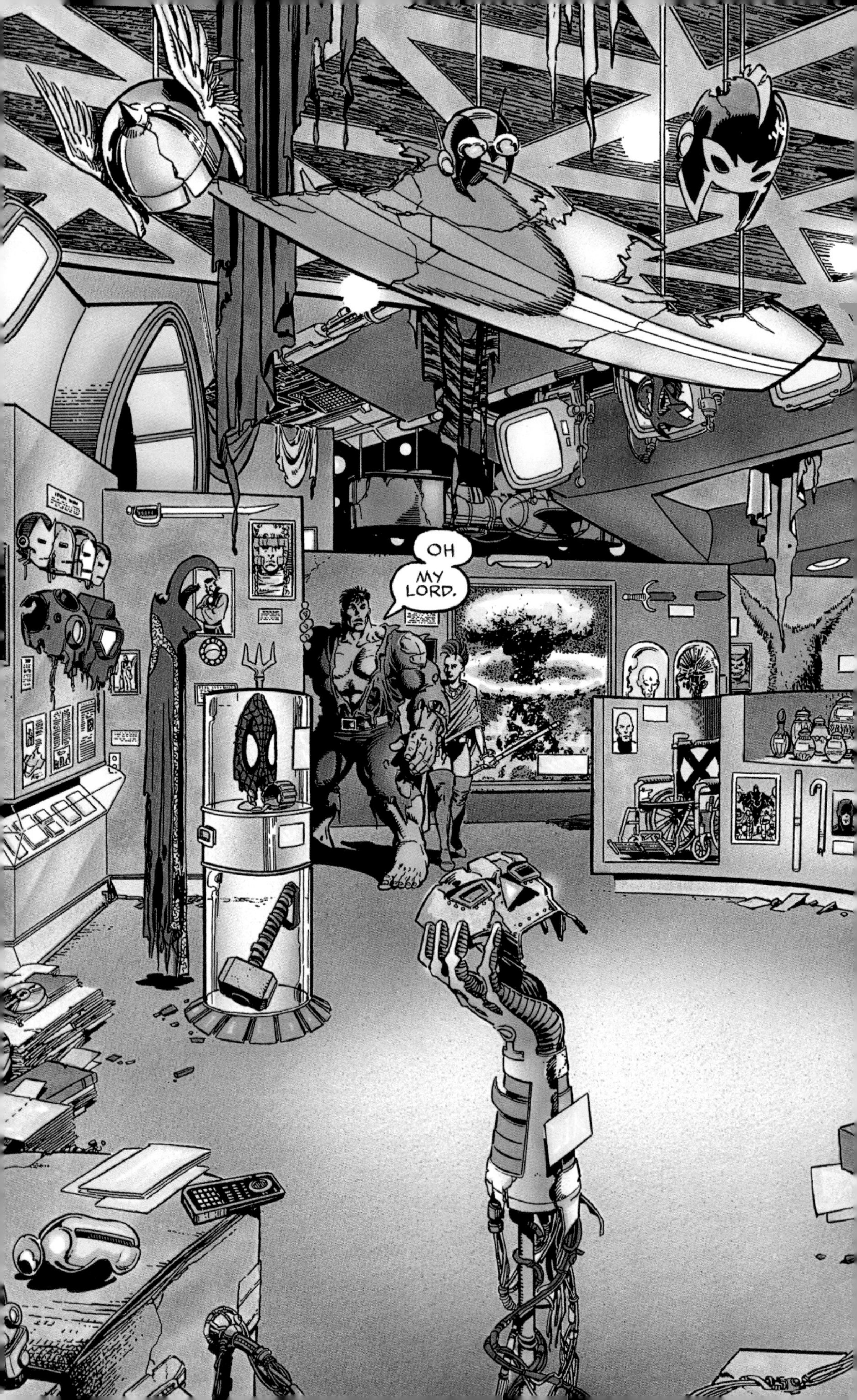
OH MY LORD.

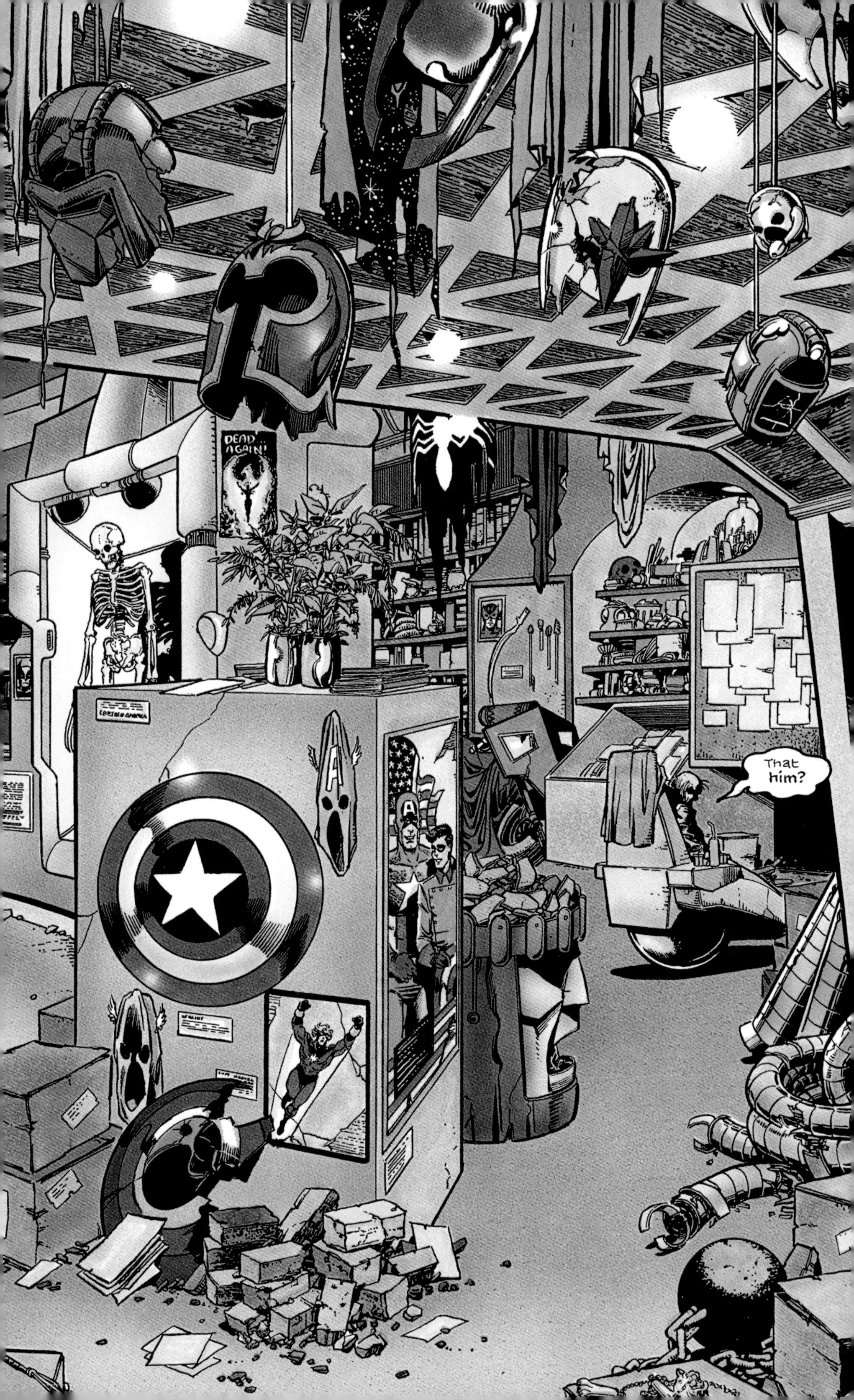
DEAD... AGAIN!
That him?

YES, GRAMPS, HE'S *HERE*.

HE TALKED AND ACTED JUST THE WAY YOU *SAID* HE WOULD, EVERY STEP OF THE WAY.

THIS.... THIS ROOM.... IT'S COMPLETELY FILLED WITH--

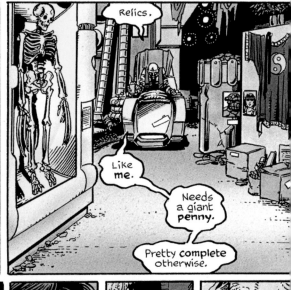

Relics.

Like me.

Needs a giant **penny**.

Pretty **complete** otherwise.

WHO *ARE* YOU, OLD MAN?

This old man.

He played one.

Play one for you.

Soon as I wet my whistle.

THAT SONG... THE ONE *HE* WAS PLAYING WHEN I--

RICK?

Bitchin', huh, Bruce.

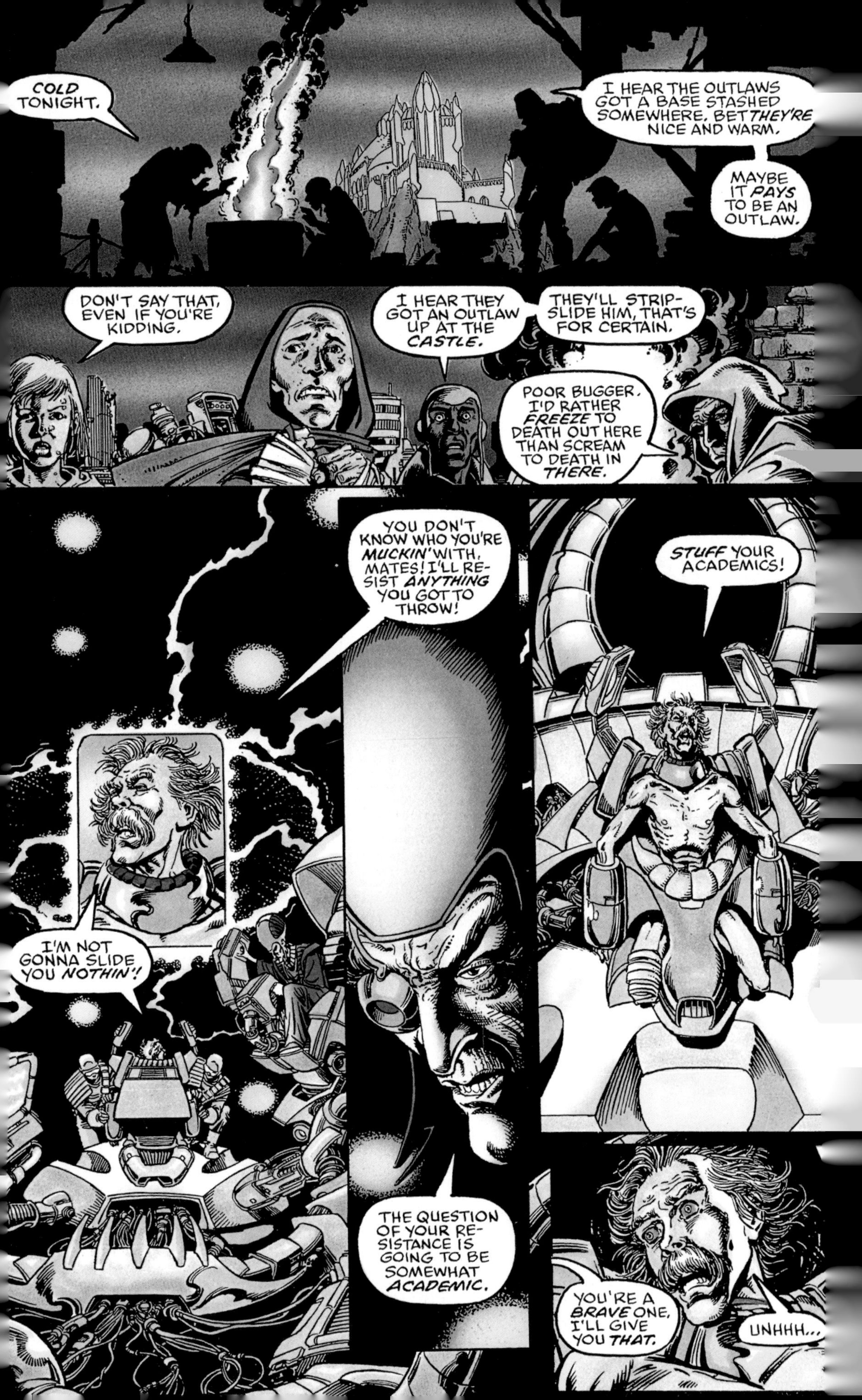
COLD TONIGHT.
I HEAR THE OUTLAWS GOT A BASE STASHED SOMEWHERE. BET THEY'RE NICE AND WARM.
MAYBE IT PAYS TO BE AN OUTLAW.
DON'T SAY THAT, EVEN IF YOU'RE KIDDING.
I HEAR THEY GOT AN OUTLAW UP AT THE CASTLE.
THEY'LL STRIP-SLIDE HIM, THAT'S FOR CERTAIN.
POOR BUGGER. I'D RATHER FREEZE TO DEATH OUT HERE THAN SCREAM TO DEATH IN THERE.
YOU DON'T KNOW WHO YOU'RE MUCKIN' WITH, MATES! I'LL RESIST ANYTHING YOU GOT TO THROW!
I'M NOT GONNA SLIDE YOU NOTHIN'!
THE QUESTION OF YOUR RESISTANCE IS GOING TO BE SOMEWHAT ACADEMIC.
STUFF YOUR ACADEMICS!
YOU'RE A BRAVE ONE, I'LL GIVE YOU THAT.
UNHHH...

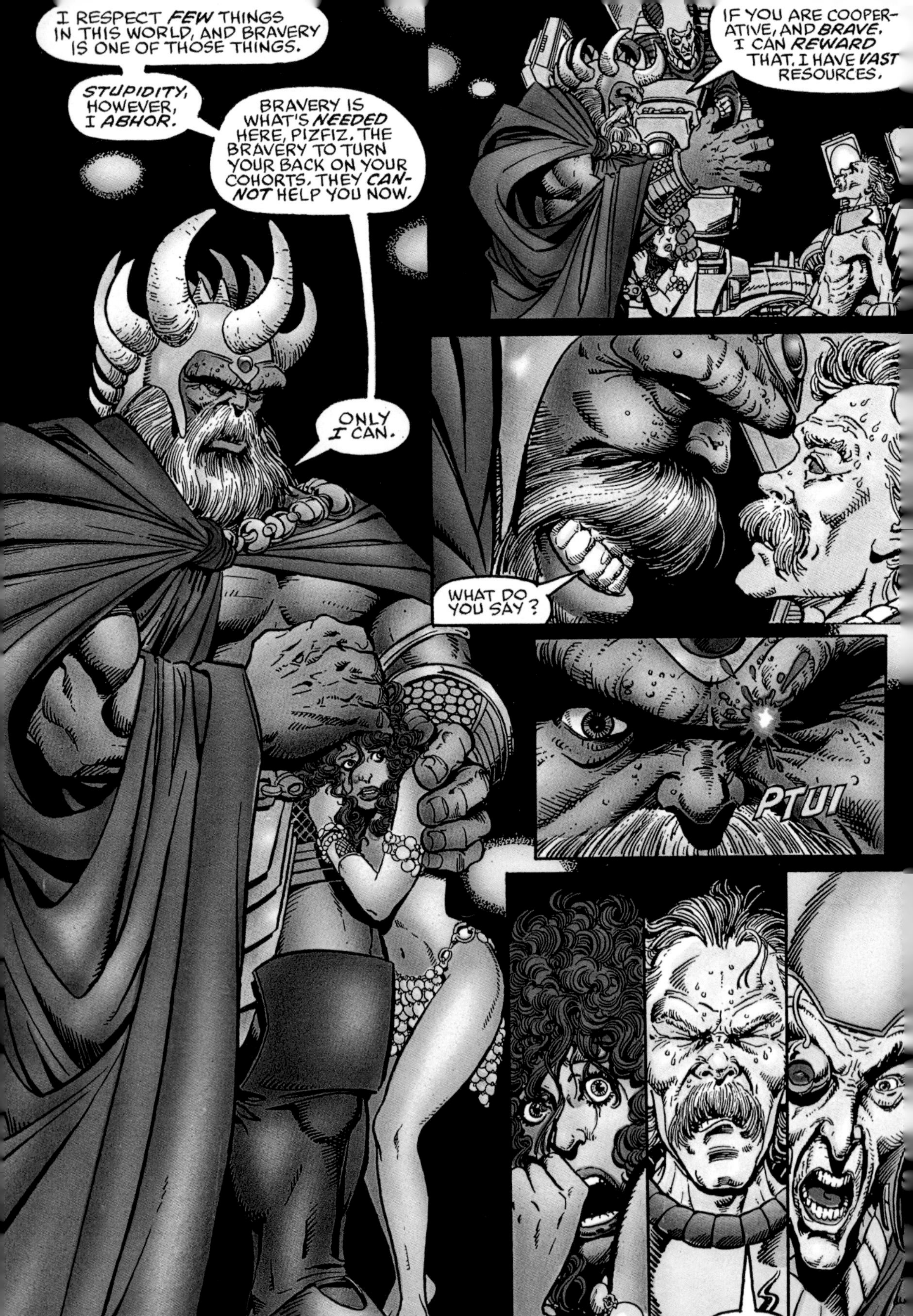
I RESPECT FEW THINGS IN THIS WORLD, AND BRAVERY IS ONE OF THOSE THINGS.
STUPIDITY, HOWEVER, I ABHOR.
BRAVERY IS WHAT'S NEEDED HERE, PIZFIZ. THE BRAVERY TO TURN YOUR BACK ON YOUR COHORTS. THEY CANNOT HELP YOU NOW.
ONLY I CAN.
IF YOU ARE COOPERATIVE, AND BRAVE, I CAN REWARD THAT. I HAVE VAST RESOURCES.
WHAT DO YOU SAY?
PTUI
FLARK YOU.

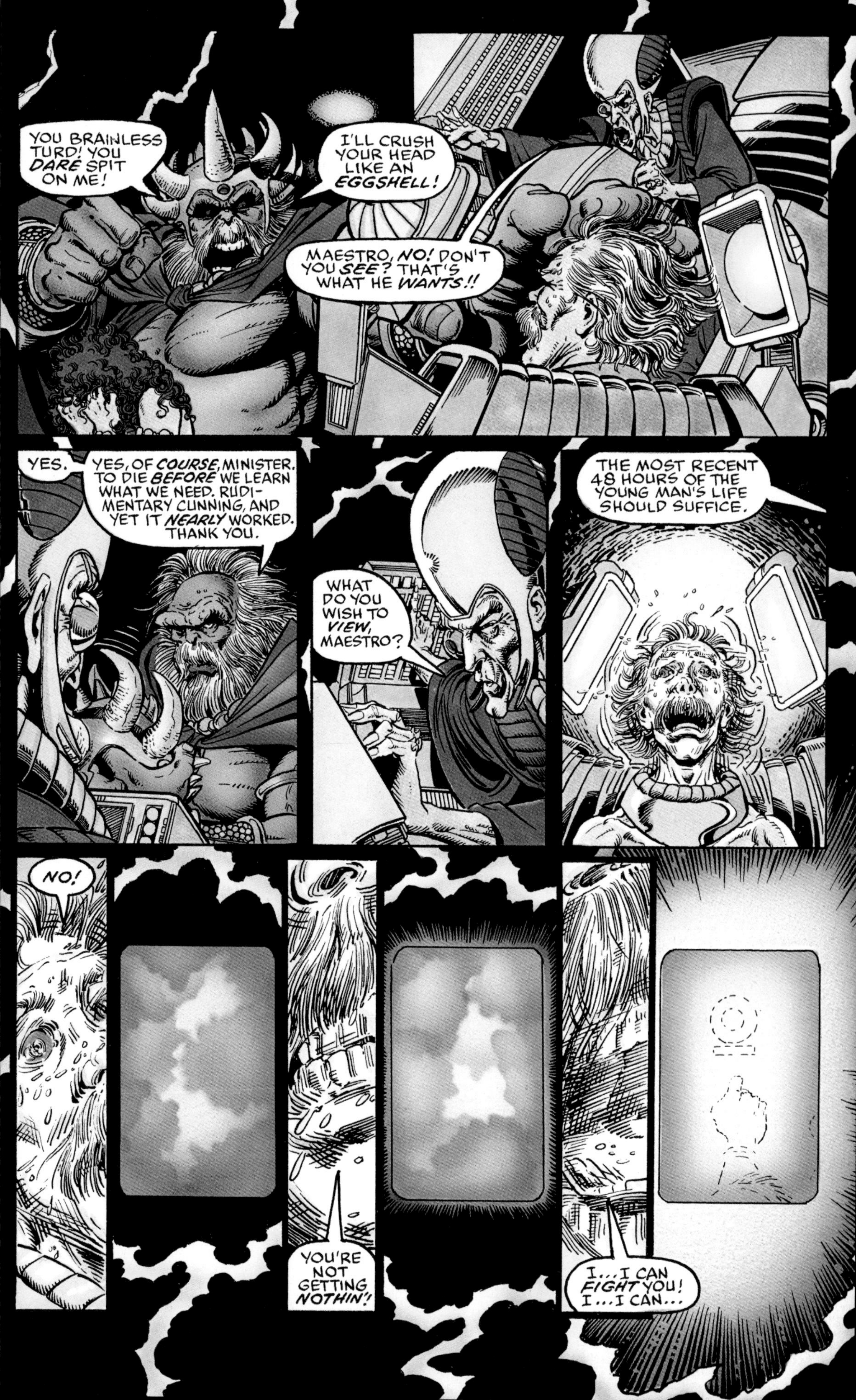
YOU BRAINLESS TURD! YOU DARE SPIT ON ME!
I'LL CRUSH YOUR HEAD LIKE AN EGGSHELL!
MAESTRO, NO! DON'T YOU SEE? THAT'S WHAT HE WANTS!!
YES.
YES, OF COURSE, MINISTER. TO DIE BEFORE WE LEARN WHAT WE NEED. RUDI-MENTARY CUNNING, AND YET IT NEARLY WORKED. THANK YOU.
WHAT DO YOU WISH TO VIEW, MAESTRO?
THE MOST RECENT 48 HOURS OF THE YOUNG MAN'S LIFE SHOULD SUFFICE.
NO!
YOU'RE NOT GETTING NOTHIN'!
I... I CAN FIGHT YOU! I... I CAN...

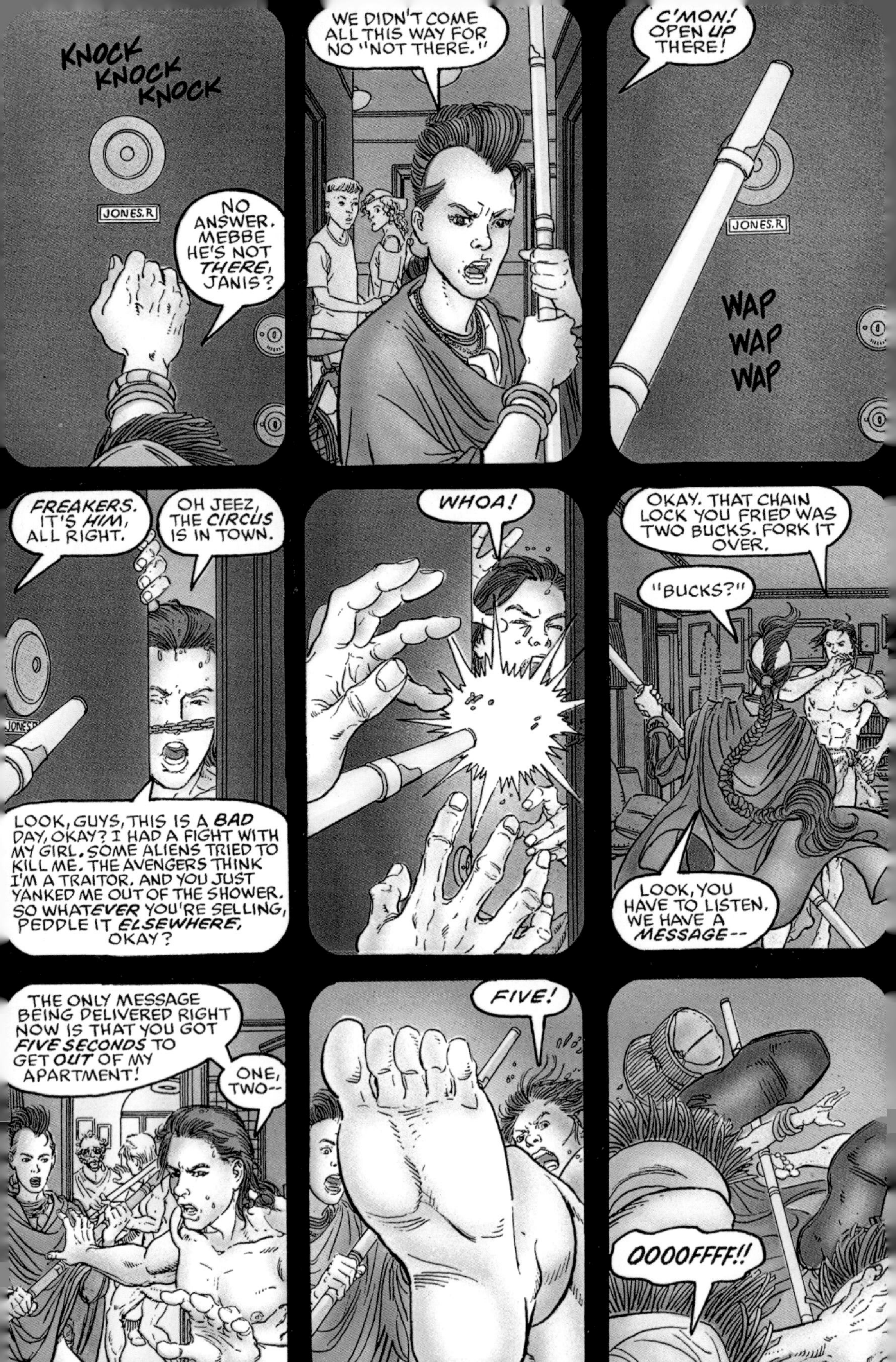
KNOCK KNOCK KNOCK
NO ANSWER. MEBBE HE'S NOT THERE, JANIS?
JONES.R
WE DIDN'T COME ALL THIS WAY FOR NO "NOT THERE."
C'MON! OPEN UP THERE!
JONES.R
WAP WAP WAP
FREAKERS. IT'S HIM, ALL RIGHT.
OH JEEZ, THE CIRCUS IS IN TOWN.
LOOK, GUYS, THIS IS A BAD DAY, OKAY? I HAD A FIGHT WITH MY GIRL. SOME ALIENS TRIED TO KILL ME. THE AVENGERS THINK I'M A TRAITOR. AND YOU JUST YANKED ME OUT OF THE SHOWER. SO WHATEVER YOU'RE SELLING, PEDDLE IT ELSEWHERE, OKAY?
WHOA!
OKAY. THAT CHAIN LOCK YOU FRIED WAS TWO BUCKS. FORK IT OVER.
"BUCKS?"
LOOK, YOU HAVE TO LISTEN. WE HAVE A MESSAGE--
THE ONLY MESSAGE BEING DELIVERED RIGHT NOW IS THAT YOU GOT FIVE SECONDS TO GET OUT OF MY APARTMENT!
ONE, TWO--
FIVE!
OOOOFFFF!!

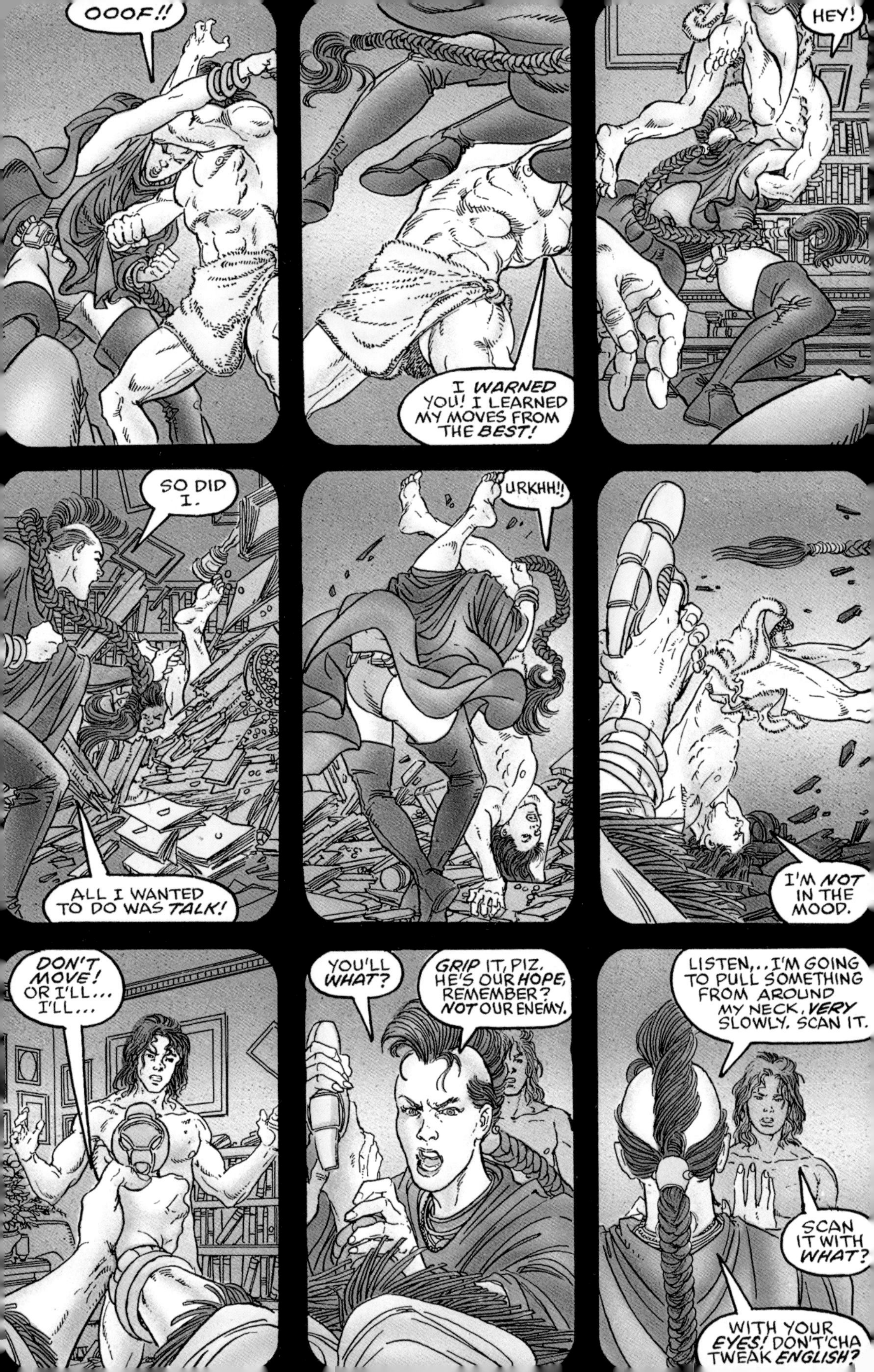

OOOF!!
I *WARNED* YOU! I LEARNED MY MOVES FROM THE *BEST*!
HEY!
SO DID I.
ALL I WANTED TO DO WAS *TALK*!
URKHH!!
I'M *NOT* IN THE MOOD.
DON'T MOVE! OR I'LL... I'LL...
YOU'LL *WHAT*?
GRIP IT, PIZ, HE'S OUR *HOPE*, REMEMBER? *NOT* OUR ENEMY.
LISTEN,.. I'M GOING TO PULL SOMETHING FROM AROUND MY NECK, *VERY* SLOWLY. SCAN IT.
SCAN IT WITH *WHAT*?
WITH YOUR *EYES*! DON'T'CHA TWEAK *ENGLISH*?

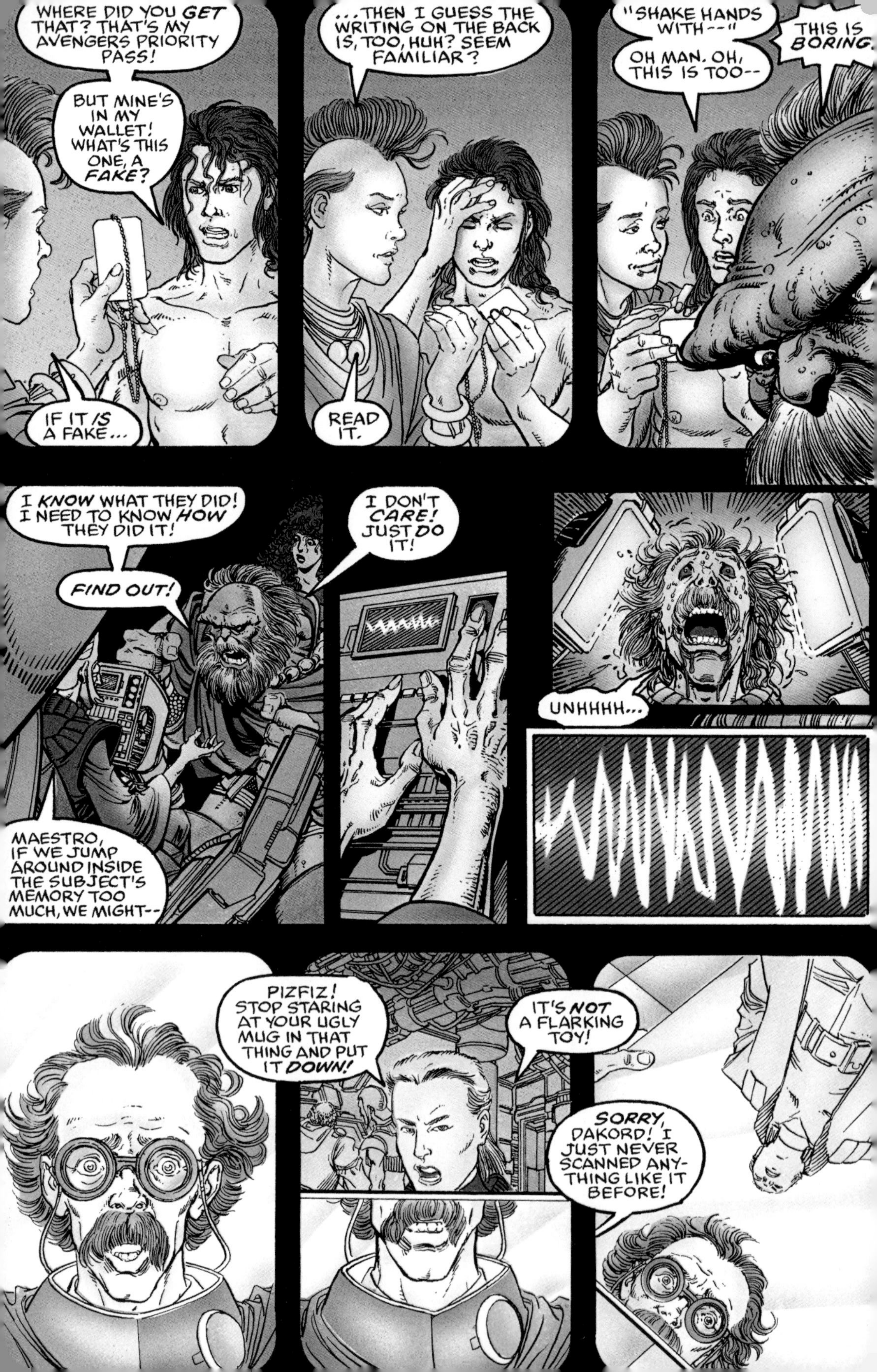
WHERE DID YOU GET THAT? THAT'S MY AVENGERS PRIORITY PASS!
BUT MINE'S IN MY WALLET! WHAT'S THIS ONE, A FAKE?
IF IT IS A FAKE...
...THEN I GUESS THE WRITING ON THE BACK IS, TOO, HUH? SEEM FAMILIAR?
READ IT.
"SHAKE HANDS WITH--"
OH MAN. OH, THIS IS TOO--
THIS IS BORING.
I KNOW WHAT THEY DID! I NEED TO KNOW HOW THEY DID IT!
FIND OUT!
MAESTRO, IF WE JUMP AROUND INSIDE THE SUBJECT'S MEMORY TOO MUCH, WE MIGHT--
I DON'T CARE! JUST DO IT!
UNHHHH...
PIZFIZ! STOP STARING AT YOUR UGLY MUG IN THAT THING AND PUT IT DOWN!
IT'S NOT A FLARKING TOY!
SORRY, DAKORD! I JUST NEVER SCANNED ANYTHING LIKE IT BEFORE!

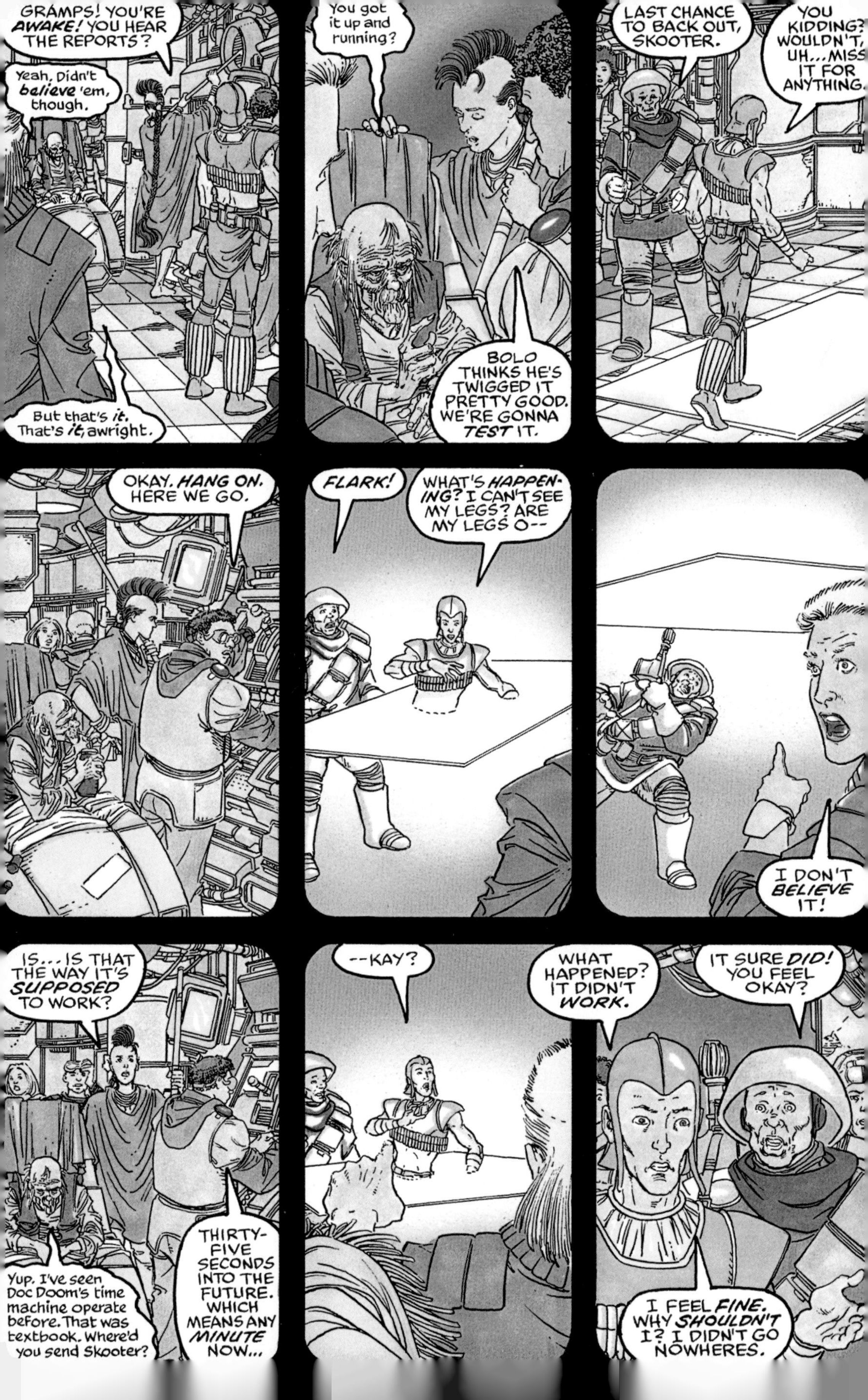
GRAMPS! YOU'RE AWAKE! YOU HEAR THE REPORTS?
Yeah, Didn't believe 'em, though.
But that's it. That's it, awright.
You got it up and running?
BOLO THINKS HE'S TWIGGED IT PRETTY GOOD. WE'RE GONNA TEST IT.
LAST CHANCE TO BACK OUT, SKOOTER.
YOU KIDDING? WOULDN'T, UH... MISS IT FOR ANYTHING.
OKAY. HANG ON. HERE WE GO.
FLARK!
WHAT'S HAPPEN-ING? I CAN'T SEE MY LEGS? ARE MY LEGS O--
I DON'T BELIEVE IT!
IS... IS THAT THE WAY IT'S SUPPOSED TO WORK?
Yup. I've seen Doc Doom's time machine operate before. That was textbook. Where'd you send Skooter?
THIRTY-FIVE SECONDS INTO THE FUTURE. WHICH MEANS ANY MINUTE NOW...
--KAY?
WHAT HAPPENED? IT DIDN'T WORK.
IT SURE DID! YOU FEEL OKAY?
I FEEL FINE. WHY SHOULDN'T I? I DIDN'T GO NOWHERES.

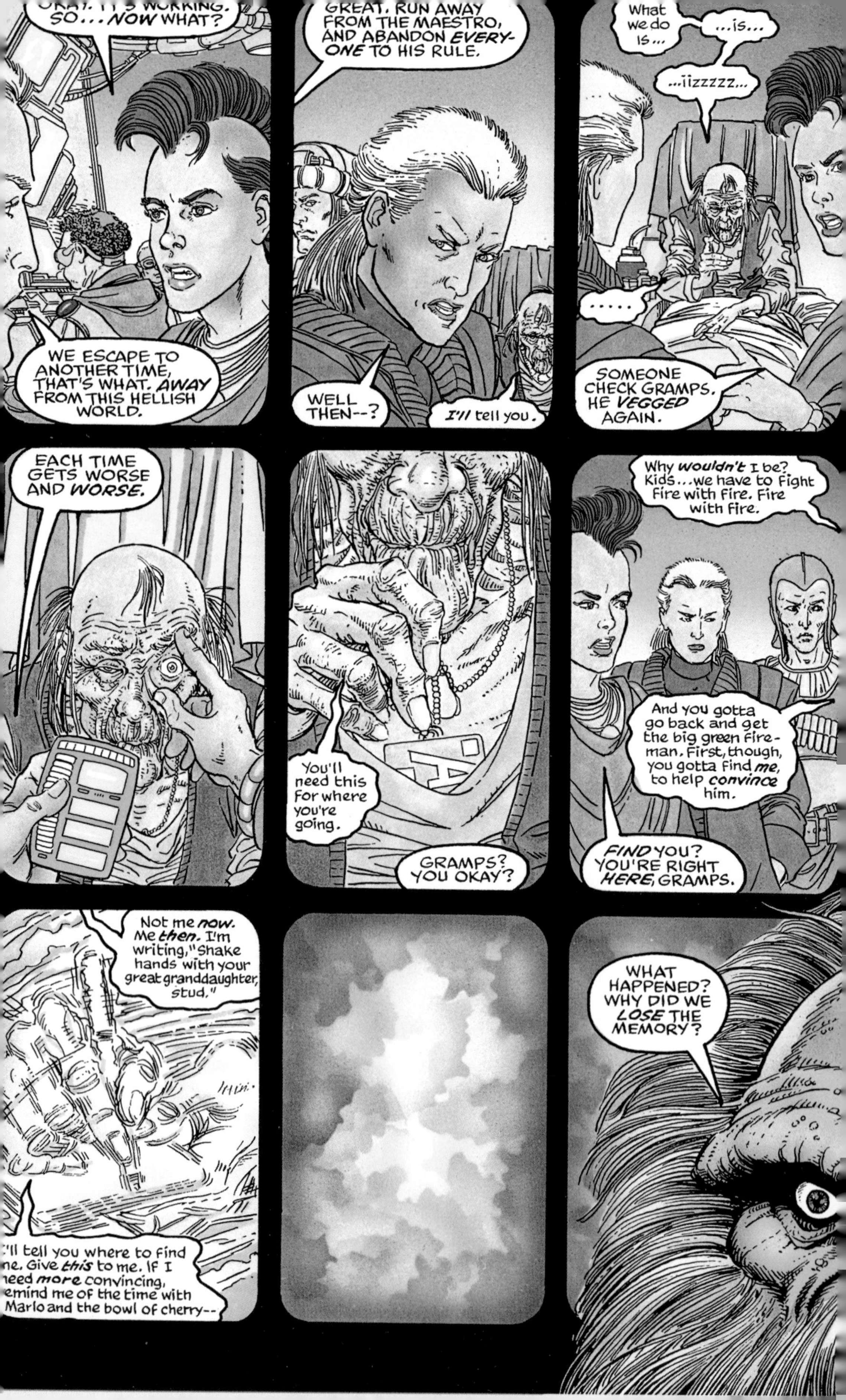
SO... NOW WHAT?
WE ESCAPE TO ANOTHER TIME, THAT'S WHAT. AWAY FROM THIS HELLISH WORLD.
GREAT. RUN AWAY FROM THE MAESTRO, AND ABANDON EVERYONE TO HIS RULE.
WELL THEN--?
I'll tell you.
What we do is...
...is...
...iizzzzz...
.....
SOMEONE CHECK GRAMPS. HE VEGGED AGAIN.
EACH TIME GETS WORSE AND WORSE.
You'll need this for where you're going.
GRAMPS? YOU OKAY?
Why wouldn't I be? Kids... we have to fight fire with fire. Fire with fire.
And you gotta go back and get the big green fire-man. First, though, you gotta find me, to help convince him.
FIND YOU? YOU'RE RIGHT HERE, GRAMPS.
Not me now. Me then. I'm writing, "Shake hands with your great granddaughter, stud."
I'll tell you where to find me. Give this to me. If I need more convincing, remind me of the time with Marlo and the bowl of cherry--
WHAT HAPPENED? WHY DID WE LOSE THE MEMORY?

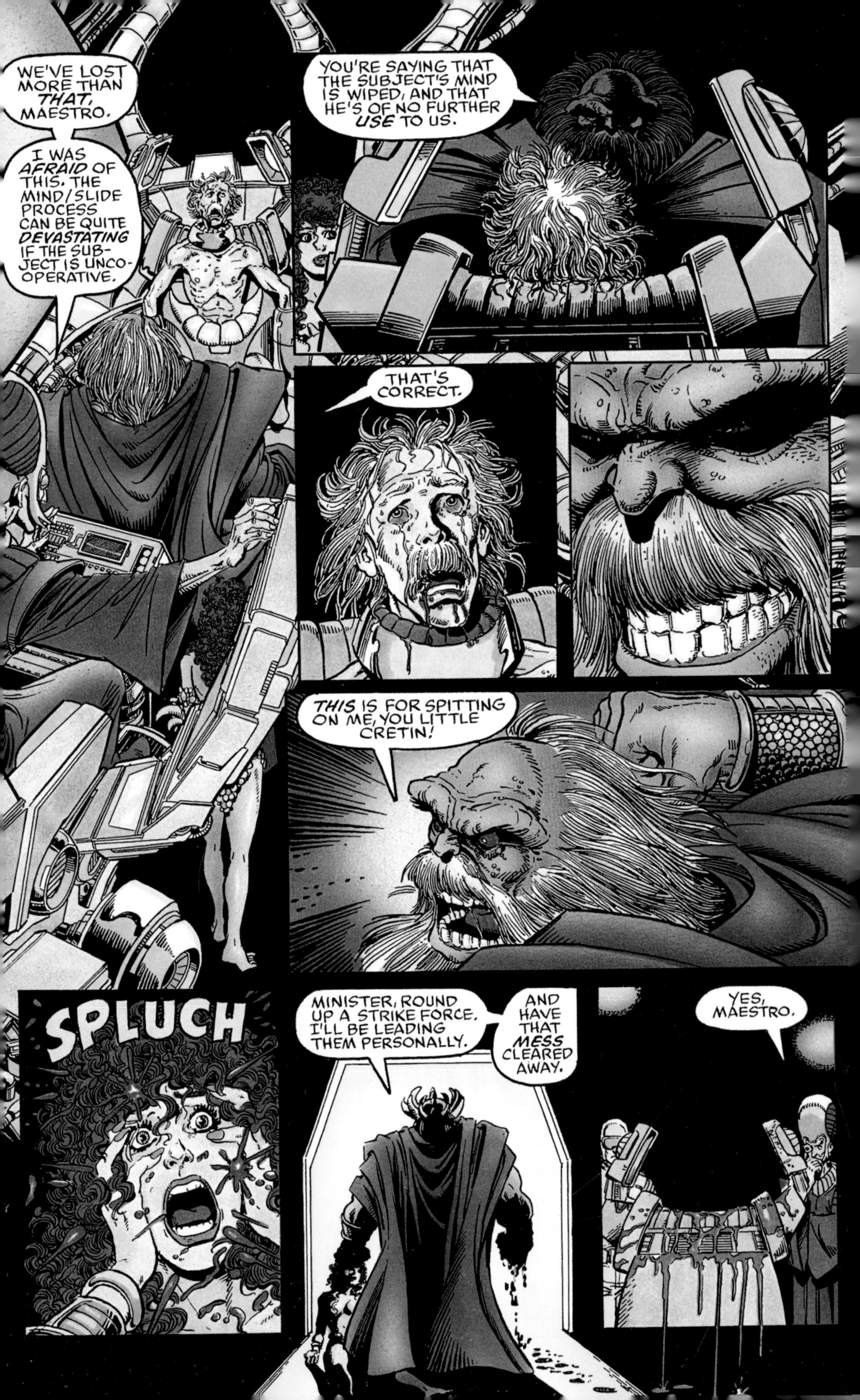
WE'VE LOST MORE THAN *THAT*, MAESTRO.
I WAS *AFRAID* OF THIS. THE MIND/SLIDE PROCESS CAN BE QUITE *DEVASTATING* IF THE SUBJECT IS UNCOOPERATIVE.
YOU'RE SAYING THAT THE SUBJECT'S MIND IS WIPED, AND THAT HE'S OF NO FURTHER *USE* TO US.
THAT'S CORRECT.
THIS IS FOR SPITTING ON ME, YOU LITTLE CRETIN!
SPLUCH
MINISTER, ROUND UP A STRIKE FORCE. I'LL BE LEADING THEM PERSONALLY.
AND HAVE THAT *MESS* CLEARED AWAY.
YES, MAESTRO.

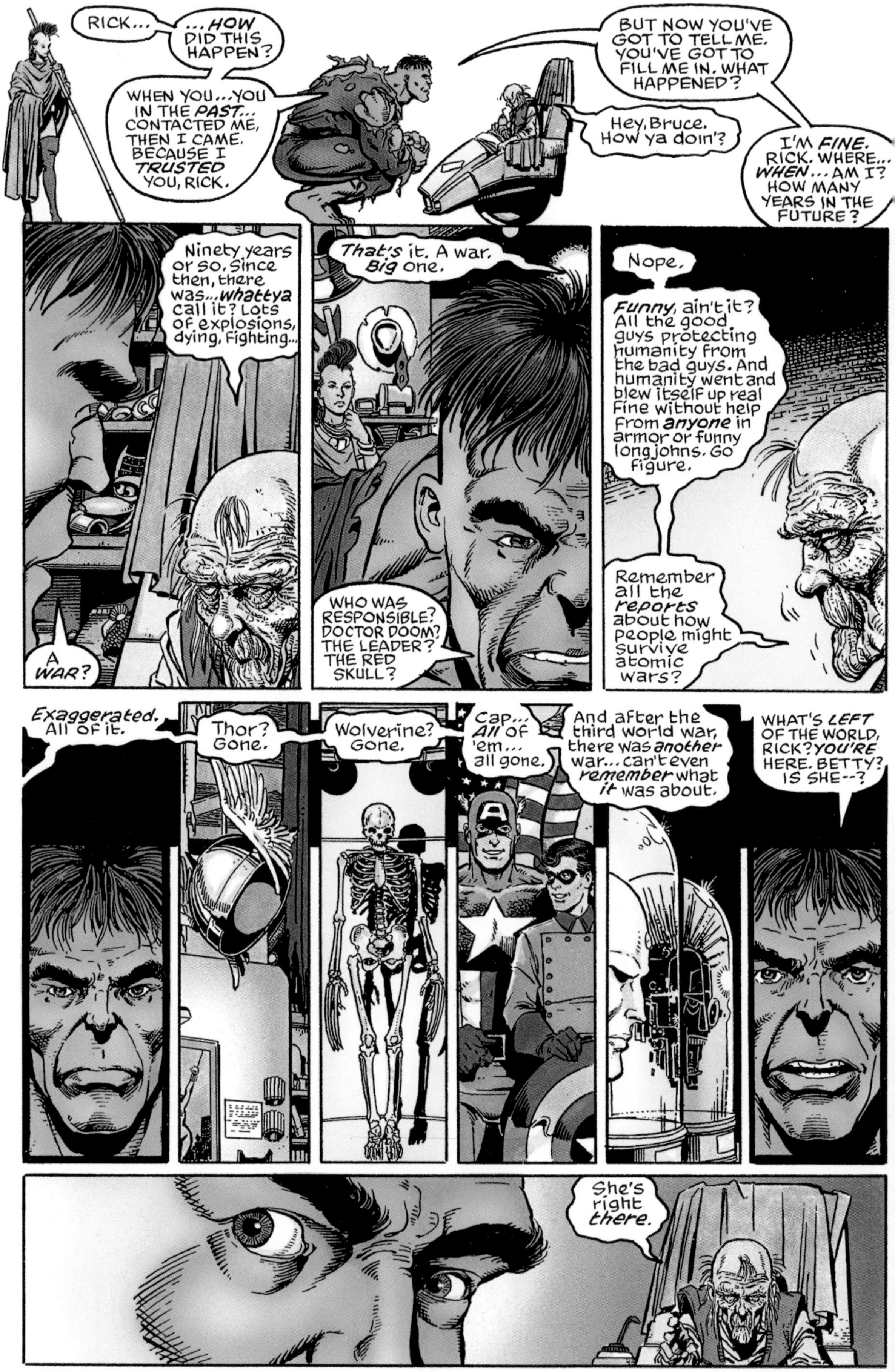
RICK...
...HOW DID THIS HAPPEN?
WHEN YOU...YOU IN THE PAST... CONTACTED ME, THEN I CAME. BECAUSE I TRUSTED YOU, RICK.
BUT NOW YOU'VE GOT TO TELL ME. YOU'VE GOT TO FILL ME IN. WHAT HAPPENED?
Hey, Bruce. How ya doin'?
I'M FINE. RICK. WHERE... WHEN... AM I? HOW MANY YEARS IN THE FUTURE?
Ninety years or so. Since then, there was...whattya call it? Lots of explosions, dying, fighting...
A WAR?
That's it. A war. Big one.
WHO WAS RESPONSIBLE? DOCTOR DOOM? THE LEADER? THE RED SKULL?
Nope.
Funny, ain't it? All the good guys protecting humanity from the bad guys. And humanity went and blew itself up real fine without help from anyone in armor or funny long johns. Go figure.
Remember all the reports about how people might survive atomic wars?
Exaggerated. All of it.
Thor? Gone.
Wolverine? Gone.
Cap... All of 'em... all gone.
And after the third world war, there was another war... can't even remember what it was about.
WHAT'S LEFT OF THE WORLD, RICK? YOU'RE HERE. BETTY? IS SHE--?
She's right there.

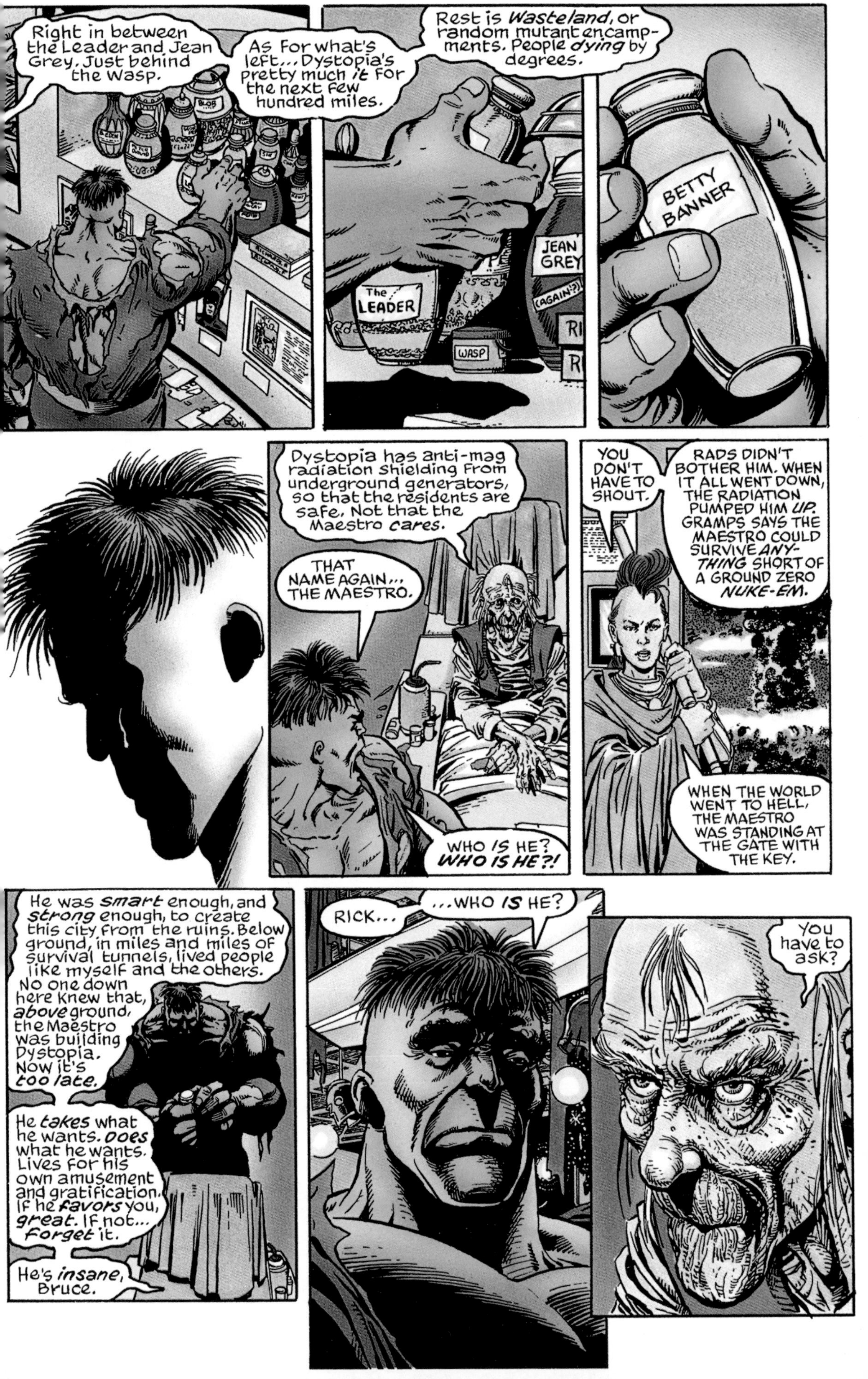
Right in between the Leader and Jean Grey. Just behind the Wasp.
As for what's left... Dystopia's pretty much it for the next few hundred miles.
Rest is Wasteland, or random mutant encampments. People dying by degrees.
The LEADER
WASP
JEAN GREY (AGAIN?)
BETTY BANNER
Dystopia has anti-mag radiation shielding from underground generators, so that the residents are safe. Not that the Maestro cares.
THAT NAME AGAIN... THE MAESTRO.
WHO IS HE? WHO IS HE?!
YOU DON'T HAVE TO SHOUT.
RADS DIDN'T BOTHER HIM. WHEN IT ALL WENT DOWN, THE RADIATION PUMPED HIM UP. GRAMPS SAYS THE MAESTRO COULD SURVIVE ANYTHING SHORT OF A GROUND ZERO NUKE-EM.
WHEN THE WORLD WENT TO HELL, THE MAESTRO WAS STANDING AT THE GATE WITH THE KEY.
He was smart enough, and strong enough, to create this city from the ruins. Below ground, in miles and miles of survival tunnels, lived people like myself and the others.
No one down here knew that, above ground, the Maestro was building Dystopia. Now it's too late.
He takes what he wants. Does what he wants. Lives for his own amusement and gratification. If he favors you, great. If not... forget it.
He's insane, Bruce.
RICK...
...WHO IS HE?
You have to ask?

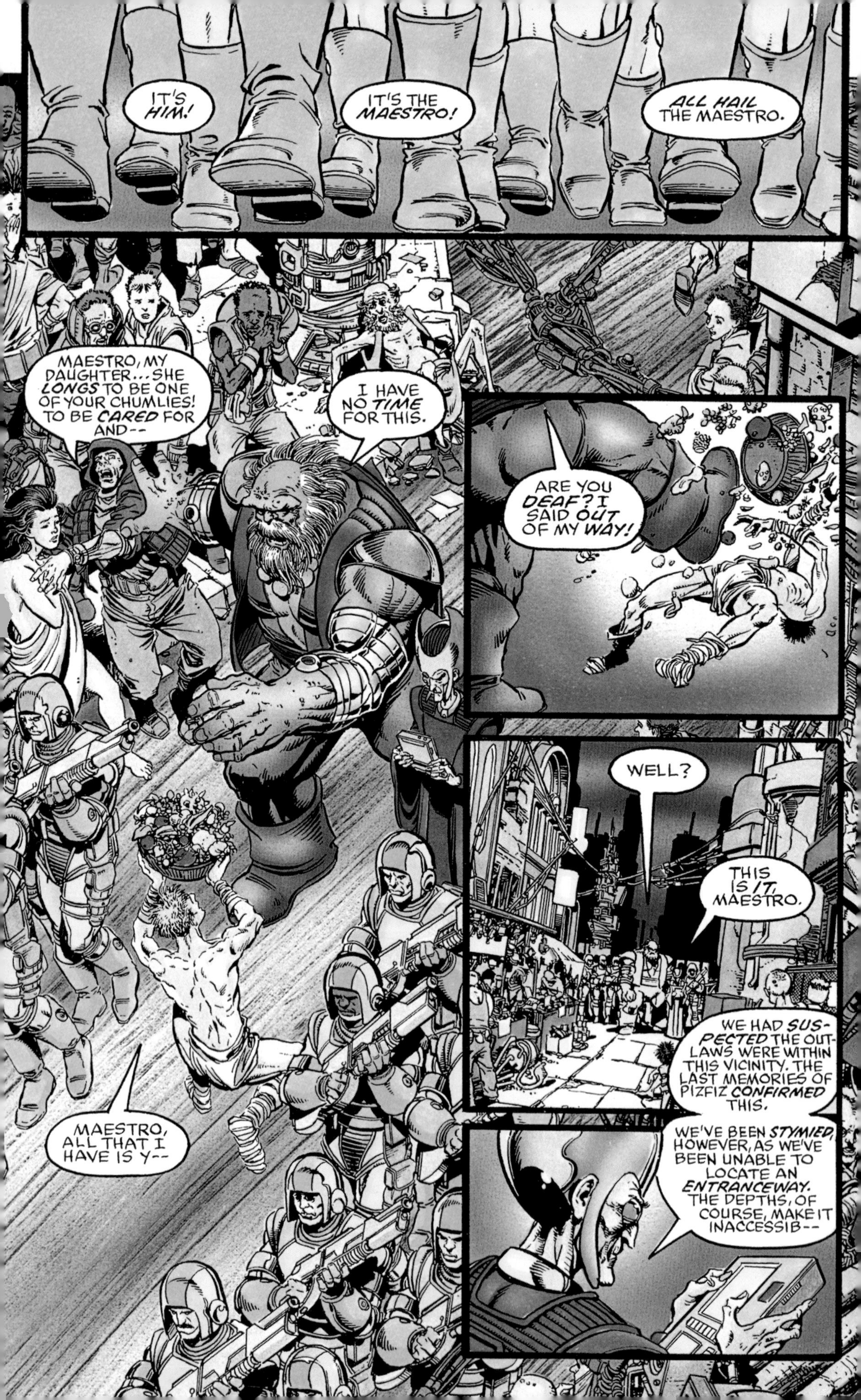
IT'S HIM!
IT'S THE MAESTRO!
ALL HAIL THE MAESTRO.
MAESTRO, MY DAUGHTER... SHE LONGS TO BE ONE OF YOUR CHUMLIES! TO BE CARED FOR AND--
I HAVE NO TIME FOR THIS.
ARE YOU DEAF? I SAID OUT OF MY WAY!
MAESTRO, ALL THAT I HAVE IS Y--
WELL?
THIS IS IT, MAESTRO.
WE HAD SUSPECTED THE OUTLAWS WERE WITHIN THIS VICINITY. THE LAST MEMORIES OF PIZFIZ CONFIRMED THIS.
WE'VE BEEN STYMIED, HOWEVER, AS WE'VE BEEN UNABLE TO LOCATE AN ENTRANCEWAY. THE DEPTHS, OF COURSE, MAKE IT INACCESSIB--

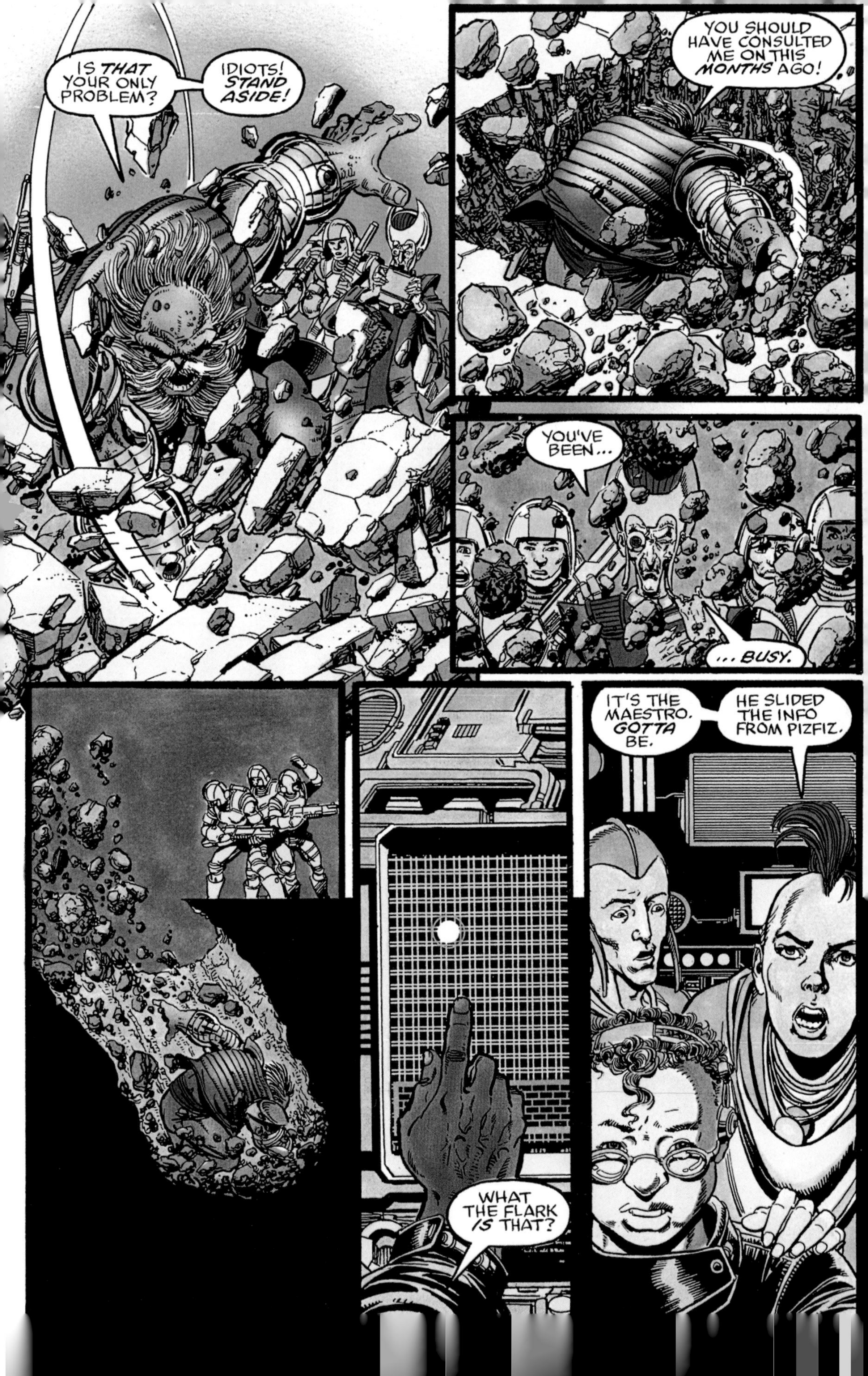
IS THAT YOUR ONLY PROBLEM?
IDIOTS! STAND ASIDE!
YOU SHOULD HAVE CONSULTED ME ON THIS MONTHS AGO!
YOU'VE BEEN...
... BUSY.
WHAT THE FLARK IS THAT?
IT'S THE MAESTRO. GOTTA BE.
HE SLIDED THE INFO FROM PIZFIZ.

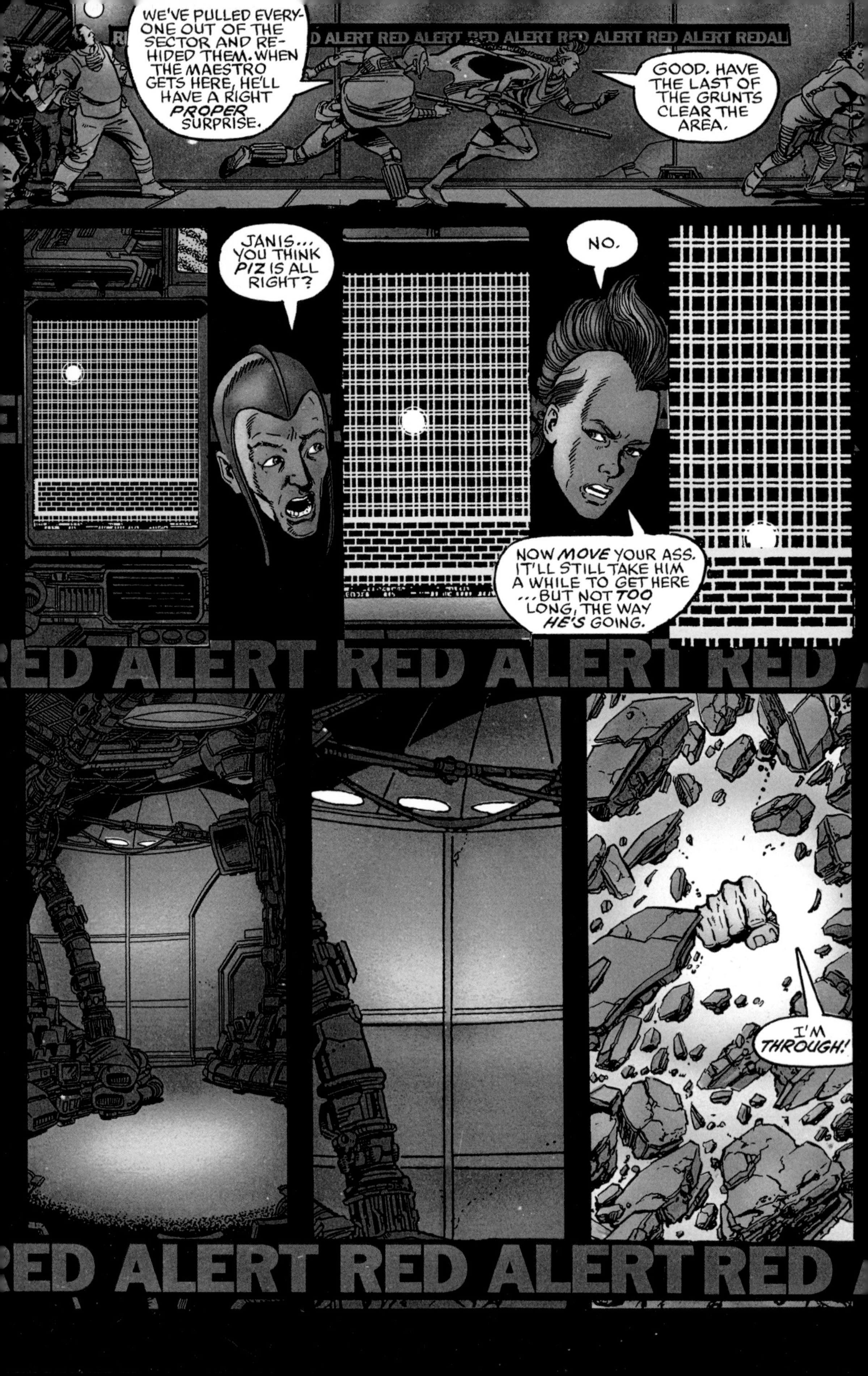

RED ALERT RED ALERT RED ALERT RED ALERT RED ALERT RED ALERT REDAL
WE'VE PULLED EVERYONE OUT OF THE SECTOR AND RE-HIDED THEM. WHEN THE MAESTRO GETS HERE, HE'LL HAVE A RIGHT PROPER SURPRISE.
GOOD. HAVE THE LAST OF THE GRUNTS CLEAR THE AREA.
JANIS... YOU THINK PIZ IS ALL RIGHT?
NO.
NOW MOVE YOUR ASS. IT'LL STILL TAKE HIM A WHILE TO GET HERE ...BUT NOT TOO LONG, THE WAY HE'S GOING.
RED ALERT RED ALERT RED
I'M THROUGH!
RED ALERT RED ALERT RED

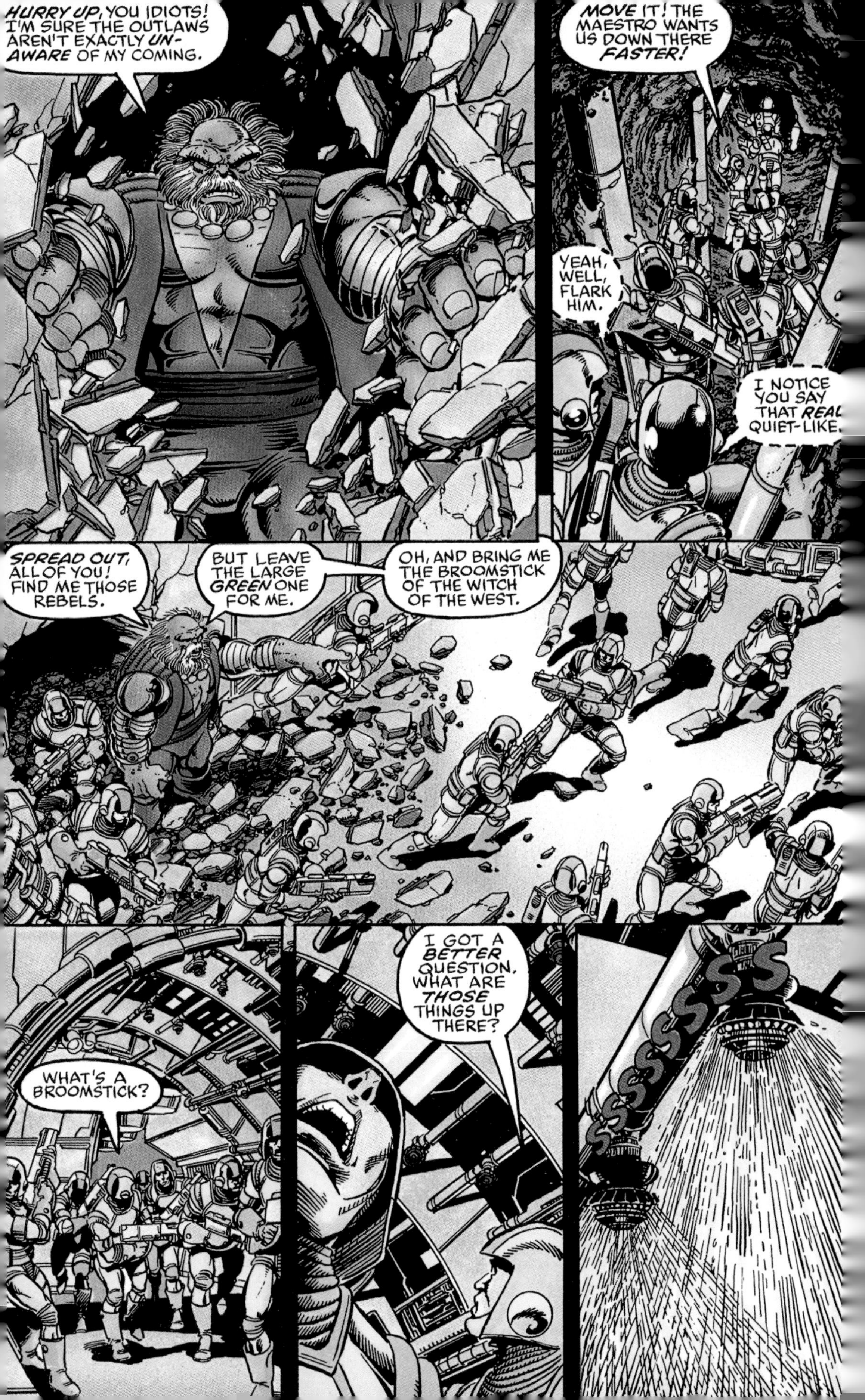
HURRY UP, YOU IDIOTS! I'M SURE THE OUTLAWS AREN'T EXACTLY UN-AWARE OF MY COMING.
MOVE IT! THE MAESTRO WANTS US DOWN THERE FASTER!
YEAH, WELL, FLARK HIM.
I NOTICE YOU SAY THAT REAL QUIET-LIKE.
SPREAD OUT, ALL OF YOU! FIND ME THOSE REBELS.
BUT LEAVE THE LARGE GREEN ONE FOR ME.
OH, AND BRING ME THE BROOMSTICK OF THE WITCH OF THE WEST.
WHAT'S A BROOMSTICK?
I GOT A BETTER QUESTION. WHAT ARE THOSE THINGS UP THERE?
SSSSSSSSS

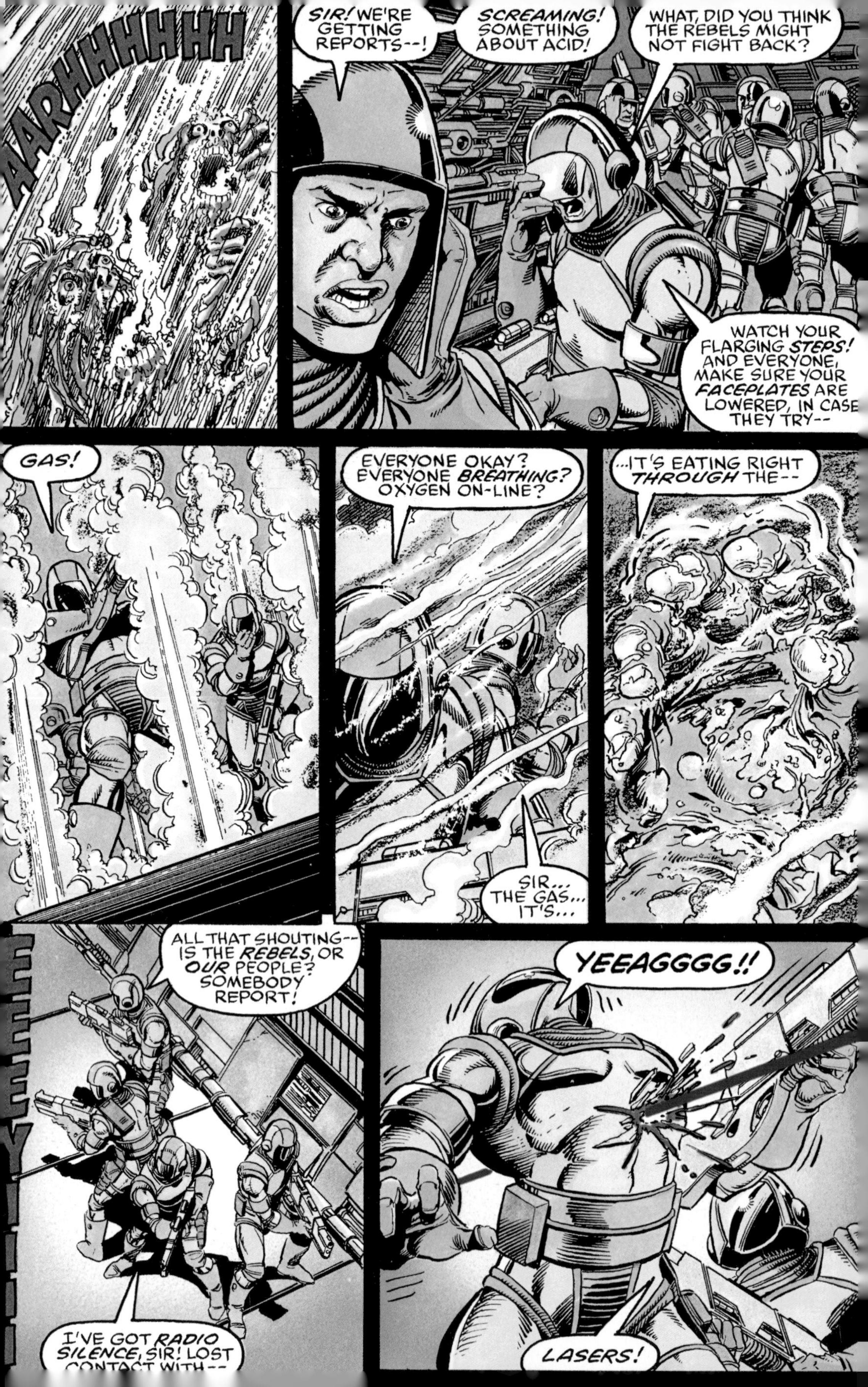
AARHHHHHHH
SIR! WE'RE GETTING REPORTS--!
SCREAMING! SOMETHING ABOUT ACID!
WHAT, DID YOU THINK THE REBELS MIGHT NOT FIGHT BACK?
WATCH YOUR FLARGING STEPS! AND EVERYONE, MAKE SURE YOUR FACEPLATES ARE LOWERED, IN CASE THEY TRY--
GAS!
EVERYONE OKAY? EVERYONE BREATHING? OXYGEN ON-LINE?
SIR... THE GAS... IT'S...
...IT'S EATING RIGHT THROUGH THE--
ALL THAT SHOUTING-- IS THE REBELS, OR OUR PEOPLE? SOMEBODY REPORT!
I'VE GOT RADIO SILENCE, SIR! LOST CONTACT WITH--
YEEAGGGG!!
LASERS!

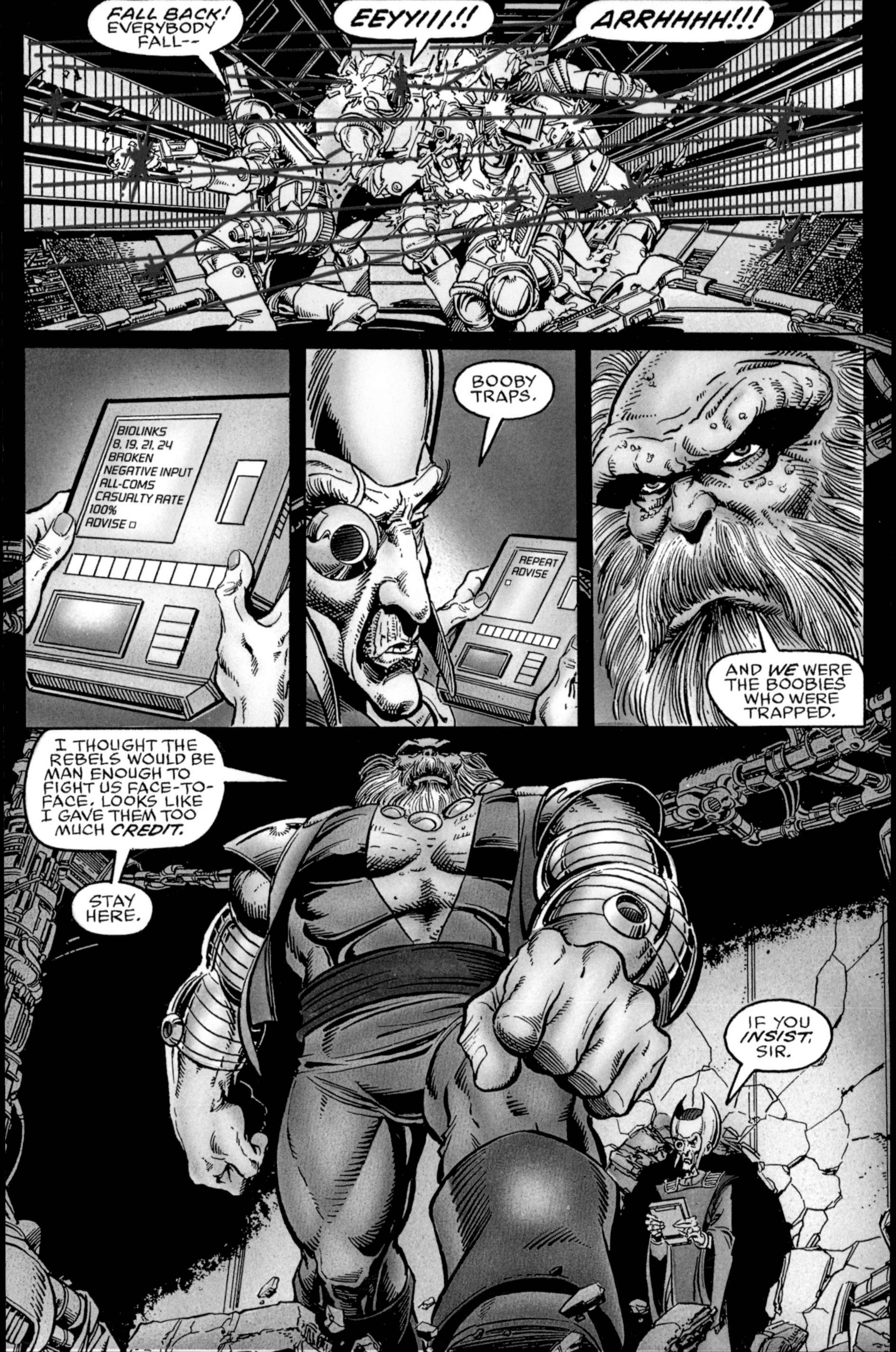
FALL BACK! EVERYBODY FALL--
EEYYIIII!!
ARRHHHH!!!
BIOLINKS
8, 19, 21, 24
BROKEN
NEGATIVE INPUT
ALL-COMS
CASUALTY RATE
100%
ADVISE
BOOBY TRAPS.
REPEAT ADVISE
AND WE WERE THE BOOBIES WHO WERE TRAPPED.
I THOUGHT THE REBELS WOULD BE MAN ENOUGH TO FIGHT US FACE-TO-FACE. LOOKS LIKE I GAVE THEM TOO MUCH CREDIT.
STAY HERE.
IF YOU INSIST, SIR.

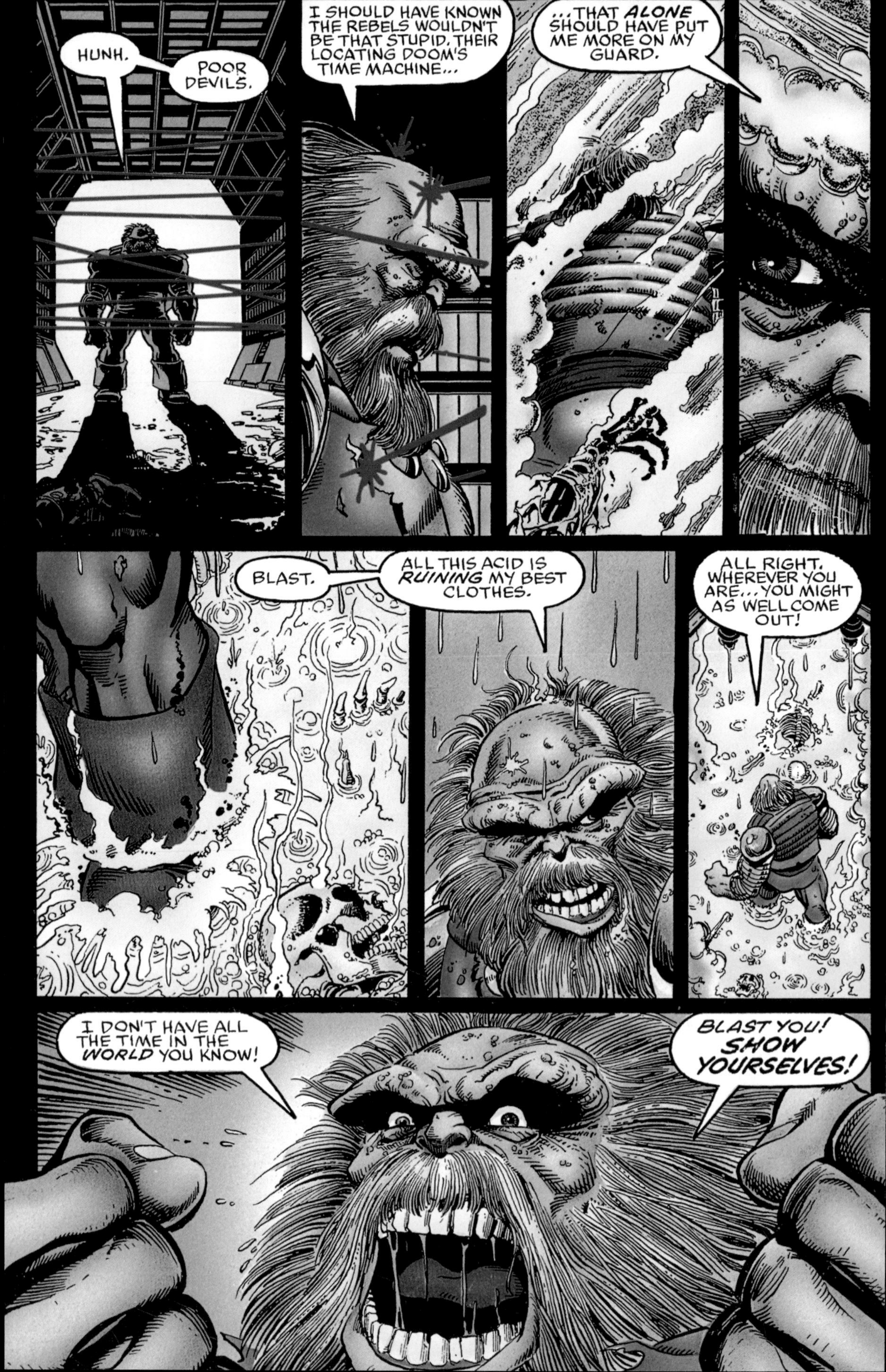
HUNH.
POOR DEVILS.
I SHOULD HAVE KNOWN THE REBELS WOULDN'T BE THAT STUPID. THEIR LOCATING DOOM'S TIME MACHINE...
...THAT ALONE SHOULD HAVE PUT ME MORE ON MY GUARD.
BLAST.
ALL THIS ACID IS RUINING MY BEST CLOTHES.
ALL RIGHT. WHEREVER YOU ARE... YOU MIGHT AS WELL COME OUT!
I DON'T HAVE ALL THE TIME IN THE WORLD YOU KNOW!
BLAST YOU! SHOW YOURSELVES!

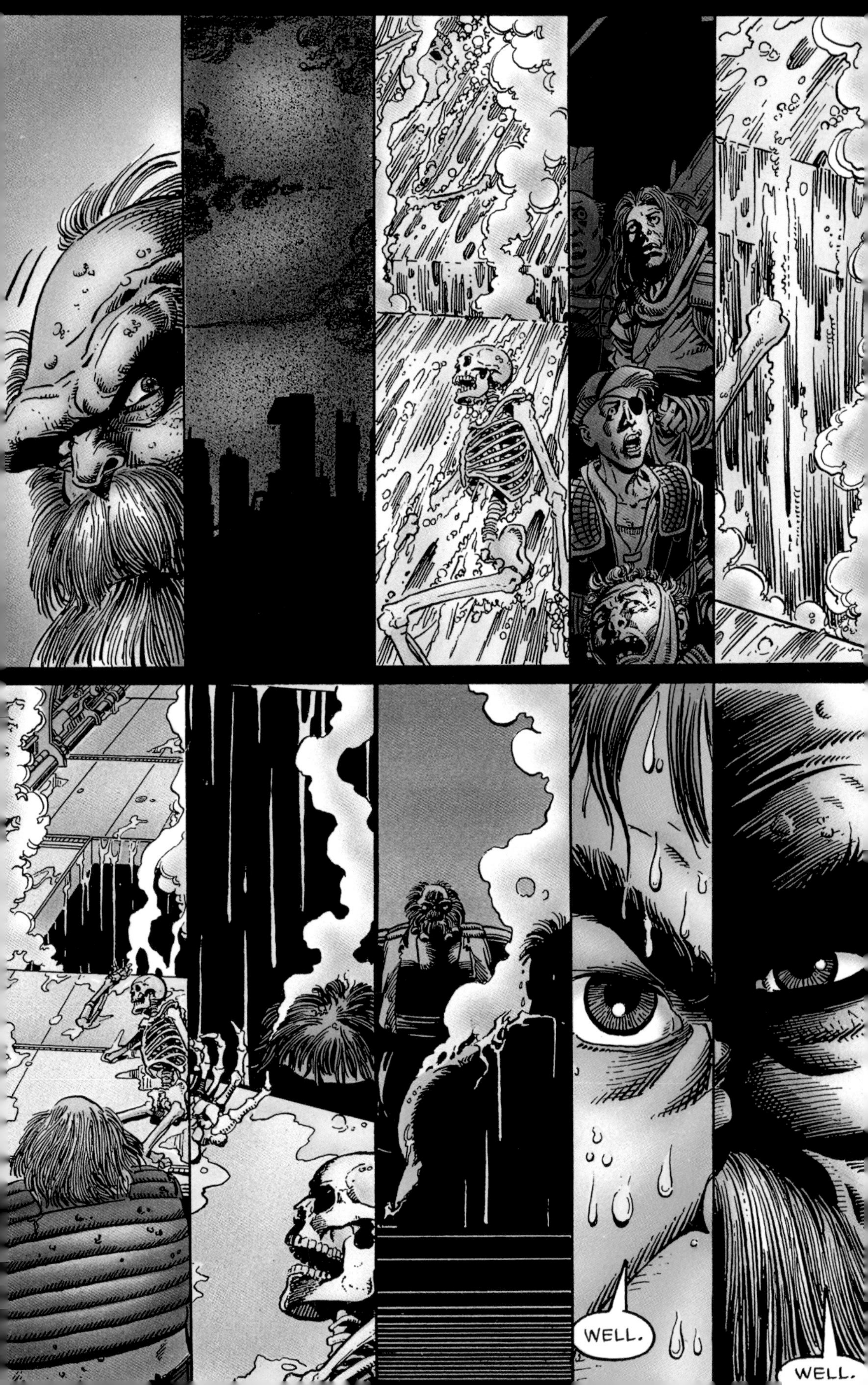
WELL.
WELL.

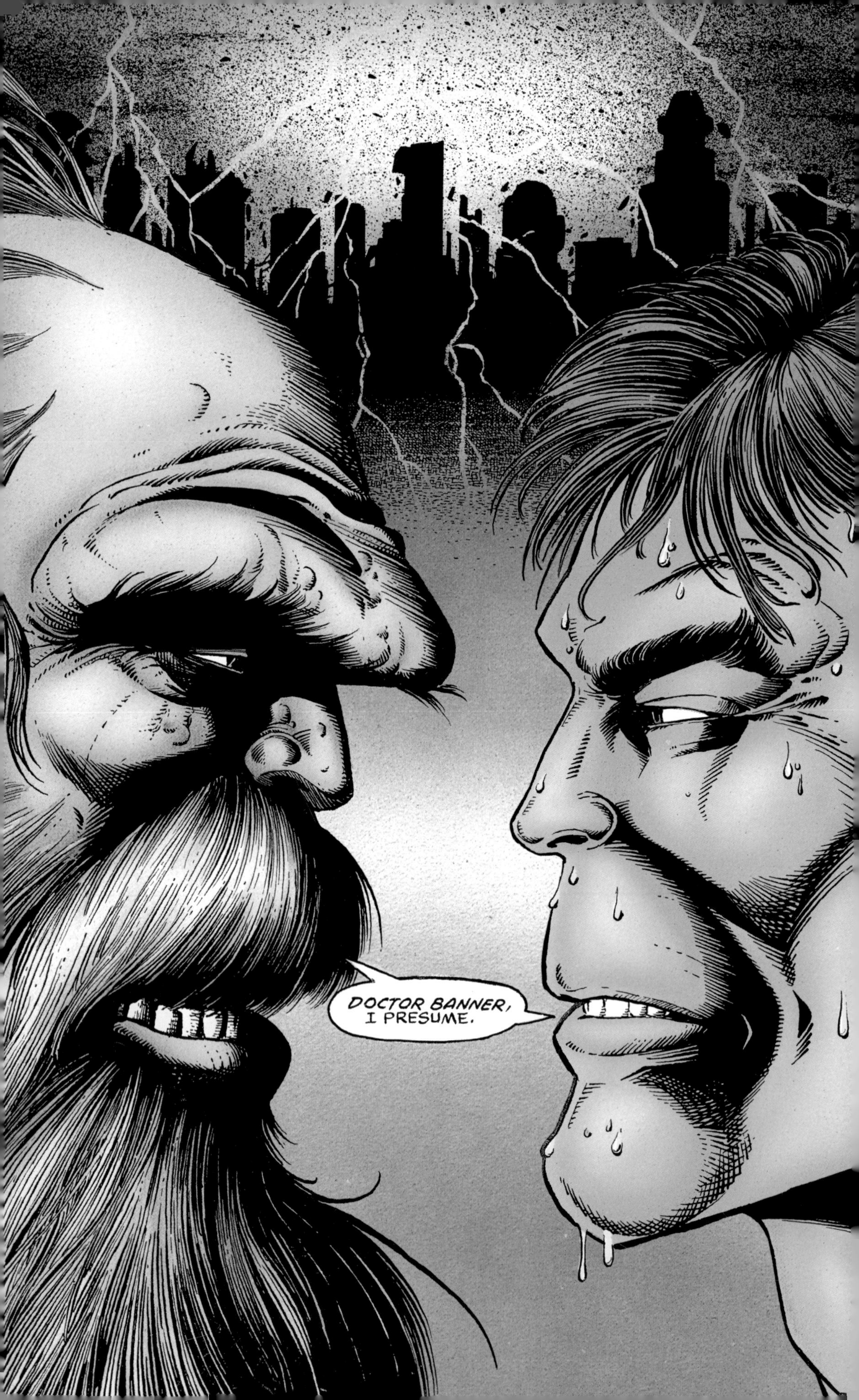
DOCTOR BANNER, I PRESUME.

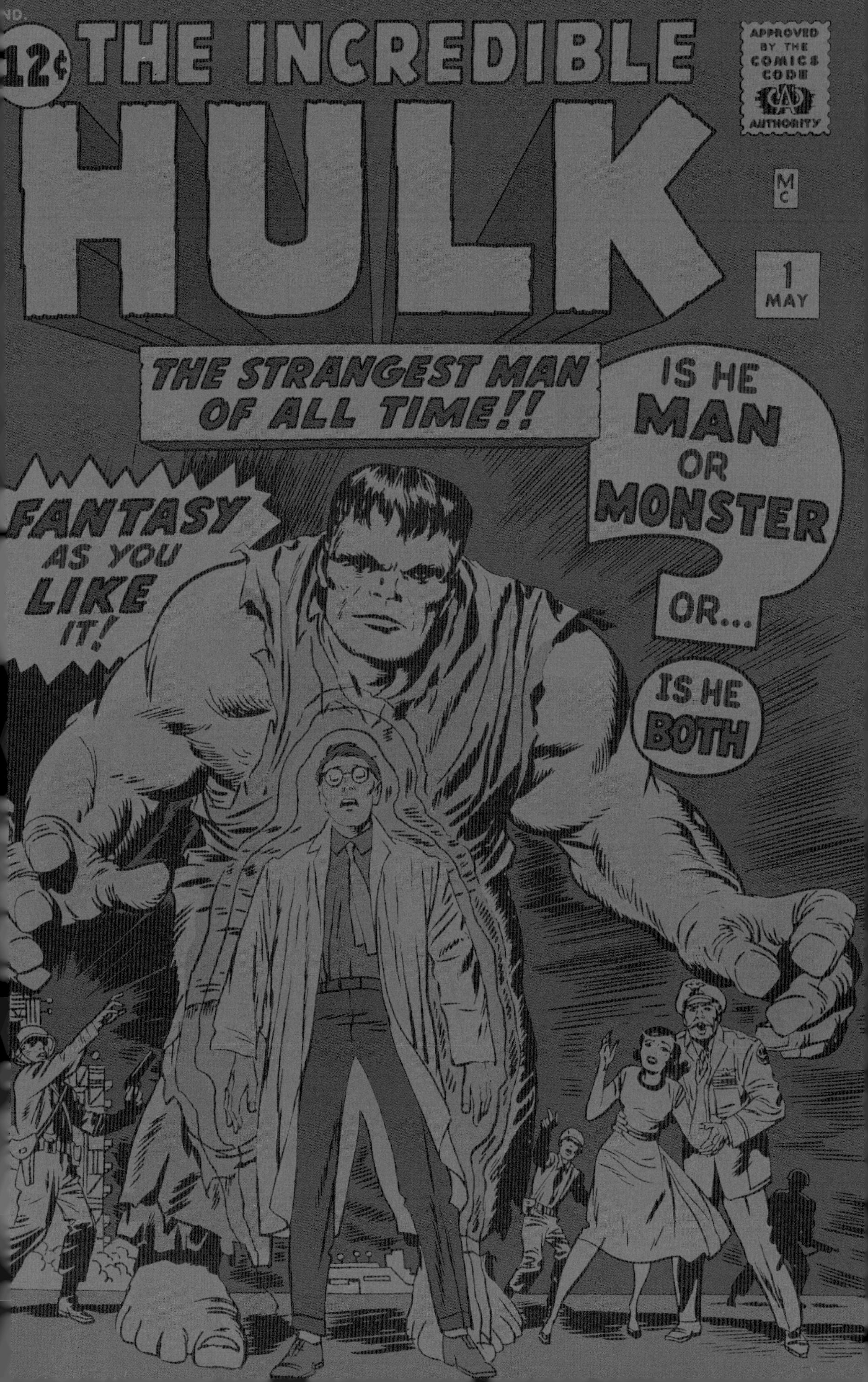
12¢
THE INCREDIBLE
HULK
APPROVED BY THE COMICS CODE AUTHORITY
MC
1
MAY
THE STRANGEST MAN OF ALL TIME!!
FANTASY AS YOU LIKE IT!
IS HE MAN OR MONSTER
OR...
IS HE BOTH

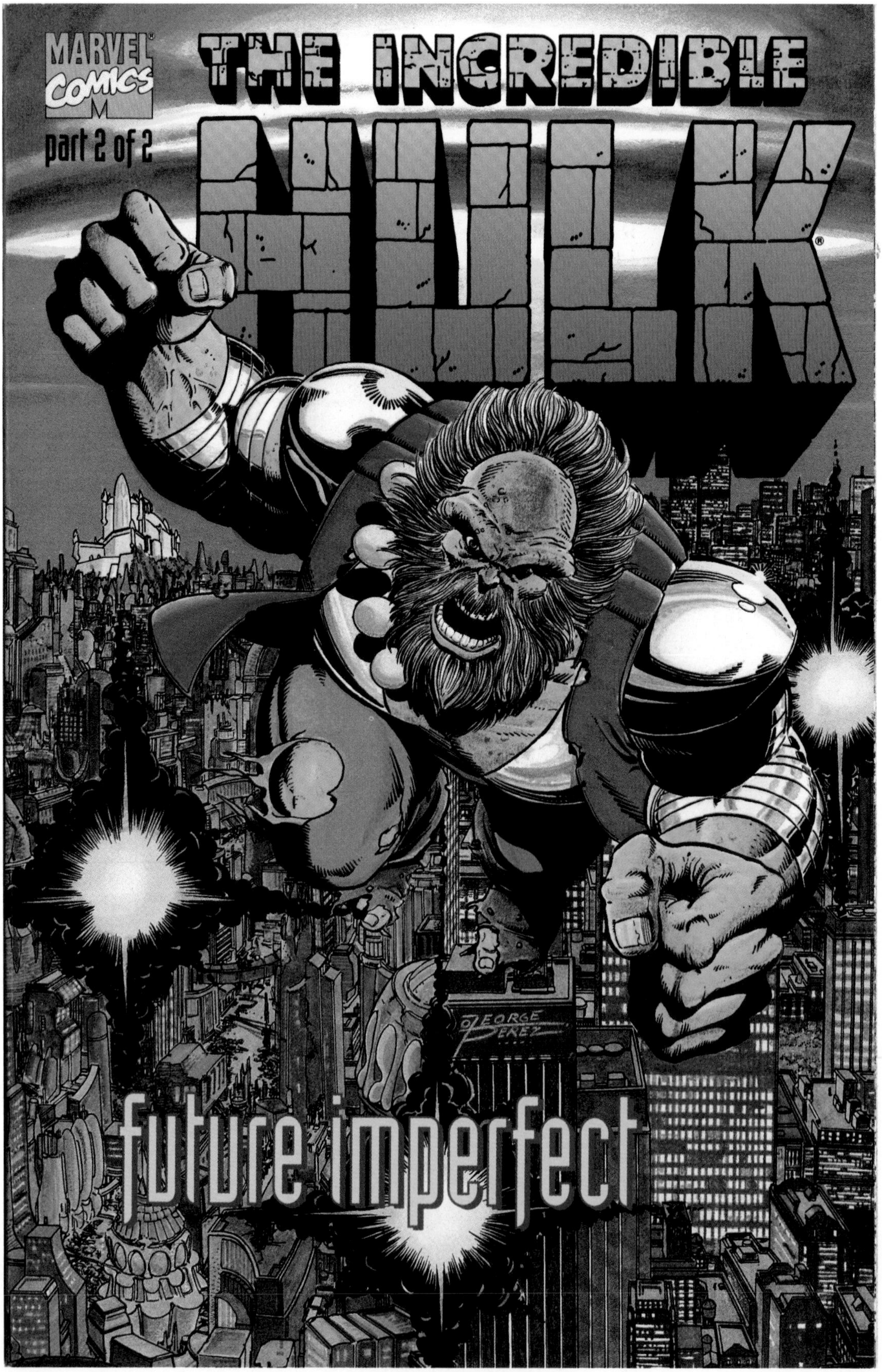
MARVEL COMICS
part 2 of 2
THE INCREDIBLE HULK
GEORGE PEREZ
future imperfect

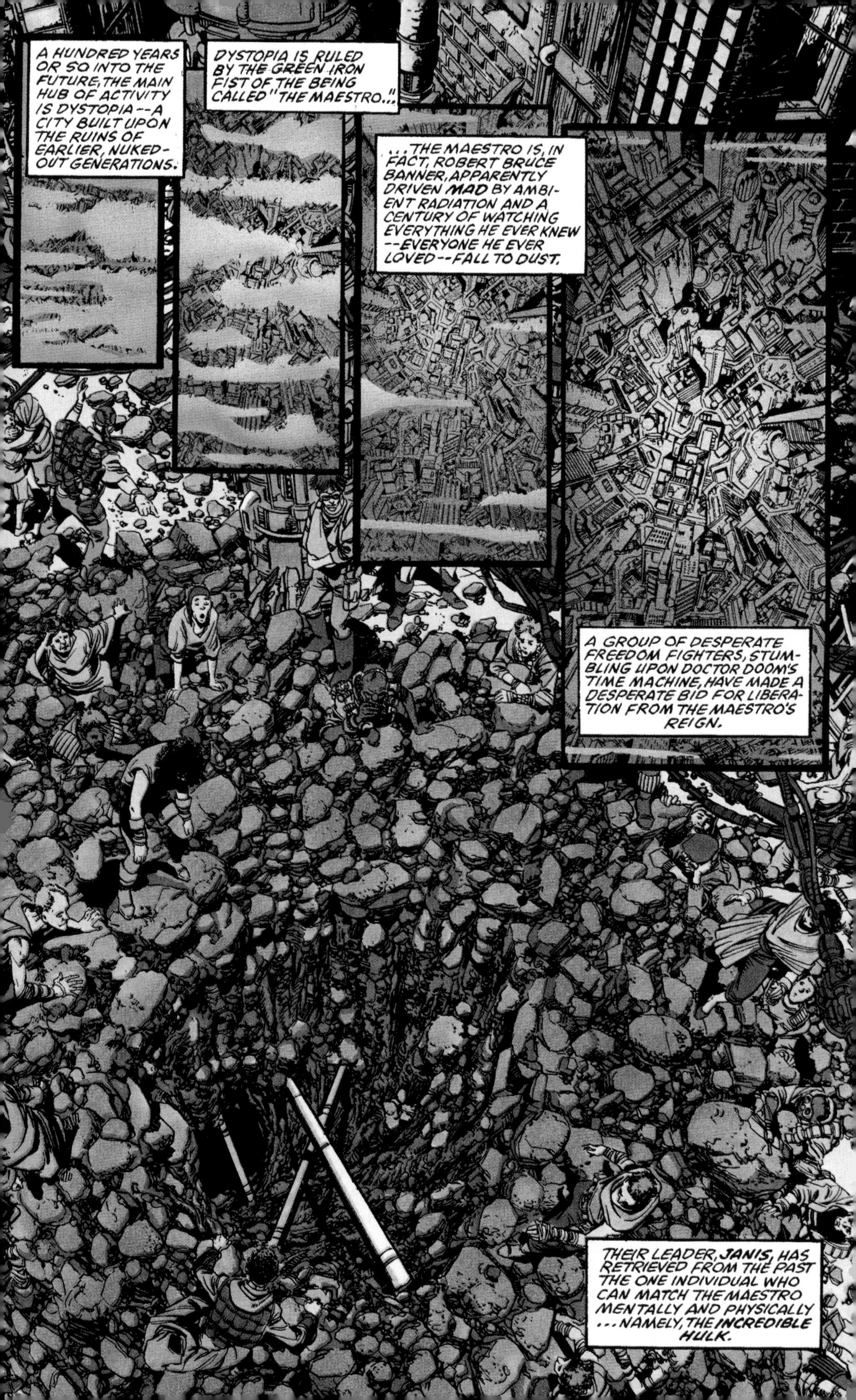
A HUNDRED YEARS OR SO INTO THE FUTURE, THE MAIN HUB OF ACTIVITY IS DYSTOPIA--A CITY BUILT UPON THE RUINS OF EARLIER, NUKED-OUT GENERATIONS.
DYSTOPIA IS RULED BY THE GREEN IRON FIST OF THE BEING CALLED "THE MAESTRO."...
...THE MAESTRO IS, IN FACT, ROBERT BRUCE BANNER, APPARENTLY DRIVEN MAD BY AMBIENT RADIATION AND A CENTURY OF WATCHING EVERYTHING HE EVER KNEW --EVERYONE HE EVER LOVED--FALL TO DUST.
A GROUP OF DESPERATE FREEDOM FIGHTERS, STUMBLING UPON DOCTOR DOOM'S TIME MACHINE, HAVE MADE A DESPERATE BID FOR LIBERATION FROM THE MAESTRO'S REIGN.
THEIR LEADER, JANIS, HAS RETRIEVED FROM THE PAST THE ONE INDIVIDUAL WHO CAN MATCH THE MAESTRO MENTALLY AND PHYSICALLY ...NAMELY, THE INCREDIBLE HULK.

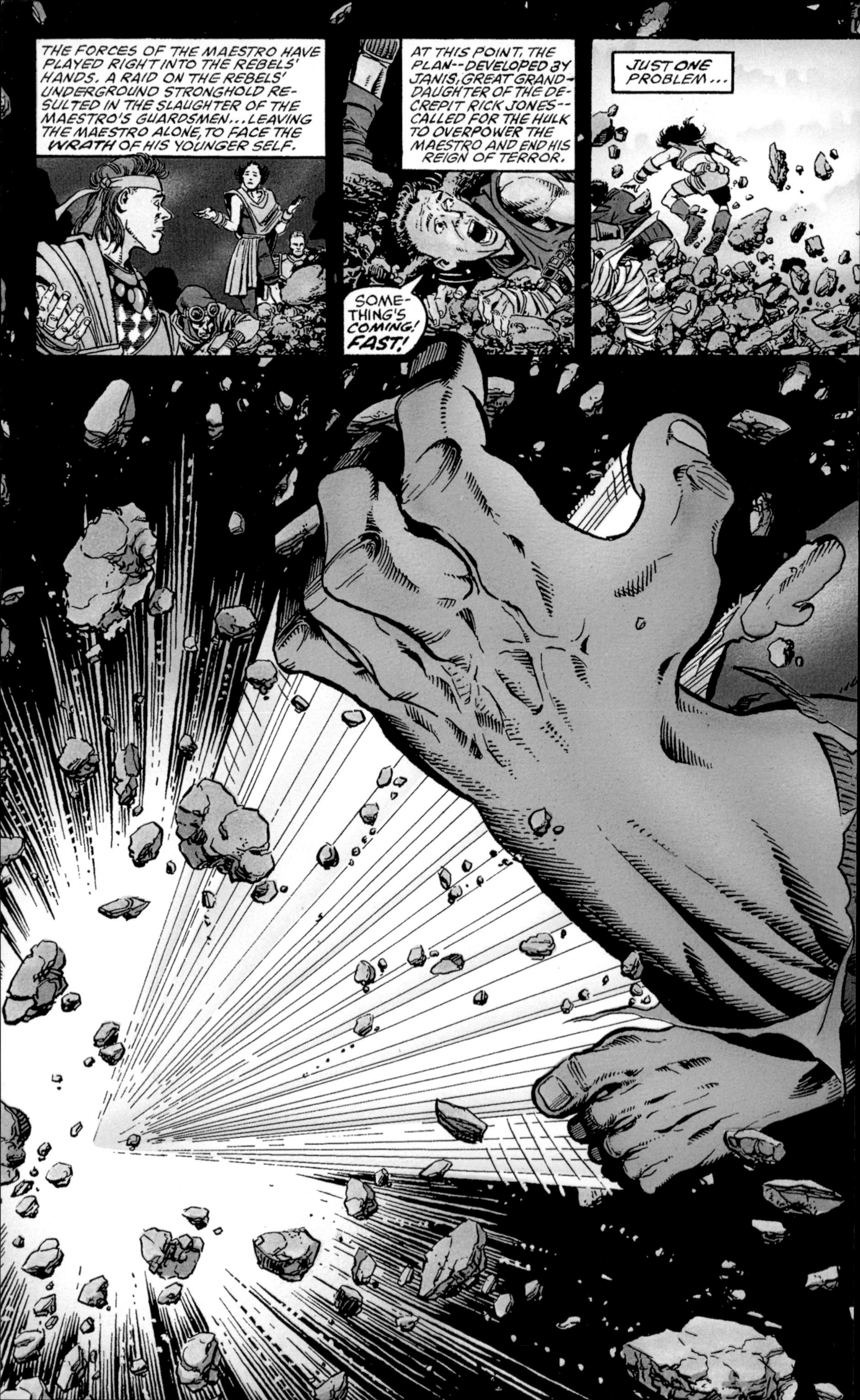
THE FORCES OF THE MAESTRO HAVE PLAYED RIGHT INTO THE REBELS' HANDS. A RAID ON THE REBELS' UNDERGROUND STRONGHOLD RESULTED IN THE SLAUGHTER OF THE MAESTRO'S GUARDSMEN... LEAVING THE MAESTRO ALONE, TO FACE THE WRATH OF HIS YOUNGER SELF.
AT THIS POINT, THE PLAN--DEVELOPED BY JANIS, GREAT GRANDDAUGHTER OF THE DECREPIT RICK JONES--CALLED FOR THE HULK TO OVERPOWER THE MAESTRO AND END HIS REIGN OF TERROR.
SOMETHING'S COMING! FAST!
JUST ONE PROBLEM...

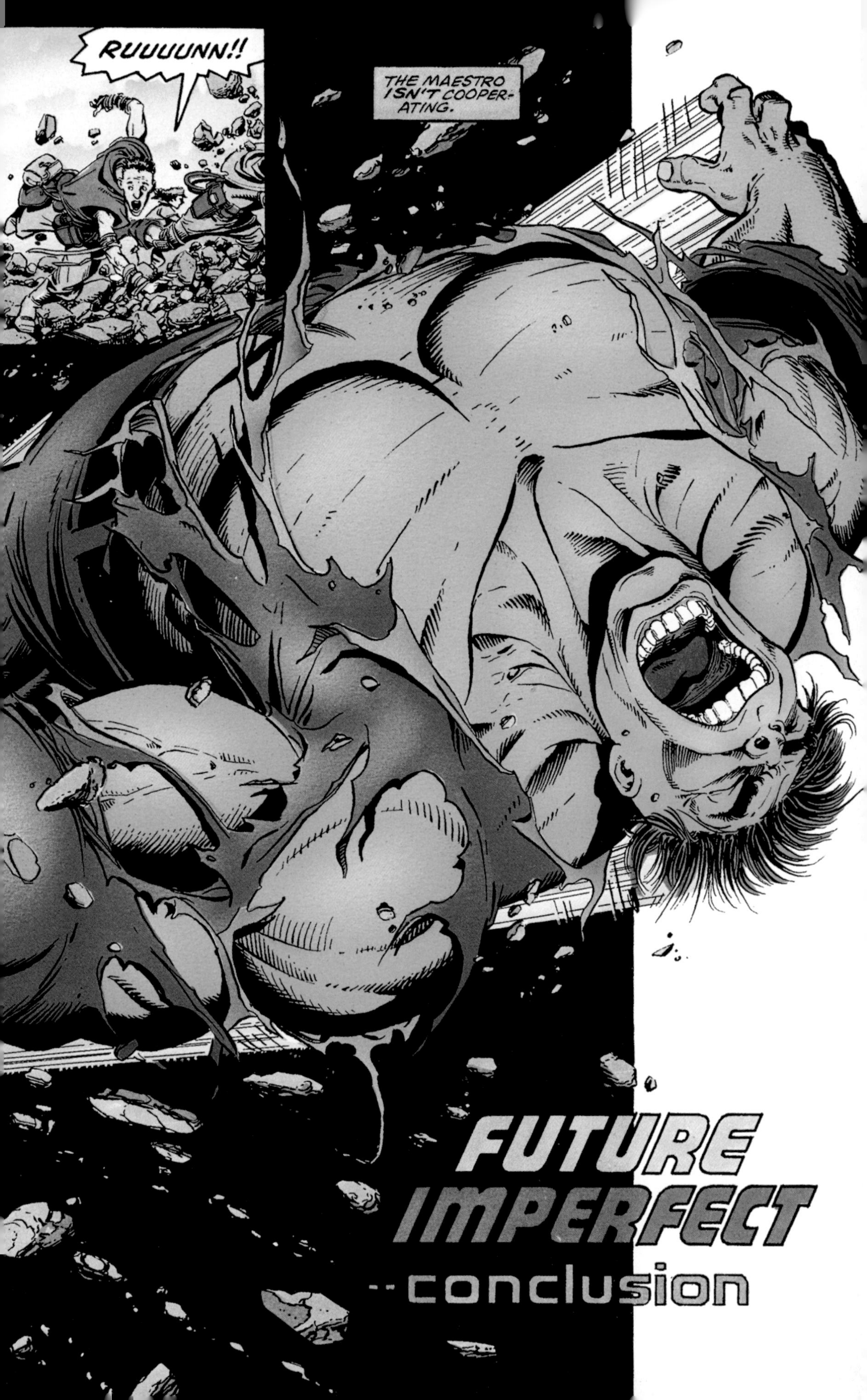
RUUUUNN!!
THE MAESTRO ISN'T COOPERATING.
FUTURE IMPERFECT
--conclusion

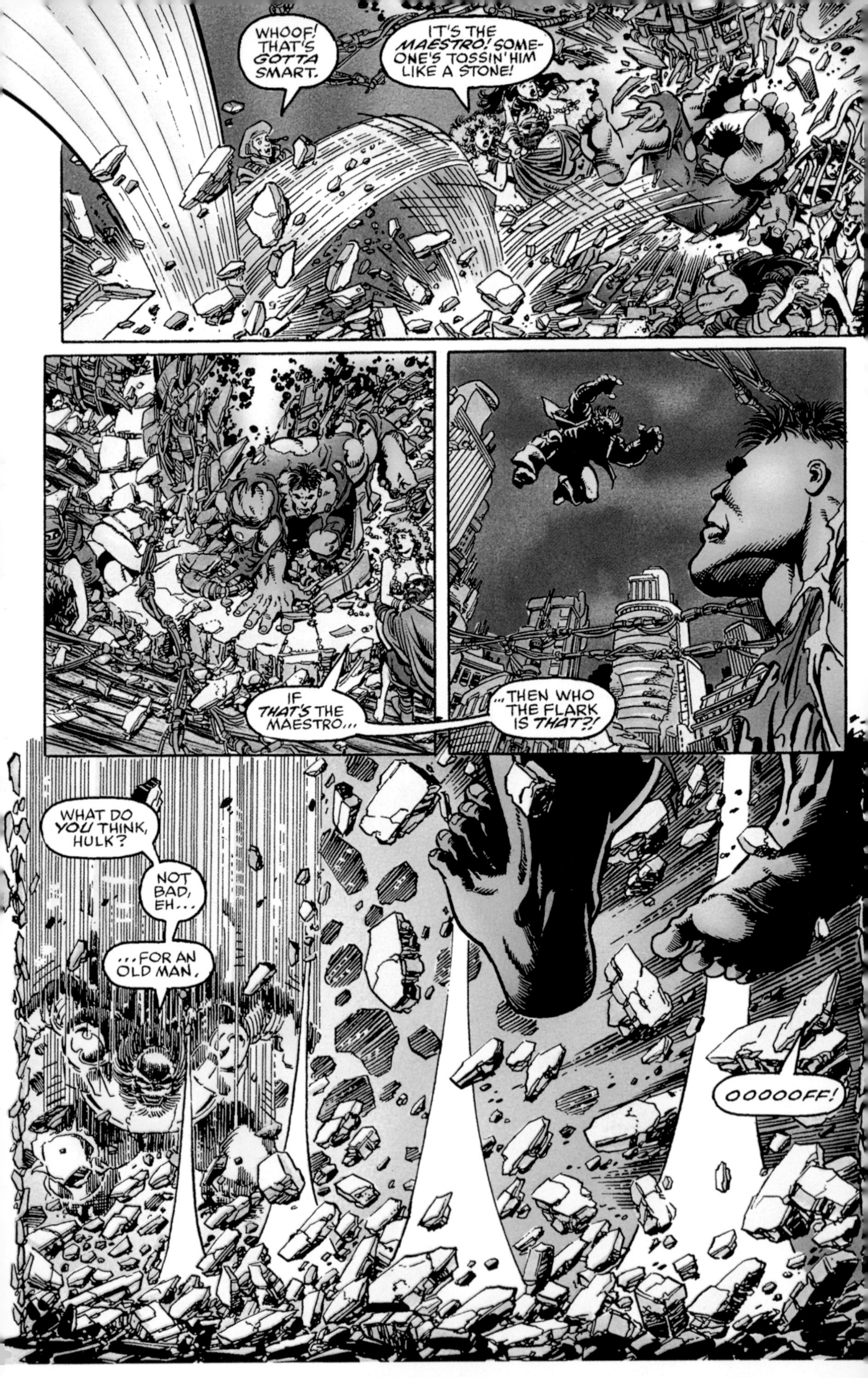
WHOOF! THAT'S GOTTA SMART.
IT'S THE MAESTRO! SOMEONE'S TOSSIN' HIM LIKE A STONE!
IF THAT'S THE MAESTRO...
...THEN WHO THE FLARK IS THAT?!
WHAT DO YOU THINK, HULK?
NOT BAD, EH...
...FOR AN OLD MAN.
OOOOOFF!

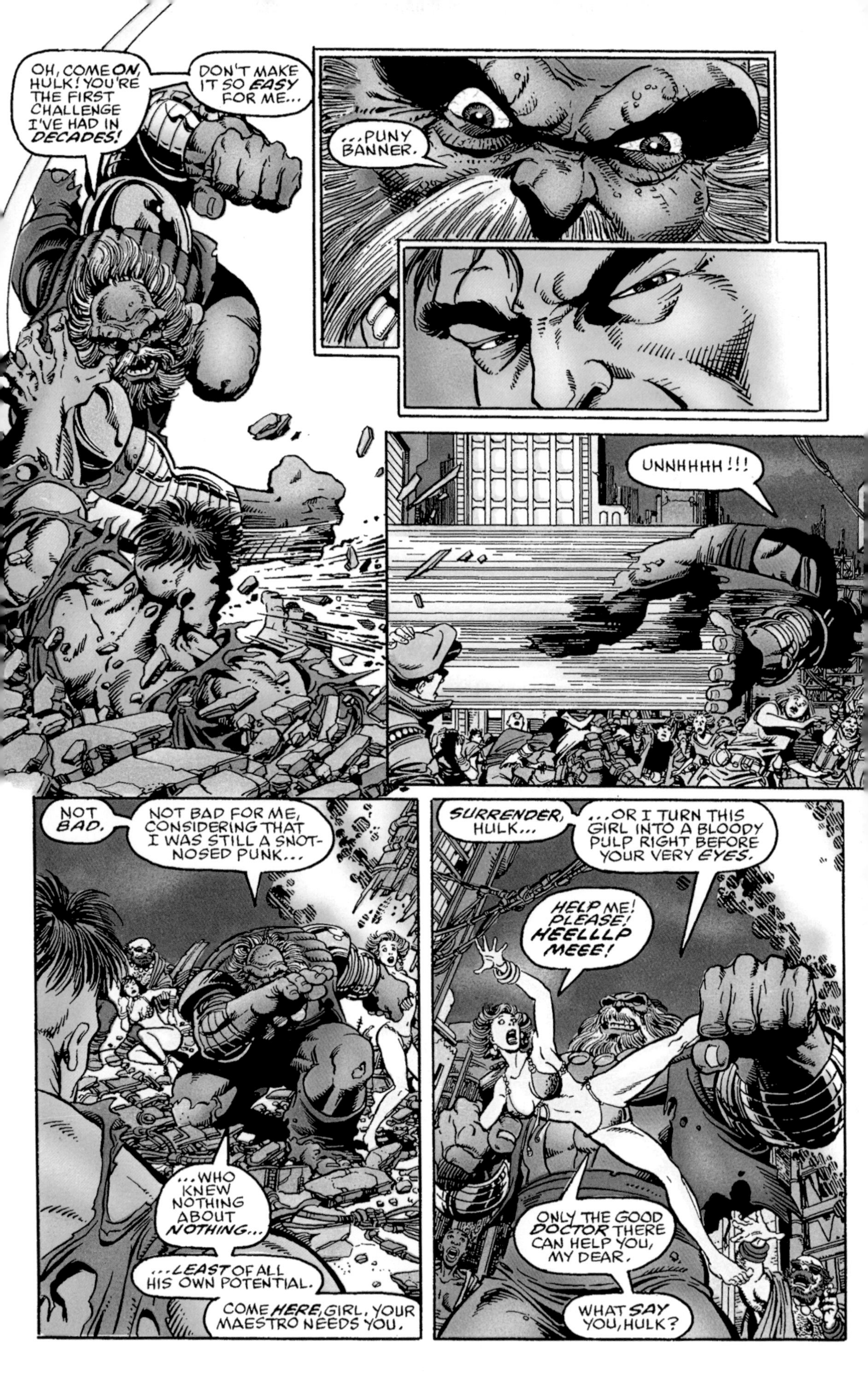
OH, COME ON, HULK! YOU'RE THE FIRST CHALLENGE I'VE HAD IN DECADES!
DON'T MAKE IT SO EASY FOR ME...
...PUNY BANNER.
UNNHHHH!!!
NOT BAD.
NOT BAD FOR ME, CONSIDERING THAT I WAS STILL A SNOT-NOSED PUNK...
...WHO KNEW NOTHING ABOUT NOTHING...
...LEAST OF ALL HIS OWN POTENTIAL.
COME HERE, GIRL. YOUR MAESTRO NEEDS YOU.
SURRENDER, HULK...
...OR I TURN THIS GIRL INTO A BLOODY PULP RIGHT BEFORE YOUR VERY EYES.
HELP ME! PLEASE! HEELLLP MEEE!
ONLY THE GOOD DOCTOR THERE CAN HELP YOU, MY DEAR.
WHAT SAY YOU, HULK?

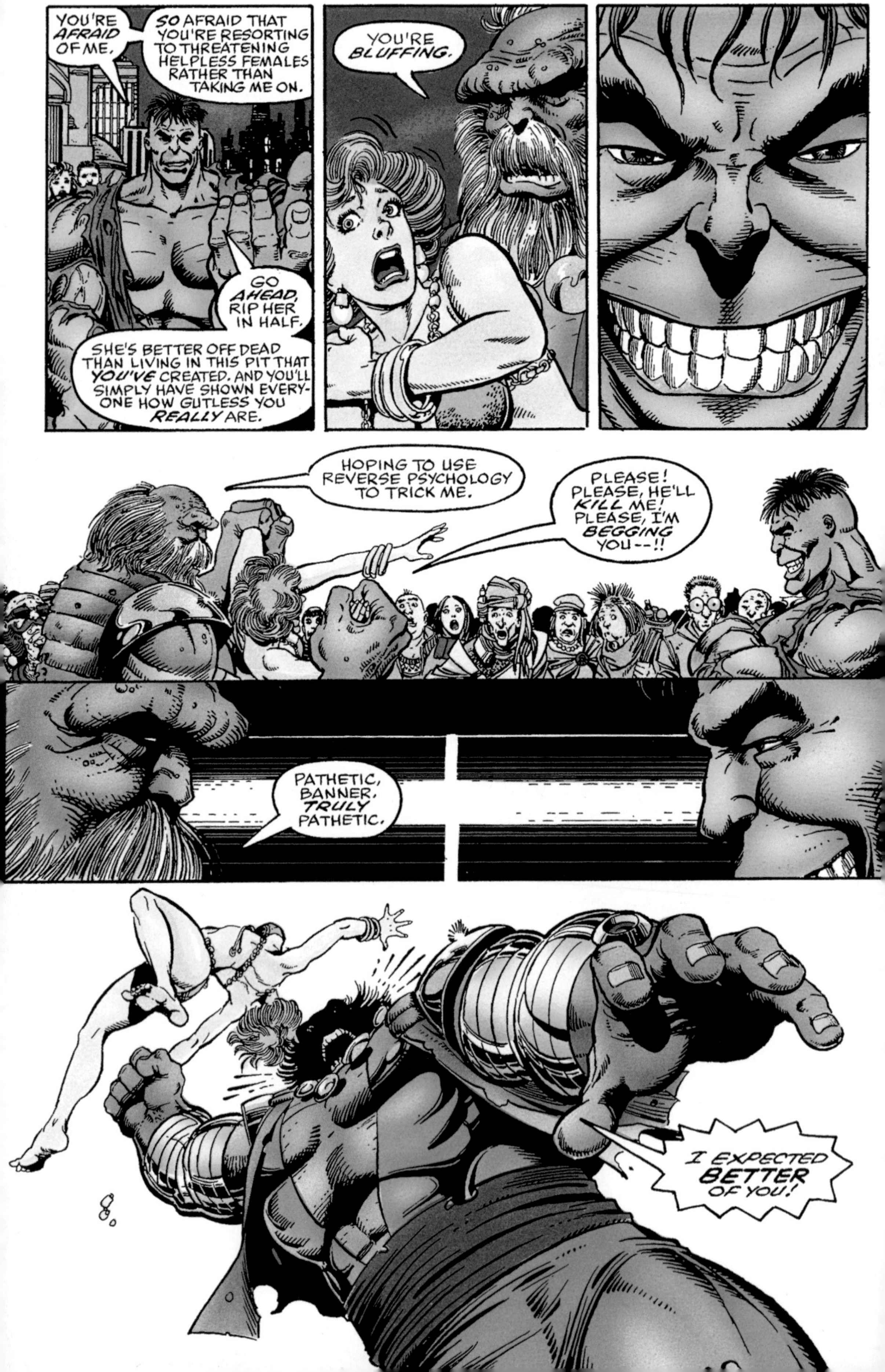
YOU'RE AFRAID OF ME.
SO AFRAID THAT YOU'RE RESORTING TO THREATENING HELPLESS FEMALES RATHER THAN TAKING ME ON.
GO AHEAD, RIP HER IN HALF.
SHE'S BETTER OFF DEAD THAN LIVING IN THIS PIT THAT YOU'VE CREATED. AND YOU'LL SIMPLY HAVE SHOWN EVERY-ONE HOW GUTLESS YOU REALLY ARE.
YOU'RE BLUFFING.
HOPING TO USE REVERSE PSYCHOLOGY TO TRICK ME.
PLEASE! PLEASE, HE'LL KILL ME! PLEASE, I'M BEGGING YOU--!!
PATHETIC, BANNER, TRULY PATHETIC.
I EXPECTED BETTER OF YOU!

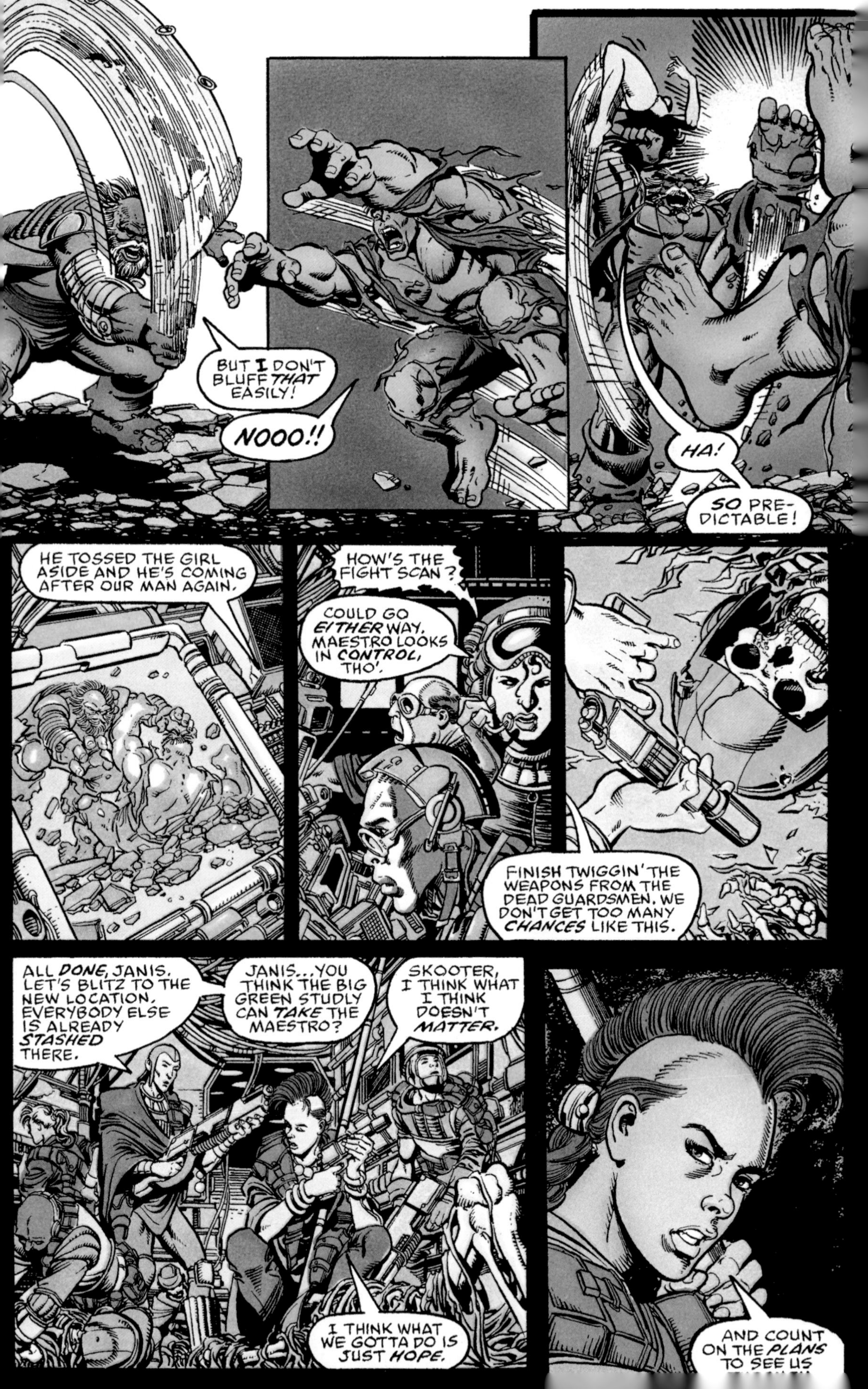
BUT I DON'T BLUFF THAT EASILY!
NOOO!!
HA!
SO PRE-DICTABLE!
HE TOSSED THE GIRL ASIDE AND HE'S COMING AFTER OUR MAN AGAIN.
HOW'S THE FIGHT SCAN?
COULD GO EITHER WAY. MAESTRO LOOKS IN CONTROL, THO'.
FINISH TWIGGIN' THE WEAPONS FROM THE DEAD GUARDSMEN. WE DON'T GET TOO MANY CHANCES LIKE THIS.
ALL DONE, JANIS. LET'S BLITZ TO THE NEW LOCATION. EVERYBODY ELSE IS ALREADY STASHED THERE.
JANIS... YOU THINK THE BIG GREEN STUDLY CAN TAKE THE MAESTRO?
SKOOTER, I THINK WHAT I THINK DOESN'T MATTER.
I THINK WHAT WE GOTTA DO IS JUST HOPE.
AND COUNT ON THE PLANS TO SEE US

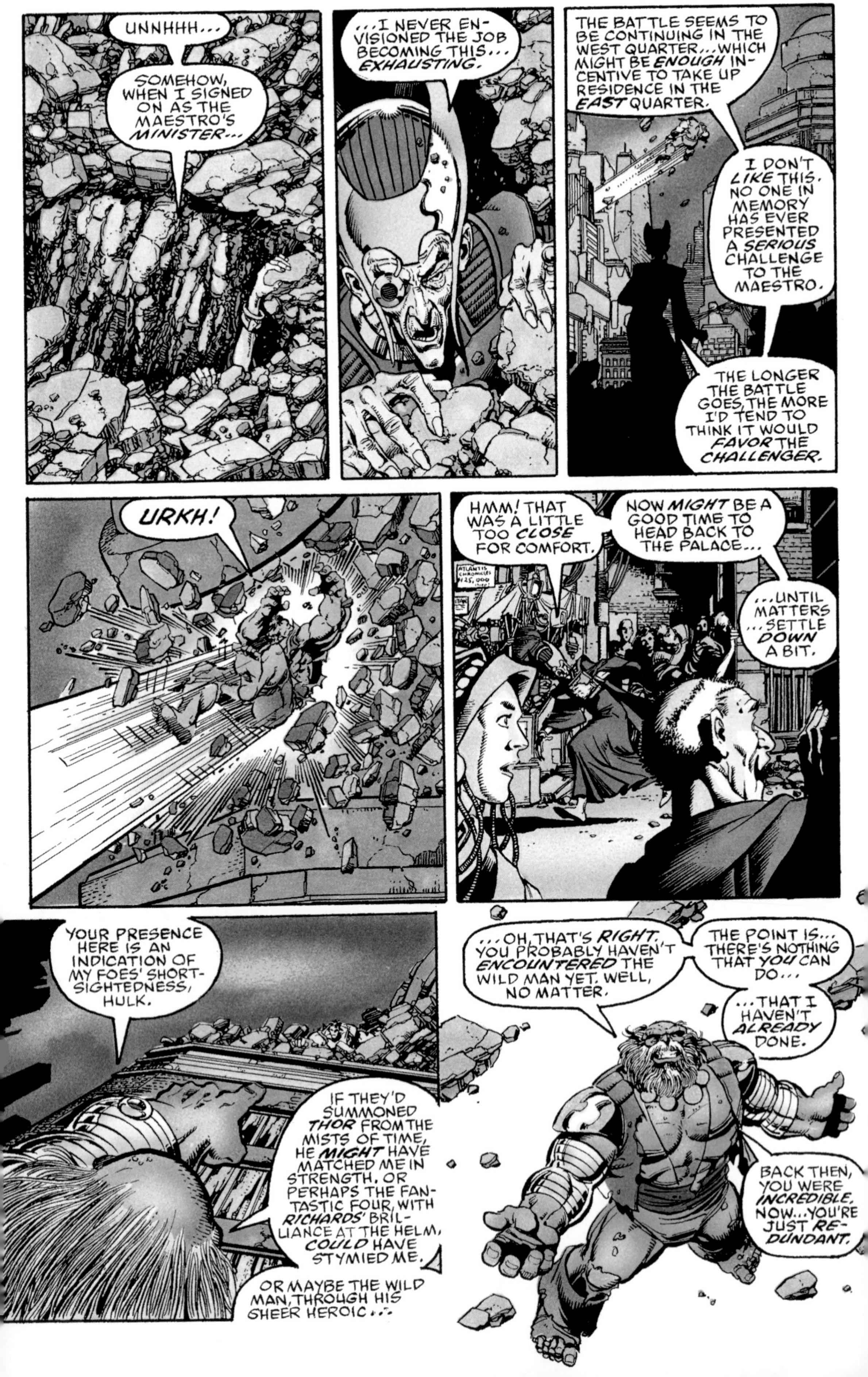
UNNHHH...
SOMEHOW, WHEN I SIGNED ON AS THE MAESTRO'S MINISTER...
...I NEVER ENVISIONED THE JOB BECOMING THIS... EXHAUSTING.
THE BATTLE SEEMS TO BE CONTINUING IN THE WEST QUARTER... WHICH MIGHT BE ENOUGH INCENTIVE TO TAKE UP RESIDENCE IN THE EAST QUARTER.
I DON'T LIKE THIS. NO ONE IN MEMORY HAS EVER PRESENTED A SERIOUS CHALLENGE TO THE MAESTRO.
THE LONGER THE BATTLE GOES, THE MORE I'D TEND TO THINK IT WOULD FAVOR THE CHALLENGER.
URKH!
HMM! THAT WAS A LITTLE TOO CLOSE FOR COMFORT.
NOW MIGHT BE A GOOD TIME TO HEAD BACK TO THE PALACE...
...UNTIL MATTERS ...SETTLE DOWN A BIT.
ATLANTIS CHRONICLES
YOUR PRESENCE HERE IS AN INDICATION OF MY FOES' SHORT-SIGHTEDNESS, HULK.
IF THEY'D SUMMONED THOR FROM THE MISTS OF TIME, HE MIGHT HAVE MATCHED ME IN STRENGTH. OR PERHAPS THE FANTASTIC FOUR, WITH RICHARDS' BRILLIANCE AT THE HELM, COULD HAVE STYMIED ME.
OR MAYBE THE WILD MAN, THROUGH HIS SHEER HEROIC...
...OH, THAT'S RIGHT. YOU PROBABLY HAVEN'T ENCOUNTERED THE WILD MAN YET. WELL, NO MATTER.
THE POINT IS... THERE'S NOTHING THAT YOU CAN DO...
...THAT I HAVEN'T ALREADY DONE.
BACK THEN, YOU WERE INCREDIBLE. NOW... YOU'RE JUST REDUNDANT.

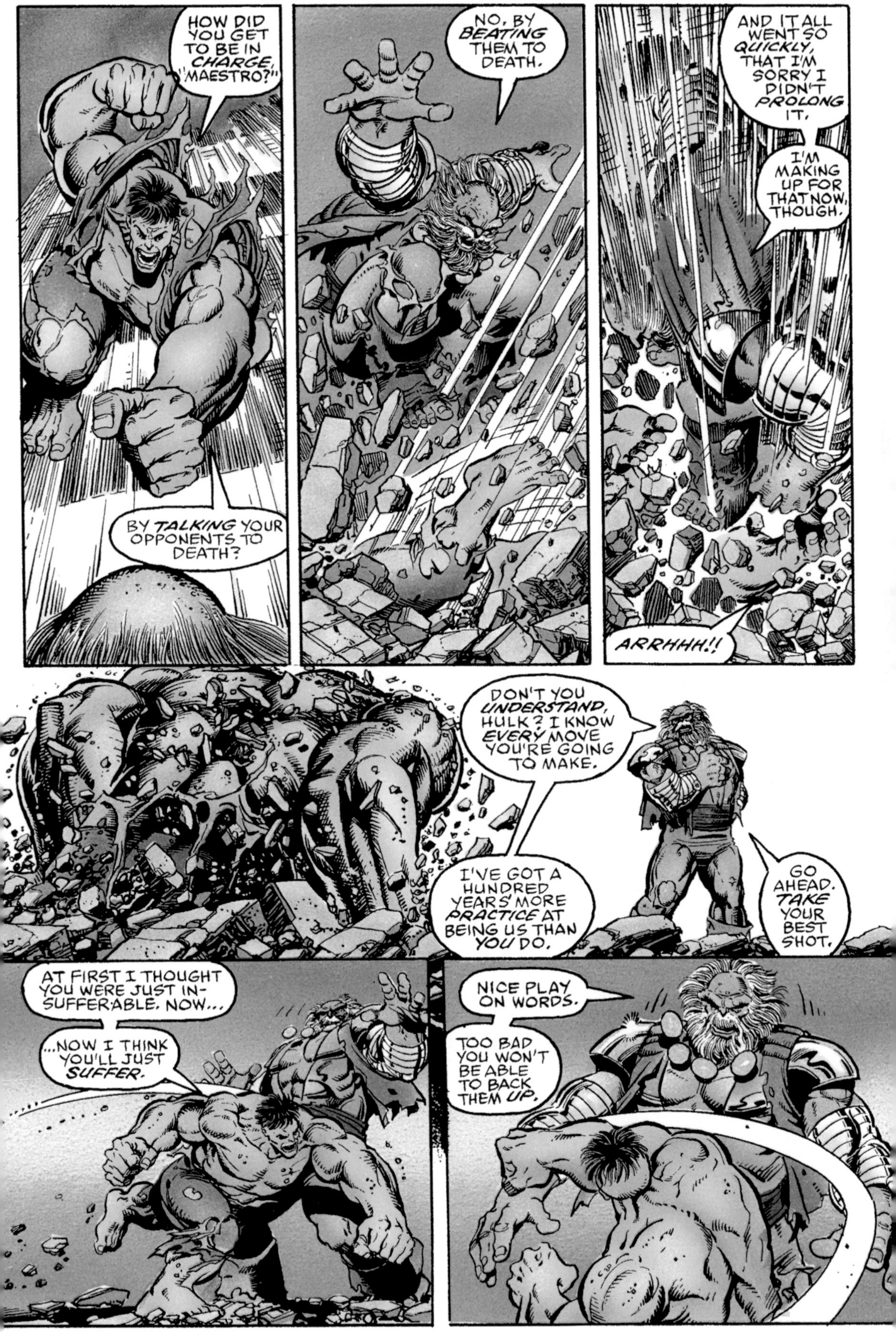
HOW DID YOU GET TO BE IN CHARGE, "MAESTRO?"
BY TALKING YOUR OPPONENTS TO DEATH?
NO, BY BEATING THEM TO DEATH.
AND IT ALL WENT SO QUICKLY, THAT I'M SORRY I DIDN'T PROLONG IT.
I'M MAKING UP FOR THAT NOW, THOUGH.
ARRHHH!!
DON'T YOU UNDERSTAND, HULK? I KNOW EVERY MOVE YOU'RE GOING TO MAKE.
I'VE GOT A HUNDRED YEARS' MORE PRACTICE AT BEING US THAN YOU DO.
GO AHEAD. TAKE YOUR BEST SHOT.
AT FIRST I THOUGHT YOU WERE JUST IN-SUFFERABLE. NOW...
...NOW I THINK YOU'LL JUST SUFFER.
NICE PLAY ON WORDS.
TOO BAD YOU WON'T BE ABLE TO BACK THEM UP.

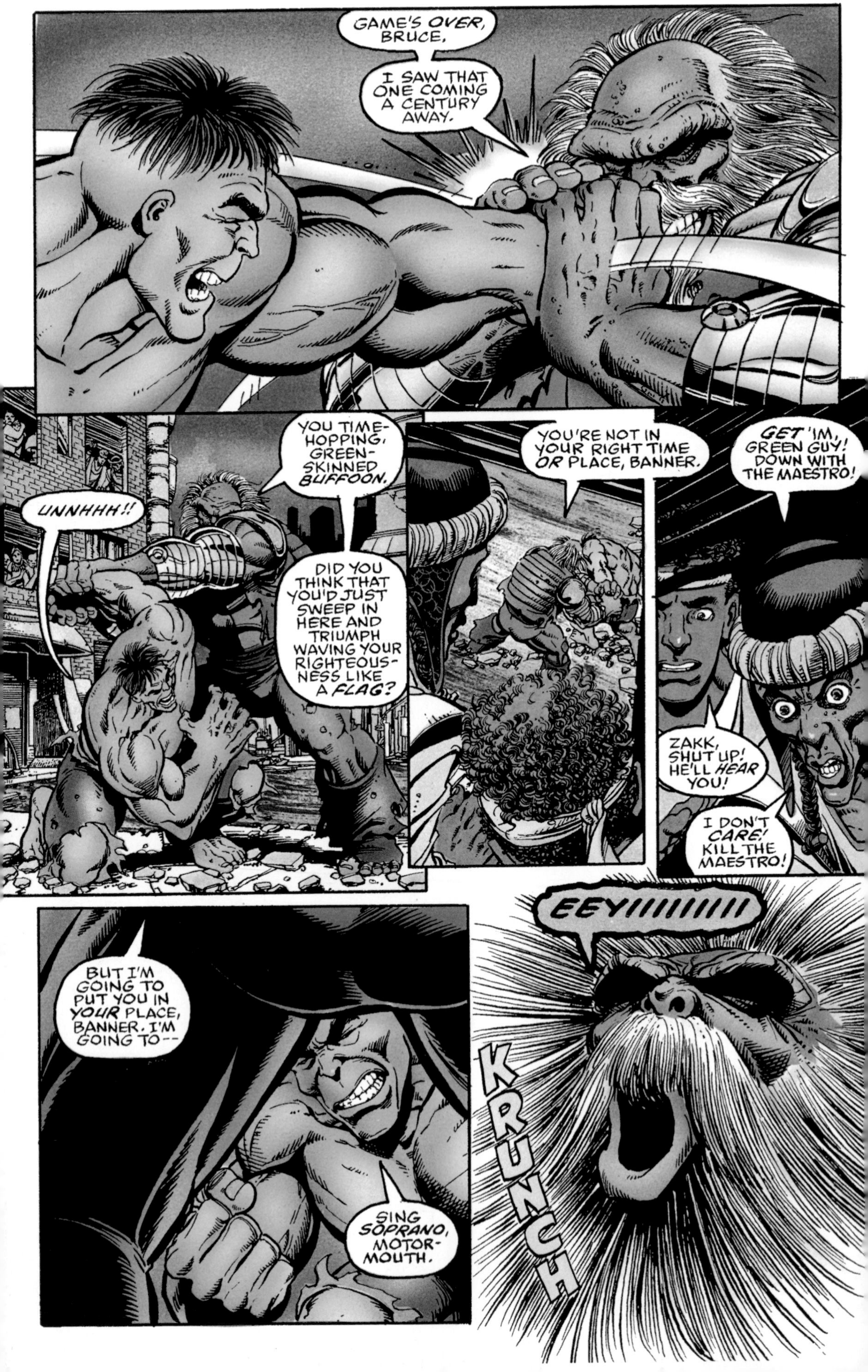
GAME'S OVER, BRUCE.
I SAW THAT ONE COMING A CENTURY AWAY.
YOU TIME-HOPPING, GREEN-SKINNED BUFFOON.
UNNHHH!!
DID YOU THINK THAT YOU'D JUST SWEEP IN HERE AND TRIUMPH WAVING YOUR RIGHTEOUS-NESS LIKE A FLAG?
YOU'RE NOT IN YOUR RIGHT TIME OR PLACE, BANNER.
GET 'IM, GREEN GUY! DOWN WITH THE MAESTRO!
ZAKK, SHUT UP! HE'LL HEAR YOU!
I DON'T CARE! KILL THE MAESTRO!
BUT I'M GOING TO PUT YOU IN YOUR PLACE, BANNER. I'M GOING TO--
SING SOPRANO, MOTOR-MOUTH.
EEYIIIIIIIIIII
KRUNCH

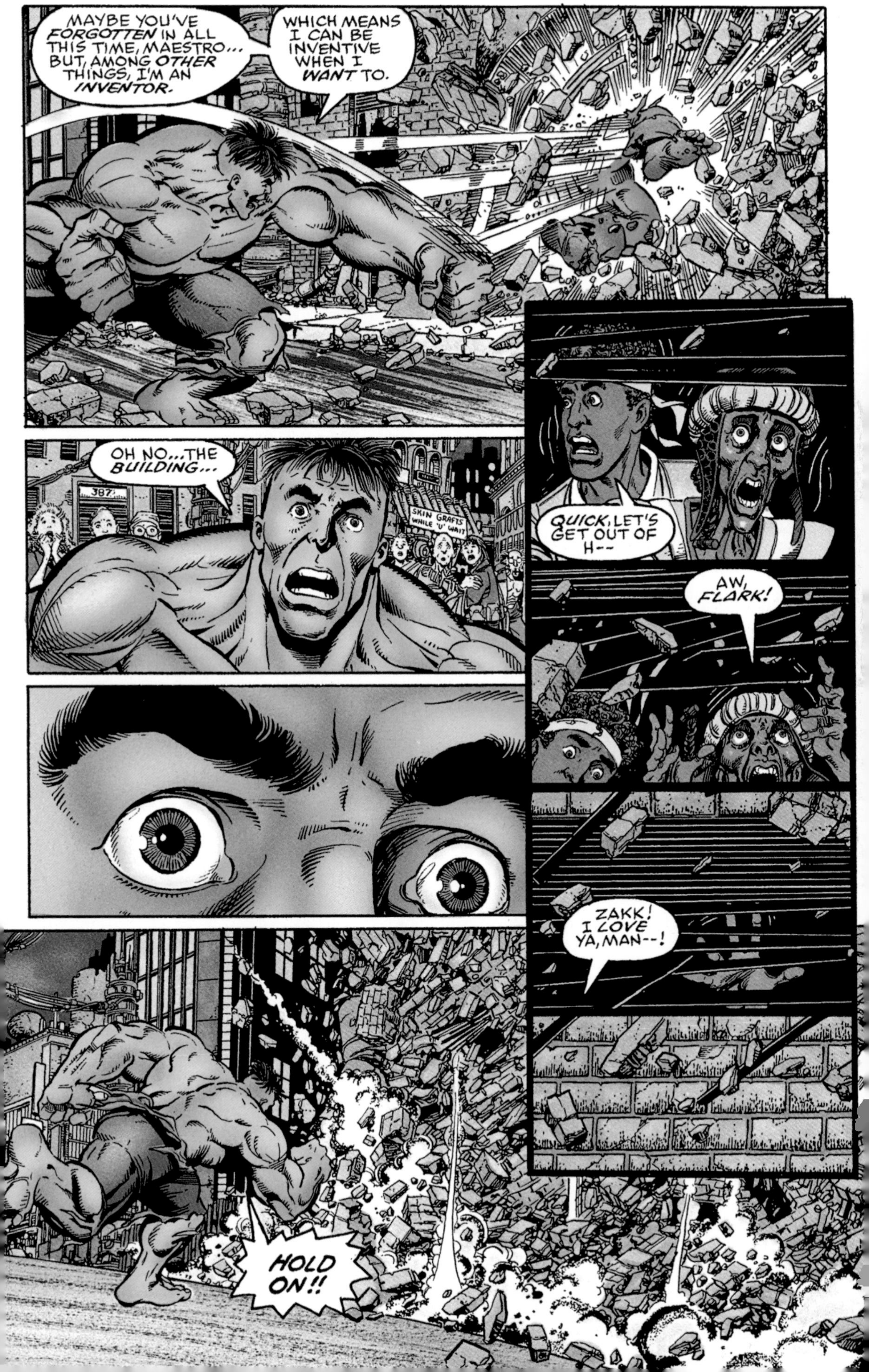
MAYBE YOU'VE FORGOTTEN IN ALL THIS TIME, MAESTRO... BUT, AMONG OTHER THINGS, I'M AN INVENTOR.
WHICH MEANS I CAN BE INVENTIVE WHEN I WANT TO.
OH NO...THE BUILDING...
387
SKIN GRAFTS WHILE 'U' WAIT
QUICK, LET'S GET OUT OF H--
AW, FLARK!
ZAKK! I LOVE YA, MAN--!
HOLD ON!!

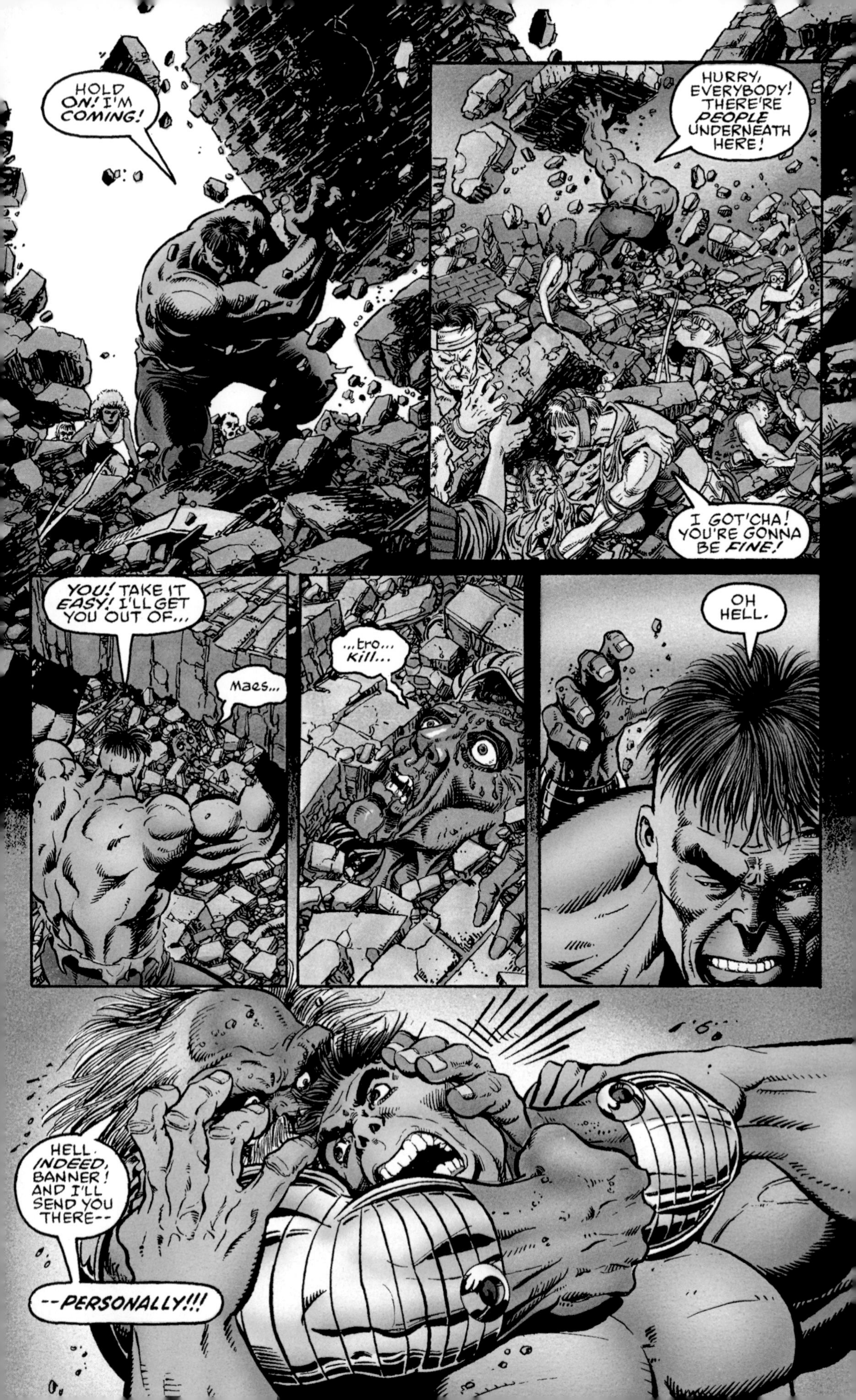
HOLD ON! I'M COMING!
HURRY, EVERYBODY! THERE'RE PEOPLE UNDERNEATH HERE!
I GOT'CHA! YOU'RE GONNA BE FINE!
YOU! TAKE IT EASY! I'LL GET YOU OUT OF...
Maes...
...tro... Kill...
OH HELL.
HELL INDEED, BANNER! AND I'LL SEND YOU THERE--
--PERSONALLY!!!

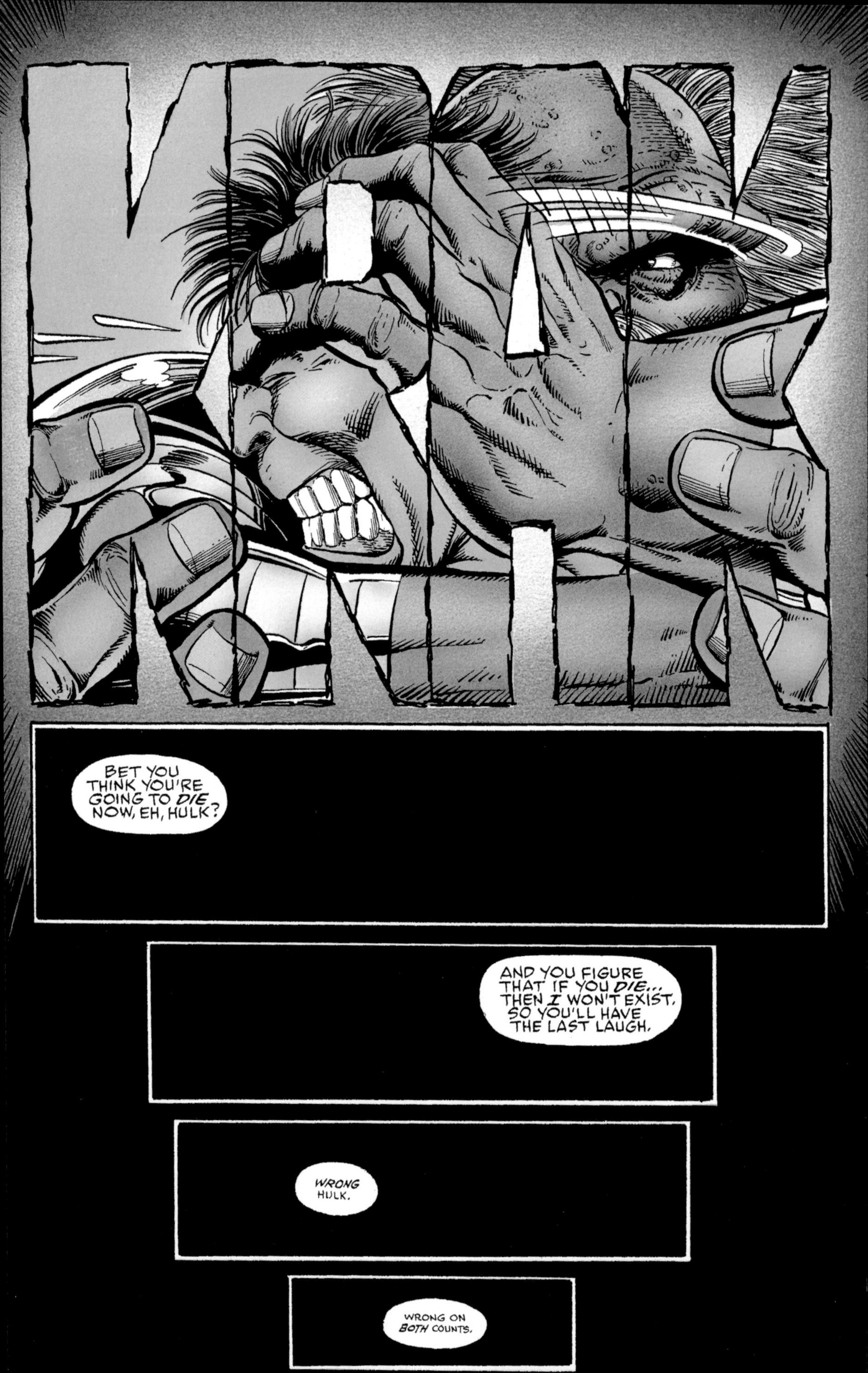

BET YOU THINK YOU'RE GOING TO *DIE* NOW, EH, HULK?
AND YOU FIGURE THAT IF YOU *DIE*... THEN *I* WON'T EXIST. SO YOU'LL HAVE THE LAST LAUGH.
WRONG HULK.
WRONG ON *BOTH* COUNTS.

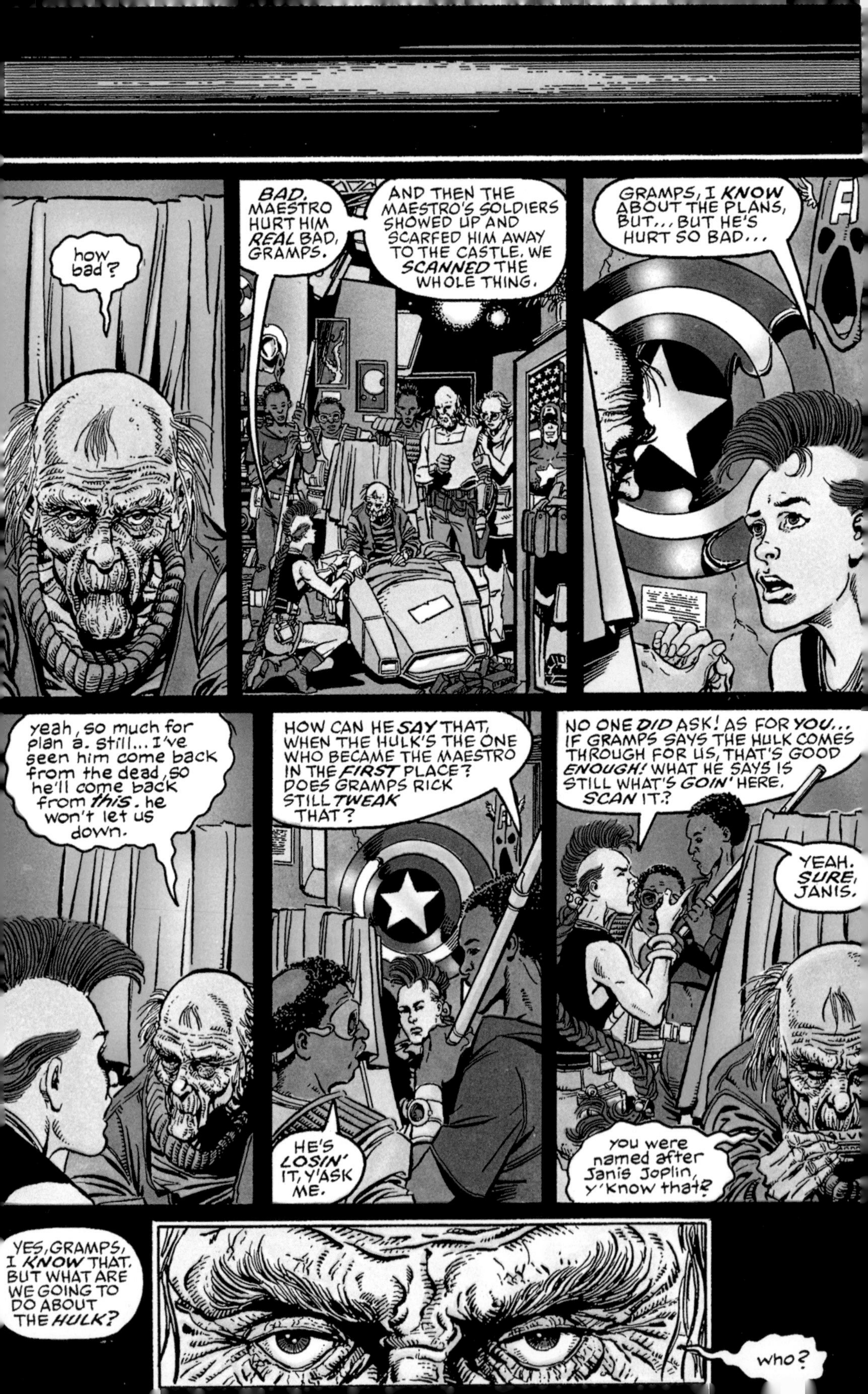
how bad?
BAD. MAESTRO HURT HIM REAL BAD, GRAMPS.
AND THEN THE MAESTRO'S SOLDIERS SHOWED UP AND SCARFED HIM AWAY TO THE CASTLE. WE SCANNED THE WHOLE THING.
GRAMPS, I KNOW ABOUT THE PLANS, BUT... BUT HE'S HURT SO BAD...
yeah, so much for plan a. still... I've seen him come back from the dead, so he'll come back from this. he won't let us down.
HOW CAN HE SAY THAT, WHEN THE HULK'S THE ONE WHO BECAME THE MAESTRO IN THE FIRST PLACE? DOES GRAMPS RICK STILL TWEAK THAT?
HE'S LOSIN' IT, Y'ASK ME.
NO ONE DID ASK! AS FOR YOU... IF GRAMPS SAYS THE HULK COMES THROUGH FOR US, THAT'S GOOD ENOUGH! WHAT HE SAYS IS STILL WHAT'S GOIN' HERE. SCAN IT?
YEAH. SURE, JANIS.
you were named after Janis Joplin, y'know that?
YES, GRAMPS, I KNOW THAT. BUT WHAT ARE WE GOING TO DO ABOUT THE HULK?
who?

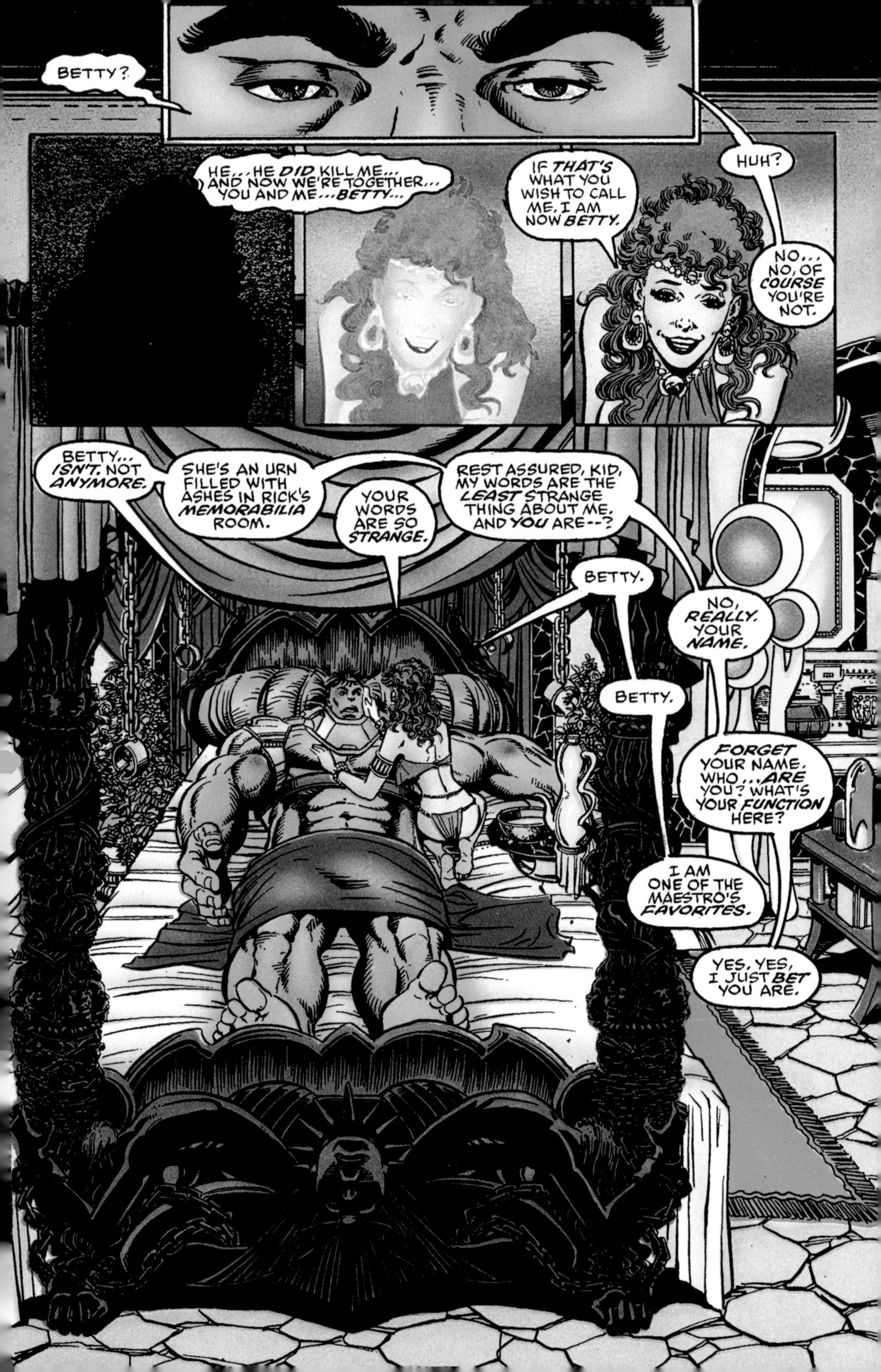
BETTY?
HE... HE DID KILL ME... AND NOW WE'RE TOGETHER... YOU AND ME... BETTY...
IF THAT'S WHAT YOU WISH TO CALL ME, I AM NOW BETTY.
HUH?
NO... NO, OF COURSE YOU'RE NOT.
BETTY... ISN'T. NOT ANYMORE.
SHE'S AN URN FILLED WITH ASHES IN RICK'S MEMORABILIA ROOM.
YOUR WORDS ARE SO STRANGE.
REST ASSURED, KID, MY WORDS ARE THE LEAST STRANGE THING ABOUT ME. AND YOU ARE--?
BETTY.
NO, REALLY. YOUR NAME.
BETTY.
FORGET YOUR NAME. WHO... ARE YOU? WHAT'S YOUR FUNCTION HERE?
I AM ONE OF THE MAESTRO'S FAVORITES.
YES, YES, I JUST BET YOU ARE.

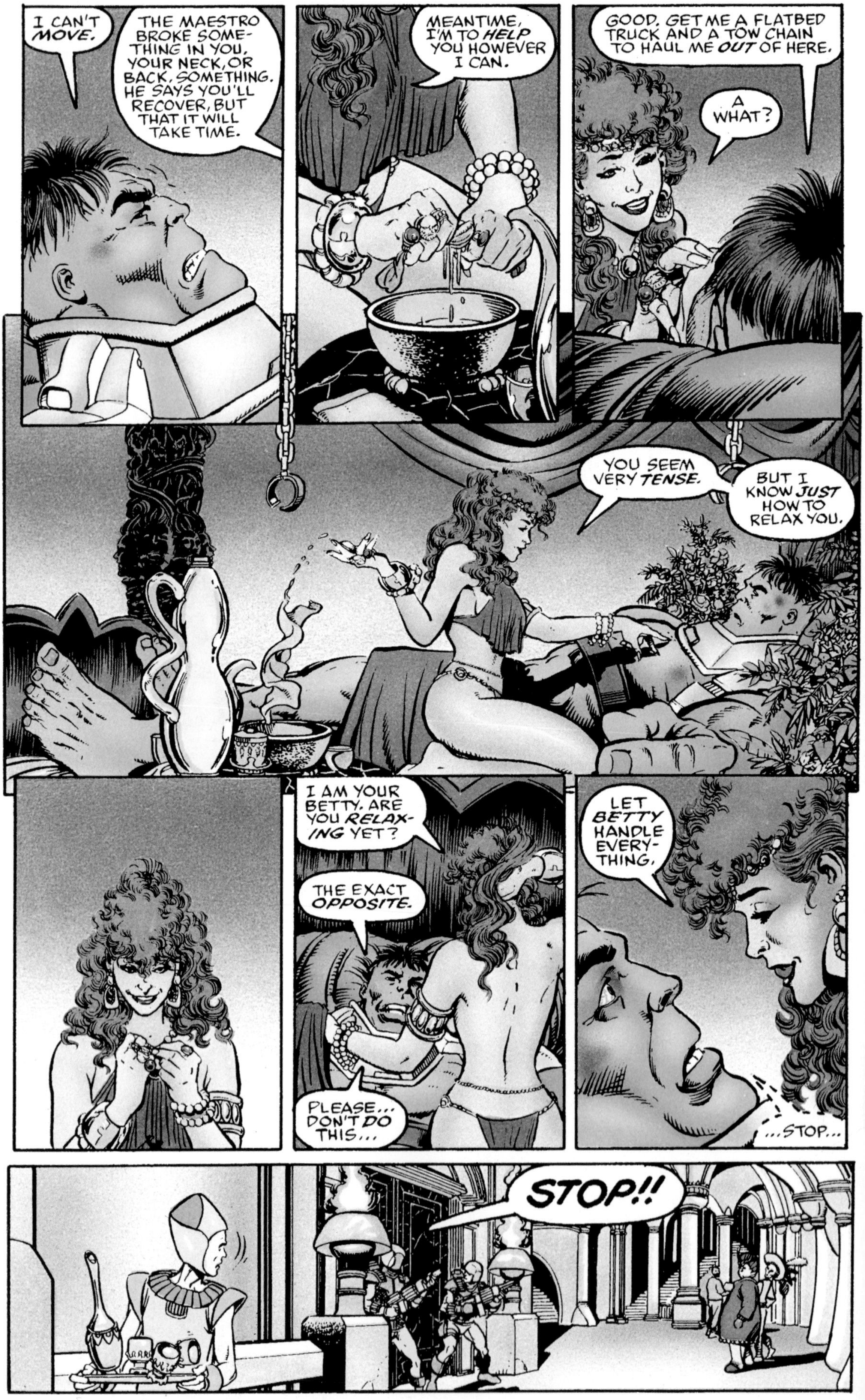
I CAN'T MOVE.
THE MAESTRO BROKE SOMETHING IN YOU, YOUR NECK, OR BACK, SOMETHING. HE SAYS YOU'LL RECOVER, BUT THAT IT WILL TAKE TIME.
MEANTIME, I'M TO HELP YOU HOWEVER I CAN.
GOOD. GET ME A FLATBED TRUCK AND A TOW CHAIN TO HAUL ME OUT OF HERE.
A WHAT?
YOU SEEM VERY TENSE.
BUT I KNOW JUST HOW TO RELAX YOU.
I AM YOUR BETTY. ARE YOU RELAXING YET?
THE EXACT OPPOSITE.
PLEASE... DON'T DO THIS...
LET BETTY HANDLE EVERYTHING.
...STOP...
STOP!!

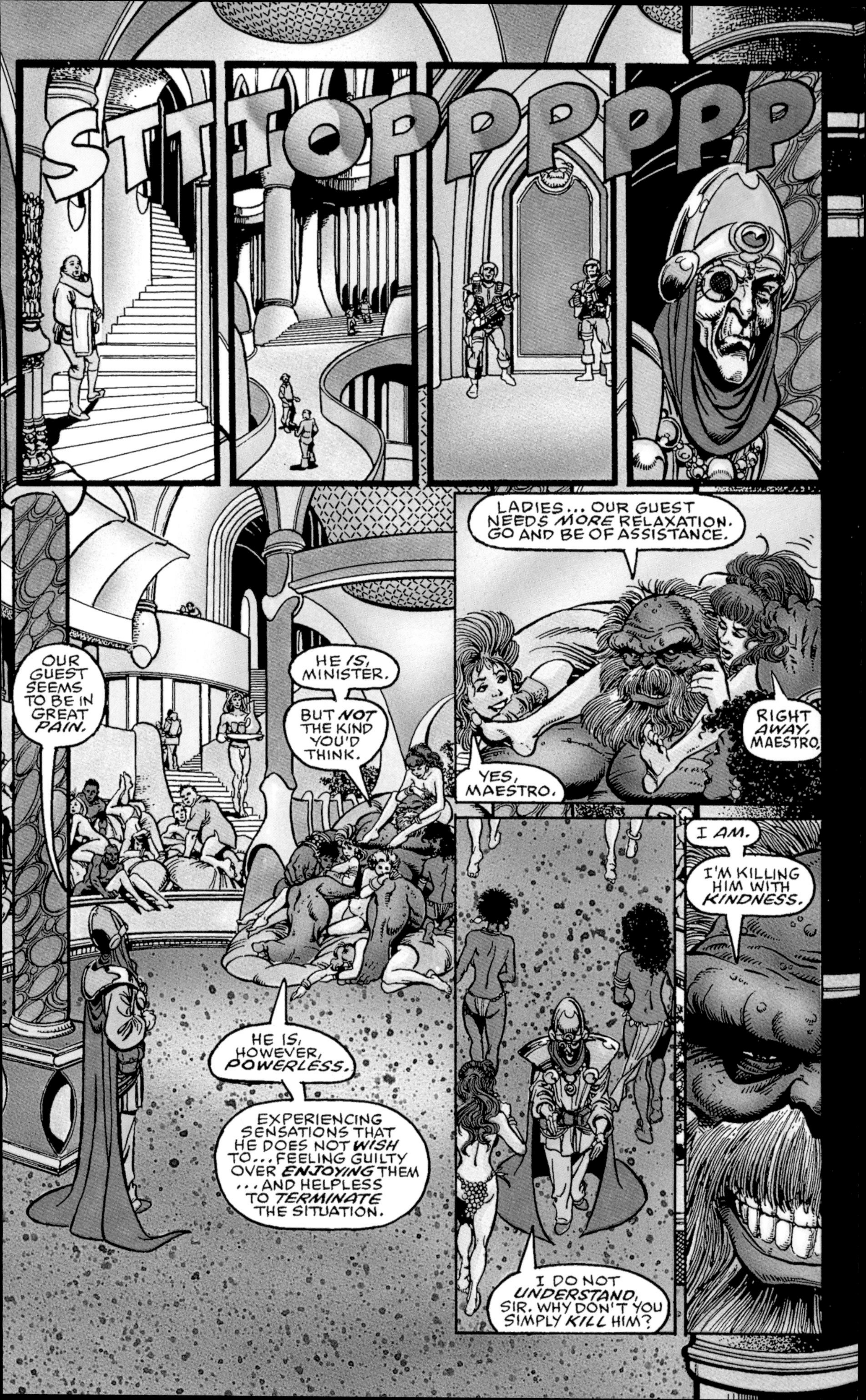
STTTOPPPPPP
LADIES... OUR GUEST NEEDS MORE RELAXATION. GO AND BE OF ASSISTANCE.
RIGHT AWAY, MAESTRO.
YES, MAESTRO.
OUR GUEST SEEMS TO BE IN GREAT PAIN.
HE IS, MINISTER.
BUT NOT THE KIND YOU'D THINK.
HE IS, HOWEVER, POWERLESS.
EXPERIENCING SENSATIONS THAT HE DOES NOT WISH TO... FEELING GUILTY OVER ENJOYING THEM ...AND HELPLESS TO TERMINATE THE SITUATION.
I DO NOT UNDERSTAND, SIR. WHY DON'T YOU SIMPLY KILL HIM?
I AM.
I'M KILLING HIM WITH KINDNESS.

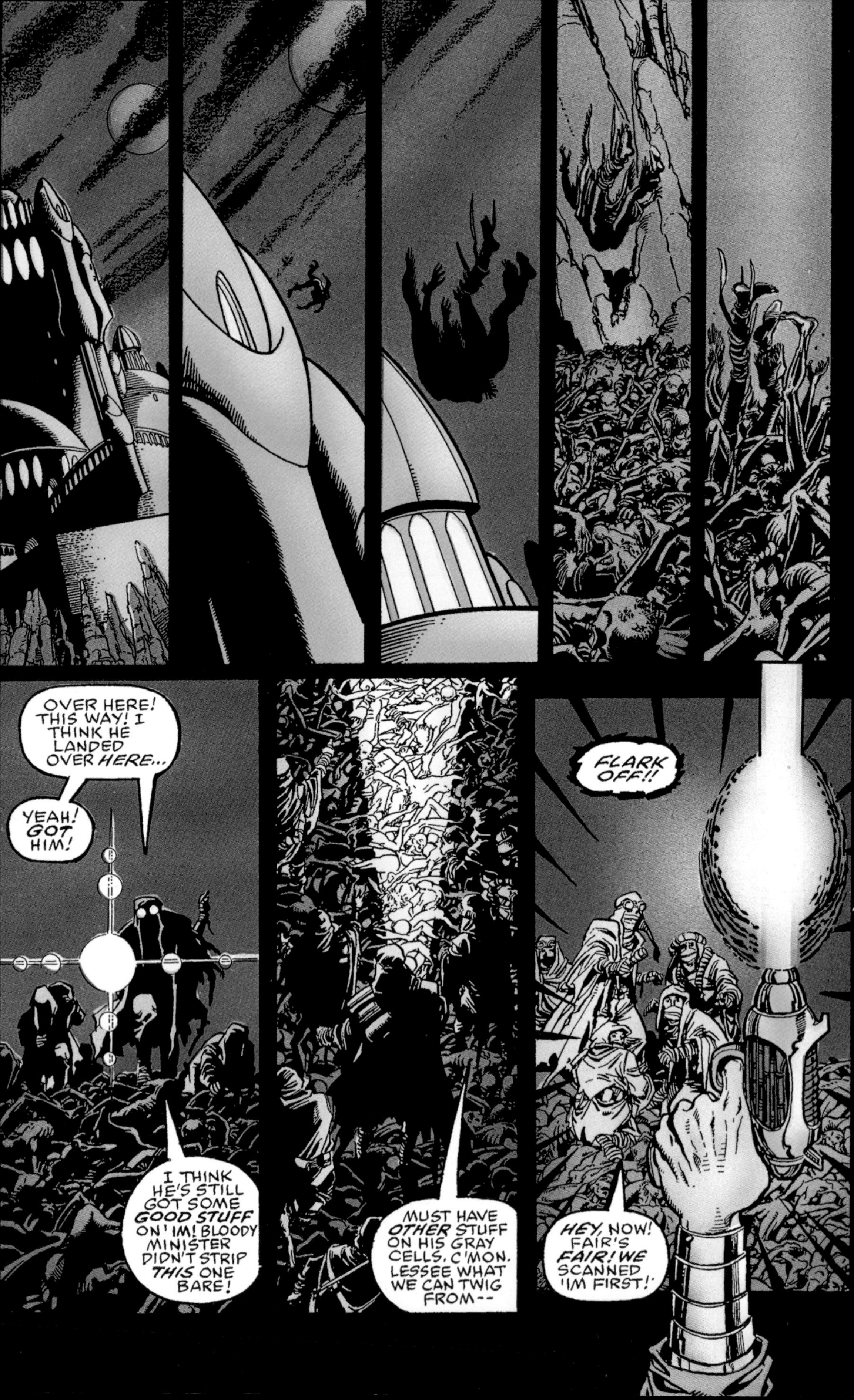
OVER HERE! THIS WAY! I THINK HE LANDED OVER HERE...
YEAH! GOT HIM!
I THINK HE'S STILL GOT SOME GOOD STUFF ON 'IM! BLOODY MINISTER DIDN'T STRIP THIS ONE BARE!
MUST HAVE OTHER STUFF ON HIS GRAY CELLS. C'MON. LESSEE WHAT WE CAN TWIG FROM--
FLARK OFF!!
HEY, NOW! FAIR'S FAIR! WE SCANNED 'IM FIRST!

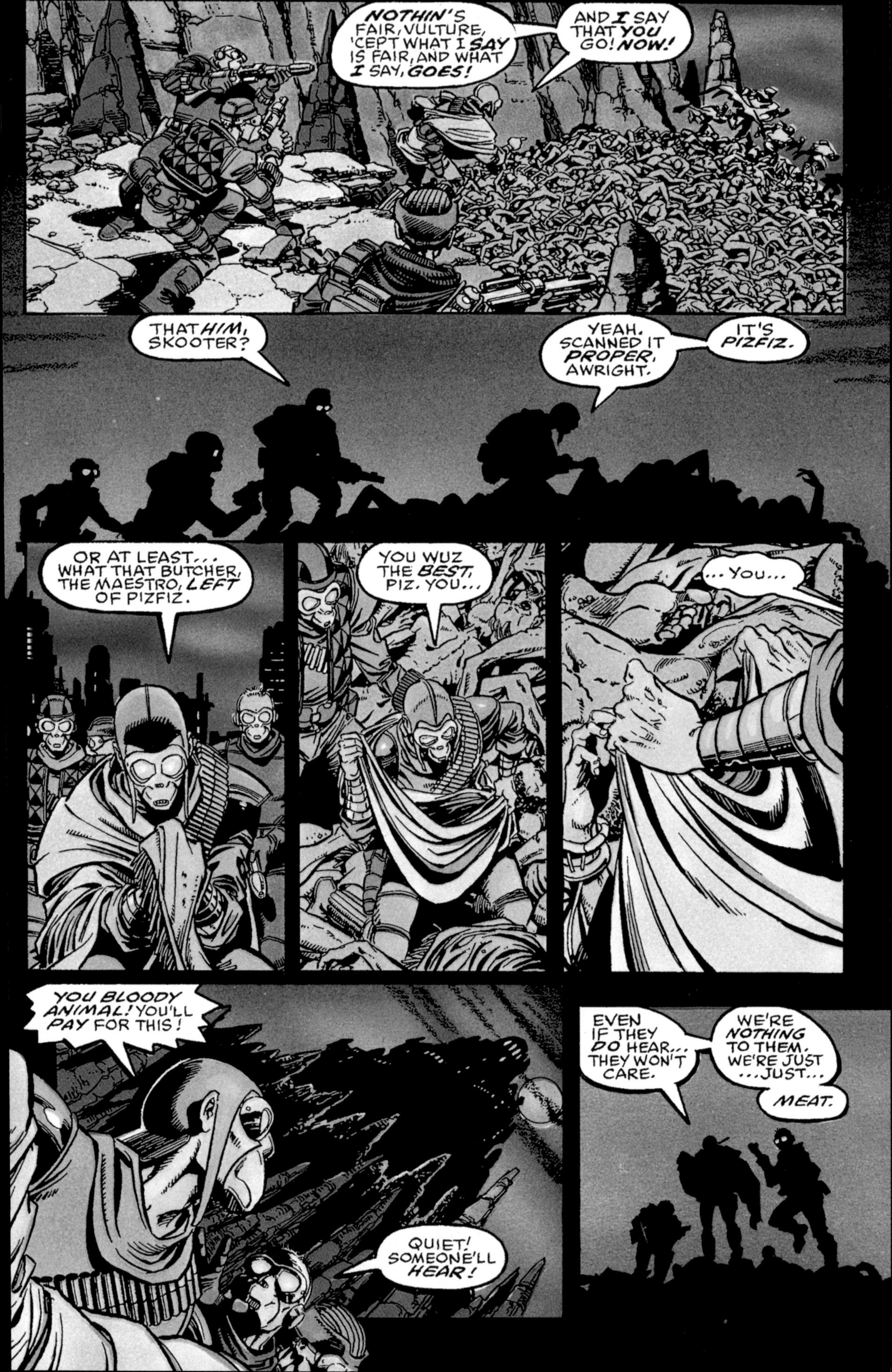
NOTHIN'S FAIR, VULTURE, 'CEPT WHAT I SAY IS FAIR, AND WHAT I SAY, GOES!
AND I SAY THAT YOU GO! NOW!
THAT HIM, SKOOTER?
YEAH. SCANNED IT PROPER, AWRIGHT.
IT'S PIZFIZ.
OR AT LEAST... WHAT THAT BUTCHER, THE MAESTRO, LEFT OF PIZFIZ.
YOU WUZ THE BEST, PIZ. YOU...
...YOU...
YOU BLOODY ANIMAL! YOU'LL PAY FOR THIS!
QUIET! SOMEONE'LL HEAR!
EVEN IF THEY DO HEAR... THEY WON'T CARE.
WE'RE NOTHING TO THEM. WE'RE JUST ...JUST...
MEAT.

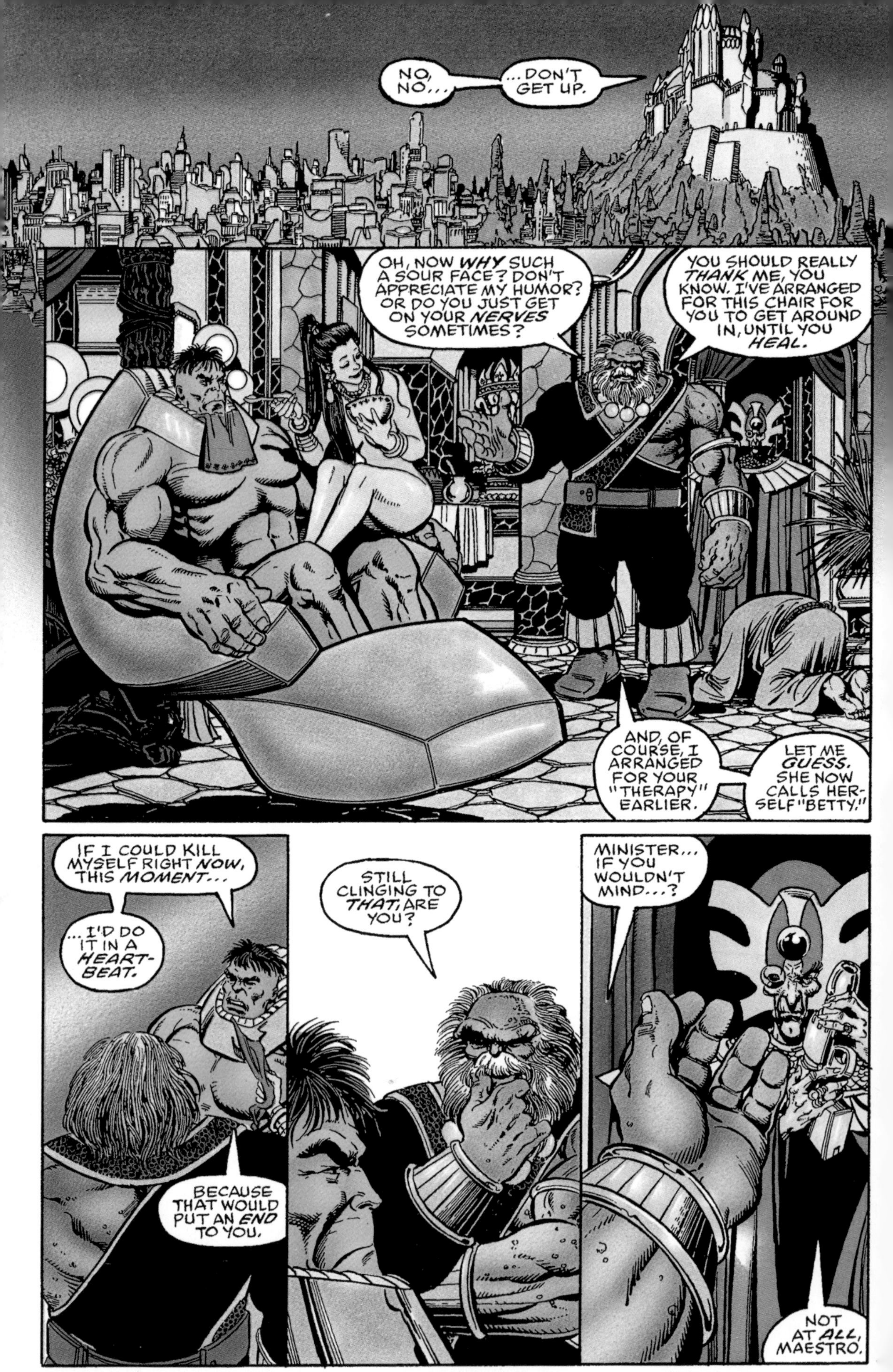
NO, NO...
...DON'T GET UP.
OH, NOW WHY SUCH A SOUR FACE? DON'T APPRECIATE MY HUMOR? OR DO YOU JUST GET ON YOUR NERVES SOMETIMES?
YOU SHOULD REALLY THANK ME, YOU KNOW. I'VE ARRANGED FOR THIS CHAIR FOR YOU TO GET AROUND IN, UNTIL YOU HEAL.
AND, OF COURSE, I ARRANGED FOR YOUR "THERAPY" EARLIER.
LET ME GUESS. SHE NOW CALLS HERSELF "BETTY."
IF I COULD KILL MYSELF RIGHT NOW, THIS MOMENT...
...I'D DO IT IN A HEARTBEAT.
BECAUSE THAT WOULD PUT AN END TO YOU.
STILL CLINGING TO THAT, ARE YOU?
MINISTER... IF YOU WOULDN'T MIND...?
NOT AT ALL, MAESTRO.

HERE, ALL YOU HAVE TO DO IS PULL THE TRIGGER. YOU HAVE ENOUGH MUSCULAR CONTROL BACK FOR *THAT*, I THINK.

TRUST ME... BLOWING YOUR BRAINS OUT IS SOMETHING THAT EVEN *OUR* FORMIDABLE HEALING ABILITIES WON'T OVERCOME.

NOW *YOU'RE* THE ONE WHO'S BLUFF-ING.

YOU WOULDN'T PUT *YOURSELF* AT RISK.

BUT I'M *NOT* AT RISK. *MY* EXISTENCE IS *ASSURED.* YOU SEE... I HAVE NO PRIOR *RE-COLLECTION* OF ANY OF THESE EVENTS.

WHEN YOUR OUTLAW PALS WENT BACK IN TIME AND BROUGHT YOU *FORWARD*, IT CREATED AN *ALTER-NATE* TIMELINE. TIME *SPLIT OFF* FROM THAT MOMENT.

ONE TIME BRANCH IS NOW THE EVENTS THAT LED TO *ME.* ALONG *ANOTHER* BRANCH ARE THE EVENTS THAT WILL NOW HAPPEN TO *YOU*... YOUR OWN "REAL FUTURE," AS IT WERE. IN OTHER WORDS: THANKS TO YOUR FRIENDS, I'M NOW ONE *POSSIBLE* FUTURE FOR DR. BRUCE BANNER, *UNHAMPERED* BY YOU. WHAT HAPPENS TO *YOU*, HULK, IS YOUR *OWN* AFFAIR.

YOU *COULD* BE *LYING.* PERHAPS ALL OF THIS ALREADY *DID* HAPPEN TO YOU. PERHAPS ALL THE THINGS YOU'RE SAYING NOW... ARE THINGS THAT YOU REMEMBER HAVING *ALREADY* HEARD, WHEN *YOU* WERE IN *MY* POSITION. AND YOU'RE HOPING THAT WHAT WORKED *ONCE* WILL WORK *AGAIN.*

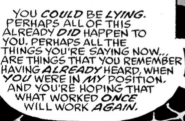

OR PERHAPS YOU SENT ME BACK TO MY OWN TIME, BUT WITH MY *MEMORY* ERASED. PERHAPS YOU'RE *NOT* AS SAFE AS YOU *THINK* YOU ARE.

I'M GETTING A HEADACHE TRYING TO FOLLOW THIS.

THAT *IS* A HAZARD WITH TIME TRAVEL THEORIZING, MINISTER.

I BELIEVE FIRMLY IN *MY* HYPOTHESIS, HULK, BUT IF YOU'RE WILLING TO RISK THROWING AWAY *YOUR* LIFE ON *YOURS*... THEN *I* WON'T STOP YOU.

GO *ON*, IF YOU'RE THAT CONFIDENT, BLOW YOUR BRAINS OUT, RIGHT HERE, RIGHT NOW.

DO IT.

GO ON.

DO IT.

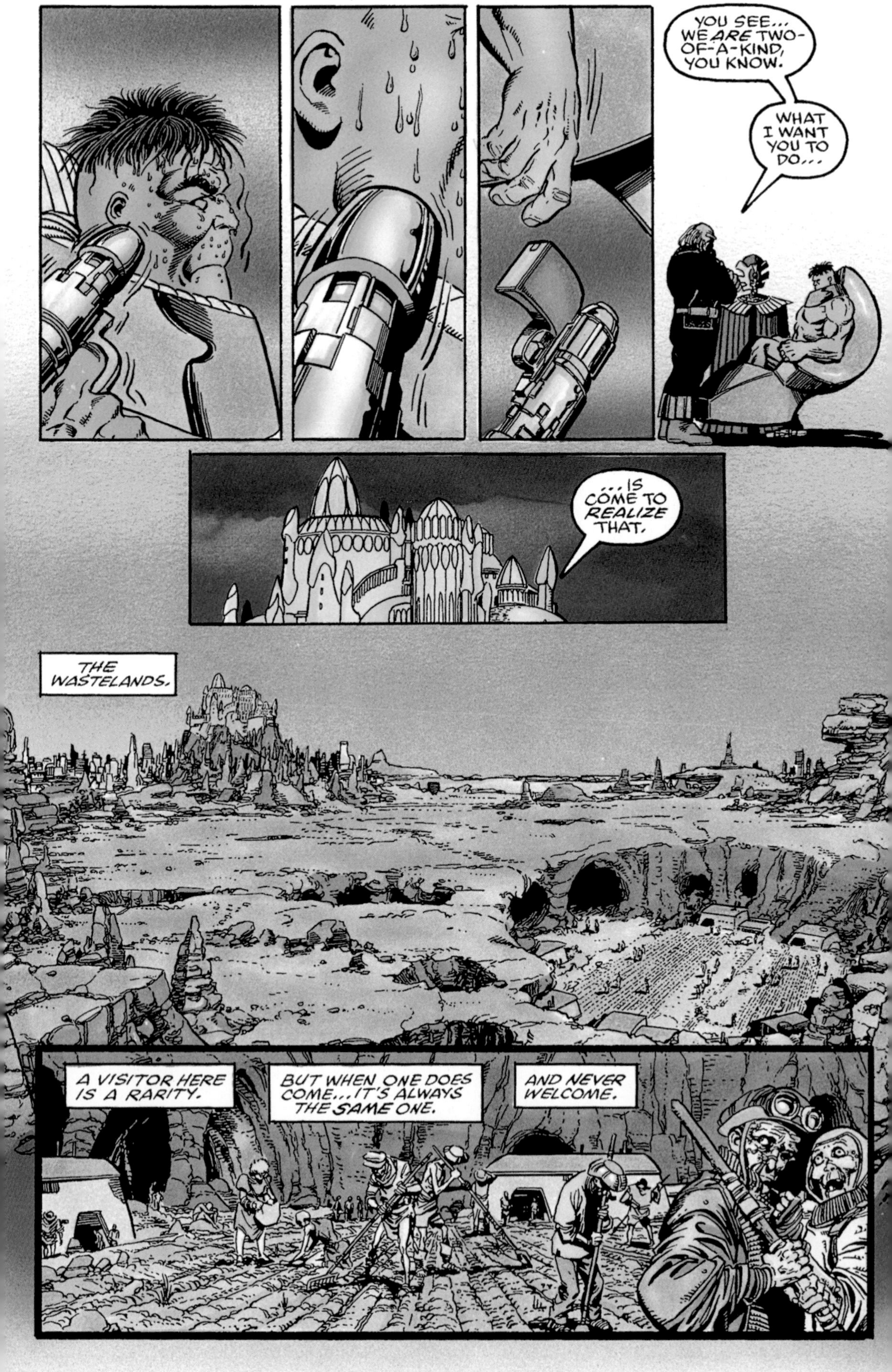
YOU SEE... WE ARE TWO-OF-A-KIND, YOU KNOW.
WHAT I WANT YOU TO DO...
...IS COME TO REALIZE THAT.
THE WASTELANDS.
A VISITOR HERE IS A RARITY.
BUT WHEN ONE DOES COME... IT'S ALWAYS THE SAME ONE.
AND NEVER WELCOME.

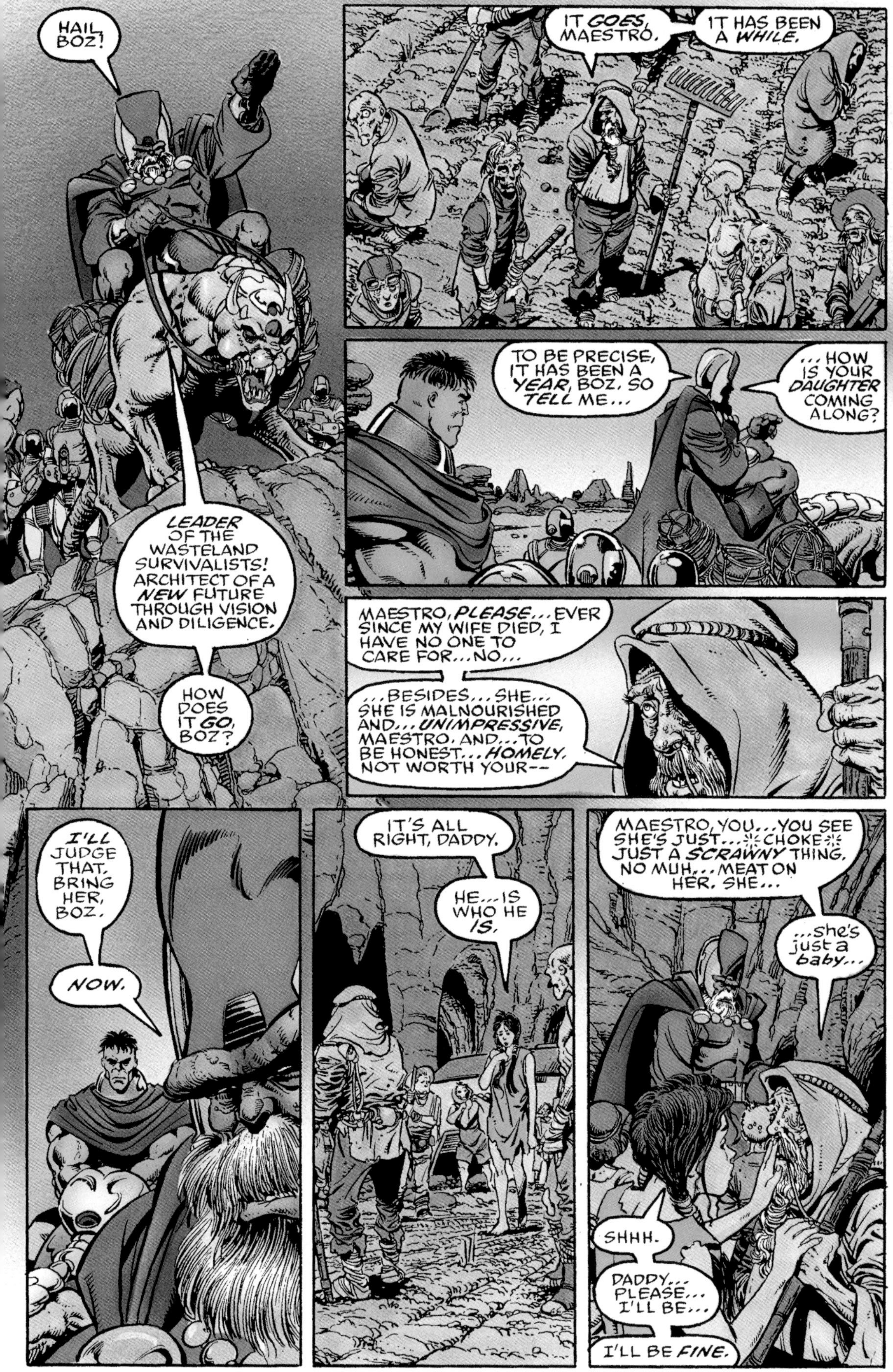
HAIL, BOZ!
LEADER OF THE WASTELAND SURVIVALISTS! ARCHITECT OF A NEW FUTURE THROUGH VISION AND DILIGENCE.
HOW DOES IT GO, BOZ?
IT GOES, MAESTRO.
IT HAS BEEN A WHILE.
TO BE PRECISE, IT HAS BEEN A YEAR, BOZ. SO TELL ME...
...HOW IS YOUR DAUGHTER COMING ALONG?
MAESTRO, PLEASE... EVER SINCE MY WIFE DIED, I HAVE NO ONE TO CARE FOR... NO...
...BESIDES... SHE... SHE IS MALNOURISHED AND... UNIMPRESSIVE, MAESTRO. AND... TO BE HONEST... HOMELY. NOT WORTH YOUR--
I'LL JUDGE THAT. BRING HER, BOZ.
NOW.
IT'S ALL RIGHT, DADDY.
HE... IS WHO HE IS.
MAESTRO, YOU... YOU SEE SHE'S JUST... *CHOKE* JUST A SCRAWNY THING. NO MUH... MEAT ON HER. SHE...
...she's just a baby...
SHHH.
DADDY... PLEASE... I'LL BE...
I'LL BE FINE.

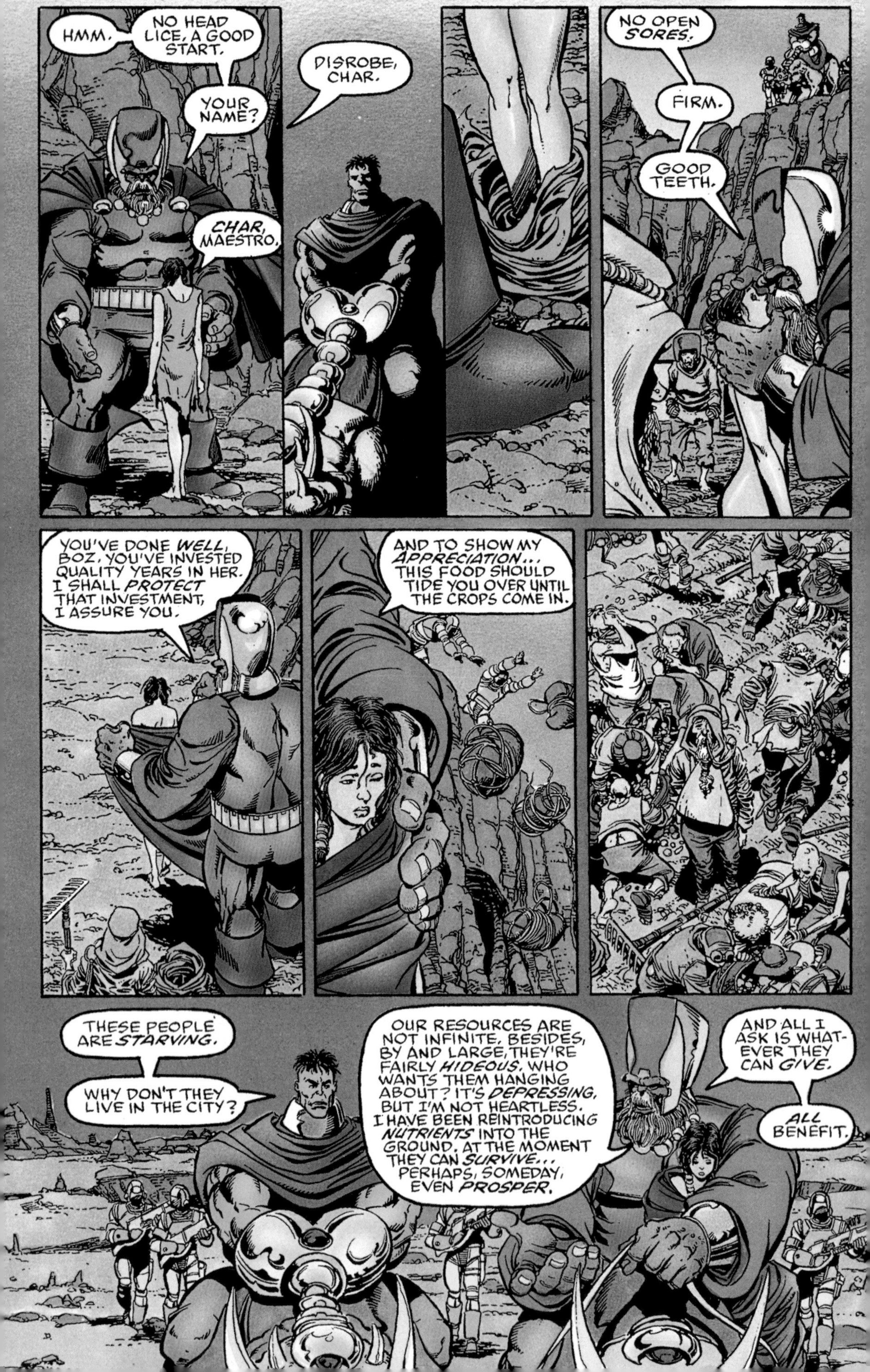
HMM.
NO HEAD LICE, A GOOD START.
YOUR NAME?
CHAR, MAESTRO.
DISROBE, CHAR.
NO OPEN SORES.
FIRM.
GOOD TEETH.
YOU'VE DONE WELL, BOZ, YOU'VE INVESTED QUALITY YEARS IN HER. I SHALL PROTECT THAT INVESTMENT, I ASSURE YOU.
AND TO SHOW MY APPRECIATION... THIS FOOD SHOULD TIDE YOU OVER UNTIL THE CROPS COME IN.
THESE PEOPLE ARE STARVING.
WHY DON'T THEY LIVE IN THE CITY?
OUR RESOURCES ARE NOT INFINITE. BESIDES, BY AND LARGE, THEY'RE FAIRLY HIDEOUS. WHO WANTS THEM HANGING ABOUT? IT'S DEPRESSING, BUT I'M NOT HEARTLESS. I HAVE BEEN REINTRODUCING NUTRIENTS INTO THE GROUND. AT THE MOMENT THEY CAN SURVIVE... PERHAPS, SOMEDAY, EVEN PROSPER.
AND ALL I ASK IS WHATEVER THEY CAN GIVE.
ALL BENEFIT.

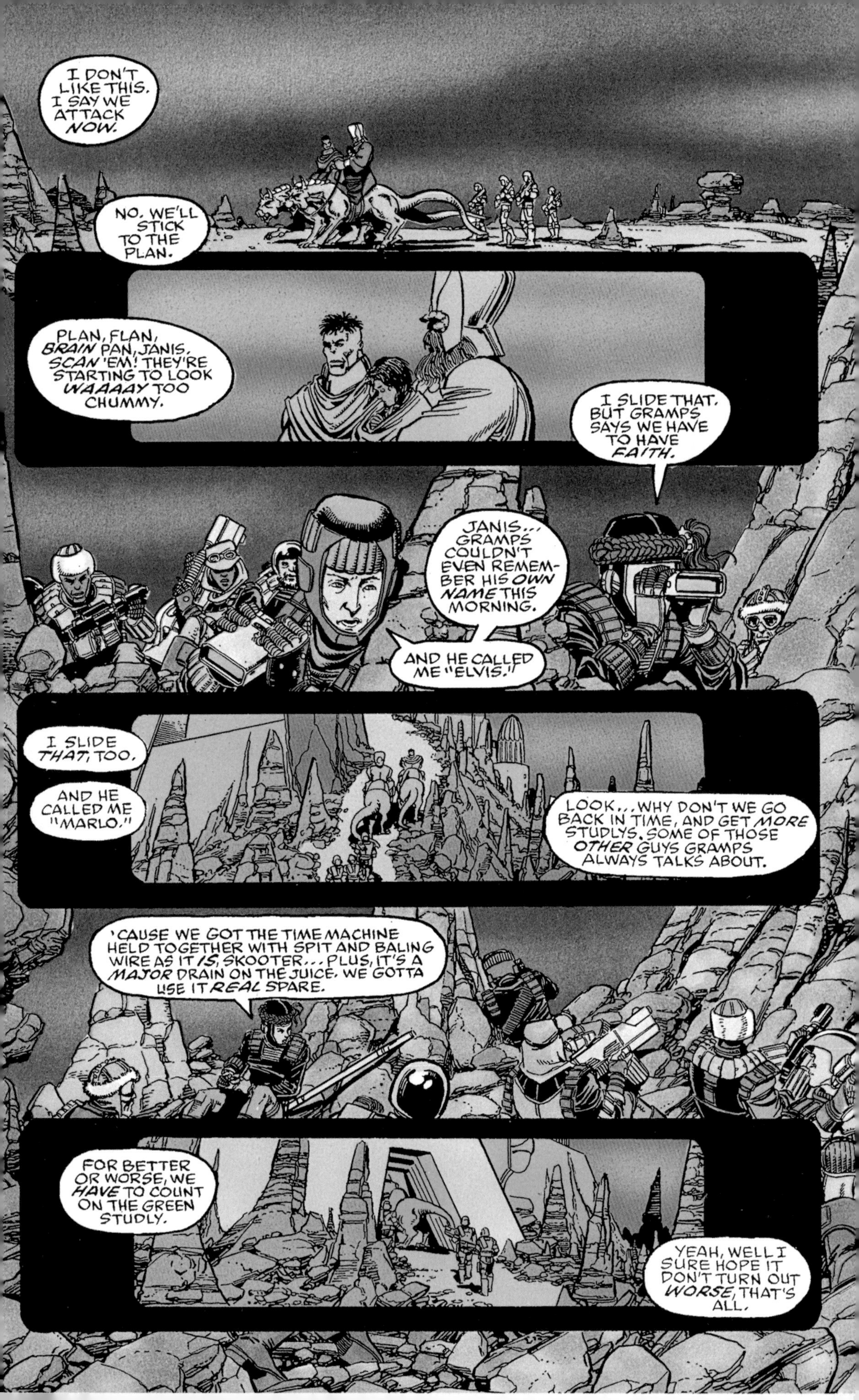
I DON'T LIKE THIS. I SAY WE ATTACK NOW.
NO. WE'LL STICK TO THE PLAN.
PLAN, FLAN, BRAIN PAN, JANIS. SCAN 'EM! THEY'RE STARTING TO LOOK WAAAAY TOO CHUMMY.
I SLIDE THAT. BUT GRAMPS SAYS WE HAVE TO HAVE FAITH.
JANIS... GRAMPS COULDN'T EVEN REMEMBER HIS OWN NAME THIS MORNING.
AND HE CALLED ME "ELVIS."
I SLIDE THAT, TOO.
AND HE CALLED ME "MARLO."
LOOK... WHY DON'T WE GO BACK IN TIME, AND GET MORE STUDLYS. SOME OF THOSE OTHER GUYS GRAMPS ALWAYS TALKS ABOUT.
'CAUSE WE GOT THE TIME MACHINE HELD TOGETHER WITH SPIT AND BALING WIRE AS IT IS, SKOOTER... PLUS, IT'S A MAJOR DRAIN ON THE JUICE. WE GOTTA USE IT REAL SPARE.
FOR BETTER OR WORSE, WE HAVE TO COUNT ON THE GREEN STUDLY.
YEAH, WELL I SURE HOPE IT DON'T TURN OUT WORSE, THAT'S ALL.

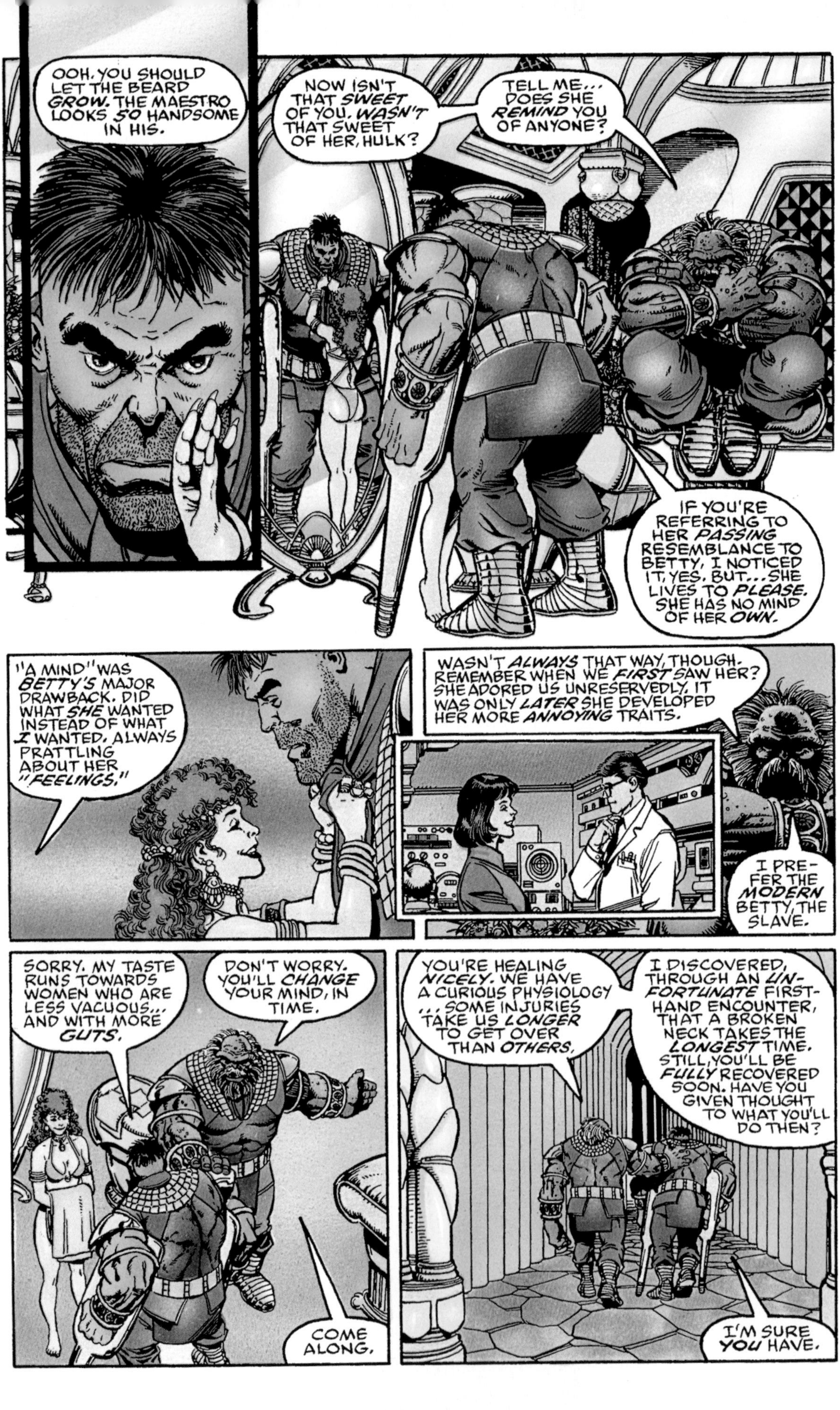
OOH. YOU SHOULD LET THE BEARD GROW. THE MAESTRO LOOKS SO HANDSOME IN HIS.
NOW ISN'T THAT SWEET OF YOU. WASN'T THAT SWEET OF HER, HULK?
TELL ME... DOES SHE REMIND YOU OF ANYONE?
IF YOU'RE REFERRING TO HER PASSING RESEMBLANCE TO BETTY, I NOTICED IT, YES. BUT... SHE LIVES TO PLEASE. SHE HAS NO MIND OF HER OWN.
"A MIND" WAS BETTY'S MAJOR DRAWBACK. DID WHAT SHE WANTED INSTEAD OF WHAT I WANTED, ALWAYS PRATTLING ABOUT HER "FEELINGS."
WASN'T ALWAYS THAT WAY, THOUGH. REMEMBER WHEN WE FIRST SAW HER? SHE ADORED US UNRESERVEDLY. IT WAS ONLY LATER SHE DEVELOPED HER MORE ANNOYING TRAITS.
I PREFER THE MODERN BETTY, THE SLAVE.
SORRY. MY TASTE RUNS TOWARDS WOMEN WHO ARE LESS VACUOUS... AND WITH MORE GUTS.
DON'T WORRY. YOU'LL CHANGE YOUR MIND, IN TIME.
COME ALONG.
YOU'RE HEALING NICELY. WE HAVE A CURIOUS PHYSIOLOGY ... SOME INJURIES TAKE US LONGER TO GET OVER THAN OTHERS.
I DISCOVERED, THROUGH AN UNFORTUNATE FIRST-HAND ENCOUNTER, THAT A BROKEN NECK TAKES THE LONGEST TIME. STILL, YOU'LL BE FULLY RECOVERED SOON. HAVE YOU GIVEN THOUGHT TO WHAT YOU'LL DO THEN?
I'M SURE YOU HAVE.

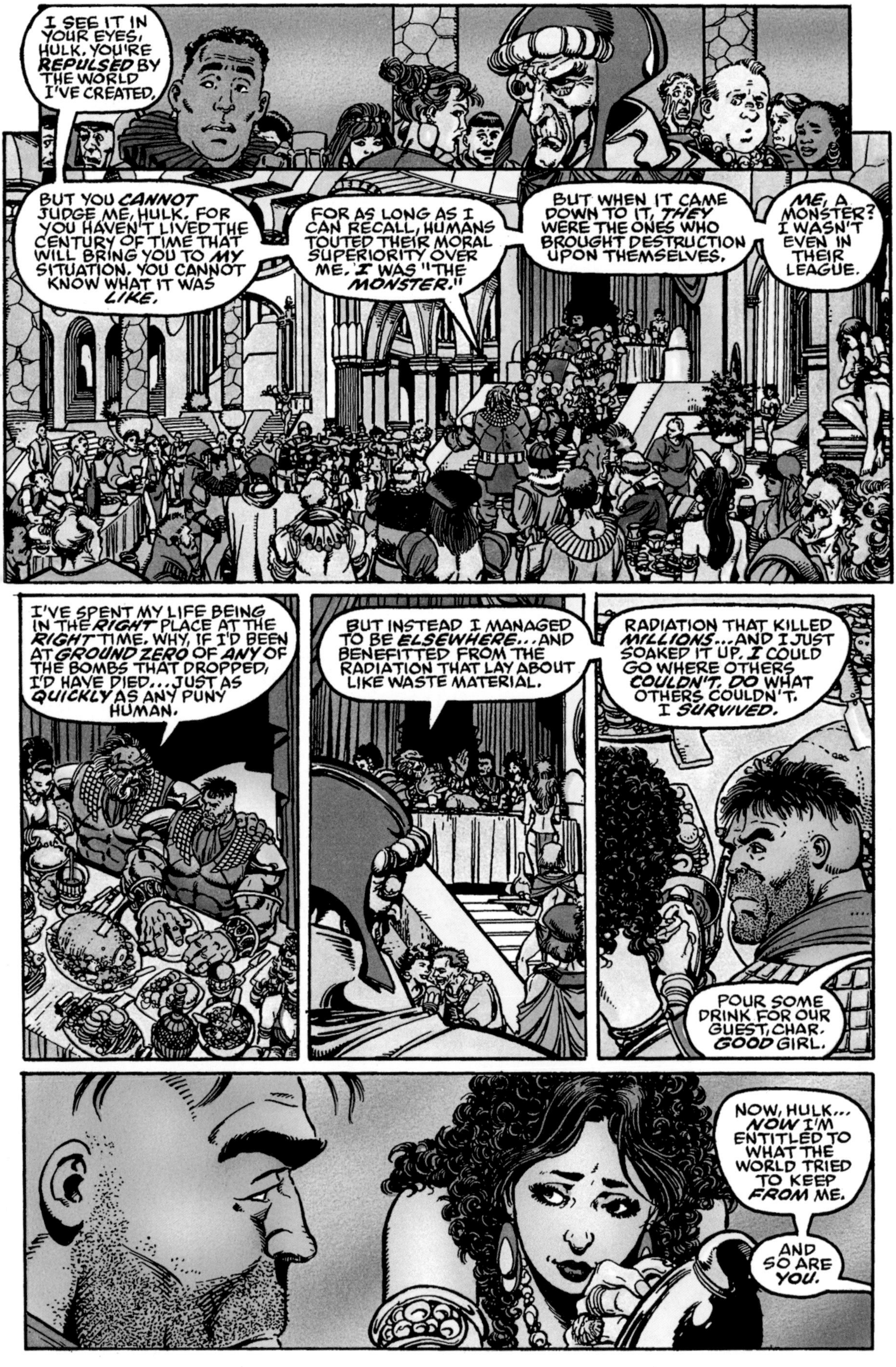
I SEE IT IN YOUR EYES, HULK. YOU'RE *REPULSED* BY THE WORLD I'VE CREATED.
BUT YOU *CANNOT* JUDGE ME, HULK. FOR YOU HAVEN'T LIVED THE CENTURY OF TIME THAT WILL BRING YOU TO *MY* SITUATION. YOU CANNOT KNOW WHAT IT WAS *LIKE*.
FOR AS LONG AS I CAN RECALL, HUMANS TOUTED THEIR MORAL SUPERIORITY OVER ME. *I* WAS "THE *MONSTER*."
BUT WHEN IT CAME DOWN TO IT, *THEY* WERE THE ONES WHO BROUGHT DESTRUCTION UPON THEMSELVES.
ME, A MONSTER? I WASN'T EVEN IN THEIR LEAGUE.
I'VE SPENT MY LIFE BEING IN THE *RIGHT* PLACE AT THE *RIGHT* TIME. WHY, IF I'D BEEN AT *GROUND ZERO* OF *ANY* OF THE BOMBS THAT DROPPED, I'D HAVE DIED... JUST AS *QUICKLY* AS ANY PUNY HUMAN.
BUT INSTEAD I MANAGED TO BE *ELSEWHERE*... AND BENEFITTED FROM THE RADIATION THAT LAY ABOUT LIKE WASTE MATERIAL.
RADIATION THAT KILLED *MILLIONS*... AND I JUST SOAKED IT UP. *I* COULD GO WHERE OTHERS *COULDN'T*. *DO* WHAT OTHERS COULDN'T. I *SURVIVED*.
POUR SOME DRINK FOR OUR GUEST, CHAR. *GOOD* GIRL.
NOW, HULK... *NOW* I'M ENTITLED TO WHAT THE WORLD TRIED TO KEEP *FROM* ME.
AND SO ARE *YOU*.

STAY *HERE.* RULE AT MY SIDE. DON'T YOU SEE, BRUCE...WE OWE HUMANS *NOTHING!* THEY'RE JUST TAKERS. THEY TAKE *ALL* WE HAVE, AND GIVE *NOTHING* BACK. THEY SPIT IN OUR FACE.

BULL. I HAVE FRIENDS, ALLIES, LOVED ONES. I HAVE...

YOU DON'T KNOW WHAT LIES AHEAD FOR YOU. *I* DO. *LISTEN* TO ME, BRUCE... THEY'RE GOING TO TAKE IT *ALL* AWAY. YOU'RE GOING TO END UP WITH *NOTHING* AND *NO ONE.* WHY GO BACK TO THAT... WHEN YOU CAN STAY HERE AND HAVE *EVERYTHING?*

YOU SAID *YOURSELF* TIME HAS SPLIT OFF. MAYBE WHAT HAPPENED TO YOU *WON'T* HAPPEN TO ME. MAYBE THINGS WILL BE *DIFFERENT.*

PERSECUTION. BETRAYAL. HATRED.

THESE THINGS *DON'T* CHANGE.

JUST TELL ME YOU'LL *THINK* ABOUT IT.

I'LL THINK ABOUT IT.

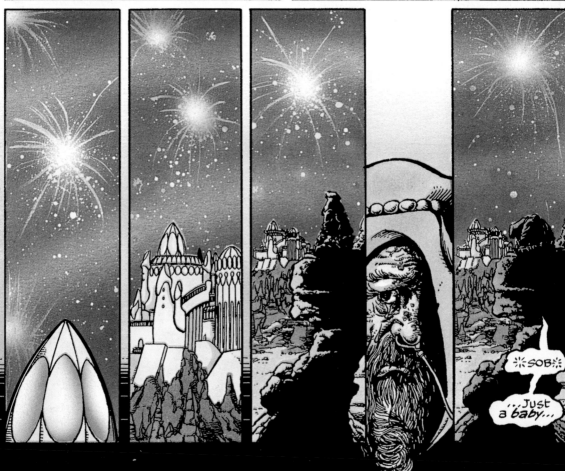

✳SOB✳

...Just a baby...

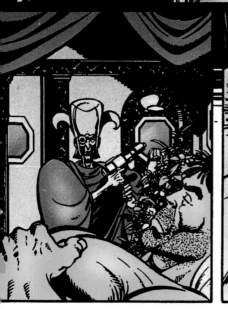

ONE OF MY DUTIES IS TO MAINTAIN THE *STATUS QUO.*

MY APOLOGIES, DR. BANNER.

YOUR BEING HERE *UPSETS* THAT.

NOT AS UPSET AS *YOU'RE* GONNA BE, SQUIRREL-EYE.

DROP IT...

...ON YOUR *OWN,* OR FROM YOUR DEAD FINGERS, MAKES *NO* DIFF TO ME.

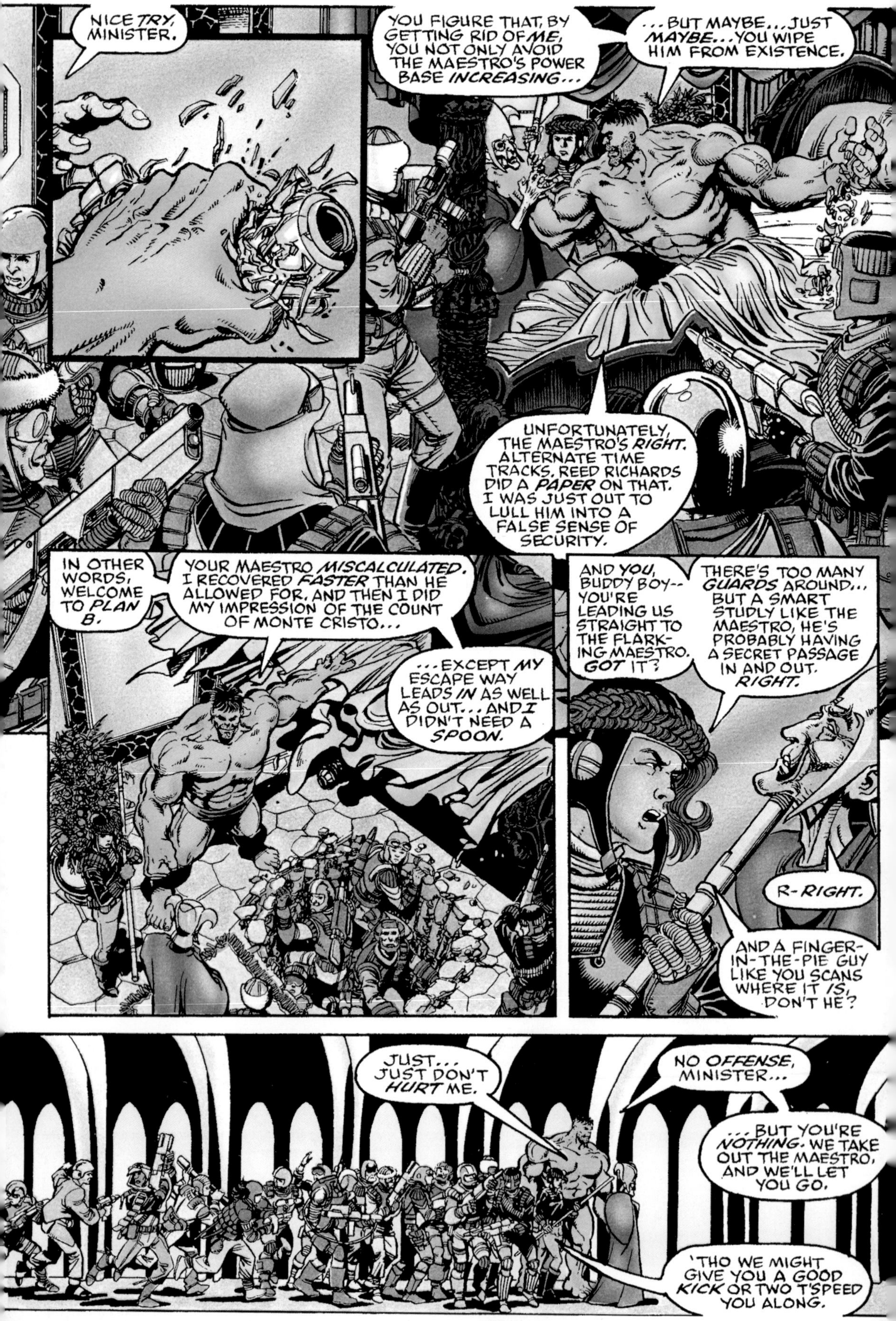
NICE TRY, MINISTER.
YOU FIGURE THAT, BY GETTING RID OF ME, YOU NOT ONLY AVOID THE MAESTRO'S POWER BASE INCREASING...
...BUT MAYBE...JUST MAYBE...YOU WIPE HIM FROM EXISTENCE.
UNFORTUNATELY, THE MAESTRO'S RIGHT. ALTERNATE TIME TRACKS. REED RICHARDS DID A PAPER ON THAT. I WAS JUST OUT TO LULL HIM INTO A FALSE SENSE OF SECURITY.
IN OTHER WORDS, WELCOME TO PLAN B.
YOUR MAESTRO MISCALCULATED. I RECOVERED FASTER THAN HE ALLOWED FOR, AND THEN I DID MY IMPRESSION OF THE COUNT OF MONTE CRISTO...
...EXCEPT MY ESCAPE WAY LEADS IN AS WELL AS OUT... AND I DIDN'T NEED A SPOON.
AND YOU, BUDDY BOY-- YOU'RE LEADING US STRAIGHT TO THE FLARKING MAESTRO. GOT IT?
THERE'S TOO MANY GUARDS AROUND... BUT A SMART STUDLY LIKE THE MAESTRO, HE'S PROBABLY HAVING A SECRET PASSAGE IN AND OUT. RIGHT.
R-RIGHT.
AND A FINGER-IN-THE-PIE GUY LIKE YOU SCANS WHERE IT IS, DON'T HE?
JUST... JUST DON'T HURT ME.
NO OFFENSE, MINISTER...
...BUT YOU'RE NOTHING. WE TAKE OUT THE MAESTRO, AND WE'LL LET YOU GO.
'THO WE MIGHT GIVE YOU A GOOD KICK OR TWO T'SPEED YOU ALONG.

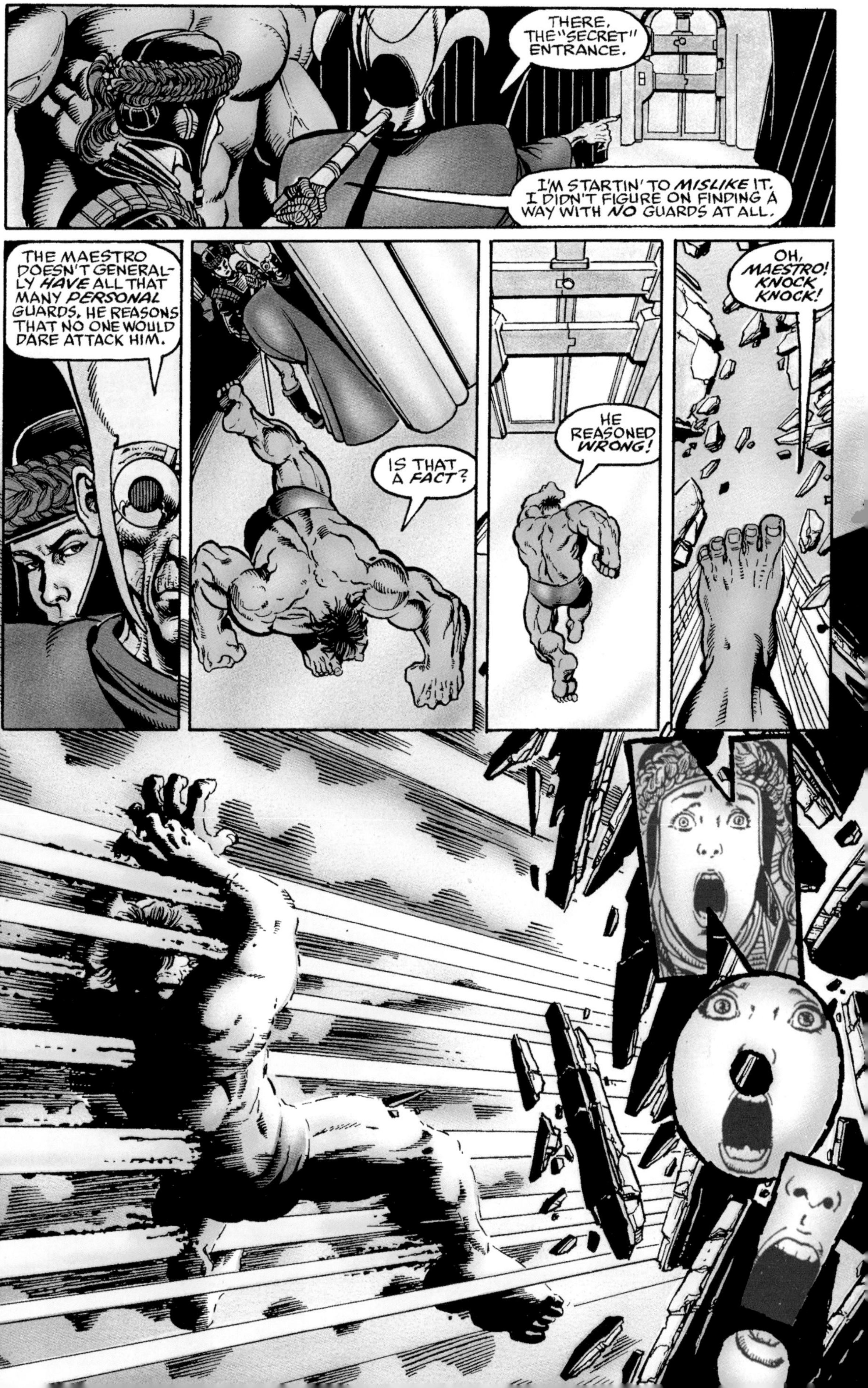
THERE, THE "SECRET" ENTRANCE.
I'M STARTIN' TO MISLIKE IT. I DIDN'T FIGURE ON FINDING A WAY WITH NO GUARDS AT ALL.
THE MAESTRO DOESN'T GENERALLY HAVE ALL THAT MANY PERSONAL GUARDS. HE REASONS THAT NO ONE WOULD DARE ATTACK HIM.
IS THAT A FACT?
HE REASONED WRONG!
OH, MAESTRO! KNOCK KNOCK!

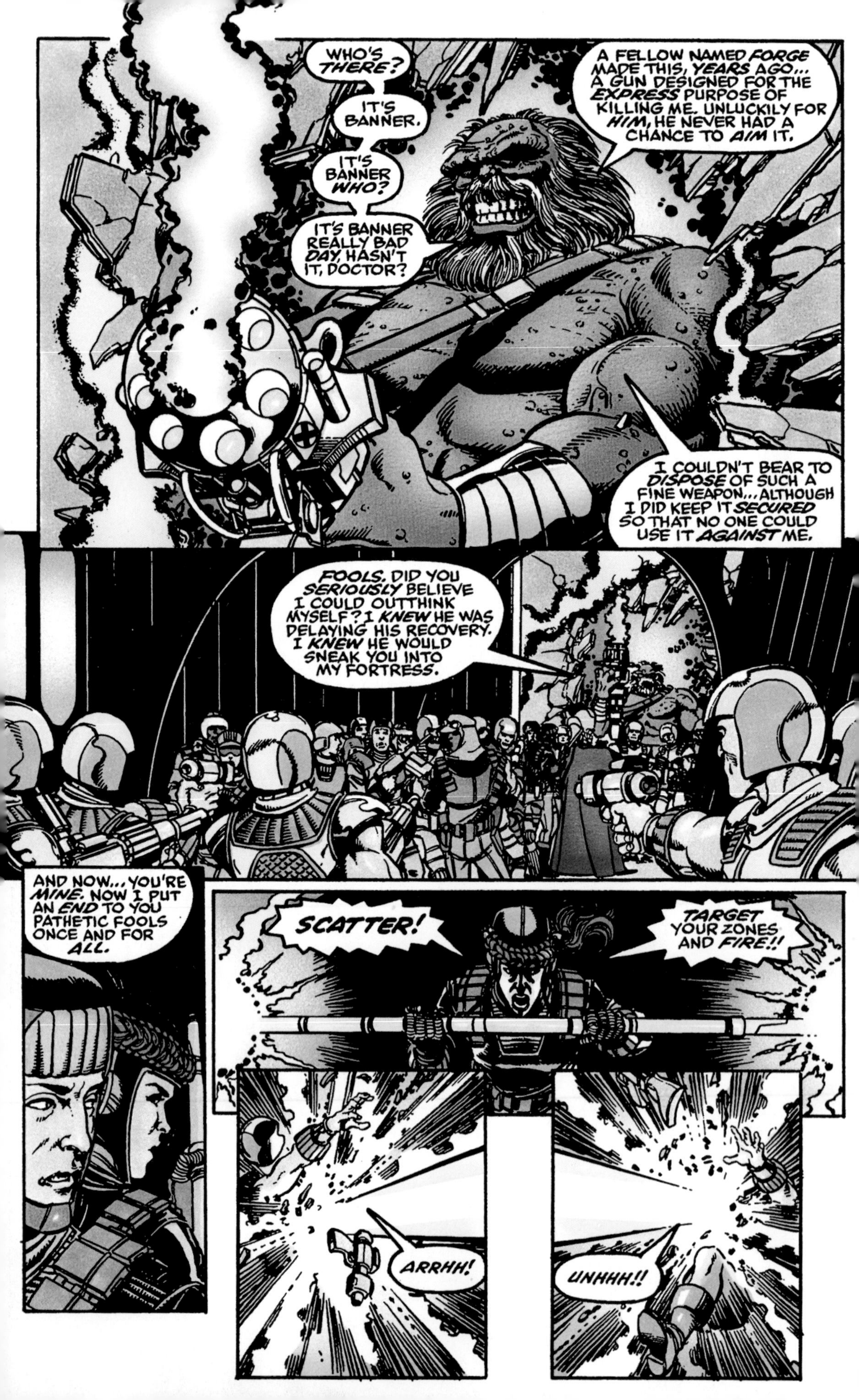
WHO'S THERE?
IT'S BANNER.
IT'S BANNER WHO?
IT'S BANNER REALLY BAD DAY, HASN'T IT, DOCTOR?
A FELLOW NAMED FORGE MADE THIS, YEARS AGO... A GUN DESIGNED FOR THE EXPRESS PURPOSE OF KILLING ME. UNLUCKILY FOR HIM, HE NEVER HAD A CHANCE TO AIM IT.
I COULDN'T BEAR TO DISPOSE OF SUCH A FINE WEAPON... ALTHOUGH I DID KEEP IT SECURED SO THAT NO ONE COULD USE IT AGAINST ME.
FOOLS. DID YOU SERIOUSLY BELIEVE I COULD OUTTHINK MYSELF? I KNEW HE WAS DELAYING HIS RECOVERY. I KNEW HE WOULD SNEAK YOU INTO MY FORTRESS.
AND NOW... YOU'RE MINE. NOW I PUT AN END TO YOU PATHETIC FOOLS ONCE AND FOR ALL.
SCATTER!
TARGET YOUR ZONES AND FIRE!!
ARRHH!
UNHHH!!

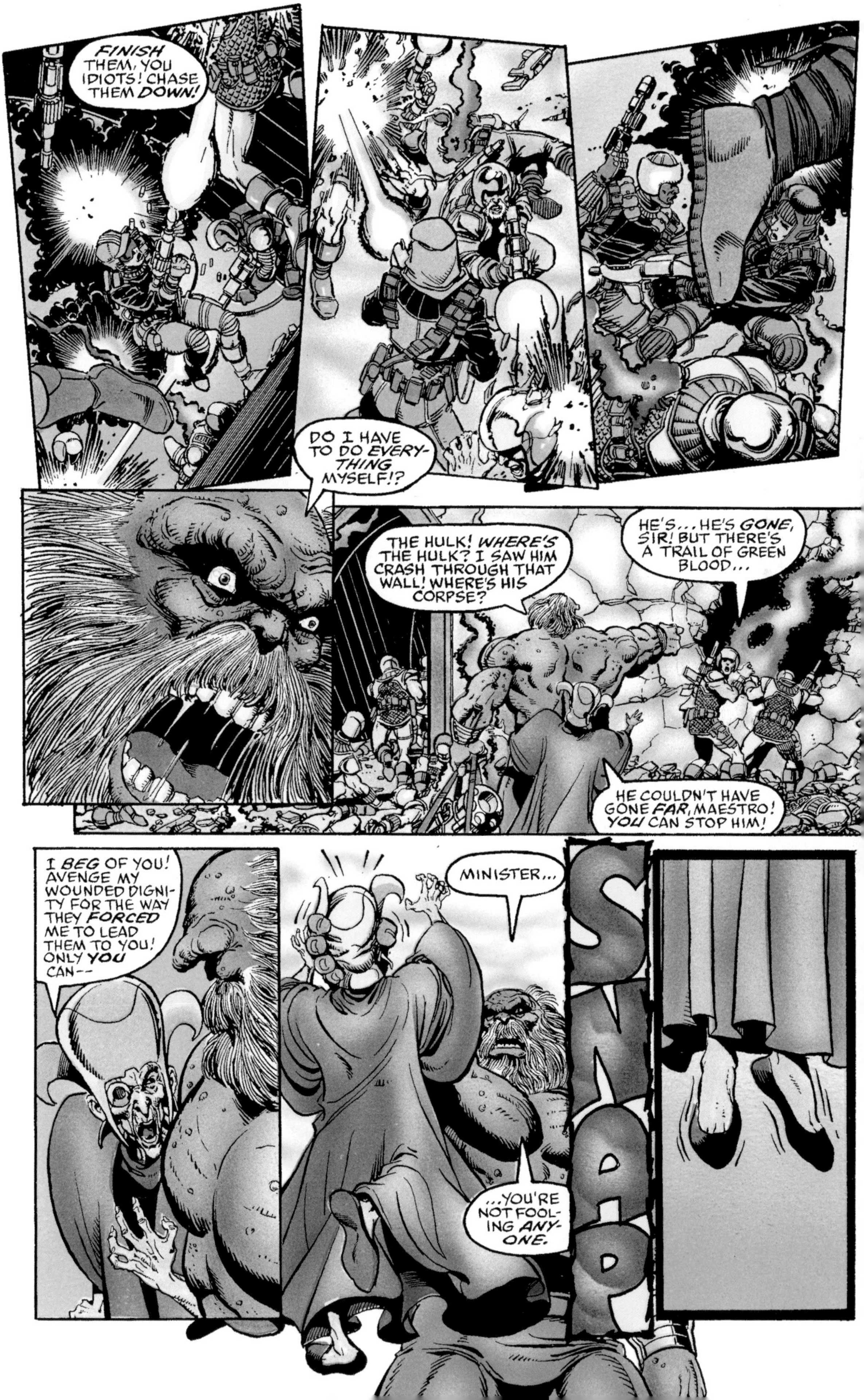
FINISH THEM, YOU IDIOTS! CHASE THEM DOWN!
DO I HAVE TO DO EVERY-THING MYSELF!?
THE HULK! WHERE'S THE HULK? I SAW HIM CRASH THROUGH THAT WALL! WHERE'S HIS CORPSE?
HE'S... HE'S GONE, SIR! BUT THERE'S A TRAIL OF GREEN BLOOD...
HE COULDN'T HAVE GONE FAR, MAESTRO! YOU CAN STOP HIM!
I BEG OF YOU! AVENGE MY WOUNDED DIGNI-TY FOR THE WAY THEY FORCED ME TO LEAD THEM TO YOU! ONLY YOU CAN--
MINISTER...
...YOU'RE NOT FOOL-ING ANY-ONE.

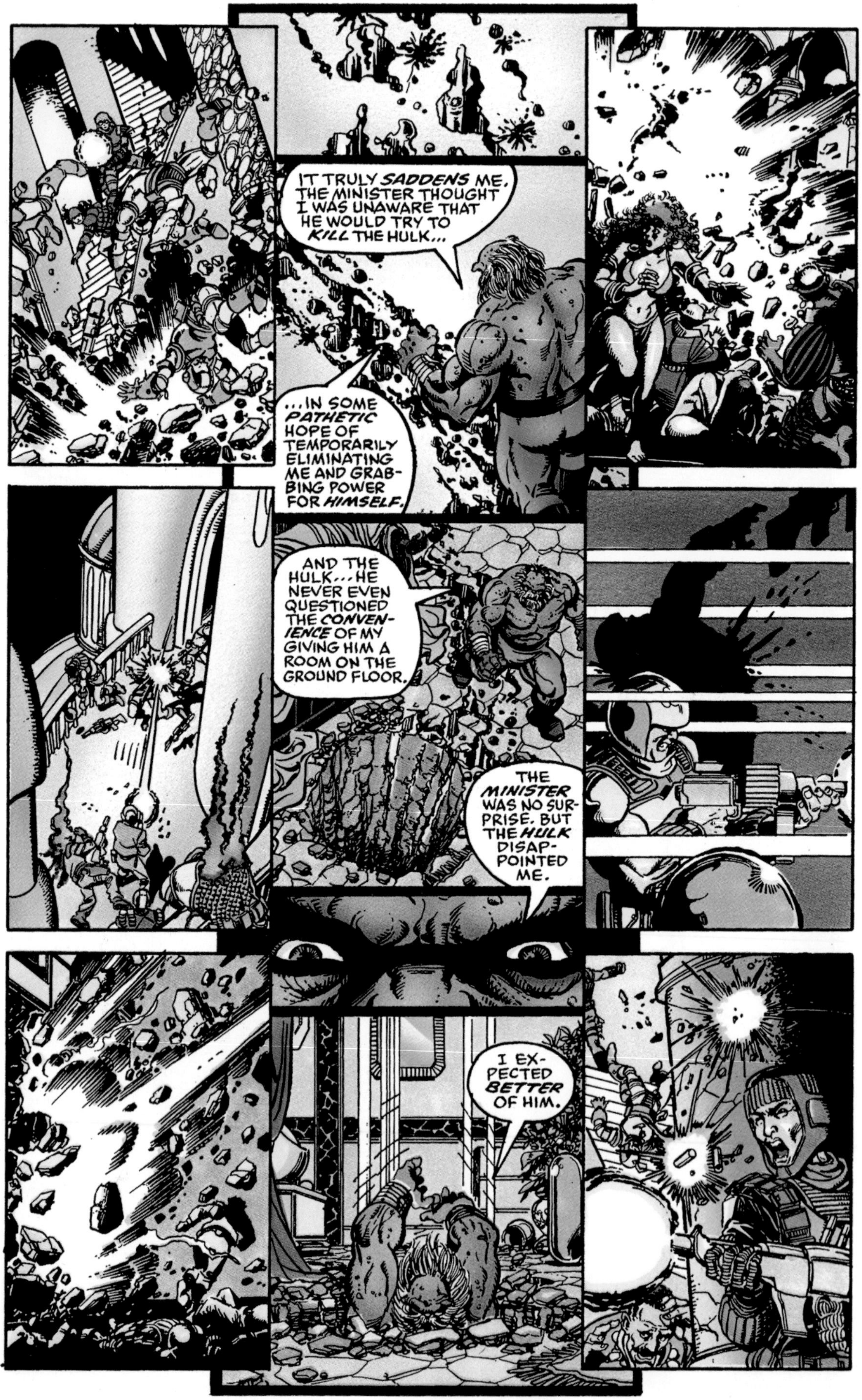
IT TRULY SADDENS ME. THE MINISTER THOUGHT I WAS UNAWARE THAT HE WOULD TRY TO KILL THE HULK...
...IN SOME PATHETIC HOPE OF TEMPORARILY ELIMINATING ME AND GRABBING POWER FOR HIMSELF.
AND THE HULK... HE NEVER EVEN QUESTIONED THE CONVENIENCE OF MY GIVING HIM A ROOM ON THE GROUND FLOOR.
THE MINISTER WAS NO SURPRISE. BUT THE HULK DISAPPOINTED ME.
I EXPECTED BETTER OF HIM.

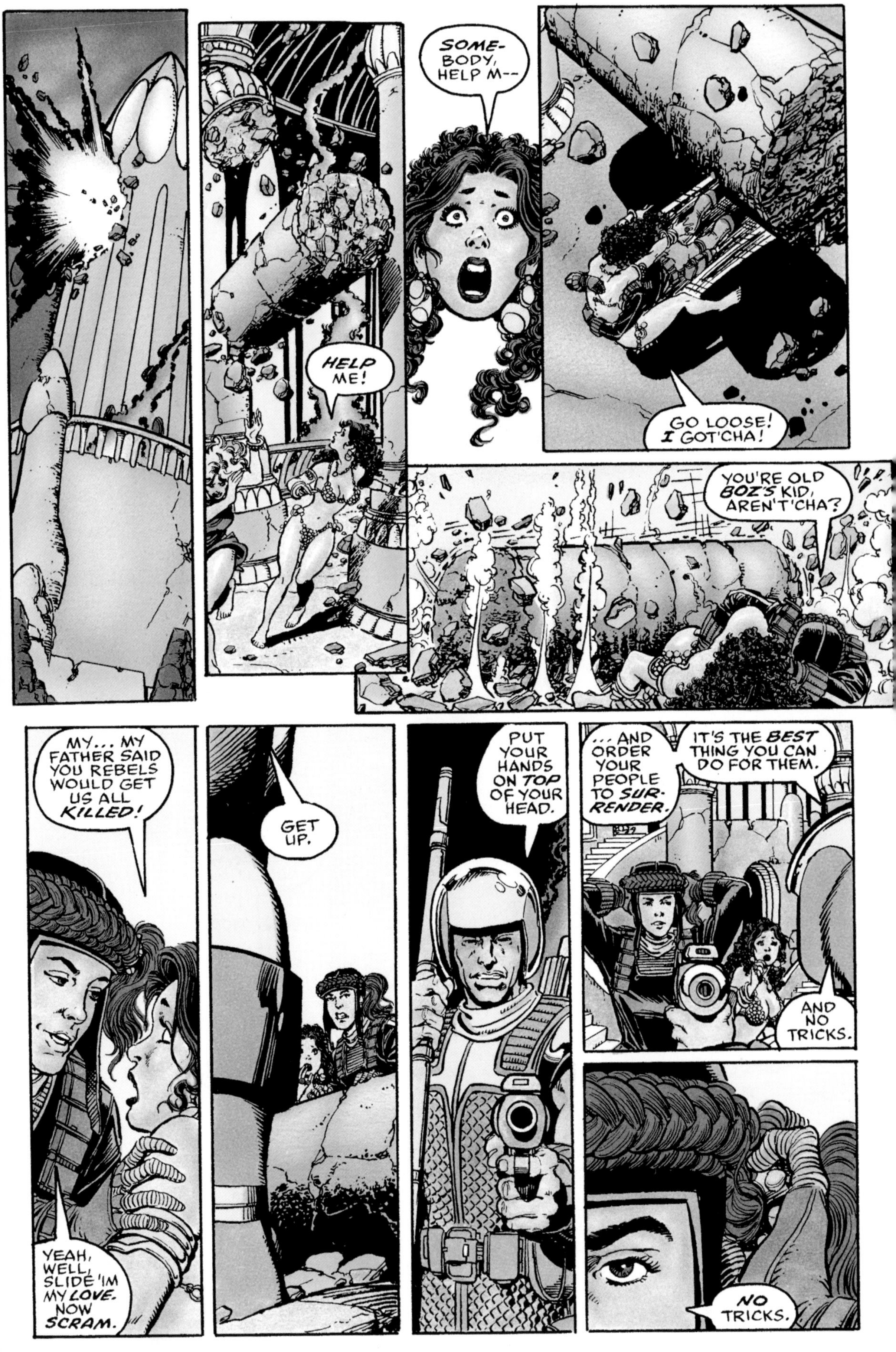
HELP ME!
SOME-BODY, HELP M--
GO LOOSE! I GOT'CHA!
YOU'RE OLD BOZ'S KID, AREN'T'CHA?
MY... MY FATHER SAID YOU REBELS WOULD GET US ALL KILLED!
YEAH, WELL, SLIDE 'IM MY LOVE. NOW SCRAM.
GET UP.
PUT YOUR HANDS ON TOP OF YOUR HEAD.
...AND ORDER YOUR PEOPLE TO SUR-RENDER.
IT'S THE BEST THING YOU CAN DO FOR THEM.
AND NO TRICKS.
NO TRICKS.

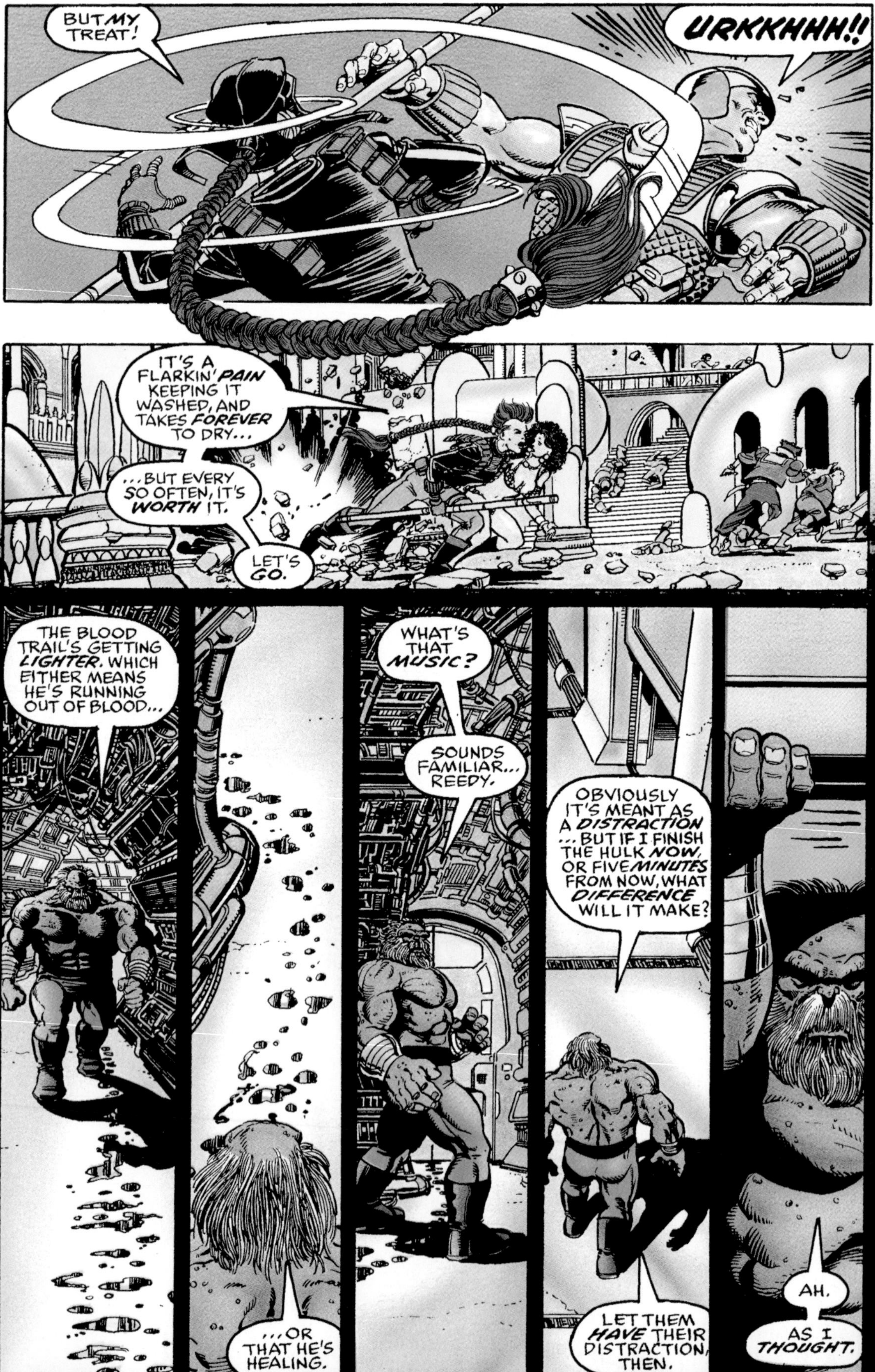
BUT MY TREAT!
URKKHHH!!
IT'S A FLARKIN' PAIN KEEPING IT WASHED, AND TAKES FOREVER TO DRY...
...BUT EVERY SO OFTEN, IT'S WORTH IT.
LET'S GO.
THE BLOOD TRAIL'S GETTING LIGHTER. WHICH EITHER MEANS HE'S RUNNING OUT OF BLOOD...
...OR THAT HE'S HEALING.
WHAT'S THAT MUSIC?
SOUNDS FAMILIAR... REEDY.
OBVIOUSLY IT'S MEANT AS A DISTRACTION ...BUT IF I FINISH THE HULK NOW, OR FIVE MINUTES FROM NOW, WHAT DIFFERENCE WILL IT MAKE?
LET THEM HAVE THEIR DISTRACTION, THEN.
AH.
AS I THOUGHT.

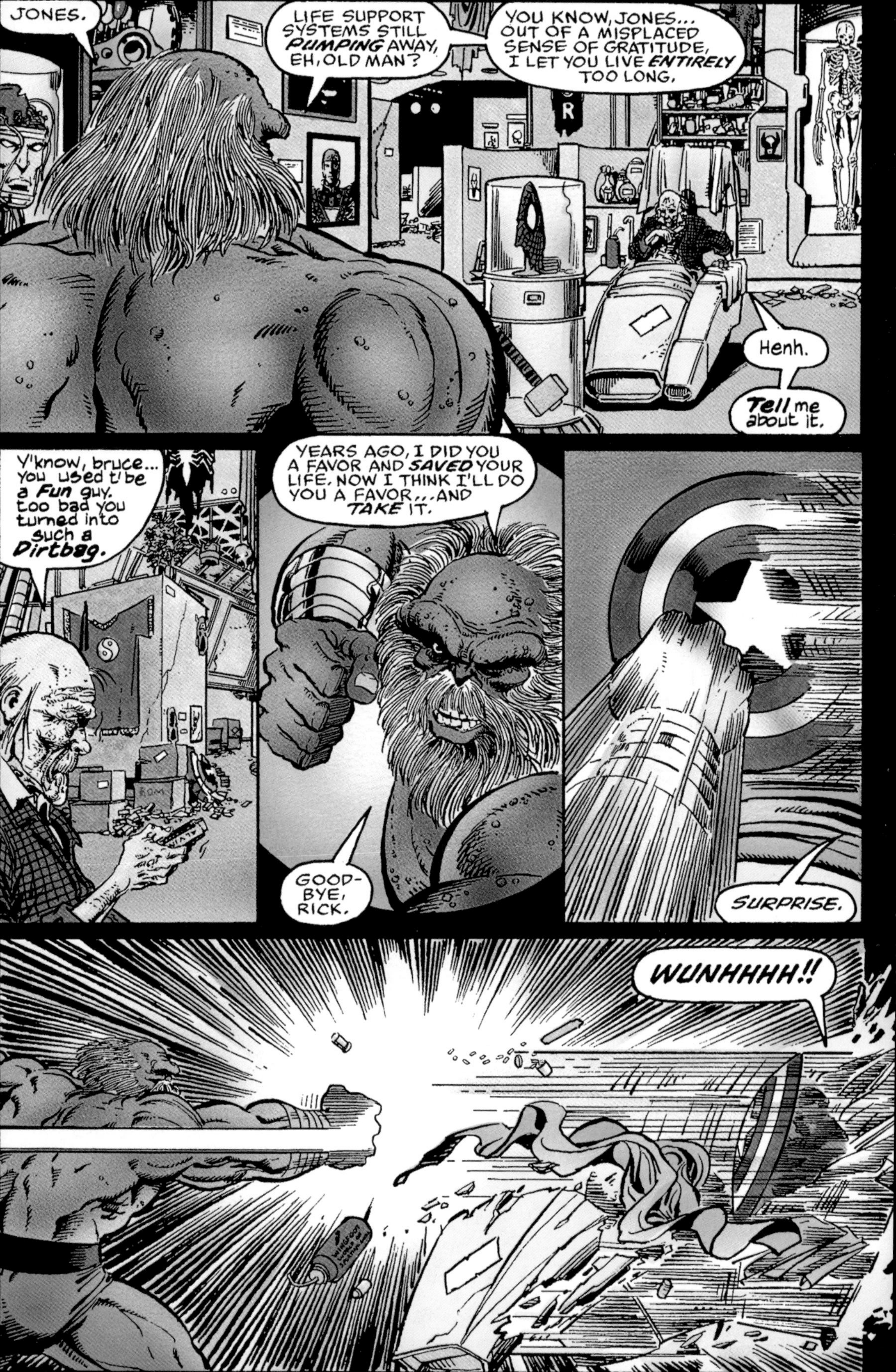
JONES.
LIFE SUPPORT SYSTEMS STILL PUMPING AWAY, EH, OLD MAN?
YOU KNOW, JONES... OUT OF A MISPLACED SENSE OF GRATITUDE, I LET YOU LIVE ENTIRELY TOO LONG.
Henh.
Tell me about it.
Y'know, bruce... you used t'be a Fun guy. too bad you turned into such a Dirtbag.
YEARS AGO, I DID YOU A FAVOR AND SAVED YOUR LIFE. NOW I THINK I'LL DO YOU A FAVOR... AND TAKE IT.
GOOD-BYE, RICK.
SURPRISE.
WUNHHHH!!

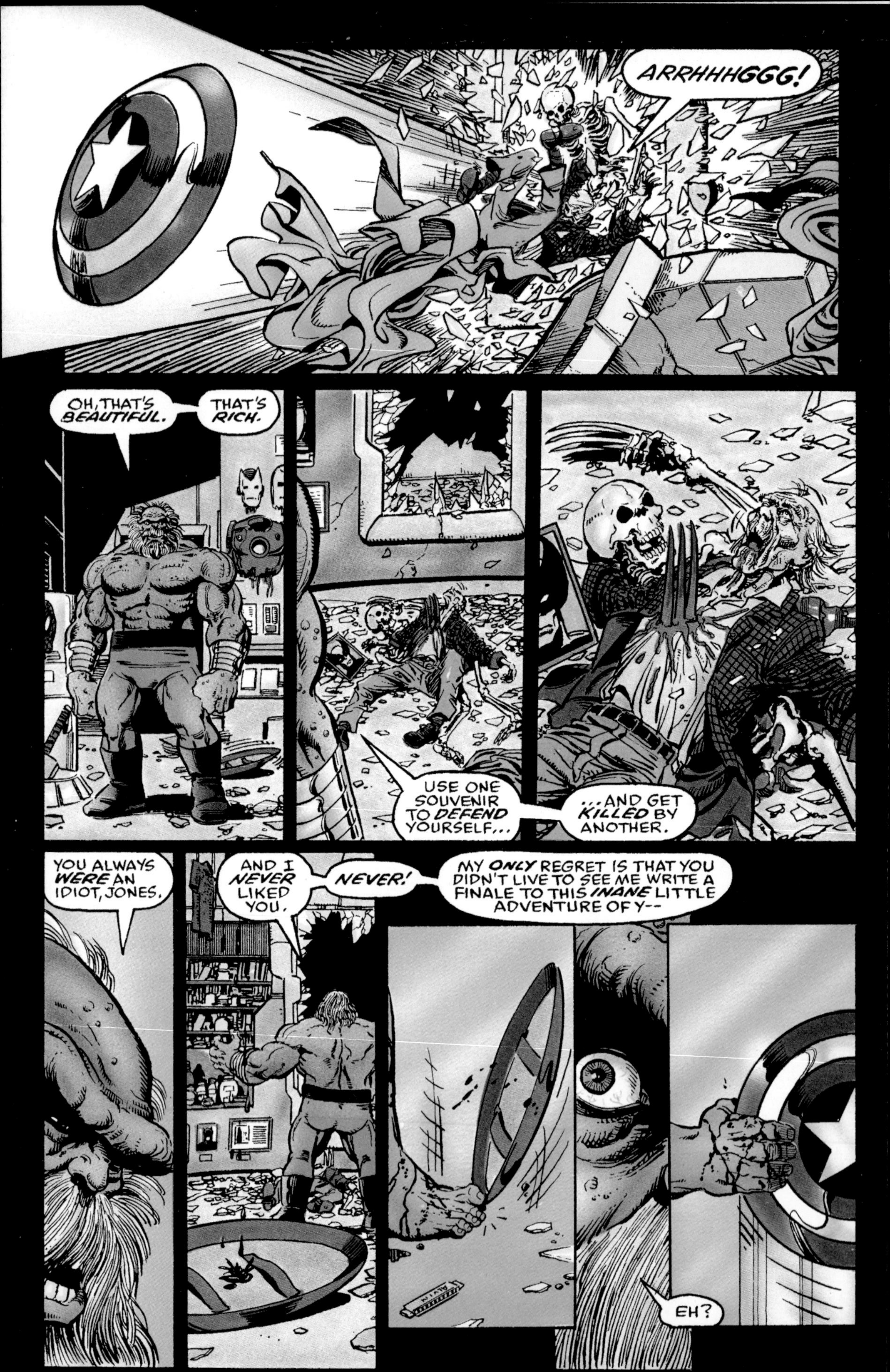
ARRHHHGGG!
OH, THAT'S BEAUTIFUL.
THAT'S RICH.
USE ONE SOUVENIR TO DEFEND YOURSELF...
...AND GET KILLED BY ANOTHER.
YOU ALWAYS WERE AN IDIOT, JONES.
AND I NEVER LIKED YOU.
NEVER!
MY ONLY REGRET IS THAT YOU DIDN'T LIVE TO SEE ME WRITE A FINALE TO THIS INANE LITTLE ADVENTURE OF Y--
EH?

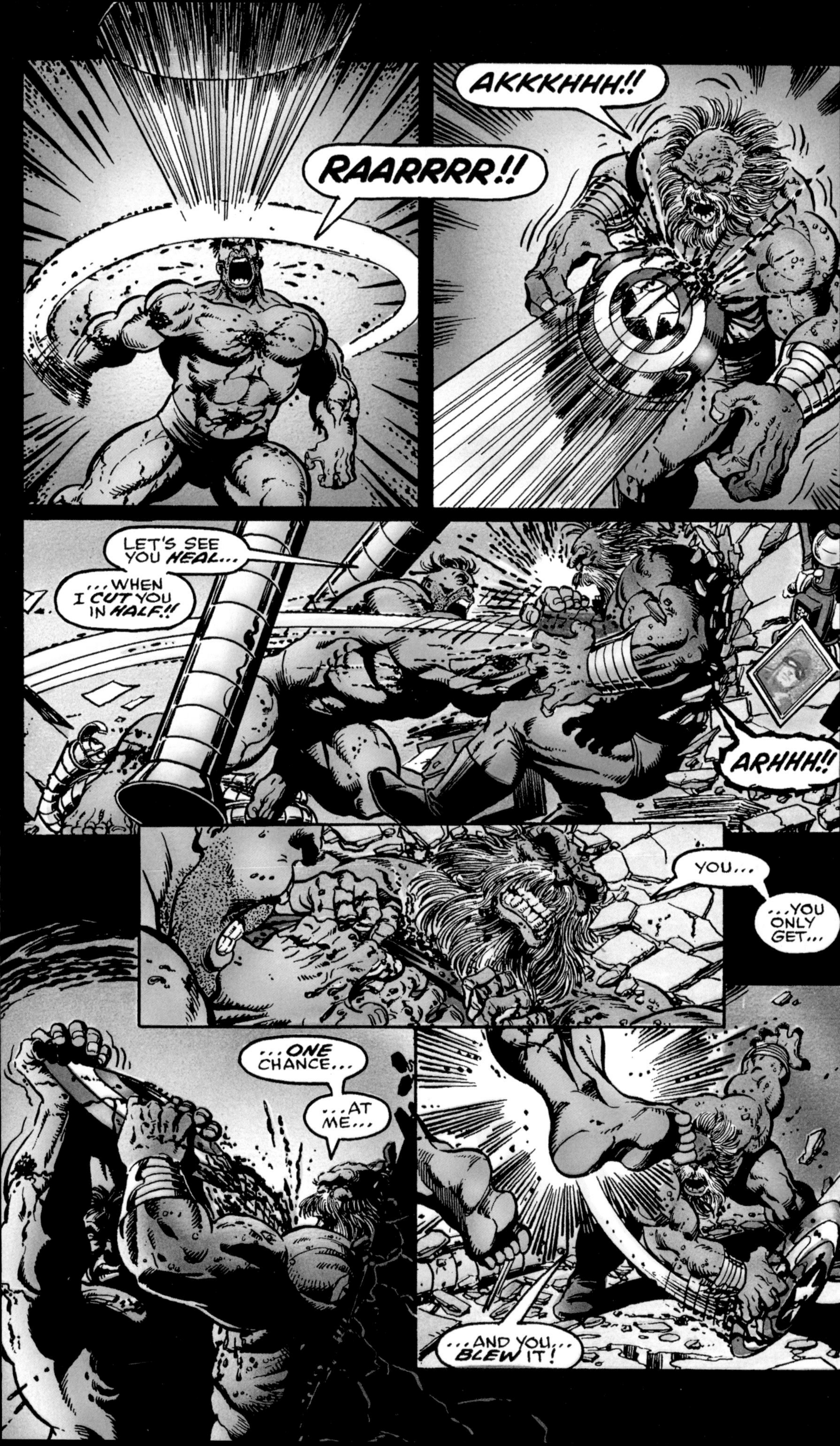
RAARRRR!!
AKKKHHH!!
LET'S SEE YOU HEAL...
...WHEN I CUT YOU IN HALF!!
ARHHH!!
YOU...
...YOU ONLY GET...
...ONE CHANCE...
...AT ME...
...AND YOU... BLEW IT!

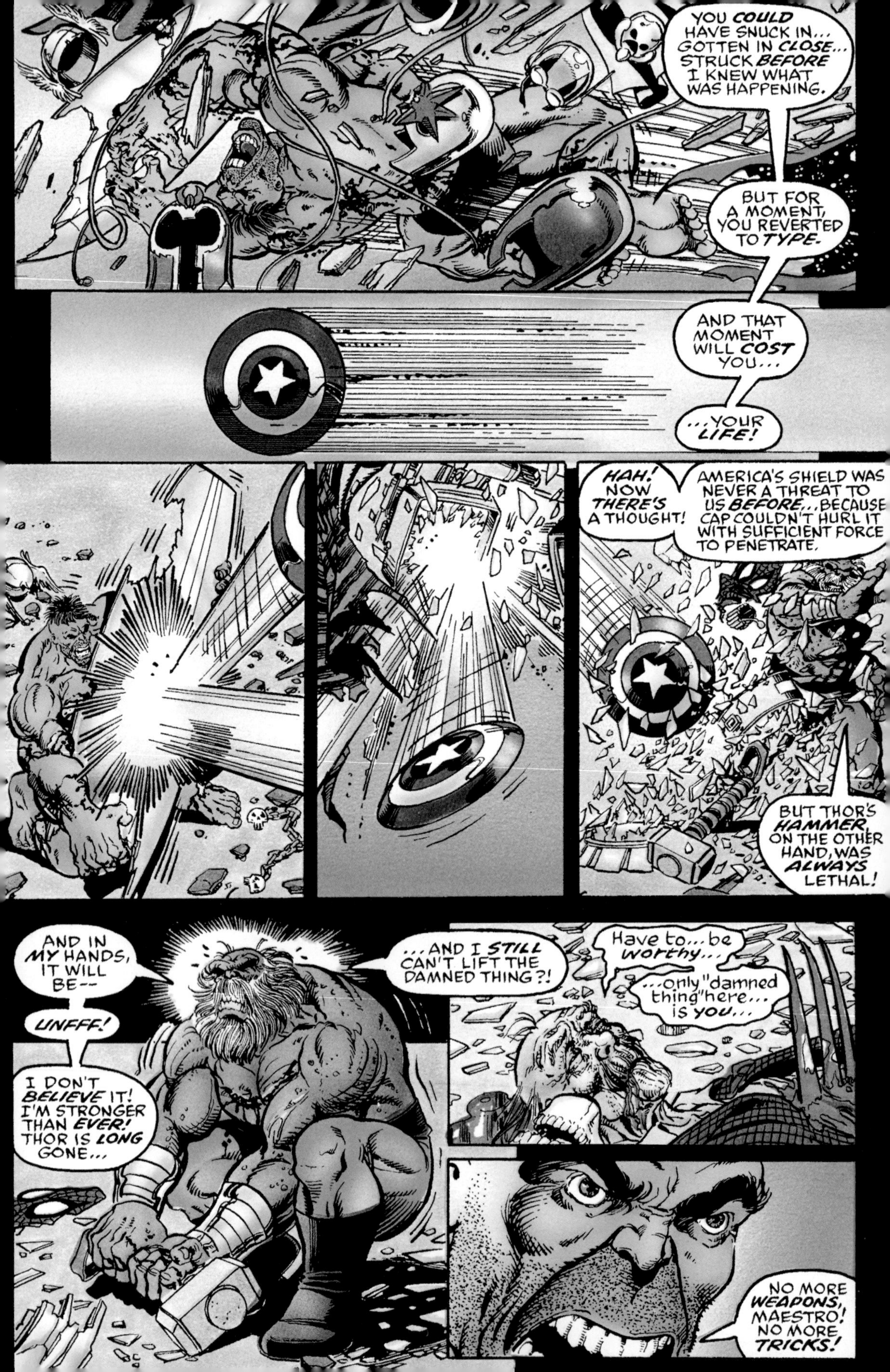
YOU COULD HAVE SNUCK IN... GOTTEN IN CLOSE... STRUCK BEFORE I KNEW WHAT WAS HAPPENING.
BUT FOR A MOMENT, YOU REVERTED TO TYPE.
AND THAT MOMENT WILL COST YOU...
...YOUR LIFE!
HAH! NOW THERE'S A THOUGHT!
AMERICA'S SHIELD WAS NEVER A THREAT TO US BEFORE... BECAUSE CAP COULDN'T HURL IT WITH SUFFICIENT FORCE TO PENETRATE.
BUT THOR'S HAMMER, ON THE OTHER HAND, WAS ALWAYS LETHAL!
AND IN MY HANDS, IT WILL BE--
UNFFF!
I DON'T BELIEVE IT! I'M STRONGER THAN EVER! THOR IS LONG GONE...
...AND I STILL CAN'T LIFT THE DAMNED THING?!
Have to... be worthy...
...only "damned thing" here... is you...
NO MORE WEAPONS, MAESTRO! NO MORE TRICKS!

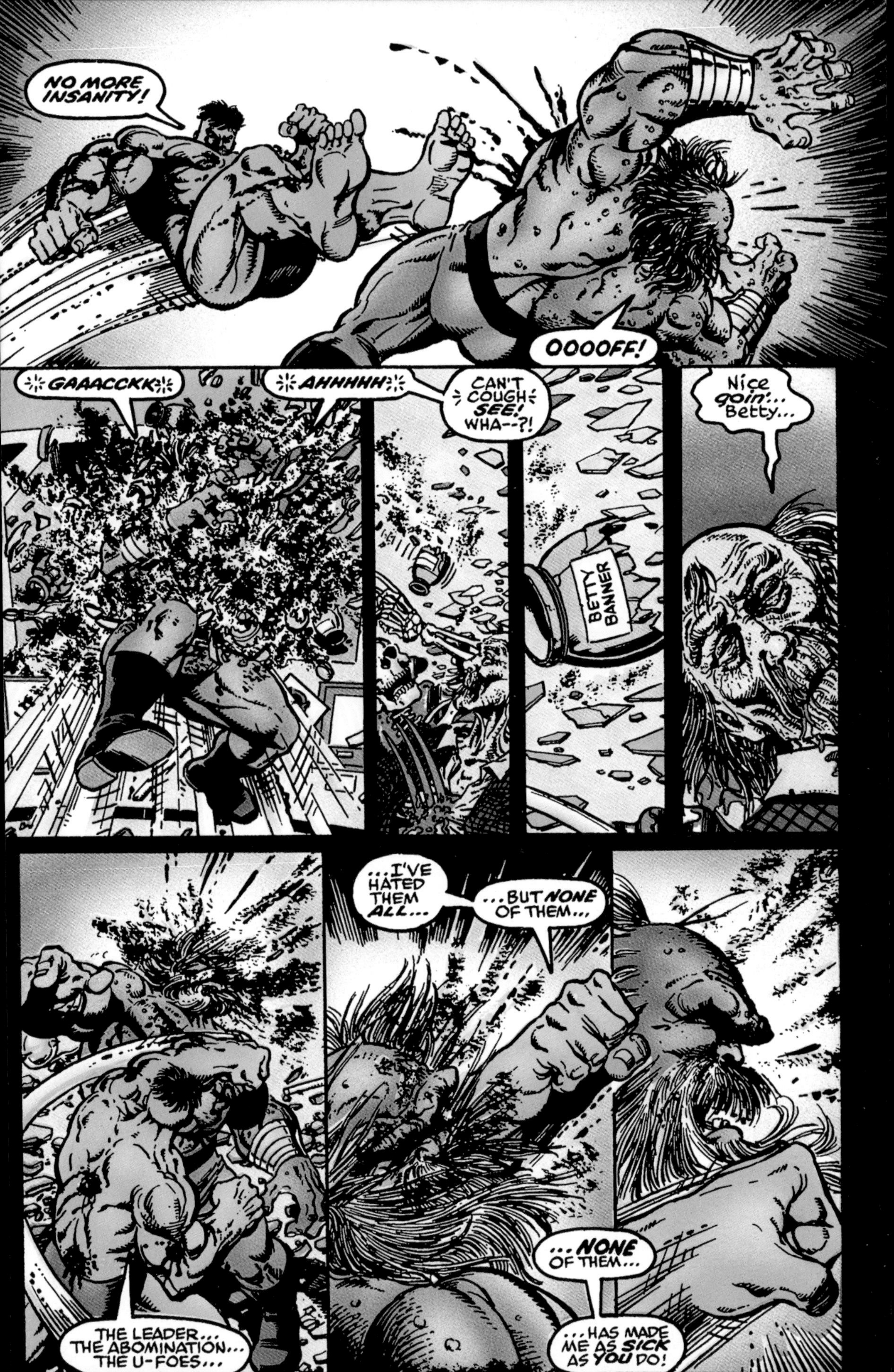
NO MORE INSANITY!
OOOOFF!
GAAACCKK
AHHHHH
CAN'T COUGH SEE! WHA--?!
Nice goin'... Betty...
BETTY BANNER
THE LEADER... THE ABOMINATION... THE U-FOES...
...I'VE HATED THEM ALL...
...BUT NONE OF THEM...
...NONE OF THEM...
...HAS MADE ME AS SICK AS YOU DO!

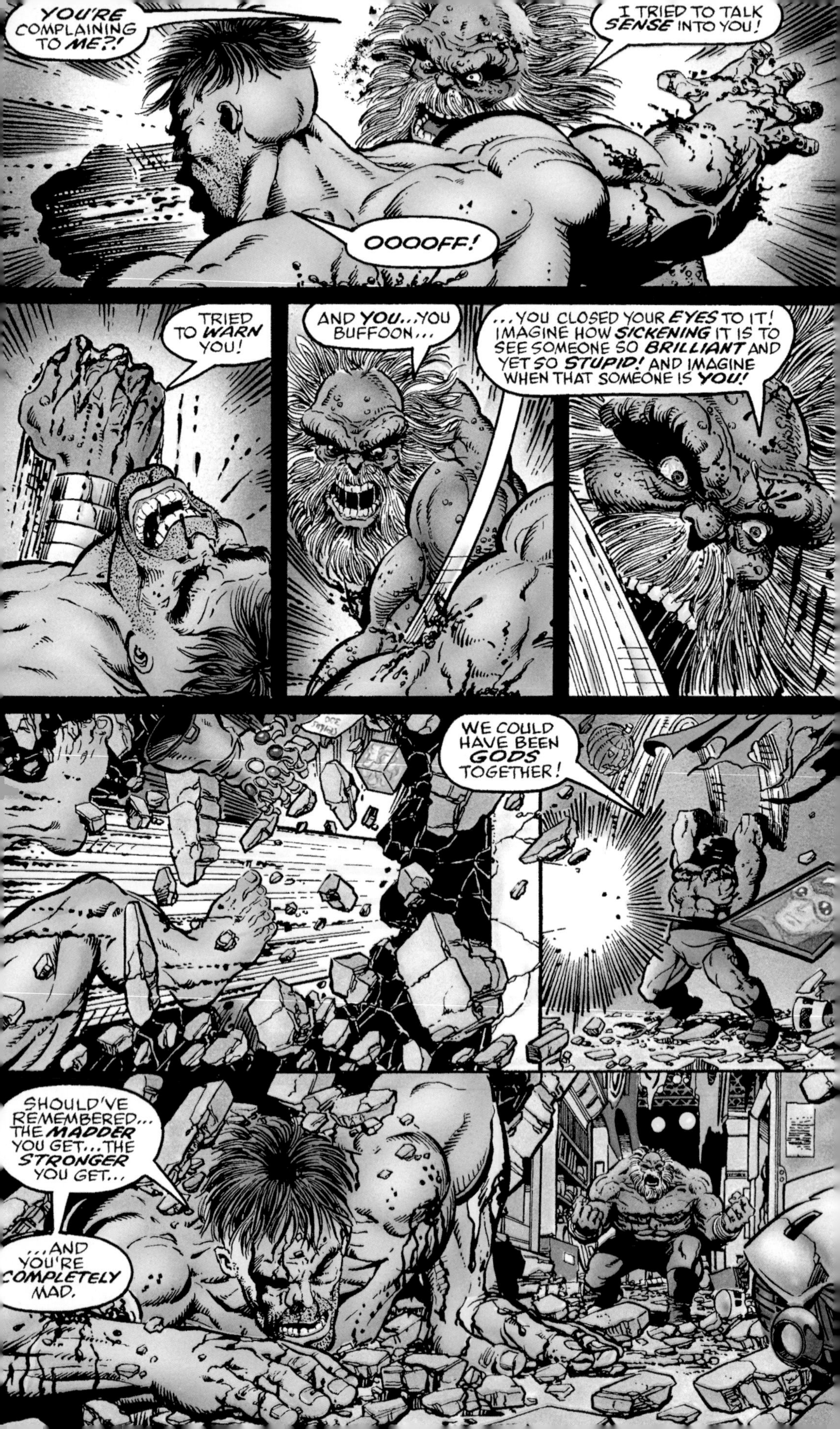
YOU'RE COMPLAINING TO ME?!
I TRIED TO TALK SENSE INTO YOU!
OOOOFF!
TRIED TO WARN YOU!
AND YOU...YOU BUFFOON...
...YOU CLOSED YOUR EYES TO IT! IMAGINE HOW SICKENING IT IS TO SEE SOMEONE SO BRILLIANT AND YET SO STUPID! AND IMAGINE WHEN THAT SOMEONE IS YOU!
WE COULD HAVE BEEN GODS TOGETHER!
SHOULD'VE REMEMBERED... THE MADDER YOU GET...THE STRONGER YOU GET...
...AND YOU'RE COMPLETELY MAD.

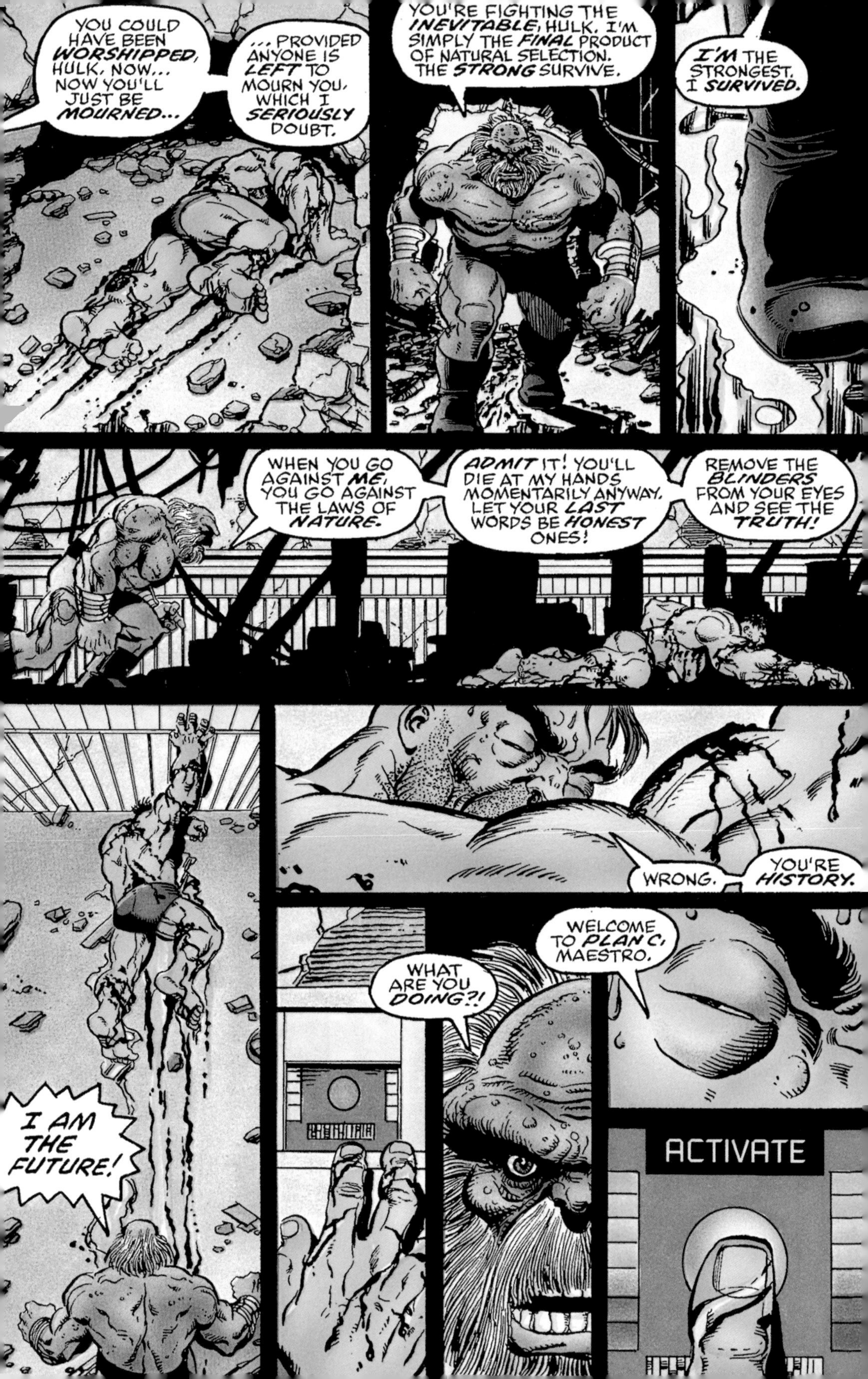
YOU COULD HAVE BEEN WORSHIPPED, HULK. NOW... NOW YOU'LL JUST BE MOURNED...
...PROVIDED ANYONE IS LEFT TO MOURN YOU, WHICH I SERIOUSLY DOUBT.
YOU'RE FIGHTING THE INEVITABLE, HULK. I'M SIMPLY THE FINAL PRODUCT OF NATURAL SELECTION. THE STRONG SURVIVE.
I'M THE STRONGEST. I SURVIVED.
WHEN YOU GO AGAINST ME, YOU GO AGAINST THE LAWS OF NATURE.
ADMIT IT! YOU'LL DIE AT MY HANDS MOMENTARILY ANYWAY. LET YOUR LAST WORDS BE HONEST ONES!
REMOVE THE BLINDERS FROM YOUR EYES AND SEE THE TRUTH!
I AM THE FUTURE!
WRONG.
YOU'RE HISTORY.
WELCOME TO PLAN C, MAESTRO.
WHAT ARE YOU DOING?!
ACTIVATE

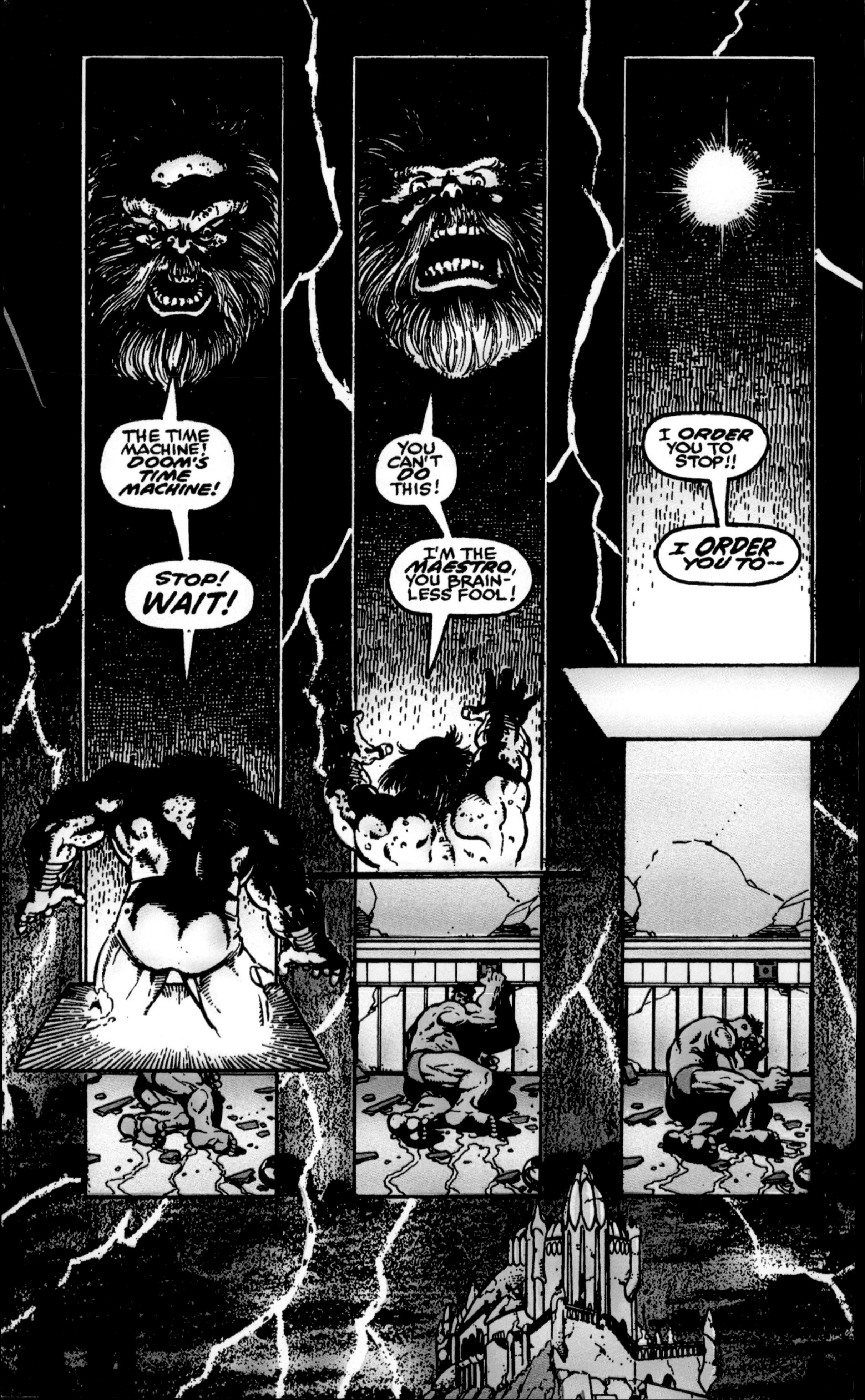
THE TIME MACHINE! DOOM'S TIME MACHINE!
STOP! WAIT!
YOU CAN'T DO THIS!
I'M THE MAESTRO, YOU BRAIN-LESS FOOL!
I ORDER YOU TO STOP!!
I ORDER YOU TO--

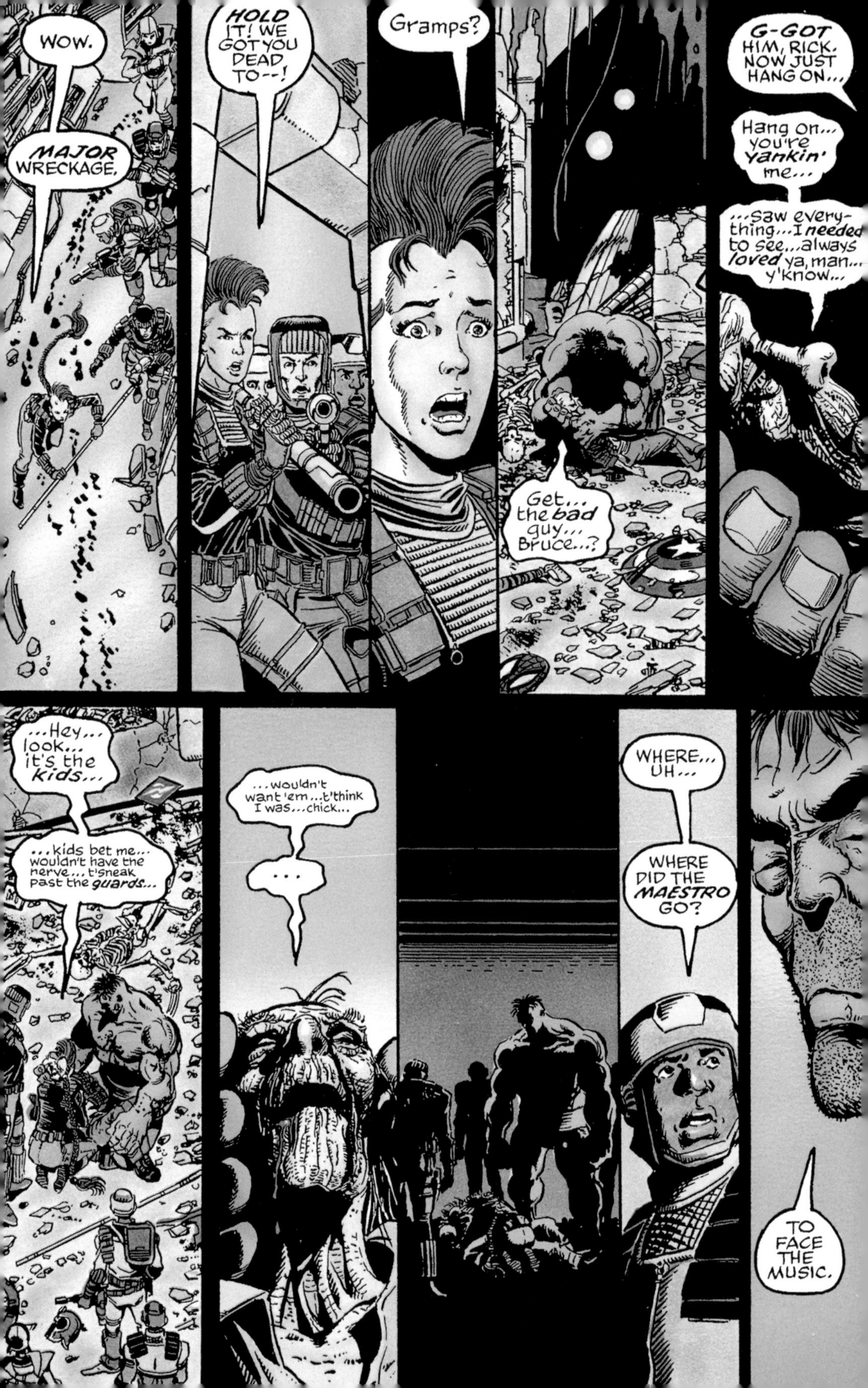
WOW.
MAJOR WRECKAGE.
HOLD IT! WE GOT YOU DEAD TO--!
Gramps?
G-GOT HIM, RICK. NOW JUST HANG ON...
Hang on... you're yankin' me...
...saw every-thing...I needed to see...always loved ya, man... y'know...
Get... the bad guy... Bruce...?
...Hey... look... it's the kids...
...kids bet me... wouldn't have the nerve... t'sneak past the guards...
...wouldn't want'em...t'think I was...chick...
...
WHERE... UH...
WHERE DID THE MAESTRO GO?
TO FACE THE MUSIC.

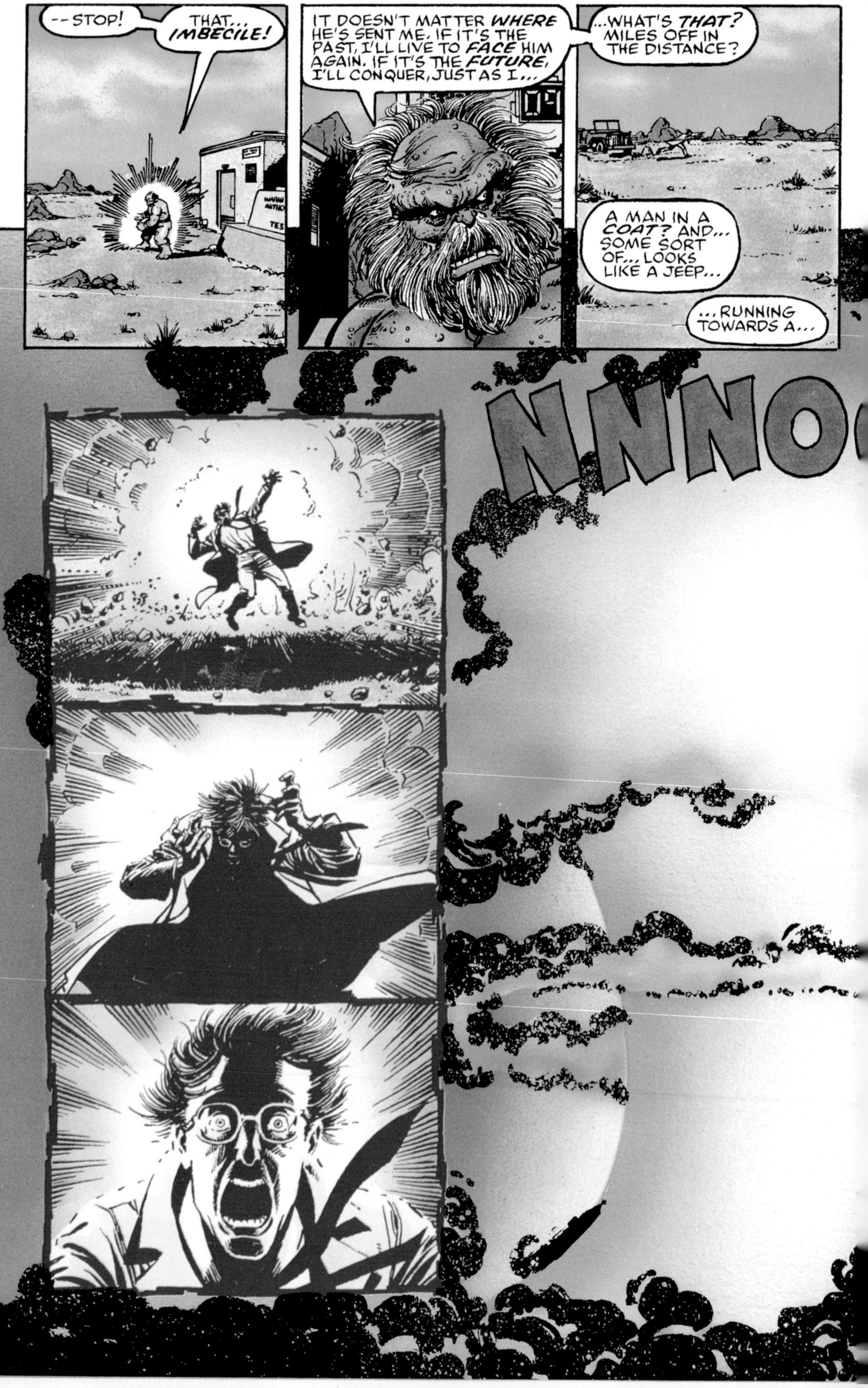
--STOP!
THAT... IMBECILE!
IT DOESN'T MATTER WHERE HE'S SENT ME. IF IT'S THE PAST, I'LL LIVE TO FACE HIM AGAIN. IF IT'S THE FUTURE, I'LL CONQUER, JUST AS I...
...WHAT'S THAT? MILES OFF IN THE DISTANCE?
A MAN IN A COAT? AND... SOME SORT OF... LOOKS LIKE A JEEP...
...RUNNING TOWARDS A...
NNNO

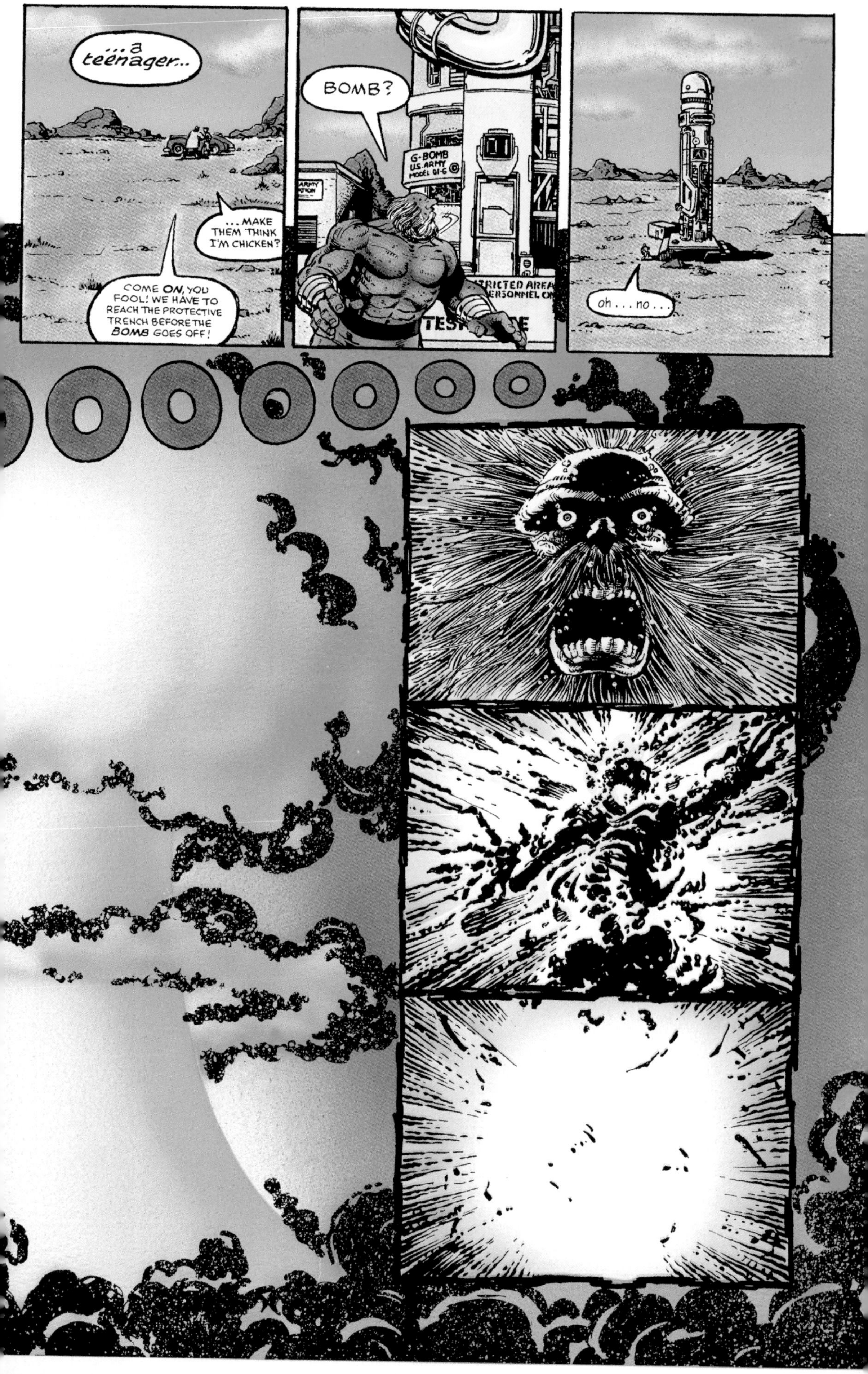
...a teenager...
...MAKE THEM THINK I'M CHICKEN?
COME ON, YOU FOOL! WE HAVE TO REACH THE PROTECTIVE TRENCH BEFORE THE BOMB GOES OFF!
BOMB?
G-BOMB U.S. ARMY MODEL 91-G ©
oh... no...

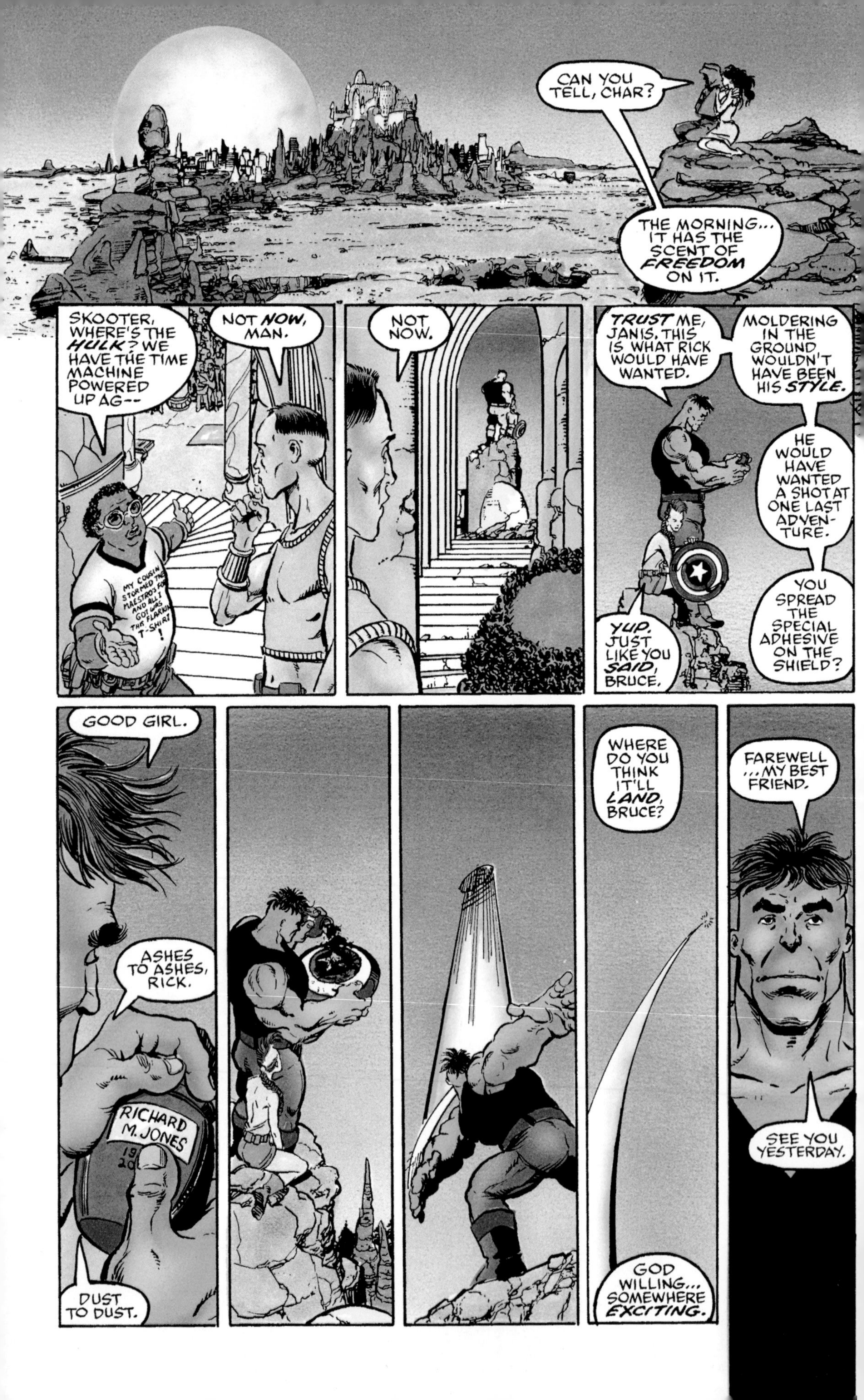
CAN YOU TELL, CHAR?
THE MORNING... IT HAS THE SCENT OF FREEDOM ON IT.
SKOOTER, WHERE'S THE HULK? WE HAVE THE TIME MACHINE POWERED UP AG--
NOT NOW, MAN.
MY COUSIN STORMED THE MAESTRO'S FOR AND ALL I GOT WAS THIS FLARKIN T-SHIRT !
NOT NOW.
TRUST ME, JANIS. THIS IS WHAT RICK WOULD HAVE WANTED.
MOLDERING IN THE GROUND WOULDN'T HAVE BEEN HIS STYLE.
HE WOULD HAVE WANTED A SHOT AT ONE LAST ADVEN-TURE.
YOU SPREAD THE SPECIAL ADHESIVE ON THE SHIELD?
YUP. JUST LIKE YOU SAID, BRUCE.
GOOD GIRL.
ASHES TO ASHES, RICK.
RICHARD M. JONES
19
20
DUST TO DUST.
WHERE DO YOU THINK IT'LL LAND, BRUCE?
GOD WILLING... SOMEWHERE EXCITING.
FAREWELL... MY BEST FRIEND.
SEE YOU YESTERDAY.

MARVEL® GRAPHIC NOVEL THE INCREDIBLE HULK (Vol. 3) #25

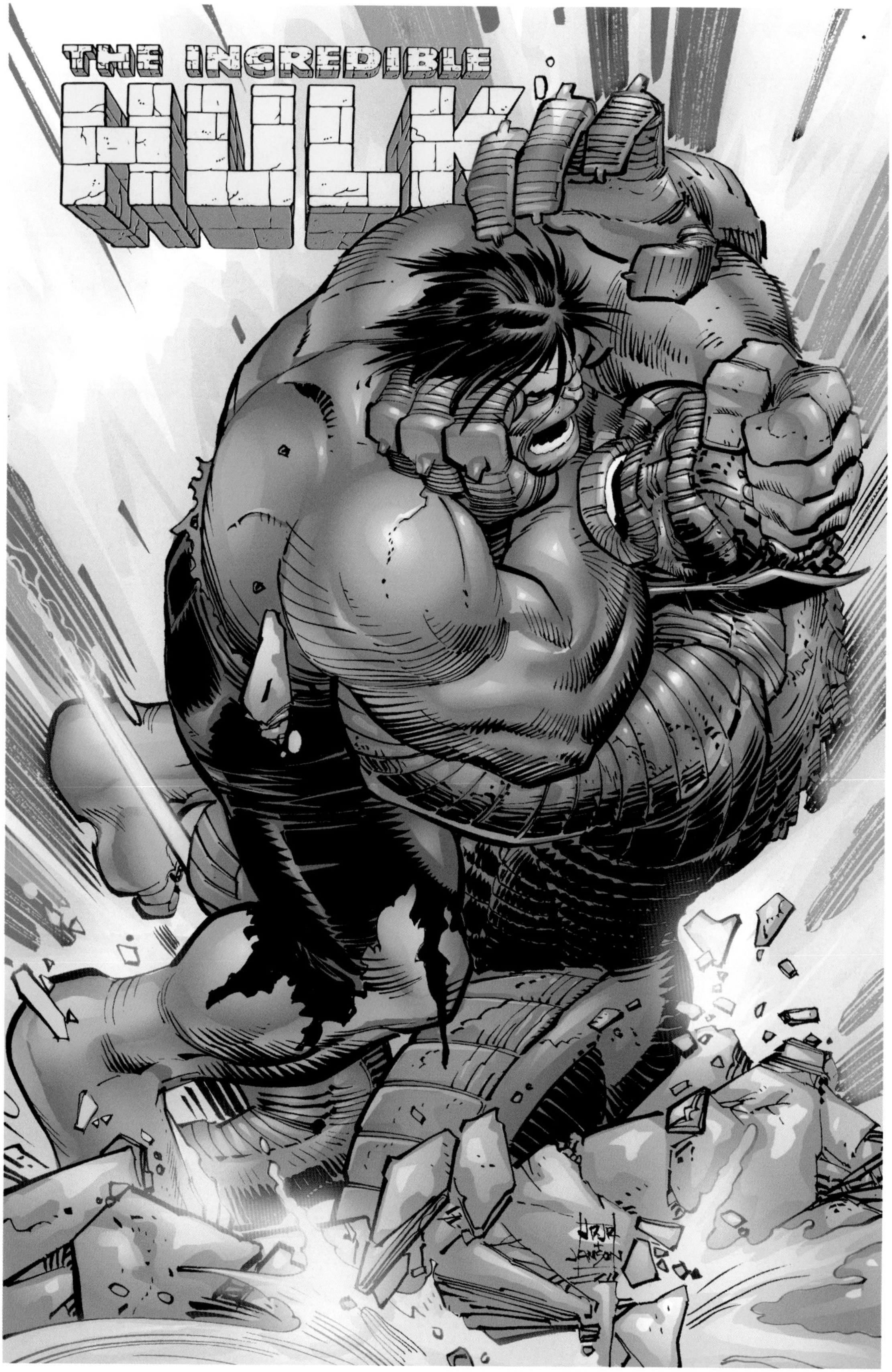
THE INCREDIBLE
HULK

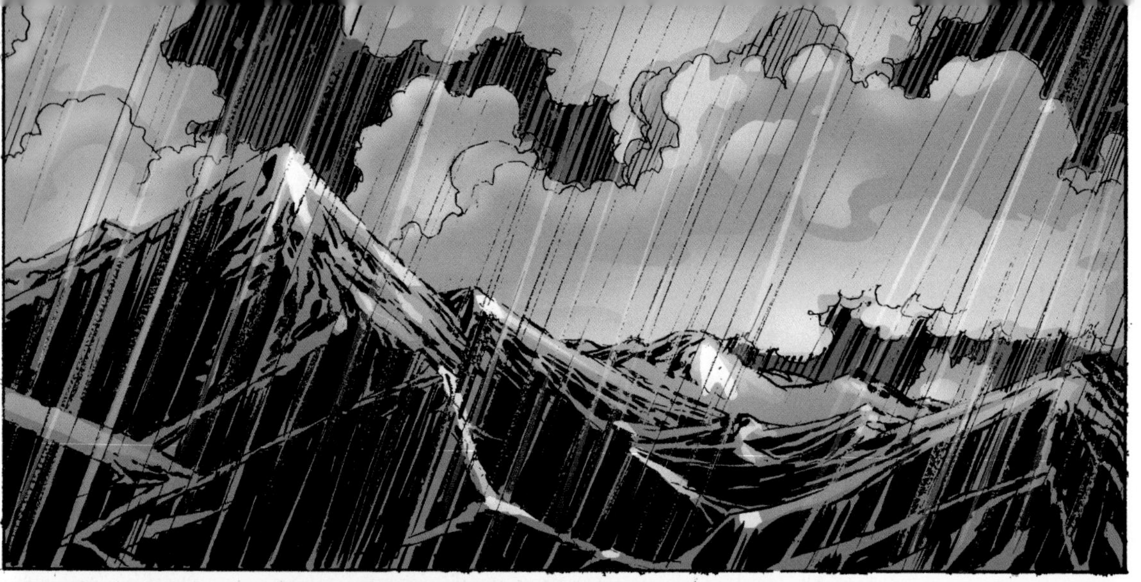

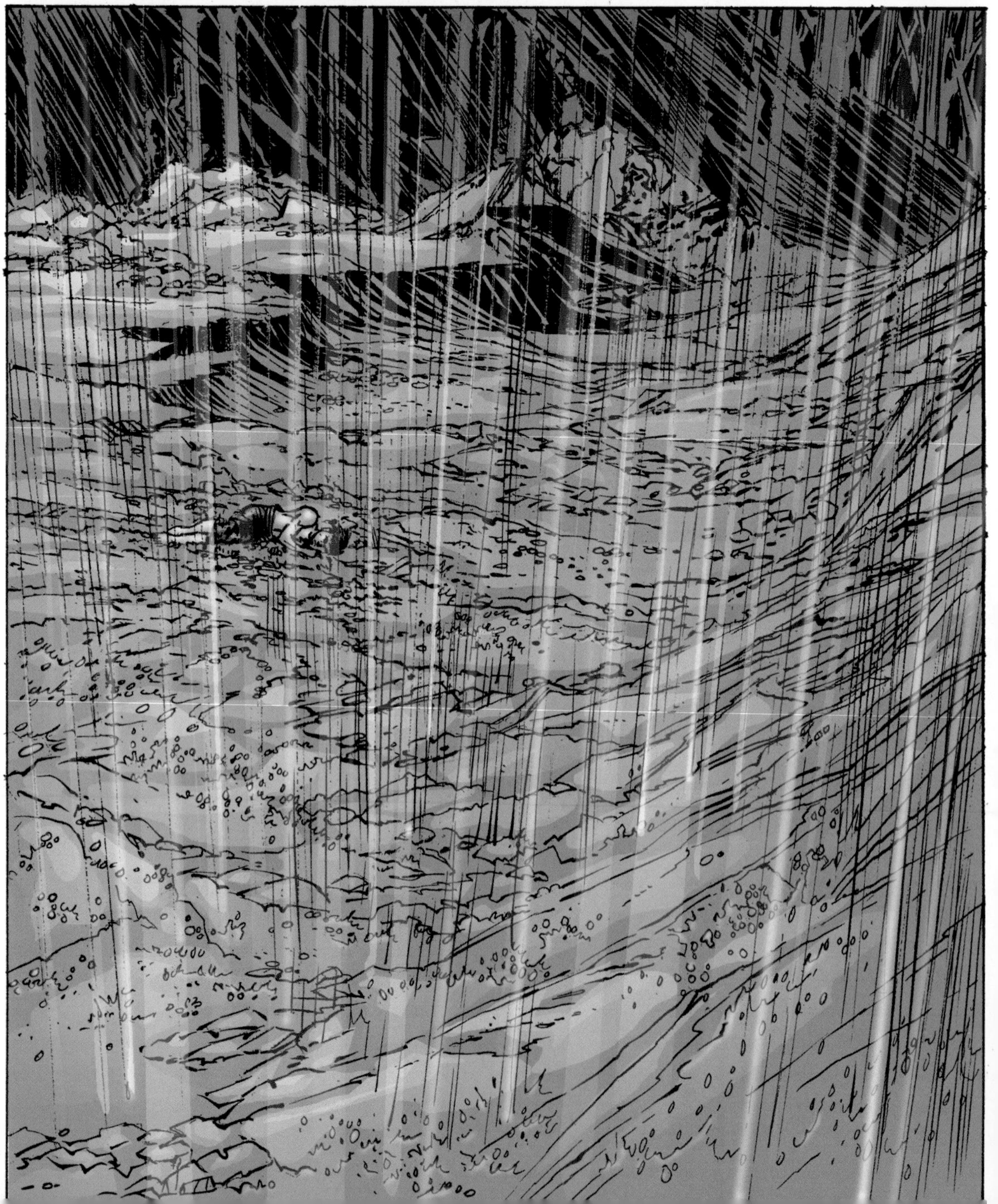

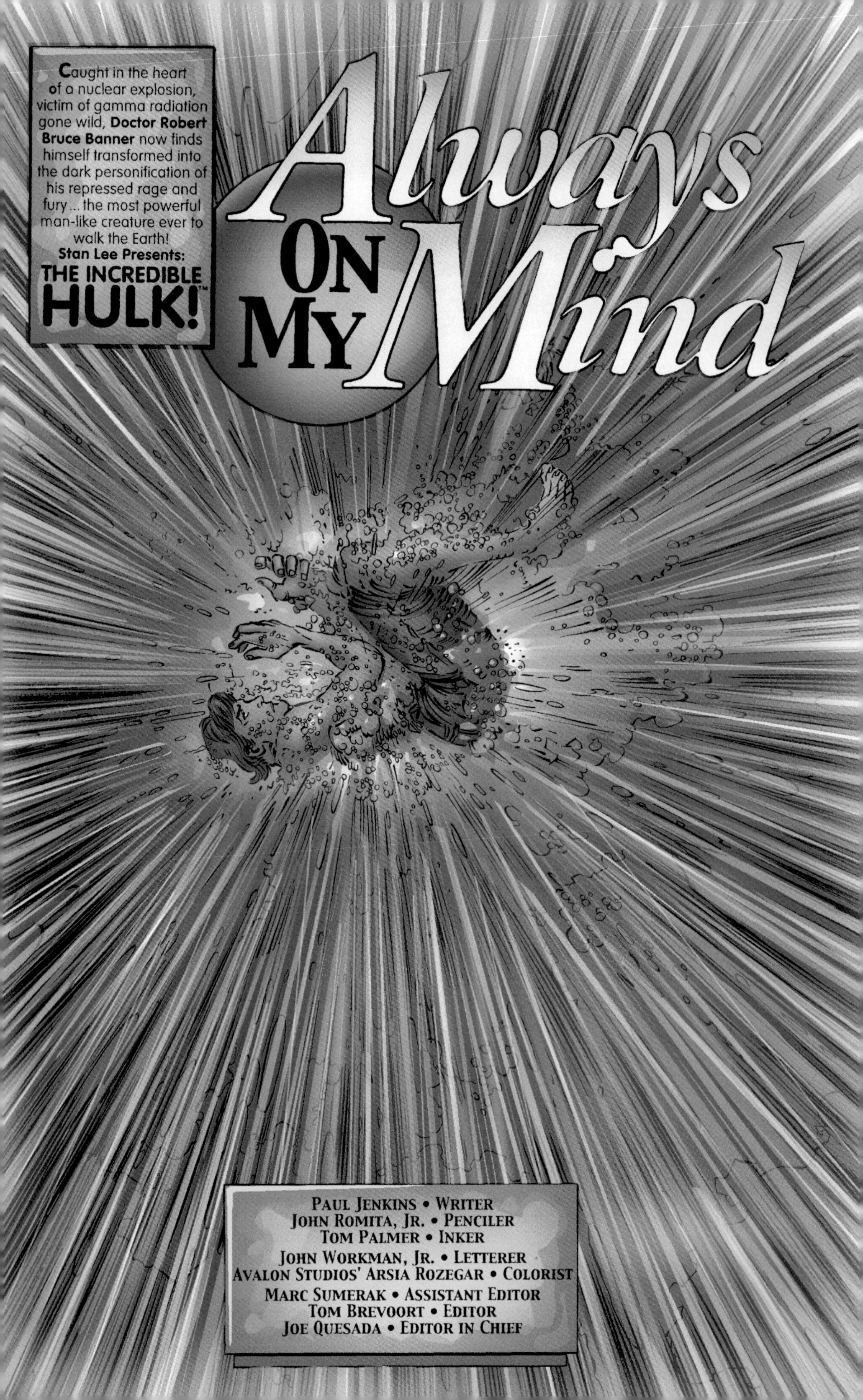
Caught in the heart of a nuclear explosion, victim of gamma radiation gone wild, Doctor Robert Bruce Banner now finds himself transformed into the dark personification of his repressed rage and fury ... the most powerful man-like creature ever to walk the Earth!
Stan Lee Presents:
THE INCREDIBLE HULK!™
Always On My Mind
PAUL JENKINS • WRITER
JOHN ROMITA, JR. • PENCILER
TOM PALMER • INKER
JOHN WORKMAN, JR. • LETTERER
AVALON STUDIOS' ARSIA ROZEGAR • COLORIST
MARC SUMERAK • ASSISTANT EDITOR
TOM BREVOORT • EDITOR
JOE QUESADA • EDITOR IN CHIEF

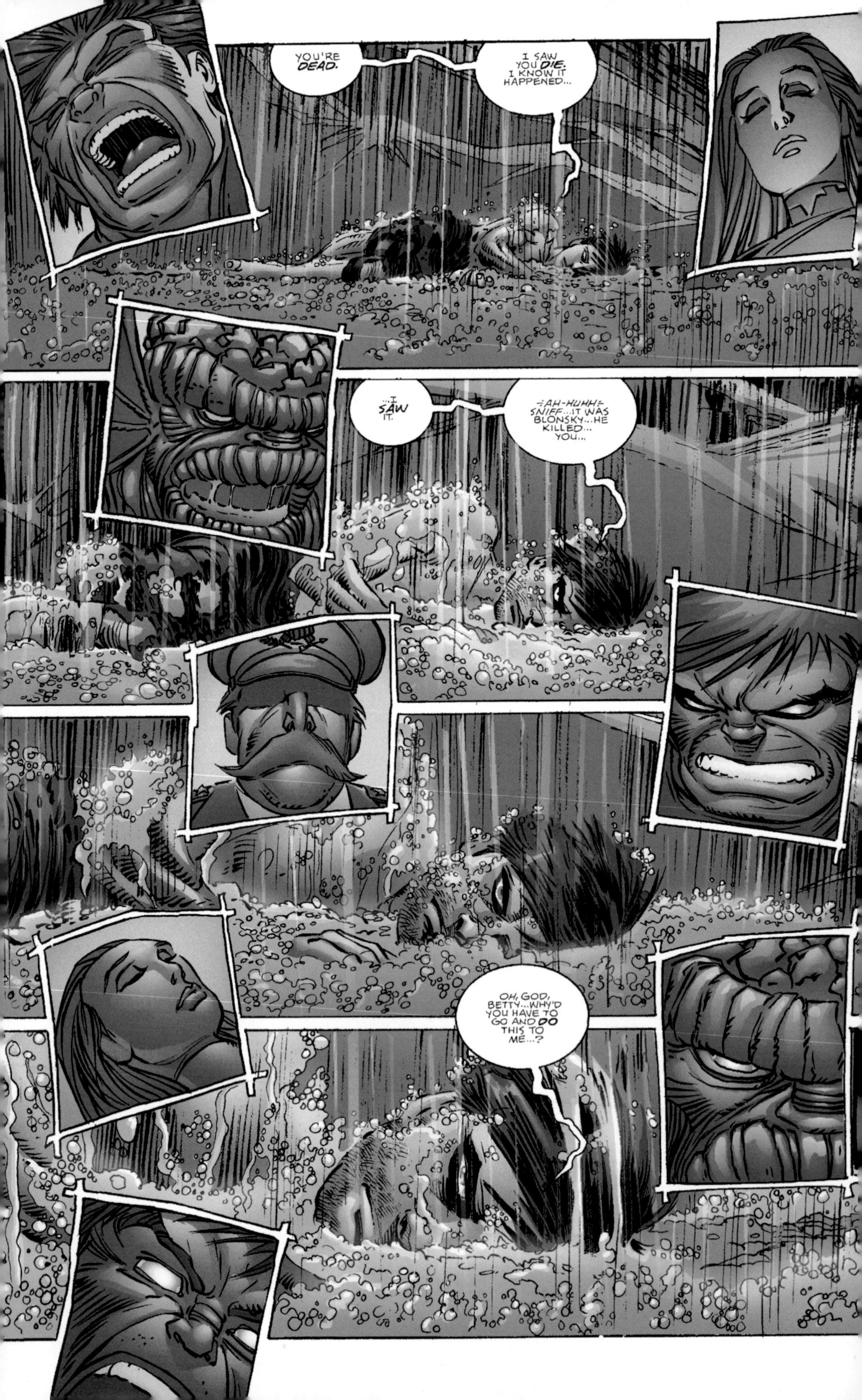
YOU'RE DEAD.
I SAW YOU DIE. I KNOW IT HAPPENED...
...I SAW IT.
-AH-HUHH- SNIFF...IT WAS BLONSKY...HE KILLED... YOU...
OH, GOD, BETTY...WHY'D YOU HAVE TO GO AND DO THIS TO ME...?

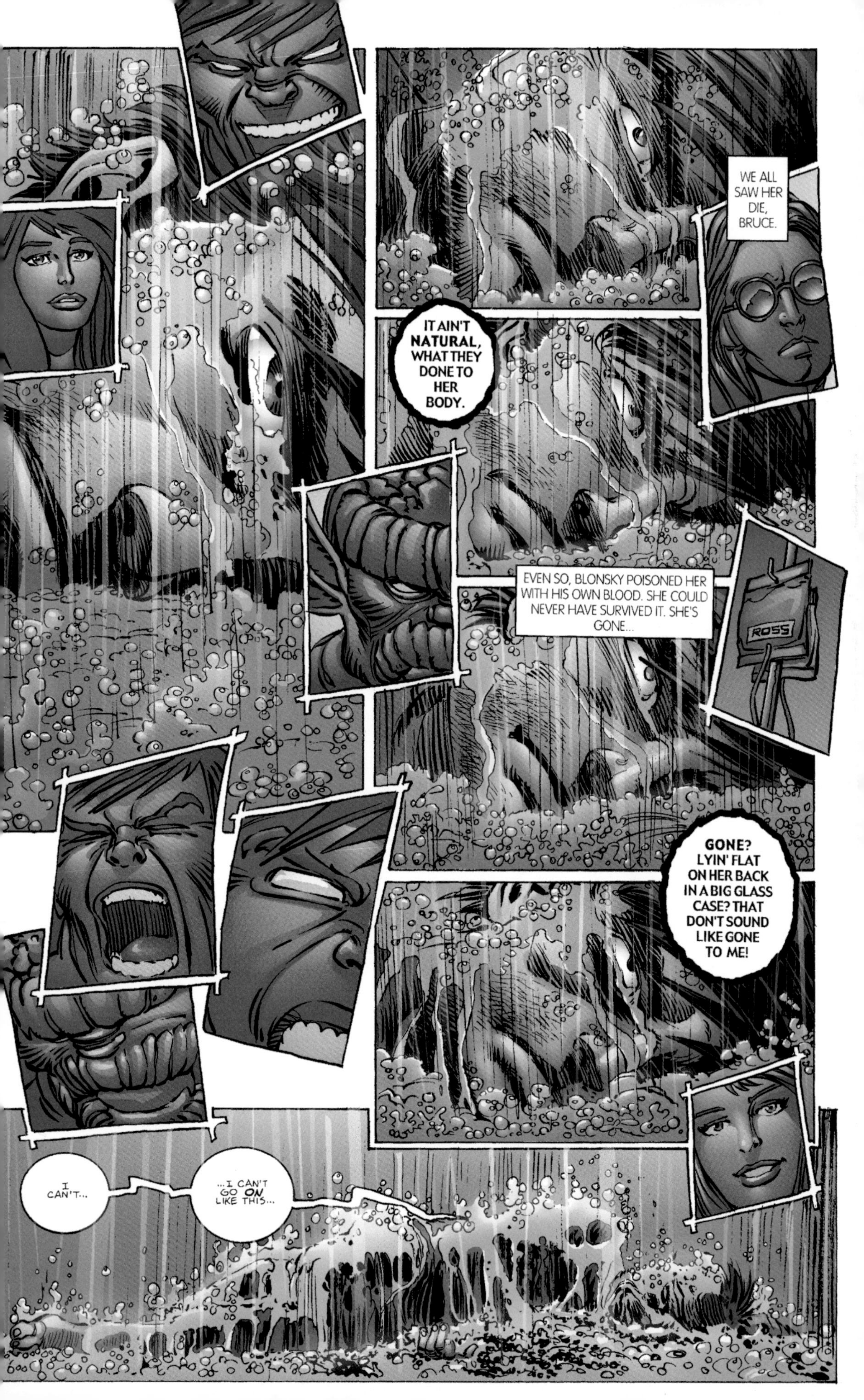
WE ALL SAW HER DIE, BRUCE.
IT AIN'T NATURAL, WHAT THEY DONE TO HER BODY.
EVEN SO, BLONSKY POISONED HER WITH HIS OWN BLOOD. SHE COULD NEVER HAVE SURVIVED IT. SHE'S GONE...
ROSS
GONE? LYIN' FLAT ON HER BACK IN A BIG GLASS CASE? THAT DON'T SOUND LIKE GONE TO ME!
I CAN'T...
...I CAN'T GO ON LIKE THIS...

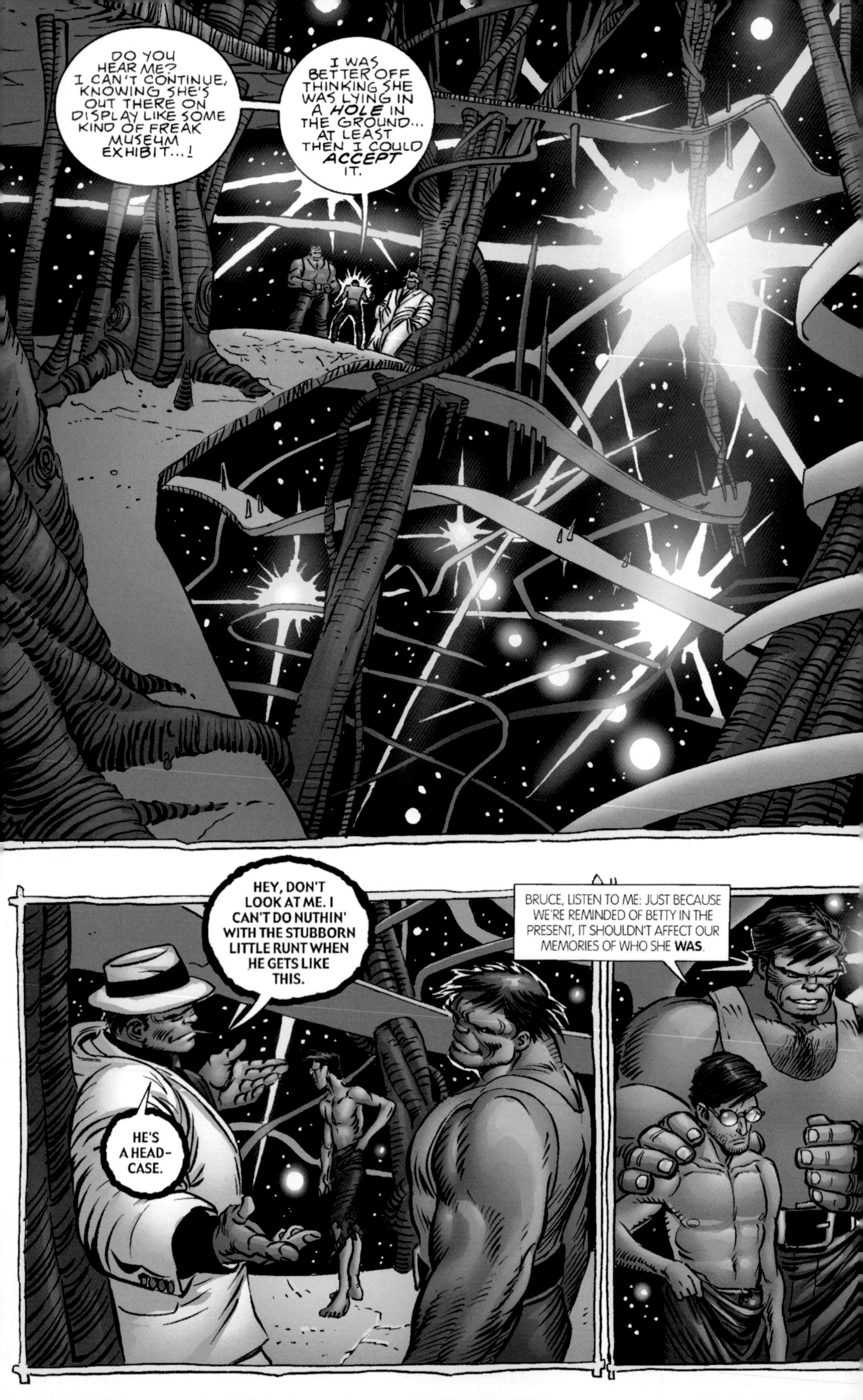
DO YOU HEAR ME? I CAN'T CONTINUE, KNOWING SHE'S OUT THERE ON DISPLAY LIKE SOME KIND OF FREAK MUSEUM EXHIBIT...!
I WAS BETTER OFF THINKING SHE WAS LYING IN A HOLE IN THE GROUND... AT LEAST THEN I COULD ACCEPT IT.
HEY, DON'T LOOK AT ME. I CAN'T DO NUTHIN' WITH THE STUBBORN LITTLE RUNT WHEN HE GETS LIKE THIS.
HE'S A HEAD-CASE.
BRUCE, LISTEN TO ME: JUST BECAUSE WE'RE REMINDED OF BETTY IN THE PRESENT, IT SHOULDN'T AFFECT OUR MEMORIES OF WHO SHE WAS.

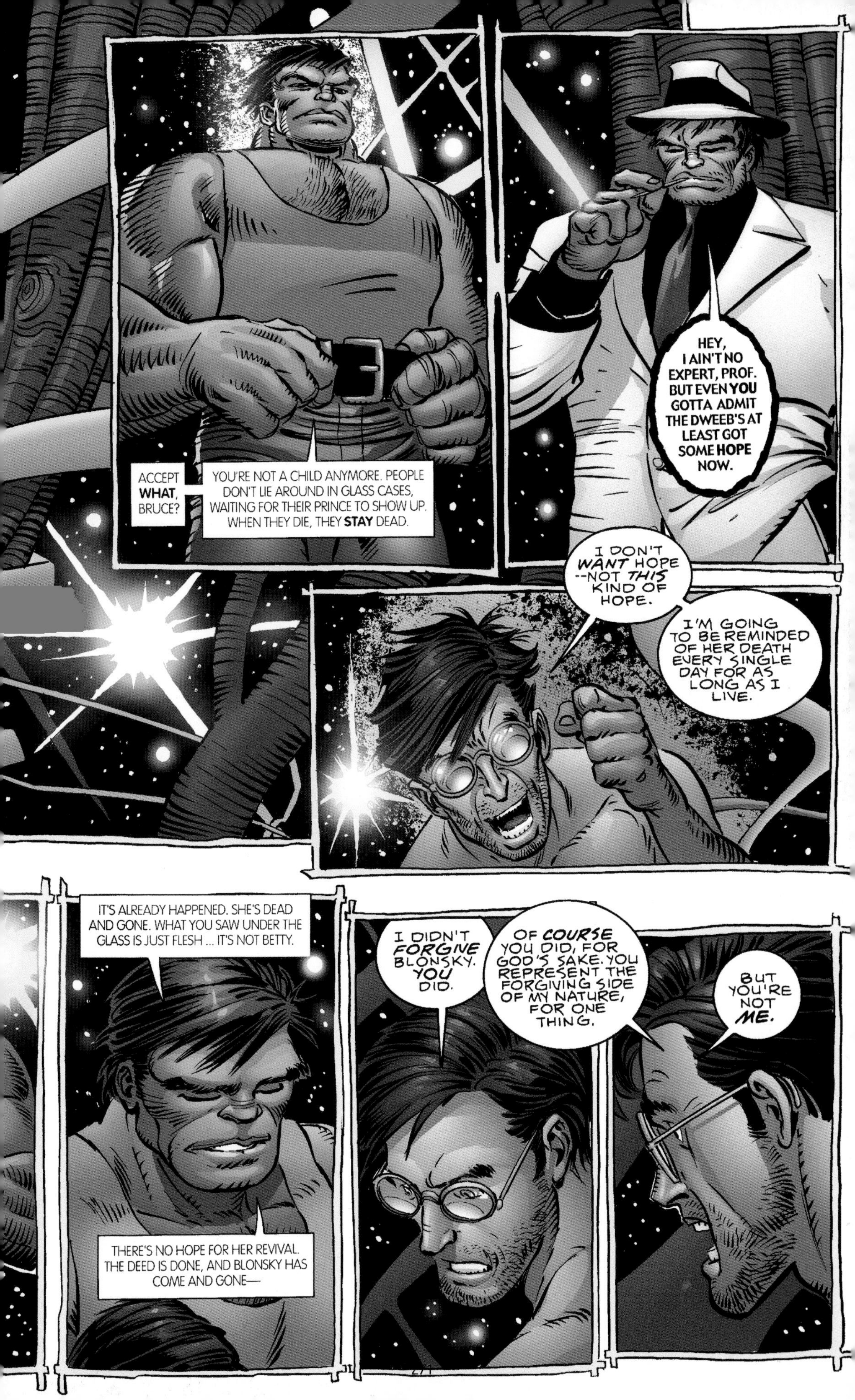

ACCEPT **WHAT**, BRUCE?
YOU'RE NOT A CHILD ANYMORE. PEOPLE DON'T LIE AROUND IN GLASS CASES, WAITING FOR THEIR PRINCE TO SHOW UP. WHEN THEY DIE, THEY **STAY** DEAD.
HEY, I AIN'T NO EXPERT, PROF. BUT EVEN **YOU** GOTTA ADMIT THE DWEEB'S AT LEAST GOT SOME **HOPE** NOW.
I DON'T *WANT* HOPE --NOT *THIS* KIND OF HOPE.
I'M GOING TO BE REMINDED OF HER DEATH EVERY SINGLE DAY FOR AS LONG AS I LIVE.
IT'S ALREADY HAPPENED. SHE'S DEAD AND GONE. WHAT YOU SAW UNDER THE GLASS IS JUST FLESH ... IT'S NOT BETTY.
THERE'S NO HOPE FOR HER REVIVAL. THE DEED IS DONE, AND BLONSKY HAS COME AND GONE—
I DIDN'T *FORGIVE* BLONSKY. *YOU* DID.
OF *COURSE* YOU DID, FOR GOD'S SAKE. YOU REPRESENT THE FORGIVING SIDE OF MY NATURE, FOR ONE THING.
BUT YOU'RE NOT *ME*.

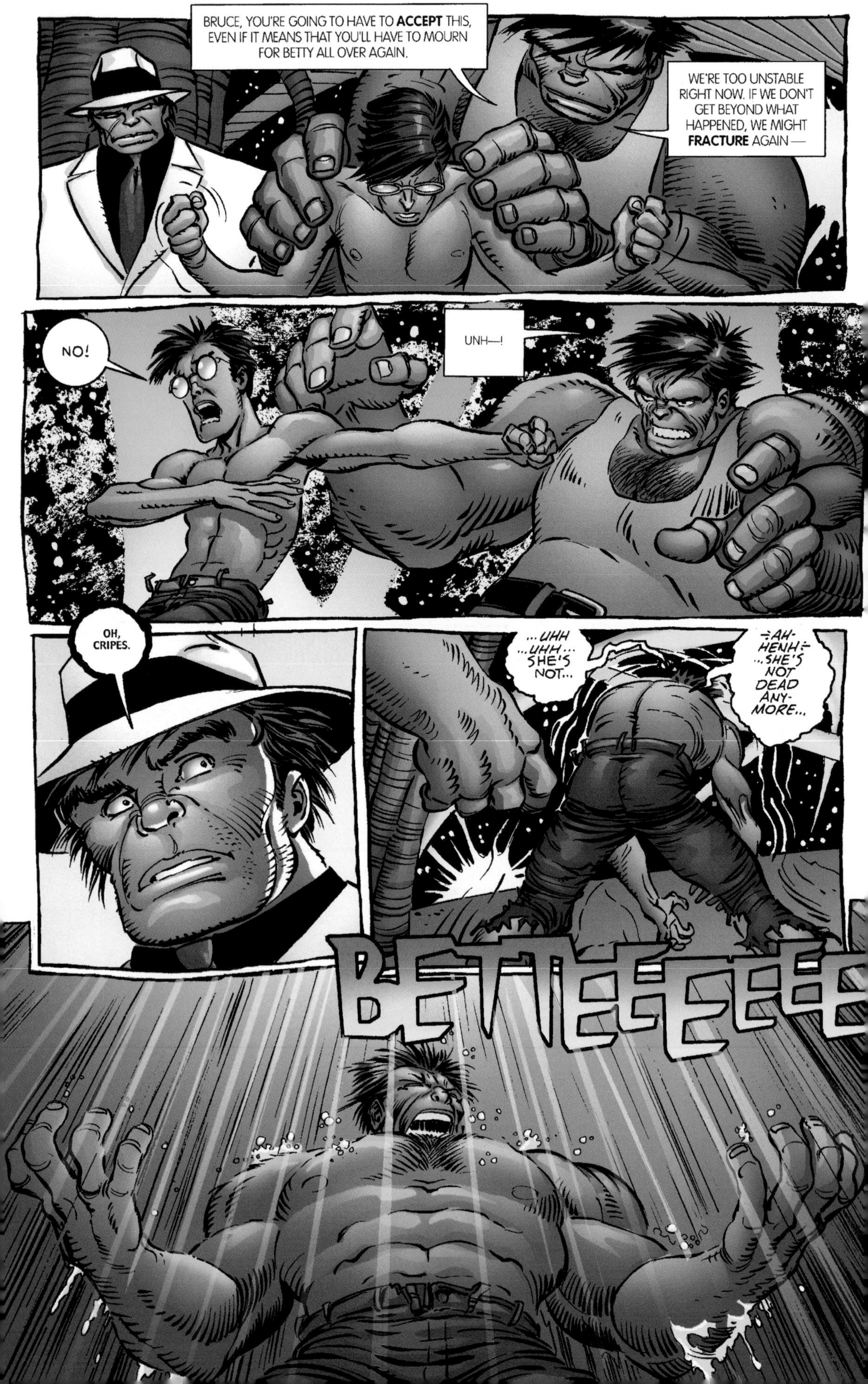
BRUCE, YOU'RE GOING TO HAVE TO ACCEPT THIS, EVEN IF IT MEANS THAT YOU'LL HAVE TO MOURN FOR BETTY ALL OVER AGAIN.
WE'RE TOO UNSTABLE RIGHT NOW. IF WE DON'T GET BEYOND WHAT HAPPENED, WE MIGHT FRACTURE AGAIN —
NO!
UNH—!
OH, CRIPES.
...UHH ...UHH... SHE'S NOT...
AH-HENH ...SHE'S NOT DEAD ANY-MORE...
BETTEEEEE

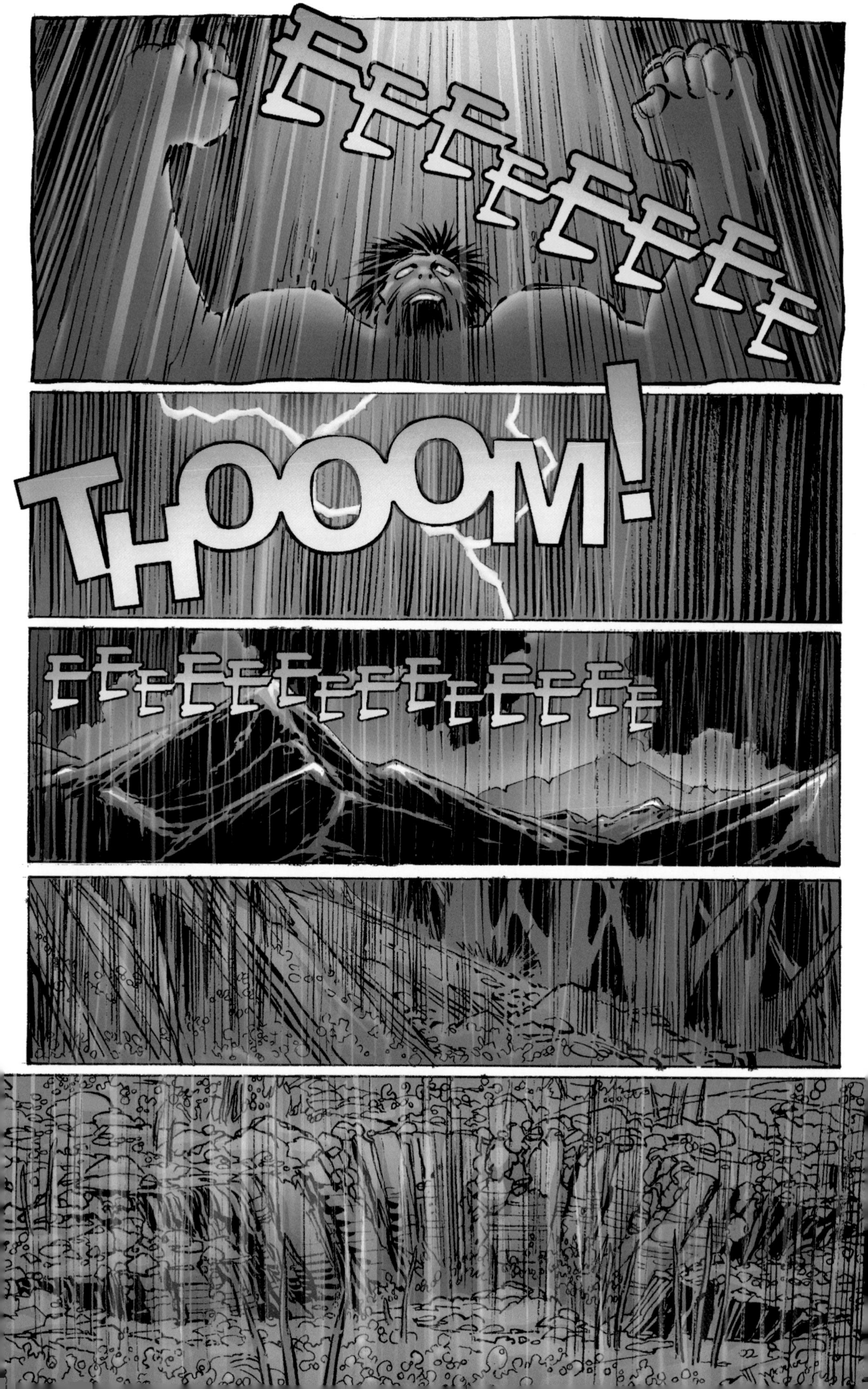
EEEEEEEE
THOOOM!
EEEEEEEEEEEEEE

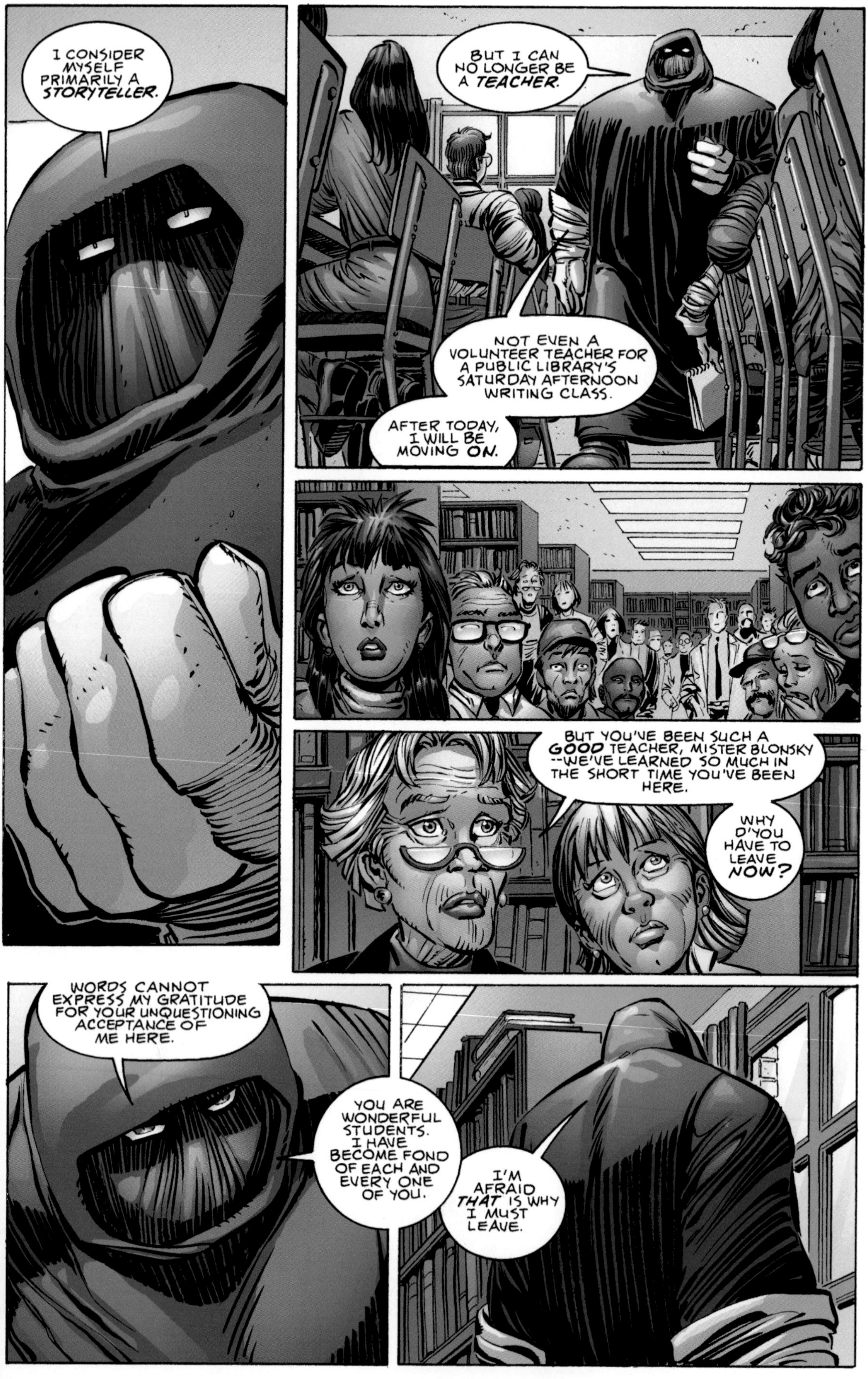

I CONSIDER MYSELF PRIMARILY A STORYTELLER.
BUT I CAN NO LONGER BE A TEACHER.
NOT EVEN A VOLUNTEER TEACHER FOR A PUBLIC LIBRARY'S SATURDAY AFTERNOON WRITING CLASS.
AFTER TODAY, I WILL BE MOVING ON.
BUT YOU'VE BEEN SUCH A GOOD TEACHER, MISTER BLONSKY --WE'VE LEARNED SO MUCH IN THE SHORT TIME YOU'VE BEEN HERE.
WHY D'YOU HAVE TO LEAVE NOW?
WORDS CANNOT EXPRESS MY GRATITUDE FOR YOUR UNQUESTIONING ACCEPTANCE OF ME HERE.
YOU ARE WONDERFUL STUDENTS. I HAVE BECOME FOND OF EACH AND EVERY ONE OF YOU.
I'M AFRAID THAT IS WHY I MUST LEAVE.

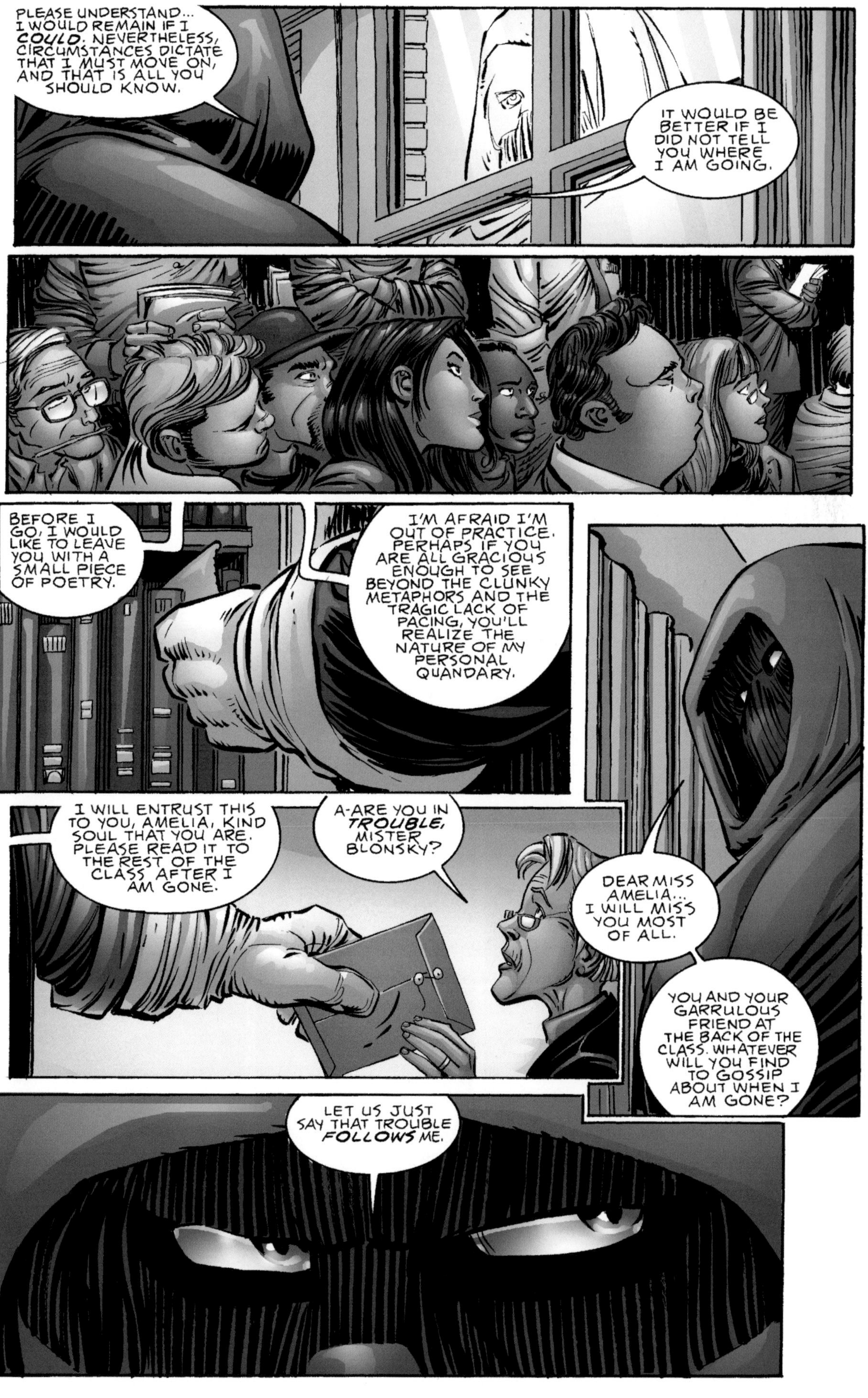
PLEASE UNDERSTAND... I WOULD REMAIN IF I COULD. NEVERTHELESS, CIRCUMSTANCES DICTATE THAT I MUST MOVE ON, AND THAT IS ALL YOU SHOULD KNOW.
IT WOULD BE BETTER IF I DID NOT TELL YOU WHERE I AM GOING.
BEFORE I GO, I WOULD LIKE TO LEAVE YOU WITH A SMALL PIECE OF POETRY.
I'M AFRAID I'M OUT OF PRACTICE. PERHAPS IF YOU ARE ALL GRACIOUS ENOUGH TO SEE BEYOND THE CLUNKY METAPHORS AND THE TRAGIC LACK OF PACING, YOU'LL REALIZE THE NATURE OF MY PERSONAL QUANDARY.
I WILL ENTRUST THIS TO YOU, AMELIA, KIND SOUL THAT YOU ARE. PLEASE READ IT TO THE REST OF THE CLASS AFTER I AM GONE.
A-ARE YOU IN TROUBLE, MISTER BLONSKY?
DEAR MISS AMELIA... I WILL MISS YOU MOST OF ALL.
YOU AND YOUR GARRULOUS FRIEND AT THE BACK OF THE CLASS. WHATEVER WILL YOU FIND TO GOSSIP ABOUT WHEN I AM GONE?
LET US JUST SAY THAT TROUBLE FOLLOWS ME.

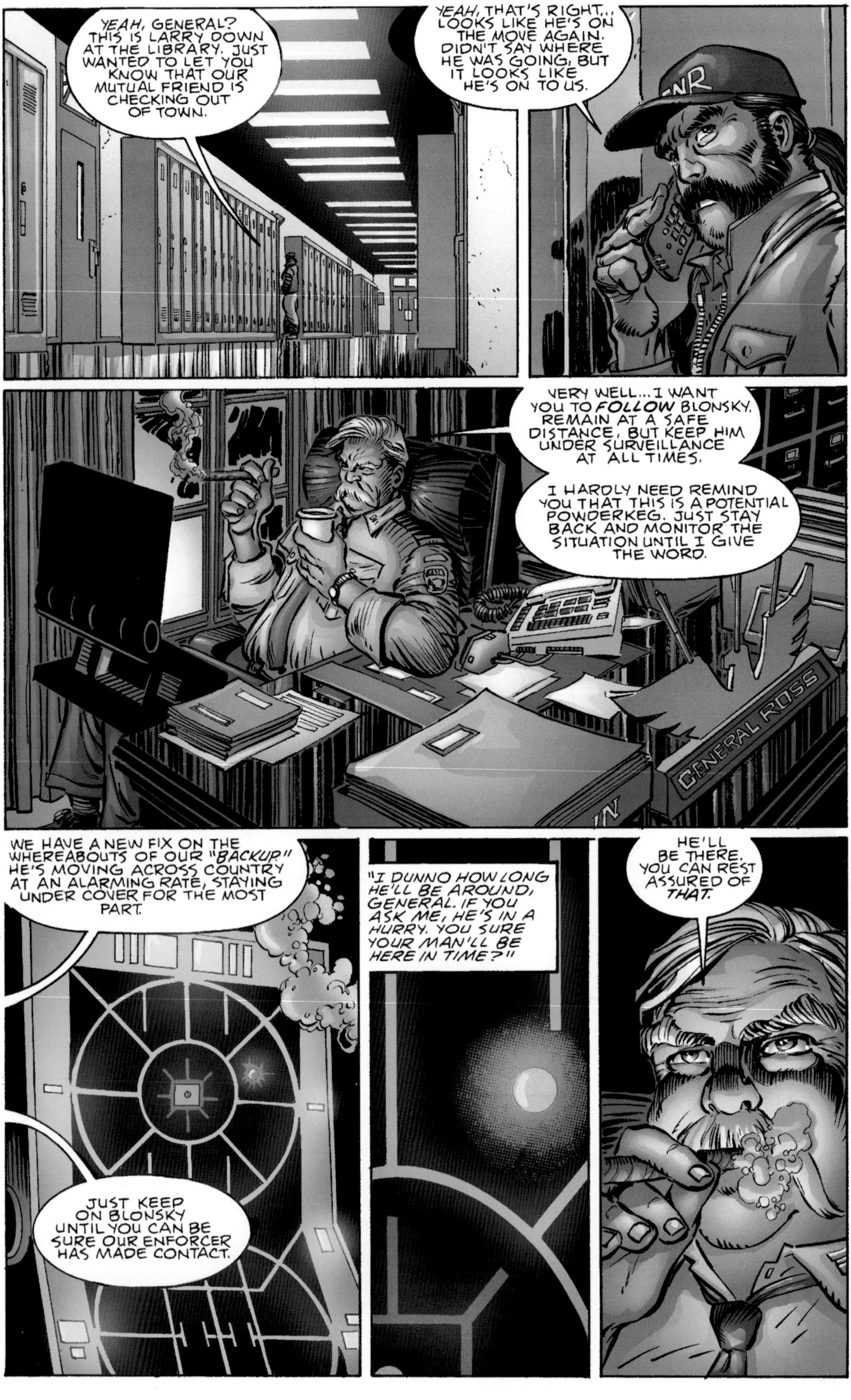
YEAH, GENERAL? THIS IS LARRY DOWN AT THE LIBRARY. JUST WANTED TO LET YOU KNOW THAT OUR MUTUAL FRIEND IS CHECKING OUT OF TOWN.
YEAH, THAT'S RIGHT... LOOKS LIKE HE'S ON THE MOVE AGAIN. DIDN'T SAY WHERE HE WAS GOING, BUT IT LOOKS LIKE HE'S ON TO US.
VERY WELL... I WANT YOU TO FOLLOW BLONSKY. REMAIN AT A SAFE DISTANCE, BUT KEEP HIM UNDER SURVEILLANCE AT ALL TIMES.
I HARDLY NEED REMIND YOU THAT THIS IS A POTENTIAL POWDERKEG. JUST STAY BACK AND MONITOR THE SITUATION UNTIL I GIVE THE WORD.
GENERAL ROSS
WE HAVE A NEW FIX ON THE WHEREABOUTS OF OUR "BACKUP." HE'S MOVING ACROSS COUNTRY AT AN ALARMING RATE, STAYING UNDER COVER FOR THE MOST PART.
JUST KEEP ON BLONSKY UNTIL YOU CAN BE SURE OUR ENFORCER HAS MADE CONTACT.
"I DUNNO HOW LONG HE'LL BE AROUND, GENERAL. IF YOU ASK ME, HE'S IN A HURRY. YOU SURE YOUR MAN'LL BE HERE IN TIME?"
HE'LL BE THERE. YOU CAN REST ASSURED OF THAT.

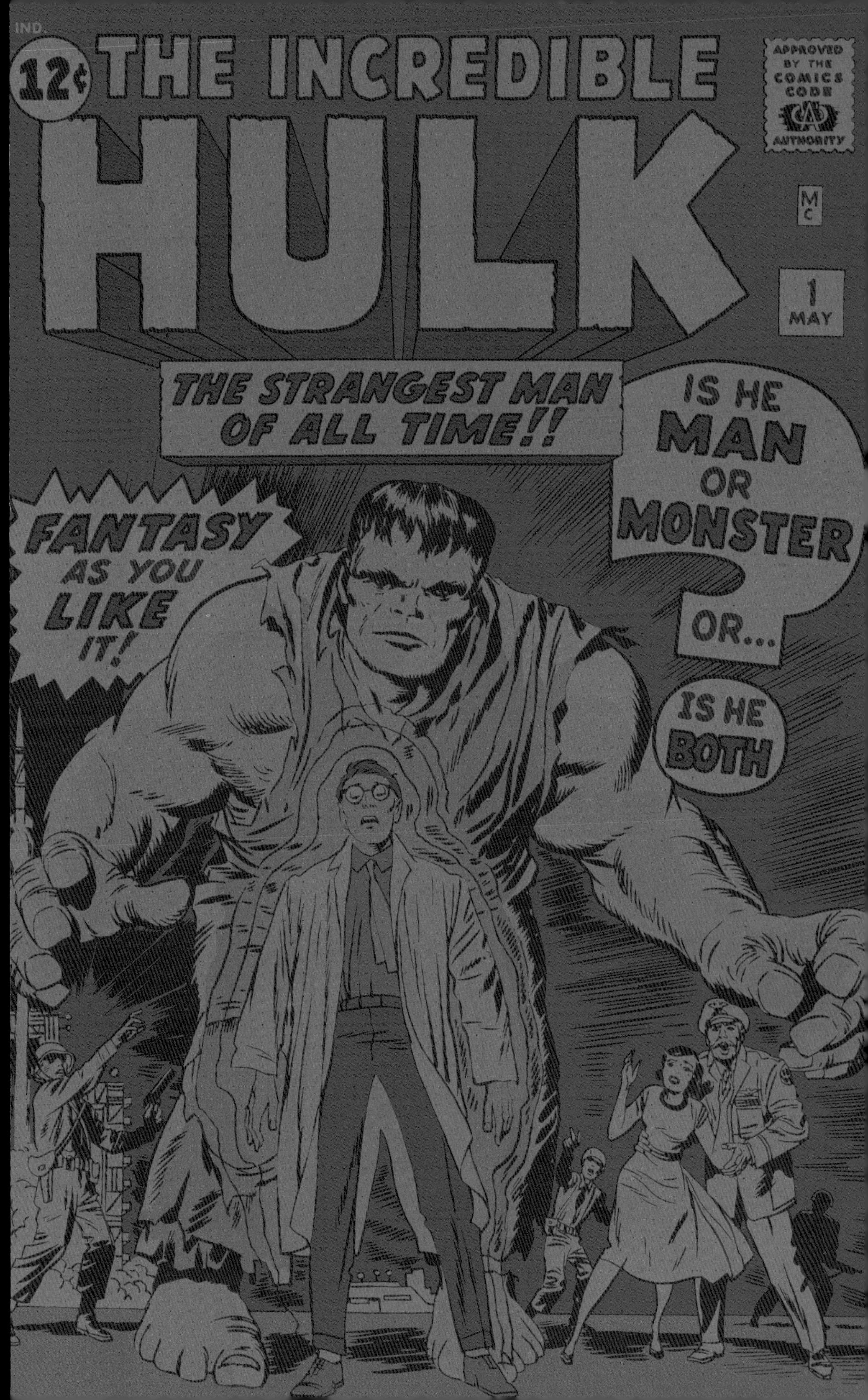
IND.
12¢
THE INCREDIBLE
HULK
APPROVED BY THE COMICS CODE AUTHORITY
MC
1
MAY
THE STRANGEST MAN OF ALL TIME!!
IS HE MAN OR MONSTER
OR...
IS HE BOTH
FANTASY AS YOU LIKE IT!

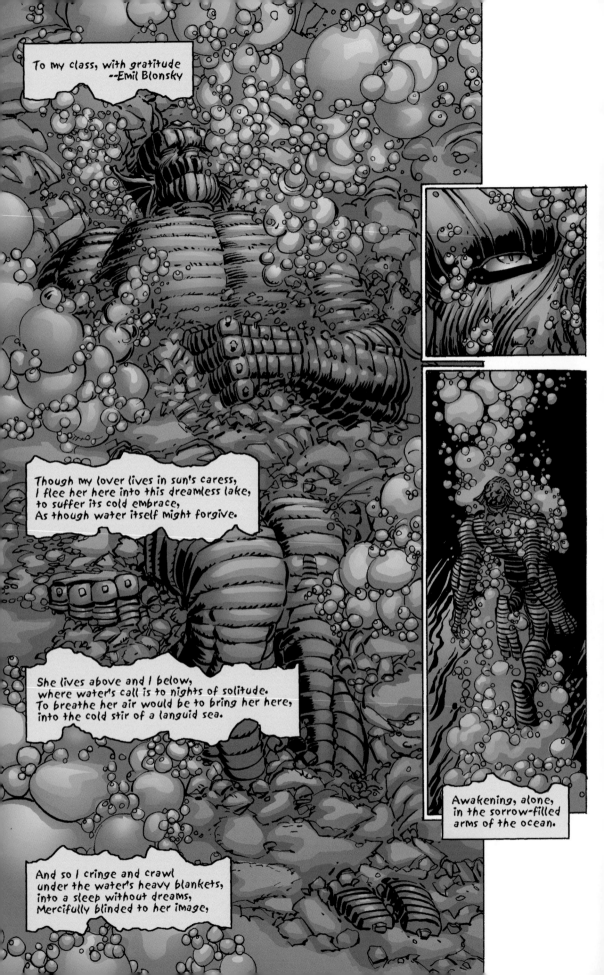

To my class, with gratitude
--Emil Blonsky

Though my lover lives in sun's caress,
I flee her here into this dreamless lake,
to suffer its cold embrace,
As though water itself might forgive.

She lives above and I below,
where water's call is to nights of solitude.
To breathe her air would be to bring her here,
into the cold stir of a languid sea.

And so I cringe and crawl
under the water's heavy blankets,
into a sleep without dreams,
Mercifully blinded to her image,

Awakening, alone,
in the sorrow-filled
arms of the ocean.

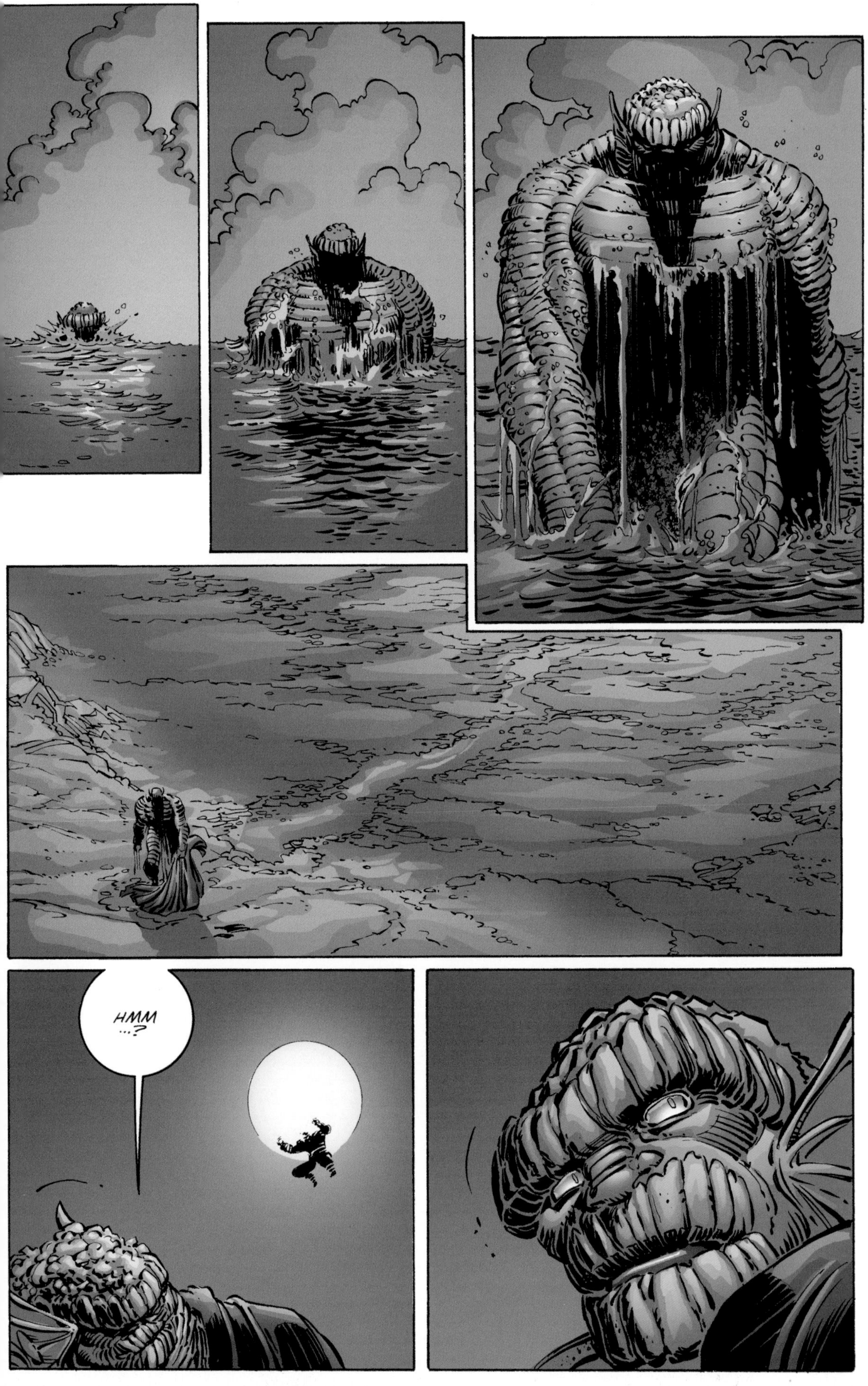
HMM ...?

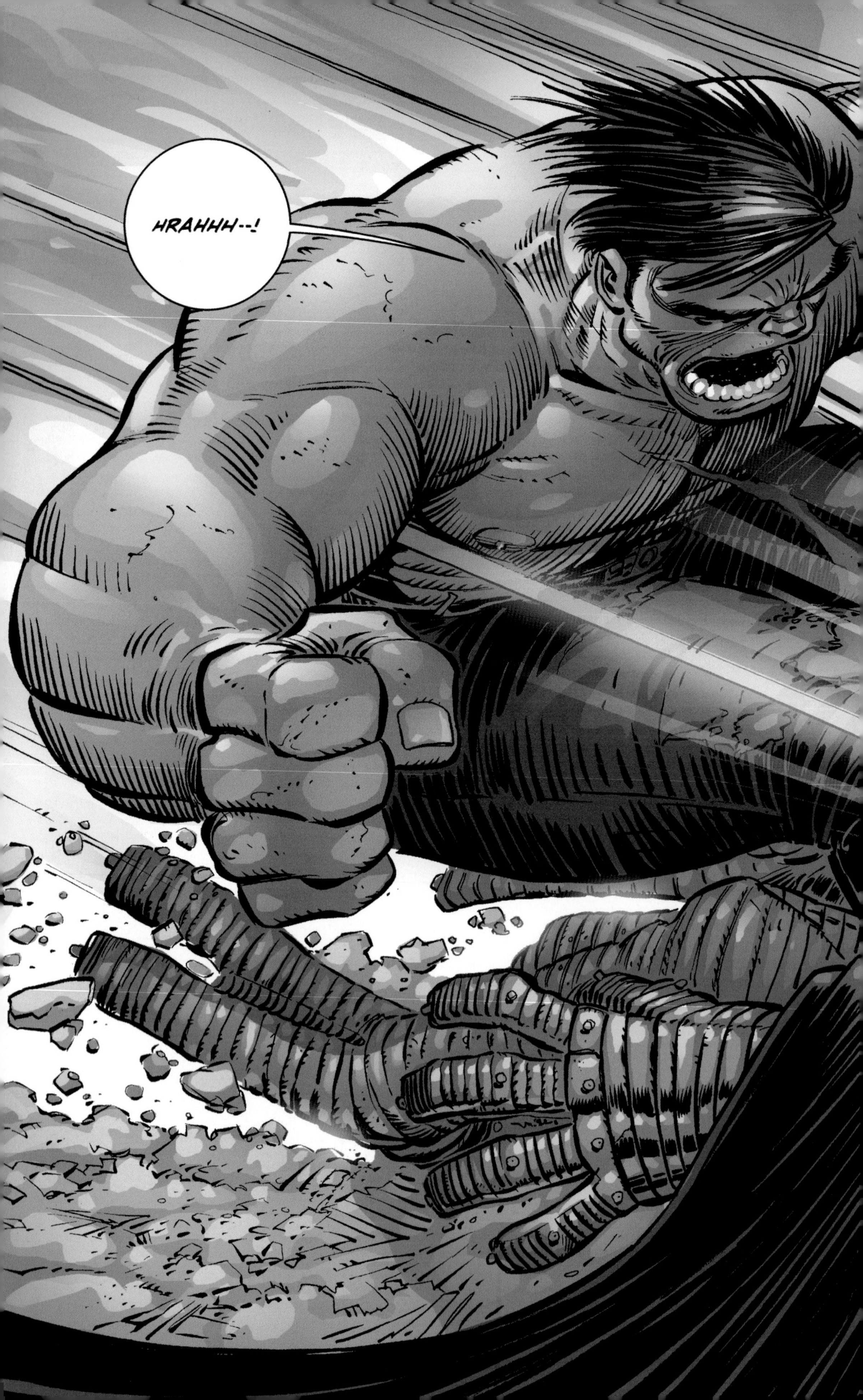
HRAHHH--!

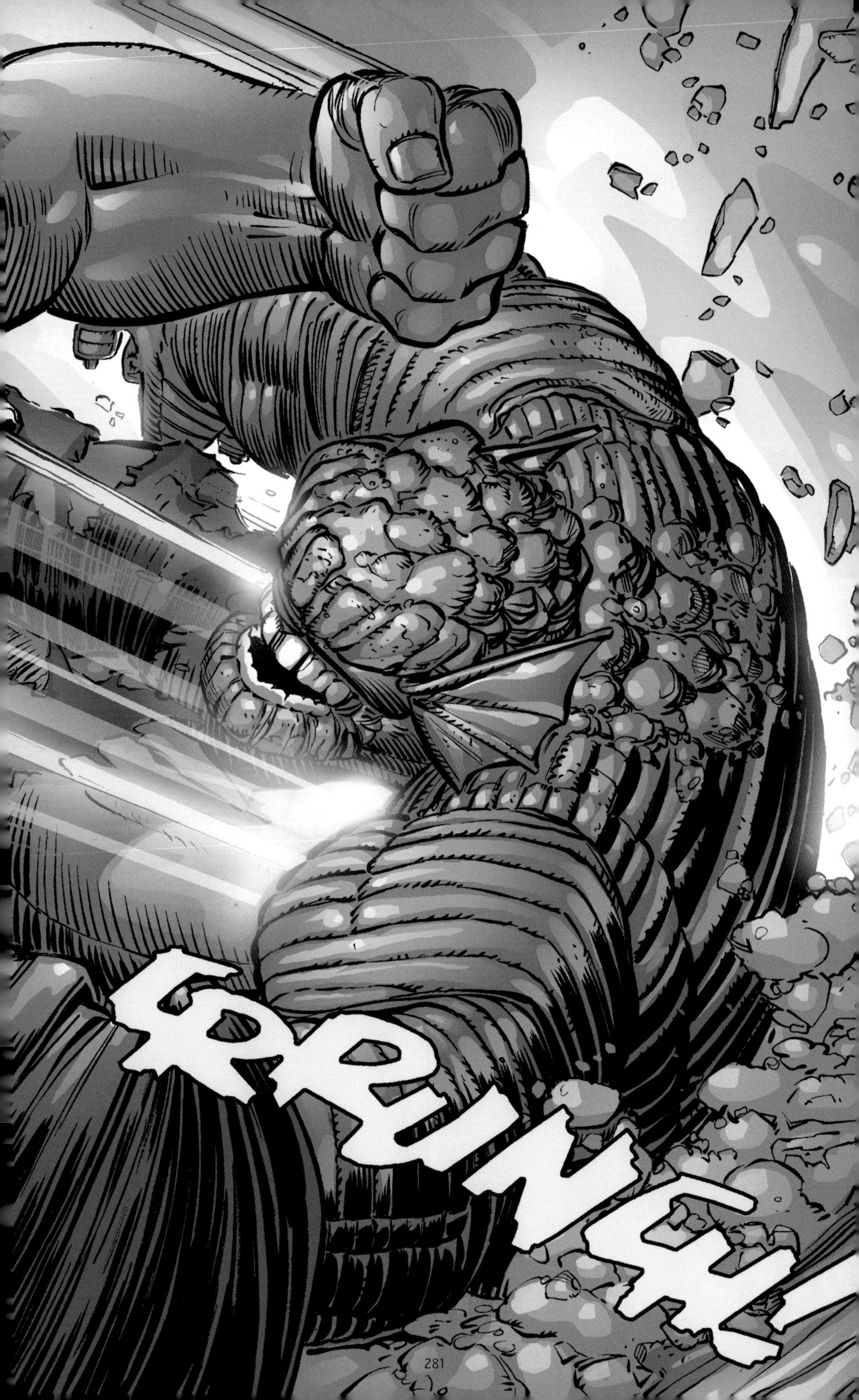
KRUNCH!

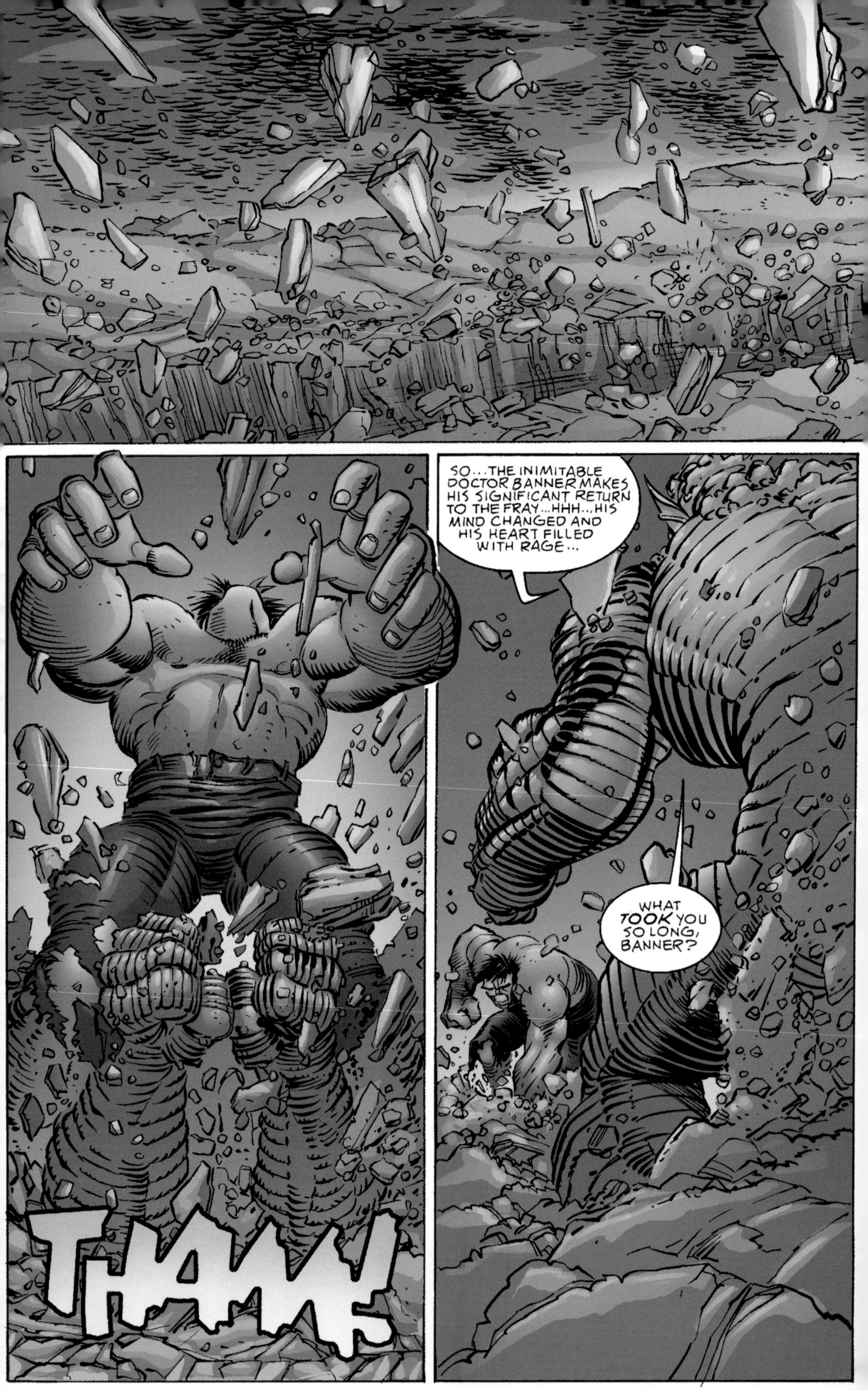
THAMS
SO... THE INIMITABLE DOCTOR BANNER MAKES HIS SIGNIFICANT RETURN TO THE FRAY... HHH... HIS MIND CHANGED AND HIS HEART FILLED WITH RAGE...
WHAT TOOK YOU SO LONG, BANNER?

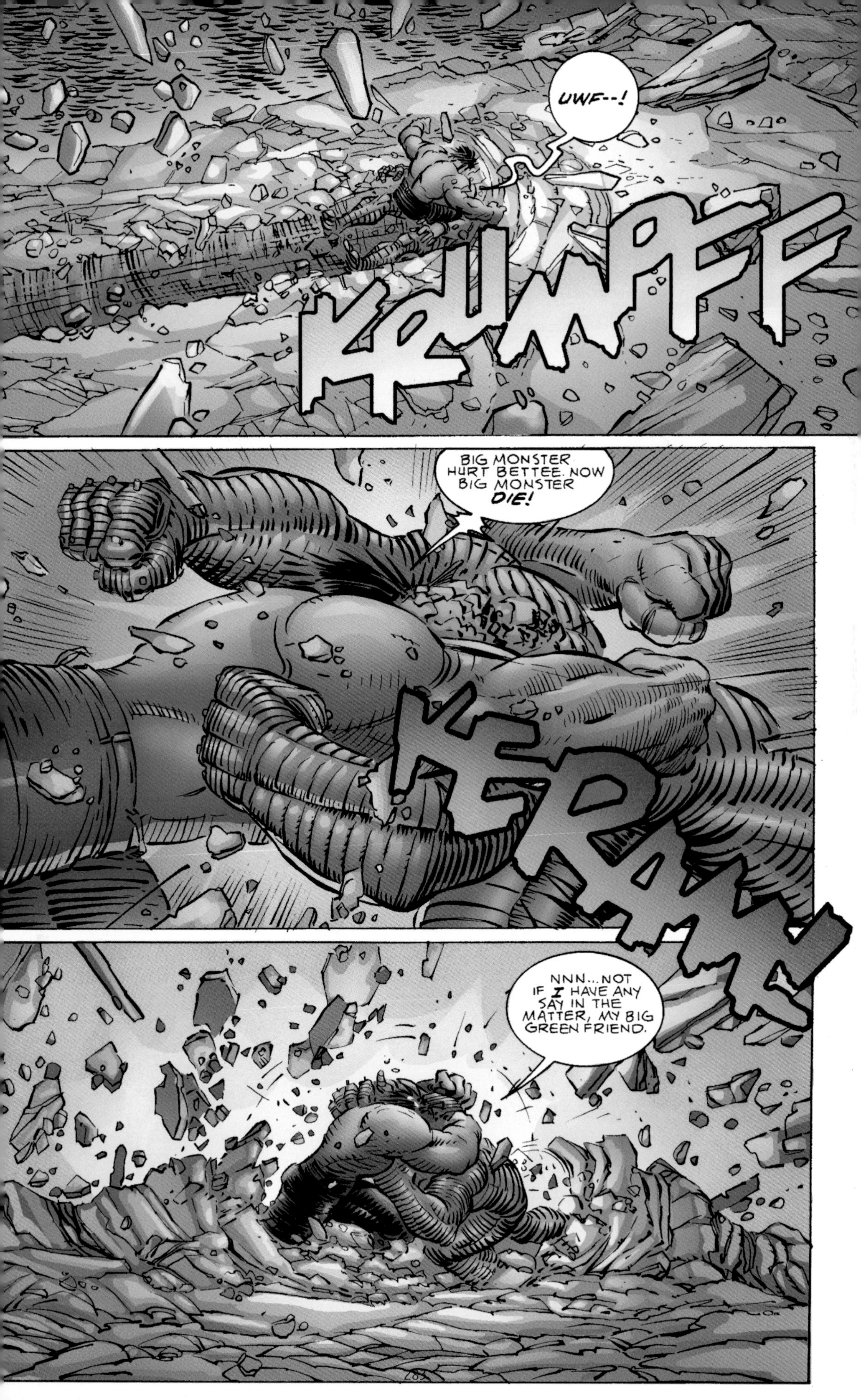
UWF--!
KRUMPFF
BIG MONSTER HURT BETTEE. NOW BIG MONSTER DIE!
KERAK!
NNN...NOT IF I HAVE ANY SAY IN THE MATTER, MY BIG GREEN FRIEND.

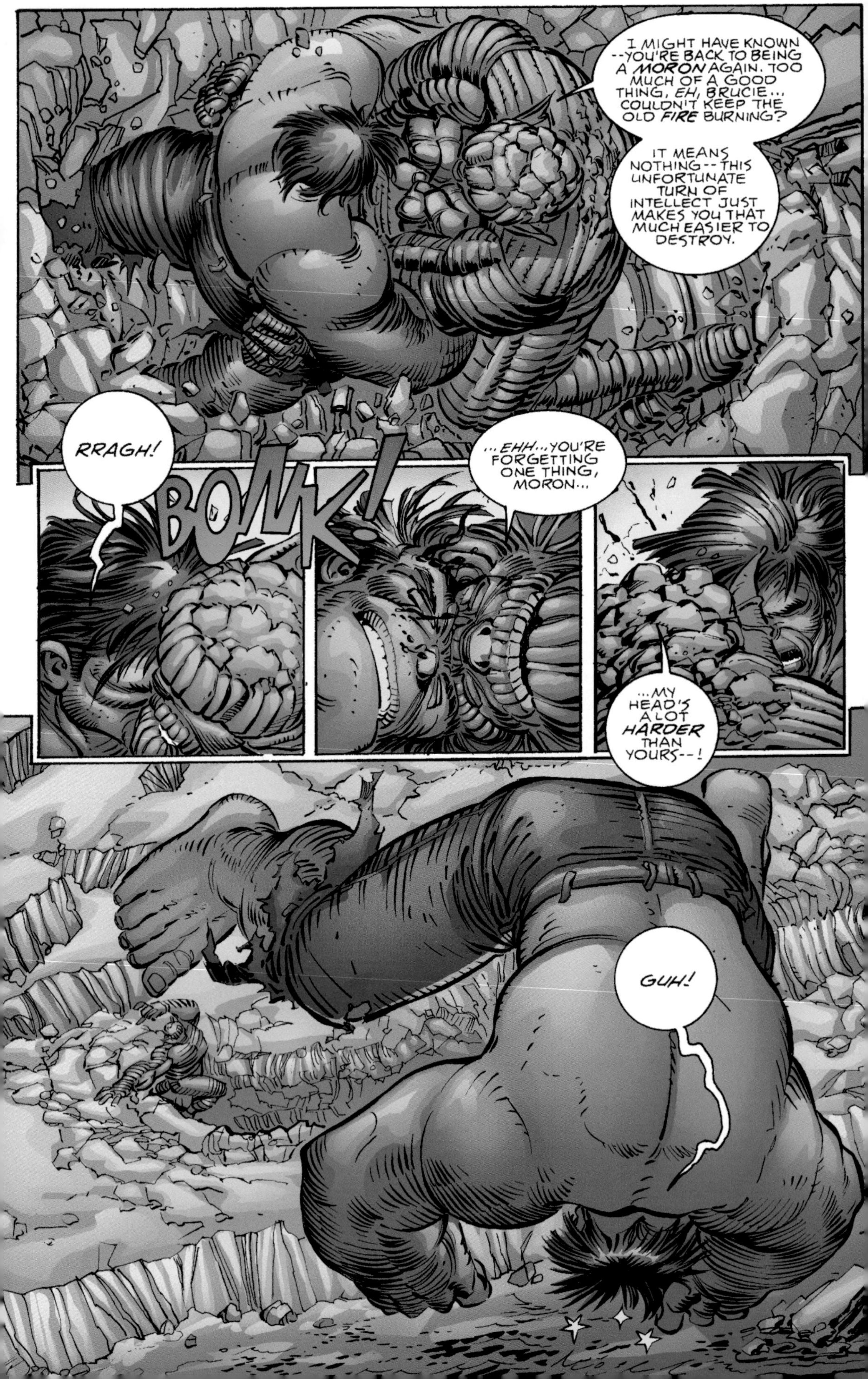
I MIGHT HAVE KNOWN --YOU'RE BACK TO BEING A MORON AGAIN. TOO MUCH OF A GOOD THING, EH, BRUCIE... COULDN'T KEEP THE OLD FIRE BURNING?
IT MEANS NOTHING-- THIS UNFORTUNATE TURN OF INTELLECT JUST MAKES YOU THAT MUCH EASIER TO DESTROY.
RRAGH!
BONK!
...EHH...YOU'RE FORGETTING ONE THING, MORON...
...MY HEAD'S A LOT HARDER THAN YOURS--!
GUH!

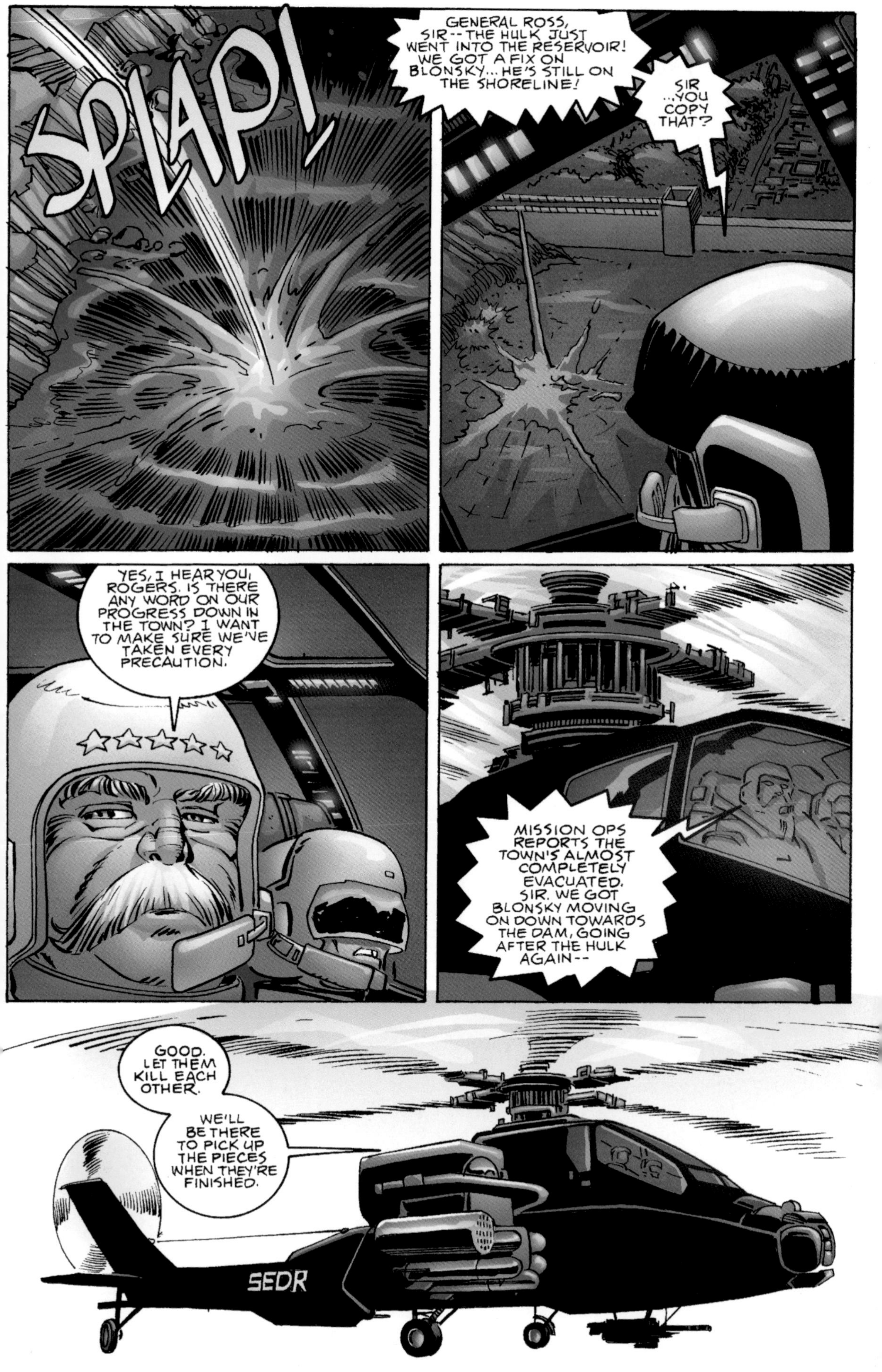
SPLAP!
GENERAL ROSS, SIR -- THE HULK JUST WENT INTO THE RESERVOIR! WE GOT A FIX ON BLONSKY... HE'S STILL ON THE SHORELINE!
...SIR ...YOU COPY THAT?
YES, I HEAR YOU, ROGERS. IS THERE ANY WORD ON OUR PROGRESS DOWN IN THE TOWN? I WANT TO MAKE SURE WE'VE TAKEN EVERY PRECAUTION.
MISSION OPS REPORTS THE TOWN'S ALMOST COMPLETELY EVACUATED. SIR, WE GOT BLONSKY MOVING ON DOWN TOWARDS THE DAM, GOING AFTER THE HULK AGAIN--
GOOD. LET THEM KILL EACH OTHER.
WE'LL BE THERE TO PICK UP THE PIECES WHEN THEY'RE FINISHED.
SEDR

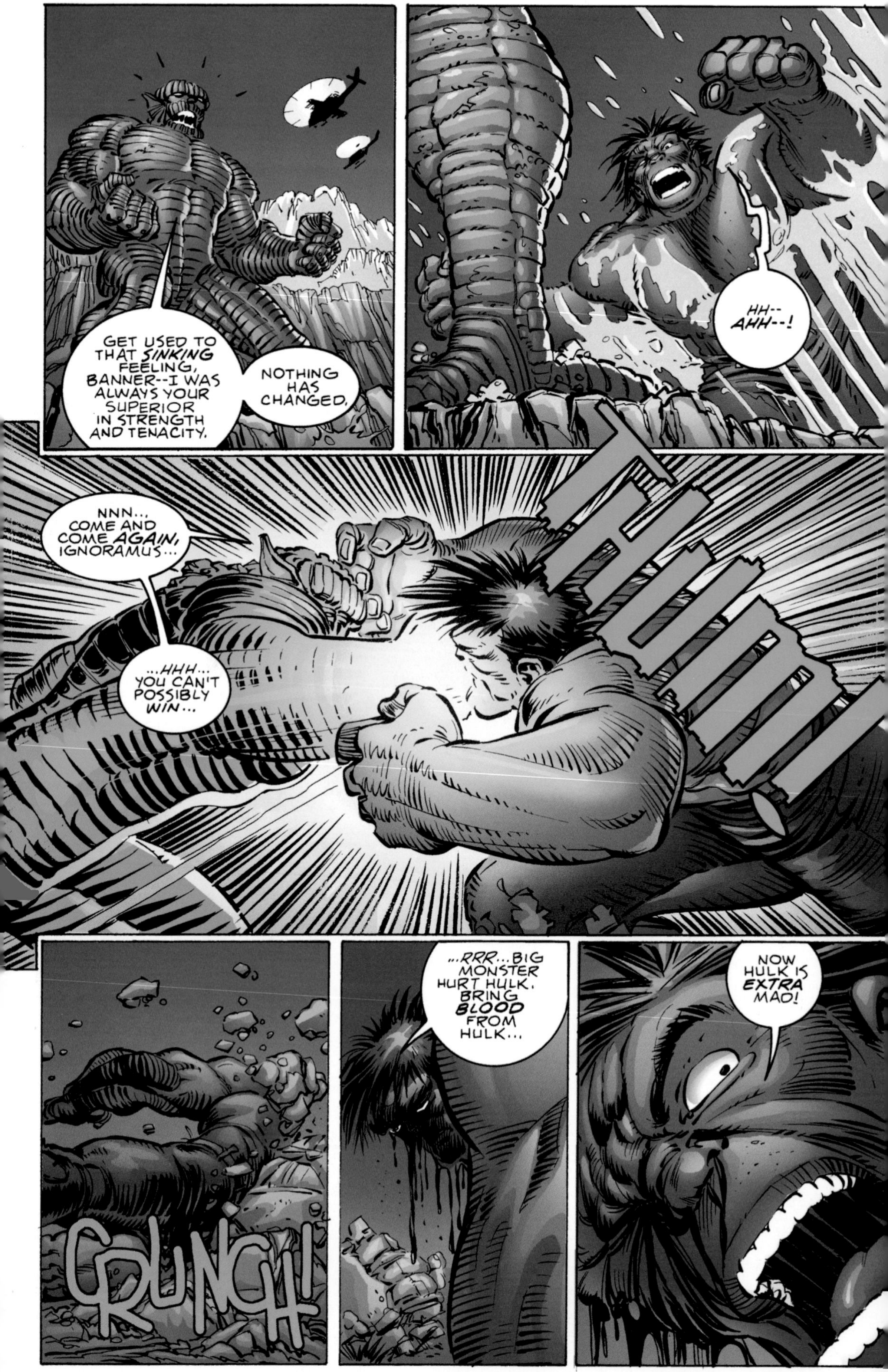
GET USED TO THAT SINKING FEELING, BANNER--I WAS ALWAYS YOUR SUPERIOR IN STRENGTH AND TENACITY.
NOTHING HAS CHANGED.
HH-- AHH--!
THUMM
NNN... COME AND COME AGAIN, IGNORAMUS...
...HHH... YOU CAN'T POSSIBLY WIN...
CRUNCH!
...RRR... BIG MONSTER HURT HULK. BRING BLOOD FROM HULK...
NOW HULK IS EXTRA MAD!

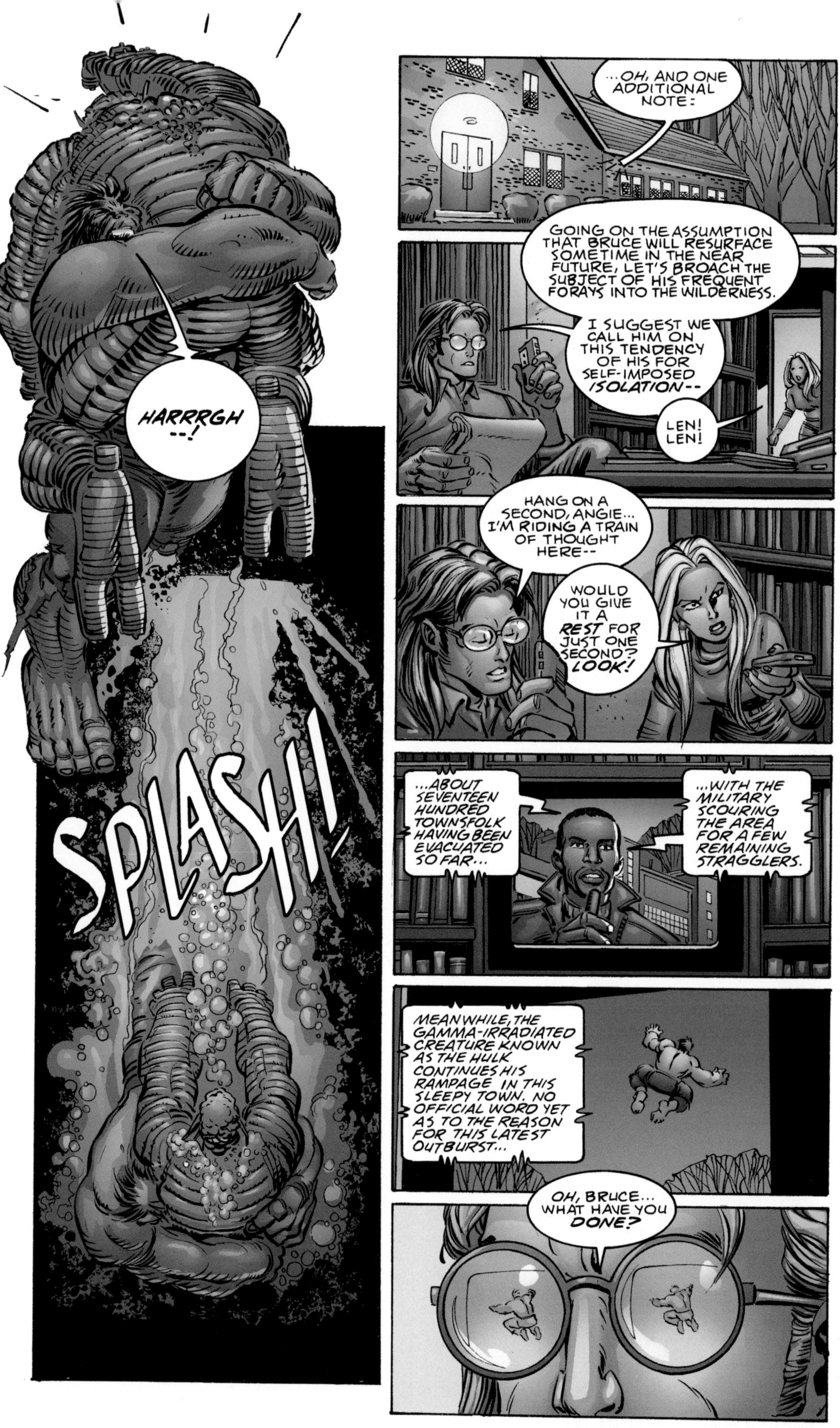
HARRRGH--!
SPLASH!
...OH, AND ONE ADDITIONAL NOTE:
GOING ON THE ASSUMPTION THAT BRUCE WILL RESURFACE SOMETIME IN THE NEAR FUTURE, LET'S BROACH THE SUBJECT OF HIS FREQUENT FORAYS INTO THE WILDERNESS.
I SUGGEST WE CALL HIM ON THIS TENDENCY OF HIS FOR SELF-IMPOSED ISOLATION--
LEN! LEN!
HANG ON A SECOND, ANGIE... I'M RIDING A TRAIN OF THOUGHT HERE--
WOULD YOU GIVE IT A REST FOR JUST ONE SECOND? LOOK!
...ABOUT SEVENTEEN HUNDRED TOWNSFOLK HAVING BEEN EVACUATED SO FAR...
...WITH THE MILITARY SCOURING THE AREA FOR A FEW REMAINING STRAGGLERS.
MEANWHILE, THE GAMMA-IRRADIATED CREATURE KNOWN AS THE HULK CONTINUES HIS RAMPAGE IN THIS SLEEPY TOWN. NO OFFICIAL WORD YET AS TO THE REASON FOR THIS LATEST OUTBURST...
OH, BRUCE... WHAT HAVE YOU DONE?

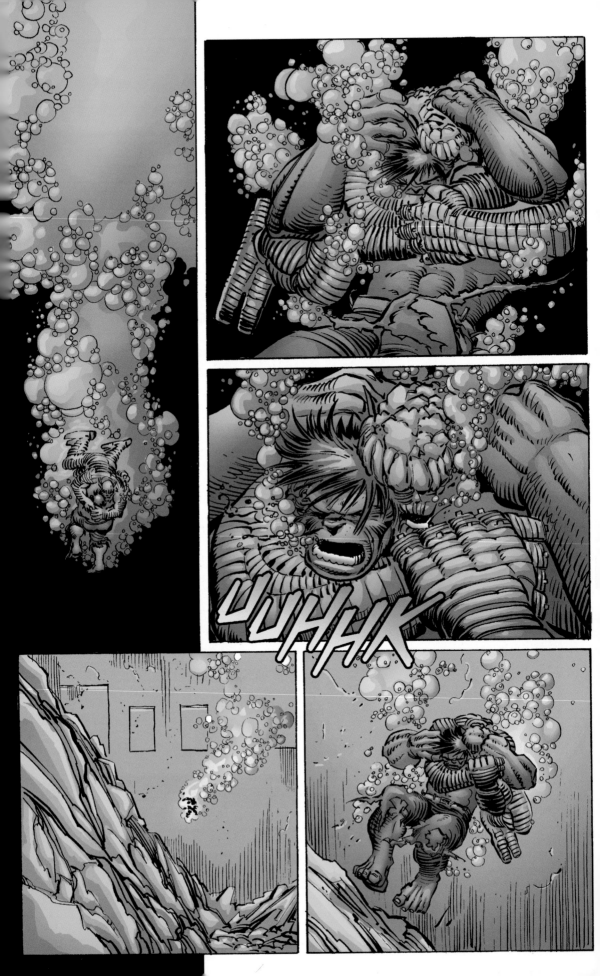

UUHHK

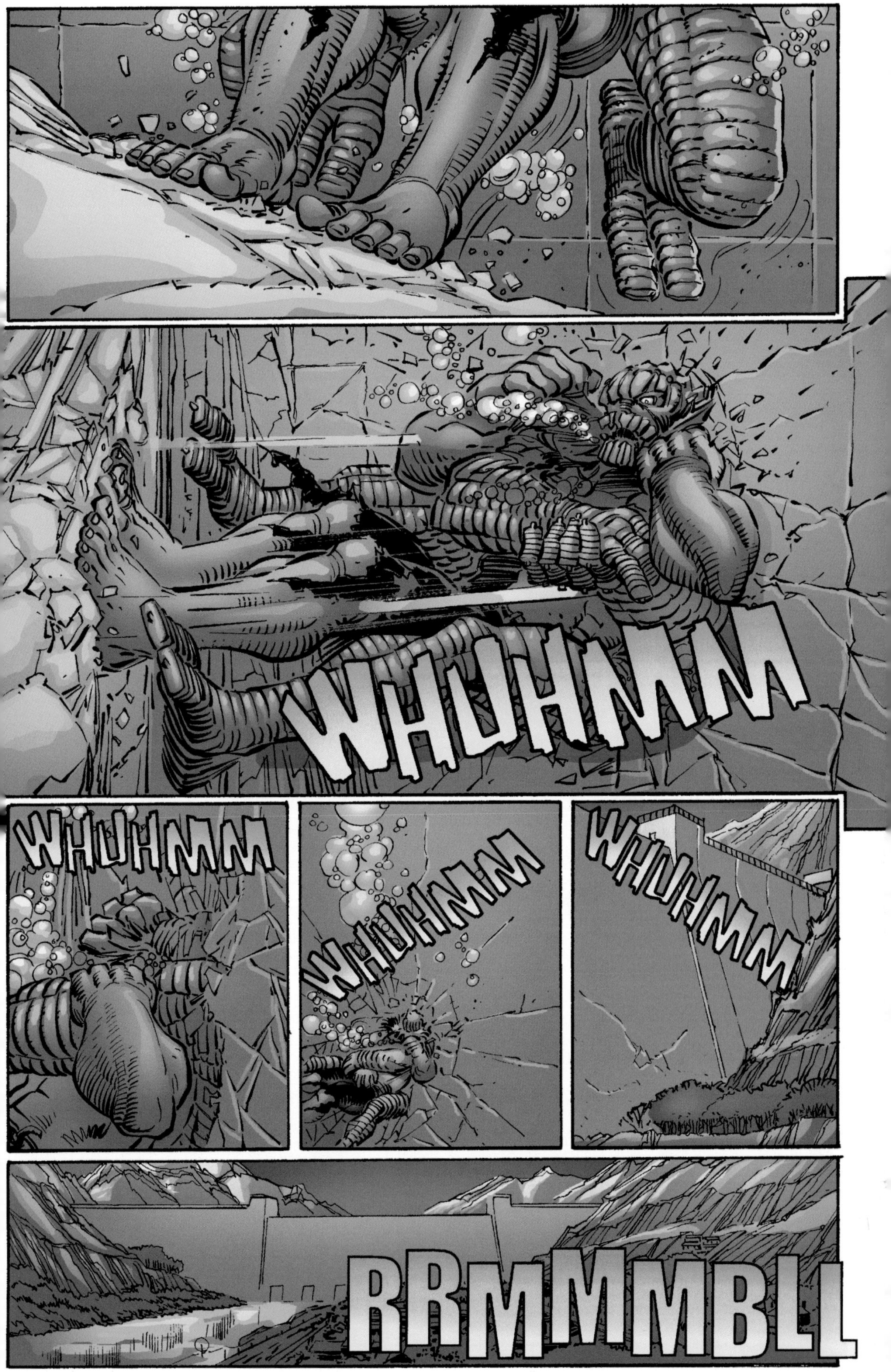
WHUHMM
WHUHMM
WHUHMM
WHUHMM
RRMMMBLL

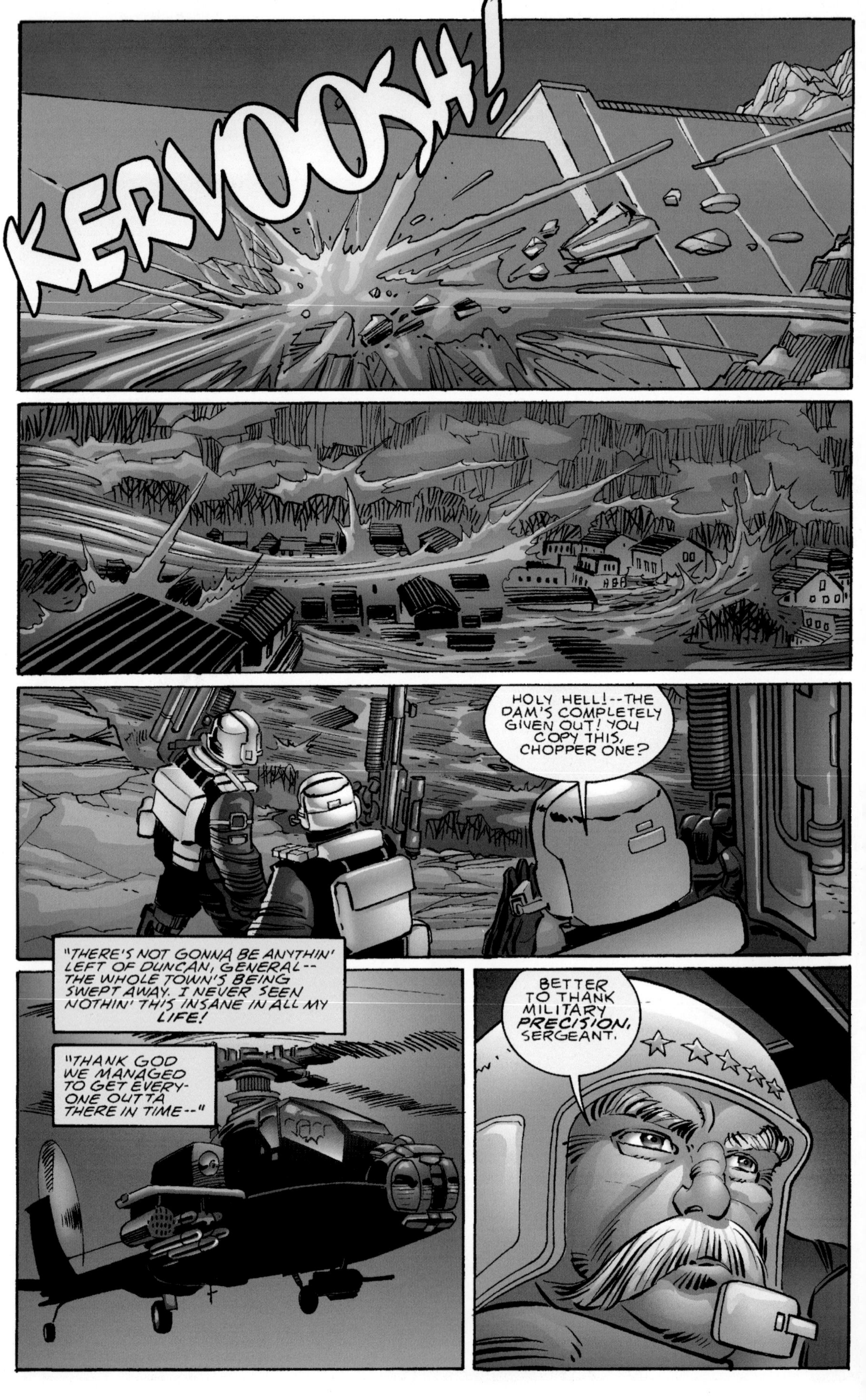
KERVOOSH!
HOLY HELL!--THE DAM'S COMPLETELY GIVEN OUT! YOU COPY THIS, CHOPPER ONE?
"THERE'S NOT GONNA BE ANYTHIN' LEFT OF DUNCAN, GENERAL-- THE WHOLE TOWN'S BEING SWEPT AWAY. I NEVER SEEN NOTHIN' THIS INSANE IN ALL MY LIFE!
"THANK GOD WE MANAGED TO GET EVERY-ONE OUTTA THERE IN TIME--"
BETTER TO THANK MILITARY PRECISION, SERGEANT.

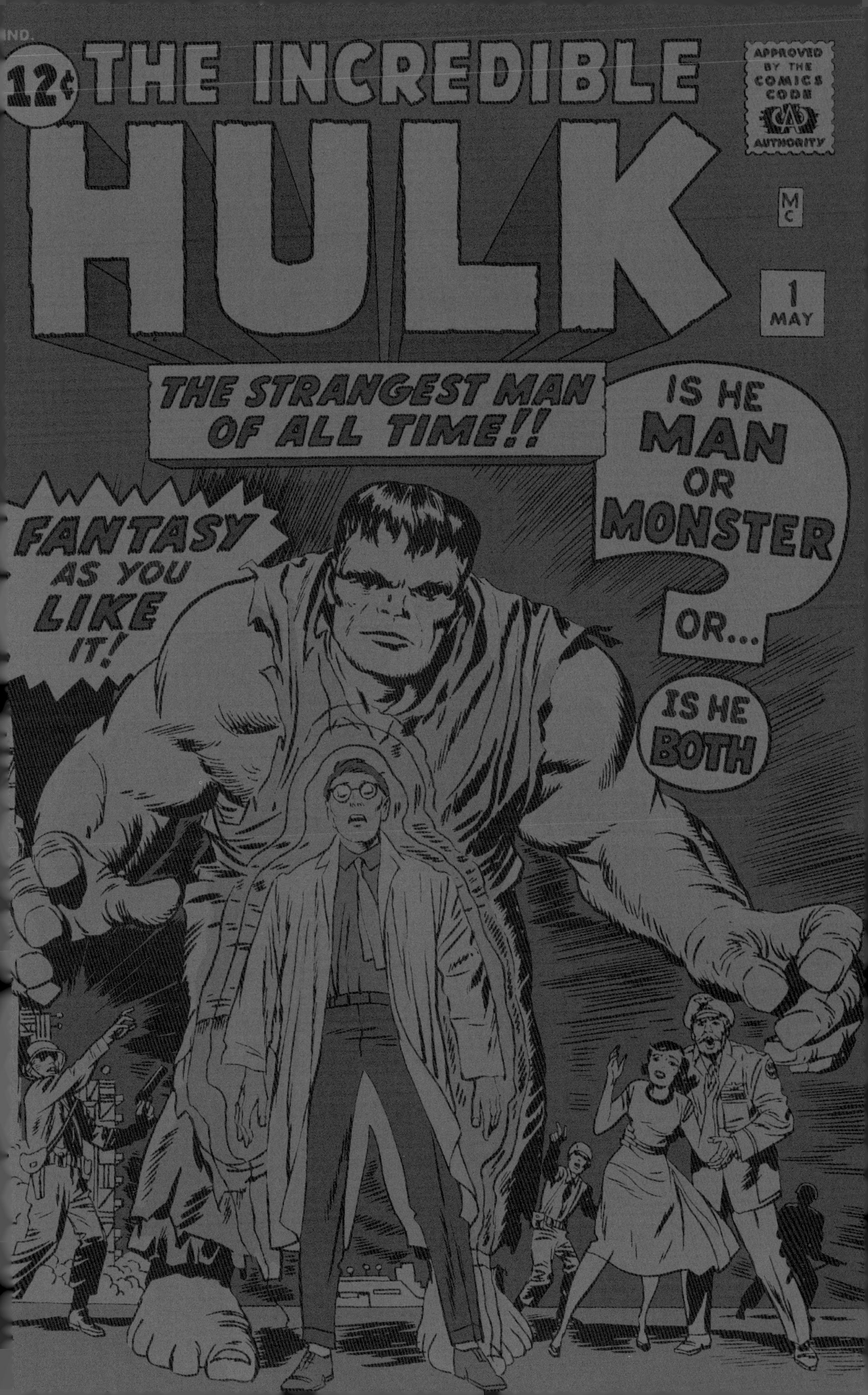
IND.
12¢
THE INCREDIBLE
HULK
APPROVED BY THE COMICS CODE AUTHORITY
MC
1
MAY
THE STRANGEST MAN OF ALL TIME!!
IS HE MAN OR MONSTER OR...
IS HE BOTH
FANTASY AS YOU LIKE IT!

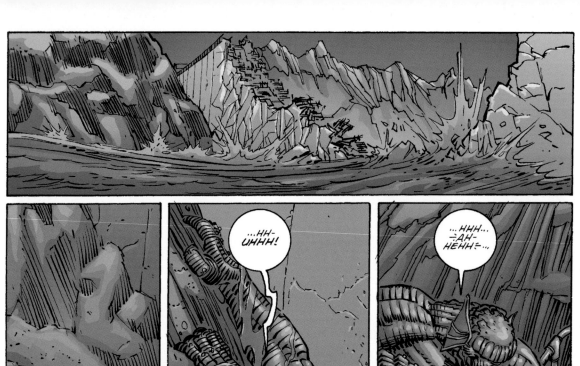

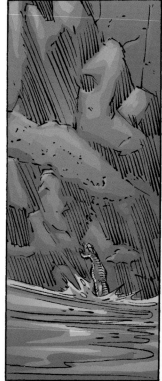

...HH-UHHH!

...HHH... ÷AH-HEHH÷...

...÷UHH÷...
I HOPE
YOU CAN *HEAR*
ME DOWN
THERE, HULK--
WHEREVER
YOU ARE
...I HOPE YOUR
EARS BURN LIKE
HELLFIRE, EVEN
AS YOUR LUNGS
COLLAPSE...

...DON'T THINK...
÷HH-UHH÷...DON'T
THINK HUMANITY
WILL EVER SHED
A TEAR FOR *YOUR*
LONELY DEMISE...

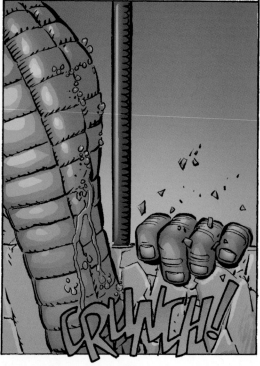

CRUNNCH!

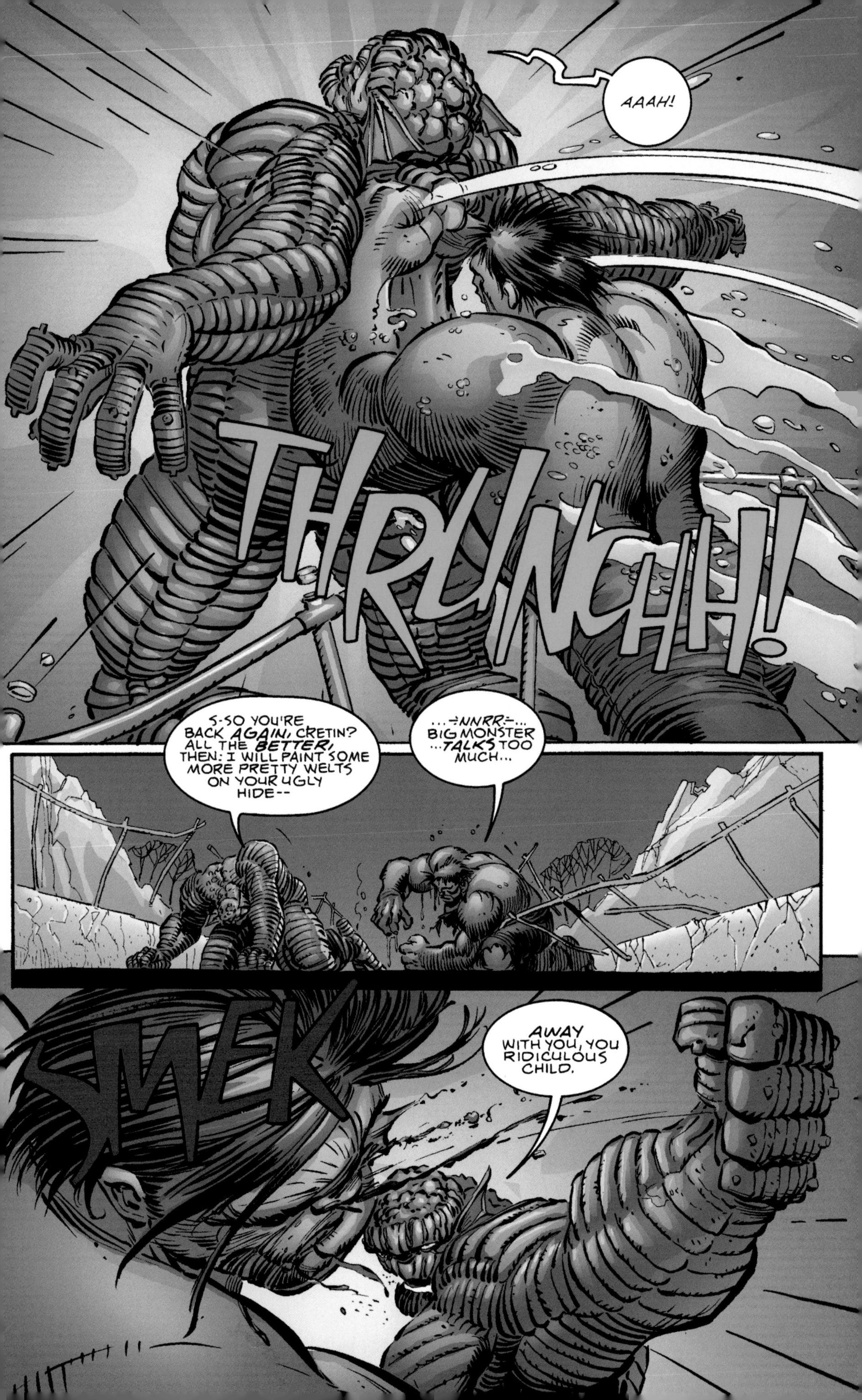
AAAH!
THRUNCHH!
S-SO YOU'RE BACK AGAIN, CRETIN? ALL THE BETTER, THEN: I WILL PAINT SOME MORE PRETTY WELTS ON YOUR UGLY HIDE--
...=NNRR=... BIG MONSTER ...TALKS TOO MUCH...
SMEK
AWAY WITH YOU, YOU RIDICULOUS CHILD.

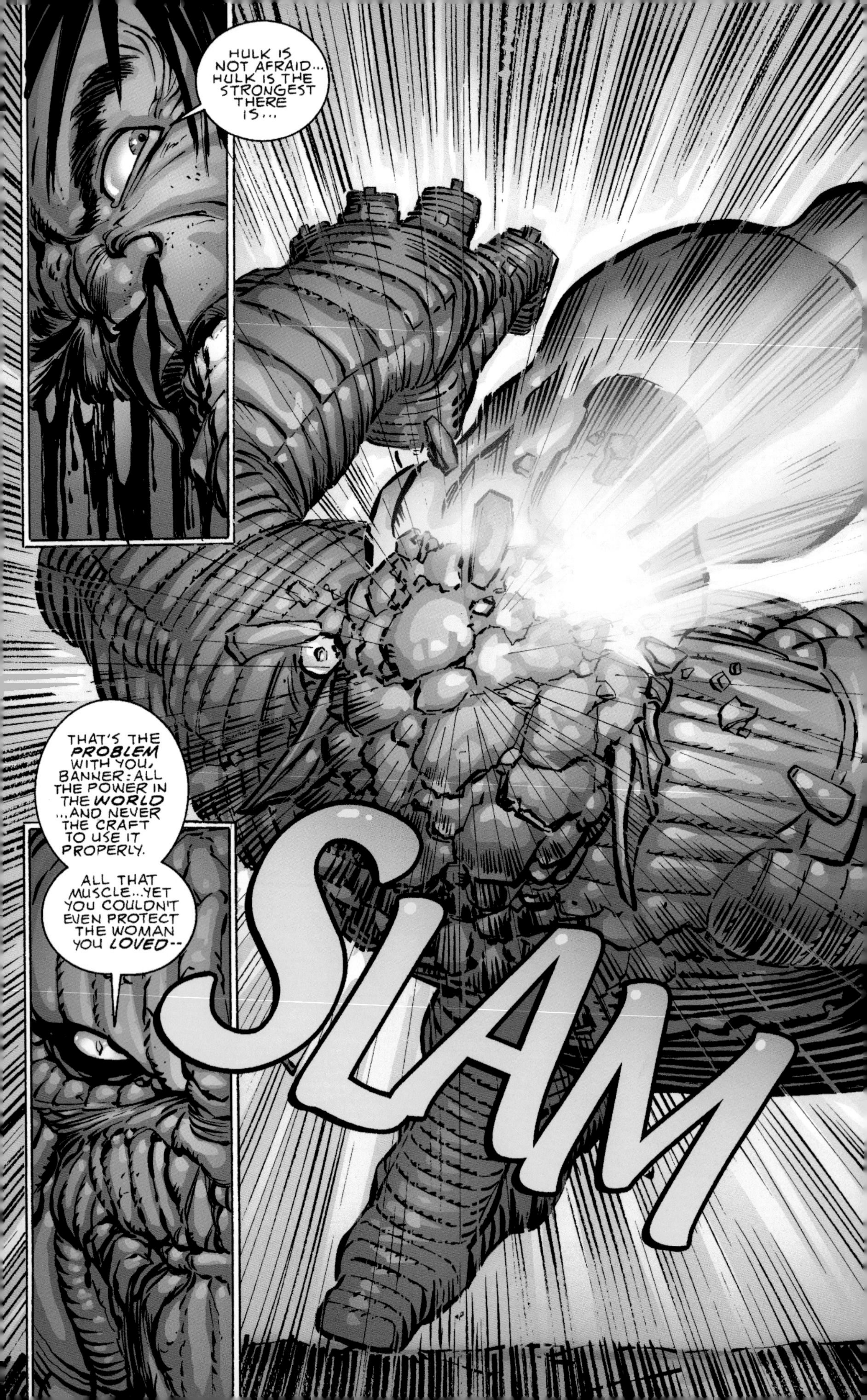
HULK IS NOT AFRAID... HULK IS THE STRONGEST THERE IS...
THAT'S THE PROBLEM WITH YOU, BANNER: ALL THE POWER IN THE WORLD ...AND NEVER THE CRAFT TO USE IT PROPERLY.
ALL THAT MUSCLE...YET YOU COULDN'T EVEN PROTECT THE WOMAN YOU LOVED--
SLAM

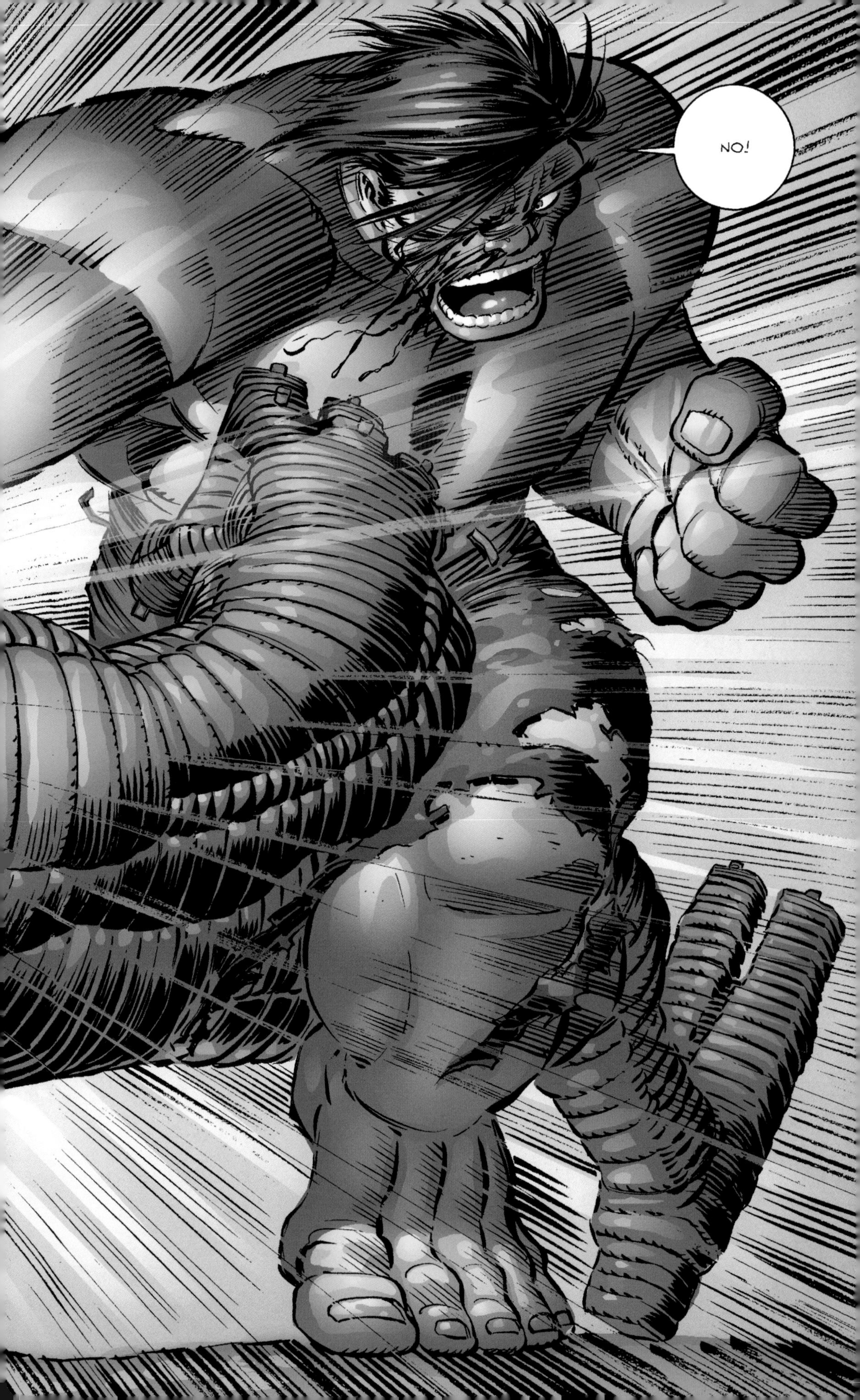
NO!

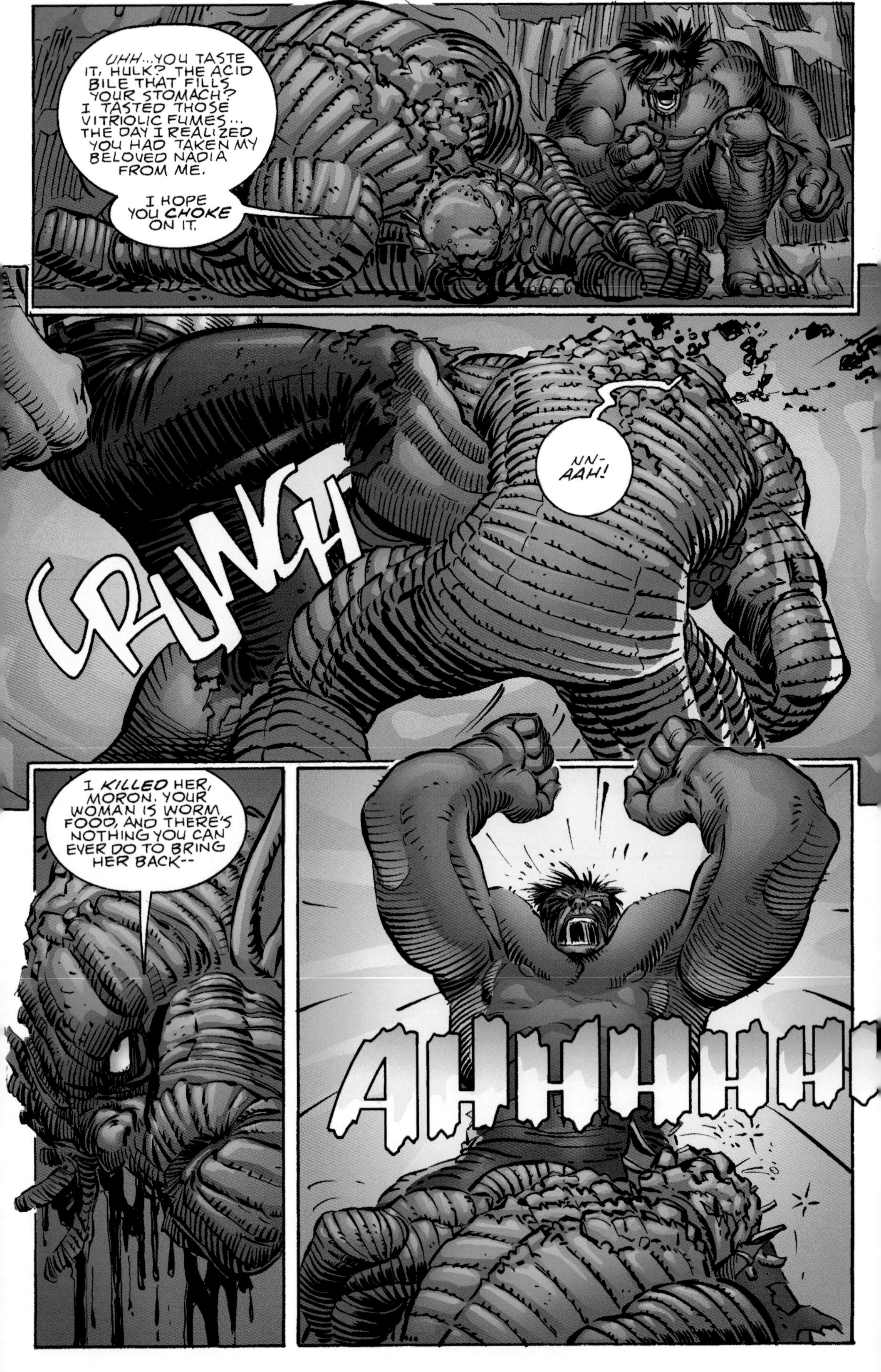

UHH...YOU TASTE IT, HULK? THE ACID BILE THAT FILLS YOUR STOMACH? I TASTED THOSE VITRIOLIC FUMES... THE DAY I REALIZED YOU HAD TAKEN MY BELOVED NADIA FROM ME.
I HOPE YOU CHOKE ON IT.
NN-AAH!
CRUNCH
I KILLED HER, MORON. YOUR WOMAN IS WORM FOOD, AND THERE'S NOTHING YOU CAN EVER DO TO BRING HER BACK--
AHHHHHH

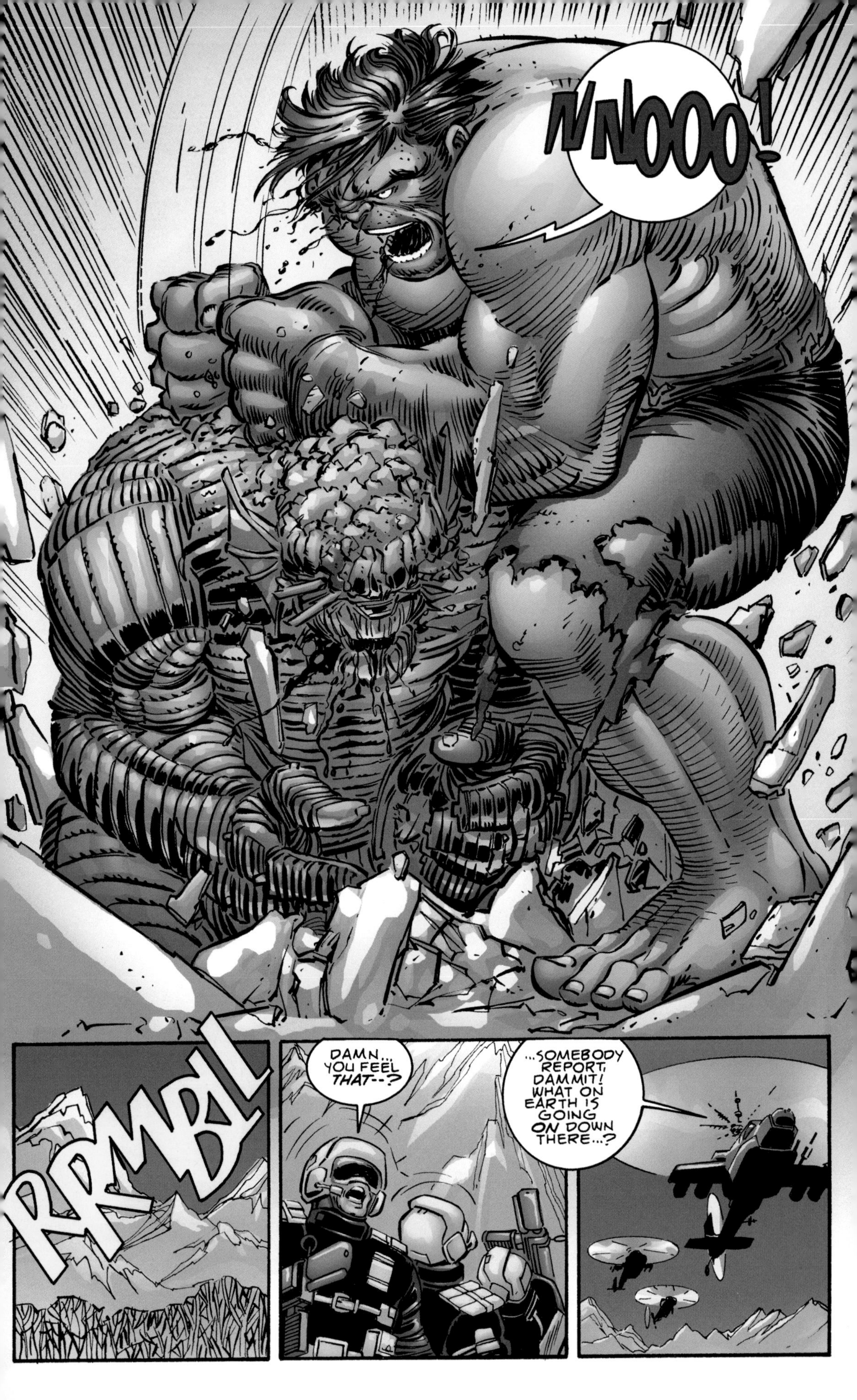
NNOOO!
RRMBL
DAMN... YOU FEEL THAT--?
...SOMEBODY REPORT, DAMMIT! WHAT ON EARTH IS GOING ON DOWN THERE...?

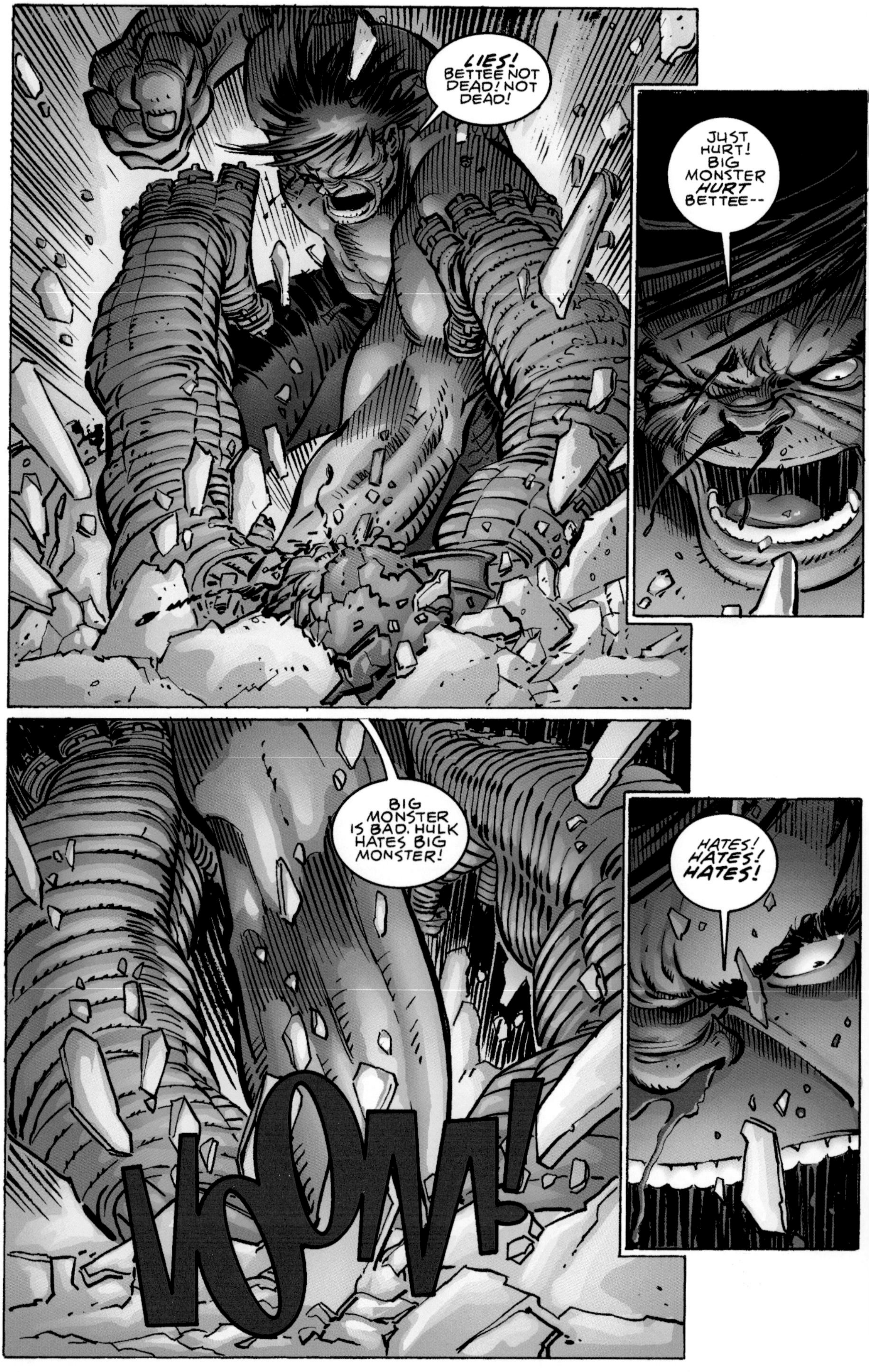
LIES! BETTEE NOT DEAD! NOT DEAD!
JUST HURT! BIG MONSTER HURT BETTEE--
BIG MONSTER IS BAD. HULK HATES BIG MONSTER!
HATES! HATES! HATES!
VOOM!

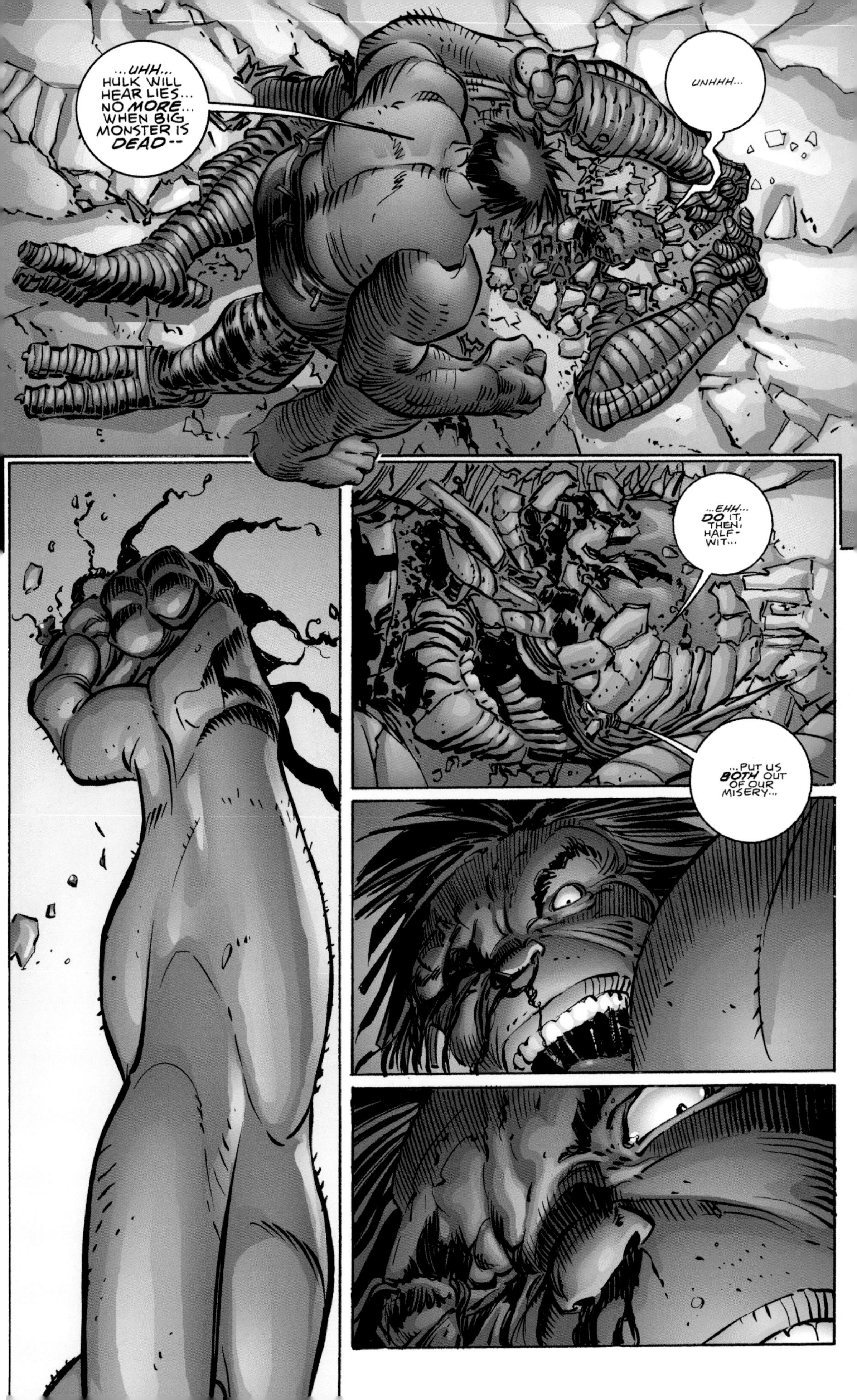
...UHH... HULK WILL HEAR LIES... NO MORE... WHEN BIG MONSTER IS DEAD--
UNHHH...
...EHH... DO IT, THEN, HALF-WIT...
...PUT US BOTH OUT OF OUR MISERY...

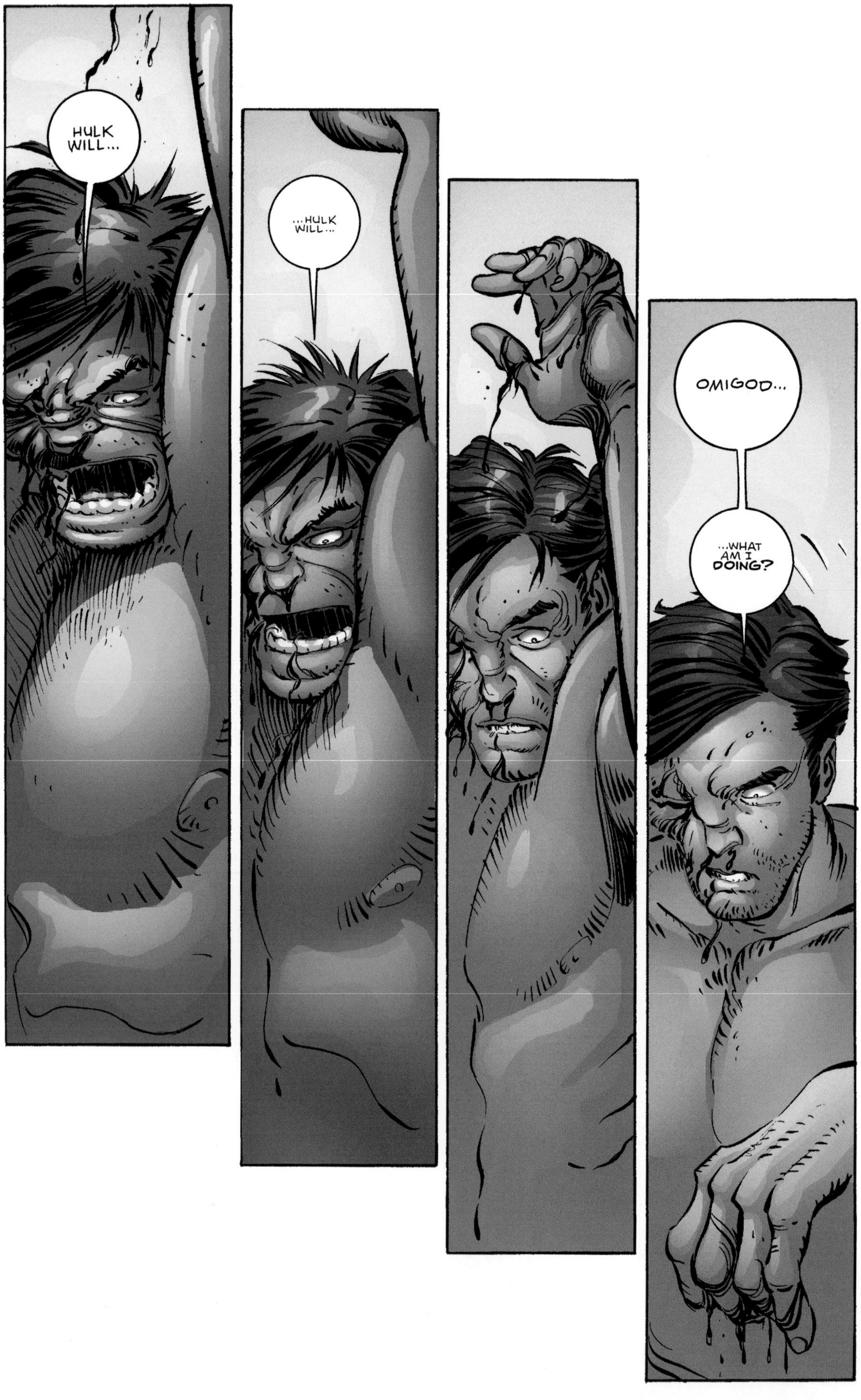
HULK WILL...
...HULK WILL...
OMIGOD...
...WHAT AM I DOING?

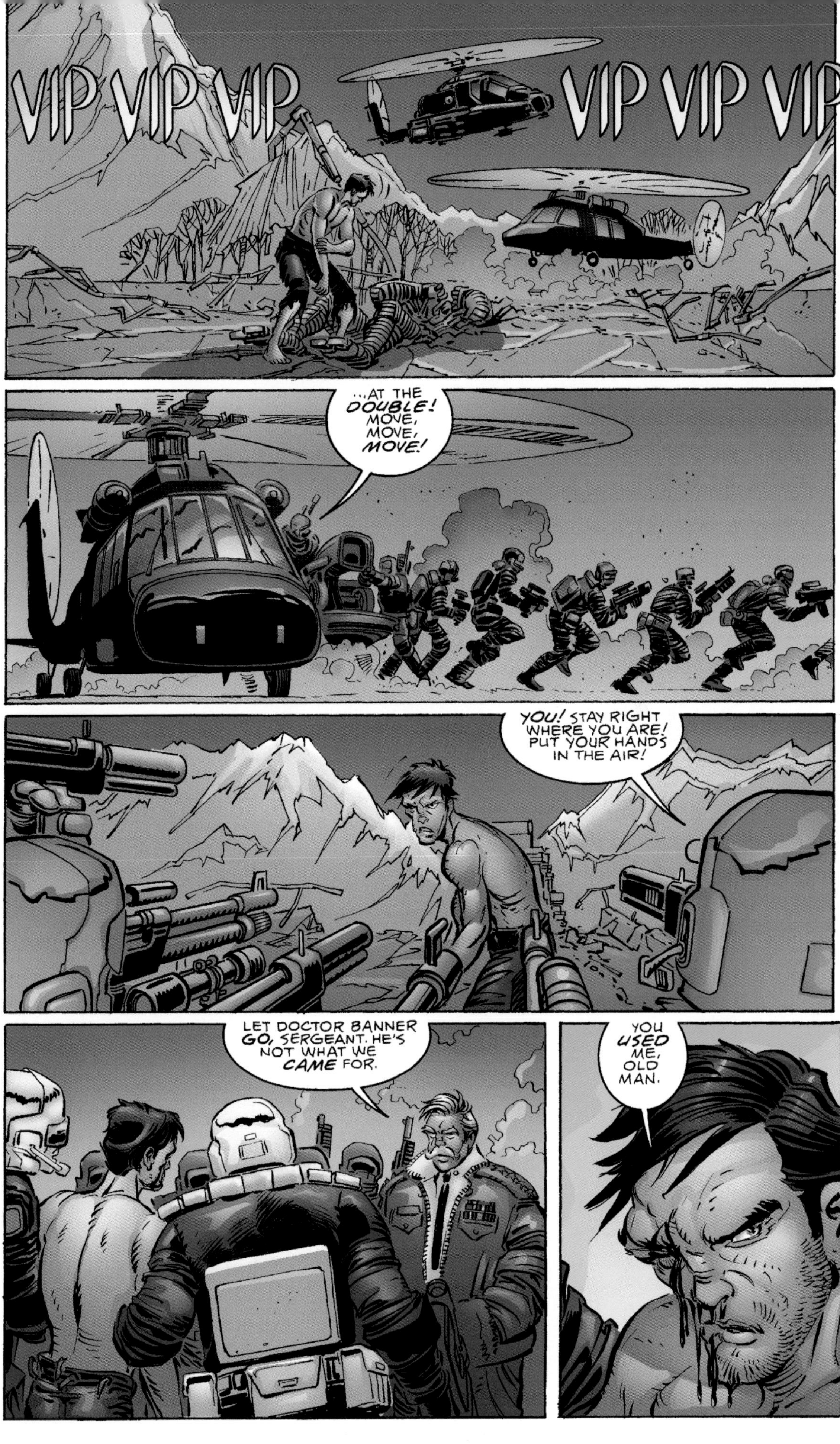
VIP VIP VIP
VIP VIP VIP
...AT THE DOUBLE! MOVE, MOVE, MOVE!
YOU! STAY RIGHT WHERE YOU ARE! PUT YOUR HANDS IN THE AIR!
LET DOCTOR BANNER GO, SERGEANT. HE'S NOT WHAT WE CAME FOR.
YOU USED ME, OLD MAN.

YOU *ALLOWED* YOURSELF TO BE USED. YOU LET YOUR HATRED FOR BLONSKY PROVIDE YOU WITH A GOOD EXCUSE, WHETHER YOU WANT TO ADMIT IT OR NOT.

ASK ANY OLD SOLDIER, BANNER: THERE'S A TIME, A PLACE, AND A *USE* FOR EVERYTHING, EVEN HATRED. THERE'S A LITTLE PIECE OF THE DEVIL IN ALL OF US.

YOU PESTILENT OLD *TROLL*-- YOU DIDN'T SHOW BETTY TO ME BECAUSE YOU CARED...YOU DID IT BECAUSE YOU KNEW I'D GO AFTER BLONSKY.

DON'T YOU EVER PRESUME TO *JUDGE* ME, BOY. I DON'T HAVE TO ANSWER TO YOU OR TO *ANYBODY* IF IT MEANS WE GOT THE BASTARD WHO MURDERED MY DAUGHTER.

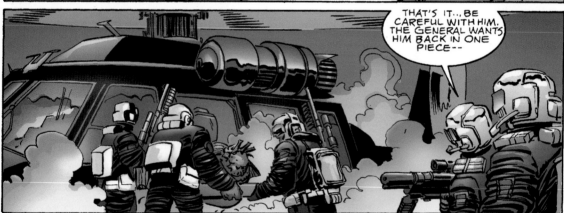

THAT'S IT..., BE CAREFUL WITH HIM. THE GENERAL WANTS HIM BACK IN ONE PIECE--

SO, YOU GOT WHAT YOU WANTED AFTER ALL, ROSS? *HEHH*... Y'KNOW, IT'S TIMES LIKE THIS WHEN I CAN BE THANKFUL THAT I LIVE IN *MY* SKIN-- HULK OR NO HULK.

THANKFUL --?

AT LEAST I DON'T HAVE TO SLEEP WITH YOUR CONSCIENCE.

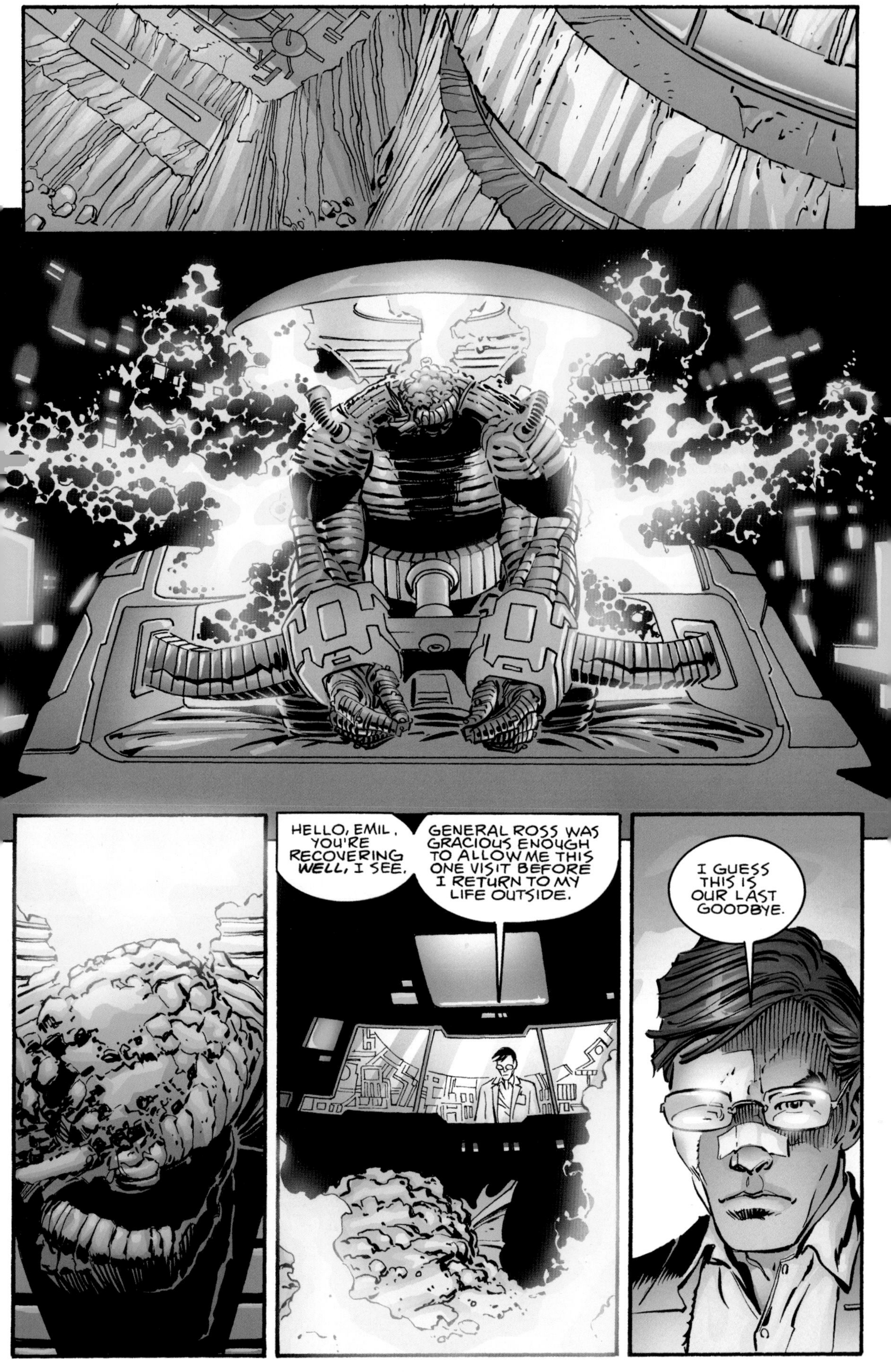
HELLO, EMIL. YOU'RE RECOVERING WELL, I SEE.
GENERAL ROSS WAS GRACIOUS ENOUGH TO ALLOW ME THIS ONE VISIT BEFORE I RETURN TO MY LIFE OUTSIDE.
I GUESS THIS IS OUR LAST GOODBYE.

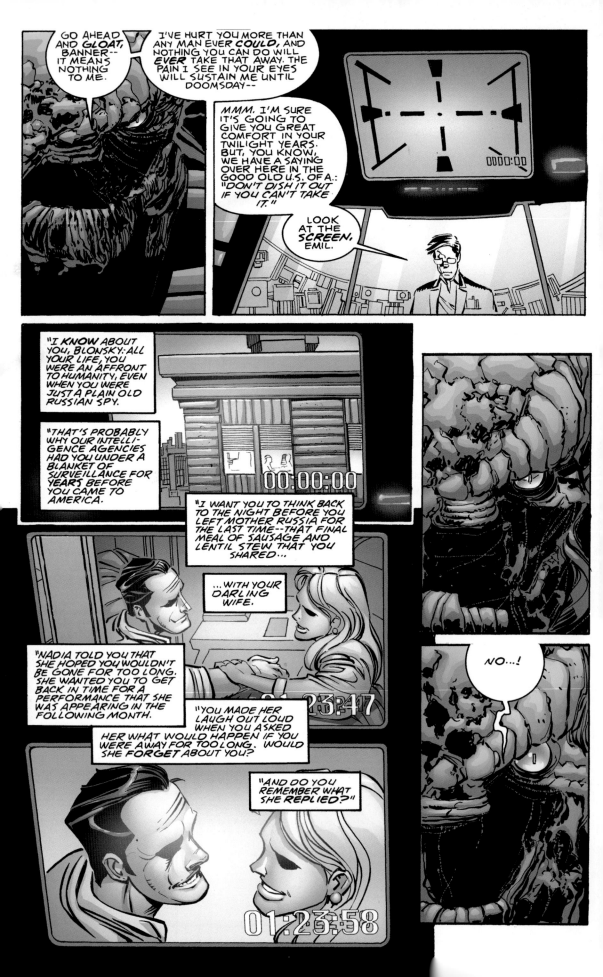

GO AHEAD AND *GLOAT*, BANNER-- IT MEANS NOTHING TO ME.

I'VE HURT YOU MORE THAN ANY MAN EVER *COULD*, AND NOTHING YOU CAN DO WILL *EVER* TAKE THAT AWAY. THE PAIN I SEE IN YOUR EYES WILL SUSTAIN ME UNTIL DOOMSDAY--

MMM. I'M SURE IT'S GOING TO GIVE YOU GREAT COMFORT IN YOUR TWILIGHT YEARS. BUT, YOU KNOW, WE HAVE A SAYING OVER HERE IN THE GOOD OLD U.S. OF A.: *"DON'T DISH IT OUT IF YOU CAN'T TAKE IT."*

0000:00

LOOK AT THE *SCREEN,* EMIL.

"*I KNOW* ABOUT YOU, BLONSKY: ALL YOUR LIFE, YOU WERE AN AFFRONT TO HUMANITY, EVEN WHEN YOU WERE JUST A PLAIN OLD RUSSIAN SPY.

"THAT'S PROBABLY WHY OUR INTELLI-GENCE AGENCIES HAD YOU UNDER A BLANKET OF SURVEILLANCE FOR *YEARS* BEFORE YOU CAME TO AMERICA.

00:00:00

"I WANT YOU TO THINK BACK TO THE NIGHT BEFORE YOU LEFT MOTHER RUSSIA FOR THE LAST TIME--THAT FINAL MEAL OF SAUSAGE AND LENTIL STEW THAT YOU SHARED...

...WITH YOUR DARLING WIFE.

"NADIA TOLD YOU THAT SHE HOPED YOU WOULDN'T BE GONE FOR TOO LONG. SHE WANTED YOU TO GET BACK IN TIME FOR A PERFORMANCE THAT SHE WAS APPEARING IN THE FOLLOWING MONTH.

"YOU MADE HER LAUGH OUT LOUD WHEN YOU ASKED HER WHAT WOULD HAPPEN IF YOU WERE AWAY FOR TOO LONG. WOULD SHE *FORGET* ABOUT YOU?

"AND DO YOU REMEMBER WHAT SHE *REPLIED?"*

NO...!

01:23:47

01:23:58

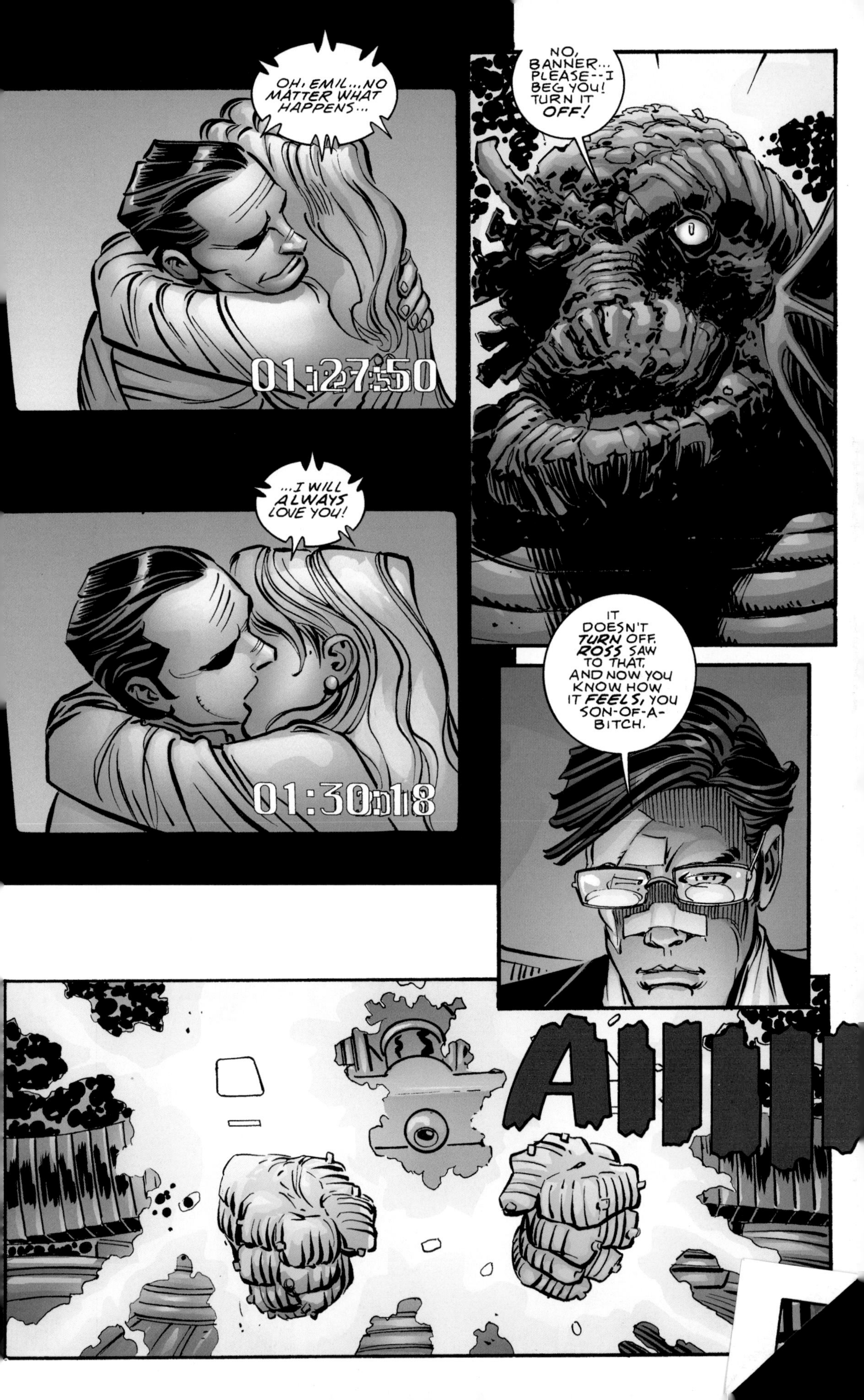
OH, EMIL...NO MATTER WHAT HAPPENS...
01:27:50
...I WILL ALWAYS LOVE YOU!
01:30:18
NO, BANNER... PLEASE--I BEG YOU! TURN IT OFF!
IT DOESN'T TURN OFF. ROSS SAW TO THAT. AND NOW YOU KNOW HOW IT FEELS, YOU SON-OF-A-BITCH.
AIIII

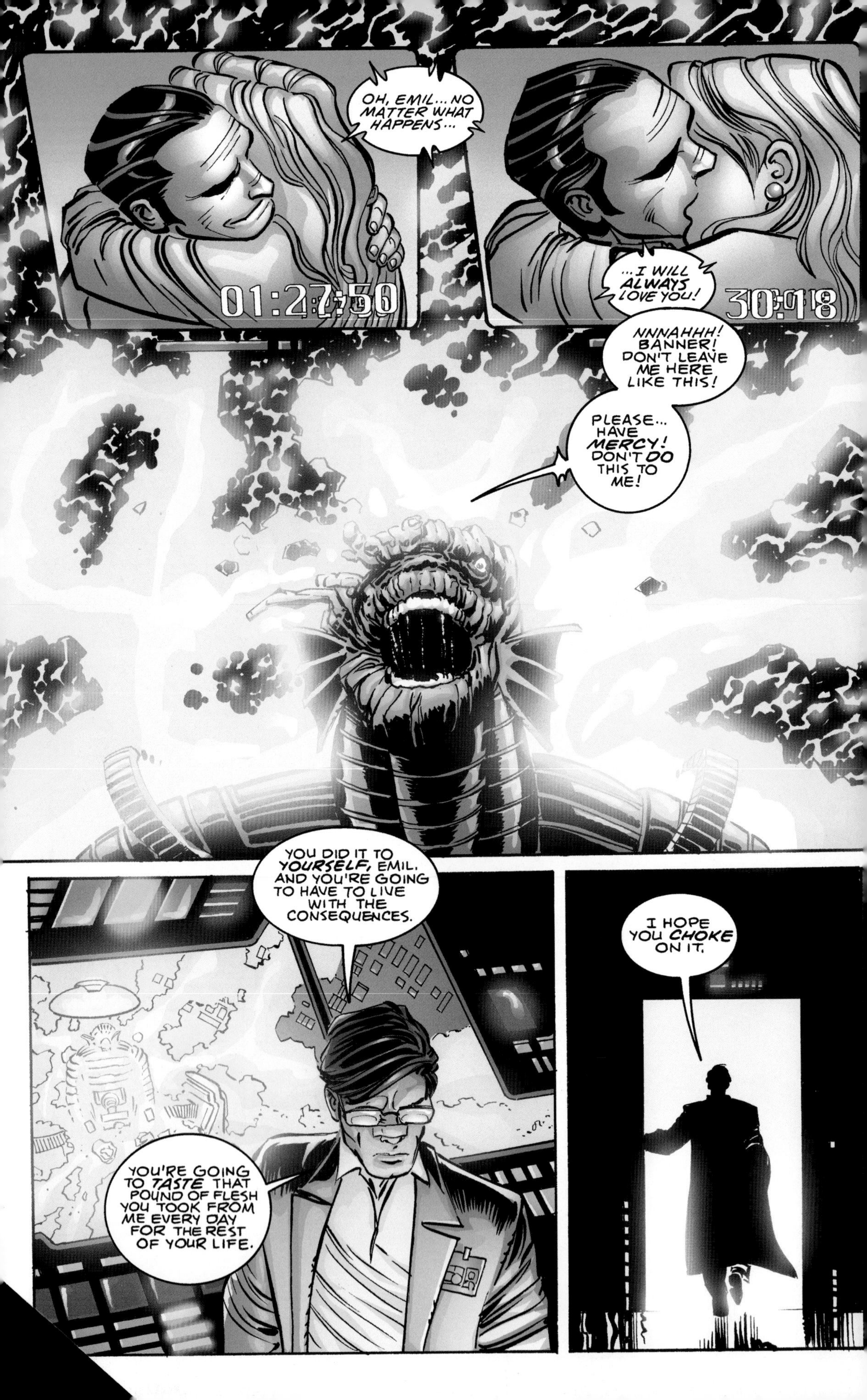
OH, EMIL... NO MATTER WHAT HAPPENS...
...I WILL ALWAYS LOVE YOU!
NNNAHHH! BANNER! DON'T LEAVE ME HERE LIKE THIS!
PLEASE... HAVE MERCY! DON'T DO THIS TO ME!
YOU DID IT TO YOURSELF, EMIL. AND YOU'RE GOING TO HAVE TO LIVE WITH THE CONSEQUENCES.
YOU'RE GOING TO TASTE THAT POUND OF FLESH YOU TOOK FROM ME EVERY DAY FOR THE REST OF YOUR LIFE.
I HOPE YOU CHOKE ON IT.

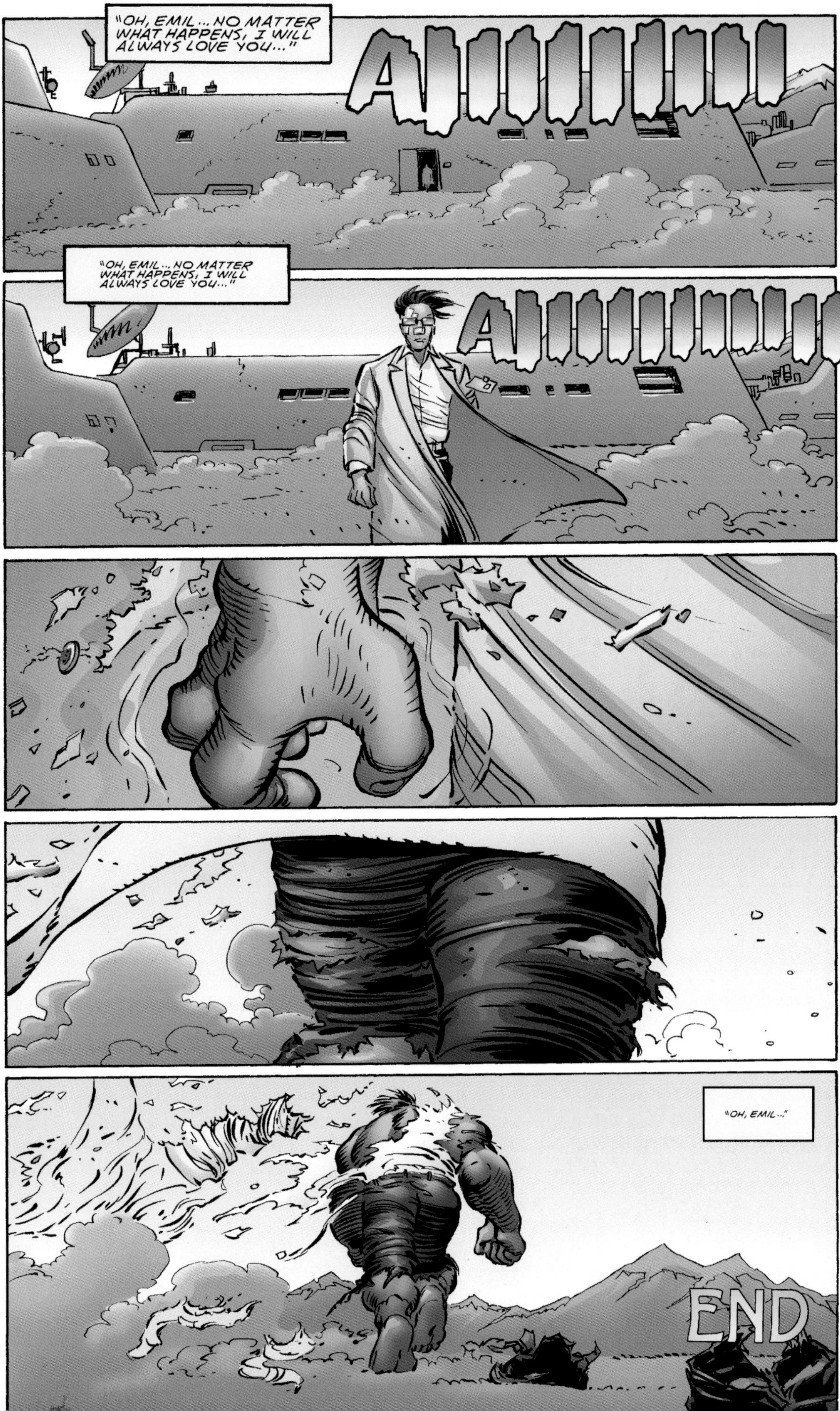
"OH, EMIL... NO MATTER WHAT HAPPENS, I WILL ALWAYS LOVE YOU..."
AIIIIIIIII
"OH, EMIL... NO MATTER WHAT HAPPENS, I WILL ALWAYS LOVE YOU..."
AIIIIIIIIII
"OH, EMIL..."
END

HULK

Art by **Dale K**eown with John Byrne

REAL NAME: Robert Bruce Banner

ALIASES: Green King, Green Scar, Holku, Sakaarson, Green One, Eye of Rage, World Breaker, Harkanon, Haarg, Once-Savage, Two-Minds, Captain Universe, Professor, War, Maestro, Joe Fixit, Mr. Fixit, Annihilator, Mechano; Bruce Barnes, Bruce Smith, Glenn Summers, Ross Oppenheimer, Bob Danner, Bruce Ross, Bruce Jones, Bruce Roberts, Mr. Bergen, Bruce Franklin, Bruce Green, Bruce Bancroft, Bruce Baxter, Bruce Davidson, David Bannon, Robert Baker, Bruce Bixby, David Banner, David Bixby, numerous other aliases to disguise identity; "Two-Hands," "Greenskin," "Mr. Green," "Jade Jaws," "Green Goliath," "Jade Giant," "Gray Goliath," "Mighty Bob," "Anti-Hulk," "Friday," "Green Golem," "Golem"

IDENTITY: Publicly known; it is not publicly known that Joe Fixit was the Hulk

OCCUPATION: Warrior; former ruler of Sakaar, rebel leader, gladiator/slave, adventurer, nuclear physicist, mechanic, leader of the Pantheon, enforcer, research scientist, stable hand, banker, ship's crewman, farmhand, steelworker, assistant at special needs children's school, waiter, dishwasher, carnival worker, ore miner, construction worker, janitor, coal miner

CITIZENSHIP: USA, wanted for crimes (several past pardons); Sakaar

PLACE OF BIRTH: Dayton, Ohio

KNOWN RELATIVES: Caiera (wife, deceased), Elizabeth "Betty" Ross Talbot Banner (wife), Brian and Rebecca Banner (parents, deceased), Bruce (paternal grandfather, presumed deceased), unidentified paternal grandmother (presumed deceased), Susan (maternal grandmother, presumed deceased), William Morris Walters (uncle), Elaine Banner Walters (aunt, deceased), Susan Elizabeth Banner (formerly Susan Drake; paternal aunt, possibly deceased), Jennifer Walters (She-Hulk, cousin), Thaddeus E. "Thunderbolt" Ross (father-in-law)

GROUP AFFILIATION: Warbound; formerly Defenders, Order, Apocalypse's Horsemen, Secret Defenders, alternate Fantastic Four (Ghost Rider/Dan Ketch, Spider-Man/Peter Parker, Wolverine/James Howlett), Pantheon, Titans Three, Avengers, Hulkbusters of Franklin Richards' Counter-Earth (as the Hulk); formerly the Hulkbusters (as Banner)

EDUCATION: Ph.D. in nuclear physics and two other fields

FIRST APPEARANCE: Incredible Hulk #1 (1962)

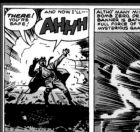

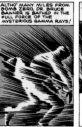

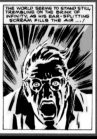

HISTORY: Robert Bruce Banner was the son of atomic physicist Dr. Brian Banner and his wife, Rebecca. Although Rebecca deeply loved Bruce, who returned her affection, Brian hated the child. An alcoholic, Brian Banner had himself been abused by his alcoholic father. He was insanely jealous of Rebecca's love for Bruce. In addition, Brian had become convinced that his work in Los Alamos to produce clean nuclear power had altered his own genes, resulting in what he saw as a mutant offspring. Bruce's early demonstrations of phenomenal intelligence only served to reinforce this belief, and Brian became increasingly abusive to Bruce, as well as to Rebecca when she defended Bruce. When Rebecca finally tried to take Bruce and flee, Brian murdered her. Having witnessed this, Bruce was intimidated by Brian into keeping silent during the ensuing trial. Brian, however, was overheard bragging how he had browbeaten Bruce into lying, and he was arrested and sent to Bellmore Psychiatric Institute in San Francisco, California.

Already a quiet intellectual youth, Bruce became even more withdrawn, internalizing his great pain and rage over his childhood sufferings. He was initially raised in Charlestown, Ohio by his aunt Susan Drake. Among his few childhood joys were the summers spent with his younger cousin, Jen Walters. By the time Bruce and his aunt (who retook her maiden name, Banner) moved to Modesto, California, Bruce had developed a separate personality to express his hidden feelings, regarding it as his imaginary friend, Hulk (or at least remembering it as so in retrospect years later). While in high school, Bruce received a severe beating after coming between an aggressive boy and his girlfriend. Enraged, the Hulk persona took control of Bruce during his sleep and he planted a bomb in the school boiler room. Realizing what had happened, Bruce rushed to the school and deactivated the timer, but was discovered, beaten again and kicked out of school. Though the bomb had been defective, Bruce's efforts were noticed by the US military, who hoped that he might become a weapons designer for them in the future. Unknown to Banner, they had Air Force General Thaddeus "Thunderbolt" Ross pressure the school not to press criminal charges as long as Bruce and Susan left town.

After graduating from Science High School, with the military's support Bruce studied nuclear physics in Navapo, New Mexico, at Desert State University (DSU) as the star

THERE! YOU'RE SAFE!
AND NOW I'LL---
AHHH
ALTHO' MANY MILES FROM BOMB ZERO, DR. BRUCE BANNER IS BATHED IN THE FULL FORCE OF THE MYSTERIOUS GAMMA RAYS!
THE WORLD SEEMS TO STAND STILL, TREMBLING ON THE BRINK OF INFINITY, AS HIS EAR-SPLITTING SCREAM FILLS THE AIR...!

Art by Jack Kirby

student of professors Herbert Josiah Weller, Max Christiansen and his mentor Geoffrey Crawford. He roomed with classmate Peter Corbeau, who would remain a long-term friend, and later with pre-law student Randy Cantor. Bruce was also classmates with Raoul Stoddard. Despite his introverted nature, Bruce was allegedly three-time dart champion. Following a brief relationship with Sally Moore, Bruce dated classmate Susan Jacobson, who tried to bring the withdrawn Banner out of his shell. When he finally did respond to her, however, his emotions exploded forth and he grabbed and terrified the girl, who broke up with him. Shortly thereafter, he had a brief fling with Susan's wilder friend Nicky. Bruce also studied for a time at Pennsylvania State University, where he met Walter Langkowski (later Sasquatch).

Bruce initially attended medical school but quit to return to his true calling. He obtained his doctorate in nuclear physics at the California Institute of Technology, alongside Phillip Sterns (later Madman) and Rikky Keegan. After a number of failed relationships, Bruce finally found happiness at CIT with medical student Angela Lipscombe; however, when Angela won a research grant and Bruce's proposals were turned down by multiple organizations, he became jealous and left her. Bruce corresponded with Charles Xavier on the gamma ray treatment of mental exhaustion and wrote a paper on particle physics, and was colleagues with Ronald Jenkins, Dimitri Solzyn and HectorDeVasquez. Unable to get work from anyone else, Banner was ultimately forced to turn to the military. Around this time Brian Banner was released from the mental hospital, and he confronted Bruce, tormenting him with the knowledge of his actions and

Art by Tim Sale

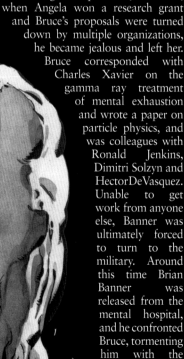

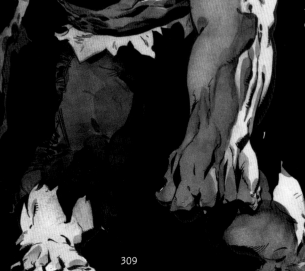

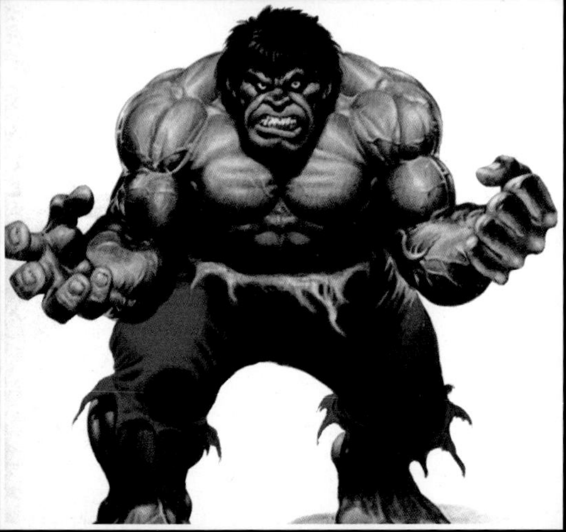

Art by Joe Jusko

threatening to kill him. Bruce fought back in self-defense, striking his father, who fell backwards, struck a tombstone and was killed. Bruce repressed his memory of this incident for many years to come.

Bruce went to work for the United States Defense Department nuclear research facility at Desert Base, New Mexico under the secret oversight of General John Ryker. There Banner finally met General "Thunderbolt" Ross, now the officer in command of the base, and his daughter, Betty. Banner and Betty eventually fell in love with each other, and Bruce also befriended cropduster Hank Stazinksi, becoming godfather to his daughter, Polly. Banner designed and oversaw construction of the "gamma bomb" or "G-bomb," a nuclear weapon with a high gamma radiation output. During the gamma bomb's first test detonation, Bruce observed from the instrumentation bunker that a civilian had breached security and entered the restricted test area. Banner told his colleague, Igor Starsky, to delay the countdown while he got the civilian to safety; however, Starsky was secretly Russian agent Igor Drenkov, and he allowed the countdown to continue, certain Banner would die in the explosion, ending the project. Reaching the civilian, Rick Jones, Banner threw him into a protective trench; but before Bruce could get himself to safety, the gamma bomb detonated and Banner was irradiated with highly charged radioactive particles. Banner was not killed by the radiation, which instead caused him to transform before Jones' eyes that very night, becoming a gray, monstrous and powerful creature that rampaged through the base. One of the soldiers seeing the creature referred to him as a "hulk," which became the name the military adopted for him; ironically this was the same name Banner had used for his persona representing his inner rage and anger, and the creature adopted this name for itself.

After the Hulk and Rick encountered, exposed and defeated Igor as he tried to steal Banner's notes, the Hulk was drawn to Betty, which led to more Army conflicts. He returned to Banner's form and mind at daybreak, but continued to transform back and forth. Realizing the Hulk's threat, Banner established a hidden desert laboratory in a cave near Desert Base. It included a small rock chamber in which Rick could seal Banner each night to contain the Hulk, and was the first of several such desert bases Banner established in the surrounding desert. Enraged by the Hulk's interest in Betty, Ross aggressively pursued the Hulk, once even aided by the new hero Iron Man (Tony Stark), to no avail. Meanwhile, though imprisoned, Igor transmitted a message to his superiors who informed the mutated genius Gargoyle (Yuri Topolov) of the Hulk's existence. Initially intending to prove his superiority, Gargoyle captured the Hulk and Rick Jones via will-sapping pellets and brought them to his Russian base; upon seeing the Hulk's transformation into Banner, Gargoyle — himself a radiation mutate — worked with Banner to achieve a cure for his own condition. Grateful, Topolov set Banner and Jones free and blew up his own base, sacrificing himself to strike back against the government that had mutated and exploited him, dying as a man.

The first of the many variations of Banner's transformations manifested as the Hulk became green, the color he would generally keep and the hue most often seen in other gamma mutates. At first Banner kept his affliction secret from everyone except Rick Jones, who was grateful to Banner for saving his life and has remained his friend and confidant ever since. Though Banner and Hulk soon defeated the invading alien Tribbitites ("Toad Men"), Banner's unexplained presence aboard their ship led to early suspicions of Banner being a traitor; these were further inflamed by Banner's frequent unexplained absences. The military regarded the Hulk as a menace and constantly hunted him, often on the orders of General Ross. For instance, the General's "Plan H" launched the Hulk into space aboard a missile, but Rick returned the missile to Earth. Space radiation transmitted back through its controls on Earth somehow enabled Rick to control Hulk via verbal commands for some time thereafter; in addition, the Hulk stopped turning back into Banner, and he would rampage while Rick slept. After Rick helped Hulk stop the Ringmaster and his Circus of Crime, he daringly used Banner's desert lab gamma ray projector to turn Hulk back into Banner, who then fine-tuned the projector, allowing him to turn into the Hulk at will while retaining his intelligence; however, Hulk remained easily provoked and violent,

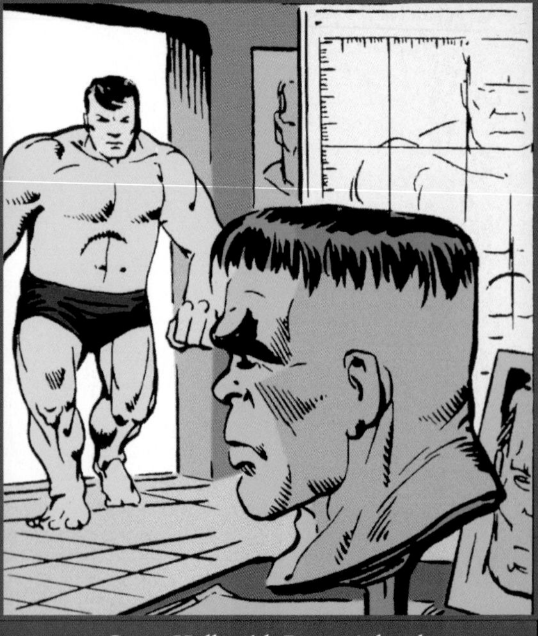

Art by Steve Ditko

Green Hulk with Banner's head.

and Banner was left weakened after his transformations. The Hulk confronted the seemingly alien conqueror Mongu, revealed to be Russian agent Boris Monguski, whose Russian soldiers tried to capture the Hulk so their scientists could make an army with his strength. The Hulk drove off the Russians but was nonetheless suspected of being involved in Mongu's hoax. As the Hulk's rampages continued, groups such as Green Cross were established to provide victims disaster relief.

General Ross unwittingly assigned Banner to stop the Hulk, whose defeats of subterranean warlord Tyrannus and Asian invader General Fang went largely unrecognized. Continued gamma exposure affected Banner, rendering his normal form briefly super-strong and once leaving Banner's normal head atop the Hulk's body, forcing him to wear a Hulk mask; the transformations eventually stabilized with Banner becoming the Hulk in times of stress, though gamma ray exposure often caused the change. Framed for destruction of U.S. technology, Hulk battled the Fantastic Four before the Wrecker (Karl Kort) was exposed as the true culprit. The Hulk redeemed himself in the government's eyes by defeating the alien Metal Master, earning a presidential pardon. Soon after, however, he was duped by the Asgardian god Loki into destroying a train trestle; though he saved the oncoming train, he was nonetheless blamed. Hearing of this, Rick Jones attempted to contact the Fantastic Four to locate Hulk, but Loki redirected the message to reach Loki's hated brother, Thor. Iron Man, Ant-Man (Hank Pym) and the Wasp (Janet Van Dyne) also received the message, joining forces to track the fugitive Hulk, who was posing as a robot named Mechano in the Kiebler Circus (apparently unaware that several Circus of Crime members were also hiding out there). Locating Hulk via Ant-Man's ants, the four heroes briefly fought the Hulk until Loki's duplicity was exposed. Following Loki's defeat, the Hulk helped the other heroes found the Avengers; however, his new teammates distrusted him due to his dangerous temper. The other-dimensional shape-shifting Space Phantom exploited this distrust by impersonating the Hulk and turning the others against him. The deception was exposed, but the Hulk, feeling he was hated by the other Avengers, quit the group.

As the Hulk's savage personality became more ascendant, he became a public menace once again, continually hunted by the military; the implacable General Ross would even form a specialized military team of "Hulkbusters" devoted to targeting the monster. Namor the Sub-Mariner briefly teamed with Hulk against the Avengers, but their alliance — uneasy due to Namor's arrogance and the Hulk's volatility — was short-lived; the Hulk turned back into Banner in mid-fight and fled. The Hulk found a recurring foe in the Leader, a gamma-enhanced intellect who repeatedly sought to defeat or exploit the Hulk. One of the Hulk's few true friends at this time was the Sentry (Robert Reynolds), whose solar energy soothed the otherwise savage beast. For a time the Hulk stayed at the Sentry's Watchtower, teaming with him against the General, Danny Boy, the Leader, Living Nuke and the Lobster People. Eventually, however, the Sentry's dark side, the Void, returned and assaulted the Hulk, psychically tormenting him and sending him on a rampage; the Hulk soon returned to his wanderings, more alone than ever. The Hulk's somewhat random travels have spanned the globe, including many nations across each continent. He has also visited numerous planets, various dimensions and past and future eras.

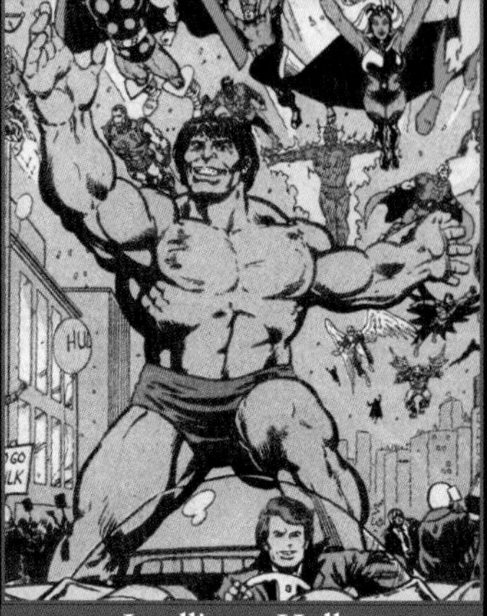
Intelligent Hulk.

Art by Sal Buscema

For a surprisingly long time, Banner concealed his double identity from virtually everyone but Rick Jones; however, during a time when the Hulk was missing and presumed dead, Jones told General Ross's aide, Major Glenn Talbot, that Banner was the Hulk, and Banner's secret inevitably became public knowledge. Aided by the Fantastic Four's Reed Richards, Banner again placed his mind in control of the Hulk. Believing his problems over, Banner proposed to Betty, who accepted; but the Leader, seeking vengeance on the Hulk, sent the Rhino to disrupt the wedding and used a gamma weapon to restore the savage Hulk. When General Ross was injured in the subsequent battle, the Hulk's nature caused a long-term rift between Bruce and Betty. Soon after, Kang the Conqueror captured the Hulk and sent him back in time to 1917 to rid himself of Banner by arranging the death of Banner's grandfather (or possibly great-grandfather) — a French World War I soldier — to prevent Banner's birth, but the Hulk instead fought attacking German soldiers, foiling Kang's plot. Banner later returned to DSU where Raoul Stoddard used his Gammatron to cure Banner, separating Banner and Hulk into two beings. The Gammatron was subsequently used to remerge them in the erroneous belief that the Hulk might stay submerged within Banner.

Rick had previously left the Hulk, who, not surprisingly, had few other long-term friends. Young Jim Wilson became a close friend, staying by Hulk's side for several lengthy periods. Mogol, agent of Tyrannus also befriended the Hulk, who angrily smashed Mogol to pieces upon learning he was a robot. Hulk formed another brief friendship with the homeless "Crackajack" Jackson, who taught him to read, but Jackson was killed by the criminals Hammer and Anvil. Rick Jones would return to the Hulk's side for long periods in the future. The Hulk also found friends and allies as a member of the Defenders, an informal super-hero group where his long-term teammates included Dr. Strange, Namor, Silver Surfer, Valkyrie, Nighthawk, Hellcat and others; however, the general public was mostly unaware of the Defenders' existence and activities during Hulk's membership, so he was still widely regarded as a menace. Others who befriended the Hulk during his journeys included Morvania's Rachel Dresden and her family, who believed the Hulk to be the legendary Golem; the benevolent New Men of the High Evolutionary's Counter-Earth; the Brickford family of Lucifer Falls, West Virginia; Siberia's Katrina Palkov; Angus & Sarah MacTavish of Scotland's Loch Fear; Bob & Carol Hickman, son-in-law and daughter of the Locust (August Hopper); an orphaned deer "Bambi" that was later possessed by Chondu the Mystic; orphan Ricky Anderson with whom he attended Florida's wonderland amusement park; Joe Timms (the Glob); the cavewoman Tanna; the uncivilized Rock People; the "Circus of Lost Souls;" "Robinson Crusoe" (aka David Purvis); Todd Gregory, whom the Hulk helped save from paternal abuse; Canadian "witch doctor" Passing Cloud; Fred Sloan and Trish Starr; Cherokee Chief John; alien exile Zgorian; and the poisoned world's symbiont "Sym."

Similarly, Banner has made numerous friends and acquaintances, such as Abby Davis, a Crystal Falls, Colorado waitress; Jungfrau, Switzerland's Katrina Euler, whom he referred to colleagues for treatment of an illness; British Columbia's Maureen Friesen; Africa's Paradise Island's Thaddeus Hatcher; Manhattan hippy Clear Marks; the mentally challenged Earl Slocum; Suzette Classon; Las Vegas singer Jimmy Martin; Faulkner, Missouri's sheriff Jonas Tolliver and his daughter Emma; St. Louis, Missouri's Jerome Able; Manhattan's Pam Grayson; and London sorceress Patricia Freeman. Some of the above proved friends to both Banner and the Hulk. Banner has also enjoyed a number of short-lived romances, such as Daily Bugle reporter Dawn Michaels, Manhattan businesswoman Alice Steinfeld and the Nightmerican Chrissie Cutler. Unfortunately, the savage Hulk's limited intellect has also rendered him the pawn of numerous evildoers who earned his alliance via promises of friendship or vengeance against those who had harmed him. Though the Fantastic Four's freakish strongman Thing has sympathized with the Hulk's plight, the two have just as often met as foes, and one effort to cure the Hulk instead resulted in a temporary switching of their minds. The feral mutant Wolverine has shared a similar ally/enemy role with the Hulk.

For years Betty Ross continued to love Banner, despite her knowledge of his double identity; however, Banner's feelings were divided after the Hulk fell in love with Jarella, queen of K'ai in an unidentified extradimensional "micro-world" whose green-skinned natives welcomed the Hulk. K'ai's Sorcerers Triad allowed Banner's brain to control the Hulk and he nearly became king, but he was always pulled back to Earth before long. Betty eventually married Glenn Talbot and Jarella was accidentally killed while living on Earth, but Betty still harbored a secret love for Banner. Banner continued efforts to cure himself aided by experts such as his former mentor Geoffrey Crawford, but never achieved any lasting success. While Banner was visiting his cousin Jennifer Walters in Los Angeles, she was shot by an agent of gangster Nicholas Trask. To save his cousin's life Banner improvised an emergency blood transfusion. The transfusion of Banner's blood mutated Walters, causing her to become the She-Hulk. Betty eventually divorced Glenn Talbot, General Ross went mad and Gamma Base was shut down. During this same time, the Hulk briefly became a pawn of the mystic realm Tunnelworld's dread sorcerer the Unnameable — who drew power from

Art by Sal Buscema

"Mindless" Hulk.

and controlled all those who knew its true name — but Dr. Strange ultimately duped the Unnameable into drawing all of its power into the Hulk and then trapping it within a sealed section of the Hulk's brain. Banner subsequently befriended Manhattan's Ruby Barclay who took him to the mystic Baba Shanti, who turned out to be Bruce's old roommate Randy Cantor seeking to guide others in the path of enlightenment he had attained to some degree. Glenn Talbot was ultimately slain in a desperate effort to destroy the Hulk.

Sometime later, repeated gamma radiation exposure during several adventures caused Bruce to retain Banner's mind in Hulk form and gave him control of his transformations. When this information became public knowledge, the US president pardoned the now heroic Hulk. Bruce briefly enjoyed the companionship of the alien Bereet, who had filmed his adventures as the Hulk from her home planet. Banner then returned to his career as a scientist, working out of Northwind Observatory, constructing the artificial assistant and companion Recordasphere and initiating a romantic relationship with his assistant, Kate Waynesboro. While Kate proved to be a SHIELD agent sent to monitor Banner to ensure he remained in control, she did end up falling in love with him. "Sphere" was destroyed by the Abomination, and Banner was very upset to learn Kate's secret. Banner's anxiety was exacerbated by the demon Nightmare, who sought to provoke him into becoming the savage Hulk once again to increase humanity's fear (and nightmares) of him. Despite his best efforts, Banner began to lose control over the Hulk. Former mobster Max "Hammer" Stryker kidnapped Kate, coercing Banner to use his gamma device to cure Stryker's cancer. The Hulk was transported to Battleworld by the Beyonder to participate in the "Secret Wars" struggle. Upon returning, he saw Stryker mutate into a Hulk-like creature. When the enraged Stryker attacked him, the only way Banner could fight the creature's brutal attack was to allow the savage Hulk personality to gain ascendance. Broken by having and then losing control, Banner retreated further into himself, allowing the Hulk to become more and more mindless and violent. Ultimately, Banner requested that the sorcerer Dr. Strange transform him into the Hulk in his mind to free himself from his tormented existence.

The now virtually mindless Hulk was too dangerous to be allowed to rampage across the Earth, and Dr. Strange did not want to kill his old friend. He found the solution in the Crossroads, a dimension that was a portal to countless other dimensions. The Hulk could go anywhere he wanted, and would be returned to the Crossroads as soon as he became dissatisfied with his location. During this time the Hulk found that there were many beings whose power dwarfed even his own. In the Crossroads the Hulk made a friend in the Puffball Collective, another entity that had been banished there; however, the Puffball was revealed to be an agent of the N'Garai demons, and had only befriended the Hulk to escape the Crossroads. Shortly after revealing itself, the Puffball was slaughtered by the N'Garai, and the Hulk returned to the Crossroads. The Collective's attention to the Hulk had begun to reawaken Banner's mind, which first manifested itself as the Triad: Goblin (his id and emotions), Guardian (his ego and sense of self-preservation) and Glow (his superego and intellect). The Triad began to guide the mindless Hulk into rediscovering himself, and on one world a wounded Hulk transformed back into Banner.

The Hulk was unwittingly returned to Earth by the Canadian super-team Alpha Flight. Seeking a monstrous form to house the disembodied intellect of Walter Langkowski (formerly Sasquatch), they unwittingly snared the Hulk with an energy harpoon. The Hulk regressed back into a violent mindless state upon returning to Earth, rampaging across the continent. Doc Samson eventually captured the Hulk and succeeded in separating Banner's psyche and atomic structure from that of the Hulk, making them separate beings. The mindless Hulk escaped and, no longer restrained by Banner's subconscious identity, became a greater menace than ever before. Banner organized a new group of Hulkbusters to capture the Hulk, for whom he still felt responsible. Nonetheless, thinking himself free from his half-existence as the Hulk, Banner at last married Betty Ross. But Banner's health sharply declined because of his having been so divided. As a result, the android Vision facilitated the reintegration of Banner and the Hulk into a single physical being. General Ross, then descending into madness, interfered with Doc Samson's subsequent attempt to cure the Hulk, causing him to revert back to his original gray state and personality — less strong and more intelligent than the traditional Hulk, but ruthless and cruel. In the process, Rick was exposed to the Hulk's energies and began turning into his own version of the savage Hulk for a brief time before being cured.

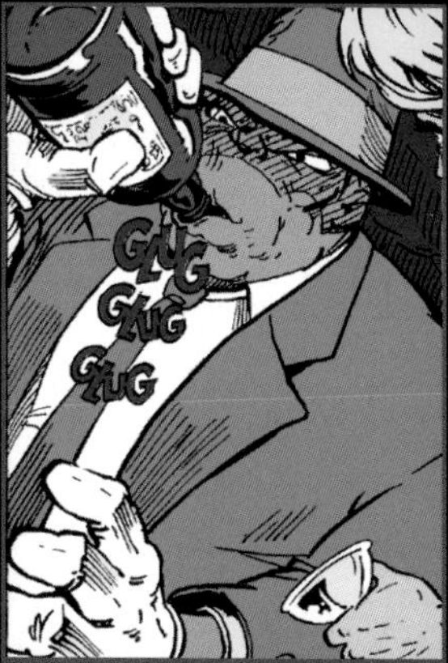
GLUG
GLUG
GLUG
Mr. Fixit.

Art by Jeff Purves

Banner initially kept the return of his Hulk transformations a secret, but his condition inevitably became public knowledge again. The gray Hulk worked alongside Rick Jones and SHIELD agent Clay Quartermain during the search for a missing gamma bomb. The quest culminated with the Leader detonating the bomb in the city of Middletown, Arizona with the Hulk at the center of the explosion. Seemingly dead, the Hulk was actually saved by wizards of Jarella's world, who brought him to their planet to overthrow the mad Grand Inquisitor. The Hulk enjoyed the resultant worship he received and decided to stay there, but the wizards sent him home so they could rule instead. Upon returning to Earth, the still gray Hulk took the identity of Joe Fixit and became an enforcer for Las Vegas casino Coliseum owner Michael Berengetti. Fixit kept his Hulk identity secret, pretending instead to have a bizarre skin condition that was sensitive to sunlight. A spell from the alien sorcerers allowed Fixit to remain in Hulk form for months without reverting, but eventually the spell wore off. Fixit briefly dated the statuesque Marlo Chandler, but eventually it became clear that he was the Hulk; Berengetti terminated his employment due to the heat the Hulk was continually bringing to his business.

The Hulk's transformation began to destabilize, and he would intermittently become Fixit and the green savage Hulk. Eventually Doc Samson partially diagnosed Banner's identity disorder and, by working with the Ringmaster's hypnosis, merged Banner's mind with that of Fixit and the savage Hulk, creating a new form, which possessed the greatest aspects of each of the splinter personalities, later nicknamed the Professor. Now mentally stable in his Hulk form, Banner was soon recruited to join covert disaster-prevention group the Pantheon, which he came to lead for a length of time. During this period he was pulled forward in time to encounter his dark future self, the Maestro; the knowledge of his potential future greatly troubled the Hulk, as did one particular encounter in which one of the Maestro's "Betties" had sex with the Hulk while he was paralyzed with a broken neck. The Pantheon also helped the Hulk free his old girlfriend Susan Jacobson, who had been imprisoned as a spy. Later, when an internal war developed in the Pantheon, the Hulk became so angry that he triggered a subconscious fail-safe he had created for himself. Fearful of his mindless form's destructive capacity, he transformed back into Banner upon becoming too angry. In addition, while in Banner's form, he possessed the mind of the savage Hulk. This created an Achilles' heel for Banner in that one of his greatest assets, his anger, became his greatest weakness.

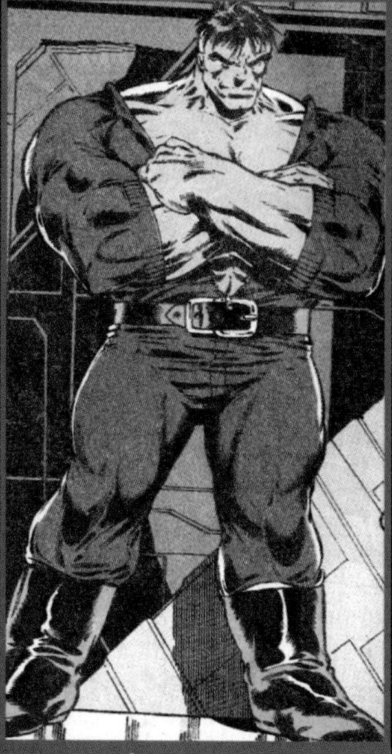
Pantheon Costume.

Art by Dale Keown

The Hulk left the Pantheon, working briefly as a mechanic under his old instructor, Max Christiansen. Later, Banner received a piece of shrapnel in his brain, and only transformation into the Hulk saved his life. The shrapnel caused the Hulk to become darker and more violent, seemingly beginning the degeneration

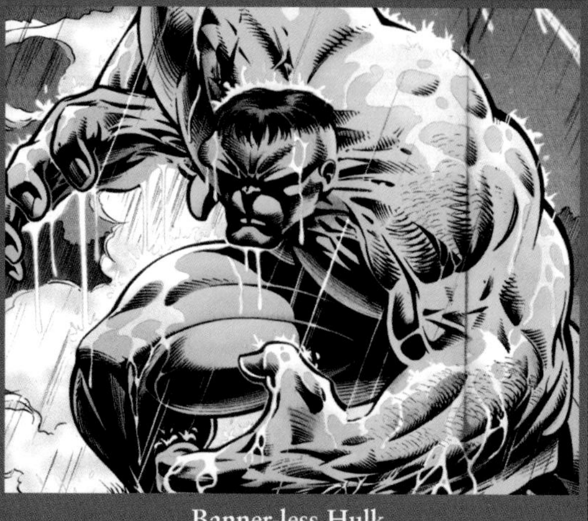
Banner-less Hulk.

Art by Mike Deodato Jr.

Art by Ed Benes

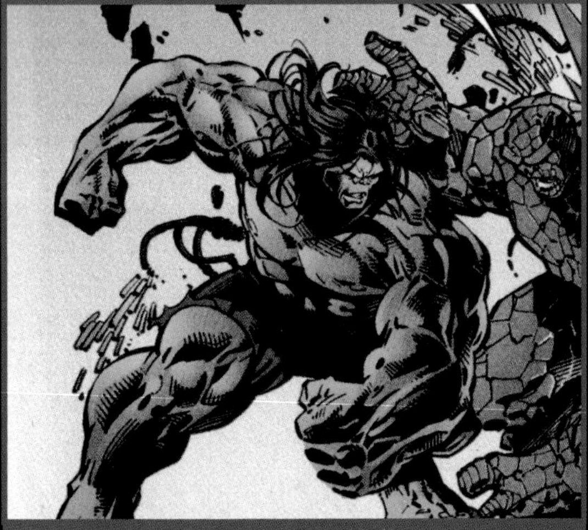
Counter-Earth Hulk.

that would lead to his becoming the Maestro. When the Hulk opposed the malevolent psychic entity Onslaught, a portion of Banner was sent to the alternate world created by Franklin Richards that eventually became known as Counter-Earth; that fragment was reborn as a fledgling Hulk with his past memories suppressed. Maintaining a connection with his Counter-Earth fragment, the Hulk initially mutated and shed massive amounts of radiation before stabilizing. Sensing that he was lacking something, the Hulk sought to gain "more," though he did not know what he truly wanted. For a time he was joined by Janis Jones (time-displaced possible future great-granddaughter of Rick Jones and Marlo Chandler), and his interdimensional connections served as a nexus attracting otherdimensional beings, such as the Hulk of Reality-9722 who had slain that timeline's Maestro and ruled his Dystopia for a time. Bereft of Banner's mental blocks, the Hulk also began to rediscover his suppressed memories of his father and his death, and he was sometimes plagued by the seeming ghost of his father. During this time the Hulk fell under the influence of the immortal mutant Apocalypse, who used a laser to destroy the shrapnel in the Hulk's brain. The Hulk briefly became Apocalypse's Horseman War, wearing a helmet intended to block out his father; however, when War injured Rick Jones, the Hulk was again plagued by guilt and his father's taunts, and he rejected Apocalypse's programming and regained his own mind.

Eventually the two Hulk fragments were remerged, restoring the status quo of the savage Hulk splitting its existence and time with Banner. The Hulk then faced and again defeated the Maestro, who had eventually absorbed enough gamma radiation from his past self to re-form. Bruce once again established a healthy relationship with his wife Betty, but he suffered a devastating blow when Betty died of radiation poisoning after his old enemy the Abomination injected her with some of his own blood; Banner initially assumed Betty had died from chronic exposure to his own radioactive body. Shortly thereafter, Banner's influence was usurped by Tyrannus, who sent the Hulk on senselessly destructive rampages that Banner could not recall. Tyrannus also briefly captured Banner and used a Tyrannoid Subterranean mutated into Hulk form to replace him. The Tyrannoid-Hulk went on even more destructive rampages, bringing down a passenger airplane, killing everyone aboard. The Hulk ultimately halted Tyrannus' plot and cleared his name.

Banner then began to suffer from the degenerative neurological disease Amyotrophic Lateral Sclerosis (ALS, aka Lou Gehrig's Disease). Banner's condition deteriorated severely, and he worked with his old college girlfriend, neurologist Angela Lipscombe, to develop a cure. During this time, the Hulk, Dr. Strange, Namor and the Surfer fell prey to a spell of their enemy Yandroth that cursed them to be drawn together as the Defenders whenever evil threatened Earth. Following being targeted and briefly captured by the nefarious General John Ryker, the Hulk was ultimately treated by Lipscombe, Reed Richards and Ant-Man (Scott Lang), who repaired Bruce's nervous system via implanting DNA from Brian Banner's corpse. Obliquely indebted to him for his continued life, Bruce at last made his peace with his memories of his father. Soon after, Yandroth's spell — which drew on the Earth goddess Gaea's power — caused the four Defenders to become increasingly self-righteous and violent, eventually establishing themselves as the Order and seeking to conquer Earth. Empowered by their violence, Yandroth nearly gained the power to destroy the world before the Order realized his plan and ceased all hostilities, dissipating his power and essence again.

Bruce was then contacted by the mysterious Mr. Blue — actually Betty Banner, secretly resurrected and surgically altered by a mysterious agency known only as the Team — who trained him to use self-hypnosis to better control his transformations. Soon after, the Leader initiated his most complex plot yet against his old foe. The Hulk was framed for the seeming death of Ricky Myers, and Bruce had to go into hiding. On the run once again, the Hulk was pursued by various agents of the covert organization Home Base, who sought his blood to create an army of super-powered warriors. Some of these agents, such as Pratt, Sandra Verdugo and the mysterious S-3, had been granted extensive regenerative powers. Both Banner and the Hulk were pursued relentlessly in a series of ever more complicated plots, though Banner continued to receive aid from Mr. Blue and Doc Samson. Verdugo was actually Ricky Myer's mother by Samson, and she

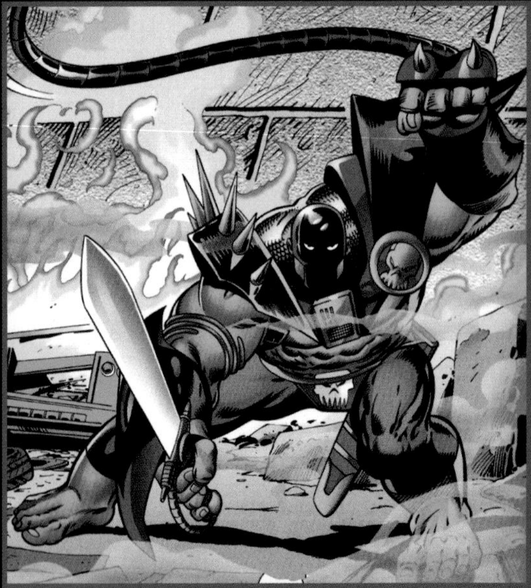
The Hulk as Apocalypse's Horseman War.

Art by Adam Kubert

had been promised to be reunited with her son if she brought the Hulk to Home Base. Realizing that Home Base would slay Ricky as soon as they had the Hulk, she instead turned against her partner, Jink Slater, arranging his death and convincing the Hulk to help rescue Ricky. Pratt successfully obtained a sample of Hulk blood but was injected with it before he could return it to Home Base. Despite being mutated by this exposure, Pratt was ultimately destroyed by the Hulk. Bruce then seemed to happen upon a New Mexico desert supply store and shared a romance with its owner; this turned out to be yet another Home Base plot, as the owner was Nadia Dornova Blonsky, the Abomination's ex-wife, who had joined with Home Base to gain revenge on her abusive former spouse. Nadia, however, developed true feelings for Banner, revealed her plot to him, and confronted the Abomination herself, intending to destroy him with a Home Base-implanted weapon. Home Base double-crossed her with an ineffective weapon, but the Hulk saved her and defeated the Abomination.

Seeking peace in Mistassini, Canada, Banner instead encountered Wolverine and the assassin Shredder before saving coral-snake-bite victim Kyle Hatcher with a transfusion of his own blood. Relocating to Manhattan, Banner befriended advertising agent Pam Grayson, who helped him defeat a psychically powered Absorbing Man. Banner was then guided back to New Mexico by Home Base and arrived to save Nadia and the recently arrived S-3 from the Home Base's Krill — lizard-like androids designed to deliver Hulk blood to Home Base. Despite her facial reconstruction, the Hulk instantly recognized S-3 as Betty, a former double agent within Home Base as well as the enigmatic Mr. Blue, and they were soon joined by Samson and Verdugo. In a seemingly final confrontation with Home Base, Sandra perished in its self-destruct nuclear explosion, while the Hulk saved the others from a Home Base Banner/Hulk clone, which he was forced to eviscerate to prevent its regeneration. During that conflict, only Nadia believed that Bruce was himself and not the clone, and Banner left all of them to be alone, though he did leave behind a supply of the Hulk's blood that Betty might use to save herself from the cancer she had obtained during the Team's treatments. Relocating to California, the Hulk was captured by the clairvoyant Even Matthews; Matthews released Banner and tried to trick Banner into killing him to prevent his dying from cancer, though Banner recognized the ruse and refused. Tony Stark drafted Banner into helping him develop a gamma-radiation-proof suit of armor, and both Banner and the Hulk were needed to save Stark from radiation toxicity after Stark elevated the radiation exposure levels in efforts to prove the armor's value.

Exhausted by his recent non-stop adventures, Banner at last fell prey to the Leader, who forced the Hulk into a somnambulant state, drawing him to his base. Left a disembodied head by his recent experiences, the Leader forced the Hulk to set his controls to establish a link between their minds, and the Leader intended to transfer his mind into the Hulk's brain, permanently ousting Banner's mind. Samson, Betty and Nadia came to the rescue, and Samson smashed the Hulk into the Leader's tank, severing his linkage to the Hulk and leaving his head to die in the open air. Nadia, however, perished saving Betty from a piece of flying glass from the shattered tank, taking it through the chest instead.

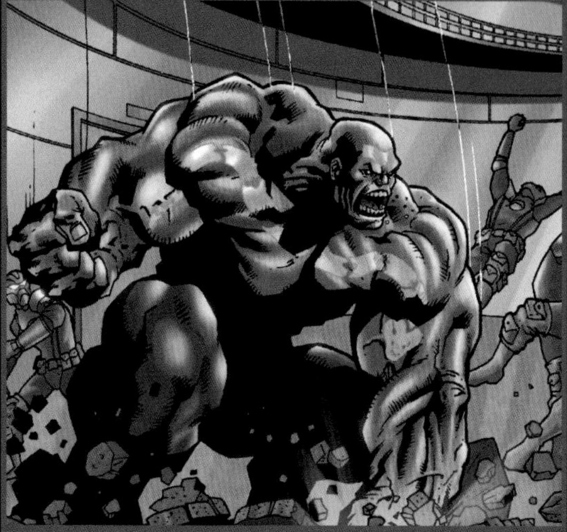

House of M reality Hulk.

Art by Jorge Lucas

Enraged and confused, the Hulk savagely beat Samson until Betty condemned the Hulk as a destructive monster and caused him to flee.

The Hulk was subsequently enlisted by Strange against the extradimensional sorcerer Dormammu, who turned Hulk to stone. Restored and seduced by Dormammu's sorcerous sister, Umar, the Hulk then joined her, Strange and Namor in stripping Dormammu of power he had usurped from the cosmic Eternity, power Umar claimed herself. Summoned to Nightmare Island, the Hulk was beset by extradimensional Mindless Ones in illusory form via the demon Nightmare, but he ultimately saw through the deceptions, decapitated Nightmare and left his new acquaintance Daydream (Nightmare's half-human daughter) behind. In London, Bruce briefly befriended the sorceress Patricia Freeman, helping her spirit track down her killer, Tom Perkins, before she faded from existence.

When the Scarlet Witch overwrote existence with the "House of M" reality, Banner and the Hulk both found themselves an accepted part of the True People tribe of Aborigines in Australia. The Hulk joined forces with AIM (Advanced Idea Mechanics) — including Monica Rappaccini, Scorpion (Carmilla Black/Thasanee Rappaccini), Professor Aaron Isaacs and his robot creation Adam — in toppling the mutant Exodus' dictatorship, which was rounding up humans for slaughter. Now ruling Australia, Banner had a relationship with Monica, learning she was Nicky from his college days. Even after discovering and neutralizing Monica's cyborg army program (developed from unwilling recruits captured by government agents) and overcoming her efforts to have him killed, Banner kept Monica by his side, refusing to surrender his new position even under instruction from the mighty Magneto who ruled that reality. Soon after, however, this reality faded from existence and the status quo was restored. The "Old Man" of the True People, whose mysticism had allowed him to see beyond the reality changes, invited "Two-Minds" (his name for Banner and the Hulk) to stay with them, but Banner realized his violent ways would be a constant threat to them. Sometime later, while passing through Jackalope, New Mexico, the Hulk fought off a SHIELD helicopter pursuing Amadeus Cho, earning the young ultra-genius' fierce loyalty.

Art by Carlo Pagulayan

THEY SENT HIM UP TO SAVE THEIR WORLD.
AND NOW IT'S TIME TO COME HOME.
BUT HIS SHIP IS SAILING THE WRONG WAY.
HIS FRIENDS TALK AND TALK. SO CALM. SO REASONABLE.
TIME AND TIME AGAIN, YOUR ANGER AND POWER HAVE THREATENED THE ENTIRE PLANET.
SO WHEN WE LEARNED THAT FURY SENT YOU INTO SPACE, WE HAD TO SEIZE THE OPPORTUNITY.
EXPLAINING THEIR TRICK.
SOON HE CAN'T HEAR THEIR WORDS. ONLY THE ANNOYING BUZZING OF THEIR PUNY HUMAN VOICES.
I HAVE ALWAYS THOUGHT OF US AS FRIENDS, BRUCE. SO I AM TRULY, GENUINELY SORRY.
BUT FOR YOUR SAKE AND OURS, WE'RE SENDING YOU AWAY. IT'S THE ONLY WAY WE CAN BE SURE.
DROWNED OUT BY THE BLOOD SURGING THROUGH HIS BODY.

The Illuminati betray the Hulk.

Enlisted to foil a plot by the terrorist group Hydra, the Hulk was exposed to a gamma bomb explosion, which rendered him delusional and left him in his gray form, but with his full strength. The Hulk rampaged in Las Vegas, battling the Human Torch and Thing at length until the former's nova flame restored his sanity. This rampage, however, had been noticed by the "Illuminati" — a secret elite cabal of super-beings who sought to keep Earth's paranormal affairs under control. Despite the objections and violent departure of Namor, the remaining Illuminati members — Iron Man, Mr. Fantastic (Reed Richards), Dr. Strange and the Inhuman monarch Black Bolt — plotted the permanent elimination of Hulk's threat to Earth. As Strange and the others had all been Hulk's friends at some point, they sought not to slay him, but instead to banish him to another world where he might live in peace. Banner had relocated to northwestern Alaska, living a solitary existence as a fisherman, but was tracked by a Nick Fury LMD (Life Model Decoy) and enlisted to destroy the Godseye, an alleged Hydra creation that threatened Earth. Banner agreed and the Hulk went up in space, risking his life and destroying the Godseye, but not before he learned it was actually a SHIELD creation. Planning to take this up with Fury, the Hulk instead fell victim to the "Illuminati" plot and was sent flying off into space with no ability to control his ship as it headed for an uninhabited planet. A parting message from his four former friends explaining their actions played out as he realized his fate.

The "Illuminati" plot went awry when the SHIELD ship carrying the Hulk was pulled into the Great Portal, a wormhole created by the Shadow People of the planet Sakaar that brought beings and objects from around the universe to their world in hopes of helping the planet and its people. Greatly weakened by the passage and subsequent crash, the Hulk was captured and auctioned off to gladiator trainer Primus Vand. Drawing early attention after slaughtering a group of immensely powerful "great devil corkers," the Hulk then targeted Sakaar's ruler, the Red King (Angmo II). Intrigued, the battle-armored King confronted the Hulk, delivering several wounds but receiving a sword slash to his face in return. The Hulk was subdued by the King's Death's Head Warguards, implanted with a control disk and sent to the training camp known as the Maw where it was believed he would perish.

Overcoming various challenges, the Hulk was placed in a group with fellow survivors the insectoid Miek (whom he had saved from the Corkers in the previous battle), a nameless Brood female, the Kronan Korg, Hiroim of the Shadow People, and the Imperials (natives of the same ruling class as the Red King) Lavin Skee and Elloe Kaifi. During their first group gladiatorial combat, an enthusiastic announcer nicknamed Hulk the "Green Scar" for a wound he received fighting the Red King. After proving themselves in combat, the gladiators were invited to join the Sakaar Democratic Insurgency; though the Hulk and others refused, Elloe sided with the rebel Insurgency, who were swiftly captured by Warguards. Recognizing the Hulk as extremely dangerous, the Red King's bound Shadow Warrior, Caiera the Oldstrong, attempted to buy him and take him out of combat, but he refused. The Red King subsequently had a bomb dropped on the gladiators, but the Hulk saved them, taking the full hit himself and then flattening the attacking Warguard, though Lavin Skee fell in combat. The remaining gladiators then joined together as Warbound, vowing loyalty to each other. Interestingly, in spots where the Hulk's blood touched the soil of Sakaar, Eleha'al vines began to grow, leading some to believe the Hulk was the Sakaarson, a being long prophesized as the savior of Sakaar.

The Warbound's next challenge was the Silver Surfer, who had also passed through the Great Portal and been enslaved by the Red King as the "Silver Savage." Surprised by his former ally's attack, the Hulk recovered and shattered the Surfer's control disk but nonetheless angrily beat him senseless. The Red King then offered

Art by Ladronn

Hulk finds himself forced to fight in the gladiatorial contests on the alien planet Sakaar.

the Warbound their freedom — as was custom after surviving three such combats — but only if they slew their former member Elloe. The Warbound refused despite the King's threats of destruction, and the Surfer then destroyed every control disk in the arena, allowing the Warbound, Surfer and others to break out and escape into the wilderness. The Surfer offered to take the Hulk with him as he departed, but the Hulk declined, having at last found friendship and a life he could enjoy.

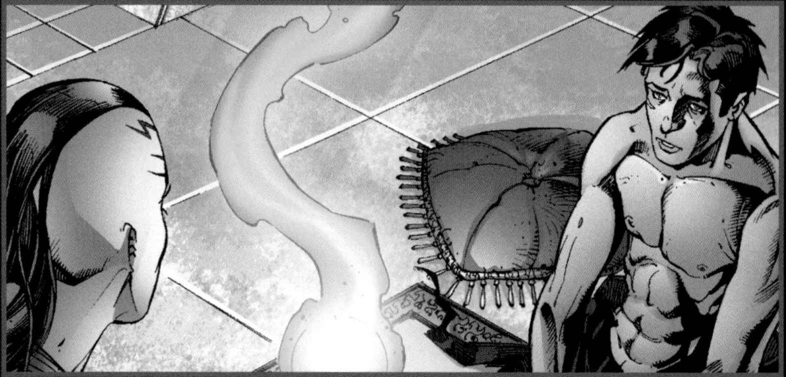

The Hulk reveals Banner to his wife Caiera.

Art by Aaron Lopresti

Via sage advice from Hiroim and Korg, the Hulk evaded multiple attacks by the King's warriors, and his following grew steadily as Miek located a number of his insectoid brethren (thought long dead) and then liberated those in the Maw. The Hulk considered leaving his allies as he feared that he was not the Sakaarson, but instead another prophecy, the apocalyptic World Breaker; however, after Miek evolved into a much more powerful form as ruler of the insectoids, Hulk decided to continue to lead the rebels. Hoping to save Sakaar from prolonged war, Caiera met the Hulk in single combat, her Old Power proving an even match for his gamma-spawned might. The Red King, however, caring little for his people and wishing to end the Hulk's threat by any means possible, unleashed the Spikes — parasitic menaces whom his father had long ago banished to one of Sakaar's moons, able to infect and assimilate organic beings into their number — freeing them to slaughter the Warbound, his own troops (including Caiera) and even the innocent civilians nearby. The Hulk proved resistant to infection, and after the Red King had an entire city of civilians slaughtered by missile attack to destroy his enemies, Caiera vowed vengeance on him and joined the rebellion.

Seeking allies, the Hulk was denied the aid of the Shadow People but did claim their stone starship to aid the rebellion. Surprising all involved, the Hulk made an alliance with the elder Spikes, learning they only sought freedom from Sakaar's environment since it deprived them of stellar energy and drove them mad with hunger. The Hulk finally met and overpowered the Red King, who mercilessly slaughtered his own people during the battle, and cast him into the wilderness where he was consumed by Wildebots. The Hulk was pronounced the new king of Sakaar and he swiftly enforced peace between the formerly warring Imperials and insectoid Natives, after which he chose Caiera as his queen, undergoing her Shadow ritual and revealing his Banner form to her. Having sustained the Spikes with his own power, the Hulk had them sent back into space, and they gratefully returned the spirits of the lives they had unintentionally absorbed on Sakaar, allowing those spirits' loved ones closure and the knowledge that they had achieved peace. By only the third day of his rule, the Hulk had earned massive approval and was making steps towards peace with long-time enemies of the Imperials when the warp core on the ship that had brought him to Sakaar exploded. The unleashed energies caused a chain reaction that shattered Crown City of Sakaar and slew the vast majority of the population, including Caiera, who was bearing the Hulk's child. Infuriated beyond comprehension and empowered even further by the explosion's energies, Hulk led Sakaar's few known survivors, including his Warbound and robot pilot Arch-E, in boarding the stone starship and heading to Earth for vengeance on the "Illuminati."

Arriving first on the moon, the Hulk savagely beat Black Bolt and then sent a transmission to Earth ordering Manhattan's evacuation that he might meet Iron Man, Dr. Strange and Reed Richards in combat. Iron Man faced him in a set of Hulkbuster armor but met a crushing defeat that shattered much of Avengers Tower as well. Overpowering all who tried to stop him — including Doc Samson, She-Hulk and two Avengers contingents — the Hulk then took down the entire Fantastic Four to get Richards. Despite his violent methods, the Hulk gained allies when Amadeus Cho organized the Renegades to assist him. Dr. Strange met Bruce Banner on the astral plane, but the Hulk crushed his hands, reducing his spell-casting ability. Tearing the roof off of Madison Square Garden, the Hulk made this his new gladiatorial arena, using Sakaarian slave disks to control the captured heroes and forcing his former banishers to fight each other. Strange then used a potion to obtain monstrous-strength via the immensely power magical entity Zom.

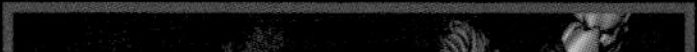

The Hulk unleashes his rage on New York's Super Heroes.

Art by David Finch

While Cho planned to gift the Hulk with his own land surrounding New Mexico's desert Base as a sanctuary, it seems the Hulk will not be content with anything but blood vengeance for the loss of his wife, his unborn child and his people. It remains to be seen what level of violence will satisfy him or if anyone can stop him. He has long said, "The madder Hulk gets, the stronger Hulk gets;" and the Hulk has never been more enraged than he is now.

HEIGHT: (Banner) 5'9½"; (gray Hulk) 6'6"; (green/savage Hulk) 7' — 8'; (green/Professor Hulk) 7'6"
WEIGHT: (Banner) 128 lbs.; (gray Hulk) 900 lbs.; (green/savage Hulk) 1040 — 1400 lbs. (green/Professor Hulk) 1150 lbs.
EYES: (Banner) Brown; (gray Hulk) gray; (green Hulk) green
HAIR: (Banner) Brown; (gray Hulk) black; (green Hulk) green

ABILITIES/ACCESSORIES: The Hulk possesses the capacity for superhuman strength ranging beyond the limits of virtually any other known humanoid being. The gamma radiation that mutated his body fortified his cellular structure and added, from some as yet unknown (presumably extradimensional) source, several hundred pounds of bone, muscle and other tissue. In times of stress the Hulk's adrenalin level escalates, causing a corresponding escalation of strength. Thus, the madder the Hulk gets, the stronger the Hulk gets. This is usually not accompanied by an additional gain in mass, but does appear to promote increased levels of energy efficiency. The Hulk has not yet found an endpoint to his maximum strength, so its upper limit remains a mystery. While described as Class 100 strength, the Hulk has on times proven capable of exceeding this parameter several times over; following exposure to the warp core breach on Sakaar, his baseline strength is even higher.

The Hulk periodically reverts to the human form of Bruce Banner, losing his extra mass and energy to the same source from which he derived it. The Hulk differs from many other gamma-irradiated human beings in that Banner was outside, exposed to sunlight, during his first heavy exposure to gamma radiation. This at least partially explains why the Hulk's color was initially gray, not green like most other gamma mutations. Moreover, this is also part of why Banner had transformed into the gray Hulk at nightfall and reverted to human form at the coming of dawn; however, it was later revealed that this was also partially due to Banner's shame over being the Hulk, and that he subconsciously forced himself to revert to human form in daylight to avoid being seen in his monstrous Hulk form. Though he has since managed to become the gray Hulk in daylight, he sometimes feels a burning sensation from sunlight contacting his skin.

The process by which Banner usually transforms into the Hulk has a chemical catalyst, adrenalin (aka epinephrine). As in normal human beings, Banner's adrenal medulla secretes large amounts of adrenalin in times of fear, rage or stress, which hormonally stimulates the heart rate, raises blood-sugar levels and inhibits sensations of fatigue. Whereas the secretion heightens normal physical abilities in normal human beings, in Banner's case it triggers the complex chemical-extra-physical process that transforms him into the Hulk. The total transformation takes anywhere from seconds to as long as 5 minutes, depending on the initial adrenalin surge, which is determined by the original external stimulus. Soon after the transformation, Hulk's adrenalin levels will return to more normal, reduced levels. At varying points of time in his life, Banner has been able to mentally control the change, producing or inhibiting it in either direction. At many times in the past, Banner would revert to the Hulk, regardless of the time of day or night, whenever he underwent enough excitation to induce a sufficient surge of adrenalin to trigger the transformation. Similarly, often if the Hulk relaxed to a great enough degree, his adrenalin levels would decline and he would revert to human form; however, there are many known instances in which the Hulk was very relaxed or even slept without reverting to human form.

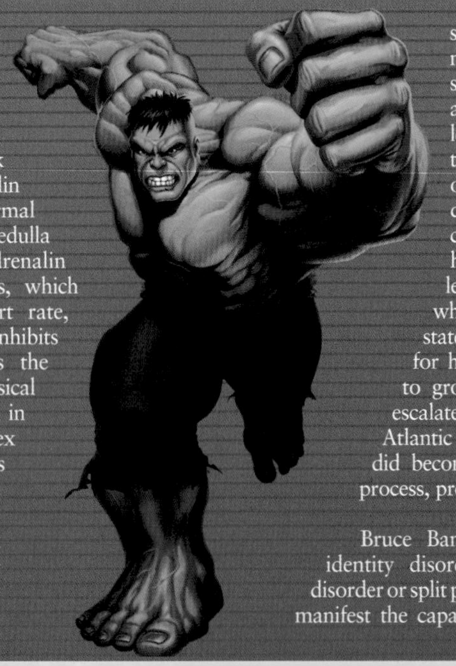

The Hulk is superhumanly durable and resistant to pain and disease. His skin can resist great heat without blistering (even tolerating the Human Torch's nova flame), great cold without freezing (down to absolute zero. -460 degrees Fahrenheit), and great impacts (he can survive direct hits by field artillery cannon shells or falls from the edge of the atmosphere). While it is possible to injure him, the Hulk also has vastly superhuman healing, enabling him to regenerate body tissue (including internal organs) within seconds to minutes; it once took him weeks to recover from a broken neck. It is not known what type of injury could kill the Hulk, but one of his alternate future counterparts was disintegrated by a nuclear level explosion, though he eventually reintegrated his form over a period of several years. The Hulk's highly efficient physiology renders him immune to all terrestrial diseases, and possibly to aging. Though Banner's form does not appear to share these immunities, some injuries will heal via transformation into the Hulk and vice versa. The Hulk can hold his breath for about an hour; his superhuman durability allows him to survive in the vacuum of space or at the ocean floor, though he would suffocate if too much time passed or if he were forced to expel his retained air. In particular, the Hulk is resistant to radiation, though in some circumstances, gamma radiation exposure has caused him to revert back into Banner. Similar effects have been achieved by draining the gamma radiation from the Hulk, or by exposing him to an uncertain type of radiation referred to as "gamma-negative rays."

The Hulk can use his superhumanly strong leg muscles to leap great distances, sometimes covering 3 miles in a single bound. He has even leapt so high into the atmosphere that he nearly achieved stable orbit. The Hulk can also produce destructive shockwaves by clapping his hands or stomping his foot. The Hulk's adrenalin levels counteract fatigue poisons; while fighting others in an enraged state, he can maintain peak output for hours on end and still continue to grow even stronger as his anger escalates. He has swum across both Atlantic and Pacific oceans, though he did become extremely exhausted in the process, presumably from lack of anger.

Bruce Banner suffers from dissociative identity disorder (aka multiple personality disorder or split personality). The Hulk's identities manifest the capacity for rage and violence that

Banner, in his human form, has repressed all of his life. The extent of Banner's disorder has only recently been appreciated, and a number of identities or personalities have been discovered. Chief among these identities are the reserved, Bruce Banner core identity, highly intelligent but virtually devoid of emotion; the "savage Hulk" identity, which has childlike levels of intelligence and curiosity, with a longing for friendship and love, and is prone to violent fits of rage (the "savage" Hulk is usually unaware that he is actually Banner, whom he sees as a different person and an enemy); the Joe Fixit identity (usually in the gray Hulk), lacking Banner's advanced intellect and scientific knowledge, is exceptionally clever and crafty, with selfish motives and desires, and similarly prone to violence; the "Professor" or "merged Hulk" identity, possessing all of Banner's intellect and the savage Hulk's strength, with normal emotional capacity, though still quite prone to violence; the "mindless" Hulk, when Banner's influence has been completely removed; and the "devil" Hulk identity, malevolent and destructive, kept submerged deep within Banner's psyche, but constantly struggling to escape and take over. By some accounts, there are dozens, if not hundreds, of different personality fragments within Banner/Hulk's psyche. The distinctions between these identities have differed significantly over time, with Banner himself having a variable capacity for emotion. At times, the Banner identity has had changing levels of control over the Hulk. Similarly, Banner's memories of his actions as the Hulk — and vice versa — vary significantly. Even the alleged "merged Hulk" seemingly proved to be yet one more splinter identity, a fragment of the whole renamed the "Professor."

His different identities produce outward effects on the Hulk's form, sometimes making him larger or smaller, gray or green, more human or more bestial in appearance, and even stronger or weaker. Among his more unusual transformations, Banner has taken on aspects of gray and green Hulks on opposite sides of his body; Banner's head has remained atop the savage Hulk's form; Banner has been trapped midway between human and Hulk forms, with changes appearing either diffusely or multifocally; and Banner's head has even poked out of the back of the savage Hulk's body. Following a transfusion from Sandra Verdugo, Banner could manifest superhuman strength and durability without transforming into the Hulk. Banner has even been physically separated from the Hulk's form on occasion, but neither form can long survive without

the other. In addition, Banner's identity disorder is a large reason why efforts to remove the Hulk's powers or to keep Banner's mind in dominance have met with failure. Under certain circumstances, different aspects of Banner and the various Hulks' personalities can communicate on some sort of psychic plane. Certain magical spells or scientific equipment — such as the Encephelo-Helmet — have allowed Banner's mind to dominate the Hulk's form for a time.

The Hulk has two powers unrelated to his physical abilities. He can see astral (spirit) forms, normally invisible to the naked eye. This ability somehow relates to his guilty conscience over his role in his father's death; he is subconsciously afraid of encountering his father's angry spirit. His other such power is a homing ability that enables him to locate the area in New Mexico where he first became the Hulk. This was actually caused by the Maestro, who had been pulled back in time and was disintegrated by the gamma bomb explosion. The Maestro psychically summoned the Hulk back to that spot to absorb gamma radiation from him, which eventually enabled the Maestro to re-form. Presumably the Hulk can still locate the site via the psychic bond, even though the Maestro is no longer exerting his influence on him.

Following the separation of most of Banner's persona into a separate Hulk on Counter-Earth, the Hulk remaining on Earth served as a walking nexus of reality and gave off increased levels of gamma radiation. His mystic nature had been enhanced by the traumatic injury to his brain and then his involvement with Onslaught. As War, the Hulk possessed heightened strength and durability, and used a highly durable sword and whip. While serving as a gladiator on Sakaar, he swiftly learned a variety of combat skills, especially with a sword or battleaxe.

POWER GRID	1	2	3	4	5	6	7
INTELLIGENCE							
STRENGTH							
SPEED							
DURABILITY							
ENERGY PROJECTION							
FIGHTING SKILLS							

POWER RATINGS

INTELLIGENCE
Ability to think and process information
1 Slow/impaired
2 Normal
3 Learned
4 Gifted
5 Genius
6 Super-Genius
7 Omniscient

STRENGTH
Ability to lift weight
1 Weak: cannot lift own body weight
2 Normal: able to lift own body weight
3 Peak human: able to lift twice own body weight
4 Superhuman: 800lbs-25 ton range
5 Superhuman: 26-75 ton range
6 Superhuman: 76-100 ton range
7 Incalculable: in excess of 100 tons

SPEED
Ability to move over land by running or flight
1 Below normal
2 Normal
3 Superhuman: Peak range: 700 MPH
4 Speed of Sound: Mach-1
5 Supersonic: Mach-2 through orbital velocity
6 Speed of light: 186,000 miles per second
7 Warp speed: transcending light speed

DURABILITY
Ability to resist or recover from bodily injury
1 Weak
2 Normal
3 Enhanced
4 Regenerative
5 bulletproof
6 Superhuman
7 Virtually indestructible

ENERGY PROJECTION
Ability to discharge energy
1 None
2 Ability to discharge energy on contact
3 Short range, short duration, single energy type
4 Medium range, duration, single energy type
5 Long range, long duration, single energy type
6 Able to discharge multiple forms of energy
7 Virtually unlimited command of all forms of energy

FIGHTING SKILLS
Proficiency in hand-to-hand combat
1 Poor
2 Normal
3 Some training
4 Experienced fighter
5 Master of a single form of combat
6 Master of several forms of combat
7 Master of all forms of combat

THE TRUE ORIGIN OF THE INCREDIBLE HULK

By Mike Conroy

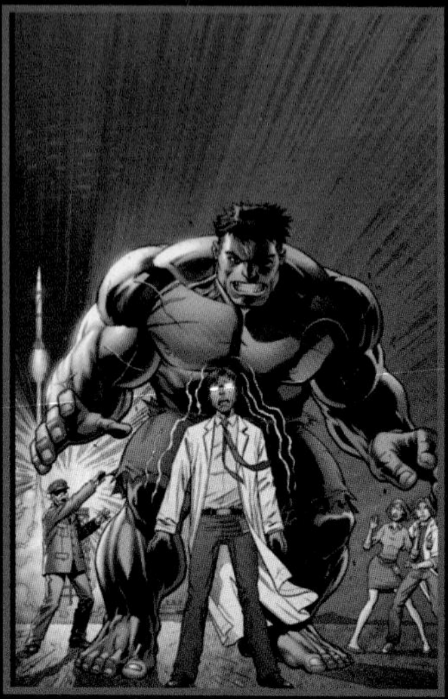

The Cold War between the USA and the Soviet Union loomed over the American people throughout the 1950s and 1960s. Fears of atomic armegeddon shaded every aspect of their lives from politics to popular culture. The Red Menace infused a wide variety of movies, among them **The Man from Planet X** (1951), **Christian Nyby's The Thing from Another World** (1951), **Invaders from Mars** (1953) and **Don Siegel's Invasion of the Body Snatchers** (1956). The apocalyptic affects of nuclear war and the fear of unfettered radiation surfaced in **The Beast From 20,000 Fathoms** (1953), **Them** (1954), **Roger Corman's The Day the World Ended** (1956), **Stanley Kramer's On the Beach** (1959), 1964's **Fail-Safe** (**Sidney Lumet**) and **Dr. Strangelove: Or How I Learned to Stop Worrying and Love the Bomb** (**Stanley Kubrick**) among others.

The pervading dread spread beyond Hollywood to include comics. At Marvel, a profusion of stories featured Communist-like alien invaders, Red (mainly Russian) antagonists or heroes menaced or transformed by radiation in such monster/fantasy titles as **Amazing Adventures, Journey into Mystery, Strange Tales, Tales of Suspense** and **Tales to Astonish.** Prior to the late 1961 publication of the first issue of **Fantastic Four,** Marvel was struggling to survive, releasing less than a dozen comics a month. Five were anthologies, published alongside such Westerns as **Gunsmoke Western, Kid Colt, Outlaw** and **Rawhide Kid** and romance/girls comics like **Millie the Model, Linda Carter, Student Nurse** and **Teenage Romance.** The influence of **Amazing Adventures** and its counterparts (all subsequently reworked into superhero titles) was evident from the coming of the Fantastic Four (themselves "victims" of radiation, albeit of the cosmic kind). Their first foe was the Mole Man's monster, fairly obviously a direct descendant of *The Crawling Creature* [from **Tales to Astonish #22,** 1961]. In fact, although the Thing is part of that sub-genre of pre-superhero Marvel monsters known as transformed humans, it takes no stretch of the imagination to place Mr Fantastic, the Invisible Girl and the Human Torch in the same category.

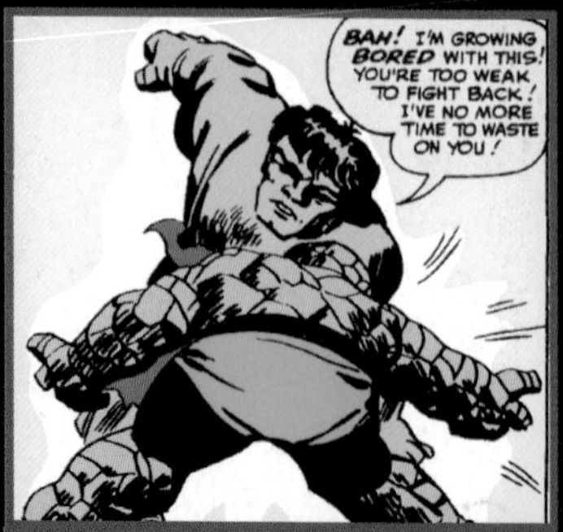
BAH! I'M GROWING BORED WITH THIS! YOU'RE TOO WEAK TO FIGHT BACK! I'VE NO MORE TIME TO WASTE ON YOU!

The Hulk vs the Thing – two of Marvel's greatest titans clash!

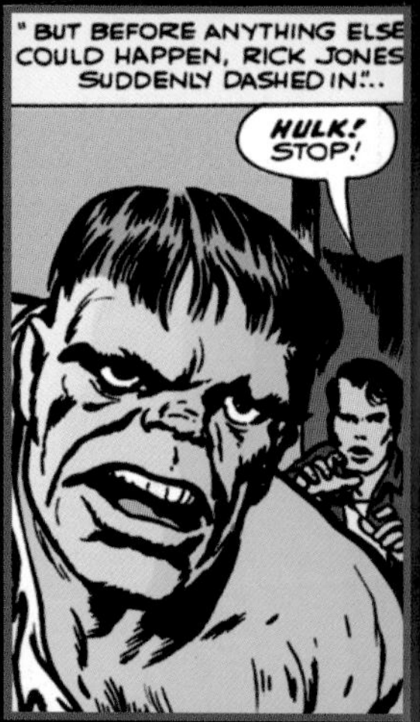
" BUT BEFORE ANYTHING ELSE COULD HAPPEN, RICK JONES SUDDENLY DASHED IN!..
HULK! STOP!

However, only the Thing's outward appearance mirrored the influence of his monstrous predecessors. When **Stan Lee** and **Jack Kirby** – the writer/artist team responsible for many of Marvel's monster stories – created a second superhero to follow the FF, they went the whole hog. Not only did their new creation look brutish but also, in the tradition of the protagonists of such stories as *Beware of... Bruttu* [**Tales of Suspense #22, 1961**], *I Found the Abominable Snowman* [**Tales to Astonish #13, 1960**] and *I am the Brute that Walks* [**Journey into Mystery #65, 1961**], he was, if not maleficent, then at least seriously misunderstood and certainly a danger to the public.

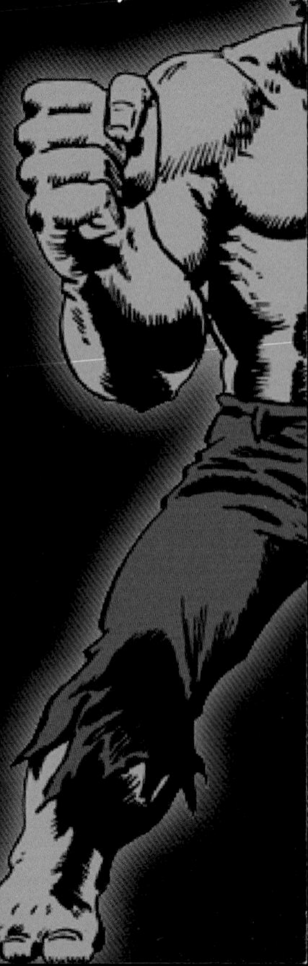

In fact, not only did Dr Bruce Banner transform into a creature that resembled *The Midnight Monster* [**Journey into Mystery #79**, 1962] but like the scientist in *Kraa the Unhuman* [**Tales of Suspense #18**, 1961], his metamorphosis into the **Hulk** came as the result of exposure to the radiation from a nuclear explosion. In his case, in a move that integrated both of America's contemporary anxieties, it was as the upshot of an "accident" contrived by Igor, a Red operative working for the Gargoyle, a Soviet scientist himself misshapen by radiation.

The Hulk – who débuted six months after the Fantastic Four – owed a great debt

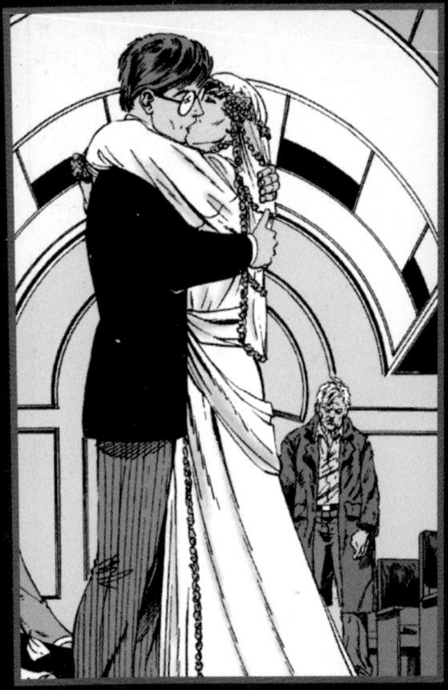

to the Marvel monsters that preceded him, but did two classic literary creatures influence his creation. While the good-by-day/bad-by-night duality of **Robert Louis Stevenson's** Dr Jekyll and Mr Hyde is evident – especially in his early appearances – the Hulk also incorporates aspects of the monster from **Mary Wollstonecraft Shelley's Frankenstein or the Modern Prometheus** [1818].

"I've always had a soft spot in my heart for the Frankenstein monster," stated Lee, who had already decided – in part because of the popularity of the Thing – to make his follow-up to the Fantastic Four an inordinately strong solo hero. "No one could ever convince me that he was the bad guy, the villain or the menace. It was he who was sinned against by those who feared him, by those whose first instinct was to strike out blindly at whatever they couldn't comprehend. He never wanted to hurt anyone; he merely groped his tortuous way through a second life trying to defend himself, trying to come to terms with those who sought to destroy him."

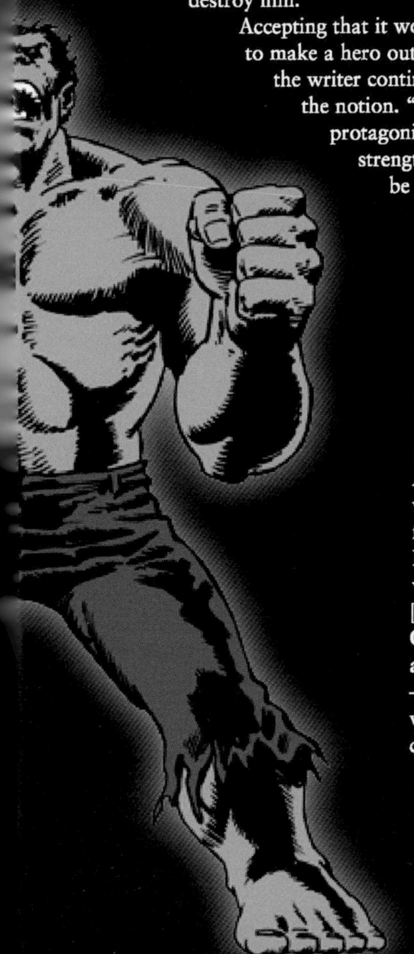

Accepting that it would be a challenge to make a hero out of a monster, the writer continued developing the notion. "We would have a protagonist with superhuman strength but he wouldn't be all-wise, all-noble, all-infallible. We would use the concept of the Frankenstein monster but update it. Our hero would be a scientist, transformed into a raging behemoth by a nuclear accident. And – since I was willing to borrow from Frankenstein, I decided I might as well borrow from [1886's **The Strange Case of**] **Dr Jekyll and Mr Hyde** as well – our protagonist would constantly change from his normal identity to his superhuman alter ego and back again."

With the character fully realised, Lee was still struggling to find a suitable name. "Racking my brain for all the appellations that would describe a gargantuan creature, a being of awesome strength coupled with a dull and sluggish thinking process, I couldn't seem to find the right word. I looked in the dictionary and the thesaurus but nothing was on target. I knew I needed a perfect name for a monstrous, potentially murderous hulking brute who... and then I stopped. It was the word 'hulking' that did it. It conjured up the perfect mental image. I knew I had found his name. He had to be... The Hulk."

Kirby then set about visualising the Hulk, who Lee had described to the artist as "a somewhat nice-looking monster, big and brutish enough to make him feared by all who met him and yet with a certain tragic appeal that would make our readers care about him and cheer him on."

Next, Lee broke one of his cardinal rules... he introduced a kid sidekick. "One of my many pet peeves has always been the young teenage sidekick of the average superhero," the writer stated. "If yours truly were a superhero there's no way I'd pal around with some freckle-faced teenager. At the very least, people would start to talk."

Although Lee made no secret of his profound dislike for these youthful staples of the superhero genre as it existed pre-Fantastic Four, he had a rationale for the creation of the teenage Rick Jones, who made his first appearance in **Incredible Hulk #1** [1962]. "We did it for a reason. He was a necessary catalyst in the creation of the Hulk and he also gave me a chance to demonstrate that it was possible to introduce a teenager into a comicbook series without making him a cloying, wimpy extension of the hero's personality."

With everything else in place, Lee decided the Hulk should be grey. He thought it would be intensely dramatic-looking and sombre. It proved to be a mistake. The printer couldn't keep a consistent shade of grey. "His skin was light grey in some places and almost black in others. There were a few panels where he seemed red and, for some reason which nobody could explain, in close-up toward the end of our little epic he was bright emerald green. As you may have already surmised, it became painfully apparent to me that grey was not the happiest colour choice I might have made."

Faced with choosing a new colour, the writer ultimately plumped for green, "mainly because there were no other emerald-skinned rampagers extant at that particular time."

Finally, two months after his first appearance and in the second issue of his own bimonthly title, the Hulk emerged as the Green Goliath the world knows and – er – loves.

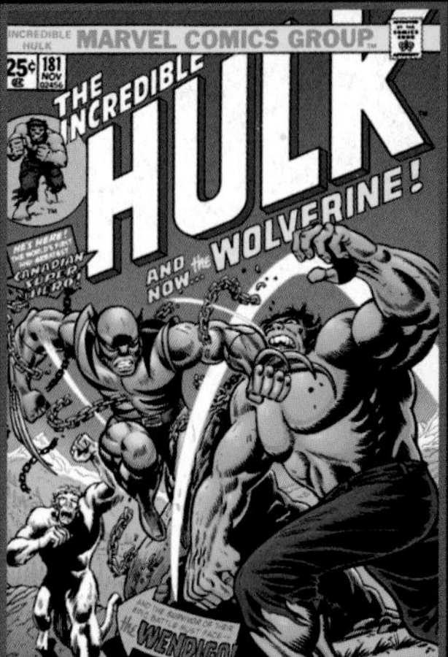
MARVEL COMICS GROUP
25¢
181
NOV
THE INCREDIBLE
HULK
AND NOW... THE WOLVERINE!
WENDIGO!

Wolverine makes his startling début in *Incredible Hulk #181* (November 1974)

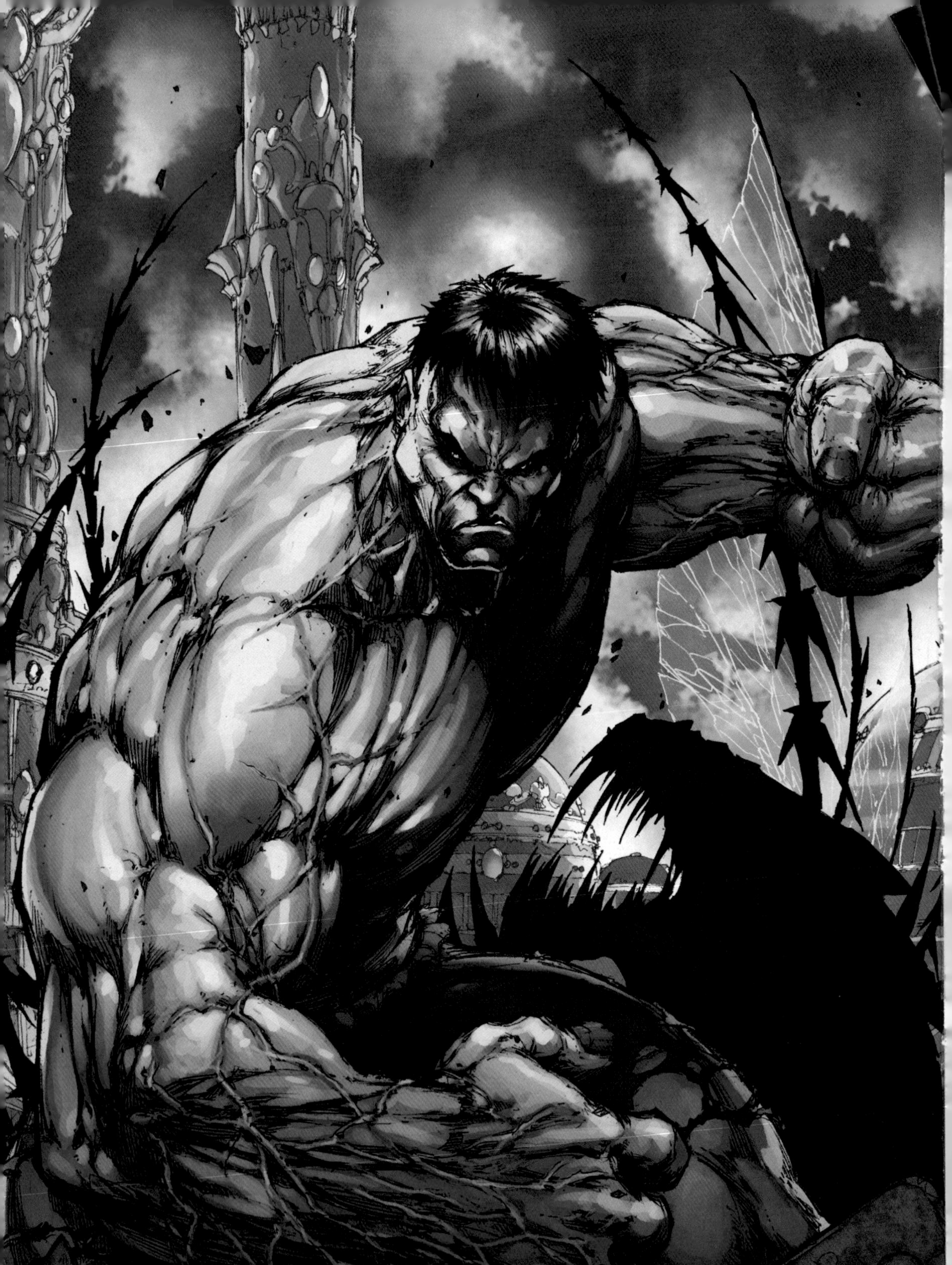
MICHAEL TURNER

ART BY MICHAEL TURNER